History–Social Science Content Standards for California Public Schools reproduced by permission, California Department of Education, CDE Press, 1430 N Street, Suite 3207, Sacramento, CA 95814.

P9-EDO-839

This book
is the property of . . .

State_____

Province_____

County_____

Parish_____

School District_____

Other_____

Enter information
in spaces to the left
as instructed

| Issued To | Year | CONDITION | |
		issued	returned

1. Teachers should see that the pupil's name is clearly written in ink in the spaces above in every book issued.
2. The following terms should be used in recording the condition of the book: New; Good; Fair; Poor; Bad.

Pupils to whom this textbook is issued must not write on any page or mark any part of it in any way, consumable textbooks excepted.

Making Thirteen Colonies

Gray Whale

Bald Eagle

Elk

Missouri River

Big Horn
Sheep

Grizzly Bear

PACIFIC OCEAN

RANGE

CASCADE

Columbia River

Mt. St. Helens

Snake River

ROCKY

MOUNTAINS

SOUTH PASS

Antelope

GREAT
PLAIN

Pla

Sea Otter

SIERRA NEVADA

Jack
Rabbit

GREAT
BASIN

Great
Salt
Lake

Mt. Whitney

MOJAVE
DESERT

Colorado River

Mountain Lion

California Sea Lion

Coyote

Rattlesnake

Road Runner

Polar
Bear

ALASKA

CANADA

Mt. McKinley

Rio Grande

Humpback Whale

Hawaiian Islands

Gulf of California

N

W   E

S

0   100   200   300 M

0   200   400 KILO

The Geography of the United States

Lake Superior

Duck

Lake Huron

Lake Ontario

St. Lawrence River

Penobscot

Beaver

Bison

Wolf

Lake Michigan

Lake Erie

HUDSON MOUNTAINS

Hudson River

White-Tailed Deer

CENTRAL PLAINS

Prairie Dog

Skunk

Ohio River

Turkey

APPALACHIAN MOUNTAINS

CUMBERLAND GAP

ATLANTIC COASTAL PLAIN

Rabbit

PIEDMONT

Black Bear

Brown Bat

Savannah River

Mississippi River

Raccoon

Red River

ATLANTIC OCEAN

Armadillo

GULF COASTAL PLAIN

Pelican

Lake Okeechobee

The Everglades

GULF OF MEXICO

Egret

Alligator

CARIBBEAN SEA

A   H I S T O R Y   O F   U S

The picture on the cover is a detail from an oil painting by Edward Hicks (1780-1849). It is called *Penn's Treaty with the Indians*; it shows William Penn and other Quakers making a peace treaty with the Indians of Pennsylvania. (To see the whole painting, turn to page 108.) Hicks was a sign painter and a Quaker preacher who began painting pictures late in life. His work became very popular. Sometimes he wrote poems and painted them around the edges of his compositions.

Oxford University Press

A HISTORY OF US

BOOK TWO

Making Thirteen Colonies

Joy Hakim

Diane L. Brooks, Ed.D.
EDUCATION CONSULTANT

Oxford University Press
New York

Oxford University Press

Oxford   New York
Auckland   Bangkok   Buenos Aires
Cape Town   Chennai   Dar es Salaam   Delhi   Hong Kong   Istanbul
Karachi   Kolkata   Kuala Lumpur   Madrid   Melbourne   Mexico City   Mumbai
Nairobi   São Paulo   Shanghai   Taipei   Tokyo   Toronto

Copyright © 1993, 1999, 2003, 2005 by Joy Hakim

Maps copyright © 1993, 1999, 2003, 2005 by Wendy Frost and Elspeth Leacock
Additional maps and illustrations for the revised third edition copyright © 2005 by Wendy Frost
First edition produced by American Historical Publications

Third Edition, Revised

Published by Oxford University Press, Inc.,
198 Madison Avenue, New York, New York 10016
Oxford is a registered trademark of Oxford University Press

Library of Congress Cataloging-in-Publication Data is available

ISBN-13: 978-0-19-518895-0   ISBN-10: 0-19-518895-0

ISBN-13: 978-0-19-518231-6   (California edition)   ISBN-10: 0-19-518231-6   (California edition)

*The illustrations used herein were drawn from many sources, including commercial photographic archives and the holdings of major museums and
cultural institutions. The publisher has made every effort to identify proprietors of copyright, to secure permission to reprint materials protected by
copyright, and to make appropriate acknowledgments of sources and proprietary rights. Sources of all illustrations and notices of copyright are
given in the picture credits at the end of the volume. Please notify the publisher if oversights or errors are discovered.*

1 3 5 7 9 8 6 4 2
Printed in the United States of America on acid-free paper

The poem on the facing page is "Indian" by Stephen Vincent Benét, from *A Book of Americans* (Holt, Rinehart & Winston). Copyright © 1933,
Rosemary & Stephen Vincent Benét. Copyright renewed © 1961, Rosemary Carr Benét. Reprinted by permission of Brandt & Brandt Literary
Agents, Inc. The lines on page 32 are from "Western Star" by Stephen Vincent Benét (Holt, Rinehart & Winston). Copyright © 1943, Rosemary
Carr Benét. Copyright renewed © 1971. Reprinted by permission of Brandt & Brandt Literary Agents, Inc.

THIS BOOK IS FOR NATALIE JOHNSON, WHO SKIS, RUNS TRACK,
CARES ABOUT PEOPLE, AND WRITES POETRY.

This engraving was done by Theodore de Bry in 1618. It is entitled "Employment for Gentlemen in New England."

Thomas Morton, an Englishman, who landed in America in 1622, was full of optimism and good cheer. He liked what he saw. This is what he wrote:

In the month of June 1622, it was my chance to arrive in the parts of New England. . . While our houses were building, I did endeavor to take a survey of the country. The more I looked, the more I liked it. And when I had more seriously considered of the beauty of the place, with all her fair endowments, I did not think that in all the known world it could be paralleled. . . in my eye 'twas nature's Masterpiece. . .

But to William Bradford, who came that same year, the land didn't look promising. Here are his thoughts:

Besides, what could they see but a hideous and desolate wilderness, full of wild beasts and wild men? And what multitudes there might be of them they knew not. . . for which way soever they turned their eye, they could have little solace (comfort). . . For summer being done, all things stand upon them with a weather-beaten face; and the whole country represented a wild and savage [way].

Contents

Puritan colonist

*Metacom, or King Philip of
the Wampanoag people*

An animal which has a head like a sucking pig...hair like a badger... the tail like a rat, the paws like a monkey, which has a purse beneath its belly, where it produces its young and nourishes them.

—LE MOYNE D'IBERVILLE, WRITING IN 1699 IN ASTONISHMENT AT AN OPOSSUM, AN ANIMAL UNKNOWN IN EUROPE

Some ten years ago being in Virginia, and taken prisoner by the power of Powhatan their chief King, I received from this great savage exceeding great courtesy, especially from his son Nantaquaua, the most manliest, comeliest, boldest spirit I ever saw in a savage, and his sister Pocahontas, the King's most dear and well beloved daughter, being but a child of 12 or 13 years of age, whose compassionate pitiful heart, of my desperate state, gave me much cause to respect her.... Jamestown she as frequently visited as her father's habitation; and during the time of two or three years, she next under God, was still the instrument to preserve this Colony from death, famine and utter confusion.

—JOHN SMITH, ADVENTURER AND CO-FOUNDER OF JAMESTOWN, VIRGINIA

Ætatis suæ 21. Aº. 1616.

...ntoaks als Rebecka daughter to the mighty Prince ...whatan Emperour of Attanoughkomouck als Virginia ...nverted and baptized in the Christian faith, and ...Wife to the wor.ll M.r Tho: Rolff.

PREFACE
Our Mixed-Up Civilization

Carved 4,000 years ago, this is the portrait of a man who ruled in Sumer around the time Abraham lived.

A long time ago—actually, it was about 4,000 years ago—in the city of Ur, there lived a boy named Abraham. Ur was in a country that is now known as Iraq but was then called Sumer.

Now you may be asking why we are in ancient Sumer when this is a book about U.S. history. Well, hold on. Abraham's story will turn out to be important—to people all over the world—and to us in America.

Abraham lived in an interesting urban center. In Sumer, between the Tigris (TY-griss) and Euphrates (yoo-FRAY-teez) rivers, people had learned to read and write and to build and govern cities (which hadn't been done much before). But something must have been wrong, because one day Abraham and his father decided to move.

Abraham moved with his whole family and his cattle and oxen. He traveled northwest, following a fingernail of green land called the Fertile Crescent. He went to a place known as Canaan (KAY-nun); he called it the land of Israel. There Abraham had two sons: Isaac and Ishmael. The descendants of those sons founded two great religions. From Isaac's children came Judaism and the Jewish people; from Ishmael's came Islam and the Muslims.

Abraham must have been a restless type, because he traveled on, to Egypt and back to Canaan. In Egypt he found a spectacular civilization, where people could also read and write. The Egyptians had built big cities and tall pyramids. They called their rulers *pharaohs* (FAIR-oze), and they kept slaves—as did many people in those days. Some of Abraham's people became slaves. Like all enslaved people, they longed to be free. Help was on its way.

This preface is a synopsis (sin OP sis; it means a brief retelling) of some ancient history. It includes stories of people from the Bible. Are they history? Many historians would say "no." We can't document those stories. But they were so widely told and believed that they influenced world history. You can't understand history if you don't know people's stories and beliefs.

Ancient Sumer is sometimes called Sumeria or Mesopotamia.

According to the biblical story, the pharaoh's daughter finds Moses. Her clothes, and her castle, don't look very ancient Egyptian. When this illustration was made, in the 15th century, artists just drew people the way they looked in their own time.

A Greek painted this vase 2,500 years ago with a scene from the *Iliad:* the Greeks and Trojans fight over the fallen body of the Greek hero Achilles *(in the middle).*

One day an Egyptian princess found a baby boy floating in a basket among the bulrushes at the edge of the river Nile. The baby was Moses. He became a great leader and led the Jewish people out of Egypt. The trip was filled with danger and adventure. It took Moses and the Jews 40 years to get to their destination: Israel. Actually, Moses didn't quite make it. You can read the story of that flight to freedom in the Hebrew Bible, which is also called the Old Testament.

Take a look at the map on page 181. Do you see Israel and Egypt? Did you notice that they are next to the Mediterranean Sea? Back in the old, old days, before cars, buses, trains, and airplanes, it was very hard traveling over land. It was much easier to get in a boat and sail away. So people who lived near the sea got around more than inland people. People living around the Mediterranean Sea traveled and traded ideas.

Greece borders the Mediterranean. More than 2,500 years ago, some very interesting people—artists, playwrights, scientists, and philosophers—lived in Greece. The most renowned Greek of those long-ago days was a blind man who had been a slave. His name was Homer and he was a poet and a storyteller. Homer's stories were so good that we still read them today. They are stories of real heroes and heroines and of mythological gods and goddesses. Homer's two adventure books, the *Iliad* and the *Odyssey,* are among the best books ever written.

The Greeks had an idea for governing people that hadn't been tried before. They called it "democracy." In the Greek language, democracy means "people's rule." In most places, kings and emperors just ruled any way they wanted to. In Athens, a Greek city-state, every citizen was expected to vote on laws and issues. The Greek democracy was limited—women and slaves couldn't vote—still, it was an amazing beginning for an idea called "self-government." In figuring out how to make their government work well, the Athenians

came up with a three-branch plan: a legislative branch to pass laws, an executive branch to carry out the laws, and a judicial branch (courts) to decide arguments about the laws.

The Romans were another Mediterranean people. A Roman writer named Virgil took Homer's stories and some other tales and rewrote them in his book, the *Aeneid* (uh NEE-id). (It's good reading.) Roman generals, like Julius Caesar, conquered much of the Mediterranean world. Then they had to govern that world. It was much more challenging than running a small city-state. They started with the Greek idea of democracy, but they didn't expect citizens to vote on every issue; citizens elected representatives to govern for them. That gave them a representative democracy, or a republic. (More than 2,000 years later, the founders of the United States studied the ideas of Greece and Rome and formed a democratic republic with a three-branch system of government.)

Rome was ruling most of the Mediterranean lands when a Jewish boy, named Jesus, was born in Israel. Jesus lived in a town called Nazareth. From his preaching and his example a great new religion grew. That religion was Christianity. The ideas of Jesus are written in the New Testament. Jesus Christ was born about the year 1. Modern history dates from the birth of Christ.

Another child was born in the land to the east of the Mediterranean. He was Mohammed, a descendant of Ishmael, and he was born in the city of Mecca in the year 570. Look at a map on page 13 and find Mecca. Mohammed founded the religion known as Islam, and his teachings are found in a book called the Koran. People who practice Islam are known as Mohammedans or Muslims.

Islam spread rapidly across Arabian lands and into North Africa and the Sudan (often through religious warfare). In the year 711 an African general, Taril ibn Ziyad, sailed an army 13 miles from

Pericles was a great Greek general and statesman. This is what he said in 431 BCE, "Our constitution does not copy the laws of neighboring states; we are rather a pattern to others than imitators ourselves. Its administration favors the many instead of the few; this is why it is called a democracy."

A Greek writer named Plato wrote a book called *The Republic*. It discussed what an ideal government might be. People still argue about Plato's ideas.

In 1947, an Arab herdsman was grazing his flock near the Dead Sea in Jordan. He went after a stray goat and stumbled into a cave, which contained some old, old jars and baskets. In them, wrapped in linen, were ancient scrolls, written in Hebrew, in Greek, and in Aramaic, an ancient language related to Hebrew and Arabic. Later more caves and scrolls were found. The Dead Sea Scrolls are the oldest known copies of parts of the Hebrew Bible; they may have been written before the birth of Christ.

In a feudal system, the peasants have to declare their loyalty to a lord and do a certain amount of work for him. In return, the lord is supposed to protect the workers and help them in bad times. Working for a lord like this was a bit better than being a slave, but not much.

Monks are men who gave up worldly goods and entered a monastery, a place where they devote their lives to religion. In the Middle Ages monasteries were big and powerful. They had their own farms, workshops, and schools, and usually didn't have to buy anything from outside.

Caravels were ships first built in the 15th century. They made long voyages possible, because they could sail into the wind.

Morocco across the mouth of the Mediterranean Sea and landed on a Spanish hill. That rocky hill became known as Jabal Taril (Taril's hill), which was soon shortened to Gibraltar.

Taril's army of Muslim Africans fought and defeated an army led by King Rodrigo of Spain. For the next seven and a half centuries much of Spain was ruled by Muslims (the Spaniards called them Moors). It was a splendid era in Spain. It was a time of religious tolerance: Jews, Muslims, and Christians lived together in harmony. The Moors built great cities with centers of learning. Agriculture flourished in Spain as it never had before or has since. These were the Middle Ages, so called because they lie between ancient days and modern times. In the Middle Ages, most Europeans were Roman Catholic Christians.

It was a time when knights, lords, and ladies lived in splendid feudal castles. And religious crusaders set off for Israel to recapture the Holy Land from the Muslims. Some managed to plunder and murder as they went.

Most people weren't lords or knights, and most didn't go on crusades. Most were peasants. They worked on the land, and their lives were short and hard. They couldn't read, they didn't get a chance to travel, and they didn't know much. Books were kept in monasteries and were read only by monks. Most Europeans had forgotten the arts and learning of the Greeks and Romans.

It was different in Spain. Remember, Arabs, Jews, and Christians had brought their scholarship, arts, and energy to that land. Spain was thriving. Then the Moors started fighting among themselves. Christian armies soon entered the fray. By 1250, Muslims controlled only one Spanish region, Granada. When they lost that in 1492, Christian kings and armies held Spain. Jews had to convert or

THE MEDITERRANEAN WORLD

leave the country immediately. The Moors were also thrown out, but more gradually.

Meanwhile, in the places that would become France, England, Germany, and Italy, cities were growing and trade was expanding. The Middle Ages were being replaced by a Renaissance (REN-uh-sahnce)—a rebirth of learning and art. It was the forgotten ideas of the ancient Greeks and Romans that were being reborn. The Renaissance began in Italy and soon was inspiring thinkers all through Europe. At the same time, travelers were describing the fabulous civilizations in the Far East. Before people could even digest all the fresh ideas, two whole new continents—South and North America—were discovered. And seagoing explorers proved, beyond anyone's doubt, that the world was round. As if that weren't enough, the Catholic Church was rocked by reformers (people who wanted to change the Church); that led to a host of new Christian Churches, called "Protestant." At the same time, the European nations (that we know today) were being formed. As you can see, it was an exciting time, but confusing, too.

The ideas of all these peoples—with all their religions and cul-

Marco Polo, a trader from Venice, went to China in the years 1275–1292. He saw wonderful things, met the Grand Khan, and came back and wrote a book about it all.

13

This sign was the Totem of the Five Nations. In 1570, five Indian tribes, the Oneida, Mohawk, Cayuga, Seneca, and Onondaga, united in an Iroquois confederation.

A Great Mystery

A Dakota Indian named Luther Standing Bear thought about the meeting of Native Americans and Europeans and wrote:

While the white people had much to teach us, we had much to teach them, and what a school could have been established upon that idea!...Only the white man saw nature as a "wilderness," and only to him was the land "infested" with "wild" animals and savage people. To us it was tame. Earth was bountiful and we were surrounded with the blessings of the Great Mystery.

tures—made up an idea pool, a kind of cultural stew, that sailed to America across the ocean from Europe. (Both the good ideas and the bad came to America. One bad idea was slavery. Some of all the peoples we have talked about kept slaves.)

In America there were already civilizations as ancient as those that had begun in Ur and Egypt and Greece. The Indian civilizations surprised the Europeans. To begin with, they weren't all alike. Some Native Americans were ruled by powerful lords. Some practiced slavery. But others lived democratically. The Iroquois had a government of the people. Women were important in Iroquois society, and there was much freedom.

There were no democracies in Europe. Mostly there were kings and emperors. Many of the European newcomers were impressed with the free life the Indians led. They thought about that free life and added it to their idea pool.

Unfortunately, many of the newcomers didn't understand the Native American cultures. Because they were different, the Europeans thought them inferior. They called the Indians "savages."They destroyed much of the Indian heritage before they came to appreciate it.

The European newcomers learned more from the Native Americans than they realized. They learned ways of planting, harvesting, and hunting. They added Indian words to their languages. They exchanged foods, animals, diseases, and even weeds. Indian ways enriched the new culture that was forming. That culture became a mixture: Africans came—in chains—but that didn't stop them from adding ideas, energy, stories, music, and knowledge of agriculture. Then people came from Asia, bringing the wisdom of ancient religions and cultures.

Out of that worldwide mixture a nation developed—our nation, the United States—and a new civilization, an American civilization, where peoples of East and West and of many races and religions now live together and share ideas.

What does that mixing do for us? It makes life in the United States very interesting. People in America eat pizza, chow mein, and pita bread—sometimes in the same meal. In America, children whose ancestors left England in tiny wooden boats go to school with children who themselves left Vietnam in tiny wooden boats. In America, children who worship in a church go to school with children who worship in a mosque or temple or synagogue or kiva. In America, people who have their own beliefs—rather than those of an organized religion—are given respect.

Our nation began as an experiment. Nothing like it had ever been tried before. The citizens of most other countries couldn't even imagine living with people who seemed different from them. Can people who don't look alike build a free and equal society together? Read on, and see for yourself.

1 A Sign in the Sky

Experts disagree about whether Halley's was the comet seen in 1066. Some say it was; others say it may not have been the same comet.

A Comets Blaze

In 1607 a dazzling comet lit the sky over Europe. "A comet, a comet!" people cried and pointed to the heavens. In those days almost everyone could name the bright stars and planets. They knew the constellations and the mythical stories of their forming. Mothers and fathers showed their children the stars named for the dog Sirius, or Draco the Dragon, or Cygnus the Swan.

Pollution and city lights had not yet dimmed the skies. Nor was there much else in the evening to capture attention. Few could afford costly candles. So when something out of the ordinary appeared in the night sky, people saw it and wondered at its meaning.

These were times when most questions were answered by religious faith or superstition. Modern science was just being born. Stars were thought to be the lights of heaven, and comets were said to be messengers sent to foretell danger and dire change.

Many who watched the bold comet were frightened. They might have been even more fearful had they known this was the very comet that had been seen in 1066, when the Norman kings invaded England from France. Those French conquerors had changed England, and the English language, for all time.

But you didn't need a comet in 1607 to see that Europe was changing. The old religion—Catholic Christianity—had broken apart. England had become Protestant, then Catholic, then Protestant again. Now some people, called Puritans, were saying that the country wasn't Protestant enough. It was all very disturbing to people used to a secure faith. To make matters worse, there were economic problems, too.

In the great Catholic nation of Spain, the government was bankrupt. Although nobody knew it, Spain's glory days were over. Would

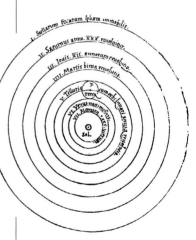

This is a diagram from Copernicus's *On the Revolution of the Celestial Spheres*. It was the first time ever (1543) that the sun *(Sol)* was shown at the center of the solar system.

15

Even when Galileo was made to recant (deny) his belief that the earth moved around the sun, he didn't really deny it. Afterward, it is said, he muttered quietly, "And yet, it moves."

Galileo (pictured above and on the opposite page) was disgraced by the Catholic Church and put under house arrest for saying that the earth moves around the sun. Galileo was lucky. The great scholar Giordano Bruno (1548–1600) was burned alive by Italian authorities when he said that the universe was infinite. Yet by the end of the 17th century, most of the new scientific beliefs about the earth and skies were commonly accepted.

that arrogant little Protestant island—that England—become Europe's new leader? Now that England's magnificent Queen Elizabeth was dead, no one knew where England was heading.

In this world that had once seemed orderly, ideas were changing. New thinkers, like the Italian scientist Galileo Galilei, were actually saying that Aristotle, the greatest of scientists, had some ideas that were wrong! Galileo even whispered that Nicholas Copernicus might be right. Copernicus, a Polish astronomer, had said the sun, not the earth, was the center of our universe. How could that be? Everyone knew that the planets and stars and sun all revolved around the earth. If that idea was wrong then the Pope and all of Europe's rulers were wrong.

Of course, that disturbing idea got Galileo into a lot of trouble. It ended up changing everything people believed. Change is troublesome, especially to those in power. And yet the new ideas, like germs, seemed to travel on invisible wings. The epidemic of thought was soon out of control.

In 1609, just two years after the comet appeared, Galileo built one of the world's first telescopes. (It was a lot stronger and therefore more useful than the few made before it.) Galileo took much of the mystery from the skies and replaced it with scientific order. When the comet of 1607 came again, in 1682, an English scientist named Edmond Halley tracked it and learned that it takes more than 75 years to complete its trips around the sun. Halley predicted that the comet would return in 1758, and he was right.

But in 1607 people knew none of that. They didn't know the year 1607 was to become famous. That very year the seeds of a new nation—a new way of governing, a new way of looking at the world—were being planted on the North American continent by a small group of English men and boys.

The message that some people read in the comet was right: the world was in for astonishing changes. Would they be changes for the better? Not for those people called Indians, who would soon meet the pale-skinned English. For them the changes were tragic.

But for England, and the rest of the world, 1607 marked the beginning of what turned out to be an awesome, momentous, earth-shaking experiment. An experiment that would lead to democracy and to a government dedicated to liberty and the pursuit of happiness.

Let's watch the United States happen. Take yourself to the beginning of the 17th century, to England, where some brave men are getting ready to travel to a place they call the New World. They have no idea what is ahead of them. They'll bring along their Old World ideas—good and bad. Pack a bag, we're going to join them.

You don't need Galileo's telescope to see Halley's comet. It's the only comet that passes close enough to earth to be seen easily with the naked eye. It has been observed 30 times since 467 B.C.E. *Above:* Halley's orbit through our solar system in 1985, its most recent visit. At the far end of its path, away from the sun, the comet goes outside the orbit of Neptune. It will be back in 2061.

Galileo Galilei

2 Across the Ocean

English ships of the 17th century were sturdy but tiny. An ocean voyage in one seemed endless.

To **embark** means to "set off."

On the docks of the river Thames (TEMS), near London, a group of Englishmen readied themselves for a trip across the vast ocean. They were brave men, as they had to be to embark on an adventure such as they had in mind. They were going to a New World, where there were strange animals, deep forests, and people said to be wild.

There was also gold. They were sure of that. A play, popular in London, told of Virginia. It said:

> *I tell thee, gold is more plentiful there than copper is with us....*
> *Why, man, all their dripping pans and their chamber pots are*
> *pure gold...and as for rubies and diamonds, they go forth on holy*
> *days and gather them by the seashore, to hang on their*
> *children's coats and stick in their caps.*

Of course the authors of that play had never been to Virginia, but people believed them. Everyone knew there was gold in America. Hadn't the Spaniards found mountains of gold? And wasn't England now the greatest of nations? Her time had come.

About 144 men actually set sail for America, but the sailors weren't counted because they returned to England.

Of the 105 men who stood on the docks, more than half listed themselves as "gentlemen". In England, gentlemen were not expected or trained to work. They lived on family money. They had time for adventure; they hoped to find riches.

Most brought their best clothes for the trip: their puffed knee pants, their silk stockings, their feathered hats, their gaudy blouses.

Gaudy means "showy and brightly colored."

Those in plainer clothes were the gentlemen's servants; a few were carpenters and bricklayers; four of them were boys—probably orphans or runaways. The boys were called "younkers" and were ex-

18

In dirty, crowded London it was easy to imagine that America was an untouched Garden of Eden. It had to be full of animals known to Europeans only from myths—but which most people firmly believed existed somewhere.

A *peril* is a danger or risk. A *privateer* was a pirate with a government license. Privateers split their loot with the king.

pected to climb the rigging, high on the ship's mast, help set the sails, and keep a lookout for land and danger. If a younker fell in the ocean and was lost—well, too bad. That was one of the perils of sea travel.

Ocean travel was risky—they all knew that. They also knew that their captain, Christopher Newport, was one of England's finest sailors. As a privateer, he had sailed the New World's seas. Queen Elizabeth had encouraged English captains to prey on Spanish ships. And Newport had led an expedition that destroyed or captured 20 Spanish vessels and sacked four towns in the West Indies and Florida. He was an English hero. What the Spaniards thought of him is something else.

But the men and boys who climbed onto three small ships and set sail down the river Thames felt confident with Newport in command. What surprised them all were contrary winds.

They sailed into the Atlantic, and the winds blew them back to England. Out they went again—and back. For six weeks those strange winds blew, while the voyagers ate their precious food and got nowhere. Now there were grumblings. Some wished they'd never come. Do you think they were scared? Do you think they thought of turning back? Pretend you are a younker. Are you excited? Or afraid? Or both?

Short Rations

The ships of the day were brightly painted with striped masts, banners, and flags. But there was never really enough food aboard for the six- or eight-week voyage. Those who made it across were usually weak and hungry when they landed—if not dead or sick with scurvy. A sailor's song went like this:

We ate the mice, we ate the rats,
And through the hold we ran like cats.

This is supposed to be a three-toed sloth. The artist had probably never been to America, let alone seen a sloth, so he made up an idea of it from someone else's description.

Abundance means "plenty."

Ballast is a heavy substance carried in a boat to make it more stable in rolling seas. ("Ballast" is a good word to know; a dictionary will give you additional meanings.) The early ships that sailed to America carried soil as ballast. When they arrived in America, sailors dumped the ballast to make room for "New World" cargo. Scientists are now studying the long-term effects of that introduction of foreign beetles, worms, and bacteria into the American ecosystem. (What's an ecosystem?)

They had boarded ship in December 1606, but it was February of 1607 when, finally, they lost sight of England. Captain Newport soon had them in the Canary Islands, where the three ships took on fresh water and food. Then they were off to the islands of the West Indies, where they rested and prepared themselves.

For they understood, when they left the West Indian island of Martinique, that they were heading for little-known territory. They were to do something Englishmen had not done before: they were to start a colony on the mainland. Spain had grown rich because of her colonies. England would beat Spain at that game. These Englishmen were determined to enrich England—and themselves, too.

For a few of the voyagers there may have been something else besides gold that drew them to America: that was its beauty and abundance. Those who had seen the land wrote of birds and flowers and fish more gorgeous than one could imagine. A poet called Virginia "earth's only Paradise."

England seemed crowded. Timber was scarce and getting scarcer. Farmland was disappearing. London's streets were filled with beggars.

Might America's land and trees and soil be as valuable as the gold nuggets the adventurers thought they were sure to find? Could this New World become a land of hope and opportunity? There were some in England who thought so.

The colonists were certainly headed for a new life in Virginia—but not always a good one. Fliers like these were put out to attract more settlers. Sometimes they weren't very truthful.

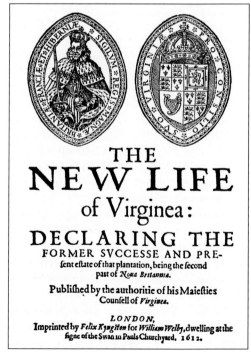

THE
NEW LIFE
of Virginea:
DECLARING THE
FORMER SVCCESSE AND PRE-
sent estate of that plantation, being the second
part of *Noua Britannia*.

Published by the authoritie of his Maiesties
Counsell of *Virginea*.

LONDON,
Imprinted by *Felix Kyngston* for *William Welby*, dwelling at the
signe of the Swan in Pauls Churchyard. 1612.

3 The First Virginians

The Powhatan had about 9,000 subjects; his land stretched from what is now Washington, D.C., to northern North Carolina.

When English parents told stories to their children, they often spoke of monsters, trolls, wild beasts, and witches. Those were savage stories, strange and disturbing. Since everyone knew there was a savage side to life, the stories had a kind of realness to them, even when they were make-believe.

But those weren't the only stories they told. There were tales of splendor and goodness, too. Every child heard the Bible's first story, which is of a Garden of Eden. Eden was a place of great beauty, a paradise. Many of the goodness stories were about sweet, simple people who lived in harmony with nature. And those stories seemed real, too, because there was much goodness in the world.

Did you know that the stories you read in childhood stay with you all your life? They influence adults more than most of them realize. So when English men and women learned of a land of great beauty, where people lived close to nature, many of the English thought of that land as paradise. They called the natives "savages," but meant the word kindly. The first English visitors to the New World described the Indians as "courteous" and "gentle" and "great."

But, later, when others met those great savages, they found they didn't always act as people do in storybooks. Soon some were calling them worse names than "savages." They called them "beasts." Some said they were servants of the devil. Others said they were part animal and part human.

But those people—the Indians—were just real people, like the English. They lived in families, in towns, governed by leaders. They farmed, hunted, played games, and fashioned beautiful objects.

Earthly Paradise

We have discovered... the goodliest soil under the cope of heaven, so abounding with sweet trees, that bring such sundry rich and pleasant gums, grapes of such greatness, as France, Spain, nor Italy have no greater....the continent is of huge and unknown greatness, and very well peopled and towned, though savagely, and the climate so wholesome, that we had not one sick since we landed here.

It was letters like this one, written by Ralph Lane in 1585, that made people want to go to the New World. Lane was a member of Raleigh's Roanoke Colony.

An **estuary** (ESS-tew-air-ee) is the body of water where the mouth of a river meets the sea.

The bear grease that the Indians rubbed on their bodies made their brown skin shine with a reddish glow. Europeans thought it really was red, and that was how the name "redskin," which many Europeans once used for Native Americans, came to be. It's based on a *misperception*, which is an error in the way things are seen.

Remember, horses first came to America with the Spanish conquistadors. Even 100 years later they were still a rarity.

Some of them were wise and some were foolish. Some were kind and some were mean. But most were a bit of all those things.

One of the most interesting Indians the English would meet was the Powhatan, the ruler or emperor of eastern Virginia. His real name was Wahunsonacock, and he had inherited an empire of five tribes. Through daring, strength and leadership, Powhatan soon held sway over dozens of villages and thousands of Indians. The English would call the Indians of his empire Powhatan Indians.

They were Woodland Indians, who spoke Algonquian (al-GON-kwee-un) dialects and hunted, fished, and farmed in a region of great abundance. The area surrounded the Chesapeake Bay and went west to mountain foothills and south to what would someday be North Carolina's border. It was a land of rivers, bays, and estuaries; of ducks, geese, wild turkeys, and deer; of fertile soil, fish, and shellfish; of wild berries, nuts, and grapes.

Powhatan's people raised vegetables—corn, beans, squash, and pumpkins—which was more than half the food they ate. Because they farmed, they lived in settled villages. Corn was their most important food. They ground it and made it into flat pancakes that served as bread or rice does in many other cultures. Aside from corn, the food they ate changed with the seasons: fresh vegetables in summer and fall; game in winter; and fish, stored nuts, and berries in the spring. (Spring was when corn supplies ran low and they sometimes went hungry.)

There was much small game in the region: raccoon, opossum, squirrel, turkey, and rabbit. But it was deer these Indians relied on most for food and clothing. Unfortunately, like people elsewhere, they overhunted; deer became scarce. And they knew if they roamed outside the Powhatan's territory—looking for better hunting grounds—they risked war with other tribes.

It was the men who hunted, fished, and fought. Women farmed. Men and women had set roles in this society and rarely changed them. Children helped their parents, played, and didn't go to work until they were young adults.

The boys often played in scarecrow houses that stood in the middle of the fields. From there they threw stones at rabbits or other animals that might nibble on the crops. It trained their throwing arms, and that helped when they became hunters. Little girls played with clay, made pots, and helped their mothers plant and cook. Boys and girls played running games. There were no horses (they hadn't arrived in this part of the New World yet), so fast runners were prized. Sometimes they would dress up like their parents—painting their bodies and wearing necklaces and bracelets of shells and beads and animal bones.

Men and women tattooed beautiful designs all over their bodies. Men sometimes hung animal claws, birds' wings, bats, even live green snakes around their necks. They rubbed themselves with bear grease—it repelled mosquitoes, kept them warm, and made their skin glisten in the sunshine. Most of the year these Indians needed little clothing, although in winter they wore deerskin garments and, sometimes, cloaks of feathers or fur.

Captain John Smith would never have been able to make this map of Virginia without help from the local Algonquian Indians, the Powhatans. You'll hear more about John Smith in Chapter 5.

Werowance is a Delaware Indian word that means, literally, "he is rich."

Powhatan was said to have 100 wives. One-third of his 9,000 subjects were warriors. Powhatan gave his decorated deerskin to Captain Christopher Newport. It is now in a museum in Oxford, England.

The Chesapeakes lived on land that is now included in the cities of Virginia Beach, Norfolk, Portsmouth, and Chesapeake.

The great Powhatan had a beautiful deerskin sewed with designs in lustrous pearls. Powhatan had stacks of deerskins and a store-house of corn, and he had copper and pearls. The tribes brought all this and more to him. It was tribute given to a ruler.

Each tribe had its own leader, called a *werowance* (WEER-ah-wunts), and also priests and healers and others with power. But the Powhatan was special. All those who met him noted it. He knew how to command, when to be stern and unforgiving and when to be understanding. The story was told of the time he visited the Potomacs (puh-TOW-mucks), who were under his rule. The young Potomac warriors came before him, and each told of awesome deeds of valor against fierce enemies or wild beasts of the forest.

Finally one young man stood before Powhatan and said, "I, my lord, went this morning into the woods and valiantly killed six muskrats. While that may be no more than boys do, it is true, while much you have heard is fable." When Powhatan heard that, he broke into laughter and gave a reward to the truth teller.

Powhatan's priests had foretold that his mighty empire would one day be destroyed by men from the east. The Chesapeakes, who lived by the ocean, were the easternmost of his tribes. Perhaps that is why, just before the 16th century turned into the 17th (in the European method of reckoning), Powhatan fought the mighty Chesapeake Indians and left them weak and powerless.

Powhatan didn't yet know that three small ships were heading for his realm. They were coming across the ocean from an island far to the east.

Virginian Indians cooking a stew of corn, fish, and beans. This picture was drawn at the end of the 16th century by John White.

24

4 English Settlers Come to Stay

The crown and coat of arms on the Virginia Company's seal show that it was granted by the king.

In Virginia, April is a sweet month. Strawberries and white dogwoods blossom below the green of tall pines. Redbuds are emerging, and so are grape leaves, honeysuckle, and wild roses.

It was thus in April of 1607, when three small ships landed at the mouth of the Chesapeake Bay. The ships were the *Susan Constant,* the *Discovery,* and the *Godspeed*, and they had been sent from England by a business corporation called the London Company.

They were the same three ships that left the docks on the river Thames. The voyagers had been told to look for gold and a river or passage that would go through the country to China and Japan. They were also to see if there were other ways to make money on this unknown continent.

The ships anchored near an elbow of beach they named Cape Henry (in honor of young Henry, the king's oldest son). Some of the mariners rowed to shore and set out exploring. "We could find nothing worth the speaking of, but fair meadows and goodly tall trees, with such fresh waters running through the woods, as I was almost ravished at the first sight thereof," wrote George Percy, who was one of the gentlemen adventurers.

On their way back to the ship the Englishmen were attacked by Indians, who came "creeping upon all fours...like bears, with their bows in their mouths," but when "they felt the sharpness of our shot, they retired into the woods with a great noise."

The local Indians knew about white men, and they didn't want them around. Spain—England's old enemy—had tried to start two colonies in the Chesapeake Bay area. An Indian prince from the re-

From the instructions *of the London Company to the First Settlers:* "When it shall please God to Send you on the Coast of Virginia you shall Do your best endeavour to find out a safe fort in the Entrance of some navigable River making Choice of Such a one as runneth furthest into the Land, and if you happen to Discover Divers [diverse] portable [navigable] Rivers and amongst them any one that hath two main branches if the Difference be not Great make Choice of that which bendeth most towards the Northwest for that way shall You soonest find the Other Sea."

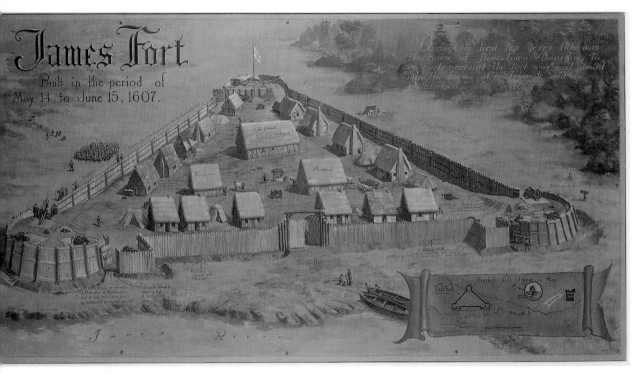

Jamestown, as it looked in 1607. The settlement is protected by a ditch and palisade (a high fence made of stakes) . A baking oven is outside the wall (why outside?). In the center is a church. Most of the houses have thatched roofs made from river grass or reeds, but some are covered with tree bark (an idea borrowed from the Indians). Today the place where Jamestown once stood is an active archaeological site. Archaeologists have located evidence of all three sides of the fort. You can also visit a reconstructed Jamestown nearby.

gion had been taken to Spain, baptized a Christian, educated, and returned to his people. That prince had far more schooling than most of the Englishmen who now wished to invade his land. The Englishmen didn't seem to know any of that. They thought of the Indians as savages.

The Englishmen spent a few weeks exploring the bay area. They feasted on strawberries ("four times bigger and better than ours in England"), ate oysters ("which were very large and delicate in taste"), and noticed grapevines ("in bigness as a man's thigh"). The oysters and mussels "lay on the ground as thick as stones; we opened

John Smith's portrait labels him "Admiral of New England." (Today *admiral* is spelled with one *l*. Do you see any other old-fashioned spellings?) Even if this wasn't an official title bestowed by the king, Smith deserved it: he not only explored and mapped Virginia but charted the New England coast from Cape Cod to Maine.

some, and found in many of them pearls…as for sturgeon [there were so many of these fish] all the world cannot be compared to it."

They planted a cross at Cape Henry, thanked God for their safe voyage, and watched as Captain Newport opened a sealed metal box. The box had been entrusted to him by the London Company. (Newport would soon sail back to England.) He opened the box and read six names and his own. They were to be members of a council and elect a president. One of the names was a surprise. It was John Smith; he was locked up in the ship's belly.

Smith was of yeoman (YO-mun) stock—and feisty; he was not one of the gentlemen. He had angered some of those gentlemen and they had put him in chains. They were planning to send him back to England. Now they would have to work with him.

The instructions in the box said they were to go inland, up a river, and find a suitable place for their colony. So they left the mouth of the Chesapeake Bay and sailed up a river they called the James, to a site they named Jamestown.

Several men, including John Smith and Christopher Newport, went on, up the James River, in search of a passage to China. They had no idea of the size of the country. When they saw breaking waves, they were sure they had found the western coast and the Pacific Ocean. John Smith wrote in his log of the "ocean ahead."

They soon discovered that the waves were caused by water tumbling over rapids in the river. They were at a site that would someday be the city of Richmond. The river would not let them go farther.

All those Jameses—the James River and Jamestown—were named to honor the new king, James I. When Queen Elizabeth died in 1603, still unmarried and childless, her cousin James was brought from Scotland to become king of the United Kingdom of Scotland and England.

King James had worked out a kind of deal with the Spaniards. It went like this: we English will stop raiding your ships if you Spaniards will promise not to attack our settlers. So the new settlers weren't as worried about Spanish attackers as they might have been in the 16th century. As it turned out, there may have been Spanish spies among them.

But it was gold that was on their mind when they reached Jamestown, and they soon began searching for it. They also built rough huts for shelter and a triangular fort for protection.

Jamestown was almost an island, with a narrow sandbar link to the mainland. It would be easy to defend against Indian raids or against ships, just in case the Spaniards did decide to come up the river. Besides, deep water touched the land. They could sail right up to the site and tie their ships to trees.

A *yeoman* was a small farmer who cultivated his own land (it was the area of land that was small, not necessarily the farmer). John Smith came from a yeoman background—he himself did other things with his life.

James I wasn't a bad man. He was very learned about many subjects, but couldn't deal with people very well. He was kind and generous to his friends, but tactless with those he didn't know. He disapproved of tobacco smoking because he thought it filthy and disgusting, but he never washed himself—and he had terrible table manners.

Christopher
Newport sailed back to England. The adventurers were on their own in America. Newport thought he had gold when he took a barrel of shiny earth back to England. It turned out to be "fool's gold" (iron pyrites).

From The Proceedings of the English Colony in Virginia, 1612: "There was no talk, no hope, no work, but dig gold, wash gold, refine gold, load gold, such a bruit [noise] of gold, as one mad fellow desired to be buried in the sands, lest they should by their art make gold of his bones."

As it turned out, they couldn't have picked a worse spot. The land was swampy, the drinking water was bad; it was hot in summer and bone-chilling in winter. The mosquitoes drove the settlers crazy and carried malaria germs.

They might have handled all that if they had been a decent bunch. But, for the most part, they were lazy and vain and fought among themselves. And their first two leaders were incompetent—which means they made a mess of the job.

All were men; they brought no women. Remember, most were gentlemen, with no training or taste for hard work. To be fair, they had been misled about the New World. They expected to find gold at their feet, and they wasted valuable time looking for it. And there wasn't a farmer among them.

To make things worse, the London Company, which had paid for the voyage, showed poor sense. It gave all the colonists salaries and did not allow them to own property. No one had a reason to work hard, because the hard workers got the same pay as those who did nothing.

Besides all that, they had bad luck—lots of bad luck. The worst may have been that they brought some English germs across the sea. One was a typhoid fever germ that killed many of them. Tidewater Virginia had other germs (especially dysentery germs) that made some sicken and die. The Indians killed still others. Some starved. What happened to those eager men and boys who had stood on London's docks in December? Fewer than half of them saw another December.

Yet the news wasn't all bad. This was the first English colony that survived in the New World. A few things had to go right to make that happen. One man, more than any other, helped make things go right. He was short, scrappy, red-bearded John Smith—who had come to Virginia in chains. He was Jamestown's third president and a born leader, even though many of the voyagers didn't like him.

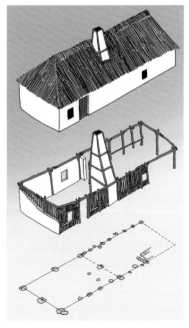

The settlers built small houses of wattle and daub—sticks and clay. They finished just in time to stave off their first Indian attack on May 26, 1607.

5 John Smith

Smith's Turk's head coat of arms. The Latin motto means "Vanquish and live."

The Jamestown colony might not have survived without Captain John Smith. He was a tough, no-nonsense man who worked hard and expected everyone else to do the same. Some people admired him; others hated him.

Pocahontas admired him and saved his life—twice. She was a bright-eyed Indian princess who was about 12 years old when the settlers first came to Virginia. The pale-skinned men and their strange ways intrigued her and she came to visit them often. Sometimes she just turned cartwheels in the middle of the Jamestown settlement; sometimes she brought food. It was John Smith who seemed to interest her most. In him she recognized a person whose intelligence and curiosity matched her own. Like her father, the great Powhatan, Smith seemed fearless.

Many of the settlers hated Smith, but they recognized that he was a leader. When he went back to England, even his enemies missed him. They said he was a braggart and that he couldn't possibly have done all the things he said he had done. He might have exaggerated a bit, but he really did do those things—like selling his schoolbooks and running away to sea. Or going off to Hungary to fight the Turks. There, on one bloody afternoon, Smith beheaded three Turks. A grateful Hungarian prince granted him a coat of arms with three Turks' heads emblazoned on it.

He wasn't a Hungarian hero for long; he was captured and sent as a slave to Constantinople, where a Turkish woman bought him. But her relatives didn't think much of him, and he was sold again. This time he killed his master, escaped, got thrown into the Mediterranean Sea, wandered through Russia, Poland, and Germany doing heroic things, and ended up in North Africa fighting pirates.

That first summer in Jamestown the settlers barely made it. "Our drink was water, our lodging, castles in the air," they reported. "With this lodging and diet, our extreme toil in bearing and planting palisades strained and bruised us….From May to September those that escaped lived upon sturgeon and sea crabs. Fifty in this time were buried."

In a page from John Smith's *Generall Historie of Virginia*, Smith lies captive before the Powhatan while Pocahontas pleads for his life to be spared.

Naturally someone who liked adventure the way John Smith did would be attracted to the adventure of a new world. Besides, like Sir Walter Raleigh, he had an idea that America could someday be an English land. He understood that there was more to be gained in the New World than gold. He realized that there were great opportunities for men and women with energy and courage.

John Smith was 28 when he took over the leadership of the Jamestown colony, and things were in a bad way. This was his motto: "If any would not work, neither should he eat." There were some grumblers, but everyone wanted to eat. So everyone worked.

Smith went and got food from the Indians. He learned their language and he learned the ways they hunted and fished. He had been a soldier and he was tough, but he was also fair and honest; the Powhatans soon understood that. They respected him and he respected them. They called him "werowance," or chief, of Jamestown. And that was what he was.

The Native Americans seemed undecided about how to act toward these strangers on their land. What would you have done if you were a Powhatan? How would you have treated the English leader, John Smith?

He had goods they wanted—axes and shovels and blankets—so they traded with him. He was a natural trader. He took his English goods to their villages and he came back to Jamestown with boatloads of corn. They told him of the prediction: that men from the east would destroy their villages. He told them he came in peace. Still, the Indians couldn't seem to make up their minds.

Sometimes they entertained Smith with dances and feasting. Other times they tried to kill him. Once he was brought before an Indian werowance and he expected to die. He pulled out his compass, showed how it worked, talked about the heavens and the earth, and soon had a tribe of friends. Another time he was taken to the great Powhatan, who seemed to have several Indian warriors ready to beat his brains out. But Pocahontas, who was the Powhatan's favorite daughter, came to his rescue. She

King Powhatan comands C: Smith to be flayne, his daughter Pokahontas beggs his life his thankfullne and how he subiected 30 of their kings, reade ye history,

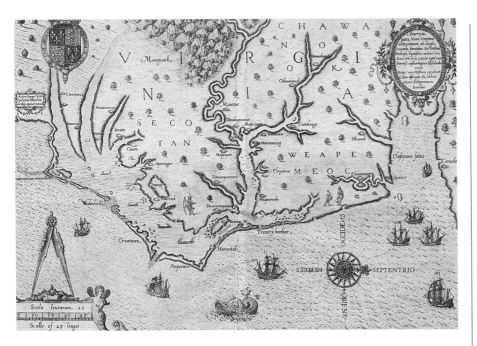

This engraving is a copy of a 1587 map of "Virginia" by John White that influenced mapmakers for decades. The area shown is now part of the Carolinas. At the mouth of the big river in the middle is Roanoke ("Roainac") Island.

put her head on Smith's, and Powhatan let him live. Was it a pre-arranged ceremony, or did Pocahontas actually save his life? No one knows for sure, but the Indians ended up adopting Smith into their tribe and making him an honorary chief. Now he was a member of Pocahontas's family.

When some other Indians tried to ambush Smith, Pocahontas warned him of the trap. Cats are supposed to have nine lives. John Smith had even more. While exploring the Chesapeake Bay, he was stung by a deadly stingray and was in such agony that he had his grave dug. He recovered—and ate the stingray. (The place where this happened, near the mouth of the Rappahannock River in Virginia, is now called Stingray Point.)

John Smith was asleep in his boat when some gunpowder exploded. It "tore the flesh from his body and thighs nine to ten inches square....To quench the tormenting fire, frying him in his clothes, he leaped over board in the deep river, where...he was near drowned." Smith was so badly wounded that he had to return to England. Pocahontas was told he was dead.

John Smith never got back to Virginia. But he did get to New England, which he named, and he mapped its coast as he had mapped much of Virginia. He wrote many books and became famous because of them. "I am no compiler by hearsay, but have been a real actor," he said. And so he was. We still read his books today, because they are so interesting.

Rough Justice

In some parts of our country, when a criminal is found guilty of a serious crime, such as murder, he can be sentenced to death by the judge. A death sentence is called capital punishment. How did capital punishment start in this country? The English brought the tradition with them. (Some Indian tribes practiced capital punishment, too.)

It didn't take long for the settlers to use capital punishment—a few months. The first execution was in the Jamestown colony in 1607. The victim was not a common criminal, but a member of a prominent English family and one of the seven-man ruling council of the Jamestown colony. His name was Captain George Kendall. His crime was treason. The colonists believed Kendall was a spy for the Spanish. Kendall tried to escape aboard the ship *Discovery,* but was captured and condemned to die. He was executed by a firing squad.

6 The Starving Time

It didn't matter how many pigs there were if you couldn't get out to kill them.

Before John Smith left for England, he counted the food in the storehouses at Jamestown. "Ten weeks' provisions in the stores," he wrote. It was October of 1609. Was there enough food to get through the winter? Smith seemed to think so. He expected the Indians to supply corn, as they had before. Besides, the settlers had hens, chickens, and goats—and so many pigs that a nearby island was called Hog Island. In addition to all that, the woods abounded with deer, rabbit, and squirrel; the river was thick with fish, frogs, and oysters.

There were new people in Jamestown, brought from England by Captain Newport. Two were women: Mrs. Thomas Forrest, the wife of a settler, and her maid, Anne Burras. Anne Burras's arrival led to a happy event, which a poet, Stephen Vincent Benét, imagined three and a half centuries later:

> —And the first white wedding held on Virginia ground
> Will marry no courtly dame to a cavalier
> But Anne Burras, lady's maid, to John Laydon, laborer,
> After some six weeks' courtship—a Fall wedding
> When the leaves were turning and the wild air sweet,
> And we know no more than that but it sticks in the mind,
> For they were serving-maid and laboring man
> And yet, while they lived (and they had not long to live),
> They were half of the first families in Virginia.

The Laydons soon had a baby. Can you guess what they named her?

Still more colonists arrived. Now there were many mouths to feed, but most people were optimistic. Everyone thought Jamestown had seen the worst of its troubles.

The Laydons named their baby Virginia.

Everyone was wrong. That winter of 1609–1610 was as awful a time as any in American history. It was called the Starving Time.

Captain George Percy, who was now governor of the Jamestown colony, said the settlers felt the "sharp prick of hunger which no man can truly describe but he who hath tasted the bitterness thereof."

They ate "dogs, cats, rats and mice," said Percy, as well as "serpents and snakes" and even boots and shoes.

> There were never Englishmen left in a foreign country in such misery....Our food was but a small can of barley, sod in water, to five men a day...our men night and day groaning in every corner of the fort most pitiful to hear...some departing out of the world, many times three or four in a night; in the morning their bodies trailed out of their cabins like dogs to be buried.

What happened? Some historians say the Starving Time was an Indian war against the English invaders. The Powhatan may have decided to get rid of the settlers by starving them. He wouldn't trade with them. He laid siege to Jamestown. That means armed Indians wouldn't let anyone in or out. The settlers couldn't hunt or fish. They could hardly get to their chickens and pigs. The gentlemen ate the animals that were inside the stockade—without much sharing. That made the others angry. Soon there was nothing for anyone to eat.

A few escaped. "Many of our men this Starving Time did run away unto the savages, whom we never heard of after," Percy wrote.

In London the Spanish ambassador learned of the misery in Virginia. (Some said there was a Spanish spy at Jamestown, but a spy wasn't needed; the disaster was common news in London.) The ambassador urged the Spanish king to send a ship and finish off the English colony. The Spaniards could have done it easily. So could the Indians, who never went that far. (What do you think American history might have been like if either of those things had happened?)

Finally, in May 1610, two English ships tied up at Jamestown's docks. Of the 500 people who were in Jamestown in October, when John Smith left for London, only 60 were still alive.

Would Powhatan have behaved differently if John Smith had been around? This is one of those historical questions that are interesting to think about.

When the new governor, Sir Thomas Gates, arrived in Jamestown after the terrible winter, it looked to him "rather as the ruins of some ancient fortification than that any people living might now inhabit it."

The Indians had power, the settlers were starved (although they look well-fed in this picture). One man was so hungry he seems to have eaten his dead wife.

7 A Lord, A Hurricane, A Wedding

A modern study of cypress tree rings in Tidewater, Virginia shows stunted growth between 1606 and 1612. It was the worst drought in nearly 800 years and not the best time to try and grow crops.

A *flotilla* is a group or small fleet of ships. *Unholsome* is the old spelling. Today we would write it as *unwholesome*. (See opposite page.)

On board ship the expression *all hands* means "all people."

Shakespeare wrote a play, *The Tempest*, after reading about the storm that wrecked the *Sea Venture* off Bermuda.

The people who walked off the two English ships in May of 1610 were horrified by what they saw. Jamestown was a wreck. Fear of Indians had kept everyone inside the fort through the cold winter. The settlers had been forced to burn their buildings to keep warm. By spring there were hardly any buildings left. The few survivors looked like skeletons. "We are starving!" they gasped.

Those on the ships had been through an ordeal themselves. On their way to Jamestown yellow fever broke out. There was no treatment for the disease then, so people died and their bodies had to be thrown overboard. They were barely over the epidemic when they ran into a fierce Atlantic hurricane.

Do you know what a hurricane at sea is like? Here it is: phenomenal, roaring winds; towering, crashing waves; fierce, crackling lightning; ear-splitting thunder. One ship, the *Catch,* went down; all hands lost. The *Sea Venture,* with sturdy Christopher Newport as captain, was wrecked on coral rocks. Luckily the rocks were within wading distance of the island of Bermuda. If you have to be shipwrecked, Bermuda is not a bad place to be. The voyagers set to work and built two new ships, the *Patience* and the *Deliverance.* They were eager to get to Jamestown and start a new life there. They imagined that the colony was thriving.

You know what they found at Jamestown. Are you surprised that they decided to leave? They had had enough of this New World. On June 7, 1610, everyone marched out of the wretched settlement, climbed aboard ship, said, "Goodbye, Jamestown," and headed for England.

They didn't get far. Lord de la Warr (what state is named for him?) was on his way up the James River with a big flotilla and 300 settlers. He was the new governor, and a good one. He made them turn around and start Jamestown again.

Lord de la Warr called Jamestown "a very…unholsome place." Still, he stayed. The colonists set to work. They cleaned, fixed, and built. The Indians continued to make their lives miserable, but now the settlers fought back. Then a few Indians and a few colonists began to trade. Some Englishmen began going up the rivers to trade with distant tribes. Tom Savage, who had lived as an adopted son of the Powhatan, was able to interpret for both peoples.

More ships came. Artisans and laborers arrived, together with "gentlemen of quality" and more livestock.

And still many died, not from starvation but from the diseases that abounded in the damp atmosphere at Jamestown.

Ætatis suæ 21. Aº. 1616.

Matoaks als Rebecka daughter to the mighty Prince Powhatan Emperour of Attanoughkomouck als Virginia converted and baptized in the Christian faith, and Wife to the wor.ll M.r Tho: Rolff.

Lord de la Warr was one of those who got sick. He went back to England, and Sir Thomas Dale took command. Dale understood the need for a healthier settlement. So one was built at a great bend of the James River, near the falls that John Smith had mistaken for the Pacific Ocean. The new settlement was named Henrico, for Henry, the king's oldest son. It had "two fair rows of houses," three "store houses," a hospital, and a "fair and handsome church." All of it was constructed in four months—Thomas Dale saw to that. Dale was a stern man, strict and religious. Anyone who swore, broke a rule, or didn't work got whipped. Three offenses and you were executed. You can see why everyone worked.

Henrico soon had a visitor. Unfortunately she was dragged there. Her name was Pocahontas.

The Indian princess was visiting some Potomac Indians when an Englishman, on a trading expedition, lured her onto his ship and wouldn't let her off. He took Pocahontas as a hostage to Henrico,

Pocahontas had two names. Her real name was Matoax. It means "little snow feather." Pocahontas, her nickname, means "playful." Then Pocahontas married John Rolfe. She was baptized and given a third name: Rebecca.

What is a hostage? *Where do we hear the word today?*

35

English noblemen like Lord
de la Warr *(above)* often have
two names: a title (such as
Lord de la Warr) and their
own given and family names.
Lord de la Warr's name was
Thomas West.

held her there, taught her the Christian religion, and gave her a new name, Rebecca.

Now it happened that a young Englishman named John Rolfe had a plantation nearby. He fell in love with the beautiful Indian princess and she fell in love with him.

Rolfe wrote to Governor Dale, asking to marry Pocahontas "to whom my heart and best thoughts are, and have a long time been so entangled, and enthralled in so intricate a labyrinth, that I was even wearied to unwind myself thereout."

It was a fine wedding, and it took place in the church at Jamestown. The Powhatan wouldn't come. Perhaps he feared a trap, or perhaps he was sad to see his daughter leave the Indian world. He sent two of her brothers and her uncle, Chief Opechancanough. They came wearing handsome garments of leather, furs, feathers, and beads. Pocahontas's marriage helped bring peace between Indians and colonists.

Soon Pocahontas had a baby and John Rolfe was so proud he took his family to England. There Pocahontas charmed everyone—even King James. (And King James didn't charm easily; he was a bit of a grouch.) The English people called her Lady Rebecca and treated her as the princess that she was. People fussed over her and pointed to her when she walked down the street. She was a celebrity. But she must have longed for a familiar face, someone she could talk to in her native language. And then she learned that John Smith was alive! She expected him to come and see her at once, but he didn't. She waited and waited. Finally, when he did come, she was so hurt that at first she wouldn't even talk to him.

John Smith had been honored by her father. He was a member of her family. How could he ignore her? But Smith seemed different, and awkward. Perhaps he didn't know how to be her brother now that she wore a long dress like a proper Englishwoman. Perhaps Pocahontas herself didn't know in which world she belonged. When John Rolfe decided to go back to Virginia, she didn't want to go. She didn't feel at all well when they boarded a ship and sailed down the Thames River. Before they reached the open sea, she was so sick that her husband took her off the ship. It was smallpox. Pocahontas died, and was buried in the churchyard at Gravesend, a town that is now part of London, but in those days was in the country. She was 22.

Let's take ourselves back in time to Jamestown. The Powhatan has not yet learned that his beloved daughter is dead. When he does, the peace will be finished. The Indians will attack. They will kill settlers, burn their homes, and try to drive them from the land. But now, for a while, there is calm.

8 A Share in America

Indian corn and an "Indian" jaybird illustrated a booklet advertising the New World's attractions.

More English ships sail for Jamestown…and more settlers…and more again. An English poet writes:

> *God will not let us fail.*
> *Let England know our willingness,*
> *For that our work is good;*
> *We hope to plant a nation*
> *Where none before hath stood.*

English men and women begin to spread out beyond Jamestown. They are settling in the New World.

It seems as if everyone in England wants to be part of the American adventure. And everyone can be part of it by giving money to the Virginia Company—the new name of the London Company—the outfit that is paying for all the exploration. The Virginia Company is a stock company, just like stock companies today. You can buy shares in the company; your money helps pay the company's expenses; if there are profits you will get your share of them.

Lords, knights, gentlemen, merchants, and plain citizens buy shares in the Virginia Company. The Archbishop of Canterbury, the Earl of Pembroke, famous Londoners, and unknown squires—all are among the investors.

The Spanish ambassador in London writes to King Philip that "fourteen earls and barons have given 40,000 ducats, the merchants give much more, and there is no poor little man nor woman who is not willing to subscribe something… much as I have written to your Majesty of the determina-

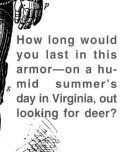

How long would you last in this armor—on a humid summer's day in Virginia, out looking for deer?

37

The early promoters of the Virginia settlements had an uphill job, for everyone in England had heard of the terrible experiences of the first Jamestown colonists.

Class System

To some extent, the English will succeed in bringing their class society to Virginia. An upper class of landowning aristocrats will be the leaders. There will be a middle class of yeomen owning small farms. The lower class will be made up of indentured servants and slaves. The Virginia aristocracy will differ from the English aristocracy in an important way: the idea that gentlemen should not work will be rejected in the New World.

tion they have formed here to go to Virginia, it seems to me that I still fall short of the reality."

Some of those people expect to make money from the gold that they are sure will be found. Many just want to take part in a great national venture. Some want to save the North American Indians from the Spaniards. In England people have read stories about the way some Spaniards treat the Indians: how they make them dig gold, how they starve them, how they make slaves of them. Good people are horrified.

They don't realize that English men and women are just like Spanish men and women. Some are good, some are not so good.

Some of the not-so-goods come to Jamestown. It is understandable that they would. Some people leave England because they are brave and curious; some are looking for riches or a better life. But others come because they are criminals and unwanted in England.

An Englishman named William Tucker arranges a powwow with the Pamunkey Indians. He tells them he wants to sign a peace treaty. The Indians give him corn and sign the treaty. Then Tucker suggests they all celebrate by drinking wine. He doesn't tell them he has poisoned the wine: 200 Indians die.

Other Englishmen attack and burn Indian villages, sometimes for no apparent reason, sometimes to revenge the Starving Time.

Meanwhile, back in England, some people are writing of Virginia as a place where Native Americans and Europeans can live side by side and learn about the best of each other's culture. They talk of In-

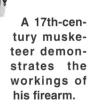

A 17th-century musketeer demonstrates the workings of his firearm.

dians going to English schools and Englishmen being trained in Indian ways. An English school for the Indians is started at Henrico.

The people who have these fine ideas aren't concerned with gold. They picture an ideal nation where people live happily tending gardens and working at jobs like blowing glass, forging iron, and making perfume.

But the people with the good ideas stay in England. They are making plans for others, and that usually doesn't work. Those who come to Virginia aren't interested in ideal societies. Most have come for adventure, or to get rich, or to get away from their problems in Europe. After they get here, they find it a lot of trouble just trying to stay alive.

Of the first 10,000 settlers who land in Virginia, only 2,000 survive. (What percentage is that?) They die of disease, Indian attack, and hunger.

Hunger? In a land of plenty? Yes, even in a land of plenty you need to know how to hunt, or fish, or raise crops, or gather food. You need to adapt yourself to new conditions. If ever you go to a strange land, try and see how the natives live. You will learn a lot. That is what John Smith did. Some of the gentlemen do not learn. They try to be Englishmen in a wilderness.

Picture Jamestown in August. If there were a thermometer it would register 98°F. The English gentlemen sometimes wear 60-pound suits of metal armor. That makes them feel safe from Indian arrows. Under the armor they wear wool clothing, because that is what they have always worn in England. Now, imagine chopping down a tree in that outfit: your hands are blistered—you've never held an ax before—and the biting flies are driving you crazy. Are you beginning to get angry? Look at the swampy ground. It's full of snakes and frogs and bugs—not the gold you were promised.

So you throw down your ax and decide to go hunting. Maybe you can kill a deer—you've seen plenty of animals. But that heavy musket is a problem. It makes a loud noise when it goes off, and you can't seem to hit anything with it, certainly not anything moving. A musket isn't accurate, like a rifle—but rifles haven't been invented yet. (A musket isn't as accurate as a bow and arrow, either.)

There is another problem I haven't mentioned. You stink. You haven't had a bath—ever. (Well, if you were daring, you may have had one last year.) Baths are considered unhealthy. Now remember, it is August and you are wearing all those clothes. Phew! If the deer aren't scared off by your loud, clanking armor, the smell will soon have them running. Indian hunters are quiet as falling leaves. They take off most of their clothes in summer; they bathe in the river. It is no wonder the Indians think the Englishmen are savages.

Tidewater Virginia's diseases are new to the Europeans and kill many of them. But the Virginia diseases are not as deadly to the newcomers as the European diseases are to the Native Americans. Tribes are being wiped out.

Wait a few chapters and you'll see: there were fewer deaths in New England. The colder climate seemed to keep some germs under control, and the community there was better organized.

9 Jamestown Makes It

Taino Indians of the Bahamas grew tobacco; Spaniards copied its Taino name, *tabaco*.

At last the settlers found gold. Gold in the form of a leaf. A leaf that dried to a golden brown and could be put in a pipe and smoked. That tobacco leaf made people rich; it made the Virginia colony prosperous.

King James hated tobacco. He thought it unhealthy and he was right. But there is a limit to what even kings can do when money is involved. Growing tobacco was very profitable, especially after John Rolfe, Pocahontas's husband, developed a sweet variety that was all the rage in England.

But there was a problem. It takes hard fieldwork to grow tobacco, and Englishmen were not anxious to work in the fields. Besides that, even the best farmers could tend only a limited number of tobacco plants. So if you wanted to get rich by growing tobacco, you had to have people working for you. The more people you had, the more tobacco you could grow. The more tobacco you sold, the richer you would get. That made servants and other workers very valuable in Virginia.

So the Virginians did everything they could think of to get people to come to America. But since most of the settlers were dying, it wasn't easy. Most of those who came were poor or in trouble with the law.

The colonists were so eager to have workers that they were willing to pay for them. Sometimes they paid so much money that ship's captains would kidnap people from the streets of London.

Many of those who came to Virginia started out as indentured servants, and usually they were very poor. Some of them were criminals who were let out of jail if they would agree to come to the colony. You can understand that most people didn't want to go to a land where so many people were dying. The indentured servants

European tobacco merchants advertised their product with fanciful pictures of the exotic New World and its inhabitants.

didn't have enough money to pay their boat fare to the New World. They had to work for the person who paid the fare. They worked from four to seven years before they were free. That was their time of indenture. Some indentured servants were treated just like slaves.

What about slaves? Were there slaves in Jamestown? Yes, there were. Slavery in the English colonies began without much thought, which is the way bad things often begin.

In 1619 a Dutch ship brought a boatload of Africans to Jamestown. These people had been kidnapped from their homes by African traders and sold to the ship's captain. He in turn sold them to the Virginia settlers. Those first African Virginians were treated like indentured servants. After a few years of working for someone else, they became free. Soon there were Africans who had land of their own—and servants, too. But some colonists got the idea of making black people into slaves. That way they wouldn't have to keep buying workers on the docks. It must have seemed a good idea to people who were desperate for workers. Tobacco agriculture demanded much labor as well as a lot of land. There was an abundance of land in America, but few people willing to do hard work in the fields.

When Indians were enslaved, they ran away. It was difficult for the blacks to run away. Where would they go? Everything was new and strange to them. Gradually laws were passed to trap black people in slavery. It was the beginning of a way of life that would bring misery to many, many innocent African-Americans.

Why did Europeans go to the trouble of importing African slaves instead of forcing Native Americans to work for them? Because the Indians didn't make good slaves. They got sick from Old World diseases, and often they just ran away.

How Tobacco Beat Out Silk

King James wanted to start a silk industry in Virginia, and the colonists needed a doctor. Dr. Lawrence Bohune was the perfect man for both tasks: he was a physician and he had scientific curiosity. He planned to experiment with silkworms and also to investigate the native herbs and plants the Indians used for healing purposes. Bohune had visited the colony in 1610 as Lord de la Warr's personal doctor, and he had impressed everyone with his good sense. So when he made plans to bring silkworms to Virginia, the king and the settlers were pleased.

In 1620, Dr. Bohune set sail for Jamestown on a ship named the *Margaret and John*. (It was the very year the Pilgrims arrived in Massachusetts Bay.) After 11 tough weeks at sea, the small ship

The silkworm is the caterpillar stage of the silk moth. The material the silkworms spin into their cocoons is what makes the silk thread.

reached the West Indies and found itself facing two armed Spanish warships. The Spaniards fired their cannons. The English ship was outclassed, a cannonball struck the good doctor, and he fell into the arms of the captain. "Oh, Dr. Bohune, what a disaster this is!" said the captain. With his last breath the doctor replied, "Fight it out, brave man, the cause is good, and the Lord receive my soul."

When the damaged ship limped into Jamestown, the doctor was dead and the silkworms had all been lost at sea. King James had hoped that silk would replace tobacco as Virginia's gold. It never did.

10 1619— A Big Year

If the colony was to survive, it had to grow. That meant sending women as well as men.

The House of Burgesses is made up of Anglican landowners elected for two year terms. (You had to own land and be a member of the Church of England to vote). They levy taxes. Collecting taxes, rather than having them controlled by the royal governor, gives the Burgesses power. They won't want to give up that power.

Some of the early laws passed by the burgesses (see the next page) of Virginia forbade pastimes that were thought immoral, like playing cards or dice. If you got caught not going to church, you were fined 50 pounds of tobacco—about a week's wages. It was against the law to swear, too.

The English found those first years in America really hard. Remember, four out of five of the first 10,000 settlers died soon after they arrived in Virginia. Most people would have given up—but not the English. The harder the challenge, the more determined they became.

The year 1619 was a turning point. After 1619 you could tell the English were in America to stay. It was a year of many firsts in Virginia:

• first boatload of Africans
• first boatload of women
• first labor strike
• first time English settlers are allowed to own land
• first elected lawmakers.

That is a lot for any year. You already know about that boatload of Africans. Now, about those women. They, too, were sold on the docks.

"Do you want a wife?"

"It will cost you 120 pounds of tobacco."

Those are the terms when a shipload of women arrives in Jamestown in 1619. These are poor women who are unable to pay the cost of their Atlantic journey. They want a new life in this new land. The lonely men want wives. There will be instant romances on the docks. What do you think of these women? Do you think they are scared? Courageous? Crazy?

A few white women have already been to Jamestown, but sending an entire boatload of them to be wives means that the English plan to stay and make homes in America. The French, who are settling in the North, are less likely to send women. Still, in 1619, the men in Jamestown outnumber the women by eight to one.

Some historians think the reason there was much violence in Jamestown was because many more men than women and children lived there. Do you think that is true? Do you think men living alone fight more than people in families? That is something to discuss.

In 1619 the Virginia Company lets the settlers have land of their own. That gives them a reason to work hard.

The first workers' strike in British America happens in 1619. Polish workers at Jamestown, who are glassmakers, demand the same rights as Englishmen. They get those rights and go back to work. There are Poles, Dutch, Germans, and Italians at Jamestown. Do you think it strange that they all want English rights? What about their own rights?

The answer to that is very simple. English men and women have more rights and freedom than people do in other European nations. They expect those same rights in America and so do people from other nations who come to the English colonies.

John Smith said no one would come to the New World "to have less freedom." The Charter of the Virginia Company said, "all and every of the persons...which shall dwell and inhabit within every or any of the said several colonies and plantations, and every of their children...shall have and enjoy all liberties...as if they had been abiding and born, within this our realm of England." That means that nobody will lose freedom if he moves from England to America.

In 1619, a group of lawmakers—known as "burgesses"—is elected to make laws. They form an assembly called the House of Burgesses. In England laws are made by Parliament. The House of Burgesses gives the Virginians their own form of Parliament. That has never happened in a colony before.

By the way, do you know what a colony is?

A colony is land controlled by a distant, or foreign, nation. In the 17th century many European nations have colonies in America as well as in other parts of the world. Those colonies are not all alike. In the Spanish colonies no Europeans except Spaniards are allowed to settle. France admits only Catholics. The English colonies have open doors.

Think about that for a minute. That decision, way back in the 1600s, to let all kinds of people settle in the English colonies, made a big difference to our country. We would become a pluralistic society. (What does that mean?)

After seven years' work, those who wanted were given their own land. Captain Smith said, "When our people were fed out of the common store, and laboured jointly together, glad was he who could slip from his labour, or slumber over his tasks, he cared not how; nay, the most honest among them would hardly take so much true paines in a week, as now for themselves they will do in a day."

A *realm* is the kingdom or country where a ruler holds sway.

Abiding means permanent or lasting.

A Hostage Swap

In 1611, Captain John Clark was a pilot on one of three ships bound for Virginia. (Like an airplane pilot, a ship's pilot is expected to guide his craft safely.) Clark and his ships (Christopher Newport was in charge of the expedition) made it to Virginia. They hadn't been there long when a Spanish ship sailed into Chesapeake Bay. A Spanish officer came ashore and was taken hostage. To get even, the Spaniards captured Clark and sailed off to Spain. Five years later the two prisoners were exchanged in London. In 1620, the Virginia Company asked John Clark to pilot a ship to Virginia. It was the *Mayflower,* and it didn't quite reach its destination.

The Virginia Company was so eager to get women to come to America that it sometimes resorted to buying girls from their families or even kidnapping them from their homes.

Now that you know about colonies, let's get back to the House of Burgesses. In the 17th century, laws for colonies were made in the home country, or by appointed governors and their councils. The House of Burgesses changed that.

England was letting colonists make laws for themselves. That was a big first in history. (An English governor did have *veto power* over the burgesses. What is a veto? Okay, you can do some work. Go to the dictionary and look that word up. The governor didn't use the veto very often.)

This is something you should remember: the House of Burgesses, formed in 1619, gave America its first representative government. It was the beginning of self-government in America.

Whoops! Hold on, that isn't quite true. Some Indian tribes had representative government. The House of Burgesses was the first representative assembly in the European colonies.

It was only a dozen years since those three small ships were tied to the trees at Jamestown and the English colonists were doing something very unusual. They were making laws for themselves.

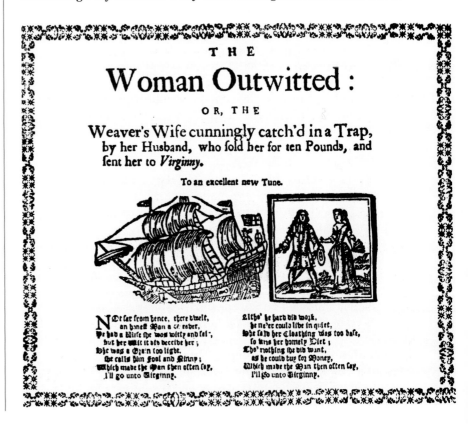

THE

Woman Outwitted:

OR, THE

Weaver's Wife cunningly catch'd in a Trap, by her Husband, who fold her for ten Pounds, and fent her to *Virginny.*

To an excellent new Tune.

11 Indians vs. Colonists

If the European settlements were to grow, they had to have the Indians' land. And the Indians weren't about to give it up easily.

The Powhatan

Indians played football with a small ball and a goal. The men played one set of rules, the women and children another. But for all the players, speed and dexterity were important. The Indians also enjoyed a game called "chunkey," which was played with a disk-shaped stone and slim poles eight or ten feet long. The idea was to roll the disk as far as possible and then throw the pole and try to hit it— or knock your opponent's pole away from its target disk.

From the time of Columbus the pattern was the same. The newcomers and the Indians would meet as friends and trade with each other. Then something would happen. Often an Indian was killed or sold into slavery, and the Indians would strike back. Sometimes they showed remarkable patience. Sometimes they were just waiting for the right moment. For the Native Americans were much like the New Americans: good and bad, fierce and gentle. Warriors on both sides went too far. The massacres were horrible.

At first the Indian leaders tried to live in peace with the settlers. But some of them realized that it would not work, that it would be the end of Indian ways. The Europeans used up land. They cut the forests and filled the land with people. Indians were hunters. To keep their way of life, the woods had to be protected. Wild animals need woods to live in, and hunters need wild animals.

Most Europeans understood that, too. One Virginia governor said, "Either we must clear the Indians out of the country, or they must clear us out." The members of the House of Burgesses ordered three expeditions to drive out the Indians "in order that they have no chance to harvest their crops or rebuild their wigwams."

There was another problem: arrogance (which means thinking you are better than others). In the 17th century arrogance was often tied to religion.

What do you think about this Native American cartoonist's version of the Pilgrims' Thanksgiving story?

Fields of Blood

Not all white people feared and hated Indians. John Lawson, a traveler in Carolina in 1700, wrote in a book about his journey: "We look upon them with Scorn and Disdain, [yet] ...for all our Religion and Education, we possess more Moral Deformities and Evils than these savages do....We make way for a Christian Colony through a Field of Blood, and defraud, and make away with those that one day may be wanted in this world." *John Lawson founded a new settlement himself. He was later captured and killed by Tuscarora Indians.*

This engraving, called *William Penn's Treaty with the Indians,* is based on a famous picture painted by Benjamin West in 1771. Edward Hicks borrowed some of West's ideas for his picture of the same event, shown on page 108.) Artists often had engravings made of their most popular works. Engraving was cheap: it allowed ordinary people who couldn't afford oil paintings to have art in their homes, and it allowed artists to reach a wider public. Why do you think this image—of whites and Indians at peace—was popular enough to be engraved?

Many Christians believed that anyone who was not Christian must be inferior. (The Aztecs believed those who weren't Aztec were inferior.)

Before long, that arrogance would become racism. Some whites believed themselves better than all Indians. Some believed themselves better than all blacks. History shows that racists are troublemakers and often the worst of their own race. There were bigots and racists in early America and they made trouble. Some of them wanted to kill all the Indians. (And some Indians wanted to kill all whites.)

However, the real problem was the fight for control of land. Even when Indians and settlers were friendly, it usually didn't last long. The newcomers wanted Indian land, and naturally the Indians didn't want to give it up. Some fair-minded white leaders respected the Indians and wanted to share the land, but they were never able to control the land-hungry settlers.

In 1737 the Delaware Indian chief Lappawinsoe signed an agreement that gave Pennsylvania colonists all the land they could cover on foot in a day and a half. Instead of walking leisurely, as the Indians expected, the colonists sent runners. Lappawinsoe was shocked and felt the Indians had been swindled.

12 Massacre in Virginia, Poverty in England

Opechancanough was a sachem, an important Indian chief and wise man.

Just when things seemed to be going well for the colonists, Pocahontas's uncle, the sachem Opechancanough, decided to try to get rid of them all. Some historians think that Opechancanough was the Indian prince who had been taken to Spain by Spanish priests, educated, and returned to his people. Whether he was or not, everyone agrees that he was intelligent and crafty, and that he hated the white men who were stealing his land.

In 1622 Opechancanough was an old man. Perhaps he thought it was his last chance to save his people. So he planned a great massacre. Indians knocked on the colonists' doors—pretending to be friendly—and then they murdered and scalped. They might have killed everyone if an Indian boy, Chanco, hadn't warned the men and women at Jamestown. Chanco had been treated kindly by the settlers and had become a Christian. The settlements outside Jamestown didn't get warned. Hundreds of English men, women, and children were killed in the Great Massacre of 1622.

King James was upset; there were too many deaths in Virginia. He set up a government investigation, and then he closed down the Virginia Company. The stockholders were wiped out; their stock was now worthless. King James took Virginia; it became a royal colony. Actually, the king didn't spend much time thinking about the Virginia colony; it was too far away. And he had problems, big problems, at home.

James believed that God had given him the right to rule—he called it "divine right." He thought that divine right meant he could do almost anything he wanted to. Parliament didn't agree, and Parliament controlled

Opechancanough never gave up. In 1644 his warriors attacked Jamestown again. He was so old and feeble he had to be carried about on a bed. Attendants held his eyelids open so he could see. But his mind had not lost its power.

To *massacre* (MASS-uh-ker) means to "kill brutally" and often in large numbers.

After the Jamestown Massacre the English had an excuse for killing Indians, and the bloodshed became intense. Killings were followed by revenge raids, more killings, and more revenge—on both sides.

In what languages was the Bible first written? See if you can find the answer.

To **dispute** means to "argue." To **harangue** means to "talk or lecture someone very forcefully." **Drivel** is stupid talk.

Bibles and Books

The King James Bible is made up of two parts: the Old Testament and the New Testament. These books, or parts of them, have other names, too. The Old Testament is also the *Hebrew Bible;* and the first five books (do you know their names?) in the Old Testament make up the Jewish *Torah.* The Greek name for the first five books is the *Pentateuch* (PEN-tuh-tewk). The first four books of the New Testament are the *Gospels.* Another name for the King James Bible is the "Authorized Version"—because its publication was authorized by the king himself.

most of the money in England. Parliament wouldn't give James the cash he wanted. Things got edgy.

James was a thoughtful man who might have made a fine professor. While he was on the throne the Bible was translated into English. That translation is called the "King James Bible." It was read in most Protestant churches in America until the 20th century. Many people think it the most beautiful translation ever.

But what England needed was a strong political leader, not a professor. One historian said King James was "two men—a witty, well-read scholar who wrote, disputed and harangued, and a nervous, drivelling idiot who acted." King Henry IV of France called him "the wisest fool in Christendom." James just wasn't the right type to be a king. He was in the wrong profession.

Let's get into a time capsule and take a look at King James's realm. Things are not going well at all. Farmers, who rent land from the rich landowning lords, are being thrown off their farms. The landlords want the land because of the new craze for sheep raising.

For some reason no one quite understands, the population is growing faster than it has ever done before. Jobs are hard to find. London and the countryside are full of beggars and starving people. Some of them climb on ships and pray for luck and a better life in the New World. Boatloads of people begin crossing the ocean.

Many of those who sail are convicts let out of jail if they will make the voyage. Englishmen write of America as a place to send their poor and troubled.

Some of the settlers are orphans. Many are very young. Heat and germs and Indians will kill most of them, yet they keep coming. Some prosper.

By midcentury (which century?) there are brick houses at Jamestown, a brick church, a fine State House, and plenty of food. For the European settlers, the American Dream has begun. Those who are tough and work hard will find in America a land of opportunity, like no land before it.

48

Opechancanough and his warriors attacked Jamestown on March 22, 1622. They killed nearly a third of the town's 1,200 inhabitants. It wasn't as one-sided as you might think from the picture. Afterwards, the settlers destroyed many of the Indians' villages, and their crops, too.

America, Land of the Free

From its beginnings, America was a land of freedom and opportunity for all. True or false?

The answer is FALSE.

For many of us, America was a land of humiliation and enslavement.

Africans came to the New World not because they wanted to but because they were taken from their homes by men with powerful weapons. When they protested, they were beaten and killed.

There was big money in it for those who stole them. There was big money in it for those who transported them. There were profits and an easy life for those who bought them.

Slavery was as old as history's records. Probably older. When Moses led the Israelites out of Egypt, they were escaping slavery. The ancient Greeks and Romans kept slaves. But in olden days, slaves were usually the booty of war. If you were captured in battle, you might end up a slave of the enemy. Slavery had nothing to do with skin color. Slaves were sometimes allowed to buy their freedom. Children of slaves were not always enslaved.

It was a Portuguese prince who got the African slave trade started in Europe. Remember Prince Henry the Navigator? In 1442 one of his ships arrived in Portugal with 10 captured Africans. The Portuguese were looking for ways to make money. Africans were good workers. Selling them as slaves would be a profitable business. Prince Henry gave those ten black Africans as a gift to the Roman Catholic Pope. The Pope gave Portugal the right to trade in Africa. But by 1455 the slave trade had become so abusive that Prince Henry tried to stop it. It was too late.

When the New World was discovered, workers were needed to mine its resources and to work its fields. Europeans didn't want those jobs; slaves had no choice.

Slavery in America developed into a terrible and degrading system. To justify that terrible system, a myth arose that blacks were inferior, that they weren't capable people.

Of course, that was just a myth. Africa had produced great cities and beautiful arts. In the 11th century the great African empire of Ghana was flourishing, with "fine houses and solid buildings," and a royal pavilion where pages held gold-tipped swords, horses gleamed in cloths of gold, and princes were "splendidly clad and with gold plaited into their hair." Slaves, in the ancient African kingdoms, were a sign of wealth. It was the way of the world. To be a slave was considered bad luck, not a wrong. The slave trade with other lands thrived—especially with Arabia, Persia, India, even China. Then the Portuguese arrived.

In America an entire way of life depended on the labor of black people. Despite harsh treatment, blacks produced writers, scientists, political leaders, musicians and many others who enriched our nation.

A famous philosopher—named George Santayana—said, "Those who cannot remember the past are condemned to repeat it." What do you think he meant? Do you think he was talking of nations, or people, or both?

One thing he didn't mean was that the same mistakes are made again and again. We will never again allow the kind of slavery we had when this nation began. But there are other forms of slavery. What about drugs? Do they enslave people's minds and bodies? Why do people sell drugs? Why did they have slaves?

In the 20th century slave-labor camps have been the scene of brutality and death for millions of Europeans and Asians. Do you know about them?

Do you know about the system of apartheid (uh-PAR-tide) that existed in South Africa?

American slavery was a horror. We should never pretend it was anything else. But the American system of government lets us correct mistakes. When you study history you see we usually do. Of that we can be proud.

13 The Mayflower: Saints and Strangers

The plaque at St. Peter's Church in Leyden, Holland, put up in memory of the *Mayflower* Pilgrims who once worshiped there.

The times were religious—and angry. To understand them we need to review some English history. Remember King Henry VIII? He was the father of Queen Elizabeth. King Henry tossed the Catholic Church out of England long before Jamestown got started. Why Henry did that is an interesting story, but you'll have to look up the details yourself. It had something to do with King Henry's wanting to get married again, and again, and again, and—whew—he had a lot of energy.

The head of the Catholic Church, the Pope, didn't approve of all that marrying. So King Henry founded the Church of England (which is sometimes called the Anglican Church) and made himself its leader.

By the 17th century most English men and women belonged to that church. (As they still do.) It was called the "established church" because it was linked to the government. Since he was king, James was head of the Church of England. The man who actually ran the church was called the Archbishop of Canterbury, and he was appointed by the king.

The Pope lived in Rome in a great palace called the Vatican. That was, and is, the control center for the entire Roman Catholic Church. The Pope is elected by bishops of the Catholic Church.

Except for that matter of control and leadership, the Anglicans and Catholics were much alike, although they didn't think so and often hated and persecuted each other. As I said, the times were

In December 1620 the *Mayflower* was anchored in Cape Cod harbor. Before the Pilgrims disembarked for good at Plymouth, Mistress Susanna White gave birth on board the ship to the first English baby born in New England, a boy whom she named Peregrine (PAIR-uh-grin). Here is his cradle.

John Smith offered to hire himself out to the Pilgrims as their guide. They told him his book was "better cheap" than he was.

Changing Times

James I brought "new ideas, new goings, new measures, new paces, new heads for your men, for women new faces," according to a poem of the times. It was a time of increasing lawlessness, of new riches for some, of poverty for others. There was growing interest in individual rights; less in community values. People began to focus on material riches rather than religion. All that was confusing and disturbing to many. Have you heard people you know complain about politics and government and the times? The Pilgrims didn't like the politics of their England, so they left.

not only religious, but also intolerant. People took their differences very seriously. Wars were fought over them.

Some Englishmen wanted the differences between Catholics and Protestants to be greater. They felt that King Henry VIII didn't go far enough when he outlawed the Catholic Church. They didn't want the Anglican church service to be at all like the Catholic service. They said they wanted to "purify" the Church of England, so they were called Puritans.

Others wanted to go even further. They believed people could speak directly to God without a priest or bishop at all. They wanted to separate themselves from the Church of England and form congregations of their own. They called themselves "Saints." Other people called them "Separatists." Some people called them troublemakers.

King James would not let the Separatists practice their religion. They had to go to the Church of England or go to jail. Their religion was more important to them than their homes—and sometimes than life itself. Some of the Separatists, especially a group from a village in northeast England called Scrooby, decided to move to Holland, where they were promised religious freedom.

And they got religious freedom in Holland—but they didn't feel at home with the Dutch. They were English, and they liked their own customs and language and villages. When their children started speaking Dutch and forgetting English ways, the people from Scrooby decided it was time to move again. They read John Smith's book, *Description of New England,* and they said, "This time to America."

Anyone who takes a trip for religious purposes is a *pilgrim.* So now these Scrooby people who were called Separatists or Saints had a new name: Pilgrims. They were the first of many, many boatloads of pilgrims who would

The Pilgrims in Holland board ship at Leyden for the first leg of their journey to religious freedom in the New World.

PILGRIMS' ROUTE, 1620

NORTH AMERICA

Atlantic Ocean

ENGLAND
SCROOBY
HOLLAND

PLYMOUTH

DUGOUT at PLYMOUTH

PLYMOUTH

CAPE COD

PILGRIMS

come to America to be free to believe whatever they wanted to believe. They, however, were pilgrims with a capital P: *the* Pilgrims.

The year is 1620. The boat they take is named the *Mayflower*. Of the 102 on board, only about half are Saints; the Scrooby people call the others "Strangers." The Strangers are leaving England for adventure, or because they are unhappy or in trouble. Saints and Strangers have many things in common. Most are from the lower classes; most have a trade; they expect to work hard; they are ambitious; and they can't stand the new ideas that are changing England. All want a better life, but the Saints hope to build a society more perfect than any on earth.

Among the Strangers are 10 indentured servants, a professional soldier, a barrelmaker, four orphans indentured, or "bound," to work without pay until they are 21, and a man soon to be convicted of murder.

Among the Saints is William Bradford, who will be elected as the colony's second governor and will write their story.

It is a terrible voyage, taking 66 days. The ship is small, wet, and foul. The smells are horrid. There is no place to change or wash clothes. Each adult is assigned a space below deck measuring seven by two and a half feet. Children get even less room. None of the passengers is allowed on deck; there is little fresh air below and many are sick. Fresh food soon runs out and then there is hard bread and dried meat that is wet and moldy. But the Pilgrims have onions, lemon juice, and beer to keep them from getting the dreaded scurvy. Amazingly, only one person dies. He is replaced on the roster by a

The word *indentured* originally came from the paper that the contract between master and servant was written on. After they signed it, the paper was torn in half, so that each piece had an *indentation* that fitted into the other piece. The master kept one piece and the servant kept the other. That was the proof of their agreement.

Scurvy is a disease resulting from lack of vitamin C. It makes people bleed easily and causes their teeth to fall out.

53

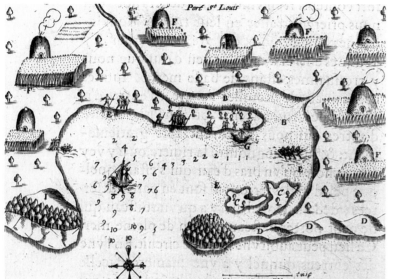

Port S.t Louis

The Pilgrims weren't the first Europeans to land at Plymouth Bay. Fishermen, trappers, and explorers, such as the Frenchman Samuel de Champlain, had been there before. Champlain drew this map, showing the Patuxet Indians' villages, in 1605.

Although the *Mayflower* was cramped and uncomfortable, one thing about it was an improvement over many ships. The *Mayflower* had carried wine barrels, and the hold smelled of the wine that had leaked out. Most 17th-century ships stank of garbage.

baby born at sea, Oceanus (ohshee-ANN-us) Hopkins. Another child, Peregrine White, is born just before they dock.

When they first sight American land, it is at Cape Cod. They planned to go to Virginia, but they are exhausted. Bradford describes Cape Cod as a "hideous and desolate wilderness, full of wild beasts and men." They sail around the cape to a place they see on Smith's map. He has called it Plymouth, after a town in England.

Before they get off the ship, there are matters to attend to. There has been trouble between Saints and Strangers, and it needs to be settled. They must live together peacefully. They need rules and laws and leaders. So they draw up a plan of government, the Mayflower Compact, which establishes a governing body:

> to enact, constitute, and frame such just and equal laws, ordinances, acts, constitutions, offices…for the general good of the Colony; unto which, we promise all due submission and obedience.

That Mayflower Compact is one of the great documents of American history. Here is a group of settlers able to govern themselves; reasonable people who agree to live together under a government of laws. The king doesn't realize what is in the future. This breed of people will not allow others to rule them for long.

Then, wrote Bradford, "being thus arrived in a good harbor, and brought safe to land, they fell upon their knees and blessed the God of Heaven who had brought them over the vast and furious ocean."

When they land, they find empty fields cleared for planting. They will learn that smallpox, caught from white fishermen, has wiped out many of New England's Indians. The Pilgrims believe that God has made the land theirs for the taking.

But it is December—too late to plant crops. Many will hunger and die before spring comes. Fewer than half of the 102 who land will survive the first winter. But no one wants to return to England. These are sturdy folk who intend to start a nation. William Bradford writes of the colony "as one small candle may light a thousand, so the light here kindled hath shone unto many, yea in some sort to our whole nation."

14 Pilgrims, Indians, and Puritans

One way of cooking a turkey on an open fire was in a roasting pan with a tight lid: "For turkey braised, the Lord be praised."

Like the Jamestown colonists, the Pilgrims have picked a poor site. The New England coast is cold and wind-whipped; the land is rocky, the soil is thin. But these industrious people will use the sea and the forest to sustain themselves. Soon they will be shipping fish, furs, and lumber back to England.

Without the Indians they might not have survived. Picture this scene: Pilgrims are struggling to find ways to live in this difficult region, when out of the woods strides a tall man in deerskin clothes. They are astounded when he greets them. "Welcome, Englishmen," he says. His name is Samoset, and he has learned some English from fishermen and traders.

Samoset returns with 60 Indians, a chieftain named Massasoit, and an Indian whom the settlers name Squanto. Squanto speaks English well. He had been kidnapped by sailors, taken to London, befriended by a London merchant, and then returned to his native land.

Trumpet and drums are played as the Pilgrims' governor, John Carver, leads Massasoit to his house, kisses his hand (as is proper to a king), offers refreshments, and writes a treaty of peace between the Indians and the English. While Massasoit is alive, the peace will be kept.

Squanto stays with the settlers. To the Pilgrims he was "a special instrument sent of God for their good beyond their expectation....He directed them how to set [plant] their corn, where to take [catch] fish, and to procure other commodities, and was also their pilot to bring them to unknown places."

Squanto's real name is Tisquantum. These Native Americans are Algonquians of the Wampanoag tribe, who live in what is now Rhode Island. *Wampanoag* means "eastern people." They hunt, fish, dig for clams, and gather berries and nuts. They are good cooks; they make venison (deer) steak, fish chowders, succotash, cornbread, and maple sugar.

Edward Winslow was a printer and a clever man. He traveled a lot to London to trade and negotiate for the Pilgrims. On his first trip back to Plymouth he brought something very important: cattle.

Not all the early colonists dressed in somber styles and colors. Only the Saints insisted on plain, dark clothes.

One of America's first folk songs praised the humble but essential pumpkin.

For pottage and puddings and custards and pies
Our pumpkins and parsnips are common supplies.
We have pumpkin at morning and pumpkin at noon,
If it were not for pumpkin,
We should be undone.

In 1621, after the first harvest, the Pilgrims invite their Indian friends to a three-day feast of Thanksgiving. In one year they have accomplished much.

The Pilgrims are frugal, but the celebration is unusually generous. They will need their food to get through the winter and to help feed the new colonists who are beginning to arrive.

William Bradford, who is elected governor when John Carver dies suddenly, keeps a record of the arrivals. When the ship *Fortune* docks he writes, "there was not so much as biscuit-cake, neither had they any bedding...nor pot, or pan."

Abraham Pearce, a black indentured servant, is one of those who comes in 1623. A few years later he will own land, vote, and be a respected member of the community.

The new arrivals bring reports from England that are not good. Now the Puritans are in trouble. The Puritans are also called Saints, but they are more moderate than the Pilgrims. Remember, Puritans don't want to separate themselves from the Church of England, they want to purify the church. What they really want is to control the Church of England; of course, King James and those in charge don't want that at all.

The Puritans can't stand King James and he doesn't like them either. Of the Puritans he says, "I will make them conform themselves, or else I will harry [harass] them out of the land." The Puritans can see that King James isn't good for England's economy. First there is inflation and then a depression. James has brought his big-spending friends to England from Scotland, where he is also king. They are getting special favors. The Puritans are not.

And so a group of Puritans gathers at Cambridge University, where most of them have gone to college, and makes plans to sail to America. The Puritans are better educated than the Pilgrims—and richer, too. John Winthrop, their leader, is a lawyer, born on a manor, with servants and tenants.

When King James dies, in 1625, and Charles I becomes king, things get even worse for the Puritans.

GOOD
NEWES
7. FROM NEW-ENGLAND:
OR
A true Relation of things very remarkable at the Plantation of *Plimoth* in NEW-ENGLAND.

Shewing the wondrous providence and goodnes of GOD, in their preservation and continuance, being delivered from many apparant deaths and dangers.

Together with a Relation of such religious and civill Lawes and Customes, as are in practise amongst the Indians, adjoyning to them at this day. As also what Commodities are there to be raysed for the maintenance of that and other Plantations in the said Country.

Written by E. W. who hath borne a part in the fore-named troubles, and there lived since their first Arrivall.

Whereunto is added by him a briefe Relation of a credible intelligence of the present estate of *Virginia*.

LONDON
Printed by I. D. for *William Bladen* and *John Bellamie*, and are to be sold at their Shops, at the *Bible* in *Pauls*-Church-yard, and at the three *Golden Lyons* in *Corn-hill*, neere the *Royall Exchange*. 1624.

Edward Winslow wrote this pamphlet to encourage more colonists to come to New England.

Giving Thanks

The story that the first American Thanksgiving was held at Plymouth Colony is a real turkey. In 1540, long before the Pilgrims sat down to their big dinner, Francisco Vasquez de Coronado and his men conducted a thanksgiving service in their camp at Palo Duro Canyon in what is now known as the Texas Panhandle.

Half a century before the Pilgrims landed, French Huguenots settled near today's Jacksonville, Florida. They "sang a psalm of Thanksgiving unto God, beseeching Him...to continue his accustomed goodness toward us." Unfortunately for the French, the goodness did not continue. Their colony was wiped out by Spanish raiders. Still, some Floridians claim that as the first American Thanksgiving.

A group of English Catholics arrived in Maine in 1605, said prayers of thanks, faced a year of Maine weather, changed their minds about living in America, and sailed back to England. But some Mainiacs (yes, that's what they are called) say their state had the first Thanksgiving.

Two years before the feast in Massachusetts, the settlers at Berkeley Hundred, on the James River in Virginia, decreed that the day of their landing, December 4, 1619, "shall be yearly and perpetually kept holy as a day of Thanksgiving." Did they have a feast? It depends on whom you ask at Berkeley Plantation. (There is no documented record of one.)

Now, to give the Pilgrims their due: they did eat a big meal, and one of them—Edward Winslow—wrote six sentences about it. None of the other claimants can say that.

Those Pilgrims needed a good meal. Fewer than half of the 102 passengers who came on the *Mayflower* in 1620 survived their first American winter. The local Indians weren't in good shape either. They had been hit—hard hit—by diseases brought by French fishermen, who had made contact four years earlier.

The English colonists wouldn't have survived at all—and they knew it—if it hadn't been for corn and other help from the Indians. And Massasoit was forever grateful to Winslow, who made a nourishing broth that helped him recover from a serious illness. Good will, necessity, and plain good sense seem to have made them all good neighbors.

So when harvest time arrived in 1621, the Pilgrims had much to be thankful for. They had made a start at the beaver trade, they lived in peace with the Native Americans, 11 houses had been built, and, thanks to Squanto, the corn harvest was good. They had celebrated harvest time in Holland; they wished to continue that tradition.

They invited Massasoit to join them. He came with 90 hungry Indians. They might have wiped out the larder, but the Indians "went and killed five deer, which they brought to the plantation and bestowed on our governor," Winslow writes.

We don't know exactly what the Pilgrims cooked, but ducks, geese, turkey, clams, eels, lobster, squash, wild grapes, dried fruit, and cornbread are all good guesses, along with watercress and other "sallet herbes." Winslow says, "Our governor sent four men on fowling, that so we might after a special manner rejoice together after we had gathered the fruit of our labors. They four in one day killed as much fowl as, with a little help beside, served the company almost a week." That's as detailed as he gets, with this addition: "for three days we entertained and feasted."

That's all we know? That's it. Except for a brief word from Governor William Bradford, who doesn't write specifically about a feast with the Indians, but does say that "they began now to gather in the small harvest they had....All summer there was no want; and now began to come in store of fowl, as winter approached, of which this place did abound....And besides wa-

(continued on p.58)

terfowl there was great store of wild turkeys, of which they took many, besides venison, etc. Besides, they had about a peck of meal a week to a person, or now since harvest, Indian corn in that proportion."

Did they eat cranberries, which were thick in the nearby bogs? Or pumpkin pie? Not likely. You need sugar for those dishes, and they didn't have any.

As devout Christians, the Pilgrims gave thanks before each meal. But this was a harvest festival, not, primarily, a celebration of thanks to God. And it probably came at the end of September. Still, all in all, the spirit was the same as at today's November festival where we give thanks, we re-member, we enjoy—and we eat!

The first national Thanksgiving was actually proclaimed by George Washington in 1789. But Thanksgiving was not cele-brated officially again until Abraham Lincoln (urged on by a magazine editor, Sarah J. Hale) decreed a national holiday in 1863. Since then it's been turkey all the way.

This is the first Thanksgiving dinner celebrated by the Pilgrims and Native Americans, as pictured by the artist J.L.G. Ferris (1863-1930). No one really knows if they ate outdoors or not.

15 Puritans, Puritans, and More Puritans

John Winthrop was a lawyer who lost his job because of his religion. In 1630 he came to America.

In 1630, the first Puritan ship, the *Arbella,* sets out for the New World. By summer's end 1,000 Puritans have landed in New England. They bring a charter from the king: the Charter of the Company of the Massachusetts Bay in New England. King Charles is happy to see the Puritans leave England.

The charter is a document written by lawyers, setting the rules that tell how the colony will be run. It allows the colonists to govern themselves. It is important to remember that, from the beginning, English settlers expected to govern themselves. It is important to remember that each colony had a charter: a written set of rules. Those charters would evolve into constitutions.

Can you guess what might happen in a community without a charter or constitution? Would you like to live in a country without laws? Would you want to write your own laws or have someone write them for you?

You can think about those questions and then get back to the Puritans, who are beginning to pour out of England. Most of them go to the Caribbean islands, where sugar is creating great fortunes. But, between 1630 and 1640, 20,000 Puritans sail for New England. Think about all those people risking their lives to cross the ocean and settle in an unknown land. It is almost as if tens of thousands of people today decided to live in outer space.

Why did they come? Many came because they really cared about their religion and wanted to practice it in peace. They wanted to build a holy community, where people would live by the rules of the Bible. Puritans believed the Bible was the whole word of God. They tried to follow its every direction, which means they tried to live very good lives.

Sweet Success

Sugar was a much-desired luxury in Europe. The West Indies (with its tropical climate) turned out to be a perfect place to grow sugarcane. Christopher Columbus brought the cane to the Caribbean on his second voyage. Soon the native trees were cut down and sugarcane plantations filled the islands.

Sugarcane grew wild in Asia. In Sanskrit, the ancient language of India, sugar was *sarkara*. That became *sukkar* in Arabic, *sakhar* in Russian, *sucre* in French, *Zucker* in German, and *sugar* in English.

Here is the first page of the Charter of the Massachusetts Bay Colony, setting out the rules by which the colonists could govern themselves. At the top left is King William III.

Once a woman got to the New World, she was expected to start having babies—that's what the Puritans on the left are telling the couple to do.

At first, the name *Quaker* was used to make fun of people; so, too, was the word *Puritan*. Then both groups decided to be proud of those words and use them themselves.

Although the Puritans tried hard to be good, things didn't work out as they wished. They expected their colony to be an example for all the world. John Winthrop, who was chosen as governor, said, "We must consider that we shall be as a city upon a hill. The eyes of all people are upon us."

One thing they didn't understand at all was the idea of *toleration*. Puritans came to America to find religious freedom—but only for themselves. They didn't believe in the kind of religious freedom we have today. But don't be too hard on them. Almost no one else believed in it either. And how many people do you know who are willing to devote their lives to an idea they believe to be right?

In those days each nation had its own church, and everyone was expected to pay taxes for its support. Suppose you didn't believe in the ideas of that religion. Too bad. You had to keep quiet, leave the country, go to jail, or maybe get hanged.

Pretend you are a Puritan. You think that yours is the only true religion, so you believe the Reverend John Cotton when he says toleration is "liberty…to tell lies in the name of the Lord."

Since you are convinced that only you Puritans are right, you think it is wrong to let anyone practice another religion. You believe that is helping the devil. You especially dislike Quakers. Your leaders call them a "cursed sect." You use the name *Quaker* to describe religious people who call themselves "Friends." Friends believe that each person has an inner light that leads him to God. People with an inner light do not have to rely on a minister to tell them what is godly. The inner light is available to everyone. This is a highly democratic idea, and most Europeans thought it very dangerous. They were used to kings and priests and ministers. It seemed reasonable to them to persecute Quakers. When Quakers came to New England or Virginia, they were whipped, sent away, and even hanged.

Remember, you are a Puritan and you've left your home and everything you know and love. You've crossed a fierce ocean to live as you wish. You don't want people with strange ideas bothering you. Democracy is another strange idea. "If the people be governors, who shall be governed?" the Reverend Cotton asks. John Winthrop, the beloved Puritan governor, who always tries to do what is best, calls

democracy the "meanest [lowest] and worst" form of government.

And yet the Puritans do practice a kind of democracy—but only for male church members. Once a year they form a General Court and vote to elect the governor and council. The General Court is a lot like the House of Burgesses, or Parliament, or Congress.

Some people call the Massachusetts Bay Colony a "theocracy" (thee-OCK-ruh-see), government by church officials in the name of God. But they are wrong. It is not a theocracy. The ministers are the most important people in the colony, but they are not allowed to hold political office. They do not govern. It is a small step toward the idea of the separation of church and state. Someday that idea will be a foundation of American liberty.

At Puritan church services women sat at the back or upstairs. At a Quaker meeting *(above)* everyone sat together.

61

What's in a Word?

We had better stop and go over some words, otherwise this book will get confusing. You've been reading about democracy and theocracy. Here's an explanation of those ideas, and some others, too.

If you keep reading history you will learn about Abraham Lincoln. He said that democracy was government "of the people, by the people, and for the people." That's a good definition.

Democracy is based on people power. Think of a pyramid with the leader on top and all the people on the bottom. The leader is picked from the bottom row and raised to the top. Power goes from the bottom to the top. You'll see in a minute that in some kinds of government, power goes the other way.

Democracy comes in two varieties: direct democracy and representative democracy.

When you choose someone to vote for you, you have *representative democracy*. The members of the House of Burgesses at Jamestown represented the colonists and made laws for them. Our Congress does the same thing for us today. We live in a representative democracy based on law. We are ruled by laws made by congressmen and congresswomen whom we elect.

Some New England towns have *direct democracy.* All the people in the town get together at a town meeting and vote directly on important issues. No one votes for them.

It is possible, with modern technology, that we will have more direct democracy in the future. We may be able to vote directly for certain laws through our TV sets. However, we will always need representatives who can take the time needed to make decisions on complicated issues.

Autocracy is the opposite of democracy. It is government by a single authority with unlimited power. In autocracies, power starts at the top of the pyramid.

A *dictator* is an autocrat. If a dictator doesn't like you, he can have you killed without consulting anyone or giving you a trial. Autocrats don't have to be bad. There have been a few good ones in history—but only a few. If a dictator is terrible, the people are stuck with him (or her). They have no power—except, sometimes, brute force. In the old days, kings and queens were autocrats. Today they usually share power with a parliament.

A *theocracy* is...if you don't remember that, go back and read the last chapter. Just kidding, you don't have to do that. A theocracy (remember?) is government by a church in the name of God.

An *aristocracy* is government by a small group of privileged people. England was an aristocracy in the 17th century. The king and the landowning aristocrats (who controlled Parliament) ruled.

Hold on. This is tough, and may be a bit boring, but it is important.

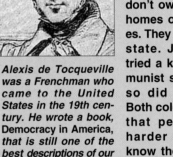

Alexis de Tocqueville was a Frenchman who came to the United States in the 19th century. He wrote a book, Democracy in America, *that is still one of the best descriptions of our system ever published.*

Democracy, autocracy, theocracy, and aristocracy are all words that tell you about political power and who has it.

Here are two words that tell about economic or money power: *communism* and *capitalism.*

In a communist country the state owns most of the land and property and shares them with its citizens. (Remember, the word *state* sometimes means "nation." That can be confusing, but that's the way it is.) People don't own their own homes or businesses. They work for the state. Jamestown tried a kind of communist system, and so did Plymouth. Both colonies found that people work harder when they know they can own land or a business. (In the 20th century, Russia and most of Eastern Europe tried and rejected communism.) People often need to be forced to be communists.

In a capitalist country you can own capital: capital is money and property. The United States is a nation that practices capitalism. In a capitalist country goods are distributed through a free market. Capitalism has disadvantages, too: wealth often piles up for a few people, while others don't have enough.

Whew, that's a lot to absorb! Now let's get back to history, which is much more exciting.

16 Of Towns and Schools and Sermons

Women who nagged or talked too much—scolds—were considered a curse in the 17th century and could be made to wear a *scold's bridle*.

At first the New England settlers built their homes behind high fences called "stockades." They were fearful of the unknown—of Indians and animals.

Soon they began spreading out, beyond the fences, into small towns with names like Greenfield, Springfield, and Longmeadow. The names described the land. Many of those early settlements were just a row of houses strung alongside abandoned Indian fields that the English settlers found and took. They lived with Indians as neighbors, although their animals sometimes made that difficult.

The Native Americans hunted animals; they had no horses, cows, sheep, or hogs. The Indians soon discovered that those English grazing animals could destroy their cornfields. In 1653 the people of the town of New Haven agreed to work for 60 days to build fences around fields planted by neighboring Indians. New England's courts ordered colonists to pay the Indians for damage done to their fields by wandering animals.

As the colonists began to prosper, they built towns in America that were something like the villages they left behind in Europe. They were compact, easy to defend, and friendly. Castles and manor houses dominated European towns; in New England's villages it was the meetinghouse that stood out. The meetinghouse was used as a church, a town hall, and a social center. It was usually placed at one end of a big field that was called a common, because everyone used it in common. Sometimes, when there were sheep to chew the field's grass and keep it short and green, the common was called a green. Houses were built around the green. The houses nearest the meet-

People in New England villages were usually friendly and neighborly to each other. They had to be. A family needed the neighbors' help to clear rocks out of a field or raise a barn roof. There was one cowman who looked after everybody's cows. But if a stranger came hanging around with no invitation from a local family, he was chased out of town.

Chairs were rare and costly in the 17th century. This one belonged to Governor Endicott.

The Puritans had so many rules and laws that they were often broken. Another popular punishment, especially for scolding women, was the ducking stool. The sinner was tied on and lowered into the stream or village pond.

Puritans liked to give their children names that were reminders of goodness and holiness. Some we still find occasionally, like Constance, Faith, or Hope; and some seem strange: Joy-from-Above, Kill-sin, Fear, Patience, Wrestling-with-the-Devil.

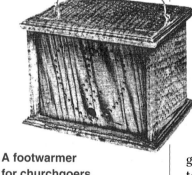

A footwarmer for churchgoers.

inghouse belonged to the most important people in town: the minister and the church leaders.

Many villages had a stream. The tumbling water of the stream turned a big wheel, and that provided power for the mills where wood was sawed and wheat ground into flour.

As the town grew other buildings were added: a general store, a blacksmith's shop, a furniture maker's shop, a candle maker's.

If the town was large enough, there might be an inn. Almost always there was a school.

The Puritans cared about schooling. By 1636 they had founded Harvard College. It was amazing that they had a college so soon after they arrived, although Harvard did get off to a rocky start. The first teacher beat his students, fed them spoiled meat, and ran off with college money.

Then they got a college president, Henry Dunster. He was so good that students began coming to study with him from Virginia and

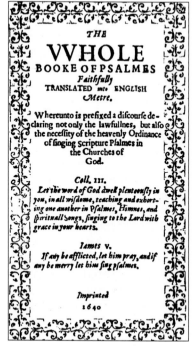

The *Whole Booke of Psalmes*, also known as the Bay Psalm Book, was the first book ever printed in the English colonies.

Bermuda and even England itself. Of course, they were all Puritans.

Because of their religion, Puritans weren't allowed to attend college in England. That was one reason it was so important to have Harvard succeed. To do that it had to have a supply of students. So, in 1642, the Massachusetts Bay Colony passed a law saying that parents must teach their children to read.

The Puritans wanted everyone to be able to read the Bible, even those who weren't going to Harvard. So the next thing they did was pass a law that said:

> It is therefore ordered, that every township in this jurisdiction, after the Lord has increased its number to 50 householders, shall then forthwith appoint one within their town to teach all such children as shall resort to him to write and read, whose wages shall be paid either by the parents or masters of such children, or by the inhabitants in general.

In plain English, that means that every town with 50 or more families must have a schoolteacher.

Do you see something unusual in that law? Read that bit at the end, "shall be paid...by the inhabitants in general." Do you know what that means? It means that everyone in the town has to pay for the education of the children. Not just the parents. That is what public education is all about. It guarantees that every child, not just those with wealthy parents, can go to school. In America, it all began with that school law in 1647.

I know what you're thinking. Why did they have to go and do it? Who needs school anyway? But you don't really mean it. It isn't fun to be ignorant.

In the 17th century much teaching was done by parents, or in church, or, if you were an apprentice, by your master. But the Puritans could see that sometimes that wasn't enough. Some parents just weren't good teachers, even though many Puritans were highly educated themselves. The Puritans thought it important that everyone read the Bible. In Boston and the larger towns some children were ac-

Blowing Thy Nose

Many little Puritan boys and girls had to study a book called *The School of Good Manners*. It reminded them to "stand not wriggling with thy body hither and thither, but steady and upright," or that "when thou blowest thy nose, let thy handkerchief be used." Naughty children were whipped with a birch stick or cane. "Spare the rod and spoil the child" was a firm belief even of kind parents and teachers.

Harvard College *(above)* had a very English class consciousness for many years. Until 1769 the roster of students was not listed in alphabetical order, but according to social status. That meant that if you were from an important family, you were listed ahead of somebody of lowly rank.

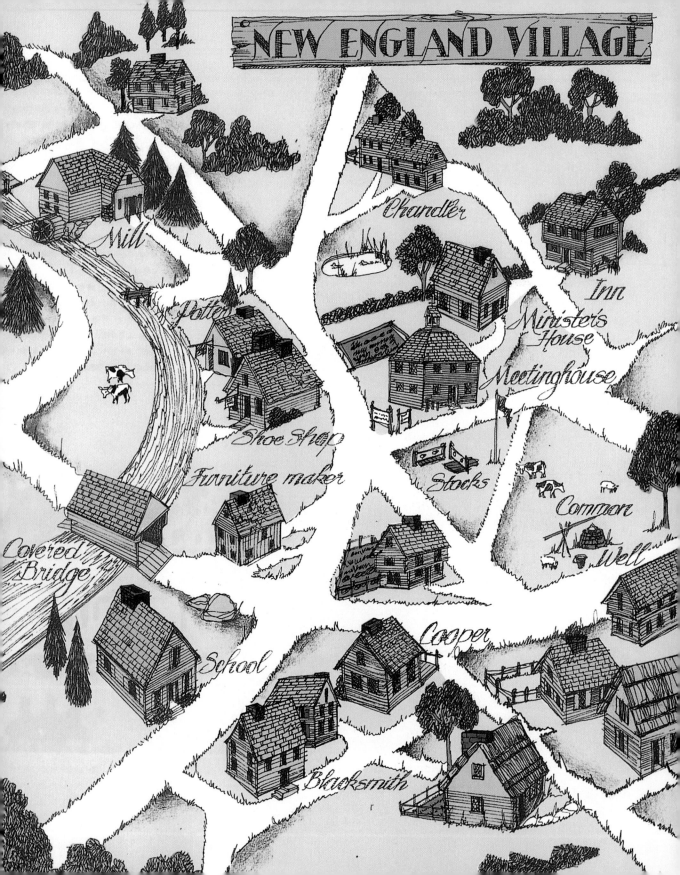

Several generations learned their ABCs from the *New England Primer (right)*, which used rhymes to help children remember letters. This might be all you got if you were a girl—very few had as much schooling as boys.

tually taught to read the Bible in its original languages. So little Puritan boys and girls of six and seven learned to read Latin and Greek, and a few learned Hebrew, too. That sounds hard, and it was, but learning languages is good training for the mind. Many of this nation's greatest thinkers came from Puritan stock.

Try and take yourself back to Puritan times, and see what you think of Sunday churchgoing. Those Puritan ministers gave sermons that lasted for hours and hours. Sometimes there was an intermission for lunch, and then everyone went back to hear more. There was no heat in the meetinghouse, and New England can get very cold. People brought warming boxes with hot coals in them to keep their feet from freezing. Sometimes they brought their dogs to church for the same reason.

A church official held a tickling rod to wake up anyone who looked as if he might be falling asleep. The dog whipper took out dogs who barked. If you were a troublemaker and wiggled and made noise you could get locked up in the town stocks. You'd have to sit there with your hands and feet stuck into a wooden contraption and everyone would make fun of you.

We know you wouldn't like that kind of life, but maybe things weren't so bad for the Puritan boys and girls. Maybe some of them even looked forward to the sermons. Remember, in Puritan Massachusetts there were no movies and no TVs. At first, there were no newspapers, no magazines, and only a few books. The Puritans were intelligent people who could read and think well. Maybe that will help you understand why everyone tried to listen to the weekly sermon and why Puritans sometimes spent all week talking about it.

Feeling Blue

Rules banning work, trade, and playing on Sundays—the Sabbath—are still called "blue laws," because the Puritans wrote the laws in books bound in blue paper. You could be fined or punished for doing these things on Sunday: running, cooking, making a bed, or shaving. A man was whipped for saying that the minister's sermon was boring. Another was put in the stocks after kissing his wife on his return home from three years at sea. And celebrating Christmas was forbidden. It was "popish"—something that Roman Catholics did. Most Puritans worked on Christmas—unless, of course, it happened to fall on a Sunday.

17 Roger Williams

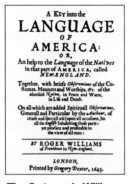

A KEY into the
LANGUAGE
OF
AMERICA:
OR,
An help to the *Language* of the *Natives*
in that part of AMERICA, called
NEW-ENGLAND.

Together, with briefe *Observations* of the Customes, Manners and Worships, &c. of the aforesaid *Natives*, in Peace and Warre, in Life and Death.

On all which are added Spirituall *Observations*, Generall and Particular by the *Authour*, of chiefe and speciall use (upon all occasions) to all the *English* Inhabiting those parts; yet pleasant and profitable to the view of all men:

BT ROGER WILLIAMS
of *Providence* in *New-England.*

LONDON,
Printed by *Gregory Dexter*, 1643.

The first words Williams translated in his guide to the Narraganset language were *I love you.*

The Puritans, who were victims of intolerance in England, were not tolerant themselves. Although they preached the Golden Rule—do unto others as you would have them do unto you—most never understood that they were breaking that rule. Roger Williams did.

Williams was a Puritan minister who came to Massachusetts seeking a "pure" religious community. Like the other Puritans, he was a serious Christian. Like the others, he disapproved of Catholic and Quaker ideas. Like the others, he thought the Indian religions were pagan.

But that's where "like the others" stops.

He didn't believe in forcing anyone to believe as he did. He believed that killing or punishing in the name of Christianity was sinful. He thought that church members—not general taxes—should pay the bills at each church. He respected the beliefs of others. Those were strange ideas in 17th-century Massachusetts.

The Puritans didn't know what to do with Roger Williams. He was a Puritan, he was brilliant, he was a minister, and he was so nice that even his opponents had a hard time disliking him.

But what an ungrateful young man he seemed! The Puritans had offered him good jobs, as teacher and minister, and he thanked them by criticizing their practices.

Governor Winthrop was shocked. So was John Cotton, the minister who took a job that Williams refused. They were especially shocked when Williams wrote a book saying it was wrong to persecute people for their beliefs. Williams called his book *The Bloody Tenet.* (The blood was from those killed because of their religious ideas.) John Cotton wrote his own book. He called it *The Bloody*

Catholics, Quakers, and Puritans were all Christians, but they each interpreted Christianity in a different way. To the Puritans—and to most Christians—pagan religions were not "real" religions, as Christianity was.

Tenet Washed and Made White. Of course that didn't end it. Williams's next book was *The Bloody Tenet Made Yet More Bloody by Mr. Cotton's Endeavor to Wash It White in the Blood of the Lamb.*

When Roger Williams started preaching that land shouldn't be taken from the Indians—that the king had no right to charter land that didn't belong to him—that was too much. The officers of the Massachusetts Bay Colony made arrangements to ship Williams back to England. They sent armed men to put him on a boat.

Roger Williams's wife heard the verdict of the court—that he was to be arrested and banished—and began to cry. Williams told her, "Fifty good men did what they thought was just." Roger Williams didn't hold grudges.

But he wasn't about to let himself get shipped back to England, and so he fled from Massachusetts. It was January 1636, he was sick, and the weather was freezing. Later, when he was an old man, Roger Williams would still remember that terrible winter. He was always thankful to the Narraganset Indians, who helped him survive the cold. He learned to love them as they loved him.

He bought land from the Indians and started a colony called Providence. It became the capital of Rhode Island and soon attracted many of those who were not wanted elsewhere. Someone described Providence as the place where "all the cranks of New England" go.

There were plenty of cranks in Providence. But there were also many who were searching for what Williams called "freedom of conscience."

When Roger Williams said *freedom of conscience,* he meant the freedom of each person to follow his own mind and heart and choose his own religion. That was to become an important right in America.

Roger Williams welcomed everyone who wished to come to Rhode Island, including Quakers and Catholics. And, while he continued to disagree with those religions, he never let that stop him from liking some of the people who practiced them. Jews, who were often persecuted elsewhere, were welcome in Rhode Island. Atheists were welcome, too.

Williams believed that state governments should not have any connection with a church. We call that

In 1763, thanks to the atmosphere of tolerance that Roger Williams fostered, Rhode Island became the home of the first permanent Jewish house of worship in America, the Touro Synagogue.

John Cotton *(above)* and most Puritans thought Williams's ideas of toleration were wrong. Maybe they thought he was crazy, too.

A *tenet* (TEN-it) is a basic idea, a fundamental concept. *Atheists* believe there is no God.

69

The poet means "meat" when he says **flesh**. When he says **they part to friends**, he means "they share with friends." He means "to lack humanity" when he says **to want humanity**. Languages keep changing, and some English words were different in the 17th century.

separation of church and state. It was a very new idea at the time.

He knew that people could be forced to go to church, but that no one's mind could be forced to believe. "Forced worship stinks in God's nostrils," said Roger Williams.

He learned the language of the Narraganset Indians and wrote a book so that others could learn it, too. In it he included these rhymes about the Indians:

> *Sometimes God gives them fish or flesh,*
> *Yet they're content without.*
> *And what comes in, they part to friends*
> *And strangers round about.*
>
> *If nature's sons both wild and tame*
> *Humane and courteous be,*
> *How ill becomes its sons of God*
> *To want humanity!*

When the great Narraganset chief Canonicus (kuh-NON-ih-kuss) was dying, he called for Roger Williams to be with him. White men had destroyed the Indian chief's kingdom, and he hated most of them. But Williams and Canonicus had something in common. Each was able to judge people by their character, not by their skin color or religion. They loved and respected each other.

Edmund S. Morgan, who wrote a book about Roger Williams, said "We may praise him...for his defense of religious liberty and the separation of church and state. He deserves the tribute...but it falls short of the man. His greatness was simpler. He dared to think."

Roger Williams

Church and State

The Puritans forced some Indians to become Christians. Roger Williams wrote a letter to the Massachusetts governor. "Are not the English of this land generally a persecuted people from their native land?" he asked. How could those who had been persecuted persecute others, he wondered? He said that the Indians should "not be forced from their religions."

Roger Williams didn't think anyone should be compelled to follow a religion. Besides, he knew it never works to try that. You can make people do things, but you can't make them believe what they don't want to believe.

Williams said that it was "against the testimony of Christ Jesus for the civil state to impose [force] upon the souls of the people a religion."

Most Puritans didn't agree with Roger Williams. They thought it was the job of the government leaders to tell people what to believe.

But Roger Williams's ideas won out. They helped bring about the separation of church and state that is one of the most important of all of America's governing ideas. In Europe and the rest of the world, millions of people have died in wars over religion, but that has not happened in this country.

Roger Williams, a devout Puritan, wrote, "Jesus never called for the sword of steel to help the sword of spirit."

18 "Woman, Hold Your Tongue"

Anne Hutchinson's clothes were plainer than these. But still she had to wear underskirts and petticoats. Imagine wash day, and no washing machine.

Anne Hutchinson was another troublemaker. At least that is what some Puritans thought. Here was a woman with 14 children who was interpreting the Bible. No one objected to that, until she began to question some of the ministers' beliefs. Soon she was trying to reach everyone with her ideas about God. Governor Winthrop was outraged. Didn't Mistress Hutchinson have enough to do, with all those babies to feed?

What was worse, in Winthrop's view, was that people were listening to her. Even men were listening. There was a reason: Anne Hutchinson had a fine mind, and she loved God. Besides, what she was saying made sense. Winthrop admitted that she was "a woman with a ready wit and bold spirit." Before long, Massachusetts was split between people who believed what Anne Hutchinson said and those who believed the ministers. She claimed God was guiding her; the ministers said they were doing God's work on earth.

Finally, the Puritans held a trial. You can read the court records for yourself. You may agree that Mrs. Hutchinson was smarter than her accusers, but that didn't help her a bit. She was kicked out of Massachusetts and out of the Puritan church, too. She moved to Rhode Island. Later Anne Hutchinson moved to New York and was killed by Indians. Governor Winthrop saw it as the judgment of God.

In those days, women, like children, were expected to be seen but not heard. They belonged to their husbands. The word for them

From Me to Thee

Puritans and Quakers used the words *thou* and *thee* instead of "you," and *thy* and *thine* instead of "your" and "yours." They are old-fashioned words that people used when talking to a child, a close friend or family member, a servant—or God. What the Puritans were saying with those words was that we are all close; we are all brothers and sisters.

No More Diapers

You might think that Anne Hutchinson had a terrible lot of diapers to change with all those children. But as soon as a baby could sit up its tight swaddling bands were taken off. In warm rooms and climates, babies didn't wear anything—though sometimes a mother wrapped a "baby clout" (probably just a piece of linen) around a baby's bottom when it sat on somebody's lap. In colder weather, babies and little kids mostly just wore a shirt—with nothing underneath. When toddlers had to go to the bathroom, their mothers plunked them down outside. Not very hygienic, maybe, but simple.

Quaker Catherine Marbury Scott had enough of life in Massachusetts after the trial and exile of her sister Ann Marbury Hutchinson, so she decided to move with her family to Rhode Island. Twenty years later, "a grave, sober, ancient woman," she returned to protest when the Puritans punished another Quaker named Christopher Holder by cutting off his ear. The Puritans imprisoned her, had her whipped with a "threefold corded knotted whip," and threatened to kill her should she return again. She said: "If God calls us, woe be to us if we come not, but He whom we love will make us not to count our lives dear unto ourselves for the sake of his name." Governor John Endicott replied: "And we shall be as ready to take away your lives as ye shall be to lay them down."

was *chattel*. That means a "piece of property." A husband could sell his wife's labor and keep the wages. If she ran away, she was accused of stealing herself and her clothing. Her husband even owned her clothes.

Female Power in Massachusetts

In 1649 and 1650, six petitions—all from Massachusetts women—were submitted to the magistrates on behalf of a midwife named Alice Tilley (midwives deliver babies). Tilley had been accused and convicted—by the male authorities—of some kind of medical malpractice (no exact account survives). Four of the women's petitions asked that Mistress Tilley be allowed to leave jail to tend her patients. Two asked that "her innocencie may be cleared."

According to historian Mary Beth Norton, "female Bostonians begged the judges to "heare the cryes of mothers, and of children yet unborn." They wanted Tilley to deliver babies. "The astonishing aspect of the petitions," says Norton, "was the total number of signatures (294)." The women won; Alice Tilley was released from prison and presumably went back to work.

From a Massachusetts Court Record, 1637

ANNE HUTCHINSON: Therefore take heed how you proceed against me, for I know that for this you go about to do me, God will ruin you and your posterity, and this whole state.

MR. NOWELL: How do you know that it was God that did reveal these things to you, and not Satan?

MRS. HUTCHINSON: How did Abraham know that it was God that bid him offer [sacrifice] his son, being a breach of the sixth commandment?

DEPUTY-GOVERNOR DUDLEY: By an immediate voice.

MRS. HUTCHINSON: So to me by an immediate revelation.

DEPUTY-GOVERNOR: How! an immediate revelation?

MRS. HUTCHINSON: By the voice of his own spirit to my soul.

GOVERNOR JOHN WINTHROP: Daniel was delivered by miracle; do you think to be delivered so too?

MRS. HUTCHINSON: I do here speak it before the Court. I look that the Lord should deliver me by his providence....

GOVERNOR WINTHROP: The Court hath already declared themselves satisfied concerning the things you hear, and concerning the troublesomeness of her spirit, and the danger of her course amongst us, which is not to be suffered. Therefore, if it be the mind of the Court that Mrs. Hutchinson, for these things that appear before us, is unfit for our society, and if it be the mind of the Court that she shall be banished out of our liberties, and imprisoned till she be sent away, let them hold up their hands.

All but three held up their hands.

GOVERNOR WINTHROP: Those that are contrary minded, hold up yours.

Mr. Coddington and Mr. Colburn only.

MR. JENNISON: I cannot hold up my hand one way or the other, and I shall give my reason if the Court require it.

GOVERNOR WINTHROP: Mrs. Hutchinson, you hear the sentence of the Court. It is that you are banished from out our jurisdiction as being a woman not fit for our society. And you are to be imprisoned till the Court send you away.

MRS. HUTCHINSON: I desire to know wherefore [why] I am banished.

GOVERNOR WINTHROP: Say no more. The Court knows wherefore, and is satisfied.

Here's a Pilgrim house that you can visit at Plimoth Plantation in Massachusetts. There you will see a whole village reconstructed to seem just as if it were 1627. Big open hearths like this were the center of every Pilgrim home.

A Home for Prayer

Religious fervor also swept through parts of Germany in the 17th century, and some of these people—who were often considered bizarre in the Old World—headed across the ocean to search for a home where they could be free to follow their beliefs. One such group was called "The Woman in the Wilderness." (The *woman* was the true church.) Johannes Kelpius was its leader, and he settled near Philadelphia and built a big, log-walled monastery to house his 40 fellow worshipers. There they studied mystical writings, engaged in devout meditation, conducted scientific experiments—which they hoped would prolong their lives indefinitely—and put a telescope on their roof to search for signs of God's arrival. Members of a number of sects sought salvation on American soil. Massachusetts already had its Puritans, and most of them didn't encourage other beliefs. So Pennsylvania was where many German religious groups headed.

19 Statues on the Common

This Quaker was arrested for preaching, driven out of town, and beaten with a cat-o'-nine-tails.

At Quaker meetings, the congregation sits and meditates in silence. Sometimes a member feels that God is communicating with him or her directly. The Friend might start talking aloud about this "inward light," or might shake and tremble—which was how the Quakers got their name.

Anne Hutchinson wasn't the only strong woman to trouble John Winthrop and the Massachusetts Bay Puritans. Her best friend was a problem, too.

Mary Dyer was Puritan and pious. Winthrop called her a "very proper and fair woman." That was when he first knew her. But Dyer followed the ways of Anne Hutchinson, and when Anne Hutchinson was cast out of Massachusetts, Mary Dyer and her husband, William, and other believers went with her.

Later, Mary Dyer took a trip back to England and found other truths for herself. She became a member of the Society of Friends, the people who were known as Quakers. Quakers call their church services "meetings." In a Quaker meeting everyone is equal, anyone may speak out, and there are no ministers. Now, in the 17th century equality was not fashionable. Besides, Quakers refuse to swear oaths of allegiance to anyone but God. But oaths of loyalty to king and country were expected in England and everywhere in the 17th century.

You need to understand that the church and the government were all part of one package in the Old World. It was the church

At this Quaker meeting most of the congregation sits in silent meditation while one member is inspired to speak.

that gave the king his right to govern. It was called the "divine right of kings." It was the government that gave the church support and lands. That was the way it had always been. It seemed as if people like the Quakers wanted to mess things up. The Quakers believed in toleration, and they believed each person could think for himself. What happens if you let people think for themselves? Why, the next step might be for them to say that the king's church and the king's priests weren't needed. And Quakers did say something like that when they sat in their meetings without ministers.

A hanging, like that of Mary Dyer, was a public spectacle in the 17th century. People took time off work to go and watch. They cheered, jeered, and partied.

So maybe you can see why Quakers were hated and persecuted by the authorities in England. They weren't liked any better in the colonies. The magistrates of the Massachusetts Bay Colony passed harsh laws to keep them away, but that didn't stop them. Some Quakers seemed determined to be martyrs, and Mary Dyer was one of them. She came to Boston and was sent away. She came back. This time she was tried, with two Quaker men, and all three were led to the gallows.

The men were hanged, but at the last minute Dyer was put on a horse and sent off to Rhode Island. She came back again. Now what do you do with a woman who cares so much about her religion that she will risk death to preach its message? You'd think the Puritans would have understood that devotion. Maybe they did, and that's what scared them.

The Puritans tried Mary Dyer again. This time they offered her her life if she would leave Massachusetts forever. She refused. Mary Dyer was hanged, on June 1, 1660, on the Boston Common in front of where the State House stands today. Her death was too much for some Puritans. In 1661 the law was changed. Today, statues of Mary Dyer and Anne Hutchinson can be seen on the Common.

A *martyr* (MAR-tur) is someone who would rather die than give up his or her belief. A *gallows* was the two standing poles and crosspiece from which people were hanged. Sometimes bodies were left on the gallows for a while, as a warning to others.

But most Puritans thought they had done everything they could to be fair to Mary Dyer. Remember, it was a different world then, a world just leaving the Middle Ages. A few people in Europe were beginning to question the old ideas. But those questions traveled slowly across the ocean. When people started talking of toleration, the Puritans "could hardly understand what was happening in the world," writes Perry Miller, a historian of the Puritans. "They could not for a long time be persuaded that they had any reason to be ashamed of their record of so many Quakers whipped, blasphemers punished by the amputation of ears, [dissenters] exiled...or witches executed. [According to the beliefs] in Europe at the time the Puritans had left, these were achievements to which any government could point with pride."

20 Of Witches and Dinosaurs

Everybody believed in witches. James I wrote a book that said they should be put to death.

That phrase, *city upon a hill,* is one to put in your head and remember. You'll hear it again and again when you read American history.

Do you know of other societies or times in history where neighbors spy on neighbors—sometimes, even, where children spy on their parents?

How many Puritans do you know? Don't think too hard. The answer is zero. Puritans are like dinosaurs: they are extinct.

I'll tell you what happened to them in just a minute, but don't worry, things worked out well. Many of their descendants turned into New England Yankees. Others are spread all across the nation. Many go to the Congregational church. In some ways, however, we are all descendants of the Puritans.

Now you may be shaking your head if you live in California, or Colorado, or West Virginia. If your parents came from Mexico or China, you're probably saying, "No way am I a Puritan!" But it's true. If you are an American, you are a descendant of the Puritans—at least a little bit—because many American laws and ideas come from Puritan laws and ideas, and they are some of the best we have.

You see, the Puritans hoped to build a place on earth where people could live as the Bible says they should, a place where people would be truly good. Governor Winthrop called Puritan Massachusetts "a city upon a hill." He expected it to stand tall as a symbol to the rest of the world. "The eyes of all people are upon us," he said.

The Puritans came to the New World to try and build a godly community where they could live close to perfect lives. No human beings have ever been able to do that, but the Puritans tried.

To make their community pure, the Puritans

Matthew Hopkins, England's Witch Finder General.

expected everyone to act like a spy and report any neighbor who did or said anything wrong. Can you see how that might make you a little uncomfortable around your neighbors? Maybe that helped cause the Puritans' downfall. Or perhaps it was their seriousness that did them in, or witches (we'll get to them soon), or their self-righteousness.

Self-righteous people believe they know the truth. They think that anyone who doesn't agree with them is wrong. They are apt to judge other people. Sometimes the Puritans were like that. They spent time judging their neighbors.

They read the Bible every day, but they didn't always pay attention to the passage in the New Testament that asks: "Why do you observe the speck of sawdust in your brother's eye and never notice the log in your own?" (What does that mean?)

A witch and her imps. An imp could be a monster, but more often it was an ordinary animal—even a fish—with horns or wings.

Benjamin Franklin, one of the wisest of all Americans, wrote in his *Autobiography* a warning against using words like "certainly, undoubtedly, or any others that give the air of positiveness to an opinion." Instead, said Franklin, we should say, "it appears to me, or I should think it so or so…if I am not mistaken."

The Puritans were very sure of themselves. They believed that God saves only a very few people and that the rest go to a terrible hell filled with fires. They thought that God decided when a child was born if he was saved or not. They used the word "elected" instead of saved, and they thought they were God's elect. Because of that, they thought they should act like God's elect and lead good lives. And that's why we can be happy they were among the first colonists. They really tried their best to be good. They worked hard, they believed in learning, and they did what they thought was right.

Cotton Mather

wrote: "And we have now with Horror seen the Discovery of such a Witchcraft! An Army of Devils is horribly broke in upon…our English Settlements: and the Houses of the Good People there are fill'd with the doleful Shrieks of their Children and Servants."

Witch Advice

If the cream won't turn to butter, a witch must be in the churn. Take a horseshoe, heat it red hot, and throw it into the churn. That will set the witch flying.

Nail a horseshoe over your door, and witches will stay away.

To tell if someone is a witch: tie the suspect's hands and feet. Toss him (or her) in the water. If he sinks he is innocent. If he floats he is a witch. (Which would you rather be?)

No one made pictures of the Salem witch trials while they were happening, so we can only imagine what they were like from what was written down. This artist imagined the trial of George Jacobs, the old man kneeling on the right. (Men could be witches, too.)

But the Puritans had a big problem. They were human and they made mistakes. Their ministers didn't help. The ministers said that people were naturally sinful, but if they sinned they would go to that terrible hell. That kept everyone under constant pressure to be close to perfect. No one could relax. And that may be what caused the nightmare of the witches.

The whole world believed in witches—there was nothing new about that. People thought that if you wanted to make a bargain with the devil you could do it, and then torment people and fly through the air on a broomstick, or become invisible and squeeze through keyholes. Everyone *knew* that witches could create thunder, sink ships, kill sheep, and make tables and chairs rattle.

Back in the days of Christopher Columbus, Pope Innocent VIII had issued orders that witches were to be burned. So in Switzerland, during three months in 1515, more than 500 witches went to the stake. Soon fires were lit in France and Germany and all over Europe. England's King James wrote a book about witches, but he wasn't alone. London's publishers were busy with the subject. In the 17th

Judge Samuel Sewall sentenced several witches to death. Later he apologized.

century, Parliament appointed Matthew Hopkins as witch finder. And Hopkins found a lot of witches. Anyone with a pimple or a wart or a mole was a suspect. Those were said to be devil's marks. It was amazing—after torture, many people confessed to knowing the devil.

In the colonies some men and women were hanged or drowned for witchery, but what happened in Salem, Massachusetts, was different from the usual story.

It all began with some little girls and their servant, Tituba. Now Tituba was a poor woman from the West Indies who told stories of the devil and witches and voodoo. The girls were nine-year-old Elizabeth Parris, eleven-year-old Abigail Williams, and their friends. Tituba's stories must have been scary, especially around the fire at night. But when Tituba taught the girls to bark like dogs and mew like cats and grunt like hogs, that might have been fun. Although Elizabeth's father, the Reverend Samuel Parris, didn't think it was fun at all. When he saw the children grunting and mewing and sometimes acting as if they were having fits or spasms, he remembered reading books from England about spells laid on people by witches. He became alarmed.

And then, to everyone's astonishment, on Sunday the girls spoke out during church meeting and said silly things. "There is a yellow bird on the minister's

Four witches are hanged in this 1655 picture. That is the hangman on the ladder. The man on the right is the witch finder, taking his money.

head," cried Anne Putnam. No one would interrupt a church service except the devil! So when the girls said Sarah Good, Sarah Osburn, and Tituba were bewitching them, everyone believed them. The two Sarahs denied the charge. But they were old and poor and no one listened to them, especially after Tituba said that she did indeed fly through the air on a broomstick.

The little girls might have been pretending when they started,

Evil Explained

It wasn't only people from European cultures who feared witches or killed people suspected of witchcraft. Some Native Americans did the same thing. It happened among people who—like the Puritans—were very religious, and wanted an answer to an overwhelming question.

If God is good, how do you explain evil? That is the big question that has concerned people from the beginning of time. It is a central question of great literature and philosophy and religions in all cultures.

There is an easy answer: witches. Suppose you can't explain a sudden earthquake that destroys your town. Suppose you can't explain a disease that kills the young and sweet and promising. Suppose you can't explain a blight that settles on the corn crop and destroys your winter food supply.

Witchcraft is the easy answer. Like the Puritans, the Indians of the pueblo explained the unexplainable with witches. In times of crisis they accused some among themselves of witchcraft, and then they killed the accused. Sometimes one or two witches were enough. Sometimes, as at Salem, it took as many as 20 to exhaust the people's fear.

The Reverend Cotton Mather was a minister and a member of one of Puritan New England's most important families. He was a scholar, and one of the first Americans to promote the smallpox vaccine when most thought it dangerous. Yet he believed firmly in witches and encouraged the hysteria in Salem.

but soon they were telling of torture and witchery, and perhaps they convinced themselves. (Or maybe, now, they were afraid to tell the truth.) Their stories grew longer and their screeches louder. They accused one person after another of putting spells on them. People came from all over Massachusetts to watch them squeal and grunt. What was to be done? Suddenly, anything that went wrong in that little town was the fault of a witch. Salem was mad with witch fever. Five-year-old Dorcas Good was taken to jail and chained to her mother when the girls said she was tormenting them. Then other people began talking of witches and pointing at their neighbors. A court was called to hear the evidence. The judges were scared, like everyone else. The leaders of the community, who might have done some thinking, didn't. More than 100 people were tried as witches; 20 people and two dogs were put to death. Then the Reverend Hale's wife was accused. But there was no one in Massachusetts more beloved and godly than she! Could it be that the girls were wrong? Everyone had believed them; no one had believed the victims. Were those people who had been killed innocent? Yes, an awful tragedy had occurred.

The witch trials were a shameful chapter in American history, although when one of the judges, Samuel Sewall, realized the wrong that had been done, he publicly apologized. The court cleared the names of those who had died. That does make this story better than some. It was a time of witch fear. There had been many witch hangings and burnings in Europe and America; never before was there a public apology. But something devilish did die in that little town of Salem. It was the belief in witchcraft. Most people had learned a sad lesson.

Some Hard Questions

The Puritans have a bad image today. People think of them as narrow bigots. That's not quite fair. The Puritans were sophisticated, sincere believers who thought they had found the truth. They were people who wanted to do right in what they saw as an evil world. The Puritans had left Europe because they didn't want their children tempted by worldly society. But that society followed them. There was to be no escape from the real world.

The problem—for people who believed they knew the ultimate truth—was how to react when their "truths" seemed wrong.

The witchcraft crisis was a problem. So were the hanging of Mary Dyer, the expulsion of Roger Williams, and the persecution of countless Puritans who were thought to have "sinned." Their children and grandchildren began asking questions for which there were no good answers. The old religion was not to survive in the new land.

21 Connecticut, New Hampshire, and Maine

The name Connecticut comes from a Mohican word, *quinni-tukqut*, meaning "at the long tidal river."

The New Haven colonists made their own rules. One said that every male had to have his hair "cut round."

No one is ever all bad or all good. The witch trials may have been a low point for the Puritans, but mostly these were good, strong, intelligent people. If they hadn't been, they never would have crossed the ocean; they would have stayed in England, as most English people did—even when they didn't like the way they were ruled.

Because the Puritans were independent thinkers they sometimes disagreed with each other. When they did, there was plenty of room in America. They could just start a new settlement.

Thomas Hooker was minister in a little town near Boston when, in 1636, he decided to move west; 100 of his followers went with him. He went to the beautiful valley of the Connecticut River. Today, no one is quite sure if he moved because of religious disagreements, or because the valley was fertile and farming was easier than in rocky Massachusetts. Perhaps it doesn't matter. He found good farmland and he was free to preach as he wished.

Hooker had no charter when he arrived in Connecticut. The king hadn't given him permission to be there. He moved in anyway. He had no legal right to the land in the eyes of the English (and certainly none in the eyes of the Native Americans), so the Connecticut settlers sent their governor, John Winthrop II, to England to get a charter.

When he went to see King Charles II, Winthrop wore a handsome ring that had belonged to Anne of Denmark, who happened to be Charles's grandmother. Winthrop gave the ring to Charles. The king, naturally, was delighted to have his grandmother's ring.

An artist's idea of the emigration of Rev. Hooker and his followers to Connecticut. Mrs. Hooker is in a litter—which was like a covered bed with poles to carry it by.

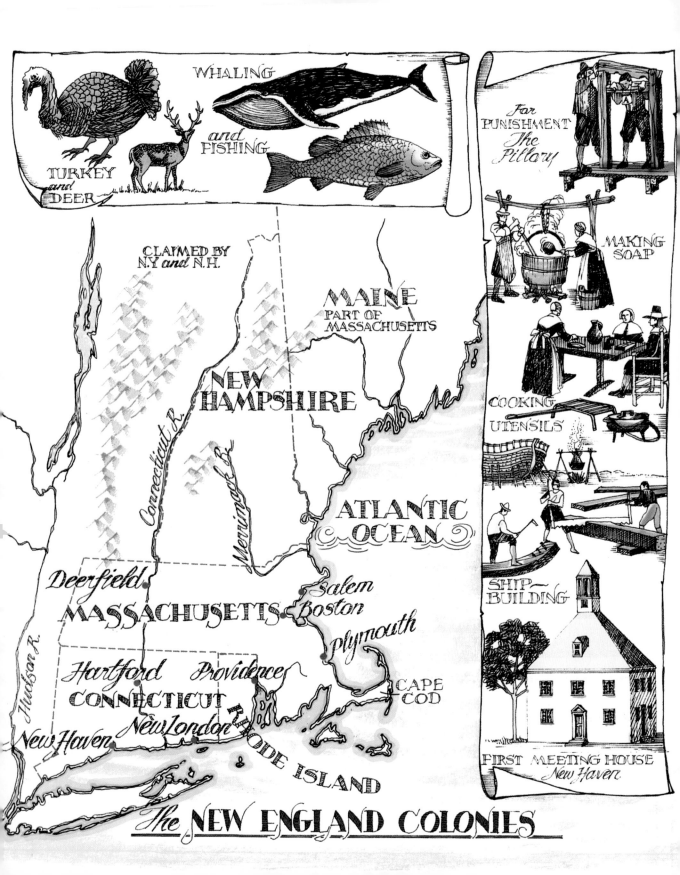

WHALING

and FISHING

TURKEY and DEER

FOR PUNISHMENT
The Pillary

MAKING SOAP

COOKING UTENSILS

SHIP-BUILDING

FIRST MEETING HOUSE
New Haven

CLAIMED BY
N.Y. and N.H.

MAINE
PART OF MASSACHUSETTS

NEW HAMPSHIRE

Connecticut R.

Merrimack R.

ATLANTIC OCEAN

Deerfield

MASSACHUSETTS

Salem
Boston
Plymouth

Hudson R.

Hartford   Providence

CONNECTICUT

New Haven   New London   RHODE ISLAND

CAPE COD

The NEW ENGLAND COLONIES

Connecticut got a charter. The land it granted stretched as far west as the Pacific Ocean (although no one knew how far that was)!

Soon Puritans were heading straight for Connecticut. Massachusetts was getting crowded and the land in Connecticut was inviting. A group settled at New Haven in 1638 and another at New London in 1646. Each town had its own minister. The New Haven colonists published a list of laws that said how you were to behave. One law said "Every male shall have his hair cut round." Another said, "Married persons must live together, or be imprisoned."

In 1639, the settlers in the Connecticut River colony had an open meeting in which they drafted a groundbreaking document known as the Fundamental Orders. It was a constitution establishing a democratic state controlled by "substantial" citizens.

While all this was going on, some people were moving north. The king had given a big piece of northern land to two friends: John Mason and Ferdinano Gorges. They divided that land: Gorges taking what became Maine, and Mason taking New Hampshire.

Mason and Gorges advertised for settlers in England, and people came.

At first, New Hampshire was part of Massachusetts, with John Mason as its proprietor. Then it became a separate colony; finally the king took it back and held it himself as a royal colony.

Maine was never a separate colony; it was part of Massachusetts until 1820, when it became the 23rd state.

As soon as colonies were established, they began competing for good land and good people. The more people who came, the more land they needed.

The big losers in this contest were the Indians. Serious colonization could not take place until the Indians had been pushed off the land. And pushed off they would be.

Mapmaker Hugo Allard drew this colorful map in 1673 to celebrate the Dutch claim to New Netherland. He got a bit carried away, and included the whole coast from Maine to Virginia.

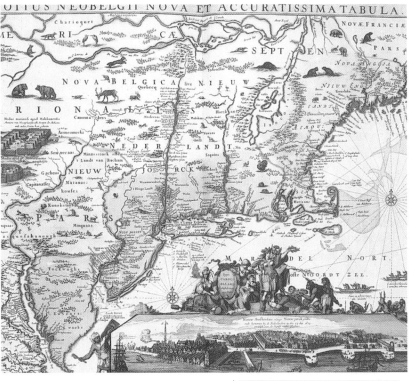

John Mason named New Hampshire after the county of Hampshire, which is on England's south coast.

Land Greed

It was the land that confused the Europeans—there was so much of it. They didn't know how to react. In Europe only the really wealthy—the aristocrats—could own land. Ordinary people didn't even dream of their own land. In America the land was so vast it would take the Europeans more than 200 years just to know how much there was. For a very long time, almost every free person who came to America could afford land.

Most Europeans couldn't quite believe their good fortune. They brought Europe's land greed with them. Each of them wanted to own land—often more than he needed. And almost as soon as the European-Americans got land, they wanted to change it, as Europe's land had been changed.

And so they looked at the beautiful forests and saw an enemy that needed conquering. And they conquered. They cut down trees, leveled hills, filled in swamps, and killed animals and birds. They didn't understand how to work with nature, as the Indians often did. They forced nature to conform to their ways and wants.

It turned out that the land wasn't endless, as they seemed to think at first. One day it would almost all be tamed. Then they would wish for some of those thick forests, some of those songbirds, some of the native animals.

There would be few of them left.

The Indians didn't accept the European idea of landownership. Their religions taught them that the land and waters and animals belonged to God. They thought land could only be shared, not owned. So at first, when they signed treaties selling land, they thought they were selling the right to share it. They didn't expect to be ordered off the land.

Their beliefs told them to live in harmony with nature. Land was to be used by a tribe as a whole, not owned by individuals. It was a way of looking at the land that did away with most greed, but not all greed. Tribes often fought each other for control of the use of land.

Of course, if large numbers of people were to live on the land it had to be changed. Millions and millions of people can't live in a forest. Cities were needed for all the people who would come to live on this bountiful land. And so we built cities and suburbs and in the process often polluted and burned and destroyed. Did we have to do that? Can we have cities and also sheltering woodlands and clean rivers and abundant wildlife? Yes, but it isn't easy. We have to care about our environment. We have to respect the natural world.

Some say one answer is to put heavy industry on space platforms. Some say high-speed trains can be put underground. Some say ideas in science-fiction books can become fact and make the environment healthier.

Can you do anything to help? Of course you can. Do you throw trash around? Does your family worry about pollution? Have you ever helped clean up your neighborhood? Do you know what *conservation* means?

This View Towards Canaan and Salisbury in Connecticut *was made in 1789, but it conveys that feeling of the early settlers—that the land in America went on forever.*

22 King Philip's War

The "entertaining" memoirs of Benjamin Church, who led colonial forces against King Philip.

Many settlers survived King Philip's War only to die of starvation because the fields were trampled or never got planted. The Massachusetts Bay Colony almost went bankrupt, and 12 towns vanished.

Massasoit was a friend of the English colonists. The first New England settlers might not have survived without his help, and they knew it. Once, when he seemed near death, a group of settlers came from Plymouth with goose soup and a broth made from the root of the sassafras tree. Massasoit got better.

Massasoit's people, the Wampanoags, were hunters and fishermen and farmers whose lives turned with the cycle of the seasons. They were peaceful people and good neighbors. When some Pilgrims visited his village, Massasoit honored them by letting them spend the night on a plank bed with himself, his wife, and two of his chiefs.

A year after the Pilgrims arrived, Massasoit signed a treaty of peace with them. For more than 50 years, while he lived, there was peace in Massachusetts. But, even before he died, there were some—Indians and English—who saw trouble ahead. Mostly it was because there were so many English men and women. At first there had been only a few of these newcomers, but soon they were pushing the natives off the land.

Massasoit's two sons were troubled. Their generation was different from that of their father. They were not awed by the English, as their father sometimes seemed. The two boys were Wamsutta and Metacom, but Massasoit had asked the General Court in Plymouth to give them English names. So they were named for ancient kings of Greece: Alexander and Philip.

When his father died, Wamsutta-Alexander became ruler. Some Englishmen feared him. They sent troops, dragged him to Plymouth, threatened him, and acted haughty and superior.

As the Indians' land shrank, King Philip *(above)* told a friend, "I am resolved not to see the day when I have no country."

Alexander became ill and died on his way home. Metacom-Philip was now leader of his people. He believed the English had killed his brother, and he wanted revenge.

Besides, Metacom saw that the new people were destroying his land. (The English now called him King Philip. Some meant it respectfully, but others were mocking when they used the title.) And so Metacom began visiting other Indian leaders trying to convince them to join him to fight the English and drive them from America. That wasn't easy. There was no history of Indian unity. The Indian peoples were as different from each other as Swedes are from Spaniards, or Chinese from Pakistanis. They were descended from different peoples who came in different waves of immigration over the Bering Strait.

Metacom wasn't ready when war began. As with many wars, it was really an accident that started things. A Christian Indian named John Sassamon was killed. Sassamon had been to Harvard and was a friend of the Plymouth colonists. Today, no one is sure who killed him, but the English executed three members of Metacom's tribe for the murder. Metacom was furious. He attacked for revenge.

King Philip's War had begun. It was fought, off and on, for two years, 1675 and 1676, and it was horrible. If you have read about Indian wars—with scalpings, torched villages, tomahawks, and war whoops— you may have been reading about this war. Both sides were incredibly brutal.

Six hundred colonists lost their lives in King Philip's War; 3,000 Indians lost theirs. Fifty of ninety English villages were attacked; many were burned to the ground. The peaceful Narraganset Indians, who had nothing to do with the war, were massacred on their own land in Rhode Island because some of the settlers now feared all Indians. Many

The Pequot War

The Pequots were Indians who lived in New England near Narragansett Bay. Settlers moved into their territory until the Pequots controlled less and less of it. The Indians got angry about this, and killed some settlers and traders. In 1636, the colonists retaliated (fought back) by destroying a Pequot village. The next year war broke out. Captain John Mason (who founded New Hampshire), and his allies from the Mohican and Narraganset tribes, attacked the Pequots' fort, near what is now West Mystic, Connecticut. The Indians inside were burned alive. Those who didn't die were sold into slavery. The Pequots were almost wiped out. It was a taste of what was to come in King Philip's War.

Colonists confront Indians during King Philip's War. Bows and arrows were faster, but guns seemed scary and noisy.

innocent white people were killed in Indian raids of revenge.

Indian disunity hurt their cause. Some tribes helped the English. In addition, Indian warriors weren't used to long wars. They knew how to attack and destroy in quick raids. When the war went on and on, many Indians got tired of it. They wanted to plant their crops and get back to normal activities. They deserted their leader. Finally Metacom was trapped in a swamp, where he was killed by an Indian who was loyal to the colonists. Metacom's head was chopped off and hung on the fort at Plymouth; there it stayed for 25 years. His wife, children, and other captured Indians were sold in the West Indies as slaves.

It was a pattern that was repeated over and over again until the Indians could fight no more.

Tomahawk comes from an Algonquian word for a war club, *tamahakan.*

This skeleton was found in a shallow grave in South Glastonbury, Connecticut. It is thought to be the remains of a Narraganset Indian shot in King Philip's War. A doctor who examined the skeleton in 1959 said that the man was a runner. He died of peritonitis, which developed as a result of his wound.

87

23 The Pueblos Win—At Least for Now

The Spaniards felt it was their duty to convert Indians to Christianity. Their missions did double duty as military forts.

The Spanish missions were small farms built around a church. Sometimes soldiers lived nearby in forts called "presidios." Sometimes the mission and the presidio were combined. Indians lived in the missions and did most of the farming and building. The priests taught them to read and write and to become Christians.

A priest, Fray Marcos de Niza, and a black man named Estebán were the first Old World explorers in New Mexico. They were looking for gold and the seven cities of Cíbola. They didn't find either.

At the very time that Metacom was fighting to free his land from the English invaders, an Indian leader, a man named Popé (poe-PAY), was preparing for the same kind of fight. Popé lived far away, thousands of miles across the continent, in a place the Spaniards called New Mexico. He was a religious leader and a great medicine man, and he would win his battle. He would drive the enemy from his country.

It is 1676 and revolution is brewing in the valley of the river that the Indians call "Big River." The white men call it "Rio Grande" (that means "big river" in Spanish).

The people of the pueblos have seen their land invaded by Spanish men and women. Their people have died mysteriously from diseases that were never known before. The Spaniards are few, but their guns and horses give them power. The Indians are forced to grow crops for the Spaniards, to pay them taxes, to clean their houses, to do their heavy work. The Spaniards take much of their land and some of their women. The pueblo people are made to worship the Spanish god. The Indians believe there is truth in all religions, so they don't mind following the ways of the Catholic Church. But the Spanish priests say that only their religion is true. They call the Indian religion evil. They say that religious freedom is the freedom to worship false gods. The Spanish priests are determined to destroy the old Indian ways. Indian dances are forbidden, the masks of the Indian priests are burned, and so are their sacred kachina dolls, important in religious ceremonies. The priests report proudly to their bishops in Spain that they have destroyed 1,600 Indian masks.

The Pueblo people pretend to do as the Spaniards wish, but, secretly, they keep to the old ways. They train their medicine men in kivas, dark rooms with hidden entries that are dug deep in the ground. Popé is one of those who is trained to be a leader.

The Spaniards have spies among the Indians. They learn of the medicine men and they are enraged. Spanish soldiers round up 47 Indian religious leaders. Four are accused of witchcraft and are hanged in the big plaza in the town called Santa Fe. The others are whipped and thrown in a dungeon.

Now the Indians are furious; even those who have converted to Christianity are enraged. Great numbers of Native Americans march to Santa Fe. (The Indians know the town as "Bead Water.") The Spaniards have killed beloved Indian leaders; they have humiliated others. The most beloved of them all is the man named Popé.

His name means "ripe squash" in the Tewa language. We know little of him except that he was wise and good, and that he inspired others.

The Indians in Santa Fe say they will leave the valley forever if the men are not released. If the Indians leave, the Spaniards will have no one to work for them and they will starve. The Spaniards open the dungeon and let Popé and all the medicine men go.

Popé has learned that the Indians have power when they unite. He must unite his people. But that will not be easy. The pueblo people of the valley speak seven different languages.

Still, he does it. Popé talks to leaders in all the pueblos. He even meets with his people's ancient enemy, the Apache. The Apaches are not pueblo people; they are nomads who have come from the Great Plains. The Apaches agree to help. Plans are made with great secrecy, for the Spaniards have spies everywhere.

In August 1680 Popé is ready. He knows the Spaniards have heard of the plans; he knows they are suspicious; he decides to mislead them. So he sends runners with a message—a message in a knotted rope. The Spaniards capture the runners and the Spanish governor forces an Indian to read the message of the knots. There are four knots and it means the revolution will come in four days.

That's what the message says, and that is what Popé wants the Spaniards to believe. But the next day, before they have time to prepare, all up and down the valley, at every Spanish settlement, at exactly the same time, Indians attack—burning, killing, and destroying. By nightfall only two Spanish communities are left: Santa Fe and Isleta.

Both of those towns are put under siege. That means that if any-

The New Mexican colony got its start in 1598 when Juan de Oñate arrived from Mexico. Oñate, a Spaniard, married a woman whose grandfather was Hernando Cortés and whose great-grandfather was the Aztec emperor Moctezuma. In 1610 the settlement is moved to Santa Fe. What is going on in Plymouth in 1610? How about at Jamestown? St. Augustine?

Though thousands of Pueblo Indians converted to Christianity, most still held on to their own beliefs and ceremonies, such as the Green Corn Dance shown here.

Nomads are people who move a lot. They settle for a while in one place, grazing their flocks. When the land is used up, or the weather changes, they move on to another spot.

Franciscans preach the gospel to two Indian leaders and their wives. One priest was asked how many "true believers" there were among his Pueblo parishioners; he said, "I don't think I have any."

one comes out, the Indians will overwhelm him. Because the plans have been made so well, there is no one to come to the Spaniards' rescue. The Indians have destroyed the other Spanish towns. Popé knows no help will come from Mexico. It usually takes a year and a half for wagons to make that trip. Besides, the winter's heavy rains have flooded the Rio Grande. A wagon train with supplies is stuck in the mud on the wrong side of the river.

Popé gives the Spanish governor a choice: he can stay in Santa Fe and starve, or he can leave the land and take his people with him.

The Spaniards leave—all of them. They march away, back to Mexico. The Indians watch peacefully and let them go. Then they burn the Spanish churches, tear down the Spanish towns, and go back to their old ways. They have won their revolution against tyranny and unfair taxes and religious persecution.

But the leaders in Spain and Mexico don't give up easily. They will return to New Mexico. It will take 12 years, and Popé will be dead, but they will be back. They will deal with the natives again. The Spaniards and the Pueblo Indians will do the same things that Englishmen and East Coast Indians are doing: they will fight, steal, trade, make peace, and misunderstand each other. These are civilizations in conflict. If there is a way for them to live in harmony, no one seems wise enough to have found it.

In 1692 the colonial Spanish leader Don Diego de Vargas *(above)* **and about 100 men reenter Santa Fe without bloodshed. This peace does not last. A year later, a fierce battle is fought for the city. The Pueblos are no longer united, and Vargas wins. The Spaniards call it** *la Reconquista—* **the "reconquest."**

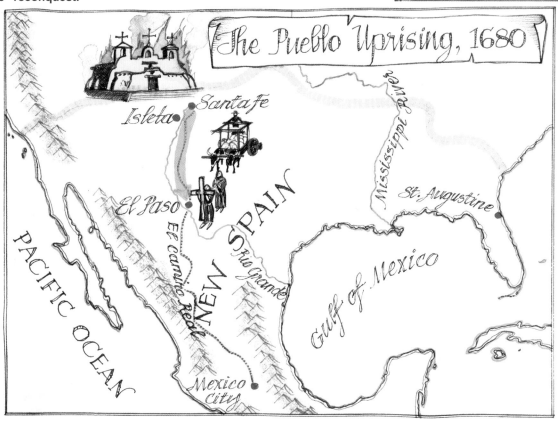

24 What's a Colony?

The Indian on the seal of the Massachusetts Bay Colony is saying "Come over and help us"— which the Indians must have found hard to believe.

Most of the colonies had no cash. They weren't supposed to mint it themselves, and England wouldn't export coins and bills. So the only way money reached the colonies was when people actually bought and sold things with it. Some colonies got so desperate for metal and paper money that they did make it themselves— or they used goods, such as tobacco, corn, and cows, instead.

Neither the landlords (Europeans) nor the renters (colonists) ever considered the Indians, who thought the land was theirs.

You may already know that England had 13 American colonies. I'll list them in just a minute.

First, do you remember what a colony is?

A colony is a place that belongs to another country. Think about a landlord and a renter. England, France, Spain, Holland, Sweden, and Portugal were all landlords in parts of America. They thought they owned the place. Then their colonists, the renters, said, "We're tired of belonging to someone else. We intend to own our own land." When that happened there were revolutions, and the landlords were forced to pack up and go home.

The east coast of North America was an English colony from 1607, when Jamestown began, until the Declaration of Independence was signed in 1776. Those were colonial times.

It was a long time. 1776 minus 1607 is…you can do the arithmetic yourself. When it comes to families, it was about seven generations. That means from son to father to grandfather to great-grandfather to great-great-

Massachusetts minted Pine Tree shillings (above). The $40 bill was backed by Spanish silver.

An artist who lived in the 19th century made this somewhat prettified portrait of an early colonial kitchen. A real 17th-century kitchen was probably barer and dirtier than this, with less furniture and fewer utensils and pots.

grandfather to great-great-great-grandfather to—whew—great-four-times-grandfather. A lot of things can happen in seven generations.

So when you read about colonial times, don't be surprised if you read different descriptions.

When the first colonists arrived, there were no friends to greet them. No houses were ready for them. They had to start from scratch—and I do mean scratch, as in scratching. The early colonists often had to live in huts of branches and dirt, or Indian wigwams, or even caves, and none of those places was bug-proof. And, of course, they had to scratch a living out of the ground.

Later colonists lived in small wooden houses with one or two rooms. Eventually, some lived in fine houses. A few lived in mansions, with beautiful furniture and paintings and dishes and silver. But no one had a bathroom like you have, or electric lights, or a furnace, or running water, or kitchen appliances. And very few people lived in mansions anyway.

You'll be reading about all 13 of the English colonies, because

In 1633, the Dutch brought a schoolmaster to the city of New Amsterdam to teach their children. He was Adam Roelantsen (ROY-lant-sun), and he founded the first school in the North American colonies. Today that school is the Collegiate School in New York City. Two years later, in 1635, Boston Latin School was opened. It was the first public school in the colonies. It, too, still exists.

ENGLISH
COLONIES
About 1740

MAINE
Part of
Massachusetts

New
Hampshire

New
York

Mass.

CLAIMED BY N.Y. and N.H.

IROQUOIS Connecticut Rhode
Island

Pennsylvania

New
Jersey

Delaware

DELAWARE
INDIANS

Appalachian Mountains

Maryland

SHAWNEE

Virginia

N

North
Carolina

CHEROKEE

South
Carolina

Georgia
CREEK

ATLANTIC
OCEAN

they turned into the United States. To get started, we need some organization. We're going to divide the colonies into three groups: north, south, and middle.

Look at the map and you'll see the New England colonies, the Middle Atlantic colonies, and the Southern colonies.

You know a whole lot about New England, so here's a test. Name the New England colonies. (Without checking on the page opposite.)

Did you get them all?

Did you goof and say Maine? Remember, Maine was not a separate colony; it was part of Massachusetts. We haven't said anything about Vermont. Today Vermont is a New England state, and a beautiful one, but it was not a separate colony.

(Remember, don't confuse states with colonies. The 13 colonies will turn into states when the Constitution is written and our nation—the United States—is formed.)

You already know about one Southern colony, Virginia. You will learn about Maryland, North Carolina, South Carolina, and Georgia. (Some people call Maryland a middle colony, but I don't.)

Coming next in this book are the Middle Colonies: New York, New Jersey, Delaware, and Pennsylvania.

First up is New York, where the Dutch are in control. It's hard for us to realize now that tiny Holland was once a great power. The Dutch had colonies all over the world. A business firm, the Dutch West India Company, owned most of the colonies, just as the Virginia and Plymouth companies owned English colonies.

Jonas Michaelius (mick-AY-lee-uss)

Sheep were very important before the colonies grew much cotton. Sheep grow heavy coats in winter, so their wool is sheared in spring.

came to New York in 1628. It was called New Netherland then, and the Dutch West India Company was in charge. That company had promised Michaelius a home in the New World. Here is part of a letter Michaelius wrote soon after he arrived:

The promise which the Lords Masters of the Company had made me to make myself a home…is wholly of no avail. For their honors well know that there are no horses, cows, or laborers to be obtained here for money….The country yields many good things for the support of life, but they are all to be gathered in an uncultivated and wild state.

The Dutch West India Company made promises that couldn't be kept. The Virginia Company did the same thing at Jamestown. (Those early Virginia settlers really expected to find gold on the ground.)

The Puritans always told the truth about their colony. So did a man named William Penn who owned a colony. (Yes, some individuals did own colonies.) We'll get to William Penn and his colony when we finish with New Netherland.

That small Dutch colony was just a trading post. The Dutch thought India—with its silks and spices—was much more important than America. But, just in case America did turn out to be valuable, they decided to do some fur trading on this continent.

The New England colonies are: Massachusetts, New Hampshire, Rhode Island, and Connecticut.

Henry Hudson: New York's Explorer

Henry Hudson knew he had found something special on a September day in 1609 when he sailed his small Dutch ship, the *Half Moon,* into the river that would bear his name. He was looking for the Northwest Passage, and the river seemed likely. It was deep and full of salmon, mullet, and other fish.

The *Half Moon* sailed jauntily, a carved red lion with a golden mane jutting out from its forward tip. The lion was splendid, and so was the whole ship. The bow (the front part of the boat) was bright green, with carved sailors' heads in shades of red and yellow. The decks—the forecastle and the poop—were painted pale blue with white clouds. The stern (the rear of the ship) was royal blue, with stars and a picture of the Man in the Moon. That wasn't all: there were glowing lanterns and flags—the Dutch flag, the flags of all seven Dutch provinces, the flag of the Dutch East India Company, and more.

Now, what would you have thought if you were a Native American standing on the shore of Manhattan Island, and this great colorful seabird appeared with men standing on its back? Remember, this was 1609, and the *Half Moon* was probably the first European ship you'd ever seen. At first the Indians thought it had come from God, and that the men aboard were his messengers. It wasn't long, however, before they realized they were just men.

95

25 Silvernails and Big Tub

New Amsterdam's coat of arms was flanked by a pair of beavers—and fur trading paid the bills.

"Old Silvernails" is what they called him, because the stick of wood that stood in place of his right leg was decorated with silver nails. He had lost the leg in a battle in the West Indies. His real name was Peter Stuyvesant (STY-viss-unt), and he was a Dutch governor and a hard-swearing, tough man. Maybe the Dutch thought Silvernails Stuyvesant was the right kind of person to run a colony in America. Maybe they didn't have any other volunteers. When it came to colonial leaders, the Dutch came up with some strange men.

They had a great piece of property, but they didn't seem to realize that. They just kind of fooled around on the North American continent. They were more serious in other parts of the globe.

Back in 1609, Henry Hudson, an Englishman sailing for the Netherlands, had gone up the river that is now called the Hudson. Because of that voyage, Holland claimed a large hunk of American land. It was land wedged between the stern Puritans in the North and the Anglican tobacco planters in the South; the Dutch called it New Netherland. (Today we know it as New York and New Jersey.)

In case you're confused: Holland, the Netherlands, and the land of the Dutch are all the same place. Why don't you find it on a map? And, while you're looking, can you find England? Can you see why both nations became sea powers? Now, cross the Atlan-

Peter Stuyvesant is still remembered in New York, where a high school is named after him.

Three early views of New Amsterdam. The big picture shows the town as seen from the village of Breukelen (today's Brooklyn Heights) across the East River. The plan at right looks down, showing the line of the city wall. The third picture shows the view from across the Hudson River, in New Jersey. In the 17th century, most of Manhattan was farmland.

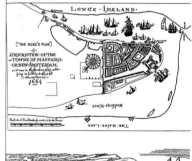

tic. Put a finger on New York Harbor. Go up the Hudson River and look for a passage to China. You'll be stopped by rapids in the river when you get to Albany. That's what happened to Henry Hudson.

In 1626 the Dutch West India Company made what may be the most famous real-estate deal in history. It bought Manhattan Island (now the center of New York City) and Long Island from the Indians who lived there for some beads and goods said to be worth $24. Since the Indians didn't think people could own land, they may have thought they were outsmarting the white men.

By this time, the Dutch had decided that American furs might be almost as good as American gold, so they set up some trading posts. People in Europe were eager to buy American furs. Beaver, bear, fox, and other fur pelts could be made into sumptuous hats, coats, and blankets. The Dutch merchants hoped to get rich in the New World.

On Manhattan Island the people from Holland built a town called New Amsterdam. At one end they put a wall because they feared wolves and because cities in Europe had walls. Today that wall is the site of a famous street. Can you guess what it is called? Outside the wall were farms, which the Dutch called *bouweries*. Today a street

You guessed it—Wall Street!

After a while, Jews in New Amsterdam were allowed to trade and own houses. But they were not allowed to build a synagogue until 1730, so they had to hold services in their homes.

Settlers in New Sweden trading with Delaware Indians. In 1643 the Swedes sold arms to the Delaware, who were fighting a Maryland tribe. Here they are making a deal to use the Indians' land for trapping furs.

Manhattan is an island 12½ miles from end to end. Broadway, its longest street, runs the length of the island.

in New York is called "the Bowery." (It doesn't look much like a farm now.)

Because of its great harbor, New Amsterdam was soon a sailor's town, bustling with people who arrived on ships from faraway places. It was said that you could hear 18 different languages being spoken in the city of New Amsterdam. Right away, in 1626, the Dutch brought slaves to New Amsterdam. You could buy a slave for about the same amount it would cost to pay a worker one year's salary. So some people thought it made good sense to own slaves. It was an economic, or money, decision.

One day a ship sailed into New Amsterdam's harbor with a group of Jews aboard. Peter Stuyvesant didn't want them to land. He was a bigot and didn't believe in religious freedom. Stuyvesant was a member of the Dutch Reformed Church and saw no reason to tolerate others. "Giving them liberty," he wrote ("them" meant the Jews), "we cannot refuse the Lutherans and Papists [Catholics]." But the Dutch West India Company said the Jews could stay, so there was nothing Stuyvesant could do.

Grouchy Old Silvernails was in charge of all of New Netherland. He was pretty good at running things, but he would stomp his wooden leg and swear at anyone who disagreed with him. When the Dutchmen who had been elected councilors objected to something he said, he called them "ignorant subjects." Another time he said he would ship them back to Holland—in pieces—if they gave him trouble.

But if you were going to run a swearing contest, Stuyvesant might lose. Johan Printz (YO-han PRINCE) had a mouth that was even more foul. He was governor of New Sweden, on the Delaware Bay, not far from New Netherland.

Printz was a whale of a man. The Indians called him Big Tub, and he may have been the biggest man on the continent. He was seven feet tall and weighed 400 pounds. Big Tub was an autocrat—an absolute ruler—and he liked to hang people who opposed him. But he did hold his colony together for 10 years, with very little help from the Swedes at home. And he introduced a new style of architecture, the log cabin, that became popular in frontier settlements.

Finally, Johan Printz got tired of trying to run things himself and went back to Sweden. The new Swedish governor decided to get tough and capture a Dutch fort, but he didn't realize what Old Silvernails was like. Stuyvesant sent seven ships, and that wiped out the Swedish colony.

That made Stuyvesant popular in New Amsterdam—but not for long. Nine years later, in 1664, the English decided to do to the Dutch what the Dutch had done to the Swedes. Old Silvernails stomped on his wooden leg, but nobody came to his rescue. The British took New Amsterdam without firing a shot. They renamed it New York.

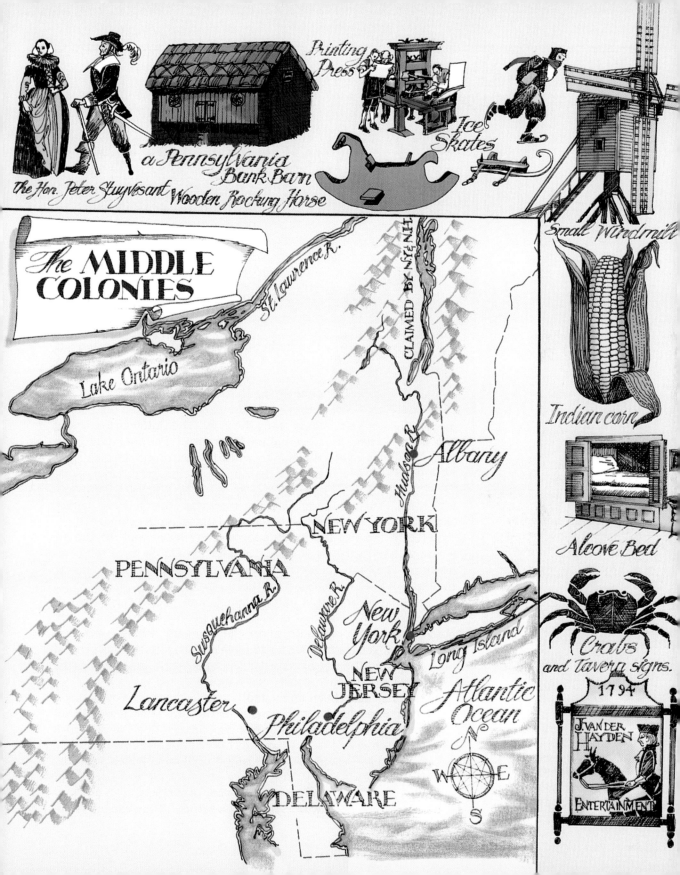

the Hon. Peter Stuyvesant

a Pennsylvania Bank Barn

Wooden Rocking Horse

Printing Press

Ice Skates

Small Windmill

The MIDDLE COLONIES

St. Lawrence R.

CLAIMED BY NY & NH

Lake Ontario

Hudson R.

Albany

NEW YORK

PENNSYLVANIA

Susquehanna R.

Delaware R.

New York

Long Island

NEW JERSEY

Lancaster

Philadelphia

Atlantic Ocean

DELAWARE

N
W   E
S

Indian corn

Alcove Bed

Crabs and Tavern signs.

1794

J. VAN DER HAYDEN

ENTERTAINMENT

26 West to Jersey

James, Duke of York, later became James II, king of England, but he was not popular.

The Netherlands pulled down its flag and left America. It was 1664, and the Dutch had been here for 50 years. During those years they had gone up the Hudson River, built a town at Fort Orange (Albany), and established big plantations along the river. The Dutch farm owners were called "patroons." People came from Holland to work the patroons' farms. They brought their tulips, their hardworking habits, their neatness, and their storytelling ways with them. (Their children's favorite story was about a fellow named Santa Claus, who visited just before Christmas, on December 6.)

Actually, most of the Dutch people didn't leave, and the British even let Peter Stuyvesant stay. They let the Dutch have religious freedom. The Netherlanders just weren't in charge anymore. It was the Duke of York who owned the place now.

The Duke of York was named James, and his brother was the king of England. York (that is what some people called James) was one of the owners of the Royal African Company, which controlled the British slave trade. It seems to have occurred to the duke that if he encouraged the use of slaves in the New World, he would make lots of money. And that is just what happened.

York must have been conceited and vain, because you can see what he named his land. Well, that isn't quite true. It wasn't all called New York. Some of it became New Jersey. The Duke of York gave a big chunk of land to two of his friends. One of them, Sir George Carteret, came from the island of Jersey, which explains why it was "New" Jersey. The duke's other friend was Lord John Berkeley. Berkeley's brother was governor of Virginia.

Those two owners were called "proprietors." They expected the people who lived on their land to pay them a tax called a "quit rent." That didn't make them very popular.

But they had good qualities all the same. They wrote a plan of government, a charter, that was the best any English colony had. It set up an assembly that represented the settlers. (Assemblies, parliaments, and congresses are all similar organizations.) The charter provided for freedom of religion. You could be a Quaker or a Puritan or an Anglican in New Jersey, and, as long as you were a man, you had the right to vote. You didn't have that freedom in Massachusetts or Virginia or most of the other colonies.

Soon people were pouring into New Jersey from all over: Finns, Swedes, Germans, English and others. In New Jersey everybody lived together in harmony.

At first New Jersey was divided into East Jersey and West Jersey. Then the king bought out the proprietors, united New Jersey, and made it a royal colony. That meant the king was now the owner of New Jersey. He sent a royal governor to take charge and collect his rents. The king allowed the colonists to keep making their own laws through the elected assembly.

For a while, New Jersey was part of the western frontier of the country. The frontier was land that was on the edge of what Europeans considered civilization. If you look at a map, you can see where the frontier of European civilization was in 1700. Is there a frontier today? Where might it be? Clue: look up.

Fort Orange, which became Albany, was established as a fur trading post before New Amsterdam.

These are rows of old Dutch houses in Albany.

27 Cromwell and Charles

Charles didn't have to lose his head, but he wouldn't give his opponents an inch. That was his downfall.

On January 30, 1649, just before he was beheaded, Charles I asked for a warmer shirt than usual, lest the cold make him tremble as though from fear. He said, "I fear not death. Death is not terrible to me. I bless my God I am prepared." When the executioner held up the head of the king, the great crowd gave out a groan. "It was such a groan," said a witness, "as I never heard before, and desire I may never hear again."

Oliver Cromwell *(right)* was a very good general who often beat the Royalists even when he was outnumbered. He wasn't a very good ruler, unfortunately.

Even though this is a book about US, you need to keep up with events in England, because what was going on there was very important to the colonists in America. And something unexpected was happening in England. A civil war was being fought. The war was between King Charles I and the Puritans. The king lost the war. Then the Puritans executed him. (Kings are never killed, they are executed.)

Are you surprised about the civil war? Are you surprised that the English would chop off their king's head? Back then a lot of people were astonished.

Some people called the new government the "Protectorate." Some people called it the pits.

Virginians were on the side of the king; people on that side were called "Cavaliers." (They got that name because the king's soldiers fought mostly on horseback, and soldiers on horseback are called "cavalry.")

The New Englanders, naturally, were for the Puritans, who were sometimes called "Roundheads." (They wore their hair short at a time when many men wore their hair long.) When they needed a haircut, Puritan men would put a bowl on their heads and cut around the bowl, as in the picture in chapter 21.)

Put 1649 in your head. Because—talking about heads—1649 was the year Charles I lost his. It was an important moment in history because

BANCKET HAVS.

it reminded people that kings could be overthrown. And, though it happened in England, it helped bring freedom to Americans.

That revolution in 1649—and it really was a revolution—was called the English Civil War. I'll say it again, because it is so important: in 1649 the Puritans won the English Civil War, and Charles I lost his head. Some people think this revolution was a failure—because, as you will soon learn, kings came back. But it wasn't a failure. The Civil War made an important point: people can change their government if they want to badly enough.

But now we're in 1649, and, since poor King Charles I is without a head, the Puritan leader, Oliver Cromwell, takes charge of the government. I would like to tell you that Cromwell does a splendid

At King Charles's trial, the judge put on a scarlet gown to read the death sentence: "Charles Stuart is a tyrant, traitor, murderer, and public enemy to the good people of this nation, and shall be put to death by the severing of his head from his body."

The first Cavaliers are swaggering young men who act as Charles's personal guard.

The Plague that devastates London in Charles II's reign ends with another disaster—the Great Fire of 1666. The fire starts in a bakery and spreads quickly. Soon most of London's old wooden houses are gone. So are the Plague germs.

job as ruler, but he doesn't. When the Puritans take power they destroy many Anglican churches, break church windows, smash statues, and burn great works of art. They even kill some Catholics and Anglicans, just because of their religion.

Oliver Cromwell tries to do what he thinks is right. He is a strong leader, and he does do many good things. But he doesn't understand that his opponents have rights, too. You could call him a tyrant and not be wrong.

One of the first things the Puritans do is to close all the theaters in London. That is going too far. London is known for its theaters and its free-speaking plays. A few of the plays in London are wicked and others mock politicians. Tyrants (wherever they are) never appreciate free speech. (Why?)

Besides, the Puritans don't have much of a sense of humor. In one of Shakespeare's plays, called *Twelfth Night,* Sir Toby Belch, a clown-like character, makes fun of Puritan behavior. Sir Toby says, "Dost thou think, because thou art virtuous, there shall be no more cakes and ale?" (What does he mean by that?) The Puritans won't even let Shakespeare's plays be seen. (Shakespeare died in 1616.)

When Cromwell dies (in 1658), his son Richard—who is known as "Tumbledown Dick"—tries to take over. Dick is a quiet man who likes farming and sports better than ruling. He can't hold on to power. Besides, the English people are tired of the stern Puritans, and they want to have fun. They want cakes and ale. So they put the old king's son on the throne. He is Charles II, and because of his good nature he is known as the "merry monarch." The time in which he rules is called the "Restoration." (You can see why it is the Restoration—kings were *restored* to power.)

But Charles isn't so merry when it comes to the Puritans. He kills some of them, and he digs up Cromwell's body and cuts off his head. Now Puritans are being mistreated. Things get so bad during the Restoration that many Puritans leave England and come to America.

Some of the king's friends come, too. When Charles II becomes king, he decides to reward friends who stayed loyal to his family while Cromwell was running things. He gives them gifts of America. As you know, he gives his brother, the Duke of York, the gift of New Netherland. (Then he sends an army to take it from the Dutch.)

He gives the Carolinas to eight of his favorite lords. He gives Pennsylvania to a young man whose religion makes it dangerous for him to live in England. In the next chapter I will tell you why.

28 William the Wise

"I have led the greatest colony into America that ever any man did upon a private credit."

William Penn was born with a silver spoon in his mouth and servants at his feet. His father was an important admiral: rich, Anglican, and a friend of King Charles II.

What did William Penn do when he grew up? He became a member of a radical, hated, outcast sect, the Society of Friends, also known as the Quakers.

What did being a Quaker do for William Penn? It got him kicked out of college when he refused to attend Anglican prayers. It got him a beating from his father, who wanted him to belong to the Church of England. It led him to jail for his beliefs—more than once. It gave him a faith that he carried through his life. And it also gave him a reason for founding an American colony.

King Charles II liked William Penn in spite of his religion. Everyone, it seems, was charmed by his sweet ways. But when Penn came before the king and refused to take off his hat—Quakers defer only to God—some people gasped and wondered if Penn's head, along with his hat, might be removed. But Charles, the "merry monarch," must have been in a good mood. As the story goes, he laughed and doffed his own hat, saying, "Only one head can be covered in the presence of a king."

Now King Charles had borrowed money from Admiral Penn, and a goodly sum it must have been, because, after the admiral died, when William asked that the debt be paid with land in America, he was given a tract of land larger than all of England. King Charles named it Pennsylvania, which means "Penn's woods."

Pennsylvania was situated midway between the pious Puritans in

An Hiſtorical and Geographical Account
OF THE
PROVINCE and COUNTRY
OF
PENSILVANIA;
AND OF
Weſt-New-Jerſey
IN
AMERICA.

The Richneſs of the Soil, the Sweetneſs of the Situation, the Wholeſomneſs of the Air, the Navigable Rivers, and others, the prodigious Encreaſe of Corn, the flouriſhing Condition of the City of *Philadelphia*, with the ſtately Buildings, and other Improvements there, The ſtrange Creatures, as Birds, Beaſts, Fiſhes, and Fowls, with the ſeveral ſorts of Minerals, Purging Waters, and Stones, lately diſcovered The Natives, Aborogines, their Language, Religion, Laws, and Cuſtoms; The firſt Planters, theDutch, Sweeds, and Engliſh, with the number of its Inhabitants; As alſo a Touch upon George Keith's New Religion, in his ſecond Change ſince he left the *QUAKERS*

With a Map of both Countries.

By GABRIEL THOMAS,
who reſided there about Fifteen Years.

London, Printed for, and Sold by A. Baldwin, at the Oxon Arms in Warwick-Lane, 1698.

Gabriel Thomas, one of the earliest settlers in Pennsylvania, wrote a pamphlet in praise of its charms—you can read his words on page 108.

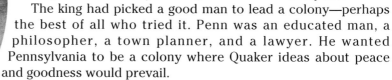

Charles II died a Catholic at heart, but he admired William Penn enough to let him practice his religion in America.

New England and the convivial Anglicans in the South. Quakers weren't wanted in either region.

Thanks to William Penn, Quakers now had their own colony. But he made it different from most of the other colonies. Penn really believed in brotherly love. He said that Pennsylvania was not just for Quakers but for everyone.

The king had picked a good man to lead a colony—perhaps the best of all who tried it. Penn was an educated man, a philosopher, a town planner, and a lawyer. He wanted Pennsylvania to be a colony where Quaker ideas about peace and goodness would prevail.

In England, Quakers seemed a threat to everyone who felt comfortable with the old, established ways of thinking. The country had beheaded a king, and that didn't work out. New ideas seemed dangerous, as they often do. Quakers had notions that would change Old England. Wealthy citizens didn't want things to change, so it was poor people, mostly, who were Quakers.

In Penn's day, some people—ministers, kings, lords, and dukes—were considered superior to the average person. They expected others to bow to them, but Quakers wouldn't. They wouldn't bow to anyone. They even refused to pay taxes to support the Church of England. Can you see a problem? The Anglicans did.

England had lords and ladies in the rich upper class, merchants and farmers in the middle class, and peasants and poor people in the lower class. It was almost impossible to rise from the lower class to the upper. The upper-class lords and earls often acted as if they were better than anyone else. It was that class system that made many ambitious people come to the New World. In America, with hard work, many poor people would rise to the top.

Because the Bible says, "Thou shalt not kill," Quakers believe all war is wrong. They won't fight even when drafted into the army. They are called "conscientious objectors," because their conscience tells them not to fight.

And they won't swear allegiance to a king or government or flag or anyone but God. That was another real problem in England, where people were expected to swear their loyalty to the king.

William Penn wanted to practice Quaker ideas in America. That

Your *conscience* is your sense of right and wrong. It's something that tells you when you're doing right and warns you when you're doing wrong. *Conscientious* means being careful to do what you know is right.

The South East Prospect of The City of Philadelphia By Peter Cooper *Painter*

meant treating all people as equals and respecting all religions. Those new ideas of "toleration" and "natural rights" were confusing. It was difficult for good people to know what was right.

Do you understand the difference between toleration and equality? Some colonies offered freedom of religion but not equality. You could practice any religion but you couldn't vote or hold office (be a mayor or sheriff) unless you belonged to the majority's church. That wasn't true in Penn's colony. While he was in charge, all religions were equal.

When Penn said all people, he meant *all* people. Quakers were among the first to object to Negro slavery and, more than anyone else, to treat Indians as equals. In 1681, William Penn wrote a letter to the Native Americans of Pennsylvania. He said:

> may [we] always live together as neighbors and friends, else what would the great God say to us, who hath made us not to devour and destroy one another, but live soberly and kindly together in the world?

Penn proposed a "firm league of peace." He continued:

> I am very sensible of the unkindness and injustice that hath been too much exercised toward you by the people of these parts of the world…but I am not such a man…I desire to win and gain your love and friendship by a kind, just, and peaceable life.

Penn was generous as well as fair. He offered land on easy terms to those who came to his colony.

On his first visit to America, he sailed up the Delaware River and picked the site of Pennsylvania's first capital, Philadelphia. Then he helped plan the city by using a pattern of crossing streets, called a "grid," that would be copied throughout the new land. He gave numbers to all the streets that went in one direction; the streets that went the other way he gave tree names, like Pine and Chestnut and Walnut. Philadelphia is still thought of as a fine example of town planning.

Penn wrote a Charter of Liberties for Pennsylvania. Penn said the charter set up a government "free to the people under it, where the

This view of Philadelphia, painted by Peter Cooper in about 1720, is the oldest surviving canvas of any American city.

William Penn planned his city, Philadelphia, without walls or fortifications, because he expected its citizens to be peaceful.

Today the capital of Pennsylvania is Harrisburg.

107

laws rule, and the people are a party to those laws."

The southeastern part of Pennsylvania was called the "Three Lower Counties." In 1704 those counties asked for their own assembly and William Penn gave it to them. In 1776 they became an independent state named Delaware.

William Penn didn't stay in America for long. He had business to attend to in England, and so he chose rulers for Pennsylvania. Since he owned the place, he had a right to do that.

Penn did not believe in democracy. (Hardly anyone did at the beginning of the 18th century.) He was an aristocrat. In those days, ordinary people were not thought to be capable of picking their own leaders. William Penn thought he was choosing good people to lead his colony. But, as it turned out, he was too trusting.

The men he picked to run his colony fought among themselves and cheated him. (He would have been better off if he had believed in democracy.) William Penn lost most of his fortune developing Pennsylvania.

But Penn did prove that freedom and fairness work. Philadelphia was soon the largest, most prosperous city in the colonies. People came from Germany, France, Scotland, and Wales—as well as England—looking for religious freedom and a good place to live. One, a boy named Benjamin Franklin, came from Boston.

William Penn and the Indians make peace, in this painting by Edward Hicks.

29 Ben Franklin

Franklin was famous for his countrified appearance. The French couldn't get over his fur hat.

Some people had problems with Benjamin Franklin. They accused him of not having any gravity. Now that doesn't mean he floated around like a weightless space voyager. *Gravity* has another meaning, as in "grave." No, not a place where you get buried, but you are getting closer. Someone who is grave is very serious, maybe a bit dull, and certainly not much fun. Ben Franklin did have a problem. He just couldn't stay serious or dull. He was always playing jokes or having fun.

The French had no trouble with Ben. They loved his jokes and admired his good mind. They were amazed by all the things he had done. He was a scientist, an inventor, a writer, and a great patriotic American.

His mind never seemed to stop for rest. Daylight saving time was his idea; and he invented bifocal glasses, the lightning rod, the one-arm desk chair, and an efficient stove. He founded the first public library, the first city hospital, and the University of Pennsylvania. He was the most famous journalist of his time, and the first editor to use cartoons as illustrations. He made electricity into a science. And that is only part of what he did.

Benjamin Franklin helped with the ideas that made this country special, and he got the French to help pay for the revolution that made us free.

But, as I said, some people had problems with Franklin. The English people didn't much like him. Well, that's not quite true. It was English politicians who didn't like him, especially when the colonies began to object to the way England was treating them.

When Ben was sent to London to represent the Americans, one Englishman wrote, "I look upon him as a dangerous engine." And Lord

Vive Franklin!

The French were fascinated by Benjamin Franklin. (Vive means "long live" in French.) One Frenchman who met him at court said:

The most surprising thing was the contrast between the luxury of our capital, the elegance of our fashions, the magnificence of Versailles...the polite haughtiness of our nobility—and Benjamin Franklin. His clothing was rustic, his bearing simple but dignified, his language direct, his hair unpowdered. It was as though classic simplicity, the figure of a thinker of the time of Plato...had suddenly been brought by magic into...the 18th century.

This poem was written in Franklin's honor:

To steal from Heaven its
sacred fire he taught;
The arts to thrive in savage
climes he brought;
In the New World the first
of Men esteem'd;
Among the Greeks a God
he has been deem'd.

109

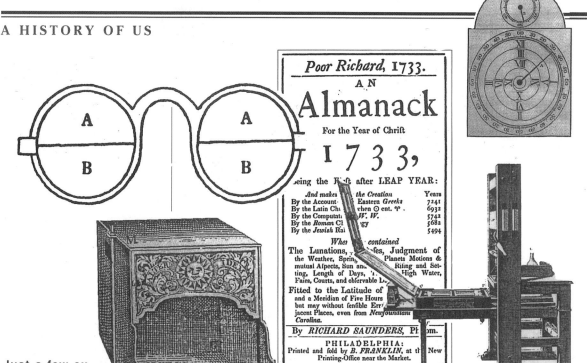

Just a few examples of Franklin's many interests. *Clockwise from lower left:* a Franklin stove, bifocals, a copy of *Poor Richard's Almanack,* a two-faced clock (the lower part tells hours and minutes, the upper part tells seconds—but it was too hard to read and never caught on), and, of course, a printing press.

Benjamin Franklin was born on January 17, 1706, and died on April 17, 1790. His life spanned the 18th century.

Sandwich (that really was his name) called him one of the "most mischievous enemies" that England ever knew. (By the way, sandwiches were named for Lord Sandwich, whose real name was John Montagu. He liked his servants to fix him a snack—meat between bread—when he played cards.)

Some Americans accused Franklin of liking the English too much; the English, of course, said he didn't like them at all. What Ben was doing was trying to be fair and also trying to prevent war. He said, "There never was a good war or a bad peace."

I think you would have liked him. And if you want to have a real hero, someone to use as a guide for ordering your life, you can't do better than Benjamin Franklin. He had what has been called a "happy balance of earnestness and humor." He made the most of what he had.

One of his biographers wrote, "He had a talent for happiness." Another said, "He hated solemn pompous people....He gave away much of his money...he set about improving himself."

But you need to know something of his life, so you can judge the man yourself.

Benjamin Franklin was born in Boston, the 15th child in a family with 17 children. He was the youngest son of the youngest son of the youngest son—back to his great-great-grandfather. His father was a hardworking candlemaker descended from Puritan stock. Young Franklin went to school for three years, and then his parents could afford no more. It was enough to get him started; he loved books and reading, and he educated himself.

One thing he didn't like was candlemaking. So his father signed him as an apprentice to Ben's older half-brother, James, who was a printer. In return for room and board (food) and training, an apprentice had to work for a certain number of years. He was not free to quit. It was something like being an indentured servant. Ben was 12 years old, and his father signed him for nine years.

He didn't get along with his brother, and what he really wanted to do was to go to sea. But he made the best of a bad situation. The print shop was a good place to learn. There were stacks of books—he read them all—and interesting people dropped by. Some wrote for the newspaper James printed and owned.

Ben wanted to write for the paper, but he knew James wouldn't publish his work. So he wrote letters to the editor and signed them with the made-up name of a woman; he called her "Silence Dogood."

The earliest portrait of Ben Franklin in existence was painted in about 1748, when he was 42 years old and the postmaster of Philadelphia.

The letters were a big hit. Silence wrote that she was "naturally very jealous for the rights and liberties of my country: and the least appearance of an incroachment on those invaluable privileges, is apt to make my blood boil exceedingly."

When Dogood wrote a description of herself, it could have been a description of Franklin: "I never intend to wrap my talent in a napkin," she wrote. "To be brief; I am courteous and affable, good-humoured (unless I am first provoked), handsome, and sometimes witty."

Everyone wanted to know who Silence Dogood was. When Ben's brother found out, he stopped printing the letters.

Ben wasn't happy, but he didn't sit around and mope. One thing Benjamin Franklin did all his life was to try and find ways to improve himself. Maybe it was his Puritan background that made him industrious.

He decide he wanted to be a writer. Ben had learned to spell at

Incroachment (which we spell *encroachment*) means "taking another's possessions gradually or slyly." Usually the word is used to describe the illegal taking of land: "He encroached on his neighbor's property."

That's Franklin on the horse in the middle. He's being honored in a parade because he helped fight off Indian attacks on the Pennsylvania frontier in 1755.

Prose is plain language not arranged as verse.

Saucy means "fresh." A *shilling* was an English silver coin, worth one-twentieth of a pound.

the printing house, but his father told him that the style of his writing was not good. So he found a friend and they wrote letters back and forth. Then he worked out exercises to improve his writing style. Sometimes he turned stories into poems, then back again into prose. It was a fine way to learn to work with words.

When Ben was 16, he read about a vegetable diet. He became a vegetarian and bought books with the money he saved by not eating meat. Soon he could talk about books with anyone. He was becoming very well educated.

But he still had problems with his brother. "Perhaps I was too saucy and provoking," said Ben. "My brother was passionate, and had often beaten me, which I took extremely amiss." Finally, at 17, Ben ran away from Boston. He sold his books and used the money to get to Philadelphia. In his *Autobiography*, Franklin described his arrival in that city:

> *I was dirty from my journey; my pockets were stuffed out with shirts and stockings; I knew no soul nor where to look for lodging. I was fatigued with traveling, rowing, and want of rest; I was very hungry; and my whole stock of cash consisted of a Dutch dollar and about a shilling in copper. The latter I gave the people of the boat for my passage, who at first refused it on account of*

my rowing; but I insisted on their taking it, a man being some-times more generous when he has but a little money than when he has plenty, perhaps through fear of being thought to have but little.

Then I walked up the street, gazing about, till near the market house I met a boy with bread. I had made many a meal on bread, and inquiring where he got it, I went immediately to the baker's he directed me to, in Second Street, and asked for biscuit, intending such as we had in Boston; but they, it seems, were not made in Philadelphia. Then I asked for a three-penny loaf, and was told they had none such. So, not considering or knowing the difference of money, and the greater cheapness nor the names of his bread, I bade him give me three-penny-worth of any sort. He gave me, according-ly three great puffy rolls. I was surprised at the quantity, but took it, and, having no room in my pockets, walked off with a roll under each arm, and eating the other. Thus I went up Market Street as far as Fourth Street, passing by the door of Mr. Read, my future wife's father; when she, standing at the door, saw me, and thought I made, as I certainly did, a most awkward, ridiculous appearance.

That awkward boy soon had a job working for a printer. Then he got a chance to go to London. He went and had adventures and learned a lot. When he returned to Philadelphia, he opened a print shop. Soon he began publishing his own newspaper. He became the best printer in Philadelphia. Because he was so good, he printed all the official papers for the colony of Pennsylvania.

Then he decided to publish an almanac. In the 17th century, al-most every colonial home had two books: one was a Bible, the other was an almanac. The almanac was very useful. It had a calen-dar; it predicted the weather; it told when the moon would be full and when it would be a sliver; it told about the ocean's tides; and it was filled with odds and ends of information. Ben Franklin, with his curiosity, had a head filled with interesting information. His al-manac, called *Poor Richard's Almanack*, became very popular. Poor Richard was always giving advice. He said things like:

Early to bed and early to rise, makes a man healthy, wealthy and wise.
God helps them who help themselves.
Three may keep a secret, if two of them are dead.

The almanac made Benjamin Franklin rich. He decided to retire, at age 42, and spend the rest of his life doing all the things he want-ed to do. He studied electricity, invented things, became a politi-cian, and was soon Philadelphia's most famous citizen. He would help found a new nation. By his example he showed that in America a poor boy could become the equal of anyone in the world.

What did Ben Franklin say when he discovered electricity?

Nothing. He was too shocked.

If you would not be forgotten,
As soon as you are dead and rotten,
Either write things worth reading,
Or do things worth the writing.
—*Benjamin Franklin*

This was Benjamin Franklin's proposal for an experiment to decide whether lightning is electricity. "On the top of some high tower or steeple, place a kind of sentry-box…big enough to contain a man and an electric stand. From the middle of the stand let an iron rod rise and pass bending out of the door, and then upright 20 feet, pointed very sharp at the end. A man standing on it, when such clouds are passing low, might be electrified." He didn't un-derstand that being elec-trified can kill you.

30 Maryland's Form of Toleration

Cecil Calvert, Maryland's owner, could make his own coins —here's his face on a 1659 silver shilling.

Did you notice that we have been traveling south? After New England we stopped in New York and New Jersey, and then Pennsylvania and Delaware. Now, if you look around, you'll see we've reached fertile, water-lapped Maryland.

Maryland is sometimes called a Southern colony and sometimes a Middle colony. During the Civil War it was a "Border colony." Can you guess why Maryland has had a hard time with its identity?

Sir George Calvert was an English lord and a real gentleman. That means he acted like one. He was not a poor boy who had to do everything for himself; he was wealthy, very wealthy. He was also energetic and daring.

Sir George made things hard for himself by becoming a Catholic. The English didn't like Catholics.

But, remember, the Spaniards, French, and Portuguese didn't like Protestants. This may seem a bit tiresome, but it was serious business back in the 17th century. You could get your head cut off if you practiced the wrong religion.

Sir George didn't get his head cut off, but he was forced to resign from his important government position. Since everyone liked him (he was a real gentleman), things worked out. The Irish—who were Catholic—were happy when the king gave him land in Ireland and named him Baron of Baltimore. Then King Charles I, who really liked Sir George, gave him a colony in America.

They named it Maryland. That was said to be in honor of the king's Catholic wife, Queen Henrietta Maria, although some say Calvert really meant to honor Mary, the mother of Jesus Christ.

Sir George dreamed of a colony "founded on religious freedom, where there would not only be a good life, but also a prosperous one, for those bold enough to take the risk." It was George Calvert's son, Cecil (SESS-ul), who actually founded the colony. He thought English Catholics could live in harmony there with Protestants.

Many Catholics did go to Maryland, but not as many as expected. Even Cecil, the new Lord Baltimore, didn't go. Cecil just stayed home and took the money that came from his colony.

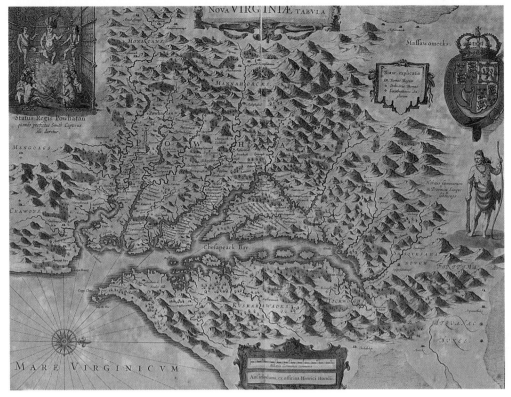

The label on this 1638 map calls the area pictured "Nova Virginiae" (New Virginia). Today it's mostly Maryland, as you can tell by comparing the picture to a modern map. Look for the Susquehanna Indian woman (the map says "Sasquesahanoug") hunting with a bow and a club. At the upper left Powhatan holds court "as he did when Captain Smith was delivered to him prisoner." If you turn back to page 23, you'll see the map by John Smith that this map is based on. What had mapmakers learned about the area in the years since Smith's map?

He sent his younger brother, Leonard, to be the first governor. He told him to be "very careful to preserve unity and peace…and treat the Protestants with as much mildness and favor as justice will permit."

The Calverts ruled well. They saw that there was representative government and that people were treated fairly. In 1649, the Calverts urged the Maryland Assembly to pass a Toleration Act. The Assembly did—it was a landmark act. Religious freedom was a new

Baltimore *(below)* was a small but thriving township by the end of the 1700s.

At top left is George Calvert, who sought freedom for Catholics in Maryland. Below is Queen Henrietta Maria, the wife of King Charles I; at right, painted in 1761, is Calvert's great-great-great-great-great grandson, Charles—and, of course, a slave.

idea that was being talked about by European philosophers, and practiced by Quakers (who still seemed peculiar to most people). But now a conservative American colony was trying out that freedom with an official act.

The Calverts were being practical. They meant to protect the Catholic minority and encourage settlement. This first-step act allowed for freedom of religion—but *only for Christians.*

Anyone who did not believe in Christ was to be hanged. That meant Jews or atheists (people who don't believe there is a God), or even some Christians who asked too many questions. Those people had to keep quiet or leave Maryland.

It was also a hanging offense to curse God. If you made fun of Christian doctrine, the law said you were to be whipped in public.

That sounds harsh—and it was—but remember the times. In the colonies controlled by France, Spain, and Portugal no Protestants, Jews, or atheists were allowed at all.

Bound Out

A big problem for early colonists in America was the shortage of labor. There weren't enough people to farm and do all the other work. One way of dealing with this was slavery—and Maryland imported many slaves. Another was by bringing over servants and apprentices who were "bound out" to an employer for a certain number of years—four or five at least, and, if you were a boy or girl, often until you were 21. The employer fed, housed, and clothed you. In return, you had to work unpaid, usually learn-ing a trade. If you had a good employer it probably wasn't a bad life; but if your employer was stingy or cruel, or just indifferent, it could be miserable. The newspapers were always full of wanted notices from employers whose bound men or apprentices had run away.

In Maryland, if you stuck the job out, the law said that when your term of service was up you were to be given 50 acres of land, a suit of clothes, an ax, two hoes, and three barrels of corn. Then, if you were a Christian white man, you could vote and be elected to the assembly.

A glassblower and his apprentice.

31 Carry Me Back to Ole Virginny

On this optimistic English tobacco label, colonists and an Indian chat happily together about the merits of the brand being advertised.

I haven't said much about Virginia since John Smith's time, and that's too bad, because some future presidents were getting born there: George Washington, Thomas Jefferson, James Madison, and James Monroe. Virginia's John Marshall, George Mason, and Patrick Henry were destined for greatness, too.

Was there something about Virginia that bred leaders? Life there was certainly different from life in Pennsylvania or Massachusetts.

Most people in 18th-century Virginia weren't Puritans or Quakers. They were Anglicans: members of the Church of England. But they were more relaxed about their religion than the Puritans. In the New England colonies the ministers were the most important people in the community; in the South, the wealthy landowners were more important.

The Virginians didn't live in towns, as people did in Massachusetts. They lived along the rivers on small farms, or on very large farms called "plantations." Living on the river made shipping easy, and that was important.

What Virginians were shipping was tobacco—to England. While a few other crops were grown, the

The slaves on a tobacco plantation don't just plant and pick and dry and cure the tobacco. The slaves do *all* the physical labor—here they're making the barrels to ship the tobacco, and packing them, too.

117

Splitting Shingles

Spinning wool

Plantation Kitchen

Tobacco

Tobacco Barn

The SOUTHERN COLONIES

Baltimore

MARYLAND

Potomac R.

Ohio R.

Appalachian Mountains

Williamsburg

James R.
Jamestown

VIRGINIA

Roanoke R.

NORTH CAROLINA

Pee Dee R.

SOUTH CAROLINA

GEORGIA

Santee R.

Savannah R.

Charleston

Savannah

Altamaha R.

Atlantic Ocean

N
W   E
S

Canvas-back Duck

Dress

Rice and Rice Hook

and Scales

Raccoon

main moneymaker was tobacco. That was a problem. When tobacco prices were high, Virginians did well. When tobacco prices fell, they were in trouble. There was no balance.

There was little industry, and most goods came from England. In this land of magnificent forests, even fine furniture and other wood products were shipped from the "mother country."

There was another problem. Tobacco uses up the soil. After a few years, nothing grows well on land that has been planted with tobacco. To succeed in a tobacco economy, you need to rest the land every few years. That means you need to own a lot of land. You also need many workers.

So tobacco growers in colonial Virginia began to buy land and workers. As you know, at first they bought indentured servants. Then they bought Africans and made them slaves. By 1750 there were more Africans in Virginia than any other single group of people. More Virginians had come from Africa than from England or Scotland.

It was a few rich white planters who held power in the colony. Most whites were small farmers, and there were thousands of them. Some owned a slave or two—or hoped to—and that made them go along with the big slave owners. Virginia was not the only place where this happened. A society built on slavery stretched from Maryland to Georgia. Slavery was not only terrible for the black slaves—it ruined many white farmers, too.

At first the South, like the North, was full of yeoman farmers. Yeomen are independent farmers who work their own land. When slave ships began bringing in large numbers of Africans, the yeomen were in trouble. The blacks, being slaves, were forced to work for nothing. The yeoman farmers couldn't compete with that. The tobacco they grew was more expensive than tobacco grown by slaves.

The yeoman farmers had these choices. They could stay in Virginia (or Maryland or the Carolinas or Georgia) and try to work their own farms. Usually that meant they would become "poor whites."

Or they could buy slaves.

Or they could head West, to the frontier, and settle new land (and perhaps fight Indians for that land). These were difficult choices.

By the 18th century most slave owners were beginning to realize that slavery was wrong. Many spoke out against it. (They also made excuses and tried to justify enslaving others. They knew that every ancient society had included slaves.) Many white people realized they were trapped in a bad system; they didn't know how to get out. George Washington, Thomas Jefferson, and many others wrote that slavery was evil—but they owned slaves. If you were a plantation owner and you freed your slaves, you might become poor. So

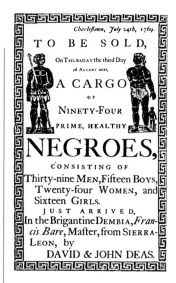

A slave auction notice. Traders usually wanted slaves to look young and healthy—they were worth more. But they didn't like slaves who looked proud and held their heads high. Such people might be troublemakers.

Divorce, Colonial Style

Dame Alice Clawson, who lived on Virginia's eastern shore in the mid-1600s, was a woman who wouldn't take nonsense from anyone. When her husband came home from a stay with the Nanticoke Indians, he brought an Indian woman home with him. Dame Alice was outraged, and hauled her two-timing husband off to the local justices. She became the first Virginia woman to obtain a divorce.

A plantation owner *(below),* a mansion, and rows of slave cabins—with dirt floors, no glass in the windows, no water (except a pump everyone shared), and smoky open fireplaces.

After seeing some slaves try to rebel against their owner, an observer from New Jersey wrote: "The ill Treatment which this unhappy part of mankind receives here, would almost justify them in any desperate attempt for gaining that *Civilitie,* & *Plenty* which tho' denied them, is here commonly bestowed on Horses!"

might your family. What would you do?

For a decent person, the problem was even more difficult than you can imagine. Many white Virginians had been very poor back in England or wherever they or their parents came from. Many had been let out of jail if they agreed to come to America. They knew what it was like to be oppressed, and many didn't want anything to do with slavery. But in some places it was against the law to free slaves. In some places it was against the law for black people to own land. It was against the law to teach black people to read. Many slave owners believed that if they freed their slaves, there would be no way for the slaves to survive. Most would not be able to find jobs. They might starve. They might be kidnapped and sold again into slavery.

A few whites did free their slaves. Some tried to end slavery. Most did nothing. What would you have done?

Imagine that you are a slave owner. You control other people's lives. You can order them around. You can have them whipped. You can taunt them. Do you think you might become mean and lazy? Do you think you might turn into a bad-tempered tyrant?

Some slave owners were all of those things. Some of them were among the meanest people in America's history. But there were others who felt great responsibility for their slaves.

There is a paradox connected with slavery. A *paradox* is a "puzzle." Something very puzzling happened in Colonial Virginia.

When it came time to write a constitution for our nation, it was the slave-owning Virginians who thought and wrote most about freedom. That is the paradox. Why do you think it was so?

32 The Good Life

For most of the 18th century wigs for the rich got fancier and fancier.

We haven't finished with paradoxical Virginia. We still haven't figured out why so many great leaders were growing up in that colony. Could it be that, for the very few lucky enough to be born wealthy, there was time to become well educated and time to be spent thinking?

By the 18th century, plantation owners live a privileged, lordly life. But it isn't as easy as some people think. To run a plantation well, you need to be intelligent and industrious. (In England, aristocrats often don't work—or want to work; that isn't true in America.)

Each plantation is like a small village owned by one family. That family lives in a great house with many rooms and many servants. The house is usually built of brick and has a long lawn that leads to the river. The kitchen is a separate small building. So is the laundry, the carpenter's shop, the spinning and weaving shed, the blacksmith's shed, and the plantation office.

The plantation's business is farming, which means stables and barns and a smokehouse are needed. The smokehouse is for smoking meats. (Smoking preserves meat; there are no refrigerators.) There is a dock where ships load and unload. And a shed where the cooper makes barrels. (Tobacco is packed into barrels, called

An English visitor wrote home in 1759: "Solomon in all his Glory was not array'd like one of these [Virginians]. I assure you, [even] the common Planter's Daughters here go every Day in finer Cloaths than I have seen content you for a Summer's Sunday. You thought...my Sattin Wastecoat was a fine best...I'm nothing amongst the Lace and Lac'd fellows...here."

This little girl lived in Maryland. She was six years old when her picture was painted in about 1710. Her clothes might be fun to dress up in— but not for climbing trees.

Dancing is part of an upper-class Southern education. In the 18th century, with no TV or stereos, people have to make their own entertainment.

Slave or Bondman?

William Byrd was a wealthy plantation owner who compared himself to men of the Bible—the patriarchs (PAY-tree-arks). That way, he made himself believe slavery was all right. He never used the word "slave." He said "bond-man" and "bond-woman." He was using a euphemism (YOO-fuh-miz-um): a "nice" word that you use because the real word is embarrassing. (Do you know some euphemisms that we use today?) Byrd thought he lived an ideal life, and he wrote about it in his diary:

I have a large family of my own, and my Doors are open to Every Body, yet I have no Bills to pay, and half-a-Crown will rest undisturbed in my Pocket

for many Moons together. Like one of the Patriarchs, I have my Flocks and my Herds, my Bond-men and Bond-women, and every Sort of trade amongst my own Servants, so that I live in a kind of Independence from everyone but Providence.

"hogsheads.") The plantation even has a kiln, where bricks are baked.

Slaves live in cabins built near the fields. The big plantations sometimes have 200 or more slaves. A man known as "King" Carter, the wealthiest Virginian, owns 10 plantations. Some other Virginians own two or three. All the people who live on a plantation have to eat. So they grow vegetables, corn, and wheat, and raise animals, too. Can you see why it is hard work to run a plantation well?

A plantation owner is like a business executive. He runs the plantation and sees that it makes a profit. He is responsible for the work and the workers (that means food, clothing, housing, and health care). He is probably a member of the House of Burgesses, and that means that he attends assembly sessions at the capital twice a year.

He may also be a court officer, called on to decide court cases. Besides, he and his wife give parties and entertain visitors, who sometimes stay for days and days or even weeks at a time. It is a busy life.

Plantation children don't live at all the way you do. Some of the ways they live are nice, but some you wouldn't like.

If you are a very rich planter's son you have to wear velvet pants and ruffled shirts and high-heeled shoes when company comes, just like your dad. That must be uncomfortable.

How do you like shaving your head so you can wear a powdered wig? Or wearing an embroidered cap when you play? (Only the very rich go in for head shaving.)

If you are a planter's daughter, you wear satin gowns with stiff petticoats. Now that is fun, because those are party dresses. Everyday clothing for boys and girls is more comfortable than these garments, but not

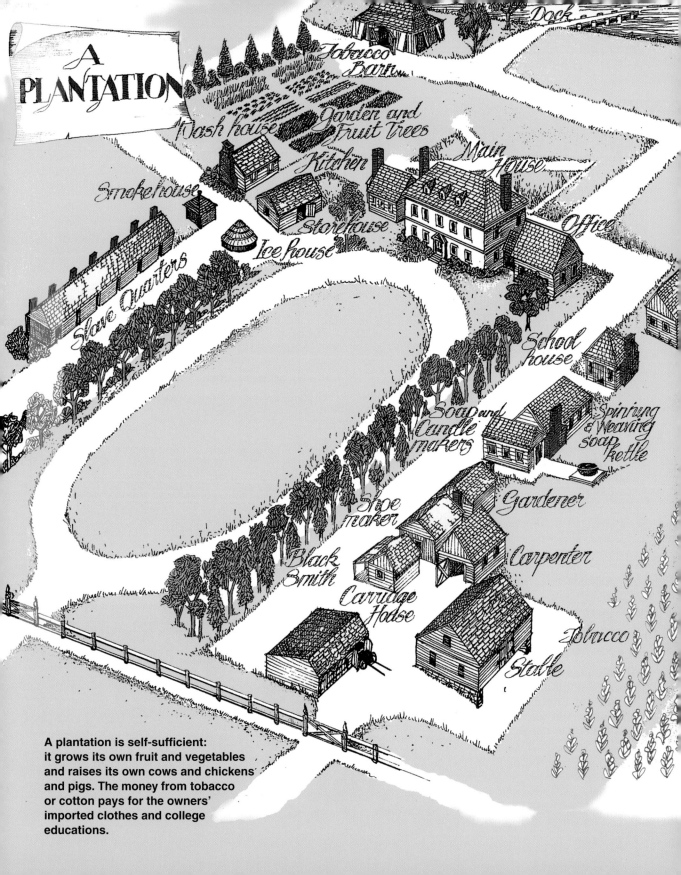

A PLANTATION

Dock

Tobacco Barn

Wash house

Garden and Fruit Trees

Kitchen

Main House

Smokehouse

Storehouse

Office

Ice house

Slave Quarters

School house

Soap and Candle makers

Spinning & Weaving

soap kettle

Shoe maker

Gardener

Black Smith

Carpenter

Carriage Hodse

Stable

Tobacco

A plantation is self-sufficient: it grows its own fruit and vegetables and raises its own cows and chickens and pigs. The money from tobacco or cotton pays for the owners' imported clothes and college educations.

Bedtime Stories

Do your parents sometimes tell you to *sleep tight*? In colonial times mattresses were laid over ropes stretched between the sides of the bed frame. When the ropes sagged, they had to be tightened with a wind-up wrench. So people really meant it when they talked about sleeping tight.

How about *climbing into bed*? Do you use that expression? And do you climb into bed, or is your bed low enough so you can just fall into it? In colonial days, there was no central heating and the floor got very cold at night. So beds were tall, and most people had to actually climb a few steps to get to bed.

Rigorous means "tough" or "demanding."

A *patrician* is an aristocrat, someone of high social rank. "Patrician" can be a noun or an adjective

like the jeans and shorts that your great (lots of "greats" here!) grandchildren will wear.

One thing you do like is horseback riding. Everyone rides horses, and everyone learns to dance, too.

If you are the child of plantation owners, you have your own schoolteacher who lives with you. Life is good to you. You study and play and go to parties. You eat big meals of meats and pies and vegetables, all home cooked. Slaves pick up after you. How do you treat them? Some boys and girls are considerate; some are not.

If you are smart and study hard, you will be taught to read the Bible in the languages in which it was written. You will learn about ancient Rome and its gladiators, poets, and politicians. You will play a musical instrument. Many Americans born after you will not have as rigorous an education.

It is a patrician life, full of special privileges. If you are a boy you may finish your schooling at Virginia's College of William and Mary or perhaps at college in England. Someday you will be expected to serve as a representative of your neighbors in the House of Burgesses. Your parents and teachers are training you to be a leader.

The College of William and Mary in Williamsburg was named for England's king and queen and was the second college in the colonies.

Even if she hates it, every little girl has to learn to sew and embroider. Girls practice on samplers like this one—it includes 12 different kinds of stitches.

33 Virginia's Capital

Virginia's enterprising Governor Alexander Spotswood started an iron industry and explored the Shenandoah Valley.

Do you remember the mosquitoes, deerflies, and snakes at Jamestown, back in John Smith's time? Well, things got better on that swampy peninsula—but not a lot better. In 1676 some frontiersmen, led by Nathaniel Bacon, marched to Jamestown. They had asked for help fighting Indians and didn't get it. They hated the governor, Sir William Berkeley (BARK-lee), who was a tyrant. Even the king called him "an old fool." The rebels burned the State House.

Almost as soon as the State House was rebuilt, it burned down again. This time it may have been an accident. Still, in 1699, when someone suggested moving the Virginia capital to Middle Plantation—eight miles away but on higher ground—most people thought it a fine idea.

Actually there were at least two "someones" who did the suggesting. One was James Blair, a Scotsman who was minister of Bruton Parish Church, the Anglican church at Middle Plantation. Reverend Blair was also the founder and first president of the College of William and Mary, which was at Middle Plantation. The other someone was Francis Nicholson, the new royal governor. Nicholson agreed that with a church and college in place, Middle Plantation would be a capital spot for the capital. But Middle Plantation wasn't much of a name for a town. A new name was needed. The king of England's name was a natural choice, and the town became Williamsburg.

That little town, born at the beginning of the 18th century, danced across the stage of history for about 80 years. Then it left the spotlight and was forgotten (until the 20th century, when it was restored and rebuilt as if it were still in the 1700s).

Governor Berkeley was a rich, selfish old man who taxed the small planters heavily. Some planters needed help. The Indians, fighting for their land, were attacking frontier farms.

Nathaniel Bacon had two plantations. One of them, near where Richmond is today, was on the edge of Indian territory. Indians attacked, killed an overseer, stole cattle, and burned tobacco. When the governor wouldn't help, Bacon led a small army against the Indians. Berkeley was furious. He gathered soldiers and planned to fight Bacon and his rebels. Bacon's army marched on Jamestown. The governor and his men ran to a warship and sailed off. Bacon burned the town and started his own government. Then he got sick and died. Berkeley came back and hanged all of Bacon's followers. This is called Bacon's Rebellion.

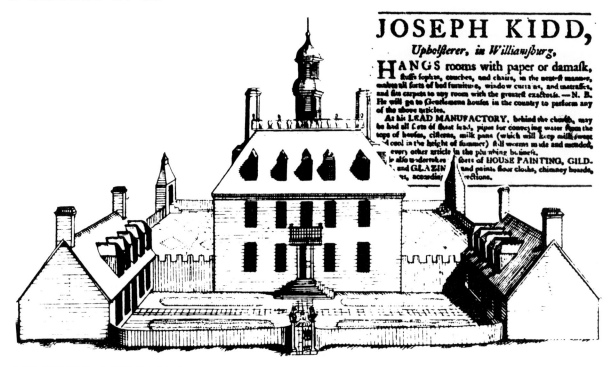

JOSEPH KIDD,

Upholsterer, in Williamsburg,

HANGS rooms with paper or damask, stuffs sophas, couches, and chairs, in the neatest manner, makes all sorts of bed furniture, window curtains, and matrasses, and fits carpets to any room with the greatest exactness. — N. B. He will go to Gentlemens houses in the country to perform any of the above articles.

At his LEAD MANUFACTORY, behind the church, may be had all sorts of sheet lead, pipes for conveying water from the tops of houses, cisterns, milk pans (which will keep milk sweet and cool in the height of summer) and worms made and mended, every other article in the plumbing business.

He also undertakes sorts of HOUSE PAINTING, GILD-, and GLAZING and paints floor cloths, chimney boards, &c. according directions.

Lord Botetourt, a popular English governor, was the first to fully occupy the Williamsburg governor's palace *(above).* His groom of the chambers, Joseph Kidd, started his own decorating business.

The word **crown**, as it is used here, means the British government.

Jamestown's land-owners didn't think moving the capital was a good idea, but most of the other plantation owners did.

Francis Nicholson arrived in Williamsburg fresh from Maryland, where he had been governor and had designed Maryland's capital, the bustling port of Annapolis. He was eager to plan Williamsburg, and he did it with care, using new ideas from France.

Williamsburg was "laid out regularly in lots…sufficient each for a house and garden and…free passage for the air which is grateful in violent hot weather." Wide, tree-lined Duke of Gloucester Street ran down the middle of the town, with the Capitol at one end and the college's Wren Building at the other end. Bruton Parish Church, with its white spire, stood proudly on the same street, along with neat houses, shops, and a grassy mall. Overlooking the mall was the finest building in the colony: the handsome, stately governor's palace. Now picture people, horses, cows, sheep, and gardens, and you have an idea of Williamsburg.

If you stand outside the governor's palace and look at the brick fence—with its stone British unicorn on top and fancy iron gates—you will be impressed. If you are lucky you may get invited inside for a musical evening. You'll sit in the candlelit ballroom, where men in starched linen blouses and women in silk brocade gowns smile and nod at each other. A display of muskets and swords in the entry is intended to leave you awed with the Crown's military might.

But, best of all, most young people agree, is a chance to lose yourself in the boxwood maze garden growing behind the palace. Almost everyone knows the ancient myth of the maze and the monstrous Minotaur on the island of Crete. The maze behind the governor's palace doesn't have any monsters—there are some peacocks strutting around—but people like to go in it and pretend they are lost, especially if there are two of them and they are in love.

Most of the year, Williamsburg is a sleepy village of 2,000 souls. Half of them are African-Americans. But in April and October, when the House of Burgesses and the courts are in session, the population doubles. Men sleep three to a bed at Christiana Campbell's tavern, where the good Mrs. Campbell, "a little old Woman, about four feet high & equally thick," keeps a popular dining room.

These are Public Times, and people come to take care of colonial business, make laws, consider court cases, see friends, and shop. You can buy a wig at the wig makers, a violin at the music shop, or a gingerbread cookie at the bakery. If you want "to put on the dog," you can have dog-hide shoes made for you at the boot makers. You

The Reverend Blair didn't like fun and games, but he took charge of William and Mary and made it a good place to go to college.

might go to an auction, a horse race, or a fair. You can see a play. (The first theater in the English colonies opens in 1717.)

One traveler writes of Williamsburg, "At the time of the assemblies and general courts, it is crowded with the gentry of the country. On those occasions there are balls and other amusements; but as soon as business is finished, they return to their plantations

Joy and Loyalty

In July 1746 news of the English army's crushing victory over rebel Scots at Culloden reached Williamsburg, and was celebrated in style, as reported in the Virginia Gazette*:*

In the Evening, a very numerous Company of Gentlemen and Ladies... after dancing some Time, withdrew to Supper... consisting of near 100 Dishes...There was also provided a great Variety of the choicest Liquors, in which the Healths of the King...and the rest of the Royal Family, the Governor, Success to His Majesty's Arms, Prosperity to this Colony, and many other Loyal Healths were chearfully drank, and a Round of the Cannon...was discharg'd at each Health, to the Number of 18 or 20 Rounds...

All the Houses in the City were illuminated, and a very large Bonfire was made in the Market-Place, 3 Hogsheads of Punch given to the Populace; and the whole concluded with the greatest Demonstrations of Joy and Loyalty.

Cooks at work in a big 18th-century kitchen like that of the governor's mansion. Dinners were huge and often consisted of a dozen courses or more—with fish, beef, and turkey all in the same meal.

and the town is in a manner deserted."

For most people a trip to Williamsburg means having a good time—unless the Reverend Mr. Blair happens to come by. Blair doesn't have a sense of humor. For 50 long years, he is a powerful force in the community. It is said that three governors have been recalled to London because of his complaints. A fourth governor remembered him as "a very vile old fellow." Blair usually gets his way. And his way is not one of tolerance. A landowning aristocracy rules Virginia and outsiders remain outside. Only Anglicans can be elected burgesses. A plan for religious liberty is hatched in Williamsburg in the second half of the 18th century, but it might not have happened if Reverend Blair had been alive.

But Blair is mortal and not typical of most Virginians. The Virginia way is gracious and courtly and easygoing. William and Mary's wise law professor, George Wythe (say *with*), will soon come to prominence in Williamsburg. He is kind

School's Out

Virginia's governor Alexander Spotswood wanted to be friends with the Indians. He sponsored the Indian Act of 1714. It created an outpost where the colonists could meet and trade with Indians. An English school was founded to teach Indian children about Christianity and English ways.

Many colonists were angry about Spotswood's ideas. Some didn't want anything to do with Native Americans. Others were afraid the Indians would sell their furs to Virginia's governor and not to them. In 1717, at the colonists' urging, the king repealed the Indian Act. The outpost and Indian school were closed.

and considerate and learned; some people call him "a walking library." George Wythe becomes mayor of Williamsburg. He frees his slaves long before he dies. He hates slavery. One of his favorite students is a young man named Thomas Jefferson.

If you had a magic wand that could waft you anywhere, you might consider landing at the Raleigh Tavern in Williamsburg on a day when George Washington, Thomas Jefferson, Patrick Henry, and Peyton Randolph are having a conversation. Just sit back and listen. Those Virginians and their friends have a rare talent for good times and serious thought. They are as splendid and energetic a group of leaders as any nation has ever produced.

They are struggling with a weighty problem: how to create a new and fair government on this gorgeous continent. And they are being pulled in two directions. There are many who think as James Blair does and want to reproduce Old England in America. One professor at the College of William and Mary writes approvingly that people in Williamsburg "behave themselves exactly like the gentry in London."

But there are others who don't behave like English gentry. They have come to America because they are unhappy with the Old World and its society of rigid classes. They want to try something new, in what they call the New World. This little village of Williamsburg will ring with debates on the purposes of government. Should individual liberty be the goal? Or is it better to preserve an orderly community where everyone has a sure place? What does "the consent of the governed" really mean? Wouldn't you like to hear what Thomas Jefferson and George Washington have to say about those questions?

George Wythe, who became one of the original signers of the Declaration of Independence, had very little proper education when he was growing up. But, with only the help of his mother, he taught himself Greek, Latin, philosophy, mathematics, and science. He even got a rabbi to teach him Hebrew.

The colonists who wanted to teach Indians didn't give up. This Indian school opened at the College of William and Mary in 1723. About a dozen Indians at a time lived and studied there. Today, the building is still in use as part of the college.

129

34 Pretend Some More

Silversmiths also made pewter items, like this tankard with its flip-up lid.

Venerate means "respect." A farmer's plow was the most important machine he owned.

You are 10 years old and indentured to Patrick Beech, a silversmith in Williamsburg. Beech was a real silversmith, we know that, but we don't know much about his servants and apprentices. We do know about the jobs they would have done and the way they might have lived. So you can pretend to be one of them. If you do, you will get an idea of what life was like for some children in the 18th century.

You have been in Virginia just a year. Your parents died of influenza in London. Since you had nowhere to go and no money, the Lord Mayor sent you and some other orphans to Virginia. Sometimes you are homesick for your friends in London, but you are beginning to like it in America. Life isn't easy, but it is better than it was in London.

Beech keeps you working from before the sun comes up until dark. Your first job in the morning is to light a fire to warm the house and another to heat the forge where silver is melted and formed. Then you clean the kitchen, run errands, and sometimes do odd jobs in the silver shop. You don't get time to play, and lately you have begun to hate Mr. Beech. He never seems to smile.

Mrs. Beech has taught you to read. She takes you to church and whips you when you are bad. She does the same with her children. She is fair but very busy. You miss your own mother.

But you do have a friend in the silver shop. His name is Tom, and he was apprenticed to a watchmaker in London before he came to the colonies. Tom says Beech is not a bad man, just worried. There isn't enough work in Williamsburg. There are too many silversmiths, and the rich planters buy their good silver in England. So Beech must make silver teeth and set them in people's mouths. He repairs watches and makes clocks, and sometimes silver cups and trays and jewelry. He has a big family to feed, along with his servants. There is enough food, but nothing extra.

Neither you nor Tom is free. The law says you must stay with Patrick Beech until you are 21. Tom is also an indentured servant. Beech paid for his passage from London: he must work for him for five years. Then, Tom tells you, he will go to Charles Town and open his own shop. He has heard the planters in South Carolina are very rich.

More than anything, you want to hunt and fish and learn to use a rifle. You have seen enough of the silversmith's work—fires and forges, pouring liquid metal, hammering silver into shape, putting teeth into the jaws of people who scream in pain. You need to be patient. Someday you will have everything you wish for—and more.

Now, pretend again. This time you are the child of a Virginia farmer. You live in a small wooden house with a big fireplace at one end. The house has only one big room with a sleeping loft. At night your parents sleep in front of the fire with the baby, and you and your brothers climb a ladder to the loft. You all sleep on straw mattresses.

The only clothes you have are those you wear, and a Sunday shirt. Tobacco and corn grow poorly on your land, because it is worn out. You have enough food, but you don't eat a balanced diet. You are sometimes sick, and you will die when you are 40.

Still, you are luckier than many children. You have had a year of schooling, and you know how to read. Your parents hope your life will be better than theirs. And it will be. At 15 you will head out to the western frontier, where you will find land and opportunity. Your schooling will help you succeed. You will marry, have 10 children, and own land enough for all of them to farm.

Most poor white boys and girls don't get to school. And there are no schools for black children. Many 18th-century Southern children never learn to read or write. It is difficult to have schools when people live so far apart on farms. It is difficult to have churches, too. Some ministers ride horseback from one church to another. The law

This is a pewter works. Pewter, which is a mixture of tin, lead, and copper or bismuth, was for people who couldn't afford silver. The apprentice is turning the wheel that drives the bellows to keep the furnace hot. If the 'prentice got fed up and ran away, his master would offer a reward for bringing him back. In the colonies, even unskilled laborers were hard to find.

No one knows who painted this picture, but it may have been done in South Carolina. The slaves may be celebrating a wedding by "jumping the broomstick." Some of their clothes look like those worn in Yoruba, which is in Nigeria in Africa. The banjo-like instrument *(above)* resembles a Yoruban *molo;* the other instrument looks like an African *gudu-gudu.*

Hoeing Cotton

From the story of a former slave, Solomon Northup:

About the first of July, when [the cotton] is a foot high or thereabouts, it is hoed the fourth and last time....During all these hoeings the overseer or driver follows the slaves on horseback with a whip.... The fastest hoer takes the lead row. He is usually about a rod in front of his companions. If one of them passes him, he is whipped. If one falls behind or is a moment idle, he is whipped. In fact, the lash is flying from morning until night.

says you must go to the Anglican church every Sunday.

Your parents hate that law, and another law that makes them pay taxes to help support the Anglican Church. They say the Anglican Church is for rich folks. They would like to join the Baptist church, but they can get in trouble if they do that. A law says their children could be taken from them if they join a free-thinking church. Since you are one of their children you agree that is a terrible law. Actually, it isn't enforced very often. Perhaps the law is meant to scare people away from new churches: like those of the Baptists and Methodists and New Light Presbyterians.

Belonging to that Anglican Church of England, as most Virginians do, makes you different from people in Massachusetts. Virginians love England and English clothing, paintings, furnishings, and ideas. They feel closer to people in England than they do to those in New England.

Now pretend that you are a slave. You don't want to? You are right. No one wants to be a slave. Some slaves, especially those who work in the fields on some big plantations, live in small huts and sleep on old blankets piled on the dirt floor. They don't eat well and they work almost all the time. Other slaves, especially those who are house servants, live in small wooden houses with beds and tables and furnishings that come from the plantation workshop or, sometimes, from the big house. Visitors from Europe will say they live better than most peasants in the Old World. (Which is probably why so many European peasants want to come to America.)

Your name is Sarah, and you live on a farm in North Carolina. There are 18 of you slaves (including children) in four families and you share two houses near the tobacco fields. A fireplace divides each house in half. Your house has a front porch, as many houses do in Africa. The porch is a nice place to rest on a hot evening. You have your own garden, which provides corn and greens and potatoes. They have made you strong and healthy. You are 11, and you can't read and never will be taught how. But you can sing and play the banjo, and that makes you popular in church. Your faith is important to you and your family. You are Christians, and you have brought your African spirituality to that religion.

35 South Carolina: Riches, Rice, Slaves

The seal of the Carolinas viewed Indians more kindly than most colonists did.

The Carolinas, North and South, were granted to eight lords proprietors by King Charles II. The lords never meant to live in America, and they didn't. They just planned to get rich by using the Carolinas to produce three products that were expensive in England: wine, silk, and olive oil.

The Carolinas worked out, but not as the lords had expected. Indigo, a plant grown for its blue dye, and rice became principal crops—not wine, silk, or olive oil. Eventually the colonies were bought back by the king. The lords lost out, and the Carolinas became royal colonies.

In South Carolina, Charles Town, named for Charles II, prospered from its beginning. No longer were there terrible starving and dying times when a colony was founded. Jamestown and Plymouth had taught the colonists what not to do.

Charleston (which was the name Charles Town turned into) soon became the busiest port in the South. It attracted younger sons of the English nobility, who gave it an aristocratic flavor.

Many of Charleston's leaders came from the tiny island of Barbados in the Caribbean Sea. In the 17th century Barbados was the wealthiest and most crowded of all English American colonies. (In 1680 Barbados's exports were more valuable

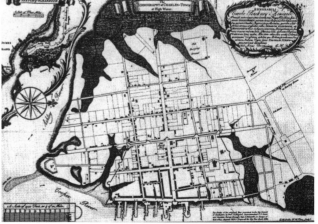

Unlike Boston or New Amsterdam, Charleston's and Philadelphia's streets were planned before any houses were built.

Here Peter Manigault, a well-known Charleston Huguenot, seems to be drinking too much. (He's the one holding a bottle on the left.) Drinking was sometimes a problem in early America. (Is it today?)

One Man's View

In 1769 "Capt. Martin a Man of War" wrote this poem about Charleston:

Black and white all mix'd together,
Inconstant, strange, unhealthful weather,
Burning heat and chilling cold
Dangerous both to young and old
Boisterous winds and heavy rains
Fevers and rheumatic pains
Agues plenty without doubt
Sores, boils, the prickling heat and gout
Musquitos on the skin make blotches
Centipedes and large cockroaches
Frightful creatures in the waters
Porpoises, sharks and alligators
Houses built on barren land
No lamps or lights, but streets of sand
Pleasant walks, if you can find 'em
Scandalous tongues, if any mind 'em
The markets dear and little money
Large potatoes, sweet as honey
Water bad, past all drinking
Men and women without thinking
Every thing at a high price
But rum, hominy and rice
Many a widow not unwilling
Many a beau not worth a shilling
Many a bargain, if you strike it
This is Charles-town, how do you like it.

than the exports of all of the North American mainland.)

South Carolina had to find ways to attract settlers. One way was to practice religious tolerance. Religious wars were making people flee from Europe. The Carolinas welcomed them, and that led to an interesting mix of peoples. Scots settled on the coast and helped fight off Spanish attacks. French Protestants, called Huguenots (HUE-guh-nots), came and proved to be just the kind of colonists the new land needed. In France they were persecuted, but France's shortsightedness was America's good fortune. The Huguenots were carpenters and blacksmiths and masons, and they believed in hard work. What John Smith would have given to have had them in Jamestown!

Field-workers were needed to plant and harvest the rice that was making the colony rich. The settlers from Barbados were used to owning slaves; they wanted slaves in America, and they encouraged it. It is an irony that Africans probably taught the white settlers how to cultivate rice, because it was rice that made slavery profitable in South Carolina. Soon there were more black people in South Carolina than whites.

South Carolina became an aristocratic colony with a few very wealthy people holding almost all the economic and political power. It was different from the other

Southern colonies in many ways, but especially because it had that important city: Charleston. In Virginia and North Carolina there was no great city. For most of the year, plantation folk in those colonies lived isolated lives. That was not the case in South Carolina. Some plantation owners in South Carolina visited their plantations only occasionally. They spent their time in Charleston, where they lived in big houses and went to fancy parties.

The Huguenots mixed and married with the English; their tastes and ideas helped create the most elegant society in the colonies.

Those who were wealthy thought life in Charleston finer than in any place on earth. But the majority of Charlestonians were not wealthy. The majority of South Carolinians were not free. They were Africans, and they worked as field hands, craftspeople, and servants. But they had their own ideas and traditions, and they brought those African ideas, songs, stories, and habits to their new home. After a while, some of those African ideas became mixed with ideas they found in America. Brer Rabbit, who started as an African, became American. In South Carolina African-Americans developed their own language, Gullah.

Some people in South Carolina speak Gullah today. They talk quickly, without a Southern accent. Gullah combines words from English, French, and a number of African languages. You may have heard some Gullah words, such as *goober* (peanut), *gumbo* (soup with okra), *juke* (as in jukebox), and *voodoo* (witchcraft). Here is a sentence in Gullah: *Shishuh tall pass una.* It means "Sister is taller than you."

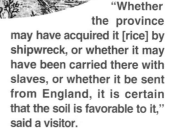

"Whether the province may have acquired it [rice] by shipwreck, or whether it may have been carried there with slaves, or whether it be sent from England, it is certain that the soil is favorable to it," said a visitor.

In 1775, Charleston was the fourth-biggest city in the colonies, with a population of 12,000. The biggest of all was Philadelphia, with 40,000 people. It was bigger than any English city except London.

These are indigo farmworkers. Indigo was an ideal second crop because it needs no work in winter, when all the hard labor of rice planting must be done. The blue dye made from the indigo plant was much prized.

36 North Carolina: Dissenters and Pirates

Many Southerners didn't want to be Anglicans. This is a Lutheran church.

North Carolina was different. It had tough land to tame, so its settlers were apt to be free-spirited small farmers. Many were outcasts and religious dissenters from aristocratic Virginia. In Virginia the rich landholders were in control, and they were Anglicans. People who wanted to join the new religious sects—the Baptists and the Methodists—were persecuted in Virginia. Some moved south to North Carolina.

North Carolina may have been the most democratic of all the colonies. Generally, North Carolinians minded their own business and left their neighbors alone, which may be why pirates made the North Carolina coast a base for their adventuring. Although some said it was because the pirates paid the North Carolina governor to leave them alone. That could be true, because it was finally a force from Virginia that got Blackbeard—the most famous and ferocious of the pirates. His real name was Edward Teach. He braided his great black beard into pigtails, wove ribbons into them,

Right: How an artist imagined Blackbeard and his ruffians enjoying themselves at their Carolina hideout. There were women who liked the pirate life, too.

136

Genuine women pirates: Mary Read *(left)* and Anne Bonney. They were friends who survived a death sentence.

and then hung smoking pieces of rope from his hat. At night the pigtails looked like coiling snakes, and the burning rope gave his face a glowing, eerie look. It was enough to scare anyone, and it did scare a lot of sailors.

Anne Bonney scared them, too. She was a tough pirate who sailed the Caribbean and Carolina coast, and had no trouble terrorizing seamen.

In 1677 some North Carolinians rebelled against England. They didn't like England's Navigation Acts, which forced them to pay

The Death of Blackbeard

In 1718 Blackbeard stationed his ship in Pamlico Sound off the North Carolina coast. No ship was permitted to pass through without paying the pirate a bribe. Governor Spotswood of Virginia decided to do something about that. He offered £100 reward for the pirate. Lieutenant Robert Maynard sailed south. In a ferocious battle, "Blackbeard received a shot in his body...yet he stood his ground and fought with great fury till he received five and twenty wounds. ...At length, as he was cocking another pistol...he fell down dead." Maynard, to prove he had killed Blackbeard, cut off the pirate's head, stuck it on his bowsprit, and sailed home.

An enterprising 12-year-old boy read about Blackbeard's death and Maynard's heroism. He was so captivated by the story that he wrote a long poem about it, set it in type, printed it on sheets of paper, and sold it in the streets of Boston. Here are the last lines:

*When the bloody fight
 was over,
we're informed by
 a Letter writ,
Teach's head was
 made a Cover
to the Jack Staff
 of the Ship:
Thus they sailed
 to Virginia,
and when the Story told,
How they killed the
 Pirates many,
they'd Applause from
 young and old.*

Can you guess the name of that boy who wrote the poem about Blackbeard on the previous page? He was a printer who became a scientist and a statesman.

A: Benjamin Franklin!

Pirate fun could be nasty. Here, pirates make captured friars give them piggyback rides, a shipboard sport called "monk-riding." One pirate wields a cat-o'-nine-tails, a cruel whip common on ships.

In 1997, some divers found a wreck off the coast of North Carolina. There were nine cannons on board, and others scattered on the ocean floor. Archaeologists believe it is Blackbeard's ship, *Queen Anne's Revenge.*

taxes to England on goods sold to other colonies. If a North Carolina tobacco grower sold some of his tobacco to a merchant in Boston, he was supposed to pay a tax to England. Did that make any sense? The colonists didn't think so.

Some North Carolinians refused to pay. They even set up their own government and tried to get free of England. They almost got away with it. They put British officials in jail, elected a legislature, and chose their leader, John Culpeper, as governor. For two years they exercised all the powers and duties of government. But the British finally got angry. They tried Culpeper for treason. He was convicted but not punished—maybe because he was so popular.

One hundred years later, in 1776, people in all the colonies were angry about English taxes. The colonists would unite, as Popé had united the Pueblo Indians—and…well, you'll see what happened.

Pieces of Eight

Money wasn't simple in colonial times. Every country had its own kind of *currency*—coins and paper money—just as they do today. So English coins, Dutch coins, French coins, Spanish coins, and Portuguese coins were all *circulating*—being used for buying and selling. That wasn't all. Colonial governments were minting coins, and private banks were, too. And even with all these different bodies making coins, there still weren't enough—so people sometimes cut them up into bits and pieces if they needed change. Paper bills weren't much used—most people preferred money made of a metal that had value, like silver or copper. (The coins we have today that we call silver and copper don't contain much of those metals. But in the 17th century they did.)

The Spanish *real* (it means "royal" in Spanish) was widely used; it became the basis for the dollar in America. Those *reales* were often cut into eight pieces. Have you read the book *Treasure Island* by Robert Louis Stevenson? The parrot that belongs to the villain of that adventure story is named Captain Flint, and he is always squawking the phrase "Pieces of eight!" Pieces of eight were eventually coins in their own right, but they began as cut-up pieces of a *real*.

That is also the reason a quarter is sometimes called *two bits*. And that Spanish heritage explains why the New York Stock Exchange quoted fractional stock prices in eighths of a dollar until January 2001 when, finally, they changed to decimals with the penny as a base.

Top: Blackbeard's head swings from the bowsprit of Lieutenant Maynard's ship. The cast bronze bell *(above)* is part of Blackbeard's treasure recovered in 1997 from his ship, *Queen Anne's Revenge.* *Left:* an archaeologist raises one of Blackbeard's cannons from the sea floor. His ship had more than 40 cannons; divers have found 13 of them.

37 Royal Colonies and a No-Blood Revolution

Sir Edmund Andros wouldn't even let the people of Cape Cod keep the oil they got from stranded whales. Whales were "royal fish."

Charles Dickens wrote *A Child's History of England.* Here is part of it. "King James the Second was a man so very disagreeable, that even the best of historians has favored his brother Charles, as becoming, by comparison, quite a pleasant character. The one object of his short reign was to re-establish the Catholic religion in England; and this he doggedly pursued with such a stupid obstinacy, that his career very soon came to a close."

I hope you don't mind, but here is some more English history. It is the year 1686 (what century is that?), and James II is king of England. You met him before, when he was the Duke of York and his brother, King Charles II, gave him New York and New Jersey.

Now Charles is dead and James wears the crown. Unfortunately, James is not the nicest of kings. And it doesn't help that he is a Catholic, because most people in England belong to the Church of England.

King James II would like to rule without Parliament. He wants to be an "absolute monarch." He believes, as did his father, Charles I, that kings have a "divine right" to rule. That means he thinks God wants him to be king. He would like to make England Roman Catholic again. He will learn that you can't force religion on people.

James tries to take charge in America, too. Before his time, the English kings hadn't bothered much with America. The colonists were mostly left alone. Now, King James wants to change that, so he sends Sir Edmund Andros to New England. Andros is a tough, take-control person who tries to tell the Puritans how to run their colony.

It is hard to tell a Puritan anything. The New England Puritans came to America to run their own affairs, and they don't want an outsider making rules for them—especially Andros. They think he is a bully.

Finally, a mob goes after Andros. He is scared. You would be, too—mobs are dangerous. Andros puts on a woman's dress and tries to escape—oops!—he forgot to change his boots. Women don't wear heavy boots. Andros is spotted and captured. The Bostonians cool down and ship him back to England.

The king is annoyed with the troublesome colonists in America.

They won't behave as they are told. But now King James has too many problems to worry much about the colonies. In England things are heating up. The English people have had enough of James II. They have another revolution—a civilized revolution. "You're not king anymore, James," is what they say. Since James isn't killed—as his father was in the English Civil War of 1649—this revolution, in 1688, is called the "Bloodless" or "Glorious Revolution." It proves that revolutions don't have to be violent.

James's Protestant daughter, Mary, and her Dutch husband, William of Orange, are asked to be rulers. They are the couple the Virginians honored when they named the College of William and Mary.

The revolution is glorious because the English people make a deal with the new king and queen. They insist that Parliament have more power than the monarchs. They also demand a Bill of Rights for the people. It is a terrible time for absolute monarchs, but a great moment for freedom. In America, the colonists find it inspiring.

Read that last paragraph again. It's important to remember that *the Glorious Revolution gave Parliament more power than the king. HOORAY!*

Do you think that makes things better for the colonies? Well, sometimes parliaments can be as pesky as kings.

When the English parliament begins to make rules for the American colonies, the colonists will get annoyed. The Americans will complain that Parliament is too powerful, especially when Parliament ignores Massachusetts's beloved charter and makes the state a royal colony with a royal governor.

The grumbling that begins in New England in 1691 will start the colonists thinking about having their own glorious revolution. They will have one—but it will not be bloodless.

Do you think that the English Bill of Rights served as an inspiration for what was to come in America?

A king and queen who helped make a peaceful revolution.

In 1687 Connecticut's charter was hidden in this Hartford oak tree to keep it out of Andros's hands. The tree blew down in 1856 and everyone who could cut a piece for a souvenir.

38 A Nasty Triangle

Men are loaded onto a slaver (slave ship) and chained together at the ankles.

You may be getting the idea that the United States began as a collection of settlements that were not much alike. And you are right.

South Carolina wasn't like Pennsylvania, and Maryland wasn't like Connecticut. The people who founded the colonies had a lot to do with those differences, and so did the conditions of the land.

Massachusetts had a special problem because of its rocky soil and cold climate. It was tough being a farmer in New England, but New Englanders were tough people who liked challenges. So they did farm, although for many it was "subsistence farming." That means they grew enough for themselves; they didn't usually have extra crops to sell. A few New England farmers were able to sell their farm products abroad but, mostly, New England's land just wasn't right for large farms—or plantations—like those in the South.

And when it came to industry, the British made things difficult. They wouldn't let the colonists manufacture goods that competed with English goods. You can understand why that caused some grumbling.

New Englanders had to find ways to earn a living. Fishing was one way. Cod became New England's gold, just as tobacco was

The people in this shed are cleaning and drying codfish, which was (and still is) an important trading commodity for New England.

The New England lumber mill cuts and splits the logs and spits them straight into the river so they can float down to the towns and ship-yards that need them for building houses and boats.

Virginia's. The Puritan settlers caught codfish and then salted and shipped and sold the fish in Europe or the Caribbean Islands. In order to do that, they needed ships. So they became shipbuilders. To make ships they needed lumber. So they harvested timber and began selling wood and wood products. They became merchants carrying goods around the world. Yankee ships were familiar sights in Singapore and Rangoon and Bristol. And New England boys, who hung around the wharfs, got a chance to touch Dutch coins, Chinese silks, or fruit from Spain. They heard tales of adventures in Tripoli and Jamaica and dreamed of becoming skippers and going to faraway places themselves.

Soon Yankees were trading all kinds of things. They might take their salted cod to Barbados and trade it for cane sugar. Then they'd go to Virginia to pick up tobacco. They'd take the tobacco and sugar to England and trade them for cash, guns, and English cloth. Then on to Africa, where they exchanged the guns and cloth for men, women, and children. From there it was back across the Atlantic Ocean to the West Indies, where the people were sold into slavery. Finally they sailed home to New England (or, sometimes, New York or Annapolis). All that was called the "triangular trade." It made some people very rich.

Between 1526 and 1870, nearly 10 million slaves were shipped from Africa to:

Europe
175,000

Spanish America
1,552,000

Brazil
3,647,000

British Caribbean
1,665,000

British North America and the United States
399,000

French America
1,600,000

Dutch America
500,000

Danish West Indies
28,000

MEN'S ROOM.   BOYS' ROOM.   WOMEN'S ROOM.

This drawing of the slave ship *Brookes* caused an uproar. It led, in 1788, to a British law limiting the number of slaves per ship's ton. The drawing was not quite accurate, but close enough: conditions were horrendous. Death rates varied, but perhaps 20% of the captured people died on shipboard in the early 17th century. The death rate for crew members—from beatings and disease—was often higher. Those who owned the slave ships sat home in comfort and profited.

Picture a triangle—a long one. Do you have three points in your mind? Now stretch the triangle across the Atlantic Ocean. Put one point on the New England coast, another in Africa, and the third in South Carolina. Are you sure you have that clearly in your mind? Now imagine a boat sailing along that triangle, from New England to Africa to South Carolina, and back to New England.

Stretch another triangle across the Atlantic. This one can start in England, go to Africa, and have a third point in Virginia. The Atlantic Ocean was once filled with ships sailing triangular routes. Most of them included a stop in the West Indies. (They were very jagged triangles; a few were rectangles.)

Let's pretend a triangle is starting at Newport, Rhode Island (near Boston). You can watch as a ship is loaded with rum and guns. (Rum is an alcoholic drink made from sugarcane.) The ship heads for Africa, where the rum and guns will be traded for African people.

The Africans have been captured by enemy tribesmen and sold to African slave traders. The slave traders bargain with the New England boat captain, who buys as many people as he can squeeze on his ship. Some of the captives are children, kidnapped from their parents.

Olaudah Equiano was one of those children. He was 11 in 1756, when he was captured in Benin. He was the youngest of seven children, a happy boy in a loving home. Like many other prosperous African families, his family had slaves. Imagine that you are Olaudah as you read his words:

One day, when all our people were gone out to their works as usual, and only I and my sister were left to mind the house, two men and a woman got over our walls, and in a moment seized us both; and without giving us time to cry out or to make any resistance, they stopped our mouths and ran off with us into the nearest wood. Here they tied our hands, and continued to carry us as far as they could, till night came

Born Free

In a graveyard at Concord, Massachusetts, stands a stone carved thus:

God wills us free—
  man wills us slaves
I will as God wills:
  Gods will be done.
Here lies the body of
  John Jack
A native of Africa
  who died March 1773,
  aged about sixty years.
Tho born in the land
  of slavery
He was born free:
Tho he lived in a land
  of liberty
He lived a slave

Till by his honest
  tho stolen labours
He acquired
  the source of slavery
Which gave him his freedom:
Tho not long before
  Death the great Tyrant
Gave him his final
  emancipation
And put him on a footing
  with kings.
Tho a slave to vice
He practised those virtues
Without which kings are
  but slaves.

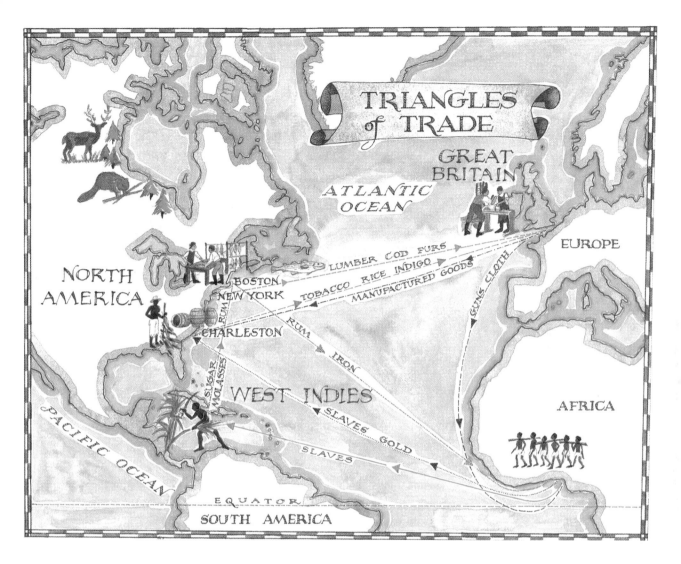

TRIANGLES of TRADE

GREAT BRITAIN

ATLANTIC OCEAN

EUROPE

NORTH AMERICA

BOSTON
NEW YORK

CHARLESTON

LUMBER COD FURS
TOBACCO RICE INDIGO
MANUFACTURED GOODS
GUNS CLOTH

RUM

RUM IRON

SUGAR MOLASSES

WEST INDIES

SLAVES GOLD

SLAVES

AFRICA

PACIFIC OCEAN

EQUATOR

SOUTH AMERICA

on, when we reached a small house, where the robbers halted for re-freshment and spent the night.

Olaudah and his sister are taken on a long journey, separated, and sold. He is passed from person to person, staying a month here, a few weeks there. Olaudah sees many parts of Africa and has many adventures. He tries to run away but is unsuccessful. Then, for the first time in his life, he sees the ocean.

> The first object which saluted my eyes when I arrived on the coast was the sea, and a slaveship, which was then riding at anchor and waiting for its cargo. These filled me with astonishment, which was soon converted into terror....When I was carried on board I was immediately handled, and tossed up to see if I was sound, by some of the crew; and I was now persuaded that I had got into a world of bad spirits, and that they were going to kill me.

There was more than one trade triangle. But all of them were tied up with slavery, and slavery was tied up with them. Most of the people who made money out of slavery didn't want to see it come to an end.

145

Olaudah is tossed below deck, where the smell is so bad he becomes sick and cannot eat. When he refuses food he is tied down and beaten. Frightened, he is at first unable to talk to anyone because the other Africans do not speak his language. Finally he meets some men who speak the language of Benin.

> I asked them if these people had no country, but lived in this hollow place [the ship]. They told me they did not, but came from a distant one....I then asked where were their women? Had they any like themselves? I was told they had. "And why," said I, "do we not see them?" They answered because they were left behind. I asked how the vessel could go? They told me they could not tell; but that there was cloth put upon the masts by the help of ropes I saw, and then the vessel went on; and the white men had some spell or magic they put in the water, when they liked, in order to stop the vessel. I was exceedingly amazed at this account, and really thought they were spirits.

Olaudah learns that he is being taken to the white men's country to work.

> I then was a little revived, and thought, if it were no worse than working, my situation was not so desperate: but still I feared I should be put to death, the white people looked and acted, as I thought, in so savage a manner; for I had never seen among any people such instances of brutal cruelty; and this is not only shown towards us blacks, but also to some of the whites themselves. One white man in particular I saw, when we were permitted to be on deck, flogged so unmercifully with a large rope near the foremast, that he died in consequence of it; and they tossed him over the side as they would have done a brute. This made me fear these people the more; and I expected nothing less than to be treated in the same manner.

Olaudah describes the scene belowdecks, where people are packed so closely they can hardly turn over. The smells, he says, are "loathsome." Women shriek, the dying groan, all is "a scene of horror."

> One day, when we had a smooth sea and moderate wind, two of my wearied countrymen, who were chained together (I was near them at the time), preferring death to such a life of misery, somehow made through the nettings, and jumped into the sea.

Olaudah is taken to Barbados in the West Indies, where he is sold. His story is different from most. He will go to sea as a slave, have many adventures, learn to read, and write his autobiography.

Africa, The Unknown Continent

North Africa was the only part of Africa the Europeans knew. And, of North Africa, they knew only the lands that touched the Mediterranean Sea. Those lands were rich in history. Egypt had once seen a civilization that produced pharaohs, pyramids, and a sphinx. That was more than 2,000 years before the birth of Christ. Much later, in the 9th century C.E., another great civilization flourished in North Africa. It was Islamic (also called "Muslim"), and it began in Arabia and spread to Morocco and Spain and Mediterranean Europe.

But what of the rest of the huge African continent? What was it like? Europeans knew almost nothing of it—although there were wild rumors of rich kingdoms and of seven lost cities.

There was a barrier of sand that kept the Europeans from learning much: the vast Sahara desert. A few people were able to cross those blazing desert sands. They were African or Arab traders who traveled from oasis to oasis carrying gold and slaves from lands to the south. It was a very dangerous journey.

Why didn't the Europeans just sail down the African coast and discover for themselves where that gold was coming from? They wanted to, but until the 15th century they couldn't do it. You see, their boats were powered by men with oars. Those boats were fine in the calm Mediterranean, but they weren't safe in the rough Atlantic waters. It was not until the 15th century that Europeans developed sophisticated sailing technology that allowed them to build caravels that could sail into the wind.

Then they got up their courage and began going down the coast, farther and farther, until the Portuguese sailor Vasco da Gama rounded the tip of Africa in 1498 and went on to India. Now, perhaps, the Europeans could stop along the African coast and visit the rich grasslands and forests below the Sahara. They could—if the Africans would let them.

But the people who lived in Africa weren't anxious to have outsiders come and explore or settle. They welcomed the Europeans as traders with goods they could use, but that was all. The Europeans couldn't land, take over, and mine the continent's gold, as they did in America. The African warriors were too strong. The Africans let the Europeans build a few trading posts, but nothing more. Besides, there were African diseases that frightened the Europeans.

So the Europeans didn't learn much about the peoples and cultures of the African continent. For them, it remained mysterious. If they had been able to explore, they would have discovered as much vari-

These bronze sculptures were carved in Benin, the country in West Africa that Olaudah Equiano was kidnapped from.

ety in Africa as in Europe. There were sophisticated empires and primitive cultures. There were sculptures cast in bronze and gold and useful iron objects hammered by village blacksmiths and cotton that weavers turned into handsome fabrics.

On the west coast of Africa, near the continent's bulge, the three great kingdoms of Ghana, Mali, and Songhai rose and fell between the time of the Roman Empire and the settling of North

America. The ruler of Mali, Mansa Musa, was a Muslim who in 1324 took so much gold to Mecca (the center of the Muslim world) that the world price of gold tumbled. In the 15th century, Timbuktu, the leading city of Songhai, was renowned for its schools and wise men. A visitor wrote of the city's "great store of doctors, judges, priests, and other learned men that are bountifully maintained at the King's cost...and hither are brought diverse manuscripts or written books... which are sold for more money than any other merchandise."

But by the time the sailing ships were able to call at West African ports, it was trade alone that interested both peoples. The Europeans had guns, iron, cloth, kettles, and mirrors that were wanted in Africa. The Africans had workers—healthy, hardy people— who were wanted to grow crops and mine and settle the place the Europeans called a New World.

And so men and women would be traded into slavery by people, on both sides of the Atlantic, who didn't seem to worry about the consequences of their actions.

He will take a European name. It is Gustavus Vassa.

Many Africans are sent to Virginia, where they are traded for tobacco. Some are exchanged for sugar and molasses in the West Indies. Others are traded for rice in South Carolina. Then the ships head back to their home ports.

In Newport, Rhode Island, where we started this voyage, the sugar and molasses are turned into rum—and the triangle begins again. That is the way the terrible triangular trade works. Every colony is a part of it. English ships carry the greatest numbers of Africans into slavery.

In the colonies, laws are soon passed that attempt to take away the blacks' humanity. The Virginia Black Code says slaves are property—not people. New York law says runaway slaves caught 40 miles north of Albany—on the way to Canada and safety—are to be killed.

Remember when the first black people arrived as indentured servants at Jamestown? In 1725 about 75,000 blacks are living in the American colonies. By 1790 there are more than 10 times that number.

A Dutch tobacco trader from New Amsterdam. Notice the slaves unloading tobacco in the background, and the town of New Amsterdam rising in the far distance. Who do you think the female figure on the left is?

39 Four and Nine Make Thirteen

Tomochichi, leader of a Creek town near Savannah, welcomed Oglethorpe.

If you've been counting, you know I've talked about 12 colonies. Can you name them? Cover the next sentence and see if you can.

Here they are: Massachusetts, New Hampshire, Connecticut, Rhode Island, New York, New Jersey, Pennsylvania, Delaware, Maryland, Virginia, North Carolina, and South Carolina.

Finally, like a tail at the end of a kite, along came the 13th colony. Do you know what it was named? Here's a clue: It was founded in 1732, when KING GEORGE II was on the throne of England. That wasn't hard: it was Georgia.

Georgia's beginning was noble, not because of birth or wealth, but because of a noble idea. Unfortunately the idea didn't work out. Still, it was inspiring.

James Oglethorpe, who planned Georgia, wanted to solve a terrible problem. People in England who couldn't pay their bills were thrown into debtors' prisons. Once they were in those jails—and they were awful places—they couldn't work or earn money, and so they had no way to pay their debts. If they were lucky, a relative or friend came up with the cash. Otherwise they just stayed there. Many died in prison.

Oglethorpe decided to found a colony where debtors could go instead of going to jail. He wanted to make it a place where people could lead ideal lives. So he had laws passed for Georgia that made drinking liquor and keeping slaves illegal. He wanted Georgians to live on small farms, and he wanted them to do their own farming. He brought experts from Europe to teach them how.

Debtors' prisons in England stuck around for more than a century after Oglethorpe. The author Charles Dickens used his writing skills to help get rid of them. When Charles was a boy, his father had been thrown in debtors' prison—so he knew just how dreadful it was. He described those prisons in some of his novels—such as *Little Dorrit* and *Our Mutual Friend*. Those are long books, but they tell wonderful stories.

In 1734 settlers began building the town of Savannah. The tent under the tall trees in front of the houses was James Oglethorpe's.

Salzburgische Emigranten.

Nichts, als das Evangelium
Vertreibt uns ins Exilium.
Verlassen wir das Vaterland,
So sind wir doch in Gottes Hand.

These Lutherans left Austria to find freedom to worship in Georgia. The verse says their only companion is the Gospel—having left their homeland, they are in God's hands.

James Edward Oglethorpe, founder of Georgia.

Oglethorpe helped to plan a handsome capital, Savannah, a city with beautiful parks and fine public squares. It was a shame his idea didn't work out. Not many debtors wanted to come to the wilds of Georgia. To some, even prison seemed safer.

Those who came were much like the settlers in the other colonies: a mixture of peoples and religions. Anglican men and women came, German Lutherans came, Catholics came, Jews came, and so did Scotch Presbyterians.

They soon discovered that Georgia was full of Indian villages. When the first settlers arrived, they found thousands of Indian mounds. The mounds were sacred sites from the Native American past. (If you get into a helicopter and fly near Eatonton, Georgia, you can see one of those earth mounds. It is shaped like an eagle with wings that spread out for 120 feet, about the size of four average classrooms.)

The local Indians had bad memories of white people. Back in 1540, the Spanish conquistador Hernando de Soto had marched through Georgia with his army. De Soto was so cruel and evil that the Indians were still telling stories about him 200 years later.

But Oglethorpe was a fine and honorable man, and the Indians learned to trust him. They made many peace treaties with him and both he and they always kept their word.

It was the settlers who gave Oglethorpe problems. They wanted to drink liquor and have slaves, and eventually they won out. When Oglethorpe tried to force his laws and "good ideas" on others, it just didn't work.

Besides, life in Georgia wasn't easy. Spaniards and pirates gave the settlers a hard time. Pirates roamed along the Georgia coast, capturing ships of all nations. Spain controlled Florida and said Georgia and the Carolinas were also her territories. Because of that, there were constant border fights. When the Spaniards attacked, the Georgians were able to fight them off—luckily for them, because none of the other colonies helped out. It was a while before the colonies thought of uniting, or of helping each other.

Oglethorpe lost all his money trying to establish Georgia. Finally, he gave up. Georgians wanted to have rice plantations and slaves and the king's government, and that is what they got. The king made Georgia into another royal colony (in 1752). That made eight royal colonies: Virginia, Massachusetts, New Hampshire, North Carolina, New York, South Carolina, New Jersey, and Georgia. Each had a royal governor, appointed by the king.

150

Rhode Island and Connecticut had charters that allowed them to govern themselves. Their assemblies (congresses) picked their governors. Maryland, Pennsylvania, and Delaware were proprietary colonies. They were owned by individuals—the Calverts and the Penns.

All the colonies had assemblies of local leaders who made most of their laws. Later England would regret the freedom she gave the colonies and try to take some of it back. That would lead to big trouble.

But in the mid-18th century most Americans were happy to be part of the mighty British empire. The 13 colonies were like 13 children of a kindly and faraway parent. Each colony seemed to be a tiny nation, with its own government, its own habits, and its own religious ways.

They were different—one from another—but in some ways they were all a bit like Europe. Each had a measure of European class society. So, if you really wanted to be independent, if you wanted to be the equal of anyone, the place to be was on the frontier. There, it was your intelligence and your strength that made you a leader. On the frontier no one cared if you were Puritan or Baptist. It didn't make a difference if your father was a lord or a pauper. Could you be depended upon? Did you tell the truth? Could you shoot straight? Were you brave? That's what mattered on the frontier.

The frontier offered something even more important: *land*. Land meant everything in a society that lived by farming. *Owning land made you feel really free.*

People were arriving in America every day. Much of the land on the East Coast was taken. The frontier was where these newest Americans were going. They were heading to the tree-thick mountains that bordered the coastal plains—and then on, over those mountains.

A famous English poet, Alexander Pope (he wrote that "A little learning is a dangerous thing"), composed a short verse, or couplet, about Oglethorpe (they were friends):
One driven by strong benevolence of soul, Shall fly like Oglethorpe from pole to pole.
What does that mean?

James Oglethorpe (in black) brought some of his Indian friends to London. In this picture he is introducing them to the trustees of his new colony.

151

40 Over the Mountains

Look at the map of the 13 colonies on page 94 to see how the colonies hug the East Coast. You will also see the Appalachian mountains running all the way down the left boundary of the colonies, blocking the way west.

A family traveling west lights a fire. Imagine cooking dinner at night in the rain and the unknown.

Look at a map. Notice: all the early English-speaking settlements are on or near the East Coast. That's not surprising, since the settlers came by boat from Europe. Most of them stayed near the place they landed.

Yet, almost from the first, a few settlers wanted to know what the land was like to the west. They came back with tales that made others want to go, too. Some went because they thought they would find the Pacific Ocean; some went west to trade with the Indians; a few were criminals who were chased away from the settlements. Most didn't get far.

Look at the map again, and you'll see why. Do you see that long strip of mountains that runs from north to south and makes a spine down the back of the eastern United States? Those are the Appalachian Mountains, and they stretch from Quebec to Alabama.

The Appalachians are the oldest mountains in our country. They are tall, but not as tall as some of the far western mountains. The Appalachians have been rounded and smoothed by millions of years of wind and rain.

Don't be confused if you hear of White Mountains in New Hampshire, Green

The Swedish introduced log houses to the New World. They were just right for places that had a lot of trees and not much else.

Can you guess the remote location of this lonely log cabin, surrounded by thick forests? It's a few miles from Baltimore, Maryland. In the 18th century you didn't have to go far to be out in a wilderness.

Mountains in Vermont, Catskill Mountains in New York, Allegheny Mountains in Pennsylvania, and Blue Ridge, Clinch, Shenandoah, and Great Smoky Mountains in the South. All these mountains are part of the Appalachian range.

Water from Appalachian streams and snows flows in two directions. Some water goes into rivers that drain into the Atlantic; some goes to rivers that drain into the Gulf of Mexico. The spot high on the mountains where the waters change direction is called a "divide."

Have you ever climbed a mountain? It isn't easy—even today, when there are clear trails. Imagine what it was like for the first trailblazers. The pioneers who went into Vermont couldn't even take horses. They had to go on foot, because the mountains were so thick with trees that no grass could grow. So there was nothing for horses to eat. Those explorers had to go with their axes, cut down trees, plant seeds, and wait for a crop before they could bring animals.

The trailblazers were first, but they were soon followed by people looking for land to farm. Usually mountain land isn't easy to farm, so they didn't stay in the mountains. They went on, over the Appalachians, to the valleys or the flat lands beyond. There was no government where they went, so they were on their own. They had to fight Indians and other settlers for their land. They were a tough breed, those early over-the-mountain people. They had to be in order to survive.

Oh, Shenandoah

Alexander Spotswood, the Virginia governor we met earlier, was a big booster of westward expansion. In 1716 he set out with an expedition into Virginia's mountainous wilderness. They traveled 200 miles, named the Blue Ridge Mountains (a trick of the light makes them look blue), and got to the Shenandoah Valley. When they came home, Spotswood gave each expedition member a tiny gold horseshoe (because their horses had to be shod to manage the rocky mountain paths). They became known as the "Knights of the Golden Horseshoe."

Talleyrand, who was a French prince and one of the most important politicians in Europe in Napoleanic times. He is supposed to have said: "The United States has 32 religions but only one dish." He didn't think much of Yankee cooking.

Do you use the expression "I'm stumped" when you're stuck about what to do or think? In the days when westbound wagons traveled terrible roads like this one—where tree stumps stuck out of the ground—if you hit a stump, you were in trouble: "stumped."

Most didn't have time to write of their adventures, so we have to listen to others to try and understand what it must have been like. A famous French diplomat named Talleyrand visited the United States at the end of the 18th century. He wrote of a trip west. Talleyrand had a guide, and he went on horseback. This is what he saw:

I was struck with astonishment; less than 154 miles away from the capital [Philadelphia] all trace of men's presence disappeared. Nature, in all her primeval vigor, confronted us. Forests as old as the world itself...here and there the traces of former tornadoes that had carried everything before them. Enormous trees, all mowed down in the same direction, extending for a considerable distance, bear witness to the wonderful force of these terrible phenomena....To be riding through a large wild forest, to lose one's way in it in the middle of the night, and to call to one's companion in order to ascertain that you are not missing each other; all this gives impressions impossible to define....When I cried, "...are you here?" and my companion replied, "Unfortunately I am, my lord," I could not help laughing at our position.

41 Westward Ho

Daniel Boone was a "long hunter," so called because he stayed in the wilderness for weeks.

The British tried to stop them. They didn't want settlers moving west. The British were in charge, and that meant they had to keep order. If the settlers moved into Indian territory, someone had to worry about protecting them from Indian attack. Someone had to protect the Indians from rifle-happy settlers. Someone had to make treaties with the Indians and do some governing.

That cost money. Britain would have to build forts in the western territories. She would have to send soldiers to man those forts. She would have to send governors. Parliament told the colonists to stay out of Indian territory.

But there was no stopping them. Some people want to go where no one has gone before. Some people are born explorers. Some people are just restless. The Americans who headed for the frontiers were all of those things—and more.

They were people who were looking for a good life, and they hadn't found it on the East Coast. By the middle of the 18th century the best land in the East was taken, and society was already in place. These people weren't content to sit around and be second-best. They were the kind who would sail across a dangerous ocean to try their luck in a new world. That kind of person was willing to risk everything for adventure or the dream of a better life.

So they headed out—and you had to be brave to do that—into the unknown wilds. They were called frontiersmen and frontierswomen, trailblazers and pathfinders. They lived in the woods, shot the food they ate, and made their own clothes. They learned from the Indians and from each other. One of them was a man named Daniel Boone.

Daniel Boone was born in 1734, two years after James Oglethorpe

Do you know why "buck" is another word for *dollar*? It's because in the days of Daniel Boone and the Long Hunters, a buckskin was worth about a dollar—so the money was named for the deer that it bought.

Daniel was not the first Boone to seek adventure. His ancestors were Normans—soldiers and farmers from French Normandy—who conquered England in the 11th century and settled there because of the good land and opportunity. To them, then, England seemed a frontier on the edge of the world.

Women and children from settler families were sometimes kidnapped by Indians during border battles over territory. Daniel Boone's own daughter, Jemima, was carried off in 1776, but he managed to rescue her. This is an artist's rather romantic idea of the event.

Have you ever seen a picture of Daniel Boone in a coonskin cap? Well, those pictures were drawn by people who didn't know Boone. He wore a broad-brimmed hat to protect his eyes from the sun.

founded Georgia. Oglethorpe would have liked Daniel Boone, and John Smith would have like him, too. Daniel Boone didn't look for others to do his work. He grew up in Pennsylvania, with Indians for friends, and he learned their ways along with the ways of the European settlers. That was an interesting combination, and it was creating a new people, a people who were wholly American.

Daniel Boone's grandfather, George Boone, had lived in England, where he was a weaver and an independent thinker. He was both cautious and daring, a man who would do what he intended and do it well. When he was 36 years old George Boone left the Church of England and joined an outcast religion that some people called Quaker. Boone knew it as the Society of Friends.

Being a Quaker in England was hard, as we've already seen. Quakers were persecuted, but George Boone stood up for his beliefs.

Then he heard about William Penn's colony in America, where Quakers and everyone had equal rights. He also heard stories of abundant land cheap enough for anyone to buy, and that seemed almost too good to be true.

As I said, Boone was cautious. He had a wife and nine children. Before he moved his whole family, he sent his three oldest children to the New World to look around. This was what George Boone learned in a letter from Pennsylvania:

Because one may hold as much property as one wishes and pay when one wishes, everybody hurries to take up property. The far ther the Germans and English cultivate the country the farther the Indians retreat. They are agreeable and peaceable....in summer one can shoot a deer, dress the skin, and wear pants from it in twenty-four hours.

It sounded good to him. In 1717, when he was 51 years old—an old man in those days—George Boone left England and sailed for Pennsylvania. Boone's grandson, Daniel, became the most famous of all the American frontiersmen.

Daniel Boone's first adventures came in 1755, during the French and Indian War (which you'll read more about in Book 3). He fought on the side of the British, as did George Washington. Washington was an officer; Boone was a wagon driver. Sitting with soldiers around the campfire, young Boone heard John Finley, a fur trader, tell stories of a land the Indians called *kentake*, which means "meadowland." Finley said it was the most beautiful land he had ever seen, filled with high grasses, birds, buffalo, deer, and beaver. It was an Indian hunting ground, and the Indians didn't want the white men to find it.

Daniel Boone got excited about those meadowlands over the mountains. As soon as the war was over, off he went, with a sack of salt around his neck, an ax in his belt, and a rifle over his shoulder. But he never found an easy way to get over the mountains.

Then, one day, a peddler knocked on his door. It turned out to be John Finley. Finley told him of an Indian trail through the mountains.

Boone searched until he found that trail. It led to a hole through the mountains, called a gap, and that led to the rich grasslands of Kentucky. In 1775 Daniel Boone and 30 woodsmen turned that Indian trail into a road that families could travel with wagons and animals. It was called the "Wilderness Road," and it went for 300 miles. By 1790, almost 200,000 people had gone west on the Wilderness Road.

Three years after Daniel Boone first reached Kentucky, settlers were already pouring in. A man named James Harrod was laying out a town named after him. Pretty soon there was a town named after Boone, too—Boonesborough.

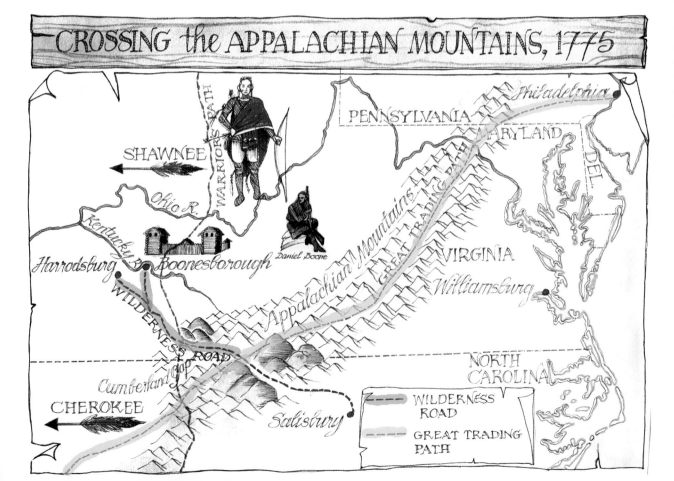

CROSSING the APPALACHIAN MOUNTAINS, 1775

SHAWNEE

PENNSYLVANIA

MARYLAND

DEL.

Philadelphia

Ohio R.

WARRIOR'S PATH

Daniel Boone

Kentucky R.

Harrodsburg

Boonesborough

Appalachian Mountains

GREAT TRADING PATH

VIRGINIA

Williamsburg

WILDERNESS ROAD

Cumberland Gap

CHEROKEE

Salisbury

NORTH CAROLINA

WILDERNESS ROAD

GREAT TRADING PATH

This bloody picture of An Attack of the Indians upon Dan'l and Squire Boone & John Stewart helped spread the legends told about Boone after his death. (Squire Boone was Daniel's brother.)

But Daniel Boone just couldn't stay settled. He was always off on one adventure or another. The Indians didn't want Boone or any whites in Kentucky. Then they hoped the settlers would at least all stay in one place. They soon learned that there was no way to keep Daniel Boone from wandering. He was a natural-born explorer, and, like a cat, he had nine (or maybe more) lives. His wife was told he was dead—more than once—and a few times he was close to it, but he always survived, whether his attackers were animals or people.

Sometimes he ran backward through the woods, and Indians following his trail went the wrong way. Once he swung 40 feet on a grapevine so Indians would lose his trail. The stories about Boone's adventures grew and grew and grew, and some of them were true: stories about how he was captured by Indians, about how he rescued his daughter from Indians, about a buffalo stampede, about how he was adopted into a tribe. Each time the stories got told, they were bigger and better.

It was said that Daniel Boone could shoot a flea off the nose of a bear. Do you think that could be true?

We would know for sure if it weren't for a canoe accident. When Daniel was an old man, he told his grandson about his adventures. His grandson wrote them all down in a book. Everyone who knew Daniel Boone agreed that he was honest, so that book must have told the real story about him. But the book was in a canoe when the Boone family moved; the canoe tipped; and the book was lost.

We do know for sure that when Daniel was a boy one of his best friends was named Abraham Lincoln. Many years later, that Abraham's grandson became a famous president. President Lincoln was proud that his grandfather had known Daniel Boone, because Daniel Boone was a real American hero.

42 The End—and the Beginning

This painting of George Washington was made when he was a young colonel in the Virginia militia—at the very beginning of what was to be an extraordinary career.

Congratulations! You have finished almost all of book 2 of *A History of US*. The 13 colonies have been formed, and are doing very well!

We have traveled into the 18th century, and those early days of hunger and hardship are now only a memory. Life is beginning to be comfortable for the settlers in this New World. It still takes courage to cross the dangerous Atlantic and begin again on a continent that is reshaping itself. But, just as the birth of a baby offers promise and hope, so, too, this vast, inviting land promises hope to all who are tired of the Old World ways.

Many people have come to America because there was no opportunity for them in that Old World. Most of those people think they have found paradise in this land of sweet-smelling flowers, abundant game, and fertile soil. In England, men are shot for hunting the king's deer. In America, deer, beaver, birds, and fish are for everyone.

Some of those who are here have a powerful dream of a free country where everyone is treated fairly. The dreamers will have the opportunity to test their ideas. They will turn 13 colonies into a nation "conceived in liberty, and dedicated to the proposition that all men are created equal."

If you keep reading our history, you will learn about the making of that nation—our nation. You will meet people like George Washington and Thomas Jefferson. You will learn more about Benjamin Franklin and Daniel Boone. The story will include war, adventure, heroism, villainy, and love. So keep on reading America's story. There is much excitement ahead.

After Words: A Cartographer Makes Maps, Not Wagons

Cartography. (car TOG ruf fee) No, it doesn't have anything to do with wagons. It is the art of making maps. It comes from Latin roots: *carta*, or *charta*, meaning paper, especially paper made from papyrus, and *graphie*, from the Greek word for "writing."

Just look out the window and you'll see: the world is flat. And yet the ancient Greeks four thousand years ago realized that the world is a sphere. (If you have any doubts about it, we now have photographs taken in space that show our beautiful green and blue globe.) The Greeks didn't have telescopes or fancy measuring devices. How did they figure out the shape of the Earth? They used their brains.

The oldest collection of maps still in existence today is a Song work from China which dates, we think, to 1099. It has 44 maps and was printed from woodblocks by a mapmaker named Shui Anli.

This original Coronelli globe, which dates from 1688, is on permanent display in the Texas Tech University Library in Lubbock, Texas.

Father Vincenzo Coronelli (vin CHEN zo CORE oh NELLY), who lived in the Republic of Venice in Italy, knew as much about the world as any person in the 17th century. (It was the century of Peter Stuyvesant, William Penn, and most of the people in this book.) That may seem surprising, because he was a Franciscan monk – a member of an order of priests (founded by Saint Francis of Assisi) who agree to a life of poverty when they join that religious order. But the Franciscans are also scholars, and Father Coronelli was among the best of them.

He spent much of his life doing one of the most important tasks of his time, or any time: making maps.

Mapmaking doesn't sound significant to you? Well, hold on, I'll try and convince you that it is.

What is a map and why is it important? Maps are sources of information. They are guides. They are usually drawings of something too big to see with a sweep of your eyes. They are a way of simplifying things too complicated to hold in your head easily. Sometimes they help you look to the future. Some people even map ideas.

The simplest maps get you from here to there. Find yourself in a new city and it helps to have a map that will guide you. That will save you time, aggravation, or maybe even disaster. Suppose you're going to a foreign land, or you're a merchant sending goods far away, or perhaps you are commanding an army on its way to battle.

Imagine that you have no map of your route or your destination. What will you pay for one? And what about the rest of the world? Do you know where you are in relation to other places?

In medieval times world maps were usually disc shaped, looking like a coin, but bigger. On most European maps, Jerusalem and the Mediterranean Sea were in the center, and Asia, Africa, and Europe surrounded them. On Japanese maps, Japan was in the center. On Korean maps, Korea was in the center. You get the idea. Maps are human creations, and we all like to think of our culture as central.

After Columbus returned from his voyage, and especially after Magellan's ship made it around the globe, Europe's view of the world was stretched. Suddenly there were new worlds to know. Lots of Europeans wanted to explore, or conquer, or invest, or exploit. Picture the excitement of the times. And the greed. The nations that won the exploration game were going to dominate the globe. But you can't explore without maps. Mapmakers, who were now in big demand and short supply, became very important people.

The best European maps of the time were based on those of the ancient Greek geographer, Ptolemy (who lived in the 2nd century C.E.), and on maps by Arabs (like the 12th-century scholar Al-Idrisi). In the 15th century, Portuguese sailors began bringing new information home. Their maps, which they treated like secret documents, were soon among the most precise in the world.

To make maps you have to be smart. Accurate maps are drawn to scale. That means a millimeter or an inch on the map needs to reflect exactly the meters or feet or miles in the real world. So mapmakers need to know mathematics. They have to be able to draw. They need to understand landforms, like mountains and valleys. They need to be aware of the latest scientific findings. The country with the best mapmakers usually has the most power and prestige. (Is it different today? What new territories are we now mapping? Who is doing it?)

How do you make a flat map of a round globe? Explorers need flat maps. They need to be able to follow a straight line from point A to point B. To understand the problem, take an orange peel. Now try and make a flat map of that peel. You can't do it. There will be tears and irregularities. There's no way to chart a direct line from one part of the skin around the whole thing after you've flat-

> Now when I was a little chap I had a passion for maps. I would look for hours at South America, or Africa, or Australia, and lose myself in all the glories of exploration. At that time there were many blank spaces on the earth, and when I saw one that looked particularly inviting on a map (but they all look like that) I would put my finger on it and say, *When I grow up I will go there. . .*
> From *Heart of Darkness*, by Joseph Conrad

Al-Idrisi, who was born in Morocco about 1100, drew this map of the world. Can you locate the Mediterranean Sea?

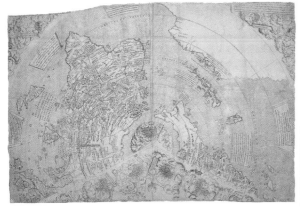

When Columbus returned from his voyage in 1493 it changed the way Europeans thought of the world. This is the first map we have that reflects that new world view and includes the Americas. The mapmaker, Giovanni Contarini, signed his name and the date, 1506. That's all we know of him. Like Columbus, Contarini thought that Asia was just beyond the New World islands. He has Brazil reach to the South Pole.

Abraham Ortelius, a 16th century Belgian, is remembered as the first cartographer to draw world maps in a uniform size, bind them together, and make an atlas. This famous map of his was published about 70 years after Columbus's voyage. It reflects a belief in a vast southern continent, Terra Australias.

Knowing latitude is easy, longitude is not. A very good book by Dava Sobel, *Longitude*, tells an exciting story of the big prize offered in the 18th century for a method to find longitude at sea.

tened it. So you have to look for a next-best solution.

In 1569 Gerhardus Mercator (GAIR har dus mer KATE er), who lived in Flanders (now parts of Belgium, France, and the Netherlands), came up with an idea. He put a stiff piece of paper around a globe. Picture the paper as a cylinder with the round Earth inside. Then Mercator projected the Earth's three-dimensional shape onto the two-dimensional paper. That projection worked fine for the areas close to the equator. But think of your orange peel flattened. In the center it's okay, but near the poles it's a torn, ragged mess. Mercator didn't want tears or gaps on his maps. He wanted to be able to draw straight lines from one place to another. So he filled in the tears and gaps by stretching the regions to the north and south, making them bigger than they actually are.

As soon as he did that he could draw straight lines of latitude and longitude on his map. That was very helpful to sailors who could look at his maps and see hazards to avoid or havens to seek. Then, if they could figure out their own longitude and latitude, they could know exactly where they were on the map.

Mercator was a poor boy whose good mind and hard-working habits took him far. He often went without sleep to study mathematics, geography, astronomy, and surveying. By the time he was 24 he was a well-known engraver and maker of scientific instruments. When he died, at 82 in 1594, he had revolutionized mapmaking and gone into the history books as one of the best mapmakers of all time. (His neighbors praised him as a modest good citizen who often helped the poor.) His maps were not only the latest scientific records of world geography, they were superb pieces of art. People everywhere wanted his maps; and the best mapmakers—like John Smith—were soon copying his methods. Most

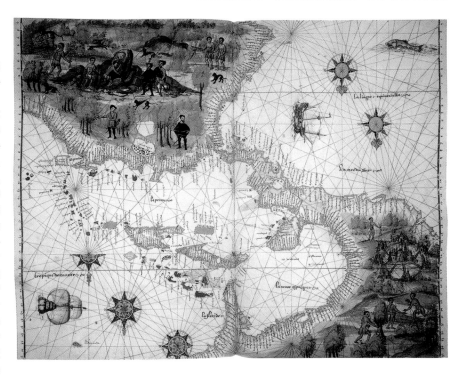

maps that you see are still based on the Mercator projection.

But keep in mind, it has a big flaw. Those stretched spaces distort the real space. Greenland, for instance, because it is near the North Pole, has to be huge on Mercator's map. Much, much bigger than Australia or South America. The truth is, it is actually much, much smaller than either of those places. There is no way to make a flat map that is an accurate picture of a globe. On page 166 you will see several approaches to the problem.

Now, finally, back to Father Vincenzo Coronelli. He lived a century after Mercator and he created some of the most gorgeous maps and globes of his time, or any time. Many of the people in this book must have known of Coronelli's maps. He built a globe for King Louis XIV of France that was 13' in diameter (think of two tall men head to head and toe to toe straddling a globe). It was the largest globe that had ever been built, and was a wonder of the time.

Coronelli, like the other Franciscans, dressed in a brown robe with a rope belt and wore sandals on his feet, but he hobnobbed with Europe's monarchs. That worked well for him and for them. In addition to supporting his work, they sent him the latest information on their conquests and explorations. It made his maps the best there were.

Coronelli put most of Australia on his globe, before anyone else did, and he filled in the interior of the other continents with rivers and bays that had rarely been marked before. He showed the St. Lawrence, the Yangtzee, the Senegal, the Paraguay, and the Zambezi rivers (which are where?). He included details on the latest exploration of the Mississippi River. And he made a special map of Siam (Thailand) based on an expedition of Jesuit Fathers sent by King Louis XIV. When he drew the seas, he added pictures of the

This gorgeous map of the Caribbean Sea and the West Indies was drawn about 1547. That finger pointing upwards from the bottom center is Florida. Mexico City is upper left. Is something wrong? Not at all. We expect North to be on top and South on the bottom. But they don't have to be that way. Turn the page around and you'll see Florida in its familiar place.

This map, printed in 1687, was color coded to mark European land claims. (No one considered Native American claims.) The mapmaker, Giovanni de Rossi, drew California as an island, So did others of his time. Rossi was pro-French. He gave everything colored pink to France.

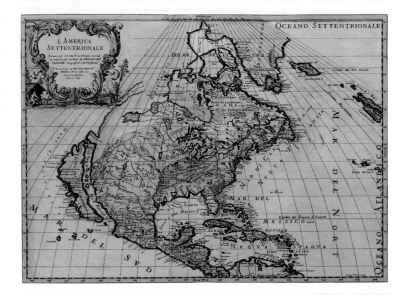

In 1688 Father Vincenzo Coronelli, working in Venice, Italy (using information sent by Catholic Jesuit priests), made this map (*right*) of the Great Lakes (then a barely explored region of western New France). Compare it with today's satellite photograph of the same area (*below*). Amazing, isn't it?

wooden ships that were bringing Europeans so much astounding new information. His maps were works of art.

In 1684, Coronelli founded the world's first geographic society: the Cosmographic Academy of the Argonauts. If you joined (it was expensive) you got world map sheets, piece by piece, as they were produced. Then you could put them together to make a globe. Sometimes you got pages of a great atlas. (It was Mercator who coined that word "atlas" for a book of maps.) The king of Poland was one of Father Coronelli's subscribers. In 1688 Coronelli put himself in a corner of a great globe he made. (I know globes don't have corners, but when the globe is flattened onto a two-dimensional page, you get corners.)

Venice, like Portugal and Spain, had been a center of world power, but Coronelli could sense the shift that was in progress. France, the Netherlands, and now England were expanding their reach—all were producing great explorers and great mapmakers; they went hand in hand.

In the late 16th century, European surveyors began using a mathematical principle, *triangulation*. If you know the length of the base of a triangle and the size of its two angles you can figure out the size of the whole triangle. This 1594 German engraving shows surveyors at work.

In Greek mythology, the Argonauts were heroes who sailed on the ship *Argo* with Jason in search of the Golden Fleece.

About Maps and the Truth

Maps lie. All of them. You just can't tell the whole truth on a flat map. When you project that three-dimensional globe onto a flat two-dimensional page, you are forced to distort. There is no way around it. Still, maps are very important and useful. And, as long as you know about distortions, you can allow for them. We've developed many kinds of projections —some do one thing, some another. No one is perfect. The important thing is to choose the right projection for your needs. The best map services, like USGS (U.S. Geological Survey) use different projections for different purposes. You can compare the projections below.

For mariners, Mercator's projection (A) used to work best. It helped bring about the Age of Exploration. Mercator knew a grid would give sailors straight lines to follow. On the globe, lines of latitude come together. To make his grid work and keep latitude lines parallel, he had to flatten the globe and stretch land and sea, especially near the polar regions. (Note Greenland, which is actually about one eighth the size of South America.) Mercator projections are still widely used.

In 1963 Arthur Robinson developed a projection (B) that is now widely used in classrooms. Although it has some distortions (check Greenland again), mostly it shows the world's land as it actu-

ally looks. Robinson turned the whole globe into a one-sided elongated ellipse (or flattened oval), so his is called an elliptical projection. The world map near the end of this book is based on a Robinson projection. It is a very useful compromise. I like it.

Maps can sometimes give you wrong ideas about geographical importance. In the 1970s, Arno Peters, a German historian, said the Mercator projection glorified Europe and North America by making them large and on top, thus diminishing the Third World. (Check Africa on Peters' projection (C). His projection gives landmasses their true size (but it distorts shape). The Peters projection is often shown with South on top, as below.

Most of the standard projections are made by putting a cylinder around a globe and projecting the globe's image on it. A conic projection (D) is made with a cone placed over a region of the Earth. You need several conic projections to capture the whole Earth.

Global gores (E) are tapered strips that, put together, make a globe. They are highly accurate, but not easy to use. You can see why.

You can get more information on maps from the USGS website, www.usgs.gov, or by calling 1-888-ASK-USGS. USGS, a government agency, belongs to you and all citizens.

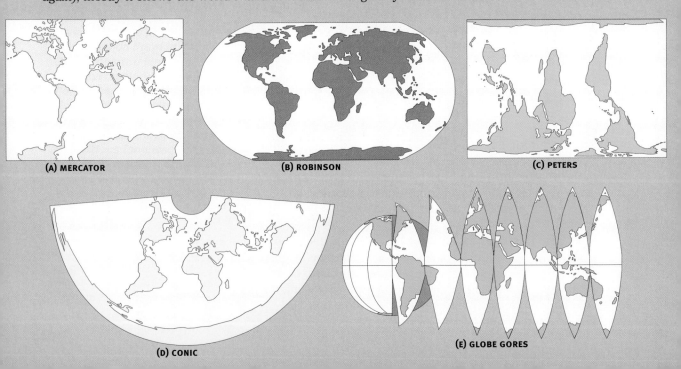

(A) MERCATOR   **(B) ROBINSON**   **(C) PETERS**

(D) CONIC   **(E) GLOBE GORES**

Some Measuring Words

Acre. (AYE kur) It's a unit of measurement used in the U.S. An acre is an area of land or sea equal to 43,560 square feet. It used to be what a yoke of oxen could plow in one day. (What's a yoke of oxen?)

Cubit. (KEW bit) In the Bible, when God gave Noah the measurements of the ark, he used cubits. For a long time, lots of people measured in cubits. It was supposed to be the distance between the elbow and the tip of the middle finger. Today a cubit is 18 inches or 45.72 cm., but the measurement is mostly a historic thing. The Latin word for "elbow" is cubitum.

Knot. Yes, it is what you get in a rope or in your hair if you aren't neat. The word actually has a number of meanings (check your dictionary). But the meaning that has to do with measuring is used by sailors. It is a measure of the speed of a ship. A knot is one nautical mile per hour (or 1,85 kilometers per hour).

League. It's a collection of baseball teams. It's also 3 miles or 4.8 kilometers. In the 17th and 18th centuries people often measured in leagues. They don't do that much today.

Light year. It is the distance that light travels in a vacuum in one year. That's about 5.88 trillion miles or 9.46 trillion kilometers. For measuring purposes you can consider space a vacuum. So if a star is 600 light years away, how far is it?

There are many other measuring words, some used today, some archaic (ar KAY ick, it means out of date). See if you can find some. (Helpful hint: check your dictionary for a measurement table.)

WORDS ABOUT THINGS (MOSTLY IMAGINARY)
USEFUL TO UNDERSTAND MAPS

Equator. An imaginary line around the middle of the earth.

Latitude. A measure of distance north and south of the equator. Latitude lines run east and west around the globe and are parallel to each other. They are measured in degrees, minutes, and seconds. There are 90 degrees of north latitude and 90 degrees of south latitude. Each degree of latitude and longitude is divided into 60 minutes (60'), and minutes into 60 seconds (60").

Prime Meridian. An imaginary line running north-south and right through Greenwich, England. The prime meridian is 0°.

Longitude. The distance, measured in degrees, east or west of the prime meridian. There are 180 degrees of west longitude and 180 degrees of east longitude. Longitude lines meet at the poles. They are not parallels.

International Date Line. An imaginary line running north-south through the Pacific Ocean, mostly along the 180th meridian. There, by international agreement, travelers change dates. Going westward one adds a day, going eastward means going back in time.

Scale. A small distance on a map represents a larger distance in the real world. Scale is the ratio of map size to actual size. Example: one half-inch on a map may represent one foot of land.

Coordinates. The numbers that tell a place's exact longitude and latitude are called its coordinates. The coordinates of Washington, D.C. are 38.54° North (latitude) and 77.2° West (longitude).

Isothermal. This word has to do with temperature. You'll find isotherm lines, showing temperatures, on climate maps.

Geology, A Storyteller's Science

Maps are snapshots of Earth at a given time. But Earth's face keeps changing. Earthquakes, volcanoes, erosion, climate, and glaciers help create that change. So do the huge tectonic plates that hold up the continents and oceans. New sea floor is constantly being formed and that pulls and tugs on the tectonic plates. Most of the United States (except the west coast and Hawaii) lies on the North American plate. The plates move along with the land that sits on them. Geological maps can help picture that activity. They add a fourth dimension — time — to cartography. One way geological maps picture time is by using different colors to show the varying ages of Earth's rock.

Here are some tidbits of U.S. geological history. How would you map them?

• The Rocky Mountains are youngsters, as mountains go (they are between 50 and 100 million years old), except for Pikes Peak—where you can find billion-year-old granite.

• Florida is an add-on to the United States. It was part of Africa until it floated our way.

• In central New York, Ice Age glaciers scoured valleys and then, when the glaciers melted, some of those valleys filled with water creating seven big Finger Lakes. (The Iroquois once believed that the fan-shaped lakes were marks from the hand of the Great Spirit.)

• Yellowstone National Park, in northwest Wyoming, lies above a hot spot or plume rising through Earth's crust from deep in the underlying mantle. Its hot springs (including Old Faithful) are souvenirs from an ancient volcano.

• The upper Rio Grande River flows south through New Mexico along a fault, the Rio Grande Rift, where lava from deep inside Earth periodically rises to the surface. Predictions are that a few million years from now, an ocean basin may spread across this area.

• About 20 million years ago, in the region that stretches from southern Oregon to western Texas, Earth's crust thinned, stretched, and broke into some 400 mountains creating the unique and often spectacular Basin and Range Region. Earth has many stories to tell. If you study geology you will learn about them.

Relief maps show the shape of the land's surface by using dark and light shadings. Leonardo da Vinci developed this technique in his drawings some 400 years ago. Artists call it *chiaroscuro* (key air oh SKYUR oh). Computers do it digitally. A computer (GIS) map can show terrain in relief across the world—a photograph is limited in its scope.

Meteorology is the study of weather and weather forecasting. Everyone knows about Ben Franklin and the lightning rod. But Ben was fascinated with the nature of weather and storms and did serious research in the field. He kept detailed records comparing wind and weather in several regions. (Imagine how excited he would be with today's satellite information gathering.)

Geologists have devised this computer-generated map showing the age of the rock that makes up the continental United States. The colors yellow to green indicate rock formed from 1 to 245 million years ago. The blue to purple shades indicate rock from 246 to 438 million years ago, and the darkening shades of red indicate rock from 449 to 2600 millions years ago.

Being Up to Date

Way back in time, when we didn't know much about the world, mapmaking was a form of artistry and maps were often gorgeous works that only the elite could afford. Then, as we explored unknown areas, more and more maps got drawn. You couldn't develop land, or settle on it, if you didn't know where you were. Accurate maps were in demand. Usually there was no time to be artistic.

Early in the 20th century, photographers climbed into airplanes and began taking aerial photographs of the land. Those photographs were not maps, but they helped make ever-more accurate maps. So did satellites when they were fired into the atmosphere, sending back stunning and precise earth portraits. Landsat 1 was the first satellite with eyes for global mapping. A single Landsat 1 scene (115 miles by 115 miles) included more than thirty million observations. Each scene took 25 seconds to complete. Landsat 1, launched in 1972, was followed by ever-more sophisticated satellites. The total amount of information sent by Landsat satellites was, and is, staggering.

But, astonishing as satellite photography is, it doesn't tell the whole story. A whole new level of cartography came along when computers entered the field. Mountains of information can be processed in a computer, making for an incredible variety of maps. Computer-based mapping is known as GIS: it stands for Geographic Information Systems. GIS maps usually have a scale of 1:1,000,000 or better. That means we can now map tiny bits of land along with vast areas of space.

Computer mapping can show earthquakes throughout history, current fault lines, weather (past and present), temperature, population. . . the possibilities are endless. Computers keyed to satellites can locate you and your vehicle wherever you are and chart a route to your destination.

Cameras sometimes distort space; computers can make corrections. Computers have done something no one expected. They have helped make maps gorgeous again. Today, cartography is a "hot" science. And you don't have to be elite to have access to great maps. Just start on the Internet with the U.S.Geological Survey maps at **http://www.usgs.gov/research/gis/title.html.**

On August 10, 2001, a member of the crew of the Space Shuttle Discovery took this picture of a satellite circling the earth.

Isaac Newton's laws of motion predict the orbits of human-made satellites. The law of gravity tells us that force changes with distance from the Earth. Knowing that lets you figure out what accelerations to expect at different altitudes. Physicist Gerry Wheeler says, "a satellite at a height of 200 kilometers should orbit the Earth in 88.5 minutes. This is close to the orbit of the satellite Vostok 6 that carried the first woman, Valentina Tereskova, into Earth orbit in June 1963."

169

Chronology of Events

WARNING: CHRONOLOGIES CAN BE DANGEROUS!

Medical reports tell of a disease—called *date-itis*—with these alarming symptoms: rapid heartbeat, heavy sweating, and frequent moaning. This disease is caused by an allergy to dates. Teachers need to be aware that this has nothing to do with dried fruit! This not-very-rare disease affects people who hate to memorize dates. If the disease is treated skillfully, recovery is possible.

NOTICE TO POSSIBLE VICTIMS OF THE DISEASE:

Before reading this page: place a glass of water in your hand, an ice pack on your head, and read rapidly. Chances are good that you will survive, and you might learn something, too.

1607: Three ships sent by the London Company land at Cape Henry, Virginia. Captain John Smith and others found Jamestown

1609: Henry Hudson sails up the Hudson River

1609–10: All but 60 of the 500 settlers in Jamestown die during the Starving Time

1610: Santa Fe founded in New Mexico

1612: Settlers plant tobacco in Virginia for the first time

1614: Pocahontas, daughter of Powhatan, marries John Rolfe in Jamestown

1619: The first African slaves arrive in Virginia, and the first representative government of the European colonies begins with Virginia's House of Burgesses

1620: The Pilgrims sail from England to Cape Cod on the *Mayflower*. They make a plan of government called the Mayflower Compact

1621: Massasoit, leader of the Wampanoag Indians, establishes peace with the Pilgrims

1622: Opechancanough leads a great massacre of English settlers around Jamestown

1626: The Dutch buy Manhattan Island from the Indians

1630–40: The Puritans keep arriving in New England and spreading through the Massachusetts Bay Colony and beyond

1632: Lord Calvert founds Maryland

1633: First school in the North American colonies founded in New Amsterdam

1636: Roger Williams founds Rhode Island; Thomas Hooker moves to Connecticut; Harvard College founded

1649: King Charles I of England is beheaded; Parliament rules

1660: Charles II restored to the English throne; Mary Dyer hanged in Massachusetts

1664: The British capture New Amsterdam and rename it New York

1665–66: London attacked first by the Great Plague and then by the Great Fire

1670: Charleston founded in South Carolina

1675–76: Massasoit's son Metacom fights New England's colonists in King Philip's War

1677: North Carolinians rebel against English taxes

1680: Pueblo Indians led by Popé attack the Spaniards and drive them out of Santa Fe

1681: William Penn founds Pennsylvania

1686: King James II sends Sir Edmund Andros to control New England colonists

1688: England's Glorious Revolution; James II deposed

1692: Witchcraft trials held in Salem, Massachusetts

1699: Williamsburg becomes capital of Virginia

1706: Birth of Benjamin Franklin in Boston

1732: James Oglethorpe founds Georgia

1734: Birth of Daniel Boone

1775: The Wilderness Road open to pioneers

More Books to Read

History and Biography

Aliki, *The Story of William Penn,* Prentice-Hall, 1964. This book is very easy to read and has colorful pictures.

Franklin Folsom, *Red Power on the Rio Grande,* Follett, 1973. The story of Popé and the Native American revolution of 1680.

Jean Fritz, *The Double Life of Pocahontas,* Putnam, 1983. Biography as it should be written: exciting and informative.

Jean Craighead George, *The First Thanksgiving,* Philomel, 1993. Just what it says: how the *Mayflower* colonists celebrated their first harvest.

Ann McGovern, *If You Lived in Colonial Times,* Scholastic, 1992. A clear, informative, colorful book. Part of a series that answers many questions about past times.

Marcia Sewall, *Thunder from the Sky,* Atheneum, 1995. What happens when the Pilgrims and the Wampanoags meet? Read this book and find out.

Historical Fiction

Patricia Clapp, *Constance: A Story of Early Plymouth,* Beech Tree Books, 1991. This is the imagined diary of a real girl, Constance Hopkins, the daughter of one of the original *Mayflower* Strangers. It's written (very well) by one of her descendants, and it is as lively and fun as Constance herself.

Rachel Field, *Calico Bush,* Macmillan, 1931. Marguerite Ledoux is a 13-year-old French orphan, bound out for six years to a family who move to the wilds of Maine in 1743. This story, written over 60 years ago, is real, fresh, and exciting. It might even make you cry.

Paul Fleischman, *Saturnalia,* HarperCollins, 1990. Fourteen-year-old William is a printer's apprentice in 1681 Boston—but he's also a captured Narraganset Indian trying to find a link with his past. This story is very well written and researched—and quite thrilling.

Sally M. Keehn, *I Am Regina,* Dell, 1991. This is based on a true story about an 11-year-old girl who was kidnapped by Indians in 1755 and lived with them for nine years before being returned to her mother and their home in western Pennsylvania.

Ann Petry, *Tituba of Salem Village,* Harper & Row, 1964. Tituba, a slave from Barbados, is sold to a minister who moves to Salem, Massachusetts. This thoughtful book tells the story of the Salem witchcraft trials from Tituba's imagined point of view.

Elizabeth George Speare, *The Sign of the Beaver,* Houghton Mifflin, 1983. Matt is alone in the woods in Maine while his father fetches his mother and sister. He's befriended by an Indian boy, Attean—and both boys learn some surprising things about each other.

Elizabeth George Speare, *The Witch of Blackbird Pond,* Dell, 1958. Seventeenth-century Connecticut is the setting for this classic tale of suspense and romance. Highly recommended.

Elizabeth Yates, *Amos Fortune: Free Man,* Dutton, 1950. Born a prince in 1710 in Africa, At-mun is captured, sold in Massachusetts, and, as Amos Fortune, works in slavery until he buys his freedom at the age of 60. He dies a respected free man in New Hampshire, aged about 90. A splendid and true story.

Poems, Folktales, a Play, Songs, and Food!

Suzanne I. Barchers and Patricia C. Marden, *Cooking Up U.S. History: Recipes and Research to Share with Children,* Teacher Ideas Press, 1991. Recipes and information about American food. You can learn how to make hasty pudding, berry ink, hardtack, snickerdoodles, gumbo, and sopapillas.

Arthur Miller, *The Crucible,* Viking, 1953. This is a play about the Salem witchcraft trials by a famous playwright. It is not hard to read.

Scott R. Sanders, *Hear the Wind Blow: American Folk Songs Retold,* Bradbury, 1985. I love this kind of book. Stories and songs and explanations.

Alvin Schwartz, *Scary Stories to Tell in the Dark: Collected from American Folklore,* Lippincott/HarperCollins, 1981. Just what the title says.

171

Picture Credits

Cover: Edward Hicks, Penn's Treaty with the Indians (detail), Gilcrease Museum, Tulsa; 5: The Granger Collection; 6–7: LOC; 8 (bottom): National Portrait Gallery, Smithsonian Institution / Art Resource; 9: Metropolitan Museum of Art, Harris Brisbane Dick Fund, 1959; 10 (bottom): Istitutuo Arti Grafiche, Bergamo; 10 (top), 11 (both): NYPL, Picture Collection; 14, 15 (bottom right): LOC; 16: NYPL, Picture Collection; 18: LOC; 19: Brown University, John Carter Brown Library; 20 (top): From André Thevet, Les Singularitéz de la France Antarctique, autrement nommé Amérique, engraved by Silvanus, printed by Christopher Plantin, Antwerp; 20 (bottom): title page from The New Life of Virginea, printed by Felix Kyngston for William Welby, London, 1612; 21: LOC; 23: The Granger Collection; 25-26 (bottom): LOC; 26: Courtesy the Association for the Preservation of Virginia Antiquities; 28: Jamestown Rediscovery; 29: LOC; 30: NYPL, Special Collections; 31: NYPL, Map Division (97-7398); 33: NYPL, Special Collections; 35: National Portrait Gallery, Smithsonian Institution / Art Resource; 36: LOC; 37 (left), 38 (top): New-York Historical Society; 38 (bottom): LOC; 40 (top): NYPL, Picture Collection; 41 (bottom): LOC; 42: NYPL, Archives and Manuscripts; 44: NYPL, Archives and Manuscripts; 45 (top): Pilgrim Hall; 45 (bottom): Joe Flying Horse, "Around the Rez" The Lakota Times (now called Indian Country Today) September 1989; 46 (both), 47: LOC; 48–49: Pilgrim Hall; 51 (left): NYPL, Picture Collection; 51 (right): LOC; 52: Harper's Weekly, March 9, 1895; 54: LOC; 55 (left): The Book of Animals; 55 (right): NYPL, Picture Collection; 56 (bottom): LOC; 58: Corbis; 59: American Antiquarian Society; 60: Massachusetts Archives; 61: Bequest of Maxim Karolik, Museum of Fine Arts, Boston; 62: NYPL, Picture Collection; 63 (left): British Library; 63 (right): LOC; 64 (bottom left): Courtesy, Winterthur Museum; 64 (top): British Museum; 64 (bottom right), 65: LOC; 67: Historical Society of Pennsylvania; 68, 69 (bottom): LOC; 69 (top): © JOHN HOPF Photography; 70: NYPL, Picture Collection; 71: Pierpoint Morgan Library; 72: Plimouth Plantation; 74 (top): from Samuel Seyer, Memoirs Historical & Topographical of Bristol, NYPL; 74 (bottom), 75: LOC; 76 (top): NYPL, Picture Collection; 76 (bottom): from Matthew Hopkins, Discoverie of Witches, NYPL; 77: British Library; 78: Courtesy, Peabody Essex Museum, Salem, Massachusetts; 79 (top): Massachusetts Historical Society; 80, 81 (left): LOC; 83: NYPL, Maps Division; 84–86, 87 (top): LOC; 87 (bottom): Hartford Courant; 88, 90 (bottom): from Pablo Beaumont, Cronica de Mechoacan, NYPL, Rare Books and Manuscripts; 90 (top; neg. no. 133131), 91 (neg. no. 11409): courtesy, Museum of New Mexico; 92: LOC; 93: NYPL, Picture Collection; 95: LOC; 96 (top): New-York Historical Society; 96 (bottom): LOC; 97: (top): New Amsterdam, Prototype View, 1650–1653, J. Clarence Davies Collection, Museum of the City of New York; 97 (middle and bottom), 98, 101–102: LOC; 103: Radio Times Hulton Picture Library; 104: from H. D. Traill, Social England, NYPL; 105 (left): LOC; 105 (right): Gabriel Thomas, Pennsylvania and West New-Jersey, published by A. Baldwin, London 1698; 106 (top): NYPL, Picture Collection; 106 (bottom): LOC; 107: The Library Company of Philadelphia; 108: Edward Hicks, Penn's Treaty with the Indians, Gilcrease Museum, Tulsa; 109: NYPL, Picture Collection; 110 (center and bottom right): LOC; 110 (top right and bottom left): Historical Society of Pennsylvania; 110 (top left): NYPL, Rare Books and Manuscripts; 111: Courtesy of the Harvard Portrait Collection, Bequest of Dr. John Collins Warren, 1856; 112: from Holley, The Life of Mr. Benjamin Franklin, 1848, Benjamin Franklin Collection, Yale University Library; 114: LOC; 115 (top): NYPL, Maps Division; 115 (bottom): LOC; 116 (left top and below): NYPL, Picture Collection; 116 (right top): Baltimore Museum of Art; 116 (bottom) art resource; 117 (top): NYPL, Picture Collection; 117 (bottom): LOC; 119: American Antiquarian Society; 120 (top): Dementi / Foster Studios, Richmond, Virginia; 120 (left): NYPL, Picture Collection; 121 (top): NYPL; 121 (bottom right): Justus Engelhardt Kuhn, Eleanor Darnall, Maryland Historical Society, Baltimore; 122: LOC (top); 122 (below): Colonial Williamsburg Foundation; 124 (right): Embroidered Sampler made by Sarah Afflick, age 7, Philadelphia Pennsylvania, 1796, silk on cotton, Cooper-Hewitt Museum/Smithsonian Institution/Art Resource, NY, Bequest of the Estate of Emily Coe Stowell; 125: LOC; 126 (below): Colonial Williamsburg Foundation; 127: Courtesy, Muscarelle Museum of Art, College of William and Mary; 128, 129: Colonial Williamsburg Foundation; 130, 131 (top): LOC; 132: Abby Aldrich Rockefeller Folk Art Center, Williamsburg, Virginia; 133 (bottom): Charleston Yearbook, 1884; 134: Louis Manigault after George Roupell, Mr. Peter Manigault and His Friends, Gibbes Museum of Art / Carolina Art Association; 135 (top): Harper's Weekly, January 5, 1867; 135 (bottom): Courtesy of The Charleston Museum, Charleston, South Carolina; 136 (top): New-York Historical Society; 136 (bottom): from Johnson, The Lives of High-Waymen and Pirates, 1736, NYPL; 137 (top two): from Johnson, Historie der Engelsche Zee-roovers, 1725, Harvard College Library, Harry Elkins Widener Collection; 137 (bottom): from Johnson, History of Pirates, 1724, Harvard College Library, Harry Elkins Widener Collection; 138, 139 (top left): Beej's Pirate Image Archive; 139 (bottom and right): Photograph by Diane Hardy, Department of Cultural Resources, North Carolina Maritime Museum; 140: LOC; 141 (top): NYPL, Picture Collection; 141 (bottom): Hartford Courant; 142 (top): Schomburg Center for Research in Black Culture; 142 (bottom): LOC; 143, 144: LOC; 147: NYPL, Picture Collection; 148: Nieu Amsterdam, NYPL, I. N. Phelps Stokes Collection; 149 (top right): Guildhall Library, London; 149, 150: LOC; 151: Courtesy, Winterthur Museum; 152 (top): Museum of Science and Industry, Chicago; 152 (bottom): Cincinnati Historical Society; 153: LOC; 154: George Tattersall, Highways and Byeways of the Forest, M. and M. Karolik Collection, Museum of Fine Arts, Boston; 155: NYPL, Picture Collection; 156, 158: LOC; 159: Washington / Curtis / Lee Collection, Washington and Lee University, Lexington, Virginia; 160: Yale University Libraries; 161: Bodeleian Library, Oxford University; 162 (top): British Library; 162 (bottom): The Granger Collection; 163: NYPL; 164 (top): The Granger Collection; 164 (middle): LOC; 164 (botom): NASA; 165: The Granger Collection; 168: USGS; 169: NASA

Index

Oglethorpe, James, 149–50, 151
Old Silvernails. *See* Stuyvesant, Peter
Oñate, Juan de, 89
Oneida Indians, 14
Onondaga Indians, 14
Opechancanough, 36, 47, 49
Ortelius, Abraham, 162

Pamunkey Indians, 38
Parliament (England), 43, 47–48, 140, 141
Parris, Samuel, 79
patroons, 100
Patuxet Indians, 54
Pearce, Abraham, 56
Penn, William, 46, 105–8
Pennsylvania, 46, 73, 104–8, 151, 156
Pequot Indians, 86
Percy, George, 33
Peters, Arno, 166
Philadelphia, Pennsylvania, 107, 108, 112–13
Philip, King, 85–87
Pilgrims, 51–58, 73. *See also* Christianity
pirates, 136–39, 150
plague, 104. *See also* disease
plantation life, 121–24
Plymouth, Massachusetts, 54, 72–73, 87
Pocahontas (Matoax), 29, 30–31, 35–36
Poor Richard's Almanack (Franklin), 113
Pope, 50, 51, 78. *See also* Catholicism
Popé, 88, 89–91
Portugal, 50, 147
Potomac Indians, 24, 35
Powhatan (chief), 21–22, 24, 30, 33, 36, 115
Powhatan Indians, 21–24, 30, 33, 45
printing, 110, 113, 117
Printz, Johan, 98
privateers, 19. *See also* pirates

Protestantism, 13, 15, 114, 115. *See also* Christianity
Providence Colony. *See* Rhode Island
Pueblo Indians, 88–91
punishment
    capital punishment, 31, 35, 102–3
    ducking stools, 64
    of Mary Dyer, 75
    of Governor Dale, 35, 36
    for religious beliefs, 116
    scold's bridles, 63
    of slaves, 146
Puritans. *See also* Christianity
    blue laws, 67
    dissatisfaction with Europe, 15, 52
    education and, 64–65
    English Civil War and, 102–4
    Anne Hutchinson, 71
    life in New England, 59–61
    religious intolerance, 56, 60, 64, 68, 77, 80, 104
    religious life, 67
    witches and, 75–80
    women and, 71–72

Quakers (Society of Friends), *See also* Christianity
William Penn and, 105–8
    persecution of, 60, 72, 74, 75, 107, 156
    in Rhode Island, 69
    women of, 61

racism, 46
Read, Mary, 137
religion. *See also* Catholicism; Christianity; specific religions and sects
    history of, 11, 13
    Islam, 9, 11, 146, 147
    Judaism, 9, 11, 12, 69, 98, 116
    Protestantism, 13, 15, 114, 115
religious tolerance and intolerance
    Catholicism, 88–91, 114–16, 116

Mary Dyer, 74–75
freedom of religion, 100, 101
in Georgia, 150
Anne Hutchinson, 71
King James II, 140
in North Carolina, 136
Puritans, 56, 60, 64, 68, 77, 80, 104
Quakers, 60, 72, 74–75, 107, 156
Catherine Marbury Scott, 72
in South Carolina, 134
of Peter Stuyvesant, 98
Roger Williams, 68–70
in Williamsburg, 128
of women, 71–72, 74–75
Restoration (England), 104
Rhode Island, 69, 86, 151
rice, 133, 135, 148
Rio Grande, 88
Roanoke Colony, 21
Robinson, Arthur, 166
Rolfe, John, 35, 36, 40
Roman Catholic. *See* Catholicism
Roundheads, 102
Royal African Company, 100

sachem, 47
Sahara desert, 146
Saints. *See* Pilgrims
Salem, Massachusetts, 78–80
Samoset, 55
Sandwich, Lord John Montagu, 110
Santa Fe, New Mexico, 89–91
Savage, Tom, 29, 35
Savannah, Georgia, 149–50
schools and education
    of colonists, 63, 64–65, 67, 93, 117, 124, 131
    of Native Americans, 39, 128, 129
Scott, Catherine Marbury, 72
Scrooby, England, 52, 53
scurvy, 19, 53. *See also* disease
Sea Venture (ship), 34
Seneca Indians, 14
Separatists. *See* Pilgrims
Sewall, Samuel, 79
Shakespeare, William, 34, 104

A Note from the Author

Imagine that we are British colonists. Most of us agree on these things:

Some people are better than others.

Some people are meant to be slaves.

Some people have a God-given right to rule.

Women are inferior to men.

We don't even question these ideas. We've grown up with them. If we are African-American or Native American we are doing some questioning. But we, too, come from cultures where slavery is practiced.

So what happened? Why do we think differently today? We're not smarter. What makes us see the world through a different prism?

I believe the answer is modern science. It opened minds. Even nonscientists began thinking in new ways.

Before 1550 there wasn't much science in the European world and its provinces. Everyone believed the earth stood still in the middle of the universe and the sun and stars moved around it. Earthquakes and lightning and tornadoes were acts of God, or the devil, and beyond human understanding.

Then, in rat-a-tat progression, along came Copernicus (ko-PUR-nih-kuss), Galileo (gal-ih-LAY-oh), Kepler, and Newton—who used their minds to search for answers to nature's puzzles. They discovered the universe has rules, and people can understand those rules.

Copernicus, Galileo, and Kepler were astronomers (worth reading about). They moved the sun into center field and set the earth orbiting around it. It wasn't an easy job. The old-style thinkers—almost everyone else—didn't like to admit they'd been wrong.

Isaac Newton explained gravity. He said gravity is a force of nature that works at a distance and keeps the moon orbiting the earth—and he proved it mathematically. That idea set off explosions in the minds of thinking people. Suddenly it made sense to ask questions, look for evidence, and seek answers: in other words, to use the scientific method.

Newton was 82 when our good friend Ben Franklin first visited England at age 18. London was buzzing with new ideas. Ben dove into science head first. He studied the course of the Gulf Stream and its warmth, and figured out that ships' captains could follow it by using a thermometer. He examined colors and learned that they absorb heat at different rates. He discovered that electricity, like gravity, is one of nature's forces; that electricity has positive and negative charges; and that lightning is a form of electricity. All these were new concepts and disturbing to some people. Ben took a lot of abuse for his "ungodly" experiments with lightning.

It was a very old tradition to ring church bells during thunderstorms. That was supposed to ward off evil spirits. But a book published in 1784 noted that in the previous 35 years, lightning had struck 386 German churches and killed 103 bell ringers—making church-bell ringing a very hazardous occupation.

Ben Franklin devised lightning rods and put them on buildings—and they worked. They made those bolts harmless by conducting them into the ground. But when an earthquake struck Boston, Ben got blamed. It was said that his rods stole lightning from the skies and drained it into the earth, where it later exploded. (Not true, but it sounded likely.)

A French priest attacked Franklin, saying it was impertinent to guard against the "thunders of heaven." Ben answered, "Surely the Thunder of Heaven is no more Supernatural than the Rain, Hail or Sunshine of Heaven, against…which we guard by Roofs and Shades."

There's a point to all this. Science makes you think. And when you begin to think about the rules of nature, you go on to think about the rules of society. When Ben was a young businessman, he went along with common practices. He owned slaves. Later, when he got to thinking and working in science, he began to change his ideas on slavery. You can trace that change—step by step. In middle age he became a leader in the antislavery movement. As an old man, he introduced a bill in Congress calling for an end to slavery throughout the new nation. Congress didn't pass it.

As always, Franklin was way ahead of most others.

When people ask me who my favorite American is, I have a hard time answering—we have a passel of amazing national ancestors. This book is filled with them: people like Roger Williams and William Penn and Anne Hutchinson. But it is hard to do better than Benjamin Franklin. Besides all that impressive thinking, he was generous-spirited and a whole lot of fun. In the next book you will read more about him.

ATLAS
Atlas's Burden, or How The Atlas Got Its Name

You've heard the term "Earth-shaking." Well, this battle really shook the Earth. It was the Titans vs. Olympians. The Titans were led by Cronus, ruler of the Universe. The Olympians, who lived on Mt. Olympus, were led by Cronus's son, Zeus. Cronus was the supreme god but feared a takeover. (It had been predicted that one of his offspring would replace him.) So Cronus ate all his children, except baby Zeus who got hidden by his mother.

Zeus wanted to be the supreme god. First he tricked his father into upchucking his brothers and sisters (those Cronus had gulped down). Then Zeus got the hundred-handed giants on his side, along with the huge one-eyed Cyclopes (SIGH klow peas), who were master metalsmiths. The Cyclopes forged a helmet of darkness for Hades (Olympian ruler of the underworld), a trident for Poseidon (Olympian ruler of the seas), and thunderbolts for Zeus. Then the fight began.

Cronus's Titans weren't pushovers. They were gigantic. As I mentioned, the Earth shook when they battled. But Zeus and the crafty Olympians won. Having won, Zeus decided to punish the vanquished. He condemned Atlas, a muscular Titan, to hold the sky on his shoulders—forever.

Now this is the mythical story the Greeks told to explain why the sky doesn't fall. It has some other details that are interesting, so you might want to see if you can read more about it. (The Greek myths are among the best stories in the world.) Atlas also came to be identified with the Atlas Mountains in northwest Africa, which extend from Morocco to Algeria to Tunisia and often seem to be holding up the sky. (They were uplifted out of the Earth at the same time as the Alps Mountains in Europe and the Canary Islands to the west. That was in the late Jurassic Age.)

But how did Atlas's name get put on map books?

It was Gerhardus Mercator, who, without meaning to, named map books "atlases." In 1595, Mercator published a book of maps with a picture of muscular Atlas on the cover. Lots of people bought the book (Gutenberg had made that possible, and Mercator was one of the most skilled and influential mapmakers ever). Because of the cover picture, Mercator's book was soon known as "the atlas"; before long, other books of maps had that title.

The next pages include a mini- atlas for you to use as you read this history, or just for your own information. Maps tell stories and answer questions, I hope you enjoy these.

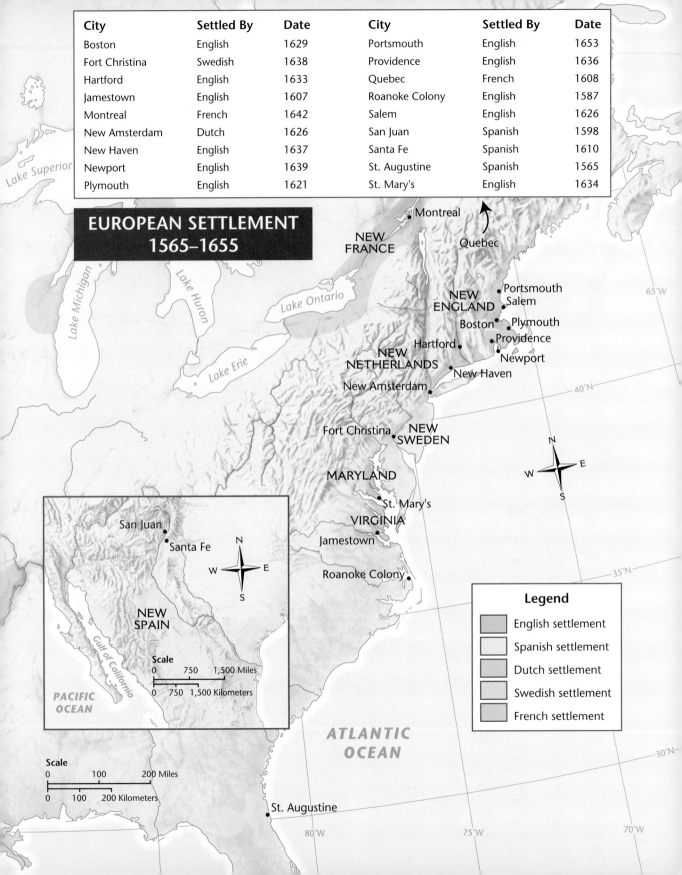

City	Settled By	Date	City	Settled By	Date
Boston	English	1629	Portsmouth	English	1653
Fort Christina	Swedish	1638	Providence	English	1636
Hartford	English	1633	Quebec	French	1608
Jamestown	English	1607	Roanoke Colony	English	1587
Montreal	French	1642	Salem	English	1626
New Amsterdam	Dutch	1626	San Juan	Spanish	1598
New Haven	English	1637	Santa Fe	Spanish	1610
Newport	English	1639	St. Augustine	Spanish	1565
Plymouth	English	1621	St. Mary's	English	1634

EUROPEAN SETTLEMENT 1565–1655

NEW FRANCE

Montreal

Quebec

NEW ENGLAND

Portsmouth
Salem
Boston
Hartford
Plymouth
Providence
Newport
New Haven

NEW NETHERLANDS

New Amsterdam

Fort Christina

NEW SWEDEN

MARYLAND

St. Mary's

VIRGINIA

Jamestown

Roanoke Colony

Lake Superior
Lake Michigan
Lake Huron
Lake Ontario
Lake Erie

65°W
40°N
35°N
30°N
80°W
75°W
70°W

San Juan
Santa Fe

NEW SPAIN

Gulf of California

PACIFIC OCEAN

Scale
0   750   1,500 Miles
0   750   1,500 Kilometers

ATLANTIC OCEAN

St. Augustine

Scale
0   100   200 Miles
0   100   200 Kilometers

Legend

	English settlement
	Spanish settlement
	Dutch settlement
	Swedish settlement
	French settlement

EUROPEAN TERRITORIES AND CLAIMS, 1714

ASIA

ARCTIC OCEAN

EUROPE

180°
140°W
80°N
100°W
60°W
20°W
Arctic Circle
40°N

Hudson Bay

NORTH AMERICA

ATLANTIC OCEAN

Gulf of Mexico

Tropic of Cancer

PACIFIC OCEAN

Caribbean Sea

Legend

	British Territory
	Claimed by Britain
	Dutch Territory
	French Territory
	Claimed by France
	Portuguese Territory
	Spanish Territory
	Claimed by Spain

Equator

0°

N
W   E
S

SOUTH AMERICA

Tropic of Capricorn

0   750   1,500 Miles
0   750   1,500 Kilometers

40°S

140°W
100°W
60°W
20°W

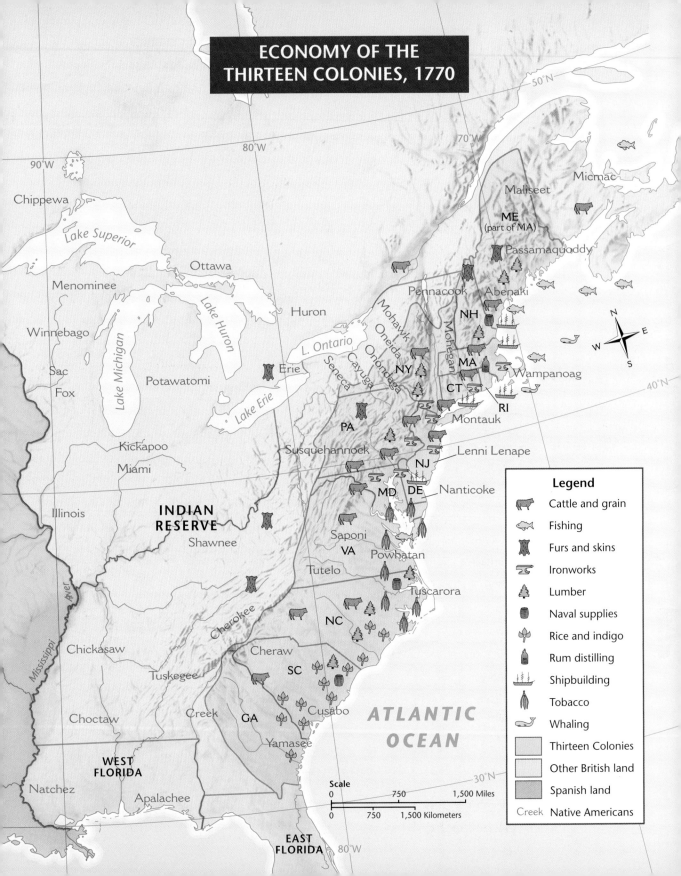

ECONOMY OF THE THIRTEEN COLONIES, 1770

50°N

90°W   80°W   70°W

Chippewa

Lake Superior

Ottawa   Maliseet

Menominee

Micmac

ME
(part of MA)

Huron   Passamaquoddy

Winnebago   Lake Huron   Pennacook   Abenaki

Lake Michigan   Mohawk   NH

Sac   L. Ontario   Oneida

Fox   Erie   Onondaga   MA

Cayuga   MOHEGAN   Wampanoag

Potawatomi   Lake Erie   Seneca   NY   CT

40°N   RI

Kickapoo   PA   Montauk

Miami   Susquehannock   Lenni Lenape

NJ

INDIAN   MD DE   Nanticoke

RESERVE   Illinois   Shawnee   Saponi

VA   Powhatan

Tutelo   Tuscarora

Cherokee   NC

Chickasaw   Cheraw

Tuskegee   SC

Choctaw   Creek   GA   Cusabo   ATLANTIC
OCEAN

Yamasee

Mississippi River   30°N

WEST
FLORIDA

Natchez   Apalachee   80°W

EAST
FLORIDA

Legend

- 🐄 Cattle and grain
- 🐟 Fishing
- Furs and skins
- Ironworks
- 🌲 Lumber
- Naval supplies
- Rice and indigo
- Rum distilling
- Shipbuilding
- Tobacco
- 🐋 Whaling
- Thirteen Colonies
- Other British land
- Spanish land
- Creek Native Americans

Scale
0   750   1,500 Miles
0   750   1,500 Kilometers

THE TRIANGULAR TRADE

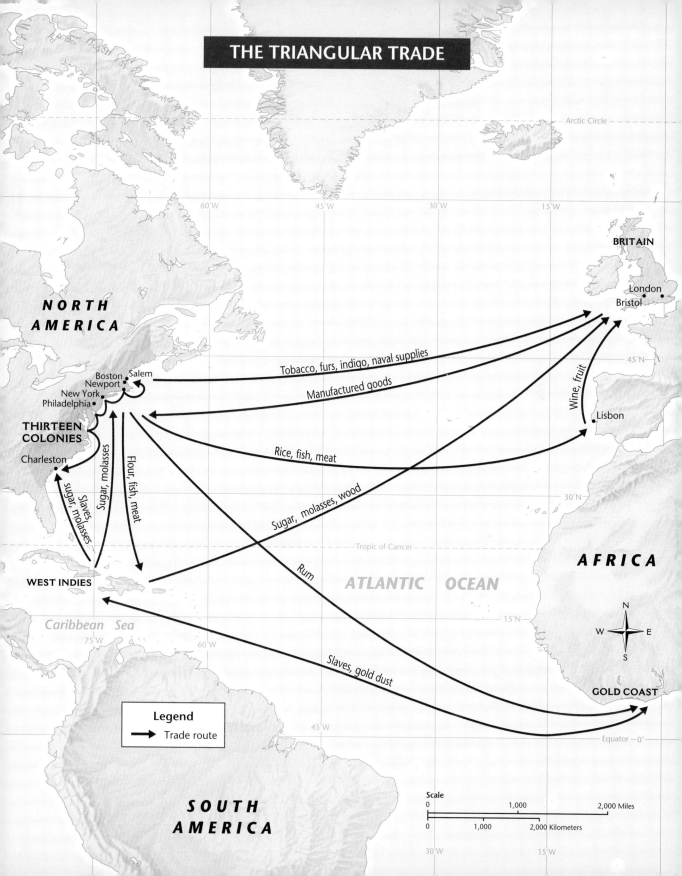

NORTH AMERICA

BRITAIN
London
Bristol

Boston
Salem
Newport
New York
Philadelphia

THIRTEEN COLONIES

Charleston

Tobacco, furs, indigo, naval supplies

Manufactured goods

Wine, fruit

Lisbon

Rice, fish, meat

Sugar, molasses

Slaves, sugar, molasses

Flour, fish, meat

Sugar, molasses, wood

Rum

WEST INDIES

AFRICA

Caribbean Sea

ATLANTIC OCEAN

Slaves, gold dust

GOLD COAST

N
W E
S

Arctic Circle

45°N

30°N

Tropic of Cancer

15°N

Equator — 0°

60°W   45°W   30°W   15°W

75°W   60°W   45°W   30°W   15°W

SOUTH AMERICA

Legend
→ Trade route

Scale
| 0 | 1,000 | 2,000 Miles |
| 0 | 1,000 | 2,000 Kilometers |

Empires Everywhere

Capture a foreign land and you have a colony. You can control its labor, resources, and wealth. Put a few colonies together and you've got an empire. But watch out: germs, goods, people, art, foods, animals, ideas, and inventions—usually travel both ways.

The Muslim Ottoman Empire is founded in Turkey in 1301; it expands into Asia, Europe and Africa, reaching a pinnacle of power and magnificence in the 16th century. It lasts until 1918.

WORLD POLITICAL

Sir Humphrey Gilbert, who was the half-brother of Sir Walter Raleigh, takes possession of Newfoundland in the name of Queen Elizabeth in 1583. (He drowns on the way home.)
In 1619 the legislature of the Netherlands gives the Dutch East India Company a monopoly. It can control all trade east of the Cape of Good Hope and west of the Straits of Magellan. (See if you can find them.) The company drives the British out of Ceylon (Sri Lanka), Indonesia, and Malaya—which leaves the Dutch with the very profitable spice trade.

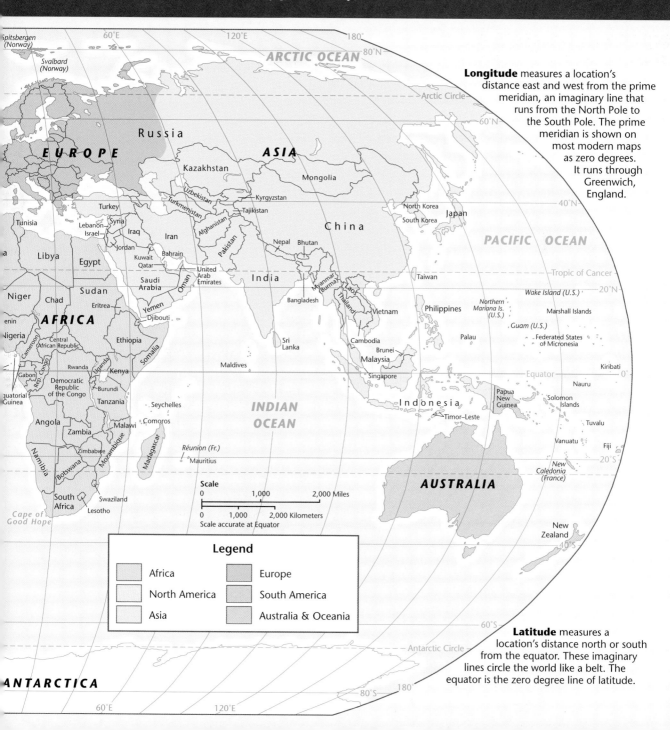

Longitude measures a location's distance east and west from the prime meridian, an imaginary line that runs from the North Pole to the South Pole. The prime meridian is shown on most modern maps as zero degrees. It runs through Greenwich, England.

Latitude measures a location's distance north or south from the equator. These imaginary lines circle the world like a belt. The equator is the zero degree line of latitude.

Scale
0   1,000   2,000 Miles
0   1,000   2,000 Kilometers
Scale accurate at Equator

Legend

	Africa		Europe
	North America		South America
	Asia		Australia & Oceania

ARCTIC OCEAN

PACIFIC OCEAN

INDIAN OCEAN

EUROPE

ASIA

AFRICA

AUSTRALIA

ANTARCTICA

Russia, Kazakhstan, Mongolia, China, India, Japan, North Korea, South Korea, Taiwan, Turkey, Iran, Iraq, Syria, Lebanon, Israel, Jordan, Saudi Arabia, Yemen, Oman, United Arab Emirates, Qatar, Kuwait, Bahrain, Uzbekistan, Turkmenistan, Tajikistan, Kyrgyzstan, Afghanistan, Pakistan, Nepal, Bhutan, Bangladesh, Myanmar (Burma), Thailand, Laos, Vietnam, Cambodia, Philippines, Malaysia, Brunei, Singapore, Indonesia, Sri Lanka, Maldives

ANALYTICAL MECHANICS

FOURTH EDITION

GRANT R. FOWLES
University of Utah

SAUNDERS GOLDEN SUNBURST SERIES
SAUNDERS COLLEGE PUBLISHING
Philadelphia   New York   Chicago
San Francisco   Montreal   Toronto
London   Sydney   Tokyo

Address orders to:
383 Madison Avenue
New York, NY 10017

Address editorial correspondence to:
West Washington Square
Philadelphia, PA 19105

Text Typeface: 10/12 Times Roman
Compositor: York Graphic Services, Inc.
Acquisitions Editor: John Vondeling
Developmental Editor: Lloyd Black
Project Editors: Maureen R. Iannuzzi, Ellen Newman
Copyeditor: Will Eaton
Art Director: Carol Bleistine
Art/Design Assistant: Virginia A. Bollard
Text Design: Caliber Design Planning, Inc.
Cover Design: Lawrence R. Didona
Text Artwork: Lawrence Ward
Production Manager: Tim Frelick
Assistant Production Manager: JoAnn Melody
Cover credit: © The Image Bank/Gabe Palmer

Library of Congress Cataloging in Publication Data

Fowles, Grant R.
  Analytical mechanics.

  Includes bibliography and index.
   1. Mechanics, Analytic. I. Title
QA807.F65   1985   531'.01'515   85-8180
ISBN 0-03-004124-4

ANALYTICAL MECHANICS   ISBN 0-03-004124-4

Library of Congress catalog card number 85-8180.

123   038   98765

Preface

This textbook is intended primarily for the undergraduate course in classical mechanics generally taken by students majoring in physics, physical science, or engineering science. It is assumed that the student has some general physics as well as a good working knowledge of differential and integral calculus. It is highly recommended that a post-calculus course in mathematics that includes some elementary differential equations and matrices be taken prior to or concurrently with this course in mechanics.

This fourth edition is basically the same in its general outline and content as the previous edition. Some new material has been introduced and many sections have been revised or expanded. The harmonic oscillator is now discussed in a separate chapter (Chapter 3) rather than as a part of the chapter on rectilinear motion of a particle.

The text begins with a brief introduction to the essentials of vector algebra and vector differentiation. The latter leads naturally to the concepts of velocity and acceleration of a particle as the first and second time derivatives of the position vector. After this mathematical preparation, Newton's laws of motion are taken up in the second chapter with particular emphasis on the one-dimensional motion of a material particle.

Chapter 3, as previously mentioned, is devoted entirely to harmonic motion and includes resonance, the nonlinear oscillator, and an application of Fourier series to the oscillator under a nonsinusoidal driving force.

The general motion of a particle in three dimensions is discussed in Chapter 4. Chapter 5, dealing with noninertial reference systems, includes the effects of the earth's rotation on projectile motion, the Foucault pendulum, and so on.

In Chapter 6 the student is introduced to celestial mechanics with emphasis on planetary and satellite motion. Systems of many particles are discussed in Chapter 7; here the conservation laws are applied to collisions and scattering of atomic particles.

The study of rigid bodies is separated into two chapters. The first of these two, Chapter 8, is the study of rotation around a fixed axis and laminar motion of a rigid body. The general case of rigid body motion in three dimensions is studied in Chapter 9, which includes such subjects as gyroscopic action and the gyrocompass.

Lagrangian mechanics is introduced in Chapter 10. Lagrange's equations are derived from Newton's laws and also from Hamilton's variational principle. The final chapter, Chapter 11, is the study of stability of equilibrium and of oscillating systems. Here Lagrange's equations are applied to find the differential equations of motion of various kinds of oscillating systems.

Metric units (either SI or cgs) are used for the most part in the numerical examples and problems. However, because nonmetric units such as the foot and the pound are so entrenched in everyday life—in the United States particularly—these units are occasionally also used.

Worked examples of problems are included at the end of nearly all sections, and problems to be worked out by the student are provided at the end of each chapter. Some problems are important theorems for which the student is asked to devise a proof. The author has always felt that the student should participate in the development of the subject, rather than merely substitute numbers into equations already derived in the text. Answers to selected odd-numbered problems are given at the end of the book. A list of mathematical helps and formulae is also included in the appendixes.

A Solutions Manual containing worked-out solutions to all problems is available to instructors upon adoption of the text.

The author wishes to express his gratitude to the users of the previous edition for the errata lists and many constructive suggestions they have provided. The following reviewers offered many valuable suggestions, and the author is deeply grateful for their help: C. Tristram Coffin, University of Michigan; Jerry S. Faughn, Eastern Kentucky University; Don E. Harrison, Jr., Naval Postgraduate School; Gerald R. Taylor, James Madison University; Charles D. Teague, Eastern Kentucky University; Gordon B. Thomson, Rutgers University; Jesse L. Weil, University of Kentucky; and Raymond J. Winkel, Jr., United States Military Academy.

GRANT R. FOWLES

Contents Overview

CONTENTS

9 Motion of Rigid Bodies in Three Dimensions,   218

10 Lagrangian Mechanics,   259

11 Dynamics of Oscillating Systems,   283

1
Fundamental Concepts. Vectors

1.1 Introduction

In any scientific theory, and in mechanics in particular, it is necessary to begin with certain primitive concepts. It is also necessary to make a certain number of reasonable assumptions. Two of the most basic concepts are *space* and *time*. In our initial study of the science of motion, mechanics, we shall assume that the physical space of ordinary experience is adequately described by the three-dimensional mathematical space of Euclidean geometry. And with regard to the concept of time, we shall assume that an ordered sequence of events can be measured on a uniform absolute time scale. We shall further assume that space and time are distinct and independent entities. According to the theory of relativity, space and time are not absolute and independent. However, this is a matter to be taken up after the study of the classical foundations of mechanics.

In order to define the position of a body in space, it is necessary to have a reference system. In mechanics we use a *coordinate system*. The basic type of coordinate system for our purpose is the *Cartesian* or *rectangular* coordinate system, a set of three mutually perpendicular straight lines or *axes*. The position of a point in such a coordinate system is specified by three numbers or coordinates, x, y, and z. The coordinates of a *moving* point change with time; that is, they are functions of the quantity t as measured on our time scale.

A very useful concept in mechanics is the *particle* or mass point, an entity that has mass[1] but does not have spatial extension. Strictly speaking the particle is an idealization that may not exist—even the proton has a finite size—but the idea is

---

[1] The concept of mass will be discussed in Chapter 2.

1

useful as an approximation of a small body, or rather, one whose size is relatively unimportant in a particular discussion. The earth, for example, might be treated as a particle in celestial mechanics.

1.2   Physical Quantities and Units

The observational data of physics are expressed in terms of certain fundamental entities called *physical quantities*—for example, length, time, force, and so forth. A physical quantity is something that can be measured quantitatively in relation to some chosen unit. When we say that the length of a certain object is, say 7 in., we mean that the quantitative measure 7 is the relation (ratio) of the length of that object to the length of the unit (1 in.). It has been found that it is possible to define all of the *unit* physical quantities of mechanics in terms of just three basic ones, namely *time, length,* and *mass.*

The Unit of Time

The basic unit for measurement of time is the *second*. It is defined in terms of the cesium atomic clock frequency standard, namely, the time required for exactly 9,192,631,770 oscillations of a particular atomic transition of the isotope cesium 133. Prior to the year 1967 the second was defined in terms of the earth's rotational period; that is, the second was equal to 1/86,400 of a mean solar day. This was abandoned in favor of the atomic standard because the earth's period of rotation is not constant.

The Unit of Length

The standard unit of length is the *meter*. This unit is now specified in terms of the velocity of light: The meter is the distance that light travels during a time interval of exactly 1/299,792,458 second. Put in another way, this establishes the velocity of light as precisely 299,792,458 meters/second. Furthermore, since the second is defined in terms of the cesium atomic clock, *both* the meter and the second are atomic-based standards. From 1967 to 1983 the meter was defined in terms of the wavelength of a certain orange spectral line of a krypton 86 lamp. Previous to 1967 the meter was defined to be the distance between two marks on a bar of a platinum-iridium alloy that was stored at the Bureau of Metric Standards, Sevres, France.

The Unit of Mass

The standard unit of mass is the *kilogram*. It is the mass of a cylinder of platinum-iridium also kept at the Bureau of Metric Standards. Copies of this primary standard are owned by the governments of most major countries of the world.

The above units comprise the basis for the Système International d'Unites or SI system.[2] The modern atomic standards of length and time in this system are not only

---

[2] Other basic and derived units are listed in Appendix A.

more precise than the former standards, but they are also universally reproducible and indestructible. Unfortunately, it is not at present technically feasible to employ an atomic standard of mass.

Actually, there is nothing particularly sacred about the physical quantities time, length, and mass as a basic set to define units. Other sets of physical quantities may be used. The so-called gravitational systems employ time, length, and *force*.

In addition to the SI system, there are other systems in common use, namely, the cgs, or centimeter-gram-second, system, and the fps, or foot-pound-second, system. These latter two systems may be regarded as secondary, because their units are specifically defined fractions of the SI units. See Appendix A.

A physical quantity that is completely specified, in appropriate units, by a single number is called a *scalar*. Familiar examples of scalars are density, volume, and temperature. Mathematically, scalars are treated as ordinary real numbers. They obey all the regular rules of algebraic addition, subtraction, multiplication, division, and so on.

There are certain physical quantities that possess a directional characteristic, such as a displacement from one point in space to another. Such quantities require a direction *and* a magnitude for their complete specification. These quantities are called *vectors* if they combine with each other according to the parallelogram rule of addition as discussed in the next section.[3] Besides displacement in space, other familiar examples of vectors are velocity, acceleration, and force. The vector concept and the development of a whole mathematics of vector quantities have proved indispensible to the development of the science of mechanics. The remainder of this chapter will be devoted largely to a study of the mathematics of vectors.

1.3   Notation. Formal Definitions and Rules of Vector Algebra

Vector quantities are denoted in print by boldface type, for example, **A**, whereas ordinary italic type represents scalar quantities. In written work it is customary to use a distinguishing mark, such as an arrow, $\vec{A}$, to designate a vector.

A given vector **A** is specified by stating its magnitude and its direction relative to some chosen reference system. A vector is represented diagrammatically by a directed line segment, as shown in Figure 1.1. A vector can also be specified by listing its *components* or projections along the coordinate axes. The component symbol $[A_x, A_y, A_z]$ will be used as an alternate designation of a vector. The equation

$$\mathbf{A} = [A_x, A_y, A_z]$$

means that the vector **A** is expressed on the right in terms of its components in a particular coordinate system. (It will be assumed that a Cartesian coordinate system is meant, unless stated otherwise.) For example, if the vector **A** represents a *displacement*

---

[3] An example of a directed quantity that does not obey the rule for addition is a finite rotation of an object about a given axis. The reader can readily verify that two successive rotations about *different* axes do not produce the same effect as a single rotation determined by the parallelogram rule. For the present we shall not be concerned with such non-vector directed quantities, however.

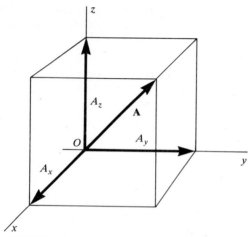

FIGURE 1.1   A vector **A** and its components in Cartesian coordinates.

from a point $P_1(x_1, y_1, z_1)$ to the point $P_2(x_2, y_2, z_2)$, then $A_x = x_2 - x_1$, $A_y = y_2 - y_1$, $A_z = z_2 - z_1$. If **A** represents a *force*, then A_x is the x component of the force, and so on. Clearly, the numerical values of the scalar components of a given vector depend on the choice of the coordinate axes.

If a particular discussion is limited to vectors in a plane, only two components are necessary. On the other hand, one can define a mathematical space of any number of dimensions. Thus the symbol $[A_1, A_2, A_3, \ldots, A_n]$ denotes an n-dimensional vector. In this abstract sense a vector is an ordered set of numbers.

We begin the study of vector algebra with some formal statements concerning vectors.

I.   *Equality of Vectors*
 The equation

$$\mathbf{A} = \mathbf{B}$$

 or

$$[A_x, A_y, A_z] = [B_x, B_y, B_z]$$

 is equivalent to the three equations

$$A_x = B_x \qquad A_y = B_y \qquad A_z = B_z$$

 That is, two vectors are equal if, and only if, their respective components are equal. Geometrically, equal vectors are parallel and have the same length, but they do not necessarily have the same position. Equal vectors are shown in Figure 1.2, where only two components are drawn for clarity. Notice that the vectors form opposite sides of a parallelogram. (Equal vectors are not necessarily equivalent in all respects. Thus two vectorially equal forces acting at *different* points on an object may produce different mechanical effects.)

II.   *Vector Addition*
 The addition of two vectors is defined by the equation

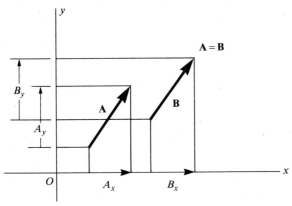

FIGURE 1.2 Illustrating equal vectors.

$$\mathbf{A} + \mathbf{B} = [A_x, A_y, A_z] + [B_x, B_y, B_z] = [A_x + B_x, A_y + B_y, A_z + B_z]$$

The sum of two vectors is a vector whose components are sums of the components of the given vectors. The geometric representation of the vector sum of two non-parallel vectors is the *third* side of a triangle, two sides of which are the given vectors. The vector sum is illustrated in Figure 1.3. The sum is also given by the parallelogram rule, as shown in the figure. The vector sum is defined, however, according to the above equation even if the vectors do not have a common point.

III. *Multiplication by a Scalar*
      If c is a scalar and $\mathbf{A}$ a vector,

$$c\mathbf{A} = c[A_x, A_y, A_z] = [cA_x, cA_y, cA_z] = \mathbf{A}c$$

The product $c\mathbf{A}$ is a vector whose components are c times those of $\mathbf{A}$. Geometrically, the vector $c\mathbf{A}$ is parallel to $\mathbf{A}$ and is c times the length of $\mathbf{A}$. When $c = -1$, the vector $-\mathbf{A}$ is one whose direction is the reverse of that of $\mathbf{A}$, as shown in Figure 1.4.

IV. *Vector Subtraction*
     Subtraction is defined as follows:

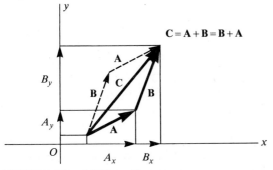

FIGURE 1.3 Addition of two vectors.

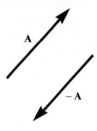

FIGURE 1.4   The negative of a vector.

$$\mathbf{A} - \mathbf{B} = \mathbf{A} + (-1)\mathbf{B} = [A_x - B_x, A_y - B_y, A_z - B_z]$$

That is, subtraction of a given vector **B** from the vector **A** is equivalent to adding $-\mathbf{B}$ to **A**.

V.   *The Null Vector*

The vector $\mathbf{O} = [0, 0, 0]$ is called the *null* vector. The direction of the null vector is undefined. From (IV) it follows that $\mathbf{A} - \mathbf{A} = \mathbf{O}$. Since there can be no confusion when the null vector is denoted by a "zero," we shall hereafter use the notation: $\mathbf{O} = 0$.

VI.   *The Commutative Law of Addition*

This law holds for vectors; that is,

$$\mathbf{A} + \mathbf{B} = \mathbf{B} + \mathbf{A}$$

since $A_x + B_x = B_x + A_x$, and similarly for the y and z components.

VII.   *The Associative Law*

The associative law is also true, because

$$\begin{aligned}
\mathbf{A} + (\mathbf{B} + \mathbf{C}) &= [A_x + (B_x + C_x), A_y + (B_y + C_y), A_z + (B_z + C_z)] \\
&= [(A_x + B_x) + C_x, (A_y + B_y) + C_y, (A_z + B_z) + C_z] \\
&= (\mathbf{A} + \mathbf{B}) + \mathbf{C}
\end{aligned}$$

VIII.   *The Distributive Law*

Under multiplication by a scalar the distributive law is valid, because, from (II) and (III),

$$\begin{aligned}
c(\mathbf{A} + \mathbf{B}) &= c[A_x + B_x, A_y + B_y, A_z + B_z] \\
&= [c(A_x + B_x), c(A_y + B_y), c(A_z + B_z)] \\
&= [cA_x + cB_x, cA_y + cB_y, cA_z + cB_z] \\
&= c\mathbf{A} + c\mathbf{B}
\end{aligned}$$

Thus vectors obey the rules of ordinary algebra as far as the above operations are concerned.

IX.   *Magnitude of a Vector*

The magnitude of a vector **A**, denoted by $|\mathbf{A}|$ or by A, is defined as the square root of the sum of the squares of the components, namely,

$$A = |\mathbf{A}| = (A_x^2 + A_y^2 + A_z^2)^{1/2}$$

where the positive root is understood. Geometrically, the magnitude of a vector is its length, that is, the length of the diagonal of the rectangular parallelepiped whose sides are A_x, A_y, and A_z, expressed in appropriate units.

X. *Unit Coordinate Vectors*

A *unit vector* is a vector whose magnitude is unity. Unit vectors are often designated by the symbol **e** from the German word *einheit*. The three unit vectors

$$\mathbf{e}_x = [1, 0, 0] \qquad \mathbf{e}_y = [0, 1, 0] \qquad \mathbf{e}_z = [0, 0, 1]$$

are called *unit coordinate vectors* or *basis vectors*. In terms of basis vectors, any vector can be expressed as a vector sum of components as follows:

$$\begin{aligned}
\mathbf{A} = [A_x, A_y, A_z] &= [A_x, 0, 0] + [0, A_y, 0] + [0, 0, A_z] \\
&= A_x[1, 0, 0] + A_y[0, 1, 0] + A_z[0, 0, 1] \\
&= \mathbf{e}_x A_x + \mathbf{e}_y A_y + \mathbf{e}_z A_z
\end{aligned}$$

A widely used notation for Cartesian unit vectors are the letters **i**, **j**, and **k**, namely

$$\mathbf{i} = \mathbf{e}_x \qquad \mathbf{j} = \mathbf{e}_y \qquad \mathbf{k} = \mathbf{e}_z$$

We shall usually employ this notation hereafter.

The directions of the unit coordinate vectors are defined by the coordinate axes (Figure 1.5). They form a right-handed or a left-handed triad, depending on which type of coordinate system is used. It is customary to use right-handed coordinate systems. The system shown in Figure 1.5 is right-handed.

Examples

1.1   Find the sum and the magnitude of the sum of the two vectors $\mathbf{A} = [1, 0, 2]$ and $\mathbf{B} = [0, 1, 1]$. Adding components we have $\mathbf{A} + \mathbf{B} = [1, 0, 2] + [0, 1, 1] = [1, 1, 3]$

$$|\mathbf{A} + \mathbf{B}| = (1 + 1 + 9)^{1/2} = \sqrt{11}$$

■

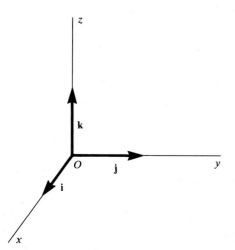

FIGURE 1.5   The unit vectors **ijk**.

1.2   For the above two vectors, express the difference in **ijk** form. Subtracting components, we have

$$\mathbf{A} - \mathbf{B} = [1, -1, 1] = \mathbf{i} - \mathbf{j} + \mathbf{k} \qquad \blacksquare$$

1.3   A helicopter flies 100 m vertically upward, then 500 m horizontally east then 1000 m horizontally north. How far is it from a second helicopter that starts from the same point rising 200 m upward, 100 m west and 500 m north? Solution: Choosing "up", "east", and "north" as basis directions, the final position of the first helicopter is expressed vectorially as $\mathbf{A} = [100, 500, 1000]$ and the second as $\mathbf{B} = [200, -100, 500]$, in meters. Hence the distance between the final positions is given by the expression

$$|\mathbf{A} - \mathbf{B}| = |[(100 - 200),(500 + 100),(1000 - 500)]|m = (100^2 + 600^2 + 500^2)^{1/2} \, m$$

$$= 787.4 \text{ m} \qquad \blacksquare$$

1.4   The Scalar Product

Given two vectors **A** and **B**, the scalar product or "dot" product, **A • B**, is the scalar defined by the equation

$$\mathbf{A} \cdot \mathbf{B} = A_x B_x + A_y B_y + A_z B_z \tag{1.1}$$

It follows from the above definition that scalar multiplication is *commutative*

$$\mathbf{A} \cdot \mathbf{B} = \mathbf{B} \cdot \mathbf{A} \tag{1.2}$$

since $A_x B_x = B_x A_x$, and so on. It also follows that it is *distributive*

$$\mathbf{A} \cdot (\mathbf{B} + \mathbf{C}) = \mathbf{A} \cdot \mathbf{B} + \mathbf{A} \cdot \mathbf{C} \tag{1.3}$$

because if we apply the definition [(1.1)] in detail

$$\mathbf{A} \cdot (\mathbf{B} + \mathbf{C}) = A_x(B_x + C_x) + A_y(B_y + C_y) + A_z(B_z + C_z)$$
$$= A_x B_x + A_y B_y + A_z B_z + A_x C_x + A_y C_y + A_z C_z$$
$$= \mathbf{A} \cdot \mathbf{B} + \mathbf{A} \cdot \mathbf{C}$$

From analytical geometry we recall the formula for the cosine of the angle between two line segments

$$\cos \theta = \frac{A_x B_x + A_y B_y + A_z B_z}{(A_x^2 + A_y^2 + A_z^2)^{1/2}(B_x^2 + B_y^2 + B_z^2)^{1/2}} = \frac{\mathbf{A} \cdot \mathbf{B}}{AB} \tag{1.4}$$

or

$$\mathbf{A} \cdot \mathbf{B} = AB \cos \theta \tag{1.5}$$

The above equation may be regarded as an alternate definition for the dot product. Geometrically, **A • B** is equal to the length of the projection of **A** on **B**, times the length of **B**.

If the dot product **A • B** is equal to zero, then **A** is perpendicular to **B**, provided neither **A** nor **B** is null.

The square of the magnitude of a vector **A** is given by the dot product of **A** with itself,

$$A^2 = |\mathbf{A}|^2 = \mathbf{A} \cdot \mathbf{A}$$

From the definitions of the unit coordinate vectors **i**, **j**, and **k**, it is clear that the following relations hold:

$$\begin{aligned} \mathbf{i} \cdot \mathbf{i} &= \mathbf{j} \cdot \mathbf{j} = \mathbf{k} \cdot \mathbf{k} = 1 \\ \mathbf{i} \cdot \mathbf{j} &= \mathbf{i} \cdot \mathbf{k} = \mathbf{j} \cdot \mathbf{k} = 0 \end{aligned} \tag{1.6}$$

Expressing Any Vector as the Product of Its Magnitude by a Unit Vector. Projection.

Consider the equation

$$\mathbf{A} = \mathbf{i}A_x + \mathbf{j}A_y + \mathbf{k}A_z$$

Multiply and divide on the right by the magnitude of **A**

$$\mathbf{A} = A\left(\mathbf{i}\frac{A_x}{A} + \mathbf{j}\frac{A_y}{A} + \mathbf{k}\frac{A_z}{A} \right)$$

Now $A_x/A = \cos \alpha$, $A_y/A = \cos \beta$, and $A_z/A = \cos \gamma$ are the *direction cosines* of the vector **A**, and α, β, and γ are the *direction angles*. Thus we can write

$$\mathbf{A} = A(\mathbf{i} \cos \alpha + \mathbf{j} \cos \beta + \mathbf{k} \cos \gamma) = A[\cos \alpha, \cos \beta, \cos \gamma]$$

or

$$\mathbf{A} = A\mathbf{n} \tag{1.7}$$

where **n** is a unit vector whose components are $\cos \alpha$, $\cos \beta$, and $\cos \gamma$. Consider any other vector **B**. Clearly, the projection of **B** on **A** is just

$$B \cos \theta = \frac{\mathbf{B} \cdot \mathbf{A}}{A} = \mathbf{B} \cdot \mathbf{n} \tag{1.8}$$

where θ is the angle between **A** and **B**.

Examples

1.4   *Component of a vector. Work*

As an example of the dot product, suppose that an object under the action of a constant force[4] undergoes a linear displacement $\Delta \mathbf{s}$, as shown in Figure 1.6. By definition, the *work* ΔW done by the force is given by the product of the component of the force **F** in the direction of $\Delta \mathbf{s}$, multiplied by the magnitude Δs of the displacement, that is,

$$\Delta W = (F \cos \theta) \Delta s$$

---

[4] The concept of force will be discussed in Chapter 2.

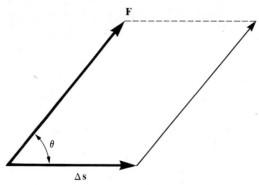

FIGURE 1.6   A force acting on a body undergoing a displacement.

where θ is the angle between **F** and Δ**s**. But the expression on the right is just the dot product of **F** and Δ**s**, that is,

$$\Delta W = \mathbf{F} \cdot \Delta \mathbf{s} \qquad \blacksquare$$

1.5   *Law of cosines*

   Consider the triangle whose sides are **A**, **B**, and **C**, as shown in Figure 1.7. Then **C** = **A** + **B**. Take the dot product of **C** with itself

$$\mathbf{C} \cdot \mathbf{C} = (\mathbf{A} + \mathbf{B}) \cdot (\mathbf{A} + \mathbf{B})$$

$$= \mathbf{A} \cdot \mathbf{A} + 2\mathbf{A} \cdot \mathbf{B} + \mathbf{B} \cdot \mathbf{B}$$

The second step follows from the application of the rules in Equations 1.2 and 1.3. Replace **A** $\cdot$ **B** by $AB \cos \theta$ to obtain

$$C^2 = A^2 + 2AB \cos \theta + B^2$$

which is the familiar law of cosines. This is just one example of the use of vector algebra to prove theorems in geometry. $\blacksquare$

1.6   Find the cosine of the angle between a long diagonal and an adjacent face diagonal of a cube. Solution: We can represent the two diagonals in question by the vectors **A** = [1, 1, 1] and **B** = [1, 1, 0]. Hence, from Equation 1.4

$$\cos \theta = \frac{\mathbf{A} \cdot \mathbf{B}}{A \, B} = \frac{1 + 1 + 0}{\sqrt{3}\sqrt{2}} = \sqrt{\frac{2}{3}} = 0.8165 \qquad \blacksquare$$

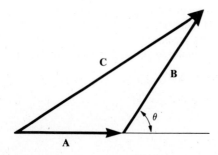

FIGURE 1.7   The law of cosines.

1.7   The vector $a\mathbf{i} + \mathbf{j} - \mathbf{k}$ is perpendicular to the vector $\mathbf{i} + 2\mathbf{j} - 3\mathbf{k}$. What is the value of a? Solution: If the vectors are perpendicular to each other, their dot product must vanish ($\cos 90° = 0$). Hence, we have

$$(a\mathbf{i} + \mathbf{j} - \mathbf{k}) \cdot (\mathbf{i} + 2\mathbf{j} - 3\mathbf{k}) = a + 2 + 3 = a + 5 = 0$$

Hence

$$a = -5 \qquad\qquad ■$$

1.5   The Vector Product

Given two vectors $\mathbf{A}$ and $\mathbf{B}$, the vector product or "cross product," $\mathbf{A} \times \mathbf{B}$, is defined as the vector whose components are given by the equation

$$\mathbf{A} \times \mathbf{B} = [A_y B_z - A_z B_y, A_z B_x - A_x B_z, A_x B_y - A_y B_x] \qquad (1.9)$$

It can be shown that the following rules hold for cross multiplication:

$$\mathbf{A} \times \mathbf{B} = -\mathbf{B} \times \mathbf{A} \qquad\qquad (1.10)$$

$$\mathbf{A} \times (\mathbf{B} + \mathbf{C}) = \mathbf{A} \times \mathbf{B} + \mathbf{A} \times \mathbf{C} \qquad\qquad (1.11)$$

$$n(\mathbf{A} \times \mathbf{B}) = (n\mathbf{A}) \times \mathbf{B} = \mathbf{A} \times (n\mathbf{B}) \qquad\qquad (1.12)$$

The proofs of these follow directly from the definition and are left as an exercise. (*Note:* The first equation states that the cross product is *anticommutative*.)

According to the definitions of the unit coordinate vectors, Section 1.3, it readily follows that

$$\begin{aligned}
\mathbf{i} \times \mathbf{i} = \mathbf{j} \times \mathbf{j} = \mathbf{k} \times \mathbf{k} = 0 \qquad\qquad (1.13)\\
\mathbf{j} \times \mathbf{k} = \mathbf{i} = -\mathbf{k} \times \mathbf{j}\\
\mathbf{i} \times \mathbf{j} = \mathbf{k} = -\mathbf{j} \times \mathbf{i}\\
\mathbf{k} \times \mathbf{i} = \mathbf{j} = -\mathbf{i} \times \mathbf{k}
\end{aligned}$$

For example,

$$\mathbf{i} \times \mathbf{j} = [0 - 0, 0 - 0, 1 - 0] = [0, 0, 1] = \mathbf{k}$$

The remaining equations are easily proved in a similar manner.

The cross product expressed in **ijk** form is

$$\mathbf{A} \times \mathbf{B} = \mathbf{i}(A_y B_z - A_z B_y) + \mathbf{j}(A_z B_x - A_x B_z) + \mathbf{k}(A_x B_y - A_y B_x)$$

Each term in parentheses is equal to a determinant

$$\mathbf{A} \times \mathbf{B} = \mathbf{i}\begin{vmatrix} A_y & A_z \\ B_y & B_z \end{vmatrix} + \mathbf{j}\begin{vmatrix} A_z & A_x \\ B_z & B_x \end{vmatrix} + \mathbf{k}\begin{vmatrix} A_x & A_y \\ B_x & B_y \end{vmatrix}$$

and finally

$$\mathbf{A} \times \mathbf{B} = \begin{vmatrix} \mathbf{i} & \mathbf{j} & \mathbf{k} \\ A_x & A_y & A_z \\ B_x & B_y & B_z \end{vmatrix} \qquad\qquad (1.14)$$

which is readily verified by expansion. The determinant form is a convenient aid for remembering the definition of the cross product. From the properties of determinants, it can be seen at once that if **A** is parallel to **B**, that is, if $\mathbf{A} = c\mathbf{B}$, then the two lower rows of the determinant are proportional and so the determinant is null. Thus the cross product of two parallel vectors is null.

Let us calculate the magnitude of the cross product. We have

$$|\mathbf{A} \times \mathbf{B}|^2 = (A_y B_z - A_z B_y)^2 + (A_z B_x - A_x B_z)^2 + (A_x B_y - A_y B_x)^2$$

With a little patience this can be reduced to

$$|\mathbf{A} \times \mathbf{B}|^2 = (A_x^2 + A_y^2 + A_z^2)(B_x^2 + B_y^2 + B_z^2) - (A_x B_x + A_y B_y + A_z B_z)^2$$

or, from the definition of the dot product, the above equation may be written in the form

$$|\mathbf{A} \times \mathbf{B}|^2 = A^2 B^2 - (\mathbf{A} \cdot \mathbf{B})^2 \tag{1.15}$$

Taking the square root of both sides of the above equation and using Equation 1.5, we can express the magnitude of the cross product as

$$|\mathbf{A} \times \mathbf{B}| = AB(1 - \cos^2\theta)^{1/2} = AB \sin\theta \tag{1.16}$$

where θ is the angle between **A** and **B**.

To interpret the cross product geometrically, we observe that the vector $\mathbf{C} = \mathbf{A} \times \mathbf{B}$ is perpendicular to both **A** and to **B**, because

$$\begin{aligned} \mathbf{A} \cdot \mathbf{C} &= A_x C_x + A_y C_y + A_z C_z \\ &= A_x(A_y B_z - A_z B_y) + A_y(A_z B_x - A_x B_z) + A_z(A_x B_y - A_y B_x) \\ &= 0 \end{aligned}$$

Similarly, $\mathbf{B} \cdot \mathbf{C} = 0$. Thus the vector **C** is perpendicular to the plane containing the vectors **A** and **B**.

The sense of the vector $\mathbf{C} = \mathbf{A} \times \mathbf{B}$ is determined from the requirement that the

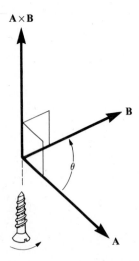

$\mathbf{A} \times \mathbf{B}$

FIGURE 1.8   The cross product of two vectors.

three vectors **A**, **B**, and **C** form a right-handed triad, as shown in Figure 1.8. (This is consistent with the previously established result that in the right-handed triad **ijk** we have **i** × **j** = **k**.) Therefore, from Equation 1.16 we see that we can write

$$\mathbf{A} \times \mathbf{B} = (AB \sin \theta)\mathbf{n} \tag{1.17}$$

where **n** is a unit vector normal to the plane of the two vectors **A** and **B**. The sense of **n** is given by the *right-hand rule,* that is, the direction of advancement of a right-handed screw rotated from the positive direction of **A** to that of **B** through the smallest angle between them, as illustrated in Figure 1.8. Equation 1.17 may be regarded as an alternate definition of the cross product.

Examples

1.8   Given the two vectors **A** = 2**i** + **j** − **k**, **B** = **i** − **j** + 2**k**, find **A** × **B**. In this case it is convenient to use the determinant form

$$\mathbf{A} \times \mathbf{B} = \begin{vmatrix} \mathbf{i} & \mathbf{j} & \mathbf{k} \\ 2 & 1 & -1 \\ 1 & -1 & 2 \end{vmatrix} = \mathbf{i}(2-1) + \mathbf{j}(-1-4) + \mathbf{k}(-2-1)$$

$$= \mathbf{i} - 5\mathbf{j} - 3\mathbf{k} \qquad\blacksquare$$

1.9   Find a unit vector normal to the plane containing the two vectors **A** and **B** above. Solution:

$$\mathbf{n} = \frac{\mathbf{A} \times \mathbf{B}}{|\mathbf{A} \times \mathbf{B}|} = \frac{\mathbf{i} - 5\mathbf{j} - 3\mathbf{k}}{[1^2 + 5^2 + 3^2]^{1/2}}$$

$$= \frac{\mathbf{i}}{\sqrt{35}} - \frac{5\mathbf{j}}{\sqrt{35}} - \frac{3\mathbf{k}}{\sqrt{35}} \qquad\blacksquare$$

1.6   An Example of the Cross Product: Moment of a Force

A particularly useful application of the cross product is the representation of moments. Let a force **F** act at a point $P(x, y, z)$, as shown in Figure 1.9, and let the vector $\overrightarrow{OP}$ be designated by **r**, that is,

$$\overrightarrow{OP} = \mathbf{r} = \mathbf{i}x + \mathbf{j}y + \mathbf{k}z$$

The moment **N**, or the *torque vector,* about a given point O is defined as the cross product

$$\mathbf{N} = \mathbf{r} \times \mathbf{F} \tag{1.18}$$

Thus the moment of a force about a point is a vector quantity having a magnitude and a direction. If a single force is applied at a point P on a body that is initially at rest and is free to turn about a fixed point O as a pivot, then the body tends to rotate. The axis of this rotation is perpendicular to the force **F**, and it is also perpendicular to the line OP.

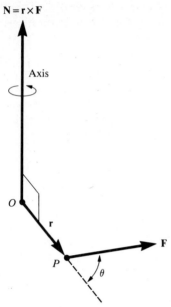

FIGURE 1.9   Illustrating the moment of a force about a point O.

Hence the direction of the torque vector **N** is along the axis of rotation.

The magnitude of the torque is given by

$$|\mathbf{N}| = |\mathbf{r} \times \mathbf{F}| = rF \sin \theta \qquad (1.19)$$

in which θ is the angle between **r** and **F**. Thus $|\mathbf{N}|$ can be regarded as the product of the magnitude of the force and the quantity $r \sin \theta$ which is just the perpendicular distance from the line of action of the force to the point O.

When several forces are applied to a single body at different points, the moments add vectorially. This follows from the distributive law of vector multiplication. The condition for rotational equilibrium is that the vector sum of all the moments is zero:

$$\sum_i (\mathbf{r}_i \times \mathbf{F}_i) = \sum_i \mathbf{N}_i = 0 \qquad (1.20)$$

A more complete discussion of force moments will be given in Chapters 8 and 9 when we study the motion of rigid bodies.

1.7   Triple Products

The expression

$$\mathbf{A} \cdot (\mathbf{B} \times \mathbf{C})$$

is called the *triple scalar product* of **A**, **B**, and **C**. It is a scalar since it is the dot product of two vectors. Referring to the determinant expression for the cross product, Equation 1.14, we see that the triple scalar product may be written

$$\mathbf{A} \cdot (\mathbf{B} \times \mathbf{C}) = \begin{vmatrix} A_x A_y A_z \\ B_x B_y B_z \\ C_x C_y C_z \end{vmatrix} \tag{1.21}$$

From the well-known property of determinants that the exchange of the terms of two rows or of two columns changes the sign but does not change the absolute value of the determinant, we can easily derive the following useful equation:

$$\mathbf{A} \cdot (\mathbf{B} \times \mathbf{C}) = (\mathbf{A} \times \mathbf{B}) \cdot \mathbf{C} \tag{1.22}$$

Thus the dot and the cross may be interchanged in the triple scalar product.

The expression

$$\mathbf{A} \times (\mathbf{B} \times \mathbf{C})$$

is called the *triple vector product*. It is left for the student to prove that the following equation holds for the triple vector product:

$$\mathbf{A} \times (\mathbf{B} \times \mathbf{C}) = (\mathbf{A} \cdot \mathbf{C})\mathbf{B} - (\mathbf{A} \cdot \mathbf{B})\mathbf{C} \tag{1.23}$$

Triple products of vectors are particularly useful in the study of rotating coordinate systems and rotations of rigid bodies, which we shall take up in later chapters. A geometric application is given in Problem 1.9 at the end of this chapter.

Examples

1.10   Given the three vectors $\mathbf{A} = \mathbf{i}$, $\mathbf{B} = \mathbf{i} - \mathbf{j}$, and $\mathbf{C} = \mathbf{k}$, find $\mathbf{A} \cdot (\mathbf{B} \times \mathbf{C})$. Using the determinant expression, Equation 1.21, we have

$$\mathbf{A} \cdot (\mathbf{B} \times \mathbf{C}) = \begin{vmatrix} 1 & 0 & 0 \\ 1 & -1 & 0 \\ 0 & 0 & 1 \end{vmatrix} = 1(-1 + 0) = -1 \qquad \blacksquare$$

1.11   Find $\mathbf{A} \times (\mathbf{B} \times \mathbf{C})$ above. From Equation 1.23 we have

$$\mathbf{A} \times (\mathbf{B} \times \mathbf{C}) = (\mathbf{A} \cdot \mathbf{C})\mathbf{B} - (\mathbf{A} \cdot \mathbf{B})\mathbf{C} = 0(\mathbf{i} - \mathbf{j}) - (1 - 0)\mathbf{k} = -\mathbf{k} \qquad \blacksquare$$

*1.8   Change of Coordinate System. The Transformation Matrix

In this section we shall show how to represent a vector in different coordinate systems. Consider the vector $\mathbf{A}$ expressed relative to the triad **ijk**

$$\mathbf{A} = \mathbf{i}A_x + \mathbf{j}A_y + \mathbf{k}A_z$$

Relative to a new triad **i′j′k′** having a different orientation from that of **ijk**, the *same* vector $\mathbf{A}$ is expressed as

*This section may be omitted without loss of continuity.

$$\mathbf{A} = \mathbf{i}'A_{x'} + \mathbf{j}'A_{y'} + \mathbf{k}'A_{z'}$$

Now the dot product $\mathbf{A} \cdot \mathbf{i}'$ is just $A_{x'}$, that is, the projection of $\mathbf{A}$ on the unit vector $\mathbf{i}'$. Thus we may write

$$A_{x'} = \mathbf{A} \cdot \mathbf{i}' = (\mathbf{i} \cdot \mathbf{i}')A_x + (\mathbf{j} \cdot \mathbf{i}')A_y + (\mathbf{k} \cdot \mathbf{i}')A_z \qquad (1.24)$$
$$A_{y'} = \mathbf{A} \cdot \mathbf{j}' = (\mathbf{i} \cdot \mathbf{j}')A_x + (\mathbf{j} \cdot \mathbf{j}')A_y + (\mathbf{k} \cdot \mathbf{j}')A_z$$
$$A_{z'} = \mathbf{A} \cdot \mathbf{k}' = (\mathbf{i} \cdot \mathbf{k}')A_x + (\mathbf{j} \cdot \mathbf{k}')A_y + (\mathbf{k} \cdot \mathbf{k}')A_z$$

The scalar products $(\mathbf{i} \cdot \mathbf{i}')$, $(\mathbf{i} \cdot \mathbf{j}')$, and so on, are called the *coefficients of transformation*. They are equal to the direction cosines of the axes of the primed coordinate system relative to the unprimed system. The unprimed components are similarly expressed as

$$A_x = \mathbf{A} \cdot \mathbf{i} = (\mathbf{i}' \cdot \mathbf{i})A_{x'} + (\mathbf{j}' \cdot \mathbf{i})A_{y'} + (\mathbf{k}' \cdot \mathbf{i})A_{z'} \qquad (1.25)$$
$$A_y = \mathbf{A} \cdot \mathbf{j} = (\mathbf{i}' \cdot \mathbf{j})A_{x'} + (\mathbf{j}' \cdot \mathbf{j})A_{y'} + (\mathbf{k}' \cdot \mathbf{j})A_{z'}$$
$$A_z = \mathbf{A} \cdot \mathbf{k} = (\mathbf{i}' \cdot \mathbf{k})A_{x'} + (\mathbf{j}' \cdot \mathbf{k})A_{y'} + (\mathbf{k}' \cdot \mathbf{k})A_{z'}$$

All of the coefficients of transformation in Equation 1.25 also appear in Equation 1.24, because $\mathbf{i} \cdot \mathbf{i}' = \mathbf{i}' \cdot \mathbf{i}$, etc., but those in the rows (equations) of Equation 1.25 appear in the columns of terms in Equation 1.24, and conversely. The transformation rules expressed in these two sets of equations are a general property of vectors. As a matter of fact, they constitute an alternative way of defining vectors.[5]

The equations of transformation are conveniently expressed in matrix notation.[6] Thus Equation 1.24 is written

$$\begin{bmatrix} A_{x'} \\ A_{y'} \\ A_{z'} \end{bmatrix} = \begin{bmatrix} \mathbf{i} \cdot \mathbf{i}' & \mathbf{j} \cdot \mathbf{i}' & \mathbf{k} \cdot \mathbf{i}' \\ \mathbf{i} \cdot \mathbf{j}' & \mathbf{j} \cdot \mathbf{j}' & \mathbf{k} \cdot \mathbf{j}' \\ \mathbf{i} \cdot \mathbf{k}' & \mathbf{j} \cdot \mathbf{k}' & \mathbf{k} \cdot \mathbf{k}' \end{bmatrix} \begin{bmatrix} A_x \\ A_y \\ A_z \end{bmatrix} \qquad (1.26)$$

The 3 by 3 matrix in the above equation is called the *transformation matrix*. One advantage of the matrix notation is that successive transformations are readily handled by means of matrix multiplication.

The reader will observe that the application of a given transformation matrix to some vector $\mathbf{A}$ is also formally equivalent to rotating that vector within the unprimed (fixed) coordinate system, the components of the rotated vector being given by Equation 1.26. Thus, finite rotations can be represented by matrices. (Note that the sense of rotation of the vector in this context is opposite that of the rotation of the coordinate system in the previous context.)

Examples

1.12   Express the vector $\mathbf{A} = 3\mathbf{i} + 2\mathbf{j} + \mathbf{k}$ in terms of the triad $\mathbf{i}'\mathbf{j}'\mathbf{k}'$ where the $x'y'$ axes are rotated $45°$ around the z axis, the z and the z' axes coinciding, as shown in Figure 1.10. Referring to the figure, we have for the coefficients of transformation, $\mathbf{i} \cdot \mathbf{i}' = \cos 45°$, and so on, hence

---

[5] See, for example, L. P. Smith, *Mathematical Methods for Scientists and Engineers*, Prentice-Hall, Englewood Cliffs, N.J., 1953.
[6] A brief review of matrices is given in Appendix H.

$$\mathbf{i} \cdot \mathbf{i}' = 1/\sqrt{2} \qquad \mathbf{j} \cdot \mathbf{i}' = 1/\sqrt{2} \qquad \mathbf{k} \cdot \mathbf{i}' = 0$$
$$\mathbf{i} \cdot \mathbf{j}' = -1/\sqrt{2} \qquad \mathbf{j} \cdot \mathbf{j}' = 1/\sqrt{2} \qquad \mathbf{k} \cdot \mathbf{j}' = 0$$
$$\mathbf{i} \cdot \mathbf{k}' = 0 \qquad \mathbf{j} \cdot \mathbf{k}' = 0 \qquad \mathbf{k} \cdot \mathbf{k}' = 1$$

These give

$$A_{x'} = \frac{3}{\sqrt{2}} + \frac{2}{\sqrt{2}} = \frac{5}{\sqrt{2}} \qquad A_{y'} = \frac{-3}{\sqrt{2}} + \frac{2}{\sqrt{2}} = \frac{-1}{\sqrt{2}} \qquad A_{z'} = 1$$

so that, in the primed system, the vector $\mathbf{A}$ is given by

$$\mathbf{A} = \frac{5}{\sqrt{2}}\mathbf{i}' - \frac{1}{\sqrt{2}}\mathbf{j}' + \mathbf{k}' \qquad\blacksquare$$

1.13   Find the transformation matrix for a rotation of the primed coordinate system through an angle ϕ about the z axis. (The previous example is a special case of this.) We have

$$\mathbf{i} \cdot \mathbf{i}' = \mathbf{j} \cdot \mathbf{j}' = \cos\phi$$
$$\mathbf{j} \cdot \mathbf{i}' = -\mathbf{i} \cdot \mathbf{j}' = \sin\phi$$
$$\mathbf{k} \cdot \mathbf{k}' = 1$$

and all other dot products are zero. Hence the transformation matrix is

$$\begin{bmatrix} \cos\phi & \sin\phi & 0 \\ -\sin\phi & \cos\phi & 0 \\ 0 & 0 & 1 \end{bmatrix} \qquad\blacksquare$$

It is clear from the above example that the transformation matrix for a rotation about a different coordinate axis, say the y axis through an angle θ, will be given by the matrix

$$\begin{bmatrix} \cos\theta & 0 & -\sin\theta \\ 0 & 1 & 0 \\ \sin\theta & 0 & \cos\theta \end{bmatrix}$$

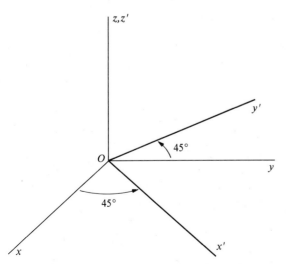

FIGURE 1.10   Rotated axes.

Consequently the matrix for the combination of two rotations, the first being about the z axis (angle ϕ) and the second being about the new y' axis (angle θ) is given by the matrix product

$$\begin{bmatrix} \cos\theta & 0 & -\sin\theta \\ 0 & 1 & 0 \\ \sin\theta & 0 & \cos\theta \end{bmatrix} \begin{bmatrix} \cos\phi & \sin\phi & 0 \\ -\sin\phi & \cos\phi & 0 \\ 0 & 0 & 1 \end{bmatrix} = \begin{bmatrix} \cos\theta\cos\phi & \cos\theta\sin\phi & -\sin\theta \\ -\sin\phi & \cos\phi & 0 \\ \sin\theta\cos\phi & \sin\theta\sin\phi & \cos\theta \end{bmatrix}$$

Now matrix multiplication is, in general, noncommutative. Hence we might expect that if the order of the rotations were reversed, and therefore the order of the matrix multiplication on the left, the final result would be different. This turns out to be the case, which the reader can verify. This is in keeping with a remark made earlier, namely that finite rotations do not obey the law of vector addition and hence are not vectors even though a single rotation has a direction (the axis) and a magnitude (the angle of rotation). However, we shall show later that infinitesimal rotations do obey the law of vector addition, and can be represented by vectors.

1.9 Derivative of a Vector

Up to this point we have been concerned mainly with vector algebra. We now begin the study of the calculus of vectors and its use in the description of the motion of particles.

Consider a vector $\mathbf{A}$, the components of which are functions of a single variable u. The vector may represent position, velocity, and so on. The parameter u is usually the time t, but it can be any quantity which determines the components of $\mathbf{A}$:

$$\mathbf{A}(u) = \mathbf{i}A_x(u) + \mathbf{j}A_y(u) + \mathbf{k}A_z(u)$$

The derivative of $\mathbf{A}$ with respect to u is defined, quite analogously to the ordinary derivative of a scalar function, by the limit

$$\frac{d\mathbf{A}}{du} = \lim_{\Delta u \to 0} \frac{\Delta\mathbf{A}}{\Delta u} = \lim_{\Delta u \to 0} \left(\mathbf{i}\frac{\Delta A_x}{\Delta u} + \mathbf{j}\frac{\Delta A_y}{\Delta u} + \mathbf{k}\frac{\Delta A_z}{\Delta u} \right)$$

where $\Delta A_x = A_x(u + \Delta u) - A_x(u)$, and so on. Hence

$$\frac{d\mathbf{A}}{du} = \mathbf{i}\frac{dA_x}{du} + \mathbf{j}\frac{dA_y}{du} + \mathbf{k}\frac{dA_z}{du} \tag{1.27}$$

The derivative of a vector, therefore, is a vector whose Cartesian components are ordinary derivatives.

It follows from the above equation that the derivative of the sum of two vectors is equal to the sum of the derivatives, namely,

$$\frac{d}{du}(\mathbf{A} + \mathbf{B}) = \frac{d\mathbf{A}}{du} + \frac{d\mathbf{B}}{du} \tag{1.28}$$

Rules for differentiating vector products will be treated later.

1.10   Position Vector of a Particle. Velocity and Acceleration in Rectangular Coordinates

In a given reference system the position of a particle can be specified by a single vector, namely, the displacement of the particle relative to the origin of the coordinate system. This vector is called the *position vector* of the particle. In rectangular coordinates, Figure 1.11, the position vector is simply

$$\mathbf{r} = \mathbf{i}x + \mathbf{j}y + \mathbf{k}z$$

The components of the position vector of a moving particle are functions of the time, namely,

$$x = x(t) \qquad y = y(t) \qquad z = z(t)$$

In Equation 1.27 we gave the formal definition of the derivative of any vector with respect to some parameter. In particular, if the vector is the position vector $\mathbf{r}$ of a moving particle and the parameter is the time t, the derivative of $\mathbf{r}$ with respect to t is called the *velocity*, which we shall denote by $\mathbf{v}$:

$$\mathbf{v} = \frac{d\mathbf{r}}{dt} = \mathbf{i}\dot{x} + \mathbf{j}\dot{y} + \mathbf{k}\dot{z} \tag{1.29}$$

where the dots indicate differentiation with respect to t. (This convention is standard and will be used throughout the book.) Let us examine the geometric significance of the velocity vector. Suppose a particle is at a certain position at time t. At a time Δt later, the particle will have moved from the position $\mathbf{r}(t)$ to the position $\mathbf{r}(t + \Delta t)$. The vector displacement during the time interval Δt is

$$\Delta \mathbf{r} = \mathbf{r}(t + \Delta t) - \mathbf{r}(t)$$

so the quotient $\Delta \mathbf{r}/\Delta t$ is a *vector* which is parallel to the displacement. As we consider

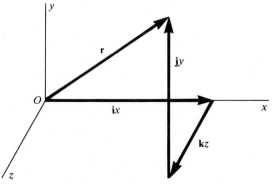

FIGURE 1.11   The position vector $\mathbf{r}$ and its components in a Cartesian coordinate system.

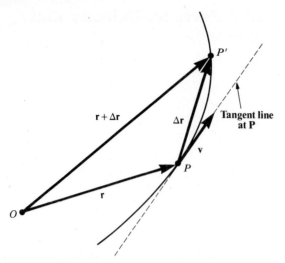

FIGURE 1.12   Velocity vector of a moving particle as the limit of the ratio $\Delta \mathbf{r}/\Delta t$.

smaller and smaller time intervals, the quotient $\Delta \mathbf{r}/\Delta t$ approaches a limit $d\mathbf{r}/dt$ which we call the velocity. The vector $d\mathbf{r}/dt$ expresses both the direction of motion and the rate. This is shown graphically in Figure 1.12. In the time interval Δt the particle moves along the path from P to P'. As Δt approaches zero, the point P' approaches P, and the direction of the vector $\Delta \mathbf{r}/\Delta t$ approaches the direction of the tangent to the path at P. The velocity vector, therefore, is always tangent to the path of motion.

The magnitude of the velocity is called the *speed*. In rectangular components the speed is just

$$v = |\mathbf{v}| = (\dot{x}^2 + \dot{y}^2 + \dot{z}^2)^{1/2} \tag{1.30}$$

If we denote the cumulative scalar distance along the path by s, then we can alternately express the speed as

$$v = \frac{ds}{dt} = \lim_{\Delta t \to 0} \frac{\Delta s}{\Delta t} = \lim_{\Delta t \to 0} \frac{[(\Delta x)^2 + (\Delta y)^2 + (\Delta z)^2]^{1/2}}{\Delta t}$$

which reduces to the expression on the right of Equation 1.30.

The time derivative of the velocity is called the *acceleration*. Denoting the acceleration by $\mathbf{a}$, we have

$$\mathbf{a} = \frac{d\mathbf{v}}{dt} = \frac{d^2\mathbf{r}}{dt^2} \tag{1.31}$$

In rectangular components

$$\mathbf{a} = \mathbf{i}\ddot{x} + \mathbf{j}\ddot{y} + \mathbf{k}\ddot{z} \tag{1.32}$$

Thus acceleration is a vector quantity whose components, in rectangular coordinates, are the second derivatives of the positional coordinates of a moving particle. The resolution of **a** into tangential and normal components will be discussed in Section 1.12.

Examples

1.14   *Projectile motion.* Let us examine the motion represented by the equation

$$\mathbf{r}(t) = \mathbf{i}bt + \mathbf{j}\left(ct - \frac{gt^2}{2}\right) + \mathbf{k}0$$

This represents motion in the xy plane, since the z component is constant and equal to zero. The velocity **v** is obtained by differentiating with respect to t, namely,

$$\mathbf{v} = \frac{d\mathbf{r}}{dt} = \mathbf{i}b + \mathbf{j}(c - gt)$$

The acceleration, likewise, is given by

$$\mathbf{a} = \frac{d\mathbf{v}}{dt} = -\mathbf{j}g$$

Thus **a** is in the negative y direction and has the constant magnitude g. The path of motion is a parabola, as shown in Figure 1.13. (This equation actually represents the motion of a projectile.) The speed v varies with t according to the equation.

$$v = [b^2 + (c - gt)^2]^{1/2} \qquad\qquad \blacksquare$$

1.15   *Circular motion.* Suppose the position vector of a particle is given by

$$\mathbf{r} = \mathbf{i}b \sin \omega t + \mathbf{j}b \cos \omega t$$

where ω is a constant.

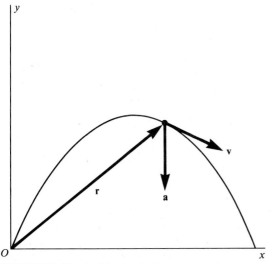

FIGURE 1.13   Position, velocity, and acceleration vectors of a particle (projectile) moving in a parabolic path.

Let us analyze the motion. The distance from the origin remains constant

$$|\mathbf{r}| = r = (b^2 \sin^2 \omega t + b^2 \cos^2 \omega t)^{1/2} = b$$

So the path is a circle of radius b centered at the origin. Differentiating $\mathbf{r}$, we find the velocity vector

$$\mathbf{v} = \frac{d\mathbf{r}}{dt} = \mathbf{i} b\omega \cos \omega t - \mathbf{j} b\omega \sin \omega t$$

The particle traverses its path with constant speed:

$$v = |\mathbf{v}| = (b^2\omega^2 \cos^2 \omega t + b^2\omega^2 \sin^2 \omega t)^{1/2} = b\omega$$

The acceleration is

$$\mathbf{a} = \frac{d\mathbf{v}}{dt} = -\mathbf{i} b\omega^2 \sin \omega t - \mathbf{j} b\omega^2 \cos \omega t$$

In this case the acceleration is perpendicular to the velocity, since the dot product of $\mathbf{v}$ and $\mathbf{a}$ vanishes:

$$\mathbf{v} \cdot \mathbf{a} = (b\omega \cos \omega t)(-b\omega^2 \sin \omega t) + (-b\omega \sin \omega t)(-b\omega^2 \cos \omega t) = 0$$

Comparing the two expressions for $\mathbf{a}$ and $\mathbf{r}$ we see that we can write

$$\mathbf{a} = -\omega^2 \mathbf{r}$$

so $\mathbf{a}$ and $\mathbf{r}$ are oppositely directed, that is, $\mathbf{a}$ always points toward the center of the circular path, Figure 1.14. ∎

1.16   *Rolling Wheel.* Let us consider the following position vector of a particle P:

$$\mathbf{r} = \mathbf{r}_1 + \mathbf{r}_2$$

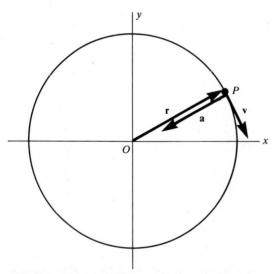

FIGURE 1.14   A particle moving in a circular path with constant speed.

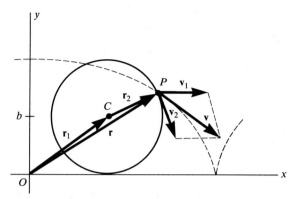

FIGURE 1.15 Cycloidal path of a particle on a rolling wheel.

in which

$$\mathbf{r}_1 = \mathbf{i}b\omega t + \mathbf{j}b$$
$$\mathbf{r}_2 = \mathbf{i}b \sin \omega t + \mathbf{j}b \cos \omega t$$

Now $\mathbf{r}_1$ by itself represents a point moving along the line $y = b$ at constant velocity, provided ω is constant, namely

$$\mathbf{v}_1 = \frac{d\mathbf{r}_1}{dt} = \mathbf{i}b\omega$$

The second part, $\mathbf{r}_2$, is just the position vector for circular motion, as discussed in the previous example. Hence the vector sum $\mathbf{r}_1 + \mathbf{r}_2$ represents a point that describes a circle of radius b about a moving center. This is precisely what occurs for a particle on the rim of a rolling wheel, $\mathbf{r}_1$ being the position vector of the center of the wheel, and $\mathbf{r}_2$ is the position vector of the particle P *relative* to the moving center. The actual path is a *cycloid* as shown in Figure 1.15. The velocity of P is

$$\mathbf{v} = \mathbf{v}_1 + \mathbf{v}_2 = \mathbf{i}(b\omega + b\omega \cos \omega t) - \mathbf{j}b\omega \sin \omega t$$

In particular, for $\omega t = 0, 2\pi, 4\pi, \ldots$, we find that $\mathbf{v} = \mathbf{i}2b\omega$ which is just twice the velocity of the center C. At these points the particle is at the uppermost part of its path. Further, for $\omega t = \pi, 3\pi, 5\pi, \ldots$, we obtain $\mathbf{v} = 0$. At these points the particle is at its lowest point and is instantaneously in contact with the ground. See Figure 1.16. ∎

1.11 Derivatives of Products of Vectors

It is often necessary to deal with derivatives of the products $n\mathbf{A}$, $\mathbf{A} \cdot \mathbf{B}$, and $\mathbf{A} \times \mathbf{B}$ where the scalar n and the vectors $\mathbf{A}$ and $\mathbf{B}$ are functions of a single parameter u, as in Section 1.9. From the general definition of the derivative, we have

$$\frac{d(n\mathbf{A})}{du} = \lim_{\Delta u \to 0} \frac{n(u + \Delta u)\mathbf{A}(u + \Delta u) - n(u)\mathbf{A}(u)}{\Delta u} \tag{1.33}$$

$$\frac{d(\mathbf{A} \cdot \mathbf{B})}{du} = \lim_{\Delta u \to 0} \frac{\mathbf{A}(u + \Delta u) \cdot \mathbf{B}(u + \Delta u) - \mathbf{A}(u) \cdot \mathbf{B}(u)}{\Delta u}$$

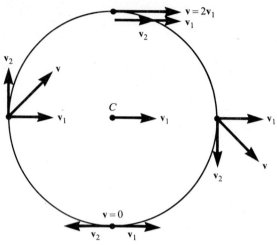

FIGURE 1.16   Velocity vectors for various points on a rolling wheel.

$$\frac{d(\mathbf{A} \times \mathbf{B})}{du} = \lim_{\Delta u \to 0} \frac{\mathbf{A}(u + \Delta u) \times \mathbf{B}(u + \Delta u) - \mathbf{A}(u) \times \mathbf{B}(u)}{\Delta u}$$

By adding and subtracting expressions like $n(u + \Delta u)\mathbf{A}(u)$ in the numerators, we obtain the following rules:

$$\frac{d(n\mathbf{A})}{du} = \frac{dn}{du}\mathbf{A} + n\frac{d\mathbf{A}}{du} \tag{1.34}$$

$$\frac{d(\mathbf{A} \cdot \mathbf{B})}{du} = \frac{d\mathbf{A}}{du} \cdot \mathbf{B} + \mathbf{A} \cdot \frac{d\mathbf{B}}{du} \tag{1.35}$$

$$\frac{d(\mathbf{A} \times \mathbf{B})}{du} = \frac{d\mathbf{A}}{du} \times \mathbf{B} + \mathbf{A} \times \frac{d\mathbf{B}}{du} \tag{1.36}$$

Notice that it is necessary to preserve the order of the terms in the derivative of the cross product. The steps are left as an exercise for the student.

1.12   Tangential and Normal Components of Acceleration

In Section 1.4, it was shown that any vector can be expressed as the product of its magnitude and a unit vector giving its direction. Accordingly, the velocity vector of a moving particle can be written as the product of the particle's speed v and a unit vector $\boldsymbol{\tau}$ that gives the direction of the particle's motion. Thus

$$\mathbf{v} = v\boldsymbol{\tau} \tag{1.37}$$

The vector $\boldsymbol{\tau}$ is called the *unit tangent vector*. As the particle moves the speed v may change and the direction of $\boldsymbol{\tau}$ may change. Let us use the rule for differentiation of the product of a scalar and a vector to obtain the acceleration. The result is

$$\mathbf{a} = \frac{d\mathbf{v}}{dt} = \frac{d(v\boldsymbol{\tau})}{dt} = \dot{v}\boldsymbol{\tau} + v\frac{d\boldsymbol{\tau}}{dt} \tag{1.38}$$

The unit vector $\boldsymbol{\tau}$, being of constant magnitude, has a derivative $d\boldsymbol{\tau}/dt$ that must necessarily express the change in the direction of $\boldsymbol{\tau}$ with respect to time. This is illustrated in Figure 1.17(a). The particle is initially at some point P on its path of motion. In a time interval Δt the particle moves to another point P' a certain distance Δs along the path. Let us denote the unit tangent vectors at P and P' by $\boldsymbol{\tau}$ and $\boldsymbol{\tau}'$, respectively, as shown. The directions of these two unit vectors differ by a certain angle $\Delta\psi$ as shown in Figure 1.17(b). It is apparent that for small values of $\Delta\psi$, the difference $\Delta\boldsymbol{\tau}$ approaches $\Delta\psi$ in magnitude. Also, the direction of $\Delta\boldsymbol{\tau}$ becomes perpendicular to the direction of $\boldsymbol{\tau}$ in the limit as $\Delta\psi$ and Δs approach zero. It follows that the derivative $d\boldsymbol{\tau}/d\psi$ is of magnitude unity and is perpendicular to $\boldsymbol{\tau}$. We shall therefore call it the *unit normal vector* and denote it by $\mathbf{n}$:

$$\frac{d\boldsymbol{\tau}}{d\psi} = \mathbf{n} \tag{1.39}$$

Next, in order to find the time derivative $d\boldsymbol{\tau}/dt$, we use the chain rule as follows

$$\frac{d\boldsymbol{\tau}}{dt} = \frac{d\boldsymbol{\tau}}{d\psi}\frac{d\psi}{dt} = \mathbf{n}\frac{d\psi}{ds}\frac{ds}{dt} = \mathbf{n}\frac{v}{\rho}$$

in which

$$\rho = \frac{ds}{d\psi}$$

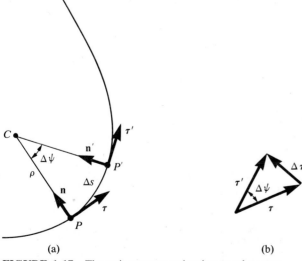

(a)   (b)

FIGURE 1.17 The unit tangent and unit normal vectors.

is the radius of curvature of the path of the moving particle at the point P. The above value for $d\tau/dt$ is now inserted into Equation 1.38 to yield the final result

$$\mathbf{a} = \dot{v}\boldsymbol{\tau} + \frac{v^2}{\rho}\mathbf{n} \qquad (1.40)$$

Thus the acceleration of a moving particle has a component

$$a_\tau = \dot{v} = \ddot{s}$$

in the direction of motion. This is the *tangential acceleration*. The other component

$$a_n = \frac{v^2}{\rho}$$

is the normal component. This component is always directed toward the center of curvature on the concave side of the path of motion. Hence the normal component is also called the *centripetal acceleration*.

From the above considerations we see that the time derivative of the speed is only the tangential component of the acceleration. The magnitude of the total acceleration is given by

$$|\mathbf{a}| = \left|\frac{d\mathbf{v}}{dt}\right| = \left(\dot{v}^2 + \frac{v^4}{\rho^2}\right)^{1/2} \qquad (1.41)$$

In particular, if a particle moves on a circle with constant speed v, as in Example 1.15, the acceleration vector is of magnitude v^2/b where b is the radius of the circle. The acceleration vector always points to the center of the circle in this case. However, if the speed is not constant but increases as a certain rate $\dot{v}$, then the acceleration has a forward component of this amount and is slanted away from the center of the circle towards the forward direction as illustrated in Figure 1.18. If the particle is slowing down, then the acceleration vector is slanted in the opposite direction.

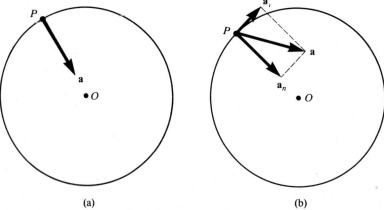

(a)   (b)

FIGURE 1.18   Acceleration vectors for a particle moving in a circular path with (a) constant speed and (b) increasing speed.

1.13   Velocity and Acceleration in Plane Polar Coordinates

It is often convenient to employ polar coordinates r, θ to express the position of a particle moving in a plane. Vectorially, the position of the particle can be written as the product of the radial distance r by a unit radial vector $\mathbf{e}_r$:

$$\mathbf{r} = r\mathbf{e}_r \qquad (1.42)$$

As the particle moves, both r and $\mathbf{e}_r$ vary, thus they are both functions of the time. Hence, if we differentiate with respect to t, we have

$$\mathbf{v} = \frac{d\mathbf{r}}{dt} = \dot{r}\mathbf{e}_r + r\frac{d\mathbf{e}_r}{dt} \qquad (1.43)$$

In order to calculate the derivative $d\mathbf{e}_r/dt$, let us consider the vector diagram shown in Figure 1.19. A study of the figure shows that when the direction of $\mathbf{r}$ changes by an amount $\Delta\theta$, the corresponding change $\Delta\mathbf{e}_r$ of the unit radial vector is as follows: The magnitude $|\Delta\mathbf{e}_r|$ is approximately equal to $\Delta\theta$, and the direction of $\Delta\mathbf{e}_r$ is very nearly perpendicular to $\mathbf{e}_r$. Let us introduce another unit vector $\mathbf{e}_\theta$ whose direction is perpendicular to $\mathbf{e}_r$. Then we have

$$\Delta\mathbf{e}_r \simeq \mathbf{e}_\theta\Delta\theta$$

If we divide by Δt and take the limit, we get

$$\frac{d\mathbf{e}_r}{dt} = \mathbf{e}_\theta\frac{d\theta}{dt} \qquad (1.44)$$

for the time derivative of the unit radial vector. In a precisely similar way, we can argue that the change in the unit vector $\mathbf{e}_\theta$ is given by the approximation

$$\Delta\mathbf{e}_\theta \simeq -\mathbf{e}_r\Delta\theta$$

Here the minus sign is inserted to indicate that the direction of the change $\Delta\mathbf{e}_\theta$ is

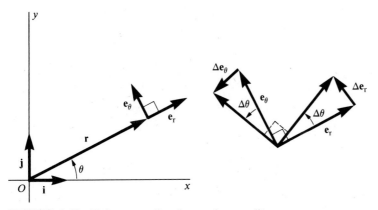

FIGURE 1.19   Unit vectors for plane polar coordinates.

opposite to the direction of $\mathbf{e}_r$ as can be seen from the figure. Consequently, the time derivative is given by

$$\frac{d\mathbf{e}_\theta}{dt} = -\mathbf{e}_r \frac{d\theta}{dt} \tag{1.45}$$

By using Equation 1.44 for the derivative of the unit radial vector, we can finally write the equation for the velocity as

$$\mathbf{v} = \dot{r}\mathbf{e}_r + r\dot{\theta}\mathbf{e}_\theta \tag{1.46}$$

Thus $\dot{r}$ is the radial component of the velocity vector, and $r\dot{\theta}$ is the transverse component.

In order to find the acceleration vector, we take the derivative of the velocity with respect to time. This gives

$$\mathbf{a} = \frac{d\mathbf{v}}{dt} = \ddot{r}\mathbf{e}_r + \dot{r}\frac{d\mathbf{e}_r}{dt} + (\dot{r}\dot{\theta} + r\ddot{\theta})\mathbf{e}_\theta + r\dot{\theta}\frac{d\mathbf{e}_\theta}{dt}$$

The values of $d\mathbf{e}_r/dt$ and $d\mathbf{e}_\theta/dt$ are given by Equations 1.44 and 1.45 and yield the following equation for the acceleration vector in plane polar coordinates:

$$\mathbf{a} = (\ddot{r} - r\dot{\theta}^2)\mathbf{e}_r + (r\ddot{\theta} + 2\dot{r}\dot{\theta})\mathbf{e}_\theta \tag{1.47}$$

Thus the radial component of the acceleration vector is

$$a_r = \ddot{r} - r\dot{\theta}^2 \tag{1.48}$$

and the transverse component is

$$a_\theta = r\ddot{\theta} + 2\dot{r}\dot{\theta} = \frac{1}{r}\frac{d}{dt}(r^2\dot{\theta}) \tag{1.49}$$

The above results show, for instance, that if a particle moves on a circle of constant radius b, so that $\dot{r} = 0$, then the radial component of the acceleration is of magnitude $b\dot{\theta}^2$ and is directed inward toward the center of the circular path. The transverse component in this case is $b\ddot{\theta}$. On the other hand, if the particle moves along a fixed radial line, that is, if θ is constant, then the radial component is just $\ddot{r}$ and the transverse component is zero. If r and θ both vary, then the general expression (1.47) gives the acceleration.

Examples

1.17   A honeybee homes in on its hive in a spiral path in such a way that the radial distance decreases at a constant rate: $r = b - ct$, while the angular speed increases at a constant rate: $\theta = kt$. Find the speed as a function of time. Solution: We have $\dot{r} = -c$, and $\ddot{r} = 0$. Thus, from Equation 1.46

$$\mathbf{v} = -c\mathbf{e}_r + (b - ct)kt\mathbf{e}_\theta$$

so

$$v = [c^2 + (b - ct)^2k^2t^2]^{1/2}$$

which is valid for $t \leq b/c$. (Larger values of t make r become negative.) Note that $v = c$ for both $t = 0$, $r = b$ and for $t = b/c$, $r = 0$.   ∎

1.18   On a horizontal turntable that is rotating at constant angular speed there is a bug crawling outward on a radial line such that the bug's distance from the center increases quadratically with time: $r = bt^2$, $\theta = \omega t$ where b and ω are constants. Find the acceleration of the bug. We have $\dot{r} = 2bt$, $\ddot{r} = 2b$, $\dot{\theta} = \omega$, $\ddot{\theta} = 0$. *Substituting into Equation 1.47, we find*

$$\mathbf{a} = \mathbf{e}_r(2b - bt^2\omega^2) + \mathbf{e}_\theta[0 + 2(2bt)\omega]$$
$$= b(2 - t^2\omega^2)\mathbf{e}_r + 4b\omega t\mathbf{e}_\theta$$

It is interesting to note that the radial component of the acceleration becomes negative for large t, in this example, although the radius is always increasing monotonically with time.   ∎

1.14   Velocity and Acceleration in Cylindrical and Spherical Coordinates

Cylindrical Coordinates

In the case of three-dimensional motion, the position of a particle can be described in cylindrical coordinates R, ϕ, z. The position vector is then written as

$$\mathbf{r} = R\mathbf{e}_R + z\mathbf{e}_z \tag{1.50}$$

where $\mathbf{e}_R$ is a unit radial vector in the xy plane and $\mathbf{e}_z$ is the unit vector in the z direction. A third unit vector $\mathbf{e}_\phi$ is needed so that the three vectors $\mathbf{e}_R\mathbf{e}_\phi\mathbf{e}_z$ constitute a right-handed triad as illustrated in Figure 1.20. We note that $\mathbf{k} = \mathbf{e}_z$.

The velocity and acceleration vectors are found by differentiating, as before. This will again involve derivatives of the unit vectors. An argument similar to that used for the plane case shows that $d\mathbf{e}_R/dt = \mathbf{e}_\phi\dot{\phi}$ and $d\mathbf{e}_\phi/dt = -\mathbf{e}_R\dot{\phi}$. The unit vector $\mathbf{e}_z$ does not change in direction, so its time derivative is zero.

In view of these facts, the velocity and acceleration vectors are easily seen to be given by the following equations:

$$\mathbf{v} = \dot{R}\mathbf{e}_R + R\dot{\phi}\mathbf{e}_\phi + \dot{z}\mathbf{e}_z \tag{1.51}$$

$$\mathbf{a} = (\ddot{R} - R\dot{\phi}^2)\mathbf{e}_R + (2\dot{R}\dot{\phi} + R\ddot{\phi})\mathbf{e}_\phi + \ddot{z}\mathbf{e}_z \tag{1.52}$$

These give the values of $\mathbf{v}$ and $\mathbf{a}$ in terms of their components in the *rotated* triad $\mathbf{e}_R\mathbf{e}_\phi\mathbf{e}_z$.

An alternative way of obtaining the derivatives of the unit vectors is to differentiate the following equations which are the relationships between the fixed unit triad **ijk** and the rotated triad:

$$\mathbf{e}_R = \mathbf{i}\cos\phi + \mathbf{j}\sin\phi \tag{1.53}$$
$$\mathbf{e}_\phi = -\mathbf{i}\sin\phi + \mathbf{j}\cos\phi$$
$$\mathbf{e}_z = \mathbf{k}$$

The steps are left as an exercise. The result can also be found by use of the rotation matrix as given in Example 1.13, Section 1.8.

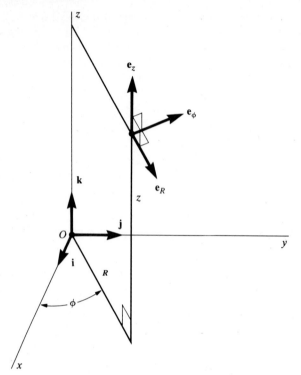

FIGURE 1.20   Unit vectors for cylindrical coordinates.

Spherical Coordinates

When spherical coordinates r, θ, ϕ are employed to describe the position of a particle, the position vector is written as the product of the radial distance r and the unit radial vector $\mathbf{e}_r$, as with plane polar coordinates. Thus

$$\mathbf{r} = r\mathbf{e}_r$$

The direction of $\mathbf{e}_r$ is now specified by the two angles ϕ and θ. We introduce two more unit vectors $\mathbf{e}_\phi$ and $\mathbf{e}_\theta$ as shown in Figure 1.21.

The velocity is

$$\mathbf{v} = \frac{d\mathbf{r}}{dt} = \dot{r}\mathbf{e}_r + r\frac{d\mathbf{e}_r}{dt} \tag{1.54}$$

Our next problem is how to express the derivative $d\mathbf{e}_r/dt$ in terms of the unit vectors in the rotated triad.

Referring to the figure, we see that the following relationships hold between the two triads

$$\begin{aligned}
\mathbf{e}_r &= \mathbf{i} \sin\theta \cos\phi + \mathbf{j} \sin\theta \sin\phi + \mathbf{k} \cos\theta \\
\mathbf{e}_\theta &= \mathbf{i} \cos\theta \cos\phi + \mathbf{j} \cos\theta \sin\phi - \mathbf{k} \sin\theta \\
\mathbf{e}_\phi &= -\mathbf{i} \sin\phi + \mathbf{j} \cos\phi
\end{aligned} \tag{1.55}$$

which express the unit vectors of the rotated triad in terms of the fixed triad **ijk**. We note the similarity between this transformation and that of the second part of Example 1.13 in Section 1.8. The two are, in fact, identical if the correct identification of rotations is made. Let us differentiate the first equation with respect to time. The result is

$$\frac{d\mathbf{e}_r}{dt} = \mathbf{i}(\dot\theta \cos\theta \cos\phi - \dot\phi \sin\theta \sin\phi)$$

$$+ \mathbf{j}(\dot\theta \cos\theta \sin\phi + \dot\phi \sin\theta \cos\phi) - \mathbf{k}\dot\theta \sin\theta$$

Next, by using the expressions for $\mathbf{e}_\phi$ and $\mathbf{e}_\theta$ in Equation 1.55, we find that the above equation reduces to

$$\frac{d\mathbf{e}_r}{dt} = \dot\phi\mathbf{e}_\phi \sin\theta + \dot\theta\mathbf{e}_\theta \qquad (1.56)$$

The other two derivatives are found by a similar procedure. The results are

$$\frac{d\mathbf{e}_\theta}{dt} = -\dot\theta\mathbf{e}_r + \dot\phi\mathbf{e}_\phi \cos\theta \qquad (1.57)$$

$$\frac{d\mathbf{e}_\phi}{dt} = -\dot\phi\mathbf{e}_r \sin\theta - \dot\phi\mathbf{e}_\theta \cos\theta \qquad (1.58)$$

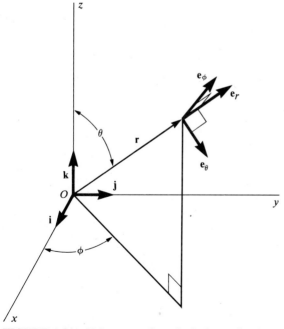

FIGURE 1.21   Unit vectors for spherical coordinates.

The steps are left as an exercise. Returning now to the problem of finding $\mathbf{v}$, we insert the expression for $d\mathbf{e}_r/dt$ given by Equation 1.56 into Equation 1.54. The final result is

$$\mathbf{v} = \mathbf{e}_r \dot{r} + \mathbf{e}_\phi r \dot{\phi} \sin \theta + \mathbf{e}_\theta r \dot{\theta} \qquad (1.59)$$

giving the velocity vector in terms of its components in the rotated triad.

To find the acceleration, we differentiate the above expression with respect to time. This gives

$$\mathbf{a} = \frac{d\mathbf{v}}{dt} = \mathbf{e}_r \ddot{r} + \dot{r} \frac{d\mathbf{e}_r}{dt} + \mathbf{e}_\phi \frac{d(r\dot{\phi} \sin \theta)}{dt} + r\dot{\phi} \sin \theta \frac{d\mathbf{e}_\phi}{dt} + \mathbf{e}_\theta \frac{d(r\dot{\theta})}{dt} + r\dot{\theta} \frac{d\mathbf{e}_\theta}{dt}$$

Upon using the previous formulas for the derivatives of the unit vectors, it is readily found that the above expression for the acceleration reduces to

$$\mathbf{a} = (\ddot{r} - r\dot{\phi}^2 \sin^2 \theta - r\dot{\theta}^2)\mathbf{e}_r + (r\ddot{\theta} + 2\dot{r}\dot{\theta} - r\dot{\phi}^2 \sin \theta \cos \theta)\mathbf{e}_\theta \qquad (1.60)$$
$$+ (r\ddot{\phi} \sin \theta + 2\dot{r}\dot{\phi} \sin \theta + 2r\dot{\theta}\dot{\phi} \cos \theta)\mathbf{e}_\phi$$

giving the acceleration vector in terms of its components in the triad $\mathbf{e}_r \mathbf{e}_\theta \mathbf{e}_\phi$.

Examples

1.19 A bead slides on a wire bent into the form of a helix, the motion of the bead being given in cylindrical coordinates by $R = b$, $\phi = \omega t$, $z = ct$. Find the velocity and acceleration vectors as functions of time. Solution: Differentiating, we find $\dot{R} = \ddot{R} = 0$, $\dot{\phi} = \omega$, $\ddot{\phi} = 0$, $\dot{z} = c$, $\ddot{z} = 0$. So, from Equations 1.51 and 1.52 we have

$$\mathbf{v} = b\omega \mathbf{e}_\phi + c\mathbf{e}_z$$
$$\mathbf{a} = -b\omega^2 \mathbf{e}_R$$

FIGURE 1.22 A rotating wheel on a rotating mount.

Thus, in this case, both velocity and acceleration are constant in magnitude, but they vary in direction because both e_ϕ and e_R change with time as the bead moves. ■

1.20 A wheel of radius b is placed in a gimbal mount and is made to rotate as follows: The wheel spins with constant angular speed ω_1 about its own axis which, in turn rotates with constant angular speed ω_2 about a vertical axis in such a way that the axis of the wheel stays in a horizontal plane and the center of the wheel is motionless. Use spherical coordinates to find the acceleration of any point on the rim of the wheel. In particular, find the acceleration of the highest point on the wheel. We can use the fact that spherical coordinates can be chosen such that $r = b$, $\theta = \omega_1 t$, and $\phi = \omega_2 t$, Figure 1.22. Then we have $\dot{r} = \ddot{r} = 0$, $\dot{\theta} = \omega_1$, $\ddot{\theta} = 0$, $\dot{\phi} = \omega_2$, $\ddot{\phi} = 0$. Equation 1.60 gives directly

$$\mathbf{a} = (-b\omega_2^2 \sin^2 \theta - b\omega_1^2)\mathbf{e}_r - b\omega_2^2 \sin \theta \cos \theta \, \mathbf{e}_\theta + 2b\omega_1\omega_2\cos \theta \, \mathbf{e}_\phi$$

The point at the top has coordinate $\theta = 0$, so at that point

$$\mathbf{a} = -b\omega_1^2\mathbf{e}_r + 2b\omega_1\omega_2\mathbf{e}_\phi$$

The first term on the right is the centripetal acceleration, and the last term is a transverse acceleration normal to the plane of the wheel. ■

PROBLEMS

1.1 Given the two vectors $\mathbf{A} = \mathbf{i} + \mathbf{j}$ and $\mathbf{B} = \mathbf{j} + \mathbf{k}$ find the following:
(a) $\mathbf{A} + \mathbf{B}$ and $|\mathbf{A} + \mathbf{B}|$
(b) $3\mathbf{A} - 2\mathbf{B}$
(c) $\mathbf{A} \cdot \mathbf{B}$
(d) $\mathbf{A} \times \mathbf{B}$ and $|\mathbf{A} \times \mathbf{B}|$

1.2 Given the three vectors $\mathbf{A} = 2\mathbf{i} + \mathbf{j}$, $\mathbf{B} = \mathbf{i} + \mathbf{k}$, and $\mathbf{C} = 4\mathbf{j}$, find the following:
(a) $\mathbf{A} \cdot (\mathbf{B} + \mathbf{C})$ and $(\mathbf{A} + \mathbf{B}) \cdot \mathbf{C}$
(b) $\mathbf{A} \cdot (\mathbf{B} \times \mathbf{C})$ and $(\mathbf{A} \times \mathbf{B}) \cdot \mathbf{C}$
(c) $\mathbf{A} \times (\mathbf{B} \times \mathbf{C})$ and $(\mathbf{A} \times \mathbf{B}) \times \mathbf{C}$

1.3 Find the angle between the vectors $\mathbf{A} = a\mathbf{i} + 2a\mathbf{j}$ and $\mathbf{B} = a\mathbf{i} + 2a\mathbf{j} + 3a\mathbf{k}$. (*Note:* These two vectors define a face diagonal and a body diagonal of a rectangular block of sides a, $2a$, and $3a$.)

1.4 Given the time-varying vector

$$\mathbf{A} = \mathbf{i}\alpha t + \mathbf{j}\beta t^2 + \mathbf{k}\gamma t^3$$

where α, β, and γ are constants, find the first and second time derivatives $d\mathbf{A}/dt$ and $d^2\mathbf{A}/dt^2$.

1.5 For what value (or values) of q is the vector $\mathbf{A} = \mathbf{i}q + 3\mathbf{j} + \mathbf{k}$ perpendicular to the vector $\mathbf{B} = \mathbf{i}q - q\mathbf{j} + 2\mathbf{k}$?

1.6 Give an algebraic and a geometric proof of the following relations:

$$|\mathbf{A} + \mathbf{B}| \le |\mathbf{A}| + |\mathbf{B}|$$
$$|\mathbf{A} \cdot \mathbf{B}| \le |\mathbf{A}| \, |\mathbf{B}|$$

1.7 Prove the vector identity $\mathbf{A} \times (\mathbf{B} \times \mathbf{C}) = (\mathbf{A} \cdot \mathbf{C})\mathbf{B} - (\mathbf{A} \cdot \mathbf{B})\mathbf{C}$.

1.8 Two vectors $\mathbf{A}$ and $\mathbf{B}$ represent concurrent sides of a parallelogram. Show that the area of the parallelogram is equal to $|\mathbf{A} \times \mathbf{B}|$.

1.9 Three vectors $\mathbf{A}$, $\mathbf{B}$, and $\mathbf{C}$ represent three concurrent edges of a parallelepiped. Show that the volume of the parallelepiped is equal to $|\mathbf{A} \cdot (\mathbf{B} \times \mathbf{C})|$.

1.10 Verify the transformation matrix for a rotation about the z axis through an angle ϕ followed by a rotation about the y' axis through an angle θ, as given in Example 1.13.

1.11   Express the vector $2\mathbf{i} + 3\mathbf{j} - \mathbf{k}$ in the primed triad $\mathbf{i'j'k'}$ in which the $x'y'$ axes are rotated about the z axis (which coincides with the z' axis) through an angle of 30°.

1.12   A racing car moves on a circle of constant radius b. If the speed of the car varies with time t according to the equation $v = ct$ where c is a positive constant, show that the angle between the velocity vector and the acceleration vector is 45° at time $t = \sqrt{b/c}$. (*Hint:* At this time the tangential and normal components of the acceleration are equal in magnitude.)

1.13   A small ball is fastened to a long rubber band and twirled around in such a way that the ball moves in an elliptical path given by the equation

$$\mathbf{r}(t) = \mathbf{i}b \cos \omega t + \mathbf{j}2b \sin \omega t$$

where b and ω are constants. Find the speed of the ball as a function of t. In particular, find v at $t = 0$ and at $t = \pi/2\omega$, at which times the ball is, respectively, at its minimum and maximum distance from the origin.

1.14   A buzzing fly moves in a helical path given by the equation

$$\mathbf{r}(t) = \mathbf{i}b \sin \omega t + \mathbf{j}b \cos \omega t + \mathbf{k}ct^2$$

Show that the magnitude of the acceleration of the fly is constant, provided b, ω, and c are constant.

1.15   A bee goes out from its hive in a spiral path given in plane polar coordinates by

$$r = be^{kt} \qquad \theta = ct$$

where b, k, and c are positive constants. Show that the angle between the velocity vector and the acceleration vector remains constant as the bee moves outward. (*Hint:* Find $\mathbf{v} \cdot \mathbf{a}/va$.)

1.16   Work Problem 1.14 using cylindrical coordinates where $R = b$, $\phi = \omega t$, and $z = ct^2$.

1.17   An ant crawls on the surface of a ball of radius b in a manner such that the ant's motion is given in spherical coordinates by the equations

$$r = b \qquad \phi = \omega t \qquad \theta = \frac{\pi}{2}[1 + \frac{1}{4}\cos(4\omega t)]$$

Find the speed of the ant as a function of the time t. What sort of path is represented by the above equations?

1.18   Prove that $\mathbf{v} \cdot \mathbf{a} = v\dot{v}$, and hence that for a moving particle $\mathbf{v}$ and $\mathbf{a}$ are perpendicular to each other if the speed v is constant. [*Hint:* Differentiate both sides of the equation $\mathbf{v} \cdot \mathbf{v} = v^2$ with respect to t. Remember that $\dot{v}$ is not the same as $|\mathbf{a}|$.]

1.19   Prove that

$$\frac{d}{dt}[\mathbf{r} \cdot (\mathbf{v} \times \mathbf{a})] = \mathbf{r} \cdot (\mathbf{v} \times \dot{\mathbf{a}})$$

1.20   Show that the tangential component of the acceleration is given by the expression.

$$a_\tau = \frac{\mathbf{v} \cdot \mathbf{a}}{v}$$

and the normal component is therefore

$$a_n = (a^2 - a_\tau^2)^{1/2} = [a^2 - \frac{(\mathbf{v} \cdot \mathbf{a})^2}{v^2}]^{1/2}$$

1.21   Use the above result to find the tangential and normal components of the acceleration as functions of time in Problems 1.14 and 1.15.

1.22   Prove that $|\mathbf{v} \times \mathbf{a}| = v^3/\rho$, where ρ is the radius of curvature of the path of a moving particle.

1.23   A wheel of radius b rolls along the ground with constant forward acceleration a_0. Show that, at any given instant, the magnitude of the acceleration of any point on the wheel is $(a_0^2 + v^4/b^2)^{1/2}$ relative to the center of the wheel, and is also $a_0[2 + 2\cos\theta + v^4/a_0^2 b^2 - (2v^2/a_0 b)\sin\theta]^{1/2}$ relative to the ground. Here v is the instantaneous forward speed, and θ defines the location of the point on the wheel, measured forward from the highest point. Which point has the greatest acceleration relative to the ground?

2
Newtonian Mechanics. Rectilinear Motion of a Particle

2.1 Newton's Laws of Motion

As stated in the introduction, dynamics is that branch of mechanics which deals with the physical laws governing the actual motion of material bodies. One of the fundamental tasks of dynamics is to predict, out of all possible ways a material system can move, which particular motion will occur in any given situation. Our study of dynamics at this point will be based on the laws of motion as they were first formulated by Newton. In a later chapter we shall study alternative ways of expressing the laws of motion in the more advanced equations of Lagrange and Hamilton. These are not different theories, however, for they can be derived from Newton's laws.

The reader is undoubtedly already familiar with Newton's laws of motion. They are as follows:

I.   Every body continues in its state of rest or of uniform motion in a straight line, unless it is compelled by a force to change that state.
II.   Change of motion is proportional to the applied force and takes place in the direction of the force.
III.   To every action there is always an equal and opposite reaction, or, the mutual actions of two bodies are always equal and oppositely directed.

Let us now examine these laws in some detail.

Newton's First Law. Inertial Reference Systems

The first law describes a common property shared by all matter, namely *inertia*. The law states that a moving body travels in a straight line with constant speed unless some influence called *force* prevents the body from doing so. Whether or not a body moves in a straight line with constant speed depends not only upon external influences (forces) but also upon the particular reference system that is used to describe the motion. The first law actually amounts to a definition of a particular kind of reference system called a Newtonian or *inertial* reference system. Such a system is one in which Newton's first law holds. Rotating or accelerating systems are not inertial. These will be studied in Chapter 5.

The question naturally arises as to how it is possible to determine whether or not a given coordinate system constitutes an inertial system. The answer is not simple. In order to eliminate *all* forces on a body it would be necessary to isolate the body completely. This is impossible, of course, since there are always at least some gravitational forces acting unless the body was removed to an infinite distance from all other matter.

For many practical purposes not requiring high precision, a coordinate system fixed to the earth is approximately inertial. Thus, for example, a billiard ball seems to move in a straight line with constant speed as long as it does not collide with other balls or hit the cushion. If the motion of a billiard ball were measured with very high precision, however, it would be discovered that the path is slightly curved. This is due to the fact that the earth is rotating and so a coordinate system fixed to the earth is not actually an inertial system. A better system would be one using the center of the earth, the center of the sun, and a distant star as reference points. But even this system would not be strictly inertial because of the earth's orbital motion around the sun. The next best approximation would be to take the center of the sun and two distant stars as reference points, for example. It is generally agreed that the ultimate inertial system, in the sense of Newtonian mechanics, would be one based on the average background of all the matter in the universe.

Mass and Force. Newton's Second and Third Laws

We are all familiar with the fact that a big stone is not only hard to lift, but that such an object is more difficult to set in motion (or to stop) than, say, a small piece of wood. We say that the stone has more inertia than the wood. The quantitative measure of inertia is called *mass*. Suppose we have two bodies A and B. How do we determine the measure of inertia of one relative to the other? There are many experiments that can be devised to answer this question. If the two bodies can be made to interact directly with one another, say by a spring connecting them, then it is found, by careful experiments, that the accelerations of the two bodies are always opposite in direction and have a *constant ratio*. (It is assumed that the accelerations are given in an inertial reference system and that only the *mutual* influence of the two bodies A and B is under consideration.) We can express this very important and fundamental fact by the equation

$$\frac{d\mathbf{v}_A}{dt} = -\frac{d\mathbf{v}_B}{dt}\mu_{BA} \tag{2.1}$$

The constant μ_{BA} is, in fact, the measure of relative inertia of B with respect to A. From Equation 2.1 it follows that $\mu_{BA} = 1/\mu_{AB}$. Thus we might express μ_{BA} as a ratio

$$\mu_{BA} = \frac{m_B}{m_A}$$

and use some standard body as a unit of inertia. Now the ratio m_B/m_A ought to be independent of the choice of the unit. This will be the case if, for any third body C,

$$\frac{\mu_{BC}}{\mu_{AC}} = \mu_{BA}$$

This is indeed found to be true. We call the quantity m the *mass*.

Strictly speaking, m should be called the *inertial mass*, for its definition is based on the properties of inertia. In practice mass ratios are usually determined by weighing. The weight or gravitational force is proportional to what may be called the *gravitational mass* of a body. All experience thus far, however, indicates that inertial mass and gravitational mass are strictly proportional to one another. Hence for our purpose we need not distinguish between the two kinds of mass.

If m is constant, the fundamental fact expressed by Equation 2.1 can now be written in the form

$$\frac{d(m_A\mathbf{v}_A)}{dt} = -\frac{d(m_B\mathbf{v}_B)}{dt} \tag{2.2}$$

The time rate of change of the product of mass and velocity is the "change of motion" of Newton's second law and, according to that law, is proportional to the *force*. In other words, we can write the second law as

$$\mathbf{F} = k\frac{d(m\mathbf{v})}{dt} \tag{2.3}$$

where $\mathbf{F}$ is the force and k is a constant of proportionality. It is customary to take $k = 1$ and write[1]

$$\mathbf{F} = \frac{d(m\mathbf{v})}{dt} \tag{2.4}$$

The above equation is equivalent to

$$\mathbf{F} = m\frac{d\mathbf{v}}{dt} \tag{2.5}$$

---

[1] In the SI system the unit of force, is called the *newton*. Thus a force of 1 newton imparts acceleration of 1 m per sec^2 to an object of 1 kg mass. The cgs unit of force (1 g × 1 cm per sec^2) is called the *dyne*. In engineering, a common unit of force is the *pound force* which imparts an acceleration of 1 ft per sec^2 to an object of 1 *slug* mass. (1 slug = 32 pounds mass.)

if the mass is constant. (According to the theory of relativity, the mass of a moving body is not constant but is a function of the speed of the body, so that Equations 2.4 and 2.5 are not strictly equivalent. However, for speeds that are small compared to the speed of light, 3×10^8m/sec, the change of mass is negligible.)

According to Equation 2.4 we can now interpret the fundamental fact expressed by Equation 2.2 as a statement that two directly interacting bodies exert equal and opposite forces on one another:

$$\mathbf{F}_A = -\mathbf{F}_B$$

This is embodied in the statement of the third law. The forces are called *action* and *reaction*.

There are situations in which the third law fails. If the two bodies are separated by a large distance and interact with one another through a force field which propagates with a finite velocity, such as the interaction between moving electric charges, then the forces of action and reaction are not always equal and opposite.[2]

One great advantage of the force concept is that it enables us to restrict our attention to a single body. The physical significance of the idea of force is that, in a given situation, there can usually be found some relatively simple function of the coordinates, called the force function, which when set equal to the product of mass and acceleration correctly describes the motion of a body. This is the essence of Newtonian mechanics.

Linear Momentum

The product of mass and velocity is called *linear momentum* and is denoted by the symbol **p**. Thus

$$\mathbf{p} = m\mathbf{v} \tag{2.6}$$

The mathematical statement of Newton's second law may then be written as

$$\mathbf{F} = \frac{d\mathbf{p}}{dt} \tag{2.7}$$

In words, *when a single force acts on a body the force is equal to the time rate of change of linear momentum of the body.*

The third law, the law of action and reaction, can be expressed conveniently in terms of linear momentum. Thus for two mutually interacting bodies A and B, we have

$$\frac{d\mathbf{p}_A}{dt} = -\frac{d\mathbf{p}_B}{dt}$$

or

$$\frac{d}{dt}(\mathbf{p}_A + \mathbf{p}_B) = 0$$

---

[2] However, it is possible in such cases to regard the force field as a third "body" with its own action and reaction. The third law thus need not be discarded. See Section 7.1 and reference cited therein.

Accordingly

$$\mathbf{p}_A + \mathbf{p}_B = \text{constant}$$

Thus the third law implies that the total linear momentum of two interacting bodies always remains constant.

The constancy of the combined linear momentum of two mutually interacting bodies is a special case of a more general rule that we shall discuss in detail later, namely that *the total linear momentum of any isolated system remains constant in time*. This fundamental statement is known as the *law of conservation of linear momentum* and is one of the most basic rules of physics. It is assumed to be valid even in those cases in which Newtonian mechanics fails to hold.

Motion of a Particle

The fundamental equation of motion of a particle is given by the analytical statement of Newton's second law, Equation 2.4. When a particle is under the influence of more than one force, it may be regarded as an experimental fact that these forces add vectorially, namely, for constant mass

$$\mathbf{F}_{net} = \Sigma \mathbf{F}_i = m\frac{d^2\mathbf{r}}{dt^2} = m\mathbf{a} \tag{2.8}$$

If the acceleration **a** of a particle is known, then the equation of motion (Equation 2.8) gives the force that acts on the particle. The usual problems of particle dynamics, however, are those in which the forces are certain known functions of the coordinates including the time, and the task is to find the position of the particle as a function of time. This involves the solution of a set of differential equations. In some problems it turns out to be impossible to obtain solutions of the differential equations of motion in terms of known analytic functions, in which case one must use some method of approximation. In many practical applications, such as ballistics, satellite motion, and so on, the differential equations are so complicated that it is necessary to resort to numerical integration, often done on high-speed electronic computers, to predict the motion.

2.2   Rectilinear Motion. Uniform Acceleration Under a Constant Force

When a moving particle remains on a single straight line, the motion is said to be *rectilinear*. In this case, without loss of generality we can choose the x axis as the line of motion. The general equation of motion is then

$$F_x(x,\dot{x},t) = m\ddot{x}$$

(*Note:* in the rest of this chapter we shall usually use the single variable x to represent the position of a particle. To avoid excessive and unnecessary use of subscripts we shall often use the symbols v and a for $\dot{x}$ and $\ddot{x}$, respectively, rather than v_x and a_x, and F rather than F_x.)

The simplest situation is that in which the force is constant. In this case we have constant acceleration

$$\ddot{x} = \frac{dv}{dt} = \frac{F}{m} = \text{constant} = a \tag{2.9}$$

and the solution is readily obtained by direct integration with respect to time:

$$\dot{x} = v = at + v_0 \tag{2.9a}$$

$$x = \tfrac{1}{2}at^2 + v_0 t + x_0 \tag{2.9b}$$

where v_0 is the initial velocity and x_0 is the initial position (i.e., the position at $t = 0$). By eliminating the time t between Equations (2.9a) and (2.9b), we obtain

$$2a(x - x_0) = v^2 - v_0^2 \tag{2.9c}$$

The student will recall the above familiar equations of uniformly accelerated motion. There are a number of fundamental applications. For example, in the case of a body falling freely near the surface of the earth, neglecting air resistance, the acceleration is very nearly constant. We denote the acceleration of a freely falling body by **g**. (By measurement, $g = 9.8$ m per sec^2 = 32 ft per sec^2.) The downward force of gravity (the *weight*) is, accordingly, equal to $m\mathbf{g}$. The gravitational force is always present, regardless of the motion of the body and is independent of any other forces that may be acting.[3] We shall henceforth call it $m\mathbf{g}$.

Example

2.1   Consider a particle that is sliding down a smooth plane inclined at an angle θ to the horizontal, as shown in Figure 2.1(a). We choose the positive direction of the x axis to be down the plane, as indicated. The component of the gravitational force in the x direction is equal to $mg \sin \theta$. This is a constant, hence the motion is given by Equations 2.9a, 2.9b, and 2.9c where

$$\ddot{x} = \frac{F_x}{m} = g \sin \theta$$

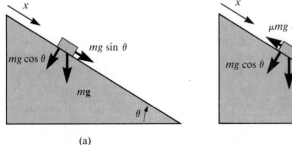
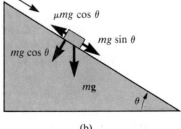

(a)   (b)

FIGURE 2.1   A block sliding down an inclined plane. (a) Smooth plane. (b) Rough plane.

[3] Effects of the earth's rotation will be studied in Chapter 5.

42

Chapter 2   Newtonian Mechanics. Rectilinear Motion of a Particle

Suppose that, instead of being smooth, the plane is rough; that is, it exerts a frictional force **f** on the particle. Then the net force in the x direction, as shown in Figure 2.1(b), is equal to $mg \sin \theta - f$. Now for sliding contact it is found that the magnitude of the frictional force is proportional to the magnitude of the normal force N, that is,

$$f = \mu N$$

where the constant of proportionality μ is known as the *coefficient of sliding or kinetic friction*.[4] In the example under discussion the normal force, as shown in the figure, is equal to $mg \cos \theta$, hence

$$f = \mu mg \cos \theta$$

Consequently, the net force in the x direction is equal to

$$mg \sin \theta - \mu mg \cos \theta$$

Again the force is constant, and Equations 2.9a, 2.9b, and 2.9c apply, where

$$\ddot{x} = \frac{F_x}{m} = g(\sin \theta - \mu \cos \theta)$$

The speed of the particle will increase if the expression in parentheses is positive, that is, if $\theta > \tan^{-1} \mu$. The angle $\tan^{-1} \mu$, usually denoted by ϵ, is called the *angle of kinetic friction*. If $\theta = \epsilon$, then $a = 0$, and the particle slides down the plane with constant speed. If $\theta < \epsilon$, a is negative, and so the particle will eventually come to rest. It should be noted that for motion *up* the plane the direction of the frictional force is reversed; that is, it is in the positive x direction. The acceleration (actually deceleration) is then $\ddot{x} = g(\sin \theta + \mu \cos \theta)$. ∎

2.3   Forces That Depend on Position. The Concepts of Kinetic and Potential Energy

It is often true that the force that a particle experiences depends on the particle's position with respect to other bodies. This is the case, for example, with electrostatic and gravitational forces. It also applies to forces of elastic tension or compression. If the force is independent of velocity or time, then the differential equation for rectilinear motion is simply

$$F(x) = m\ddot{x} \tag{2.10}$$

It is usually possible to solve this type of differential equation by one of several methods. One useful and significant method of solution is to use the chain rule and write the acceleration in the following way:

$$\ddot{x} = \frac{d\dot{x}}{dt} = \frac{dx}{dt}\frac{d\dot{x}}{dx} = v\frac{dv}{dx}$$

so the differential equation of motion may be written

[4]There is another coefficient of friction called the *static* coefficient μ_s which, when multiplied by the normal force, gives the maximum frictional force under static contact, that is, the force required to barely start an object to move when it is initially at rest. In general $\mu_s > \mu$.

$$F(x) = mv\frac{dv}{dx} = \frac{m}{2}\frac{d(v^2)}{dx} = \frac{dT}{dx} \tag{2.11}$$

The quantity $T = \frac{1}{2}mv^2$ is called the *kinetic energy* of the particle. We can now express the above equation in integral form

$$\int_{x_0}^{x} F(x)dx = T - T_0 \tag{2.11a}$$

Now the integral $\int F(x)\, dx$ is the *work* done on the particle by the impressed force $F(x)$. Thus, *the work is equal to the change in the kinetic energy of the particle*. Let us *define* a function $V(x)$ such that

$$-\frac{dV}{dx} = F(x) \tag{2.12}$$

The function $V(x)$ is called the *potential energy*; it is defined only to within an additive (arbitrary) constant. In terms of $V(x)$, the work integral is

$$\int_{x_0}^{x} F(x)dx = -\int_{x_0}^{x} dV = -V(x) + V(x_0) = T - T_0 \tag{2.13}$$

Notice that the above equation remains unaltered if $V(x)$ is changed by adding *any* constant C, because

$$-[V(x) + C] + [V(x_0) + C] = -V(x) + V(x_0)$$

We now transpose terms and write Equation 2.13 in the following form:

$$T + V(x) = T_0 + V(x_0) = \text{constant} = E \tag{2.14}$$

or equivalently

$$\frac{1}{2}mv^2 + V(x) = E \tag{2.14a}$$

This is known as the *energy equation*. We call the constant E the total energy. It is equal to the sum of the kinetic and the potential energies. In words: *For one-dimensional motion, if the impressed force is a function of position only, then the sum of the kinetic and potential energies remains constant throughout the motion.* The force in this case is said to be *conservative*.[5] Nonconservative forces, that is, those for which no potential function exists, are usually of a dissipational nature, such as friction.

The motion of the particle can be obtained by solving the energy equation (Equation 2.14a) for v

$$v = \frac{dx}{dt} = \pm\sqrt{\frac{2}{m}[E - V(x)]} \tag{2.15}$$

---

[5] A more complete discussion of conservative forces will be found in Chapter 4.

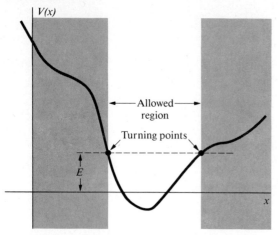

FIGURE 2.2   Graph of a one-dimensional potential energy function $V(x)$ showing allowed region of motion and the turning points for a given value of the total energy E.

which can be written in integral form

$$\int_{x_0}^{x} \frac{dx}{\pm\sqrt{\dfrac{2}{m}[E - V(x)]}} = t - t_0 \qquad (2.15a)$$

thus giving t as a function of x.

In view of Equation 2.15 we see that the expression for v is real only for those values of x such that $V(x)$ is less than or equal to the total energy E. Physically, this means that the particle is confined to the region, or regions, for which the condition $V(x) \leq E$ is satisfied. Furthermore, v goes to zero when $V(x) = E$. This means that the particle must come to rest and reverse its motion at those points for which the equality holds. These points are called the *turning points* of the motion. The above facts are illustrated in Figure 2.2.

Examples

2.2 *Free fall*. The motion of a freely falling body (discussed above under the case of constant acceleration) is an example of conservative motion. If we choose the x direction to be positive upward, then the gravitational force is equal to $-mg$. Therefore, $-dV/dx = -mg$, and $V = mgx + C$. The constant of integration C is arbitrary and merely depends on the choice of the reference level for measuring V. We can choose $C = 0$ which means that $V = 0$ when $x = 0$. The energy equation is then

$$\frac{1}{2}mv^2 + mgx = E$$

The energy constant E is determined from the initial conditions. For instance, let the body be projected upward with initial speed v_0 from the origin $x = 0$. These values give $E = mv_0^2/2 = mv^2/2 + mgx$, so

$$v^2 = v_0^2 - 2gx$$

The turning point of the motion, which is in this case the maximum height, is given by setting $v = 0$. This gives $0 = v_0^2 - 2gx_{max}$, or

$$h = x_{max} = \frac{v_0^2}{2g}$$

∎

2.3   *Variation of gravity with height.* In the preceding example it was assumed that g was constant. Actually, the force of gravity between two particles is inversely proportional to the square of the distance between them (Newton's Law of Gravity).[6] Thus, the gravitational force that the earth exerts on a body of mass m is given by

$$F_r = -\frac{GMm}{r^2}$$

in which G is Newton's constant of gravitation, M is the mass of the earth, and r is the distance from the center of the earth to the body. By definition, this force is equal to the quantity $-mg$ when the body is at the surface of the earth, so $mg = GMm/r_e^2$. Thus, $g = GM/r_e^2$ is the acceleration of gravity at the earth's surface. Here r_e is the radius of the earth (assumed to be spherical). Let x be the distance above the surface so $r = r_e + x$. Then, neglecting any other forces such as air resistance, we can write

$$F(x) = -mg\frac{r_e^2}{(r_e + x)^2} = m\ddot{x}$$

for the differential equation of motion of a vertically falling (or rising) body with the variation of gravity taken into account. To integrate we set $\ddot{x} = v\,dv/dx$. Then

$$-mgr_e^2 \int_{x_0}^{x} \frac{dx}{(r_e + x)^2} = \int_{v_0}^{v} mv\,dv$$

$$mgr_e^2 \left(\frac{1}{r_e + x} - \frac{1}{r_e + x_0} \right) = \frac{1}{2}mv^2 - \frac{1}{2}mv_0^2$$

This is, in fact, just the *energy* equation in the form of Equation 2.13. The potential energy is $V(x) = -mg[r_e^2/(r_e + x)]$ rather than mgx.
Maximum height. Escape Speed. Suppose a body is projected upward with initial speed v_0 at the surface of the earth, $x_0 = 0$. The energy equation then yields, upon solving for v^2, the following result:

$$v^2 = v_0^2 - 2gx\left(1 + \frac{x}{r_e}\right)^{-1}$$

This reduces to the result for a uniform gravitational field of the previous example if x is very small compared to r_e so that the term x/r_e can be neglected. The turning point (maximum height) is found by setting $v = 0$ and solving for x. The result is

$$x_{max} = h = \frac{v_0^2}{2g}\left(1 - \frac{v_0^2}{2gr_e}\right)^{-1} \tag{2.16}$$

---

[6] We shall study Newton's Law of Gravity in more detail in Chapter 6.

Again we get the formula of the previous example if the second term in the parentheses can be ignored, i.e., if v_0^2 is much smaller than $2gr_e$.

Finally, let us apply the exact formula (2.16) to find the value of v_0 that gives an infinite value of h. This is called the *escape speed*, and it is clearly found by setting the quantity in parentheses equal to zero. The result is

$$v_e = (2gr_e)^{1/2}$$

This gives, for $g = 9.8$ m/s^2 and $r_e = 6.4 \times 10^6$m,

$$v_e \simeq 11 \text{ km/sec} \simeq 7 \text{ mi/sec}$$

for the numerical value of the escape speed from the surface of the earth.

In the earth's atmosphere, the average speed[7] of air molecules (O_2 and N_2) is about 0.5 km per sec, which is considerably less than the escape speed, so the earth retains its atmosphere. The moon, on the other hand, has no atmosphere, because the escape speed at the moon's surface, owing to the moon's small mass, is considerably smaller than that at the earth's surface; any oxygen or nitrogen would eventually disappear. The earth's atmosphere, however, contains no significant amount of hydrogen, even though hydrogen is the most abundant element in the universe as a whole. A hydrogen atmosphere would have escaped from the earth long ago, because the molecular speed of hydrogen is large enough (owing to the small mass of the hydrogen molecule) that at any instant a significant number of hydrogen molecules would have speeds exceeding the escape speed.   ■

2.4   The Force as a Function of Time. The Concept of Impulse

If the force acting on a particle is known explicitly as a function of time, then the equation of motion, for constant mass, is

$$F(t) = m\frac{dv}{dt}$$

This can be integrated directly to give

$$\int_0^t F(t)dt = mv(t) - mv_0 \tag{2.17}$$

The integral $\int F(t)dt$ is called the *impulse*.[8] It is equal to the change of momentum imparted to a body by the force $F(t)$ acting over a certain time interval. (Here we have arbitrarily taken the initial value of t to be zero.)

The position of the particle as a function of time can be found by a second integration. First we rewrite Equation 2.17 in the form

---

[7] According to kinetic theory, the average speed of a gas molecule is equal to $(3kT/m)^{1/2}$ where $k =$ Boltzmann's constant $= 1.38 \times 10^{-16}$ erg per degree, T is the absolute temperature, and m is the mass of the molecule.

[8] The use of the impulse concept will be taken up in Chapter 7.

$$\frac{dx}{dt} = v(t) = v_0 + \int_0^t \frac{F(t)}{m} dt \tag{2.18}$$

which then gives

$$x - x_0 = \int_0^t v(t)dt = v_0 t + \int_0^t \left[\int_0^t \frac{F(t')}{m} dt' \right] dt \tag{2.19}$$

It should be noted that *only* in the case of the force being given as a function of t is the solution of the equation of motion expressible as a simple double integral. In all other cases, the various methods of solving second order differential equations must be used to find the position x as a function of t.

Examples

2.4   *Constant force.* The previously discussed case of a constant force, Section 2.2, is clearly a special case of a time-dependent force. Thus Equations 2.18 and 2.19 become

$$v(t) = v_0 + \frac{F}{m} \int_0^t dt = v_0 + \frac{Ft}{m}$$

$$x(t) = x_0 + v_0 t + \int_0^t \frac{Ft}{m} dt = x_0 + v_0 t + \frac{Ft^2}{2m}$$

which are equivalent to the case of uniform acceleration with $a = F/m$. (See Equation 2.9a and 2.9b.)

2.5   *Step force.* Suppose a body of mass m is subject to a constant force F_1 that acts for a certain length of time t_1 and then the force suddenly changes to a different (constant) value F_2. We apply the result of the previous example piecewise: For $0 \le t \le t_1$ we have $v = v_0 + F_1 t/m$ and $x = x_0 + v_0 t + (F_1 t^2/2m)$. These give the initial values of v and x at $t = t_1$ for the second interval, in which we make the substitution $t - t_1$ for t, thus

$$v(t) = v_0 + \frac{F_1 t_1}{m} + \frac{F_2}{m}(t - t_1)$$

$$x(t) = x_0 + v_0 t_1 + \frac{F_1 t_1^2}{2m} + \left(v_0 + \frac{F_1 t_1}{m} \right)(t - t_1) + \frac{F_2}{2m}(t - t_1)^2$$

for $t > t_1$. The procedure can be repeated for any number of steps in the force function. ∎

2.6   *Uniformly increasing force. The jerk.* Suppose a body of mass m is initially at rest and that at time $t = 0$ a constantly increasing force is applied: $F(t) = ct$. This might represent the effective force driving an automobile forward if the driver presses down increasingly on the accelerator. The differential equation of motion is

$$m \frac{dv}{dt} = ct$$

Then

$$v = \int_0^t \frac{ct}{m} dt = \frac{ct^2}{2m}$$

and

$$x = \int_0^t \frac{ct^2}{2m} dt = \frac{ct^3}{6m}$$

where the initial position is at the origin ($x = 0$). Thus v increases *quadratically* with time, and the displacement x increases as the *cube* of t. Note that the third derivative of x with respect to time is constant in this case: $d^3x/dt^3 = c/m$. The time-rate of change of acceleration, which is the third time derivative of displacement, has been termed the "jerk."

■

2.5   Velocity-Dependent Forces. Fluid Resistance and Terminal Velocity

It often happens that the force that acts on a body is a function of the velocity of the body. This is true, for example, in the case of viscous resistance exerted on a body moving through a fluid. If the force can be expressed as a function of v only, the differential equation of motion may be written in either of the two forms

$$F_0 + F(v) = m\frac{dv}{dt} \tag{2.20}$$

$$F_0 + F(v) = mv\frac{dv}{dx} \tag{2.21}$$

Here F_0 is any constant force that doesn't depend on v. Upon separating variables, integration then yields either t or x as functions of v. A second integration can then yield a functional relationship between x and t.

For normal fluid resistance, including air resistance, $F(v)$ is not a simple function and generally must be found through experimental measurements. However, a fair approximation for many cases is given by the equation

$$F(v) = -c_1 v - c_2 v|v| = -v(c_1 + c_2|v|) \tag{2.22}$$

in which c_1 and c_2 are constants whose values depend on the size and shape of the body. (The absolute-value sign is necessary on the last term because the force of fluid resistance is always opposite to the direction of v.) If the above form for $F(v)$ is used to find the motion by solving Equations 2.20 or 2.21, the resulting integrals are somewhat messy. But for the limiting cases of either small v or large v, respectively, the linear or the quadratic term in $F(v)$ dominates and the differential equations become somewhat more manageable.

For spheres in air, approximate values for the constants in the equation for $F(v)$ are, in SI units

$$c_1 = 1.55 \times 10^{-4}D$$

$$c_2 = 0.22\, D^2$$

where D is the diameter of the sphere in meters. The ratio of the quadratic term $c_2v|v|$ to the linear term c_1v is thus $\dfrac{0.22v|v|D^2}{1.55 \times 10^{-4}vD} = 1.4 \times 10^3|v|D$. This means that, for instance, with objects of baseball size ($D \sim 0.07$m) the quadradic term dominates for speeds in excess of 0.01 m/s(1 cm/s), and the linear term dominates for speeds less than this value. For speeds around this value *both* terms must be taken into account. (See Problem 2.13.)

Examples

2.7   *Horizontal motion with linear resistance.* Suppose a block is projected with initial velocity v_0 on a smooth horizontal surface and that there is air resistance such that the linear term dominates. Then, in the direction of the motion, $F_0 = 0$ in Equations 2.20 and 2.21 and $F(v) = -c_1v$. The differential equation of motion is then

$$-c_1v = m\frac{dv}{dt}$$

which gives, upon integrating,

$$t = \int_{v_0}^{v} -\frac{m\,dv}{c_1v} = -\frac{m}{c_1}\ln\left(\frac{v}{v_0}\right)$$

We can easily solve for v as a function of t by multiplying by $-c_1/m$ and taking the exponent of both sides. The result is

$$v = v_0e^{-c_1t/m}$$

Thus the velocity decreases exponentially with time. A second integration gives

$$x = \int_0^t v_0e^{-c_1t/m}dt$$

$$= \frac{mv_0}{c_1}(1 - e^{-c_1t/m})$$

showing that the block approaches a limiting position given by $x_{lim} = mv_0/c_1$.   ∎

2.8   *Horizontal motion with quadratic resistance.* If the parameters are such that the quadratic term dominates, then for positive v, we can write

$$-c_2v^2 = m\frac{dv}{dt}$$

which gives

$$t = \int_{v_0}^{v} \frac{-m\,dv}{c_2v^2} = \frac{m}{c_2}\left(\frac{1}{v} - \frac{1}{v_0}\right)$$

Solving for v, we get

$$v = \frac{v_0}{1 + kt}$$

where we have introduced the abbreviation $k = c_2 v_0/m$. Thus, for large values of kt the value of v diminishes like $1/t$. It is left as a problem to show that there is *no limiting position* in this case, that is, x becomes indefinitely large for large t.   ■

Vertical Fall Through a Fluid. Terminal Velocity

(a)   *Linear Case.* For an object falling vertically in a resisting fluid the force F_0 in Equations 2.20 and 2.21 is the weight of the object, namely $-mg$ for the x-axis positive in the upward direction. For the linear case of fluid resistance we then have for the differential equation of motion

$$-mg - c_1 v = m\frac{dv}{dt} \tag{2.23}$$

Separating variables and integrating, we find

$$t = \int_{v_0}^{v} \frac{m\, dv}{-mg - c_1 v} = -\frac{m}{c_1} \ln\frac{mg + c_1 v}{mg + c_1 v_0} \tag{2.24}$$

in which v_0 is the initial velocity at $t = 0$. Upon multiplying by $-c_1/m$ and taking the exponent we can solve for v:

$$v = -\frac{mg}{c_1} + \left(\frac{mg}{c_1} + v_0\right)e^{-c_1 t/m} \tag{2.25}$$

The exponential term drops to a negligible value after a sufficient time ($t \gg m/c_1$), and the velocity approaches the limiting value $-mg/c_1$. The limiting velocity of a falling body is called the *terminal velocity*; it is that velocity at which the force of resistance is just equal and opposite to the weight of the body so that the total force is zero, and so the acceleration is zero. The magnitude of the terminal velocity is the *terminal speed*.

Let us designate the terminal speed mg/c_1 by v_t, and let us write τ (which we may call the *characteristic time*) for m/c_1. Equation 2.25 may then be written in the more significant form

$$v = -v_t + (v_t + v_0)e^{-t/\tau} \tag{2.26}$$

In particular, for an object dropped from rest at time $t = 0$, $v_0 = 0$, we find

$$v = -v_t(1 - e^{-t/\tau}) \tag{2.27}$$

Thus after one characteristic time the speed is $1 - e^{-1}$ times the terminal speed, in two characteristics times it is the factor $1 - e^{-2}$ of v_t, and so on. After an interval of 5τ the speed is within one percent of the terminal value, namely $(1 - e^{-5})v_t = 0.993\, v_t$.

(b) *Quadratic case*. In this case the magnitude of $F(v)$ is proportional to v^2, and so the differential equation of motion is, remembering that we are taking the positive direction upward,

$$-mg \pm c_2 v^2 = m \frac{dv}{dt} \qquad (2.28)$$

The minus sign for the resistance term refers to upward motion (v positive), and the plus sign refers to downward motion (v negative). The double sign is necessary for any resistive force that involves an even power of v. As in the previous case, the differential equation of motion can be integrated to give t as a function of v:

$$t - t_0 = \int_{v_0}^{v} \frac{m\,dv}{-mg - c_2 v^2} = \tau\left(\tan^{-1}\frac{v_0}{v_t} - \tan^{-1}\frac{v}{v_t}\right) \qquad (rising)$$

$$t - t_0' = \int_{v_0}^{v} \frac{m\,dv}{-mg + c_2 v^2} = \tau\left(\tanh^{-1}\frac{v_0}{v_t} - \tanh^{-1}\frac{v}{v_t}\right) \qquad (falling)$$

where

$$\sqrt{\frac{m}{c_2 g}} = \tau \qquad (the\ characteristic\ time)$$

and

$$\sqrt{\frac{mg}{c_2}} = v_t \qquad (the\ terminal\ speed) \qquad (2.29)$$

Solving for v,

$$v = v_t \tan\left[\frac{t_0 - t}{\tau} + \tan^{-1}\frac{v_0}{v_t}\right] \qquad (rising) \qquad (2.30)$$

$$v = -v_t \tanh\left[\frac{t - t_0'}{\tau} - \tanh^{-1}\frac{v_0}{v_t}\right] \qquad (falling) \qquad (2.30a)$$

If the body is released from rest at time $t = 0$, then $t_0' = 0$. We have then, from the definition of the hyperbolic tangent,

$$v = -v_t \tanh\frac{t}{\tau} = -v_t\left(\frac{e^{t/\tau} - e^{-t/\tau}}{e^{t/\tau} + e^{-t/\tau}}\right) \qquad (2.31)$$

Again we see that the terminal speed is practically attained after the lapse of a few characteristic times, for example, for $t = 5\tau$, the speed is $0.99991\,v_t$. Graphs of speed versus time of fall for the linear and quadratic laws of resistance are shown in Figure 2.3. It is interesting to note that, in *both* the linear and the quadratic cases, the characteristic time is given by the same expression, namely

$$\tau = \frac{v_t}{g} \qquad (2.32)$$

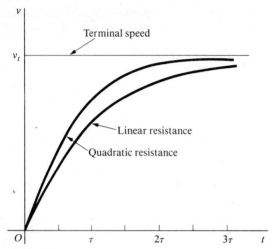

FIGURE 2.3   Graphs of speed versus time of fall for a falling body.

Example

2.9   *Falling raindrops and basketballs.* Calculate the terminal speed in air and characteristic time for (a) a very tiny spherical raindrop of diameter 0.1 mm = 10^{-4} m, and (b) a basketball of diameter 0.25 m and mass 0.6 kg. To decide which type of force law to use, quadratic or linear, we recall the expression stated earlier giving the ratio of the quadratic to the linear force for air resistance, namely $1.4 \times 10^3 |v| D$. For the raindrop this is $0.14v$, and for the basketball it is $350v$, numerically, where v is in m/s. Thus, for the raindrop v must exceed $1/0.14 = 7.1$ m/s for the quadratic force to dominate. In the case of the basketball v must exceed only $1/350 = 0.0029$ m/s for the quadratic force to dominate. We conclude that the linear case should hold for the falling raindrop, while the quadratic case should be correct for the basketball. (See also Problem 2.13.)

   The volume of the raindrop is $\pi D^3/6 = 0.52 \times 10^{-12}$ m³, so, multiplying by the density of water, 10^3 kg/m³, gives the mass $m = 0.52 \times 10^{-9}$ kg. For the drag coefficient we get $c_1 = 1.55 \times 10^{-4}D = 1.55 \times 10^{-8}$ Ns/m. This gives a terminal speed

$$v_t = \frac{mg}{c_1} = \frac{0.52 \times 10^{-9} \times 9.8}{1.55 \times 10^{-8}} \text{m/s} = 0.33 \text{ m/s}$$

The characteristic time is

$$\tau = \frac{v_t}{g} = \frac{0.33 \text{ m/s}}{9.8 \text{ m/s}^2} = 0.034 \text{ s}$$

   For the basketball the drag constant is $c_2 = 0.22D^2 = 0.22 \times (0.25)^2 = 0.0138$ Ns²/m², and so the terminal speed is

$$v_t = \left(\frac{mg}{c_2}\right)^{1/2} = \left(\frac{0.6 \times 9.8}{0.0138}\right)^{1/2} \text{m/s} = 20.6 \text{ m/s}$$

The characteristic time is

$$\tau = \frac{v_t}{g} = \frac{20.6 \text{ m/s}}{9.8 \text{ m/s}^2} = 2.1 \text{ s}$$

Thus the raindrop practically attains its terminal speed in less than one second when starting from rest, whereas it takes several seconds for the basketball to come to within one percent of the terminal value.

[For more information on aerodynamic drag the reader is referred to an article by C. Frohlich in *Am. J. Phys.*, **52**, 325 (1984), and the extensive list of references cited therein.]   ∎

PROBLEMS

2.1   Find the velocity $\dot{x}$ and the position x as functions of the time t for a particle of mass m which starts from rest at $x = 0$ and $t = 0$ subject to the following force functions:
(a) $F_x = F_0 + ct$
(b) $F_x = F_0 \sin ct$
(c) $F_x = F_0 e^{ct}$
where F_0 and c are positive constants.

2.2   Find the velocity $\dot{x}$ as a function of the displacement x for a particle of mass m which starts from rest at $x = 0$ subject to the following force functions:
(a) $F_x = F_0 + cx$
(b) $F_x = F_0 e^{-cx}$
(c) $F_x = F_0 \cos cx$
where F_0 and c are positive constants.

2.3   Find the potential energy function $V(x)$ for each of the forces in Problem 2.2.

2.4   Given that the velocity of a particle in rectilinear motion varies with the displacement x according to the equation

$$\dot{x} = bx^{-3}$$

where b is a positive constant, find the force acting on the particle as a function of x. (*Hint:* $F = m\ddot{x} = m\dot{x}\, d\dot{x}/dx$.)

2.5   Complete the last part of Example 2.8 to show that x becomes indefinitely large for large t.

2.6   An automobile of mass m is initially at rest. At time $t = 0$ a constant forward driving force F_0 is applied. After a time t_1 the force suddenly doubles to the value $2F_0$ and remains constant thereafter. Show that the total distance traveled at time $t = 2t_1$ is $(5/2)F_0 t_1^2/m$.

2.7   Do the above problem for the case in which the force has the same constant value F_0 from $t = 0$ to $t = t_1$, but then instead of doubling, the force increases *linearly* with time (constant jerk) such that at time $t = 2t_1$ the force has the value $2F_0$. In this case show that the total distance traveled at time $t = 2t_1$ is $(13/6)F_0 t_1^2/m$.

2.8   A block of wood is projected up an inclined plane with initial speed v_0. If the inclination of the plane is 30° and the coefficient of sliding friction $\mu = 0.1$, find the total time for the block to return to the point of projection.

2.9   A metal block of mass m slides on a horizontal surface which has been lubricated with a heavy oil such that the block suffers a viscous resistance that varies as the three-halves power of the speed:

$$F(v) = -cv^{3/2}$$

If the initial speed of the block is v_0 at $x = 0$, show that the block cannot travel farther than $2mv_0^{1/2}/c$.

2.10   A gun is fired straight up. Assuming that the air drag on the bullet varies quadratically with speed, show that the speed varies with height according to the equations

$$v^2 = Ae^{-2kx} - \frac{g}{k} \qquad \text{(upward motion)}$$

$$v^2 = \frac{g}{k} - Be^{2kx} \qquad \text{(downward motion)}$$

in which A and B are constants of integration, g is the acceleration of gravity, and $k = c_2/m$ where c_2 is the drag constant and m is the mass of the bullet. (*Note:* x is measured positive upward, and the gravitational force is assumed to be constant.)

2.11   Use the above result to show that when the bullet hits the ground on its return the speed will be equal to the expression

$$\frac{v_0 v_t}{(v_0^2 + v_t^2)^{1/2}}$$

in which v_0 is the initial upward speed and

$$v_t = (mg/c_2)^{1/2} = \text{terminal speed} = (g/k)^{1/2}$$

(This result allows one to find the fraction of the initial kinetic energy lost through air friction.)

2.12   A particle of mass m is released from rest a distance b from a fixed origin of force that attracts the particle according to the inverse square law

$$F(x) = -kx^{-2}$$

Show that the time required for the particle to reach the origin is

$$\pi \left(\frac{mb^3}{8k} \right)^{1/2}$$

2.13   Show that the terminal speed of a falling spherical object is given by

$$v_t = [(mg/c_2) + (c_1/2c_2)^2]^{1/2} - (c_1/2c_2)$$

when *both* the linear and the quadratic terms in the drag force are taken into account.

2.14   Use the above result to calculate the terminal speed of a soap bubble of mass 10^{-7} kg and diameter 10^{-2} m. Compare with the value obtained by using Equation 2.29.

2.15   Given: The force acting on a particle is the product of a function of the distance and a function of the velocity: $F(x,v) = f(x)g(v)$. Show that the differential equation of motion can be solved by integration. If the force is a product of a function of distance and a function of time, can the equation of motion be solved by simple integration? Can it be solved if the force is a product of a function of time and a function of velocity?

2.16   The force acting on a particle of mass m is given by

$$F = kvx$$

in which k is a positive constant. The particle passes through the origin with speed v_0 at time $t = 0$. Find x as a function of t.

3

The Harmonic Oscillator

3.1 Introduction

Of the many varieties of motional phenomena that we see in everyday life, one of the most common is *periodic motion*: a child playing on a swing, the rise and fall of the tides, the swaying of a tree in the wind, and so on. For simple systems, periodic or oscillatory motion can take place if the system has an equilibrium position, and there exists a force which tends to restore the system to equilibrium whenever it is disturbed. Owing to its singular importance, we shall devote a separate chapter to the study of oscillatory motion. We shall also have occasion to refer to our results in later chapters.

3.2 Linear Restoring Force. Harmonic Motion

The simplest and most fundamental type of restoring force is the *linear* case. An example of such a force is that exerted by an elastic cord or spring that obeys Hooke's law:

$$F = -k(X - X_e) \tag{3.1}$$

Here X is the total length of the spring, and X_e is the unstretched or equilibrium length. The constant of proportionality k is called the *stiffness*. The quantity $X - X_e$ is the displacement from equilibrium (where $F = 0$). Let us label the displacement x, so we can write Hooke's law as

$$F(x) = -kx \tag{3.2}$$

55

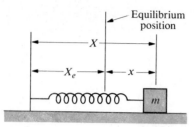

FIGURE 3.1   A model of the linear harmonic oscillator.

If such a force is exerted on a body of mass m, such as a block on a frictionless horizontal surface, as shown in Figure 3.1, Newton's second law gives $m\ddot{x} = -kx$, or

$$m\ddot{x} + kx = 0 \tag{3.3}$$

The above type of differential equation of motion is met in a wide variety of physical problems. In the particular example that we are using here, the constants m and k refer to the mass of a body and to the stiffness of a spring, respectively, and the displacement x is a distance. The same equation is encountered, as we shall see later, in the case of a pendulum, where the displacement is an angle, and where the constants involve the acceleration of gravity and the length of the pendulum. Again, in certain types of electrical circuits, this equation is found to apply, where the constants represent the circuit parameters, and the quantity x represents electric current or voltage.

  Equation 3.3 can be solved in a number of ways. It is one example of an important class of differential equations known as *linear differential equations with constant coefficients*.[1] Many, if not most, of the differential equations of physics are second-order differential equations. To solve Equation 3.3 we shall employ the trial method in which the function e^{qt} is the trial solution, where q is a constant to be determined. If $x = e^{qt}$ is, in fact, a solution, then for all values of t we must have

$$m\frac{d^2}{dt^2}e^{qt} + ke^{qt} = 0$$

which reduces, upon differentiating and canceling the common factors, to the *auxiliary equation*

$$mq^2 + k = 0$$

that is $q^2 = -k/m$, so q is imaginary:

$$q = \pm i\sqrt{\frac{k}{m}} = \pm i\omega_0$$

---

[1] The general nth-order equation of this type is

$$c_n\frac{d^nx}{dt^n} + \ldots + c_2\frac{d^2x}{dt^2} + c_1\frac{dx}{dt} + c_0x = b(t)$$

The equation is called *homogeneous* if $b = 0$. The most general solution contains n functions and n constants of integration as coefficients of the functions. *All* of these functions and n constants are required in order to fit the solution to arbitrary boundary conditions. See any standard text on differential equations.

where $i = \sqrt{-1}$, and we have introduced the abbreviation

$$\omega_0 = \sqrt{\frac{k}{m}} \tag{3.4}$$

Thus our trial method yields two solutions of the mathematical form $e^{i\omega_0 t}$ and $e^{-i\omega_0 t}$ What does this mean? To answer this question we shall digress momentarily to discuss the complex exponential function e^{iu}.

According to a theorem by Euler[2] the complex exponential is expressible in terms of ordinary trigonometric functions by the relations

$$e^{iu} = \cos u + i \sin u \tag{3.5}$$
$$e^{-iu} = \cos u - i \sin u$$

or equivalently

$$\cos u = \frac{e^{iu} + e^{-iu}}{2} \tag{3.5a}$$

$$\sin u = \frac{e^{iu} - e^{-iu}}{2i}$$

Furthermore, it is a handy property of linear differential equations that if $x_1(t)$ and $x_2(t)$ are known solutions in terms of the independent variable t, then *any* linear combination $C_1x_1 + C_2x_2$ is also a solution. The constants C_1 and C_2 are arbitrary. [This is easily verified by direct substitution: In our case we have $m\dfrac{d^2}{dt^2}(C_1x_1 + C_2x_2) + k(C_1x_1 + C_2x_2) = C_1(m\ddot{x}_1 + kx_1) + C_2(m\ddot{x}_2 + kx_2) = 0$ since x_1 and x_2 are solutions.]

The upshot of all this is that we can express the *general* solution of our differential equation of motion as a linear combination

$$x(t) = C_+e^{i\omega_0 t} + C_-e^{-i\omega_0 t} \tag{3.6}$$

or equivalently

$$x(t) = A \cos \omega_0 t + B \sin \omega_0 t \tag{3.7}$$

in which $C_+ = \dfrac{1}{2}(A - iB)$ and $C_- = \dfrac{1}{2}(A + iB)$. We want $x(t)$ and A and B to be *real*, so C_+ and C_- are conjugate complex quantities.[3] Finally, a third way of expressing our solution is found by use of the trigonometric identity $\cos(\alpha - \beta) = \cos \alpha \cos \beta + \sin \alpha \sin \beta$ which gives

$$x(t) = \mathscr{A} \cos(\omega_0 t - \varphi) \tag{3.8}$$

where $A = \mathscr{A} \cos \varphi$ and $B = \mathscr{A} \sin \varphi$, so that $A^2 + B^2 = \mathscr{A}^2 \sin^2 \varphi + \mathscr{A}^2 \cos^2 \varphi = \mathscr{A}^2$, and $B/A = \mathscr{A} \sin \varphi / \mathscr{A} \cos \varphi = \sin \varphi / \cos \varphi = \tan \varphi$.

The physical motion represented by our mathematical solution is a sinusoidal

---

[2] A proof is given in Appendix D.
[3] We shall use roman, rather than italic type, to distinguish complex quantities.

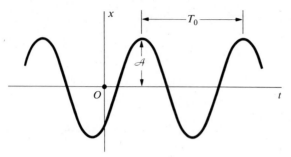

FIGURE 3.2 Graph of the displacement versus time for the harmonic oscillator.

oscillation of the displacement x, Figure 3.2. This is known as *harmonic motion*. The maximum displacement is called the *amplitude* of the oscillation; it is the constant $\mathcal{A}$ in Equation 3.8, or $(A^2 + B^2)^{1/2}$ from Equation 3.7. The coefficient ω_0 is called the *angular frequency*. The *period* T_0 of the oscillation is the time required for one complete cycle, that is, the time for which the argument of the sine or cosine terms increases by exactly 2π. Thus $T_0\omega_0 = 2\pi$, or

$$T_0 = \frac{2\pi}{\omega_0} = 2\pi\sqrt{\frac{m}{k}} \tag{3.9}$$

The *linear frequency* is defined as the number of cycles per unit of time. It is denoted by the symbol f_0, and so

$$2\pi f_0 = \omega_0 \tag{3.10}$$

$$f_0 = \frac{1}{T_0} = \frac{1}{2\pi}\sqrt{\frac{k}{m}} \tag{3.11}$$

It is common usage to employ the word "frequency" for either angular or linear frequency; which is meant is usually clear from the context. The unit of linear frequency (cycles per second or s^{-1}) is called the *hertz* (hz) in honor of Heinrich Hertz, who first demonstrated the existence of radio waves.

Constants of the Motion and Initial Conditions

The expressions for the displacement of the harmonic oscillator as a function of time, Equations 3.6, 3.7, and 3.8 each contain *two* arbitrary constants: C_+ and C_-, A and B, $\mathcal{A}$ and φ, respectively. The values of these constants are related to the initial conditions. Thus, if the block in Figure 3.1 is initially displaced by an amount x_0, and is given a velocity $\dot{x}_0$ at time $t = 0$, then in Equation 3.7 we see that $x_0 = A$. By differentiating we have $\dot{x}(t) = -A\omega_0 \sin \omega_0 t + B\omega_0 \cos \omega_0 t$, so $\dot{x}_0 = B\omega_0$, and the complete expression for the displacement is

$$x(t) = x_0 \cos \omega_0 t + \frac{\dot{x}_0}{\omega_0} \sin \omega_0 t \tag{3.12}$$

The amplitude of the oscillation is $\mathscr{A} = (A^2 + B^2)^{1/2} = \left(x_0^2 + \dfrac{\dot{x}_0^2}{\omega_0^2}\right)^{1/2}$. The com-

plex constants are then given by $C_+ = \dfrac{1}{2}\left(x_0 - i\dfrac{\dot{x}_0}{\omega_0}\right)$, $C_- = \dfrac{1}{2}\left(x_0 + i\dfrac{\dot{x}_0}{\omega_0}\right)$, and

the phase constant $\varphi = \tan^{-1}(\dot{x}_0/x_0\omega_0)$.

Effect of a Constant External Force on A Harmonic Oscillator

Suppose the same spring shown in Figure 3.1 is held in a vertical position supporting the same mass m, Figure 3.3. The total force acting is now given by adding the weight mg to the restoring force

$$F = -k(X - X_e) + mg \qquad (3.13)$$

where the positive direction is down. This equation could be written $F = -kx + mg$ by defining x to be $X - X_e$, as previously. However, it is more convenient to define the variable x in a different way, namely, as the displacement from the *new* equilibrium position X'_e obtained by setting $F = 0$ in Equation 3.13: $0 = -k(X'_e - X_e) + mg$ which gives $X'_e = X_e + mg/k$. We now define the displacement as

$$x = X - X'_e = X - X_e - mg/k$$

Putting this into Equation 3.13 gives, after a very little algebra

$$F = -kx$$

so the differential equation of motion is again

$$m\ddot{x} + kx = 0$$

and our solution in terms of our newly defined x is identical to that of the horizontal case. It should now be evident that *any* constant external force applied to a harmonic

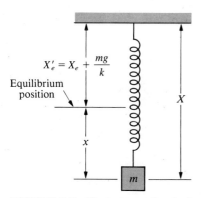

FIGURE 3.3   Vertical case for the harmonic oscillator.

oscillator merely shifts the equilibrium position. The equation of motion remains unchanged if we measure the displacement x from the new equilibrium position.

Examples

3.1 When a light spring supports a block of mass m in a vertical position, the spring is found to stretch by an amount D_1 over its unstretched length. If the block is further pulled downward a distance D_2 from the equilibrium position and released, say at time $t = 0$, find (a) the resulting motion, (b) the velocity of the block when it passes back upward through the equilibrium position, and (c) the acceleration of the block at the top of its oscillatory motion.

Solution:

First, for the equilibrium position we have

$$F_x = 0 = -kD_1 + mg$$

where x is chosen positive downward. This gives us the value of the stiffness constant:

$$k = \frac{mg}{D_1}$$

From this we can find the angular frequency of oscillation:

$$\omega_0 = \sqrt{\frac{k}{m}} = \sqrt{\frac{g}{D_1}}$$

We shall express the motion in the form $x(t) = A \cos \omega_0 t + B \sin \omega_0 t$. Then $\dot{x} = -A\omega_0 \sin \omega_0 t + B\omega_0 \cos \omega_0 t$. From the initial conditions we find

$$x_0 = D_2 = A \qquad \dot{x}_0 = 0 = B\omega_0 \qquad B = 0$$

The motion is therefore given by

(a) $$x(t) = D_2 \cos\left(\sqrt{\frac{g}{D_1}}\,t\right)$$

in terms of the given quantities. Note that the mass m does not appear in the final expression. The velocity is then

$$\dot{x}(t) = -D_2 \sqrt{\frac{g}{D_1}} \sin\left(\sqrt{\frac{g}{D_1}}\,t\right)$$

and the acceleration

$$\ddot{x}(t) = -D_2 \frac{g}{D_1} \cos\left(\sqrt{\frac{g}{D_1}}\,t\right)$$

As the block passes upward through the equilibrium position the argument of the sine term is $\pi/2$ (one-quarter period), so

(b) $$\dot{x} = -D_2 \sqrt{\frac{g}{D_1}} \qquad (center)$$

At the top of the swing the argument of the cosine term is π (one-half period), which gives

(c) $$\ddot{x} = D_2 \frac{g}{D_1} \qquad (top)$$

It is interesting to note that in the case $D_1 = D_2$ the downward acceleration at the top of the swing is just g. This means that the block, at that particular instant, is in *free fall*, that is, the spring is exerting zero force on the block.   ∎

3.2   *The simple pendulum.* The so-called simple pendulum consists of a small "bob" of mass m swinging at the end of a light inextensible string of length l, Figure 3.4. The motion is along a circular arc defined by the angle θ, as shown. The restoring force is the component of the weight $m\mathbf{g}$ acting in the direction of increasing θ along the path of motion: $F_s = -mg \sin \theta$. Treating the bob as a particle the differential equation of motion is therefore

$$m\ddot{s} = -mg \sin \theta$$

Now $s = l\theta$, and, for small θ, $\sin \theta = \theta$ to a fair approximation. So, after cancelling the m's and rearranging terms, we can write the differential equation of motion either in terms of θ or s as follows:

$$\ddot{\theta} + \frac{g}{l}\theta = 0 \qquad \ddot{s} + \frac{g}{l}s = 0$$

Although the motion is along a curved path rather than a straight line, the differential equation is mathematically identical to that of the linear harmonic oscillator, Equation 3.3, with the quantity g/l replacing k/m. Thus, to the extent that the approximation $\sin \theta = \theta$ is valid, we can conclude that the motion is simple harmonic with angular frequency

$$\omega_0 = \sqrt{\frac{g}{l}}$$

and period

$$T_0 = \frac{2\pi}{\omega_0} = 2\pi\sqrt{\frac{l}{g}}$$

It is interesting to note that the above formula gives a period of very nearly two seconds, or a half-period of one second, when the length l is one meter. More accurately, for a half-period of one second, known as the "seconds pendulum", the precise length is obtained by setting $T_0 = 2$ s and solving for l. This gives $l = g/\pi^2$, numerically, when g is expressed

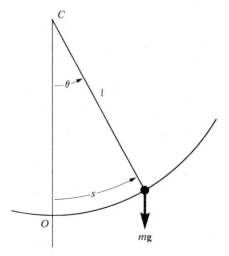

FIGURE 3.4   The simple pendulum.

in m/s^2. At sea level at a latitude of 45°, the value of the acceleration of gravity is $g = 9.8062$ m/s^2. Accordingly, the length of a seconds pendulum at that location is $9.8062/9.8696 = 0.9936$ m.   ∎

3.3   Energy Considerations in Harmonic Motion

Consider a particle under the action of a linear restoring force $F_x = -kx$. Let us calculate the work done by an external force F_{ext} in moving the particle from the equilibrium position ($x = 0$) to some position x. We have $F_{ext} = -F_x = kx$, so

$$W = \int_0^x F_{ext}\,dx = \int_0^x kx\,dx = \frac{k}{2}x^2$$

In the case of a spring obeying Hooke's law the work is stored in the spring as potential energy: $W = V(x)$ where

$$V(x) = \frac{1}{2}kx^2 \tag{3.14}$$

Thus $F_x = -dV/dx = -kx$ as required by the definition of V. The total energy, when the particle is undergoing harmonic motion, is given by the sum of the kinetic and potential energies, namely

$$E = \frac{1}{2}m\dot{x}^2 + \frac{1}{2}kx^2 \tag{3.15}$$

This equation epitomizes the harmonic oscillator in a rather fundamental way: *the kinetic energy is quadratic in the velocity variable, and the potential energy is quadratic in the displacement variable.* The total energy is constant if there are no other forces except the restoring force acting on the particle.

The motion of the particle can be found by starting with the energy equation (3.15). Solving for the velocity gives

$$\frac{dx}{dt} = \pm\left(\frac{2E}{m} - \frac{k}{m}x^2\right)^{1/2} \tag{3.16}$$

which can be integrated to give t as a function of x as follows:

$$t = \int \frac{dx}{\pm[(2E/m) - (k/m)x^2]^{1/2}} = \mp (m/k)^{1/2}\cos^{-1}(x/\mathscr{A}) + C \tag{3.17}$$

in which C is a constant of integration and $\mathscr{A}$ is the amplitude given by

$$\mathscr{A} = \left(\frac{2E}{k}\right)^{1/2} \tag{3.18}$$

Upon solving the integrated equation for x as a function of t, we find the same relationship as that of the previous section, with the addition that we now have an explicit value for the amplitude. We can also obtain the amplitude directly from the energy equation (3.15) by finding the turning points of the motion where $\dot{x} = 0$: the value of

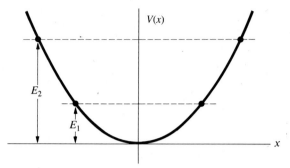

FIGURE 3.5   Graph of the parabolic potential energy function of the harmonic oscillator. The turning points defining the amplitude are indicated for two different values of the total energy.

x must lie between $(2E/k)^{1/2}$ and $-(2E/k)^{1/2}$ in order for $\dot{x}$ to be real. This is illustrated in Figure 3.5.

We also see from the energy equation that the maximum value of the speed, which we shall call v_{max}, occurs at $x = 0$. Accordingly, we can write

$$E = \frac{1}{2}mv_{max}^2 = \frac{1}{2}k\mathscr{A}^2 \tag{3.19}$$

As the particle oscillates, the kinetic and potential energies continually change. The constant total energy is entirely in the form of kinetic energy at the center where $x = 0$ and $\dot{x} = \pm v_{max}$, and it is all potential energy at the extrema where $\dot{x} = 0$ and $x = \pm \mathscr{A}$.

Example

3.3   *The energy function of the simple pendulum.* The potential energy of the simple pendulum is given by the expression

$$V = mgh$$

where h is the vertical distance from the reference level (which we choose to be the level of the equilibrium position). For a displacement through an angle θ, Figure 3.4, we see that $h = l - l\cos\theta$, so

$$V(\theta) = mgl\,(1 - \cos\theta)$$

Now the series expansion for the cosine is $\cos\theta = 1 - \dfrac{\theta^2}{2!} + \dfrac{\theta^4}{4!} - \ldots$, so for small θ we have approximately $\cos\theta = 1 - \theta^2/2$. This gives

$$V(\theta) = \frac{1}{2}mgl\,\theta^2$$

or, equivalently, since $s = l\theta$,

$$V(s) = \frac{1}{2}\frac{mg}{l}s^2$$

Thus, to a first approximation, the potential energy function is quadratic in the displacement variable. In terms of s, the total energy is given by

$$E = \frac{1}{2}m\dot{s}^2 + \frac{1}{2}\frac{mg}{l}s^2$$

in accordance with the general statement concerning the energy of the harmonic oscillator discussed above.   ∎

3.4   Damped Harmonic Motion

The foregoing analysis of the harmonic oscillator is somewhat idealized in that we have failed to take into account frictional forces. These are always present in a mechanical system to some extent. Analogously, there is always a certain amount of resistance in an electrical circuit. For a specific model let us consider an object of mass m that is supported by a light spring of stiffness k. We shall assume that there is a viscous retarding force varying *linearly* with the velocity, such as is produced by air drag at low speeds.[4] The forces are indicated in Figure 3.6.

If x is the displacement from equilibrium, then the restoring force is $-kx$, and the retarding force is $-c\dot{x}$ where c is a constant of proportionality. The differential equation of motion is therefore $m\ddot{x} = -kx - c\dot{x}$, or

$$m\ddot{x} + c\dot{x} + kx = 0 \tag{3.20}$$

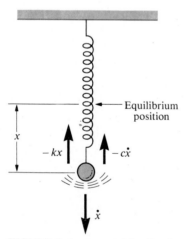

FIGURE 3.6   A model for the damped harmonic oscillator.

[4]Nonlinear drag is more realistic in many situations; however the equations of motion are very much more difficult to solve and will not be treated here.

As with the undamped case, we shall use as a trial solution the exponential function e^{qt}. This is a solution if

$$m\frac{d^2}{dt^2}e^{qt} + c\frac{d}{dt}e^{qt} + ke^{qt} = 0 \qquad (3.21)$$

for all t. This will be the case if q satisfies the auxiliary equation, obtained by performing the differentiations and cancelling the common factor e^{qt}:

$$mq^2 + cq + k = 0 \qquad (3.22)$$

The roots are given by the well-known quadratic formula

$$q = \frac{-c \pm (c^2 - 4mk)^{1/2}}{2m} \qquad (3.23)$$

Depending on the value of the discriminant $c^2 - 4mk$, there are three physically distinct cases:

I. $c^2 - 4mk > 0$ *overdamping*
II. $c^2 - 4mk = 0$ *critical damping*
III. $c^2 - 4mk < 0$ *underdamping*

We shall discuss the three cases separately.

I.   In the overdamped case there are two different real (negative) values of q, which we shall call $-\gamma_1$ and $-\gamma_2$:

$$q_1 = -\frac{c}{2m} + \left(\frac{c^2}{4m^2} - \frac{k}{m}\right)^{1/2} = -\gamma_1$$

$$q_2 = -\frac{c}{2m} - \left(\frac{c^2}{4m^2} - \frac{k}{m}\right)^{1/2} = -\gamma_2$$

The general solution is therefore a linear combination given by

$$x(t) = A_1 e^{-\gamma_1 t} + A_2 e^{-\gamma_2 t} \qquad (3.24)$$

The constants A_1 and A_2 are determined from the initial conditions. Since both terms represent exponential decay, the physical motion is also an exponential type of decay with two different decay constants. The system, given an initial displacement, returns to the equilibrium position without oscillating—the damping force dominates and prevents any periodic motion from taking place. A graph is shown in Figure 3.7.

II. In the case of critical damping the two roots are equal: $q_1 = q_2 = -c/2m = -\gamma$. Thus we have only *one* function, an exponential decay $e^{-\gamma t}$, as the solution of the differential equation of motion. We need to find another function satisfying the equation of motion in order to build up a general solution containing two different functions and constants; this is required in order that the solution may be fitted to arbitrary boundary conditions (initial displacement *and* velocity). To find the general solution we can go back to the original differential equation of motion (3.20) and rewrite it setting $c^2/4m = k = \gamma^2 m$, which is the condition

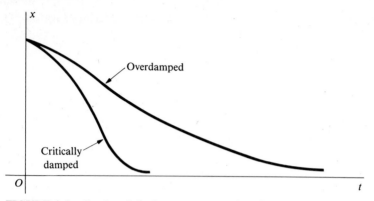

FIGURE 3.7   Graphs of displacement versus time for the overdamped and critically damped cases of the harmonic oscillator.

for equal roots for q. This gives $m(\ddot{x} + 2\gamma\dot{x} + \gamma^2 x) = 0$, which, upon deleting the m, can be factored as

$$\left(\frac{d}{dt} + \gamma\right)\left(\frac{d}{dt} + \gamma\right)x = 0$$

We now make the substitution $u = \gamma x + dx/dt$ which then gives

$$\left(\frac{d}{dt} + \gamma\right)u = 0$$

or $du/dt = -\gamma u$. This is easily integrated to give $\ln u = -\gamma t + A'$, or

$$u = Ae^{-\gamma t}$$

where A' is the constant of integration and $A = \ln A'$. Hence, from the definition of u, we have $Ae^{-\gamma t} = \gamma x + dx/dt$, or

$$A = \left(\gamma x + \frac{dx}{dt}\right)e^{\gamma t} = \frac{d}{dt}(xe^{\gamma t})$$

A second integration then yields $At + B = xe^{\gamma t}$ where B is a second constant of integration. Upon solving for x we finally arrive at the general solution:

$$x(t) = (At + B)e^{-\gamma t} = Ate^{-\gamma t} + Be^{-\gamma t} \tag{3.25}$$

Thus the other function we were seeking is the product $te^{-\gamma t}$, which also represents a decaying type of motion. Our general solution shows that the motion is nonoscillatory, as in the overdamped case. A graph is shown in Figure 3.7. Given an initial displacement, the system returns asymptotically to the equilibrium position. Critical damping, or approximately critical damping, gives an optimum return to equilibrium for certain applications, such as mechanical suspensions.

III.   If the resistance constant c is small enough so that $c^2 < 4mk$, we have the case of underdamping. In this case the quantity $c^2 - 4mk$ is negative in Equation 3.23; consequently the two values of q are complex numbers. It is convenient to express them in the form

$$q_1 = -\frac{c}{2m} + i\left(\frac{k}{m} - \frac{c^2}{4m^2}\right)^{1/2}$$

$$q_2 = -\frac{c}{2m} - i\left(\frac{k}{m} - \frac{c^2}{4m^2}\right)^{1/2}$$

Let us introduce the abbreviation

$$\omega_d = \left(\frac{k}{m} - \frac{c^2}{4m^2}\right)^{1/2} = (\omega_0^2 - \gamma^2)^{1/2} \tag{3.26}$$

where $\gamma = c/2m$ and $\omega_0 = (k/m)^{1/2}$. Then

$$q_1 = -\gamma + i\omega_d$$
$$q_2 = -\gamma - i\omega_d$$

The general solution of the equation of motion can then be expressed as the linear combination

$$x(t) = C_+ e^{(-\gamma + i\omega_d)t} + C_- e^{(-\gamma - i\omega_d)t} \tag{3.27}$$
$$= e^{-\gamma t}(C_+ e^{i\omega_d t} + C_- e^{-i\omega_d t})$$

We recognize the complex expression in parentheses as precisely the same as that obtained for the undamped harmonic oscillator, Equation 3.6, with ω_d replacing ω_0. Consequently, we can express the general solution in terms of trigonometric functions as follows:

$$x(t) = e^{-\gamma t}(A \cos \omega_d t + B \sin \omega_d t) \tag{3.28}$$

$$x(t) = e^{-\gamma t}\mathcal{A} \cos(\omega_d t - \varphi) \tag{3.29}$$

in which the constants C_+, C_-, A, B, $\mathcal{A}$, and φ are related in the same way as they were in the undamped case: $C_\pm = (A \mp iB)/2$, $A^2 + B^2 = \mathcal{A}^2$, and $\tan \varphi = B/A$.

The physical motion is perhaps best interpreted by considering Equation 3.29. We see that the motion is given by the product of an exponential decay and a sinusoidal oscillation of angular frequency ω_d. Since Equation 3.26 tells us that ω_d is less than ω_0, the presence of damping causes the oscillation to be slower than it would be in the absence of damping. The corresponding period T_d is the natural period of the freely running harmonic oscillator with damping:

$$T_d = 2\pi/\omega_d = 2\pi/(\omega_0^2 - \gamma^2)^{1/2} \tag{3.30}$$

A plot of the motion is shown in Figure 3.8. Equation 3.29 shows that the two curves given by $x = \mathcal{A}e^{-\gamma t}$ and $x = -\mathcal{A}e^{-\gamma t}$ form an envelope of the curve of motion, because the cosine factor takes on values between $+1$ and -1, including $+1$ and -1, at which points the curve of motion touches the envelope. Accordingly, the points of contact are separated by a time interval of one-half

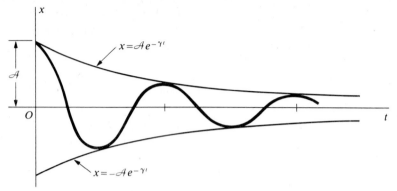

FIGURE 3.8   Graph of displacement versus time for the underdamped harmonic oscillator.

period $T_d/2$. These points, however, are not quite the maxima and minima of the displacement. It is left to the student to show that the actual maxima and minima are also separated in time by the same amount. In one complete period the amplitude diminishes by a factor $e^{-\gamma T_d}$; also, in a time $\gamma^{-1} = 2m/c$ the amplitude decays by a factor $e^{-1} = 0.3679$.

In summary, our analysis of the freely running harmonic oscillator has shown that the presence of damping of the linear type causes the oscillator, given an initial motion, to return eventually to a state of rest at the equilibrium position. The return to equilibrium is either oscillatory, or not, depending on the amount of damping. The critical condition, given by $c^2 = 4mk$, characterizes the limiting case of the nonoscillatory mode of return.

Mechanical Suspensions

Consider a mechanical system with linear damping. For fixed values of the damping constant c and stiffness k, the criterion determining the type of damping is determined by the value of the mass. If the system is critically damped for a certain critical mass m_{crit}, we have $c^2 = 4km_{crit}$. The discriminant is then

$$c^2 - 4km = 4k(m_{crit} - m)$$

so the system will be overdamped, or underdamped, respectively, depending on whether the mass is less than, or greater than m_{crit}. Thus, in an automobile suspension system (springs and shock absorbers) increasing the load (passengers) causes the system to tend to be underdamped or oscillatory, while decreasing the load results in a stiffer, nonoscillatory condition.

Energy Considerations

The total energy of the damped harmonic oscillator is given by the sum of the kinetic and potential energies

$$E = \frac{1}{2}m\dot{x}^2 + \frac{1}{2}kx^2$$

This is constant for the undamped oscillator, as stated previously. Let us differentiate the above expression with respect to t:

$$\frac{dE}{dt} = m\dot{x}\ddot{x} + kx\dot{x} = (m\ddot{x} + kx)\dot{x}$$

Now the differential equation of motion is $m\ddot{x} + c\dot{x} + kx = 0$, or $m\ddot{x} + kx = -c\dot{x}$. Thus we can write

$$\frac{dE}{dt} = -c\dot{x}^2$$

for the time rate of change of total energy. We see that it is given by the product of the damping force and the velocity. Since this is always either zero or negative, the total energy continually decreases, and, like the amplitude, eventually becomes negligibly small. The energy is dissipated as frictional heat by virtue of the viscous resistance to the motion.

Examples

3.4 An automobile suspension system is critically damped, and its period of free oscillation with no damping is one second. If the system is initially displaced by an amount x_0, and released with zero initial velocity, find the displacement at $t = 1$ s.

Solution:
  For critical damping we have $\gamma = c/2m = (k/m)^{1/2} = \omega_0 = 2\pi/T_0$. Hence $\gamma = 2\pi$ s^{-1} in our case, since $T_0 = 1$ s. Now the general expression for the displacement in the critically damped case, Equation 3.25, is $x(t) = (At + B)e^{-\gamma t}$, so, for $t = 0$, $x_0 = B$. Differentiating, we have $\dot{x}(t) = (A - \gamma B - \gamma At)e^{-\gamma t}$ which gives $\dot{x}_0 = A - \gamma B = 0$, so $A = \gamma B = \gamma x_0$ in our problem. Accordingly,

$$x(t) = x_0(1 + \gamma t)e^{-\gamma t} = x_0(1 + 2\pi t)e^{-2\pi t}$$

is the displacement as a function of time. For $t = 1$ s, we obtain $x_0(1 + 2\pi)e^{-2\pi} = x_0(7.28)e^{-6.28} = 0.0136\ x_0$. The system has practically returned to equilibrium. ∎

3.5 The frequency of a damped harmonic oscillator is one-half the frequency of the same oscillator with no damping. Find the ratio of the maxima of successive oscillations.

Solution:
  We have $\omega_d = \frac{1}{2}\omega_0 = (\omega_0^2 - \gamma^2)^{1/2}$ which gives $\omega_0^2/4 = \omega_0^2 - \gamma^2$, so $\gamma = \omega_0(3/4)^{1/2}$. Consequently

$$\gamma T_d = \omega_0(3/4)^{1/2}[2\pi/(\omega_0/2)] = 10.88$$

Thus the amplitude ratio is

$$e^{-\gamma T_d} = e^{-10.88} = 0.00002$$

This is a *highly damped* oscillator. ∎

3.6   Given: The terminal speed of a baseball in free fall is 30 m/s. Assuming a linear air drag, calculate the effect of air resistance on a simple pendulum using a baseball as the "bob".

Solution:

In Chapter 2 we found the terminal speed for the case of linear air drag to be given by $v_t = mg/c_1$ where c_1 is the linear drag coefficient. This gives

$$\gamma = \frac{c_1}{2m} = \frac{(mg/v_t)}{2m} = \frac{g}{2v_t} = \frac{9.8 \text{ms}^{-2}}{60 \text{ ms}^{-1}} = 0.163 \text{ s}^{-1}$$

for the exponential damping constant. Consequently, the baseball pendulum's amplitude drops off by a factor e^{-1} in a time $\gamma^{-1} = 6.13$ s. Note that this is independent of the length of the pendulum. Earlier, in Example 3.2, we showed that the angular frequency of oscillation of the simple pendulum of length l is given by $\omega_0 = (g/l)^{1/2}$ for *small* amplitude. Therefore, from Equation 3.30, the period of our pendulum is

$$T_d = 2\pi(\omega_0^2 - \gamma^2)^{-1/2} = 2\pi\left(\frac{g}{l} - 0.0265 \text{ s}^{-2}\right)^{-1/2}$$

In particular, for a baseball "seconds pendulum" for which the half-period is one second in the absence of damping, we have $g/l = \pi^2$, so the half-period with damping in our case is

$$\frac{T_d}{2} = \pi(\pi^2 - 0.0265)^{-1/2} \text{ s} = 1.00134 \text{ s}$$

Our solution somewhat exaggerates the effect of air resistance, because the drag function for a baseball is more nearly quadratic in the velocity, rather than linear, except at very low velocities as discussed in Section 2.5.   ∎

3.5   Forced Harmonic Motion. Resonance

In this section we shall study the motion of a damped harmonic oscillator that is driven by an external force F_{ext}. The total applied force is then the sum of three forces: the elastic restoring force $-kx$, the viscous damping force $-c\dot{x}$, and the driving force F_{ext}. The differential equation of motion is therefore $-kx - c\dot{x} + F_{ext} = m\ddot{x}$, or, upon transposing terms

$$m\ddot{x} + c\dot{x} + kx = F_{ext} \tag{3.31}$$

In particular, we are interested in the motion produced by a harmonic type of force, that is, when F_{ext} varies sinusoidally with time. We could then take $F_{ext} = F_0 \cos \omega t$ where F_0 is the amplitude and ω is the angular frequency of the driving force. Although it is quite straightforward to solve the differential equation using the above trigonometric form for the driving force, it is algebraically simpler to use the complex exponential form

$$F_{ext} = F_0 e^{i\omega t}$$

so that

$$m\ddot{x} + c\dot{x} + kx = F_0 e^{i\omega t} \tag{3.32}$$

Mathematically, the variable x is now a complex number. But that needn't bother us, because if we find a solution of the above equation, we can be sure that the real parts of both sides are equal (as well as the imaginary parts), and it is the real part that represents the physical motion.

The solution of the above linear differential equation is given by the sum of two parts: the first is the solution of the homogeneous equation $m\ddot{x} + c\dot{x} + kx = 0$, which we have already solved in the previous section; the second is any particular solution that we are able to find. As we know, the solution of the homogeneous equation represents a motion, oscillatory or nonoscillatory, which eventually decays to zero—it is called the *transient term*. We are here interested in a solution that depends on the nature of the driving force. This force is constant in amplitude and varies sinusoidally with time, so we may reasonably expect to find a solution for which the displacement x also has the same sinusoidal time dependence. Therefore, for the *steady-state* condition, we shall try a solution of the complex exponential type

$$x(t) = Ae^{i(\omega t - \varphi)} \tag{3.33}$$

where the amplitude A and phase difference φ are constants to be determined. If this "guess" is correct, we must have

$$m\frac{d^2}{dt^2}Ae^{i(\omega t - \varphi)} + c\frac{d}{dt}Ae^{i(\omega t - \varphi)} + kAe^{i(\omega t - \varphi)} = F_0e^{i\omega t}$$

hold for all values of t. Upon performing the indicated operations and cancelling the common factor $e^{i\omega t}$, we find

$$-m\omega^2A + i\omega cA + kA = F_0e^{i\varphi} = F_0(\cos\varphi + i\sin\varphi) \tag{3.34}$$

Equating the real and imaginary parts yields the two equations

$$A(k - m\omega^2) = F_0\cos\varphi \tag{3.35}$$

$$c\omega A = F_0\sin\varphi$$

Upon dividing the second by the first and using the identity $\tan\varphi = \sin\varphi/\cos\varphi$, we obtain the following relation for the phase angle

$$\tan\varphi = \frac{c\omega}{k - m\omega^2} \tag{3.36}$$

By squaring both sides of Equations 3.35 and adding and employing the identity $\sin^2\varphi + \cos^2\varphi = 1$, we find

$$A^2(k - m\omega^2)^2 + c^2\omega^2A^2 = F_0^2$$

We can then solve for A, the amplitude of the steady-state oscillation, as a function of the driving frequency

$$A(\omega) = \frac{F_0}{[(k - m\omega^2)^2 + c^2\omega^2]^{1/2}} \tag{3.37}$$

In terms of our previous abbreviations $\omega_0^2 = k/m$ and $\gamma = c/2m$, we can write the expressions in another form as follows:

$$\tan \varphi = \frac{2\gamma\omega}{\omega_0^2 - \omega^2} \tag{3.38}$$

$$A(\omega) = \frac{F_0/m}{[(\omega_0^2 - \omega^2)^2 + 4\gamma^2\omega^2]^{1/2}} \tag{3.39}$$

$$A(\omega) = \frac{F_0/m}{D(\omega)} \tag{3.39a}$$

where $D(\omega) = [(\omega_0^2 - \omega^2)^2 + 4\gamma^2\omega^2]^{1/2}$.

The above result relating the amplitude and phase of the damped harmonic oscillator under the action of a sinusoidal driving force is of fundamental importance. A plot of $A(\omega)$ versus ω (Figure 3.9) shows that the amplitude assumes a maximum value at a certain applied frequency ω_r, called the *amplitude resonant frequency*, or simply resonant frequency for short. The function $D(\omega)$ defined above is known as the *resonance denominator*.

To find ω_r we calculate $dA/d\omega$ from Equation 3.39 and set the result equal to zero. Upon solving the resulting equation for ω we finally obtain

$$\omega_r = (\omega_0^2 - 2\gamma^2)^{1/2} \tag{3.40}$$

In the case of weak damping, that is, if γ is very small compared to ω_0, then the resonant frequency differs by only a small amount from ω_0, the frequency of the freely running undamped oscillator. Also, since the angular frequency of the freely running oscillator is given by $\omega_d = (\omega_0^2 - \gamma^2)^{1/2}$, we have

$$\omega_r = (\omega_d^2 - \gamma^2)^{1/2} \tag{3.41}$$

At the extreme of strong damping, no amplitude resonance occurs if $\gamma \geq \omega_0/\sqrt{2}$,

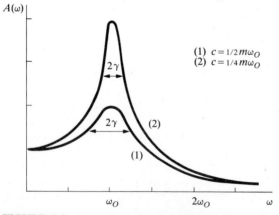

FIGURE 3.9   Graphs showing amplitude versus driving frequency for two values of the damping constant.

because the amplitude then becomes a monotonically decreasing function of ω. To see this, consider the limiting case $\gamma^2 = \omega_0^2/2$. Equation 3.39 then gives

$$A(\omega) = \frac{F_0/m}{[(\omega_0^2 - \omega^2)^2 + 2\omega_0^2\omega^2]^{1/2}} = \frac{F_0/m}{(\omega_0^4 + \omega^4)^{1/2}}$$

which clearly decreases with increasing values of ω starting with $\omega = 0$.

Amplitude of Oscillation at the Resonance Peak

The steady-state amplitude at the resonant frequency, which we shall call A_{max}, is obtained from Equations 3.39 and 3.40. The result is

$$A_{max} = \frac{F_0/m}{2\gamma\sqrt{\omega_0^2 - \gamma^2}} = \frac{F_0}{c\omega_d} \tag{3.42}$$

In the case of weak damping, we can neglect γ^2 and write

$$A_{max} \simeq \frac{F_0}{2\gamma m\omega_0} = \frac{F_0}{c\omega_0} \tag{3.42a}$$

Thus the amplitude of the induced oscillation at the resonant condition becomes very large if the damping constant c is very small, and conversely. In mechanical systems it may, or may not, be desirable to have large resonant amplitudes. In the case of electric motors, for example, rubber or spring mounts are used to minimize the transmission of vibration. The stiffness of these mounts is chosen so as to ensure that the resulting resonant frequency is far from the running frequency of the motor.

Sharpness of the Resonance. Quality Factor

The sharpness of the resonance peak is frequently of interest. Let us consider the case of weak damping $\gamma \ll \omega_0$. Then in the expression for steady-state amplitude, Equation 3.39, we can make the following substitutions:

$$\omega_0^2 - \omega^2 = (\omega_0 + \omega)(\omega_0 - \omega)$$
$$\simeq 2\omega_0(\omega_0 - \omega)$$
$$\gamma\omega \simeq \gamma\omega_0$$

These, together with the expression for A_{max}, allow us to write the amplitude equation in the following approximate form:

$$A(\omega) \simeq \frac{A_{max}\gamma}{\sqrt{(\omega_0 - \omega)^2 + \gamma^2}} \tag{3.43}$$

The above equation shows that when $|\omega_0 - \omega| = \gamma$, or equivalently, if

$$\omega = \omega_0 \pm \gamma$$

then

$$A^2 = \tfrac{1}{2}A_{max}^2$$

This means that γ is a measure of the width of the resonance curve. Thus 2γ is the frequency difference between the points for which the energy is down by a factor of $\frac{1}{2}$ from the energy at resonance, because the energy is proportional to A^2. This is illustrated in Figure 3.9.

Another way of designating the sharpness of the resonance peak is in terms of a parameter Q called the *quality factor* of a resonant system. It is defined as

$$Q = \frac{\omega_d}{2\gamma} \tag{3.44}$$

or, for weak damping

$$Q \simeq \frac{\omega_0}{2\gamma} \tag{3.44a}$$

Thus the total width $\Delta\omega$ at the half-energy points is approximately

$$\Delta\omega = 2\gamma \simeq \frac{\omega_0}{Q}$$

or, since $\omega = 2\pi f$,

$$\frac{\Delta\omega}{\omega_0} = \frac{\Delta f}{f_0} \simeq \frac{1}{Q} \tag{3.45}$$

giving the fractional width of the resonance peak. In Figure 3.9 the value of Q is 2 for curve (1) and 4 for curve (2).

Electrically driven quartz crystal oscillators are used to control such things as watches and the frequency of radio broadcasting stations. The Q of the quartz crystals in such applications is of the order of 10^4. Such high values of Q ensures that the frequency of oscillation remains accurately at the resonance frequency.

Phase Angle

The phase difference between the applied driving force and the steady-state response is given by Equation 3.38, namely $\varphi = \tan^{-1}[2\gamma\omega/(\omega_0^2 - \omega^2)]$. This relation is plotted in Figure 3.10 showing φ as a function of the driving frequency ω. At $\omega = 0$ the phase difference is zero and remains small for small ω, so the response is in phase with the driving force. Near the resonance frequency, actually at $\omega = \omega_0$, the phase angle φ increases to $\pi/2$ and so the response is 90° out of phase at this frequency. Finally, for large values of ω the value of φ approaches π, hence the motion of the system is just 180° out of phase with the driving force.

Velocity Resonance

The actual motion of the driven harmonic oscillator is given by taking the real part of both sides of Equation 3.33, namely

$$x(t) = A(\omega) \cos(\omega t - \varphi) \tag{3.46}$$

where $A(\omega)$ is given by either of Equations 3.37 or 3.39. Sometimes it is of interest to know how the velocity of the driven harmonic oscillator varies with frequency. For instance, certain types of electrical transducers employed to monitor vibrating machinery produce outputs that are proportional to the velocity, rather than the displacement.

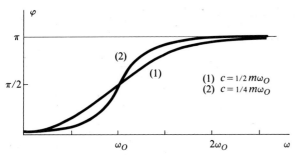

FIGURE 3.10   Graphs of phase angle versus driving frequency for two values of the damping constant.

By differentiating the above equation with respect to t, we find

$$\dot{x}(t) = -\omega A(\omega) \sin(\omega t - \varphi) \tag{3.47}$$

Thus the product $\omega A(\omega)$ can be considered to be the *velocity amplitude* of the driven harmonic oscillator, because $\dot{x}(t)$ varies between $-\omega A(\omega)$ and $+\omega A(\omega)$. Let us call it $v(\omega)$, so that

$$v(\omega) = \frac{\omega F_0/m}{[(\omega_0^2 - \omega^2)^2 + 4\gamma^2\omega^2]^{1/2}} \tag{3.48}$$

Now it is a straightforward, although somewhat tedious exercise to show that the maximum value of $v(\omega)$ occurs at $\omega = \omega_0$. Thus we can regard ω_0 as the *velocity resonant frequency*.

As stated previously, the amplitude resonant frequency ω_r differs from ω_0 by only a small amount in the case of weak damping, so that, in that case, the resonant frequencies for both velocity and amplitude are nearly equal. But, for strong damping we found that no amplitude resonance occurs when $\gamma > \omega_0/\sqrt{2}$. This is not the case with velocity resonance; the velocity amplitude function $v(\omega) = \omega A(\omega)$ exhibits a maximum at $\omega = \omega_0$ for *any* value of the damping factor γ.

Electrical-Mechanical Analogs

When an electric current flows in a circuit comprised of inductive, capacitative, and resistive elements, there is a precise analogy with a moving mechanical system of masses and springs with frictional forces of the type studied previously. Thus if a current $i = dq/dt$ (q being the charge) flows through an inductance L, the potential difference across the inductance is $L\ddot{q}$ and the stored energy is $\frac{1}{2}L\dot{q}^2$. Hence inductance and charge are analogous to mass and displacement, respectively, and potential difference is analogous to force. Similarly, if a capacitance C carries a charge q, the potential difference is $C^{-1}q$ and the stored energy is $\frac{1}{2}C^{-1}q^2$. Consequently we see that the reciprocal of C is analogous to the stiffness constant of a spring. Finally, for an electric current i flowing through a resistance R, the potential difference is $iR = \dot{q}R$, and the rate of energy dissipation is $i^2R = \dot{q}^2R$ in analogy with the quantity $c\dot{x}^2$ for a mechanical system. Table 3.1 summarizes the situation.

TABLE 3.1 Electrical-Mechanical Analogs

	Mechanical		Electrical
x	Displacement	q	Charge
$\dot{x}$	Velocity	$\dot{q} = i$	Current
m	Mass	L	Inductance
k	Stiffness	C^{-1}	Reciprocal of capacitance
c	Damping resistance	R	Resistance
F	Force	V	Potential difference

Example

3.7 The exponential damping factor γ of a spring suspension system is one-tenth the critical value. If the undamped frequency is ω_0, find (a) the resonant frequency, (b) the quality factor, (c) the phase angle φ when the system is driven at a frequency $\omega = \omega_0/2$, and (d) the steady-state amplitude at this frequency.

Solution:

(a) We have $\gamma = \gamma_{crit}/10 = \omega_0/10$, so from Equation 3.40

$$\omega_r = [\omega_0^2 - 2(\omega_0/10)^2]^{1/2} = \omega_0(0.98)^{1/2} = 0.99\omega_0$$

(b) The system can be regarded as weakly damped, so, from Equation 3.44a

$$Q \simeq \frac{\omega_0}{2\gamma} = \frac{\omega_0}{2(\omega_0/10)} = 5$$

(c) From Equation 3.38 we have

$$\varphi = \tan^{-1}\left(\frac{2\gamma\omega}{\omega_0^2 - \omega^2}\right) = \tan^{-1}\left[\frac{2(\omega_0/10)(\omega_0/2)}{\omega_0^2 - (\omega_0/2)^2}\right]$$
$$= \tan^{-1}0.133 = 7.6°$$

(d) From Equations 3.39 and 3.39a we first calculate the value of the resonance denominator

$$D(\omega = \omega_0/2) = [(\omega_0^2 - \omega_0^2/4)^2 + 4(\omega_0/10)^2(\omega_0/2)^2]^{1/2}$$
$$= [(9/16) + (1/100)]^{1/2}\omega_0^2 = 0.7506\ \omega_0^2$$

From this, the amplitude is

$$A(\omega = \omega_0/2) = \frac{F_0/m}{0.7506\ \omega_0^2} = 1.332\frac{F_0}{m\omega_0^2}$$

Notice that the factor $(F_0/m\omega_0^2) = F_0/k$ is the steady-state amplitude for zero driving frequency. ∎

3.6   The Nonlinear Oscillator. Method of Successive Approximations

When a system is displaced from its equilibrium position the restoring force may vary in a manner other than in direct proportion to the displacement. For example, a spring may not obey Hooke's law exactly; also, in many physical cases the restoring force function is inherently nonlinear, as is the case with the simple pendulum discussed in the example to follow.

In the nonlinear case the restoring force can be expressed as

$$F(x) = -kx + \epsilon(x) \tag{3.49}$$

in which the function $\epsilon(x)$ represents the departure from linearity. It is necessarily quadratic, or higher order, in the displacement variable x. The differential equation of motion under such a force, assuming no external forces are acting, can be written in the form

$$m\ddot{x} + kx = \epsilon(x) = \epsilon_2 x^2 + \epsilon_3 x^3 + \ldots \tag{3.50}$$

Here we have expanded $\epsilon(x)$ as a power series.

The above type of equation usually requires some method of approximation to arrive at a solution. To illustrate one method we shall take a particular case in which only the cubic term in $\epsilon(x)$ is of importance. Then we have

$$m\ddot{x} + kx = \epsilon_3 x^3 \tag{3.51}$$

Upon division by m and introduction of the abbreviations $\omega_0^2 = k/m$, $\epsilon_3/m = \lambda$ we can write

$$\ddot{x} + \omega_0^2 x = \lambda x^3 \tag{3.52}$$

We shall find the solution by *the method of successive approximations*.

Now we know that for $\lambda = 0$ a solution is $x = A \cos \omega_0 t$. Suppose we try a *first* approximation of the same form

$$x = A \cos \omega t \tag{3.53}$$

where, as we shall see, ω is not quite equal to ω_0. Inserting our trial solution into the differential equation gives

$$-A\omega^2 \cos \omega t + A\omega_0^2 \cos \omega t = \lambda A^3 \cos^3 \omega t = \lambda A^3 \left(\frac{3}{4} \cos \omega t + \frac{1}{4} \cos 3\omega t \right)$$

In the last step we have used the trigonometric identity $\cos^3 u = \frac{3}{4} \cos u + \frac{1}{4} \cos 3u$ which is easily derived by use of the relation $\cos^3 u = [(e^{iu} + e^{-iu})/2]^3$. Upon transposing and collecting terms we get

$$\left(-\omega^2 + \omega_0^2 - \frac{3}{4}\lambda A^2 \right) A \cos \omega t - \frac{1}{4}\lambda A^3 \cos 3\omega t = 0 \tag{3.54}$$

Excluding the trivial case $A = 0$, we see that our trial solution does not exactly satisfy the differential equation. However, an approximation to the value of ω *which is valid for small* λ is obtained by setting the quantity in parentheses equal to zero. This yields

$$\omega^2 = \omega_0^2 - \frac{3}{4}\lambda A^2 \tag{3.55}$$

for the frequency of our freely running nonlinear oscillator. As we can see, it is a function of the amplitude A.

To obtain a better solution we must take into account the dangling term involving the third harmonic, cos $3\omega t$. Accordingly, we shall take a *second* trial solution of the form

$$x = A \cos \omega t + B \cos 3\omega t \qquad (3.56)$$

Putting this into the differential equation we find, after collecting terms

$$(-\omega^2 + \omega_0^2 - \frac{3}{4}\lambda A^2)A \cos \omega t + (-9B\omega^2 + \omega_0^2 B - \frac{1}{4}\lambda A^3) \cos 3\omega t$$
$$+ \text{ (terms involving } B\lambda \text{ and higher multiples of } \omega t) = 0$$

Setting the first quantity in parentheses equal to zero gives the same value for ω found above. Equating the second to zero gives a value for the coefficient B, namely

$$B = \frac{\frac{1}{4}\lambda A^3}{-9\omega^2 + \omega_0^2} = \frac{\lambda A^3}{-32\omega_0^2 + 27\lambda A^2} \approx -\frac{\lambda A^3}{32\omega_0^2} \qquad (3.57)$$

where we have assumed that the term in the denominator involving λA^2 is small enough to neglect. Our second approximation can be expressed as

$$x = A \cos \omega t - \frac{\lambda A^3}{32\omega_0^2} \cos 3\omega t \qquad (3.58)$$

$$\omega = \omega_0\left(1 - \frac{3\lambda A^2}{4\omega_0^2}\right)^{1/2} \qquad (3.59)$$

We shall stop at this point, but the process could be repeated to find yet a third approximation, and so on.

The above analysis, although it is admittedly very crude, brings out two essential features of free oscillation under a nonlinear restoring force; that is, the period of oscillation is a function of the amplitude of vibration, and the oscillation is not strictly sinusoidal but can be considered as the superposition of a mixture of harmonics. It can be shown that the vibration of a nonlinear system driven by a purely sinusoidal driving force will also be distorted; that is, it will contain harmonics. The loudspeaker of a radio receiver or a "hi-fi" system, for example, may introduce distortion (harmonics) over and above that introduced by the electronic amplifying system.

Example

3.8 *The simple pendulum as a nonlinear oscillator.* Previously in this Chapter, Example 3.2, we treated the simple pendulum as a linear harmonic oscillator by using the approximation $\sin \theta \simeq \theta$. Actually, the sine can be expanded as a power series

$$\sin \theta = \theta - \frac{\theta^3}{3!} + \frac{\theta^5}{5!} - \cdots$$

so the differential equation for the simple pendulum, $\ddot{\theta} + (g/l) \sin \theta = 0$, may be written in the form of Equation 3.50, and, by retaining only the linear and the cubic terms in the expansion for the sine, the differential equation becomes

$$\ddot{\theta} + \omega_0^2\theta = \frac{\omega_0^2}{3!}\theta^3$$

in which $\omega_0^2 = g/l$. This is mathematically identical to Equation 3.52 with the constant $\lambda = \omega_0^2/3! = \omega_0^2/6$. The improved expression for the angular frequency, Equation 3.59, then gives

$$\omega = \omega_0\left[1 - \frac{3(\omega_0^2/6)A^2}{4\omega_0^2}\right]^{1/2} = \omega_0\left(1 - \frac{A^2}{8}\right)^{1/2}$$

and

$$T = \frac{2\pi}{\omega} = 2\pi\sqrt{\frac{l}{g}}\left(1 - \frac{A^2}{8}\right)^{-1/2} = T_0\left(1 - \frac{A^2}{8}\right)^{-1/2}$$

for the period of the simple pendulum. Here A is the amplitude of oscillation expressed in radians. Our method of approximation shows that the period for non-zero amplitude is longer by the factor $\left(1 - \frac{A^2}{8}\right)^{-1/2}$ than that calculated earlier assuming $\sin\theta = \theta$. For instance, if the pendulum is swinging with an amplitude of $90° = \pi/2$ radians (a fairly large amplitude) the factor is $\left(1 - \frac{\pi^2}{32}\right)^{-1/2} = 1.2025$, so the period is about 20 percent longer than the period for small amplitude. This is considerably greater than the increase due to damping of the baseball pendulum, treated in Example 3.6.   ∎

*3.7   Nonsinusoidal Driving Force. Fourier Series

In order to determine the motion of a harmonic oscillator that is driven by an external periodic force which is *other* than "pure" sinusoidal, it is necessary to employ a somewhat more involved method than that of the previous sections. In this more general case it is convenient to use the *principle of superposition*. The principle is applicable to any system governed by a linear differential equation. In our application the principle states that if the external driving force acting on a damped harmonic oscillator is given by a superposition of force functions

$$F_{ext} = \sum_n F_n(t) \tag{3.60}$$

such that the differential equations

$$m\ddot{x}_n + c\dot{x}_n + kx_n = F_n(t)$$

are individually satisfied by the functions $x_n(t)$, then the solution of the differential equation of motion

$$m\ddot{x} + c\dot{x} + kx = F_{ext} \tag{3.61}$$

* As in Chapter 1, sections marked with an asterisk may be omitted without loss of continuity.

is given by the superposition

$$x(t) = \sum_n x_n(t) \tag{3.62}$$

The validity of the principle is easily verified by substitution:

$$m\ddot{x} + c\dot{x} + kx = \sum_n (m\ddot{x}_n + c\dot{x}_n + kx) = \sum_n F_n(t) = F_{ext}$$

In particular, when the driving force is periodic, that is, if for any value of the time t

$$F_{ext}(t) = F_{ext}(t + T)$$

where T is the period, then the force function can be expressed as a superposition of harmonic terms according to *Fourier's theorem*. This theorem states that any periodic function $f(t)$ can be expanded as a sum as follows:

$$f(t) = \frac{1}{2}a_0 + \sum_{n=1}^{\infty} [a_n \cos(n\omega t) + b_n \sin(n\omega t)] \tag{3.63}$$

The coefficients are given by the following formulas (derived in Appendix G):

$$a_n = \frac{2}{T} \int_{-T/2}^{T/2} f(t) \cos(n\omega t)\, dt \qquad n = 0,1,2, \ldots \tag{3.64}$$

$$b_n = \frac{2}{T} \int_{-T/2}^{T/2} f(t) \sin(n\omega t)\, dt \qquad n = 1,2, \ldots$$

Here T is the period and $\omega = 2\pi/T$ is the fundamental frequency. If the function $f(t)$ is an *even* function, that is, if $f(t) = f(-t)$, then the coefficients $b_n = 0$ for all n. The series expansion is then known as a *Fourier cosine series*. Similarly, if we have an *odd* function so that $f(t) = -f(-t)$, then the a_n all vanish, and the series is called a *Fourier sine series*. By use of the relation $e^{iu} = \cos u + i \sin u$ it is straightforward to verify that Equations 3.63 and 3.64 may also be expressed in complex exponential form as follows:

$$f(t) = \sum_n c_n e^{in\omega t} \qquad n = 0, \pm 1, \pm 2, \ldots \tag{3.65}$$

$$c_n = \frac{1}{T} \int_{-T/2}^{T/2} f(t) e^{-in\omega t}\, dt \tag{3.66}$$

Thus, to find the steady-state motion of our harmonic oscillator subject to a given periodic driving force, we express the force as a Fourier series of the form of Equations 3.63 or 3.65, using formulas 3.64 or 3.66 to determine the Fourier coefficients a_n and b_n, or c_n. For each value of n, corresponding to a given harmonic $n\omega$ of the fundamental driving frequency ω, there is a response function $x_n(t)$. This function is the steady-state solution of the driven oscillator treated in Section 3.5. The superposition of all the $x_n(t)$ gives the actual motion. In the event that one of the harmonics of the driving frequency coincides, or nearly coincides, with the resonance frequency ω_r, then the response at that harmonic will dominate the motion. As a result, if the damping constant γ is very small, the resulting oscillation may be very nearly sinusoidal even if a highly nonsinusoidal driving force is applied.

Example

3.9 *Periodic pulse.* To illustrate the above theory we shall analyze the motion of a harmonic oscillator that is driven by an external force consisting of a succession of rectangular pulses:

$$F_{ext}(t) = F_0 \qquad NT - \frac{1}{2}\Delta T \le t \le NT + \frac{1}{2}\Delta T$$

$$F_{ext}(t) = 0 \qquad \text{otherwise}$$

where $N = 0, \pm 1, \pm 2, \ldots$, T is the time from one pulse to the next, and ΔT is the width of each pulse as shown in Figure 3.11. In this case $F_{ext}(t)$ is an even function of t, so it can be expressed as a Fourier cosine series. Equation 3.64 gives the coefficients

$$a_n = \frac{2}{T} \int_{-\Delta T/2}^{+\Delta T/2} F_0 \cos(n\omega t)\, dt$$

$$= \frac{2}{T} F_0 \left[\frac{\sin(n\omega t)}{n\omega} \right]_{-\Delta T/2}^{+\Delta T/2}$$

$$= F_0 \frac{2 \sin(n\pi \Delta T/T)}{n\pi} \qquad (3.67)$$

where in the last step we use the fact that $\omega = 2\pi/T$. We see also that

$$a_0 = \frac{2}{T} \int_{-\Delta T/2}^{+\Delta T/2} F_0 dt = F_0 \frac{2\Delta T}{T}$$

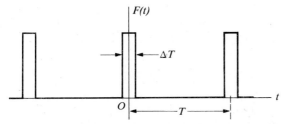

FIGURE 3.11 Rectangular-pulse driving force.

Thus, for our periodic pulse force we can write

$$F_{ext}(t) = F_0\left[\frac{\Delta T}{T} + \frac{2}{\pi} \sin\left(\pi \frac{\Delta T}{T}\right) \cos(\omega t)\right.$$ (3.68)

$$+ \frac{2}{2\pi} \sin\left(2\pi \frac{\Delta T}{T}\right) \cos(2\omega t)$$

$$\left. + \frac{2}{3\pi} \sin\left(3\pi \frac{\Delta T}{T}\right) \cos(3\omega t) + \cdots\right]$$

The first term in the above series expansion is just the *average* value of the external force: $F_{avg} = F_0(\Delta T/T)$. The second term is the Fourier component at the fundamental frequency ω. The remaining terms are harmonics of the fundamental: 2ω, 3ω, and so on.

Referring back to Section 3.5, Equations 3.38 and 3.39, we can now write down the final expression for the motion of our pulse-driven oscillator. It is given by the superposition principle

$$x(t) = \sum_n x_n(t) = \sum_n A_n \cos(n\omega t - \varphi_n)$$ (3.69)

in which the respective amplitudes are

$$A_n = \frac{a_n/m}{D_n(\omega)} = \frac{(F_0/m)(2/n\pi) \sin(n\pi\Delta T/T)}{[(\omega_0^2 - n^2\omega^2)^2 + 4\gamma^2 n^2\omega^2]^{1/2}}$$ (3.70)

and the phase angles

$$\varphi_n = \tan^{-1}\left(\frac{2\gamma n\omega}{\omega_0^2 - n^2\omega^2}\right)$$ (3.71)

Here m is the mass, γ is the decay constant, and ω_0 is the frequency of the freely running oscillator with no damping.

As a specific numerical example let us consider the spring suspension system of Example 3.7 under the action of a periodic pulse for which the pulse width is one-tenth the pulse period: $\Delta T/T = 0.1$. As before, we shall take the damping constant to be one-tenth critical: $\gamma = 0.1\,\omega_0$ and the pulse frequency to be one-half the undamped frequency of the system: $\omega = \omega_0/2$. The Fourier series for the driving force, Equation 3.68, is then

$$F_{ext}(t) = F_0[0.1 + \frac{2}{\pi} \sin(0.1\pi) \cos(\omega t) + \frac{2}{2\pi} \sin(0.2\pi) \cos(2\omega t)$$

$$+ \frac{2}{3\pi} \sin(0.3\pi) \cos(3\omega t) + \cdots]$$

$$= F_0[0.1 + 0.197 \cos(\omega t) + 0.187 \cos(2\omega t) + 0.172 \cos(3\omega t) + \cdots]$$

The resonance denominators in Equation 3.70 are given by

$$D_n = \left[\left(\omega_0^2 - n^2\frac{\omega_0^2}{4}\right)^2 + 4(0.1)^2\omega_0^2 n^2\frac{\omega_0^2}{4}\right]^{1/2} = \left[\left(1 - \frac{n^2}{4}\right)^2 + 0.01n^2\right]^{1/2}\omega_0^2$$

Thus

$$D_0 = \omega_0^2 \qquad D_1 = 0.757\omega_0^2 \qquad D_2 = 0.2\omega_0^2 \qquad D_3 = 1.285\omega_0^2$$

The phase angles, Equation 3.71, are

$$\varphi_n = \tan^{-1}\left(\frac{0.2n\omega_0^2/2}{\omega_0^2 - n^2\omega_0^2/4}\right) = \tan^{-1}\left(\frac{0.4n}{4 - n^2}\right)$$

which gives

$$\varphi_0 = 0 \qquad \varphi_1 = \tan^{-1}(0.133) = 0.132 \qquad \varphi_2 = \tan^{-1}\infty = \pi/2$$
$$\varphi_3 = \tan^{-1}(-0.24) = -0.226$$

The steady-state motion of the system is therefore given by the following series, Equation 3.69,

$$x(t) = \frac{F_0}{m\omega_0^2}[0.1 + 0.26\cos(\omega t - 0.132) + 0.935\sin(2\omega t)$$
$$+ 0.134\cos(3\omega t + 0.226) + \ldots]$$

The dominant term is the one involving the second harmonic $2\omega = \omega_0$ because ω_0 is close to the resonant frequency. Note also the phase of this term: $\cos(2\omega t - \pi/2) = \sin(2\omega t)$.

■

PROBLEMS

3.1 A guitar string vibrates harmonically with a frequency of 512 hz (one octave above middle C on the musical scale). If the amplitude of oscillation of the center point of the string is 0.002 m (2 mm), what is the maximum speed and the maximum acceleration at that point?

3.2 A piston executes simple harmonic motion with an amplitude of 0.1 m. If it passes through the center of its motion with a speed of 0.5 m/s, what is the period of oscillation?

3.3 A particle undergoes simple harmonic motion with a frequency of 10 hz. Find the displacement x at any time t for the following initial condition:

$$t = 0 \qquad x = 0.25 \text{ m} \qquad \dot{x} = 0.1 \text{ m/sec}$$

3.4 Verify the relations among the four quantities A, B, φ, and $\mathcal{A}$ given just below Equation 3.8.

3.5 A particle undergoing simple harmonic motion has a velocity $\dot{x}_1$ when the displacement is x_1 and a velocity $\dot{x}_2$ when the displacement is x_2. Find the angular frequency and the amplitude of the motion in terms of the given quantities.

3.6 On the surface of the moon the acceleration of gravity is about one-sixth that on the earth. What is the half-period of a simple pendulum of length one meter on the moon?

3.7 Two springs having stiffness k_1 and k_2, respectively, are used in a vertical position to support a single object of mass m. Show that the angular frequency of oscillation is $[(k_1 + k_2)/m]^{1/2}$ if the springs are tied in parallel, and $[k_1k_2/(k_1 + k_2)m]^{1/2}$ if the springs are tied in series.

3.8 A spring of stiffness k supports a box of mass M in which is placed a block of mass m. If the system is pulled downward a distance d from the equilibrium position and then released, find the force of reaction between the block and the bottom of the box as a function of time. For what value of d will the block just begin to leave the bottom of the box at the top of the vertical oscillations? Neglect any air resistance.

3.9 Show that the ratio of two successive maxima in the displacement of a damped harmonic oscillator is constant. [*Note:* The maxima do not occur at the points of contact of the displacement curve with the curve $Ae^{-\gamma t}$.]

3.10 The frequency f_d of a damped harmonic oscillator is 100 hz, and the ratio of the amplitude of two successive maxima is one-half. (a) What is the undamped frequency f_0 of this oscillator? (b) What is the resonant frequency f_r?

3.11 Given: The amplitude of a damped harmonic oscillator drops to $1/e$ of its initial value after n complete cycles. Show that the ratio of period of oscillation to the period of the same oscillator with no damping is given by

$$\frac{T_d}{T_0} = \left(1 + \frac{1}{4\pi^2 n^2}\right)^{1/2} \simeq 1 + \frac{1}{8\pi^2 n^2}$$

where the approximation in the last expression is valid if n is large. (See approximation formulas in Appendix D.)

3.12 Work all parts of Example 3.7 for the case in which the exponential damping factor γ is one-half the critical value, and the driving frequency is equal to $2\omega_0$.

3.13 For a lightly damped harmonic oscillator, $\gamma \ll \omega_0$, show that the driving frequency for which the steady-state amplitude is one-half the steady-state amplitude at the resonant frequency is given by $\omega \simeq \omega_0 \pm \gamma\sqrt{3}$.

3.14 Show that the quality factor Q of a lightly damped harmonic oscillator is equal to the ratio of the steady-state amplitude at the resonant frequency to that at zero driving frequency for a given value of the forcing amplitude F_0.

3.15 A damped harmonic oscillator is driven by an external force of the form

$$F_{ext} = F_0 \sin\omega t$$

Show that the steady-state solution is given by

$$x(t) = A(\omega) \sin(\omega t - \varphi)$$

where $A(\omega)$ and φ are identical to the expressions given by Equations 3.37 and 3.38.

3.16 Solve the differential equation of motion of the damped harmonic oscillator driven by a damped harmonic force:

$$F_{ext}(t) = F_0 e^{-\alpha t} \cos\omega t$$

[*Hint:* $e^{-\alpha t} \cos\omega t = \text{Re}(e^{-\alpha t + i\omega t}) = \text{Re}(e^{\beta t})$, where $\beta = -\alpha + i\omega$. Assume a solution of the form $Ae^{\beta t - i\theta}$.]

3.17 A simple pendulum of length l oscillates with an amplitude of 45°. (a) What is the period? (b) If this pendulum is used as a laboratory experiment to determine the value of g, find the error incurred in the use of the elementary formula $T_0 = 2\pi(l/g)^{1/2}$. (c) Find the approximate amount of third-harmonic content in the oscillation of the pendulum.

3.18 Verify Equations 3.65 and 3.66 in the text.

3.19 Show that the Fourier series for a periodic "square wave" is

$$f(t) = \frac{4}{\pi}\left[\sin(\omega t) + \frac{1}{3}\sin(3\omega t) + \frac{1}{5}\sin(5\omega t) + \cdots\right]$$

where

$$f(t) = +1 \quad \text{for} \quad 0 < \omega t < \pi,\ 2\pi < \omega t < 3\pi,\ \text{and so on}$$
$$f(t) = -1 \quad \text{for} \quad \pi < \omega t < 2\pi,\ 3\pi < \omega t < 4\pi,\ \text{and so on}$$

3.20 Use the above result to find the steady-state motion of a damped harmonic oscillator that is driven by a periodic square-wave force of amplitude F_0. In particular, find the relative amplitudes of the first three terms A_1, A_3, and A_5 of the response function $x(t)$ in the case that the third harmonic, 3ω, of the driving frequency coincides with the frequency ω_0 of the undamped oscillator. Let the quality factor $Q = 100$.

4

General Motion of a Particle in Three Dimensions

4.1 Introduction. General Principles

We turn our attention now to the general case of motion of a particle in space. We have already seen that the vectorial form of the equation of motion of a particle is

$$\mathbf{F} = \frac{d\mathbf{p}}{dt} \tag{4.1}$$

in which $\mathbf{p} = m\mathbf{v}$ is the linear momentum. This is essentially an abbreviation for three component equations in which the force components may involve the coordinates, their time derivatives, and the time. Unfortunately, no general method exists for finding analytical solutions in all possible cases. However, there are many physically important special types of force function for which the differential equations of motion can be attacked by relatively simple methods. Some of these will be studied in the sections to follow.

In those cases where $\mathbf{F}$ is known as an explicit function of time, the linear momentum $\mathbf{p}$ can be found by finding the impulse, that is, by integrating with respect to time, as in the one-dimensional case, namely

$$\int_0^t \mathbf{F}(t) \, dt = \mathbf{p}(t) - \mathbf{p}(0) = m\mathbf{v}(t) - m\mathbf{v}(0) \tag{4.2}$$

85

A second integration with respect to time will yield the position:

$$\int_0^t \mathbf{v}(t)\, dt = \mathbf{r}(t) - \mathbf{r}(0) \tag{4.3}$$

Although the above method is perfectly valid, it is not a typical situation in particle dynamics that the force is known in advance as a function of time. Of course, in the special case of zero force, the momentum and velocity are constant and the preceding equations are particularly simple. We shall have occasion to discuss the concept of constant momentum under zero force in a more general form when we take up the study of systems of particles in Chapter 7.

Angular Momentum

Consider the general equation of motion of a particle $\mathbf{F} = d\mathbf{p}/dt$. Let us multiply both sides by the operator $\mathbf{r} \times$ to obtain

$$\mathbf{r} \times \mathbf{F} = \mathbf{r} \times \frac{d\mathbf{p}}{dt}$$

The left-hand side of the above equation is, by definition, the moment of the force about the origin of the coordinate system. The right-hand side turns out to be the time derivative of the quantity $\mathbf{r} \times \mathbf{p}$. To prove this statement we differentiate

$$\frac{d}{dt}(\mathbf{r} \times \mathbf{p}) = \mathbf{v} \times \mathbf{p} + \mathbf{r} \times \frac{d\mathbf{p}}{dt}$$

But $\mathbf{v} \times \mathbf{p} = \mathbf{v} \times m\mathbf{v} = m\mathbf{v} \times \mathbf{v} = 0$. Thus, we can write

$$\mathbf{r} \times \mathbf{F} = \frac{d}{dt}(\mathbf{r} \times \mathbf{p}) \tag{4.4}$$

The quantity $\mathbf{r} \times \mathbf{p}$ is called the *angular momentum* of the particle about the origin. Our result, stated in words, is that *the time rate of change of the angular momentum of a particle is equal to the moment of force acting on the particle.*

The important concept of angular momentum will be found to be particularly useful in the study of planetary-type motion which we shall take up in Chapter 6, and in the study of systems of particles and rigid bodies, Chapters 7–10.

The Work Principle

In the general equation of motion $\mathbf{F} = d\mathbf{p}/dt$ let us take the dot product of both sides with the velocity $\mathbf{v}$:

$$\mathbf{F} \cdot \mathbf{v} = \frac{d\mathbf{p}}{dt} \cdot \mathbf{v} = \frac{d(m\mathbf{v})}{dt} \cdot \mathbf{v}$$

Now from the rule for differentiation of a dot product, we have $d(\mathbf{v} \cdot \mathbf{v})/dt = 2\mathbf{v} \cdot$

dv/dt. Hence, if we assume that the mass m is constant, we see that the above equation is equivalent to

$$\mathbf{F} \bullet \mathbf{v} = \frac{d}{dt}\left(\frac{1}{2}m\mathbf{v} \bullet \mathbf{v}\right) = \frac{dT}{dt} \tag{4.5}$$

in which we have introduced the kinetic energy $T = \frac{1}{2}mv^2$. Further, since $\mathbf{v}dt = d\mathbf{r}$, we can integrate to obtain

$$\int \mathbf{F} \bullet d\mathbf{r} = \int dT \tag{4.6}$$

Now the left-hand side of the above equation is a *line integral*. It represents the work done on the particle by the force $\mathbf{F}$ as the particle moves along the path of motion. The right-hand side is just the net change in the particle's kinetic energy. Hence the equation merely states that *the work done on the particle is equal to the increment in the kinetic energy.*

Conservative Forces and Force Fields

Generally, the value of a line integral, the work in this case, depends on the path of integration; see Figure 4.1. In other words, the work done usually depends on the particular route the particle takes in going from one point to another. This means that if we were given the problem of calculating the value of the work integral we would normally need to know the path of motion of the particle beforehand. However, the usual kinds of problems that are of interest in particle dynamics are those in which the path of motion is not known in advance, rather, the path is one of the things to be calculated. It would appear then that the work principle expressed by Equation 4.6 might not prove very useful for our purposes. However, it turns out that the work principle is indeed very useful in the study of the motion of a particle under the action

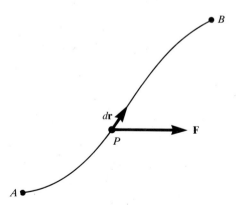

FIGURE 4.1 The work done by a force $\mathbf{F}$ is the line integral $\displaystyle\int_A^B \mathbf{F} \cdot d\mathbf{r}$.

of a particular kind of force known as *conservative force*. Fortunately, many of the physically important forces are of this type.

When the force **F** is a function of the positional coordinates only, it is said to define a static *force field*. Among the possible kinds of force fields, there is an important class for which the work integral $\int \mathbf{F} \cdot d\mathbf{r}$ is independent of the path of integration. Such force fields are conservative. Mathematically, a conservative field is one in which the expression $\mathbf{F} \cdot d\mathbf{r}$ is an *exact differential*. When a particle moves in a conservative field, the work integral and hence the kinetic energy increment can be known in advance. This knowledge can be of use in predicting the motion of the particle.

4.2   The Potential Energy Function in Three-Dimensional Motion. The Del Operator

If a particle moves under the action of a conservative force **F**, the statement that the work increment $\mathbf{F} \cdot d\mathbf{r}$ is an exact differential means that it must be expressible as the differential of a scalar function of the position **r**, namely

$$\mathbf{F} \cdot d\mathbf{r} = -dV(\mathbf{r}) \tag{4.7}$$

This is analogous to the one-dimensional case where $F_x dx = -dV$, Section 2.3. The function V is the potential energy. The work principle, Equation 4.6, then is simply expressed as $\Delta T = -\Delta V$, or

$$\Delta(T + V) = 0 \tag{4.8}$$

This implies that the quantity $T + V$ remains constant as the particle moves. We call it the total energy E, and write

$$\tfrac{1}{2}mv^2 + V(\mathbf{r}) = E \tag{4.9}$$

In the case of a nonconservative force the work increment is not an exact differential and therefore cannot be equated to a quantity $-dV$. A common example of a nonconservative force is friction. When nonconservative forces are present we can express the total force as a sum $\mathbf{F} + \mathbf{F}'$ where **F** is conservative and $\mathbf{F}'$ is nonconservative. The work increment is then given by $dT = \mathbf{F} \cdot d\mathbf{r} + \mathbf{F}' \cdot d\mathbf{r} = -dV + \mathbf{F}' \cdot d\mathbf{r}$ or

$$d(T + V) = \mathbf{F}' \cdot d\mathbf{r}$$

We see that the quantity $T + V$ is not constant, but increases or decreases as the particle moves depending on the sign of $\mathbf{F}' \cdot d\mathbf{r}$. In the case of dissipative forces the direction of $\mathbf{F}'$ is opposite to that of $d\mathbf{r}$, hence $\mathbf{F}' \cdot d\mathbf{r}$ is negative and the total energy $T + V$ diminishes as the particle moves.

Gradient and the Del Operator in Mechanics

If rectangular coordinates are employed, the statement

$$\mathbf{F} \cdot d\mathbf{r} = -dV$$

is expressed as

$$F_x\,dx + F_y\,dy + F_z\,dz = -\frac{\partial V}{\partial x}dx - \frac{\partial V}{\partial y}dy - \frac{\partial V}{\partial z}dz$$

This clearly implies that

$$F_x = -\frac{\partial V}{\partial x} \qquad F_y = -\frac{\partial V}{\partial y} \qquad F_z = -\frac{\partial V}{\partial z} \tag{4.10}$$

Stated in words, if the force field is conservative, then the components of the force are given by the negative partial derivatives of a potential energy function.

We can now express **F** vectorially as

$$\mathbf{F} = -\mathbf{i}\frac{\partial V}{\partial x} - \mathbf{j}\frac{\partial V}{\partial y} - \mathbf{k}\frac{\partial V}{\partial z} \tag{4.11}$$

This equation can be written in a convenient abbreviated form

$$\mathbf{F} = -\nabla V \tag{4.12}$$

Here we have introduced the vector differentiation operator

$$\nabla = \mathbf{i}\frac{\partial}{\partial x} + \mathbf{j}\frac{\partial}{\partial y} + \mathbf{k}\frac{\partial}{\partial z} \tag{4.13}$$

It is called the *del operator*. The expression ∇V is also called the *gradient of V* and is sometimes written grad V. Mathematically, the gradient of a function is a vector that represents the maximum spatial derivative of the function in direction and magnitude. Physically, the negative gradient of the potential energy function gives the direction and magnitude of the force that acts on a particle located in a field created by other particles. The meaning of the negative sign is that the particle is urged to move in the direction of *decreasing* potential energy rather than in the opposite direction. An illus-

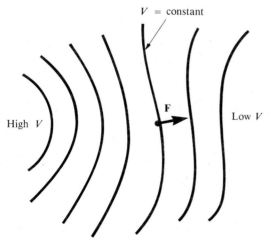

FIGURE 4.2   A force field represented by equipotential contour curves.

tration of the gradient is shown in Figure 4.2. Here the potential energy function is plotted out in the form of contour lines representing the curves of constant potential energy. The force at any point is always normal to the equipotential curve or surface passing through the point in question.

Conditions for the Existence of a Potential Function. The Curl

In Chapter 2 we found that one-dimensional motion of a particle is always conservative if the force is a function of position only. The question naturally arises as to whether or not the corresponding statement is true for the general case of two- and three-dimensional motion. That is, if the force acting on a particle is a function of the position coordinates only, is there always a function V which satisfies Equations 4.10 above? The answer to this question is *no*; only if the force components satisfy certain criteria does a potential function exist.

Let us assume that a potential function *does* exist, that is, that Equations 4.10 hold. Then we have

$$\frac{\partial F_x}{\partial y} = -\frac{\partial^2 V}{\partial y\, \partial x} \qquad \frac{\partial F_y}{\partial x} = -\frac{\partial^2 V}{\partial x\, \partial y}$$

This order of differentiation can be reversed; the two expressions are equal. Hence we can write

$$\frac{\partial F_x}{\partial y} = \frac{\partial F_y}{\partial x} \qquad \frac{\partial F_x}{\partial z} = \frac{\partial F_z}{\partial x} \qquad \frac{\partial F_y}{\partial z} = \frac{\partial F_z}{\partial y} \tag{4.14}$$

where the latter two equations are obtained in a similar manner by taking appropriate pairs of the three equations (4.10). These are the *necessary* conditions, then, on F_x, F_y, and F_z for a potential function to exist; they express the condition that $\mathbf{F} \cdot d\mathbf{r} = F_x\, dx + F_y\, dy + F_z\, dz$ is an exact differential. It is also possible to show that they are *sufficient* conditions, that is, if Equations 4.14 hold at all points, then the force components are indeed derivable from a potential function $V(x,y,z)$, and the sum of the kinetic energy and the potential energy is constant.[1]

The criteria for a force field to be conservative are conveniently expressed in terms of the del operator. In this application we introduce the cross product of the del operator:

$$\nabla \times \mathbf{F} = \mathbf{i}\left(\frac{\partial F_z}{\partial y} - \frac{\partial F_y}{\partial z}\right) + \mathbf{j}\left(\frac{\partial F_x}{\partial z} - \frac{\partial F_z}{\partial x}\right) + \mathbf{k}\left(\frac{\partial F_y}{\partial x} - \frac{\partial F_x}{\partial y}\right) \tag{4.15}$$

The cross product as defined above is called the *curl of* $\mathbf{F}$. According to Equations 4.14, we see that the components of the curl each vanish if the force $\mathbf{F}$ is conservative. Thus the condition for a force to be conservative can be written in the compact form

$$\nabla \times \mathbf{F} = 0 \tag{4.16}$$

---

[1] See any advanced calculus textbook, for example, A. E. Taylor, *Advanced Calculus*, Ginn, Boston, 1955. An interesting discussion of the conservancy criteria when the field contains singularities has been given by Feng in *Amer. J. Phys.* **37**, 616 (1969).

Mathematically, the above equation represents the condition that the expression $\mathbf{F} \cdot d\mathbf{r}$ is an exact differential, or in other words, that the integral $\int \mathbf{F} \cdot d\mathbf{r}$ is independent of the path of integration. Physically, the vanishing of the curl of $\mathbf{F}$ means that the work done by $\mathbf{F}$ on a moving particle is independent of the path of the particle in going from one given point to another.

There is a third expression involving the del operator, namely the dot product $\nabla \cdot \mathbf{F}$. This is called the *divergence of* $\mathbf{F}$. In the case of a force field, the divergence gives a measure of the density of the sources of the field at a given point. The divergence is of particular importance in the theory of electricity and magnetism.

Expressions for the gradient, curl, and divergence in cylindrical and spherical coordinates are given in Appendix F.

Examples

4.1 Given the potential energy function

$$V(\mathbf{r}) = \alpha x^2 + \beta xy + \gamma z + C$$

in which α, β, γ, and C are constants, find the force function.

Solution:

Applying the del operator, we have

$$\mathbf{F} = -\nabla V = -\left(\mathbf{i} \frac{\partial V}{\partial x} + \mathbf{j} \frac{\partial V}{\partial y} + \mathbf{k} \frac{\partial V}{\partial z} \right)$$

$$= -\mathbf{i}(2x\alpha + y\beta) - \mathbf{j}(x\beta) - \mathbf{k}\gamma$$

Notice that the constant C does not appear in the force function; as in the one-dimensional case the value of C is arbitrary. It is equal to the potential energy at the origin in this case: $C = V(0)$. ∎

4.2 Suppose a particle of mass m is moving in the above force field, and at time $t = 0$ the particle passes through the origin with speed v_0. What will the speed of the particle be if and when it passes through the point $\mathbf{r} = \mathbf{i} + 2\mathbf{j} + \mathbf{k}$?

Solution:

To answer the given question we need only to use the fact that the force is conservative (we know that a potential energy function exists) and so the total energy is constant: $T + V = E = const.$ In our case

$$E = \frac{1}{2}mv^2 + V(\mathbf{r}) = \frac{1}{2}mv_0^2 + V(0)$$

so

$$v^2 = v_0^2 + \frac{2}{m}[V(0) - V(\mathbf{r})]$$

$$= v_0^2 + \frac{2}{m}[C - (\alpha x^2 + \beta xy + \gamma z + C)]$$

$$= v_0^2 - \frac{2}{m}(\alpha + 2\beta + \gamma)$$

at the given point. ∎

4.3   Is the force field $\mathbf{F} = \mathbf{i}xy + \mathbf{j}xz + \mathbf{k}yz$ conservative? The curl of $\mathbf{F}$ is

$$\nabla \times \mathbf{F} = \begin{vmatrix} \mathbf{i} & \mathbf{j} & \mathbf{k} \\ \partial/\partial x & \partial/\partial y & \partial/\partial z \\ xy & xz & yz \end{vmatrix} = \mathbf{i}(z - x) + \mathbf{j}0 + \mathbf{k}(z - x)$$

The final expression is not zero for all values of the coordinates, hence the field is *not* conservative. ∎

4.4   For what values of the constants a, b, and c is the force $\mathbf{F} = \mathbf{i}(ax + by^2) + \mathbf{j}cxy$ conservative? Taking the curl, we have

$$\nabla \times \mathbf{F} = \begin{vmatrix} \mathbf{i} & \mathbf{j} & \mathbf{k} \\ \partial/\partial x & \partial/\partial y & \partial/\partial z \\ ax + by^2 & cxy & 0 \end{vmatrix} = \mathbf{k}(c - 2b)y$$

This shows that the force is conservative, provided $c = 2b$. The value of a is immaterial. ∎

4.5   Show that the inverse-square law of force in three dimensions $\mathbf{F} = (-k/r^2)\mathbf{e}_r$ is conservative by the use of the curl. Use spherical coordinates. The curl is given in Appendix F as

$$\nabla \times \mathbf{F} = \frac{1}{r^2 \sin \theta} \begin{vmatrix} \mathbf{e}_r & \mathbf{e}_\theta r & \mathbf{e}_\phi r \sin \theta \\ \dfrac{\partial}{\partial r} & \dfrac{\partial}{\partial \theta} & \dfrac{\partial}{\partial \phi} \\ F_r & rF_\theta & rF_\phi \sin \theta \end{vmatrix}$$

We have $F_r = -k/r^2$, $F_\theta = 0$, $F_\phi = 0$. The curl then reduces to

$$\nabla \times \mathbf{F} = \frac{\mathbf{e}_\theta}{r \sin \theta} \frac{\partial}{\partial \phi}\left(\frac{-k}{r^2}\right) - \frac{\mathbf{e}_\phi}{r} \frac{\partial}{\partial \theta}\left(\frac{-k}{r^2}\right) = 0$$

which, of course, vanishes since both partial derivatives are zero. Thus the force in question is conservative. ∎

4.3   Forces of the Separable Type. Projectile Motion

It is often the case that a Cartesian coordinate system can be chosen such that the components of a force field involve the respective coordinates alone, that is

$$\mathbf{F} = \mathbf{i}F_x(x) + \mathbf{j}F_y(y) + \mathbf{k}F_z(z) \tag{4.17}$$

Forces of this type are said to be *separable*. It is readily verified that the curl of such a force is identically zero:

$$\nabla \times \mathbf{F} = \begin{vmatrix} \mathbf{i} & \mathbf{j} & \mathbf{k} \\ \partial/\partial x & \partial/\partial y & \partial/\partial z \\ F_x(x) & F_y(y) & F_z(z) \end{vmatrix} = 0$$

The x-component is $\partial F_z(z)/\partial y - \partial F_y(y)/\partial z$, and similarly for the other components. Hence the field is conservative because each partial derivative is of the mixed type and therefore vanishes identically, since the coordinates x, y, z are independent variables.

The integration of the differential equations of motion is then very simple, because each component equation is of the type $m\ddot{x} = F_x(x)$. In this case the equations can be solved by the methods described under rectilinear motion in Chapter 2.

In the event that the force components involve the time and the time derivatives of the respective coordinates, then it is no longer true that the force is necessarily conservative. Nevertheless, if the force is separable, then the component equations of motion are of the form $m\ddot{x} = F_x(x,\dot{x},t)$ and may be solved by the methods used in Chapter 2. Some examples of separable forces, both conservative and nonconservative, will be discussed here and in the sections to follow.

Motion of a Projectile in a Uniform Gravitational Field

One of the famous classical problems of particle dynamics is the motion of a projectile. We shall study this problem in some detail because it illustrates most of the general principles that have been cited in the foregoing sections.

(*a*) *No Air Resistance*

First, for simplicity, we consider the case of a projectile moving with no air resistance. In this idealized situation there is only one force acting, namely the force of gravity. Choosing the z axis to be vertical, we have the differential equation of motion

$$m\frac{d^2\mathbf{r}}{dt^2} = -mg\mathbf{k}$$

If we further idealize the problem and assume that the acceleration of gravity g is constant, then the force function is clearly of the separable type and is also conservative since it is a special case of that expressed by Equation 4.17. We shall particularize the problem further by choosing the initial speed to be v_0 and the initial position to be at the origin at time $t = 0$. The energy equation 4.9 then reads

$$\tfrac{1}{2}m(\dot{x}^2 + \dot{y}^2 + \dot{z}^2) + mgz = \tfrac{1}{2}mv_0^2$$

or, equivalently

$$v^2 = v_0^2 - 2gz \qquad (4.18)$$

thus giving the speed as a function of height. This is all the information we can obtain directly from the energy equation.

In order to proceed further, we must go back to the differential equation of motion. This can be written

$$\frac{d}{dt}\left(\frac{d\mathbf{r}}{dt}\right) = -g\mathbf{k} \qquad (4.19)$$

It can be integrated directly. A single integration gives the velocity as

$$\frac{d\mathbf{r}}{dt} = -gt\mathbf{k} + \mathbf{v}_0 \qquad (4.19a)$$

in which the constant of integration $\mathbf{v}_0$ is the initial velocity. Another integration yields the position vector

$$\mathbf{r} = -\tfrac{1}{2}gt^2\mathbf{k} + \mathbf{v}_0 t + \mathbf{r}_0 \tag{4.19b}$$

The constant of integration $\mathbf{r}_0$ is zero in this case, since the initial position of the projectile is taken to be the origin. In components

$$\begin{aligned}
x &= \dot{x}_0 t \\
y &= \dot{y}_0 t \\
z &= \dot{z}_0 t - \tfrac{1}{2}gt^2
\end{aligned} \tag{4.19c}$$

Here $\dot{x}_0$, $\dot{y}_0$, and $\dot{z}_0$ are the components of the initial velocity $\mathbf{v}_0$. We have thus solved the problem of determining the position of the projectile as a function of time.

Concerning the path or trajectory of the projectile, we notice that if the time t is eliminated from the x and y equations, the result is

$$y = bx$$

in which the constant b is given by

$$b = \frac{\dot{y}_0}{\dot{x}_0}$$

Thus the path lies entirely in a plane. In particular, if $\dot{y}_0 = 0$, then the path lies in the xz plane. Next, if we eliminate t between the x and z equations, we find the equation of the path to be of the form

$$z = Ax - Bx^2$$

where $A = \dot{z}_0/\dot{x}_0$ and $B = g/2\dot{x}_0^2$. Hence the path is a parabola lying in the plane $y = bx$. This is shown in Figure 4.3.

(b) *Linear Air Resistance*

We now consider the motion of a projectile for the more realistic situation in

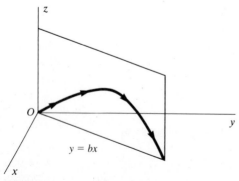

FIGURE 4.3   Path of a projectile in three dimensions.

which there is a retarding force due to air resistance. In this case the motion is not conservative. The total energy continually diminishes as a result of frictional loss.

For simplicity, let us assume that the law of air resistance is linear so that the resisting force varies directly with the velocity $\mathbf{v}$. It will be convenient to write the constant of proportionality as $m\gamma$ where m is the mass of the projectile. Thus we have two forces acting on the projectile, namely the air resistance $-m\gamma\mathbf{v}$, and the force of gravity which is equal to $-mg\mathbf{k}$, as before. The differential equation of motion is then

$$m\frac{d^2\mathbf{r}}{dt^2} = -m\gamma\mathbf{v} - mg\mathbf{k}$$

or, upon cancelling the m's, we have

$$\frac{d^2\mathbf{r}}{dt^2} = -\gamma\mathbf{v} - g\mathbf{k} \tag{4.20}$$

The integration of the above equation is conveniently accomplished by expressing it in component form as follows:

$$\ddot{x} = -\gamma\dot{x} \tag{4.20a}$$
$$\ddot{y} = -\gamma\dot{y}$$
$$\ddot{z} = -\gamma\dot{z} - g$$

We now see that the equations are separated. Hence each can be solved individually by the methods of Chapter 2. Using our results from Section 2.5, we can write down the solutions immediately, by setting $\gamma = c_1/m$, c_1 being the linear drag coefficient. The results are

$$\dot{x} = \dot{x}_0 e^{-\gamma t} \tag{4.20b}$$
$$\dot{y} = \dot{y}_0 e^{-\gamma t}$$
$$\dot{z} = \dot{z}_0 e^{-\gamma t} - \frac{g}{\gamma}(1 - e^{-\gamma t})$$

for the velocity components, and

$$x = \frac{\dot{x}_0}{\gamma}(1 - e^{-\gamma t}) \tag{4.20c}$$

$$y = \frac{\dot{y}_0}{\gamma}(1 - e^{-\gamma t})$$

$$z = \left(\frac{\dot{z}_0}{\gamma} + \frac{g}{\gamma^2}\right)(1 - e^{-\gamma t}) - \frac{g}{\gamma}t$$

for the positional coordinates. Here, as before, the initial velocity components are $\dot{x}_0$, $\dot{y}_0$, and $\dot{z}_0$, and the initial position of the projectile is taken as the origin.

The above solution of the motion of a projectile with linear air resistance can be written vectorially in the following way:

$$\mathbf{r} = \left(\frac{\mathbf{v}_0}{\gamma} + \frac{\mathbf{k}g}{\gamma^2}\right)(1 - e^{-\gamma t}) - \mathbf{k}\frac{gt}{\gamma} \tag{4.20d}$$

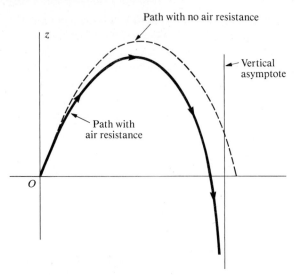

FIGURE 4.4 Comparison of the paths of a projectile with and without air resistance. Motion is shown in the plane $y = bx$.

That it is a solution of the vector differential equation of motion is easily verified by differentiation.

As in the case of zero air resistance, the path of the projectile lies in a vertical plane $y = bx$ with $b = \dot{y}_0/\dot{x}_0$. The path in this plane is not a parabola, however, but is a curve that lies below the corresponding parabolic trajectory. This is illustrated in Figure 4.4. Inspection of the x and y equations shows that, for large t, the values of x and y approach the limiting values

$$x \to \frac{\dot{x}_0}{\gamma} \qquad y \to \frac{\dot{y}_0}{\gamma}$$

This means that the complete trajectory of the projectile, if it did not hit anything, would have a vertical asymptote as shown in the figure.

In the actual motion of a projectile through the atmosphere, the law of resistance is by no means linear, but is a very complicated function of the velocity. An accurate calculation of the trajectory can be done by means of numerical integration methods aided by the use of high-speed computers. (See reference cited under Example 2.9 in Chapter 2.)

Horizontal Range

The horizontal range of a projectile with linear air drag is found by setting $z = 0$ in the third of Equations 4.20c and then eliminating t among the three equations. We shall set $\dot{y}_0 = 0$ so that the trajectory lies in the xz-plane. From the first of Equations

4.20c we have $1 - \gamma x/\dot{x}_0 = e^{-\gamma t}$, so $t = -\gamma^{-1} \ln(1 - \gamma x/\dot{x}_0)$. Thus the horizontal range x_h is given by the implicit expression

$$\left(\frac{\dot{z}_0}{\gamma} + \frac{g}{\gamma^2}\right)\frac{\gamma x_h}{\dot{x}_0} + \frac{g}{\gamma^2}\ln\left(1 - \frac{\gamma x_h}{\dot{x}_0}\right) = 0 \tag{4.21}$$

This is a transcendental equation and must be solved by some approximation method to find x_h. We can expand the logarithmic term by use of the series

$$\ln(1 - u) = -u - \frac{u^2}{2} - \frac{u^3}{3} - \cdots$$

which is valid for $|u| < 1$. With $u = \gamma x_h/\dot{x}_0$ it is left as a problem to show that this leads to the following expression for the horizontal range:

$$x_h = \frac{2\dot{x}_0\dot{z}_0}{g} - \frac{8\dot{x}_0\dot{z}_0^2}{3g^2}\gamma + \cdots \tag{4.22}$$

If the projectile is fired at angle of elevation α with initial speed v_0, then $\dot{x}_0 = v_0 \cos\alpha$, $\dot{z}_0 = v_0 \sin\alpha$, and $2\dot{x}_0\dot{z}_0 = 2v_0^2 \sin\alpha \cos\alpha = v_0^2 \sin 2\alpha$. An equivalent expression is then

$$x_h = \frac{v_0^2 \sin 2\alpha}{g} - \frac{4v_0^3 \sin 2\alpha \sin\alpha}{3g^2}\gamma + \cdots \tag{4.22a}$$

The first term on the right is the range in the absence of air resistance. The remainder is the decrease due to air resistance.

Example

4.6   *Horizontal range of a golf ball.* For objects of baseball or golf ball size traveling at normal speeds, the air drag is more nearly quadratic in v, rather than linear, as pointed out in Section 2.5. However, the approximate expression found above can be used to find the range for flat trajectories by "linearizing" the force function given by Equation 2.22, which may be written in three dimensions as

$$\mathbf{F}(\mathbf{v}) = -\mathbf{v}(c_1 + c_2|\mathbf{v}|)$$

To linearize it we set $|\mathbf{v}|$ equal to the initial speed v_0 and so the constant γ is given by

$$\gamma = \frac{c_1 + c_2 v_0}{m}$$

(A better approximation would be to take the average speed, but that is not a given quantity.) Although this method exaggerates the effect of air drag, it allows a quick "ballpark" estimate to be found easily.

For a golf ball of diameter $D = 0.042$ m and mass $m = 0.046$ kg we find that c_1 is negligible and so

$$\gamma = \frac{c_2 v_0}{m} = \frac{0.22 D^2 v_0}{m}$$

$$= \frac{0.22(0.042)^2 v_0}{0.046} = 0.0084\ v_0$$

numerically, where v_0 is in m/s. For a "chip shot" with, say, $v_0 = 20$ m/s, we find $\gamma = 0.0084 \times 20 = 0.17$ s^{-1}. The horizontal range is then, for $\alpha = 30°$,

$$x_h = \frac{(20)^2 \sin 60°}{9.8}\,\text{m} - \frac{4(20)^3 \sin 60° \sin 30° \times 0.17}{3(9.8)^2}\,\text{m}$$

$$= 35.3 \text{ m} - 8.2 \text{ m} = 27.1 \text{ m}$$

Our estimate thus gives a reduction of about one fourth due to air drag on the ball.

■

4.4   The Harmonic Oscillator in Two and Three Dimensions

Consider the motion of a particle that is subject to a linear restoring force which is always directed toward a fixed point, the origin of our coordinate system. Such a force can be represented by the expression

$$\mathbf{F} = -k\mathbf{r}$$

Accordingly, the differential equation of motion is simply expressed as

$$m\frac{d^2\mathbf{r}}{dt^2} = -k\mathbf{r} \tag{4.23}$$

The situation can be represented approximately by a particle attached to a set of elastic springs as shown in Figure 4.5. This is the three-dimensional generalization of the linear oscillator studied earlier. Equation 4.23 is the differential equation of the *linear isotropic oscillator*.

The Two-Dimensional Isotropic Oscillator

In the case of motion in a single plane, the above differential equation is equivalent to the two component equations

$$m\ddot{x} = -kx \tag{4.23a}$$
$$m\ddot{y} = -ky$$

These are separated, and we can immediately write down the solutions in the form

$$x = A \cos(\omega t + \alpha) \qquad y = B \cos(\omega t + \beta) \tag{4.23b}$$

in which

$$\omega = \left(\frac{k}{m}\right)^{1/2}$$

The constants of integration A, B, α, and β are determined from the initial conditions in any given case.

In order to find the equation of the path, we eliminate the time t between the two equations. To do this, let us write the second equation in the form

$$y = B \cos(\omega t + \alpha + \Delta)$$

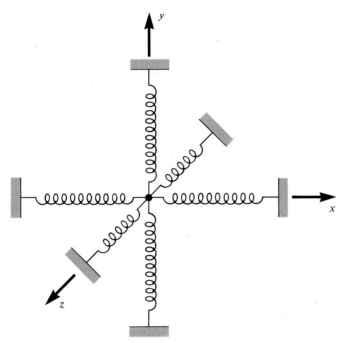

FIGURE 4.5 Model of a three-dimensional harmonic oscillator.

where

$$\Delta = \beta - \alpha$$

Then

$$y = B[\cos(\omega t + \alpha) \cos \Delta - \sin(\omega t + \alpha) \sin \Delta]$$

From the first of Equations 4.23b, we then have

$$\frac{y}{B} = \frac{x}{A} \cos \Delta - \left(1 - \frac{x^2}{A^2}\right)^{1/2} \sin \Delta$$

or, upon squaring and transposing terms, we obtain

$$\frac{x^2}{A^2} - xy\frac{2 \cos \Delta}{AB} + \frac{y^2}{B^2} = \sin^2 \Delta \tag{4.24}$$

which is a quadratic equation in x and y. Now the general quadratic

$$ax^2 + bxy + cy^2 + dx + ey = f$$

represents an ellipse, a parabola, or a hyperbola, depending on whether the discriminant

$$b^2 - 4ac$$

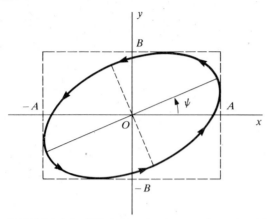

FIGURE 4.6   Elliptical path of a two-dimensional isotropic oscillator.

is negative, zero, or positive, respectively. In our case the discriminant is equal to $-(2 \sin \Delta/AB)^2$ which is negative, so the path is an ellipse as shown in Figure 4.6.

In particular, if the phase difference Δ is equal to $\pi/2$, then the equation of the path reduces to the equation

$$\frac{x^2}{A^2} + \frac{y^2}{B^2} = 1$$

which is the equation of an ellipse whose axes coincide with the coordinate axes. On the other hand, if the phase difference is 0 or π, then the equation of the path reduces to that of a straight line, namely

$$y = \pm \frac{B}{A}x$$

The positive sign is taken if $\Delta = 0$, and the negative sign if $\Delta = \pi$. In the general case, it is possible to show that the axis of the elliptical path is inclined to the x axis by the angle ψ where

$$\tan 2\psi = \frac{2AB \cos \Delta}{A^2 - B^2} \tag{4.25}$$

The derivation is left as an exercise.

The Three-Dimensional Isotropic Harmonic Oscillator

In the case of three-dimensional motion the differential equation of motion is equivalent to the three equations

$$m\ddot{x} = -kx \qquad m\ddot{y} = -ky \qquad m\ddot{z} = -kz \tag{4.26}$$

which are separated. Hence the solutions may be written in the form of Equations 4.23b or, alternately, we may write

$$x = A_1 \sin \omega t + B_1 \cos \omega t \qquad (4.26a)$$
$$y = A_2 \sin \omega t + B_2 \cos \omega t$$
$$z = A_3 \sin \omega t + B_3 \cos \omega t$$

The six constants of integration are determined from the initial position and velocity of the particle. Now Equations 4.26a can be expressed vectorially as

$$\mathbf{r} = \mathbf{A} \sin \omega t + \mathbf{B} \cos \omega t \qquad (4.26b)$$

in which the components of $\mathbf{A}$ are A_1, A_2, and A_3, and similarly for $\mathbf{B}$. It is clear that the motion takes place entirely in a single plane which is common to the two constant vectors $\mathbf{A}$ and $\mathbf{B}$, and that the path of the particle in that plane is an ellipse, as in the two-dimensional case. Hence the analysis concerning the shape of the elliptical path under the two-dimensional case also applies to the three-dimensional case.

Nonisotropic Oscillator

The above discussion considered the motion of the isotropic oscillator, wherein the restoring force is independent of the direction of the displacement. If the magnitudes of the components of the restoring force depend on the direction of the displacement, we have the case of the *nonisotropic oscillator*. For a suitable choice of axes, the differential equations for the nonisotropic case can be written

$$m\ddot{x} = -k_1 x \qquad (4.27)$$
$$m\ddot{y} = -k_2 y$$
$$m\ddot{z} = -k_3 z$$

Here we have a case of *three* different frequencies of oscillation: $\omega_1 = \sqrt{k_1/m}$, $\omega_2 = \sqrt{k_2/m}$, $\omega_3 = \sqrt{k_3/m}$, and the motion is given by the solutions

$$x = A \cos(\omega_1 t + \alpha) \qquad (4.28)$$
$$y = B \cos(\omega_2 t + \beta)$$
$$z = C \cos(\omega_3 t + \gamma)$$

Again, the six constants of integration in the above equations are determined from the initial conditions. The resulting oscillation of the particle lies entirely within a rectangular box (whose sides are $2A$, $2B$, and $2C$) centered on the origin. In the event that ω_1, ω_2, and ω_3 are commensurate, that is, if

$$\frac{\omega_1}{n_1} = \frac{\omega_2}{n_2} = \frac{\omega_3}{n_3} \qquad (4.29)$$

where n_1, n_2, and n_3 are integers, the path, called a *Lissajous* figure, will be closed, because after a time $2\pi n_1/\omega_1 = 2\pi n_2/\omega_2 = 2\pi n_3/\omega_3$ the particle will return to its initial position and the motion will be repeated. (In Equation 4.29 it is assumed that any common integral factor is canceled out.) On the other hand, if the ω's are *not* commensurate, the path is not closed. In this case the path may be said to fill completely the rectangular box mentioned above, at least in the sense that if we wait long enough, the particle will come arbitrarily close to any given point.

The net restoring force exerted on a given atom in a solid crystalline substance is approximately linear in the displacement in many cases. The resulting frequencies of oscillation usually lie in the infrared region of the spectrum: 10^{12} to 10^{14} vibrations per second.

Energy Considerations

In the preceding chapter we showed that the potential energy function of the one-dimensional harmonic oscillator is quadratic in the displacement, $V(x) = \dfrac{1}{2}kx^2$. For the general three-dimensional case it is easy to verify that

$$V(x,y,z) = \frac{1}{2}k_1x^2 + \frac{1}{2}k_2y^2 + \frac{1}{2}k_3z^2$$

since $F_x = -\partial V/\partial x = -k_1x$, and similarly for F_y and F_z. If $k_1 = k_2 = k_3 = k$, we have the isotropic case, and

$$V(x,y,z) = \frac{1}{2}k(x^2 + y^2 + z^2) = \frac{1}{2}kr^2$$

The total energy in the isotropic case is then given by the simple expression

$$\frac{1}{2}mv^2 + \frac{1}{2}kr^2 = E$$

which is similar to that of the one-dimensional case discussed in the previous chapter.

Example

4.7   A particle of mass m moves in two dimensions under the following potential energy function:

$$V(\mathbf{r}) = \frac{1}{2}k(x^2 + 4y^2)$$

Find the resulting motion, given the initial condition at $t = 0$: $x = a$, $y = 0$, $\dot{x} = 0$, $\dot{y} = v_0$,

Solution:

This is a nonisotropic oscillator potential. The force function is

$$\mathbf{F} = -\nabla V = -\mathbf{i}kx - \mathbf{j}4ky = m\ddot{\mathbf{r}}$$

The component differential equations of motion are then

$$m\ddot{x} + kx = 0 \qquad m\ddot{y} + 4ky = 0$$

The x-motion has angular frequency $\omega = (k/m)^{1/2}$, while the y-motion has angular frequency just twice that, namely $\omega_y = (4k/m)^{1/2} = 2\omega$. We shall write the general solution in the form

$$x = A_1 \cos \omega t + B_1 \sin \omega t$$
$$y = A_2 \cos 2\omega t + B_2 \sin 2\omega t$$

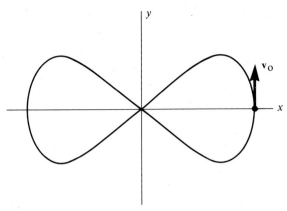

FIGURE 4.7   Lissajous figure.

To use the initial condition we must first differentiate with respect to t to find the general expression for the velocity components

$$\dot{x} = -A_1\omega \sin \omega t + B_1\omega \cos \omega t$$
$$\dot{y} = -2A_2\omega \sin 2\omega t + 2B_2\,\omega \cos 2\omega t$$

Thus, at $t = 0$, we see that the above four equations reduce to

$$a = A_1 \qquad 0 = A_2 \qquad 0 = B_1\omega \qquad v_0 = 2B_2\omega$$

These equations give directly the values of the amplitude coefficients, $A_1 = a$, $A_2 = B_1 = 0$, $B_2 = v_0/2\omega$, so the final equations for the motion are

$$x = a \cos \omega t$$

$$y = \frac{v_0}{2\omega} \sin 2\omega t$$

The path is a Lissajous figure having the shape of a "figure eight" as shown in Figure 4.7.   ∎

4.5   Motion of Charged Particles in Electric and Magnetic Fields

When an electrically charged particle is in the vicinity of other electric charges, it experiences a force. This force **F** is said to be due to the electric field **E** which arises from these other charges. We write

$$\mathbf{F} = q\mathbf{E}$$

where q is the electric charge carried by the particle in question.[2] The equation of motion of the particle is then

---

[2] In SI units F is in newtons, q in coulombs, and E in volts per meter. In cgs units F is in dynes, q in electrostatic units, and E in statvolts per centimeter.

$$m\frac{d^2\mathbf{r}}{dt^2} = q\mathbf{E} \tag{4.30}$$

or, in component form,

$$m\ddot{x} = qE_x \tag{4.30a}$$
$$m\ddot{y} = qE_y$$
$$m\ddot{z} = qE_z$$

The field components are, in general, functions of the position coordinates x, y, and z. In the case of time-varying fields (that is, if the charges producing $\mathbf{E}$ are moving) the components, of course, also involve t.

Let us consider a simple case, namely that of a uniform constant electric field. We can choose one of the axes, say the z axis, to be in the direction of the field. Then $E_x = E_y = 0$, and $E = E_z$. The differential equations of motion of a particle of charge q moving in this field are then

$$\ddot{x} = 0 \qquad \ddot{y} = 0 \qquad \ddot{z} = \frac{qE}{m} = \text{constant}$$

These are of exactly the same form as those for a projectile in a uniform gravitational field. The path is therefore a parabola, if $\dot{x}$ and $\dot{y}$ are not both zero initially. Otherwise, the path is a straight line, as with a body falling vertically.

It is shown in textbooks dealing with electromagnetic theory[3] that

$$\nabla \times \mathbf{E} = 0$$

if $\mathbf{E}$ is due to static charges. This means that motion in such a field is conservative, and that there exists a potential function Φ such that $\mathbf{E} = -\nabla\Phi$. The potential energy of a particle of charge q in such a field is then $q\Phi$, and the total energy is constant and is equal to $\frac{1}{2}mv^2 + q\Phi$.

In the presence of a static magnetic field $\mathbf{B}$ (called the magnetic induction) the force acting on a moving particle is conveniently expressed by means of the cross product, namely,

$$\mathbf{F} = q(\mathbf{v} \times \mathbf{B}) \tag{4.31}$$

where $\mathbf{v}$ is the velocity, and q is the charge.[4] The differential equation of motion of a particle moving in a purely magnetic field is then

$$m\frac{d^2\mathbf{r}}{dt^2} = q(\mathbf{v} \times \mathbf{B}) \tag{4.32}$$

The above equation states that the acceleration of the particle is always at right angles to the direction of motion. This means that the tangential component of the acceleration ($\dot{v}$) is zero, and so the particle moves with constant speed. This is true even if $\mathbf{B}$ is a varying function of the position $\mathbf{r}$ as long as it does not vary with time.

[3] For example, J. C. Slater and N. H. Frank, *Electromagnetism,* McGraw-Hill, New York, 1947.
[4] Equation (4.31) is valid for SI units: F is in newtons, q in coulombs, v in meters per second, and B in webers per square meter. In cgs units we must write $F = (q/c) (\mathbf{v} \times \mathbf{B})$, where F is in dynes, q in electrostatic units, c is the speed of light (3×10^{10} cm per sec), and B is in gauss. (See Slater and Frank, footnote 3.)

Example

4.8 Let us examine the motion of a charged particle in a uniform constant magnetic field. Suppose we choose the z axis to be in the direction of the field; that is, we shall write

$$\mathbf{B} = \mathbf{k}B$$

The differential equation of motion now reads

$$m\frac{d^2\mathbf{r}}{dt^2} = q(\mathbf{v} \times \mathbf{k}B) = qB \begin{vmatrix} \mathbf{i} & \mathbf{j} & \mathbf{k} \\ \dot{x} & \dot{y} & \dot{z} \\ 0 & 0 & 1 \end{vmatrix}$$

$$m(\mathbf{i}\ddot{x} + \mathbf{j}\ddot{y} + \mathbf{k}\ddot{z}) = qB(\mathbf{i}\dot{y} - \mathbf{j}\dot{x})$$

Equating components, we have

$$\begin{aligned} m\ddot{x} &= qB\dot{y} \\ m\ddot{y} &= -qB\dot{x} \\ \ddot{z} &= 0 \end{aligned} \tag{4.33}$$

Here, for the first time, we meet a set of differential equations of motion which are *not* of the separated type. The solution is relatively simple, however, for we can integrate at once with respect to t to obtain

$$\begin{aligned} m\dot{x} &= qBy + c_1 \\ m\dot{y} &= -qBx + c_2 \\ \dot{z} &= \text{constant} = \dot{z}_0 \end{aligned}$$

or

$$\dot{x} = \omega y + C_1 \qquad \dot{y} = -\omega x + C_2 \qquad \dot{z} = \dot{z}_0 \tag{4.34}$$

where we have used the abbreviation $\omega = qB/m$. The c's are constants of integration, and $C_1 = c_1/m$, $C_2 = c_2/m$. Upon inserting the expression for $\dot{y}$ from the second part of Equation 4.34 into the first part of Equation 4.33, we obtain the following separated equation for x:

$$\ddot{x} + \omega^2 x = \omega^2 a \tag{4.35}$$

where $a = C_2/\omega$. The solution is clearly

$$x = a + A\cos(\omega t + \theta_0) \tag{4.36}$$

where A and θ_0 are constants of integration. Now, if we differentiate with respect to t, we have

$$\dot{x} = -A\omega\sin(\omega t + \theta_0) \tag{4.37}$$

The above expression for $\dot{x}$ may be substituted for the left side of the first of Equations 4.34 and the resulting equation solved for y. The result is

$$y = b - A\sin(\omega t + \theta_0) \tag{4.38}$$

where $b = -C_1/\omega$. To find the form of the path of motion, we eliminate t between Equation 4.36 and Equation 4.38 to get

$$(x - a)^2 + (y - b)^2 = A^2 \tag{4.39}$$

Thus the projection of the path of motion on the xy plane is a circle of radius A centered at

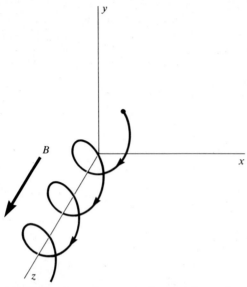

FIGURE 4.8 Helical path of a particle moving in a magnetic field.

the point (a,b). Since, from the third of Equations 4.34, the speed in the z direction is constant, we conclude that the path is a *helix*. The axis of the *winding* path is in the direction of the magnetic field, as shown in Figure 4.8. From Equation 4.38 we have

$$\dot{y} = -A\omega \cos(\omega t + \theta_0) \qquad (4.40)$$

Upon eliminating t between Equation 4.37 and Equation 4.40, we find

$$\dot{x}^2 + \dot{y}^2 = A^2\omega^2 = A^2\left(\frac{qB}{m}\right)^2 \qquad (4.41)$$

Letting $v_1 = (\dot{x}^2 + \dot{y}^2)^{1/2}$, we see that the radius A of the helix is given by

$$A = \frac{v_1}{\omega} = v_1\frac{m}{qB} \qquad (4.42)$$

If there is no component of the velocity in the z direction, the path is a circle of radius A. It is evident that A is directly proportional to the speed v_1, and that the angular frequency ω of motion in the circular path is *independent* of the speed. ω is known as the cylotron frequency. The cyclotron, invented by Ernest Lawrence, depends for its operation on the fact that ω is independent of the speed of the charged particle. ∎

4.6 Constrained Motion of a Particle

When a moving particle is restricted geometrically in the sense that it must stay on a certain definite surface or curve, the motion is said to be *constrained*. A piece of ice sliding around in a bowl, or a bead sliding on a wire, are examples of constrained motion. The constraint may be complete, as with the bead, or it may be one sided, as with the ice in the bowl. Constraints may be fixed, or they may be moving. In this chapter we shall study only fixed constraints.

The Energy Equation for Smooth Constraints

The total force acting on a particle moving under constraint can be expressed as the vector sum of the net external force $\mathbf{F}$ and the force of constraint $\mathbf{R}$. The latter force is the reaction of the constraining agent upon the particle. The equation of motion may therefore be written

$$m\frac{d\mathbf{v}}{dt} = \mathbf{F} + \mathbf{R} \tag{4.43}$$

If we take the dot product with the velocity $\mathbf{v}$ we have

$$m\frac{d\mathbf{v}}{dt} \cdot \mathbf{v} = \mathbf{F} \cdot \mathbf{v} + \mathbf{R} \cdot \mathbf{v} \tag{4.44}$$

Now in the case of a *smooth* constraint—for example, a frictionless surface—the reaction $\mathbf{R}$ is normal to the surface or curve while the velocity $\mathbf{v}$ is tangent to the surface. Hence $\mathbf{R}$ is perpendicular to $\mathbf{v}$ and the dot product $\mathbf{R} \cdot \mathbf{v}$ vanishes. Equation 4.44 then reduces to

$$\frac{d}{dt}\left(\frac{1}{2}m\mathbf{v} \cdot \mathbf{v}\right) = \mathbf{F} \cdot \mathbf{v}$$

Consequently, if $\mathbf{F}$ is conservative, we can integrate as in Section 4.2, and we find the same energy relation as Equation 4.9, namely,

$$\tfrac{1}{2}mv^2 + V(x,y,z) = \text{constant} = E$$

Thus the particle, although remaining on the surface or curve, moves in such a way that the total energy is constant. We might, of course, have expected this to be the case for frictionless constraints.

Examples

4.9   A particle is placed on top of a smooth sphere of radius a. If the particle is slightly disturbed, at what point will it leave the sphere?

The forces acting on the particle are the downward force of gravity and the reaction $\mathbf{R}$ of the spherical surface. The equation of motion is

$$m\frac{d\mathbf{v}}{dt} = m\mathbf{g} + \mathbf{R}$$

Let us choose coordinate axes as shown in Figure 4.9. The potential energy is then mgz, and the energy equation reads

$$\tfrac{1}{2}mv^2 + mgz = E \tag{4.45}$$

From the initial conditions ($v = 0$ for $z = a$) we have $E = mga$, so, as the particle slides down, its speed is given by the equation

$$v^2 = 2g(a - z)$$

Now, if we take radial components of the equation of motion, we can write the force equation as

$$-\frac{mv^2}{a} = -mg \cos \theta + R = -mg\frac{z}{a} + R$$

Hence

$$R = mg\frac{z}{a} - \frac{mv^2}{a} = mg\frac{z}{a} - \frac{m}{a}2g(a - z)$$
$$= \frac{mg}{a}(3z - 2a)$$

Thus R vanishes when $z = \frac{2}{3}a$, at which point the particle will leave the sphere. This may be argued from the fact that the sign of R changes from positive to negative there. ∎

4.10 *Constrained motion on a cycloid.* Consider a particle sliding under gravity in a smooth cycloidal trough, Figure 4.10, represented by the parametric equations

$$x = A(2\varphi + \sin 2\varphi)$$
$$z = A(1 - \cos 2\varphi)$$

where φ is the parameter. Now the energy equation for the motion, assuming no y-motion, is

$$E = \frac{m}{2}v^2 + V(z) = \frac{m}{2}(\dot{x}^2 + \dot{z}^2) + mgz$$

Since $\dot{x} = 2A\dot{\varphi}(1 + \cos 2\varphi)$ and $\dot{z} = 2A\dot{\varphi} \sin 2\varphi$, we find the following expression for the energy in terms of φ:

$$E = 4mA^2\dot{\varphi}^2(1 + \cos 2\varphi) + mgA(1 - \cos 2\varphi)$$

or, by use of the identities $1 + \cos 2\varphi = 2\cos^2 \varphi$, $1 - \cos 2\varphi = 2\sin^2 \varphi$,

$$E = 8mA^2\dot{\varphi}^2 \cos^2 \varphi + 2mgA \sin^2 \varphi$$

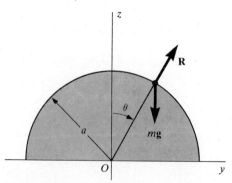

FIGURE 4.9   Particle sliding on a smooth sphere.

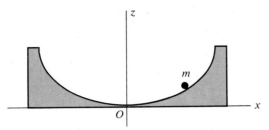

FIGURE 4.10 Particle sliding in a smooth cycloidal trough.

Let us introduce the variable s defined by $s = 4A \sin \varphi$. The energy equation can then be written

$$E = \frac{m}{2}\dot{s}^2 + \frac{1}{2}\left(\frac{mg}{4A}\right)s^2$$

This is just the energy equation for harmonic motion in the single variable s. Thus the particle undergoes periodic motion whose frequency is independent of the amplitude of oscillation, unlike the simple pendulum for which the frequency depends on the amplitude. The periodic motion in the present case is said to be *isochronous*. (The linear harmonic oscillator under Hooke's law is, of course, isochronous.)

The Dutch physicist and mathematician Christiaan Huygens discovered the above fact in connection with attempts to improve the accuracy of pendulum clocks. He also discovered the theory of evolutes and found that the evolute of a cycloid is also a cycloid. Hence, by providing cycloidal "cheeks" for a pendulum, the motion of the bob must follow a cycloidal path and the period is thus independent of the amplitude. Though ingenious, the invention never found extensive practical use. ∎

PROBLEMS

4.1 Find the force for each of the following potential energy functions:

(a) $V = cxyz + C$
(b) $V = \alpha x^2 + \beta y^2 + \gamma z^2 + C$
(c) $V = ce^{-(\alpha x + \beta y + \gamma z)}$
(d) $V = cr^n$ in spherical coordinates

4.2 By finding the curl, determine which of the following forces are conservative:

(a) $\mathbf{F} = \mathbf{i}x + \mathbf{j}y + \mathbf{k}z$
(b) $\mathbf{F} = \mathbf{i}y - \mathbf{j}x + \mathbf{k}z^2$
(c) $\mathbf{F} = \mathbf{i}y + \mathbf{j}x + \mathbf{k}z^3$
(d) $\mathbf{F} = -kr^{-n}\mathbf{e}_r$ in spherical coordinates

4.3 Find the value of the constant c such that each of the following forces is conservative:

(a) $\mathbf{F} = \mathbf{i}xy + \mathbf{j}cx^2 + \mathbf{k}z^3$
(b) $\mathbf{F} = \mathbf{i}(z/y) + c\mathbf{j}(xz/y^2) + \mathbf{k}(x/y)$

4.4 A particle of mass m moving in three dimensions under the potential energy function $V(x,y,z) = \alpha x + \beta y^2 + \gamma z^3$ has speed v_0 when it passes through the origin.

(a) What will its speed be if and when it passes through the point $(1,1,1)$?

(b)   If the point $(1,1,1)$ is a turning point in the motion $(v = 0)$, what is v_0?
(c)   What are the component differential equations of motion of the particle?

(*Note:* It is *not* necessary to solve the differential equations of motion in this problem.)

4.5   Consider the two force functions

(a) $\mathbf{F} = \mathbf{i}x + \mathbf{j}y$
(b) $\mathbf{F} = \mathbf{i}y - \mathbf{j}x$

Verify that (a) is conservative and that (b) is nonconservative by showing that the integral $\int \mathbf{F} \cdot d\mathbf{r}$ is independent of the path of integration for (a), but not for (b), by taking two paths in which the starting point is the origin $(0,0)$, and the end point is $(1,1)$. For one path take the line $x = y$. For the other path, take the x axis out to the point $(1,0)$ and then the line $x = 1$ up to the point $(1,1)$.

4.6   Show that the variation of gravity with height can be accounted for approximately by the following potential energy function:

$$V = mgz\left(1 - \frac{z}{r_e}\right)$$

in which r_e is the radius of the earth. Find the force given by the above potential function. From this, find the component differential equations of motion of a projectile under such a force. If the vertical component of the initial velocity is v_{0z}, how high does the projectile go? (Compare with Example 2.3.)

4.7   Particles of mud are thrown from the rim of a rolling wheel. If the forward speed of the wheel is v_0, and the radius of the wheel is b, show that the greatest height above the ground that the mud can go is

$$b + \frac{v_0^2}{2g} + \frac{gb^2}{2v_0^2}$$

At what point on the rolling wheel does this mud leave? (*Note:* It is necessary to assume that $v_0^2 \geq bg$.)

4.8   A gun is located at the bottom of a hill of constant slope φ. Show that the range of the gun measured up the slope of the hill is

$$\frac{2v_0^2 \cos \alpha \sin(\alpha - \varphi)}{g \cos^2 \varphi}$$

where α is the angle of elevation of the gun, and that the maximum value of the slope range is

$$\frac{v_0^2}{g(1 + \sin \varphi)}$$

4.9   Write down the component form of the differential equations of motion of a projectile if the air resistance is proportional to the square of the speed. Are the equations separated? Show that the x and y components of the velocity are given by

$$\dot{x} = \dot{x}_0 e^{-\gamma s} \qquad \dot{y} = \dot{y}_0 e^{-\gamma s}$$

where s is the distance the projectile has traveled along the path of motion, and $\gamma = c_2/m$.

4.10   Fill in the steps leading to Equations 4.22 and 4.22a giving the horizontal range of a projectile that is subject to linear air drag.

4.11 The initial conditions for a two-dimensional isotropic oscillator are as follows: $t = 0$, $x = A$, $y = 4A$, $\dot{x} = 0$, $\dot{y} = 3\omega A$ where ω is the angular frequency. Find x and y as functions of t. Show that the motion takes place entirely within a rectangle of dimensions $2A$ and $10A$. Find the inclination ψ of the elliptical path relative to the x axis. Make a sketch of the path.

4.12 A small lead ball of mass m is suspended by means of six light springs as shown in Figure 4.5. The stiffness constants are in the ratio 1:4:9 so that the potential energy function can be expressed as

$$V = \frac{k}{2}(x^2 + 4y^2 + 9z^2)$$

At time $t = 0$ the ball is given a push in the $(1,1,1)$ direction imparting to it a speed v_0 at the origin. If $k = \pi^2 m$, numerically, find x, y, and z as functions of the time t. Does the ball ever retrace its path? If so, for what value of t does it first return to the origin with the same velocity that it had at $t = 0$?

4.13 Complete the derivation of Equation 4.25.

4.14 An atom is situated in a simple cubic crystal lattice. If the potential energy of interaction between any two atoms is of the form $cr^{-\alpha}$ where c and α are constants and r is the distance between the two atoms, show that the total energy of interaction of a given atom with its six nearest neighbors is approximately that of the three-dimensional harmonic oscillator potential

$$V \simeq A + B(x^2 + y^2 + z^2)$$

where A and B are constants. [*Note:* Assume that the six neighboring atoms are fixed and are located at the points $(\pm d,0,0)$, $(0, \pm d,0)$, $(0,0, \pm d)$, and that the displacement (x,y,z) of the given atom from the equilibrium position $(0,0,0)$ is small compared to d. Then $V = \Sigma cr_i^{-\alpha}$ where $r_1 = [(d - x)^2 + y^2 + z^2]^{1/2}$ with similar expressions for $r_2, r_3,$ . . . , r_6. See approximation formulas in Appendix D.]

4.15 An electron moves in a force field due to a uniform electric field **E** and a uniform magnetic field **B** which is at right angles to **E**. Let $\mathbf{E} = \mathbf{j}E$ and $\mathbf{B} = \mathbf{k}B$. Take the initial position of the electron at the origin with initial velocity $\mathbf{v}_0 = \mathbf{i}v_0$ in the x direction. Find the resulting motion of the particle. Show that the path of motion is a cycloid:

$$x = a \sin \omega t + bt$$
$$y = a(1 - \cos \omega t)$$
$$z = 0$$

Cycloidal motion of electrons is utilized in the *magnetron*—an electronic tube used to produce high-frequency radio waves, as in microwave ovens.

4.16 A particle is placed on a smooth sphere of radius b at a distance $b/2$ above the central plane. As the particle slides down the side of the sphere, at what point will it leave?

4.17 A bead slides on a smooth rigid wire bent into the form of a circular loop of radius b. If the plane of the loop is vertical, and if the bead starts from rest at a point which is level with the center of the loop, find the speed of the bead at the bottom and the reaction of the wire on the bead at that point.

4.18 Show that the period of the particle sliding in the cycloidal trough of Example 4.10 is 4π $(A/g)^{1/2}$.

5

Noninertial Reference Systems

5.1   Accelerated Coordinate Systems and Inertial Forces

In describing the motion of a particle it is frequently very convenient, and sometimes necessary, to employ a coordinate system which is not inertial. For example, a coordinate system fixed to the earth is the most convenient one to describe the motion of a projectile, even though the earth is accelerating and rotating.

   We shall first consider the case of a coordinate system that undergoes pure translation. In Figure 5.1 $Oxyz$ are the primary coordinate axes (assumed fixed), and $O'x'y'z'$ are the moving axes. In the case of pure translation the respective axes Ox and $O'x'$, and so on, remain parallel. The position vector of a particle P is denoted by $\mathbf{r}$ in the fixed system and by $\mathbf{r}'$ in the moving system. The displacement OO' of the moving origin is denoted by $\mathbf{R}_0$. Thus, from the triangle $OO'P$, we have

$$\mathbf{r} = \mathbf{R}_0 + \mathbf{r}' \qquad (5.1)$$

Taking the first and second time derivatives gives

$$\mathbf{v} = \mathbf{V}_0 + \mathbf{v}' \qquad (5.2)$$

$$\mathbf{a} = \mathbf{A}_0 + \mathbf{a}' \qquad (5.3)$$

in which $\mathbf{V}_0$ and $\mathbf{A}_0$ are, respectively, the velocity and acceleration of the moving system, and $\mathbf{v}'$ and $\mathbf{a}'$ are the velocity and acceleration of the particle *in* the moving system.

112

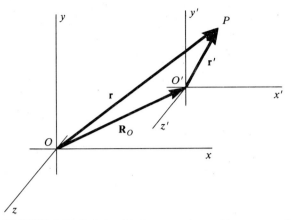

FIGURE 5.1   Relationship between the position vectors for two coordinate systems undergoing pure translation relative to one another.

In particular, if the moving system is not accelerating, so that $\mathbf{A}_0 = \mathbf{O}$, then

$$\mathbf{a} = \mathbf{a}'$$

so the acceleration is the same in either system. Consequently, if the primary system is inertial, Newton's second law $\mathbf{F} = m\mathbf{a}$ becomes $\mathbf{F} = m\mathbf{a}'$ in the moving system, that is, the moving system is also an inertial system (provided it is not rotating). Thus, as far as Newtonian mechanics is concerned, we cannot specify a unique coordinate system; if Newton's laws hold in one system, they are also valid in any other system moving with uniform velocity relative to the first.

On the other hand, if the moving system is accelerating, then Newton's second law becomes

$$\mathbf{F} = m\mathbf{A}_0 + m\mathbf{a}'$$

or

$$\mathbf{F} - m\mathbf{A}_0 = m\mathbf{a}' \tag{5.4}$$

for the equation of motion in the accelerating system. If we wish, we can write the above equation in the form

$$\text{"}\mathbf{F}\text{"} = m\mathbf{a}' \tag{5.5}$$

in which "$\mathbf{F}$" $= \mathbf{F} + (-m\mathbf{A}_0)$. That is, an acceleration $\mathbf{A}_0$ of the reference system can be taken into account by adding an *inertial term* $-m\mathbf{A}_0$ to the force $\mathbf{F}$ and equating the result to the product of mass and acceleration in the moving system. Inertial terms in the equations of motion are sometimes called *inertial forces* or *fictitious forces*. Such "forces" are not due to interactions with other bodies, rather, they stem from the choice of the reference system. Whether or not one wishes to call them forces is purely a matter of terminology. In any case, inertial terms are present if a noninertial coordinate system is used to describe the motion of a particle.

Example

5.1   A block of wood rests on a rough horizontal table. If the table is accelerated in a horizontal direction, under what conditions will the block slip? Let μ_s be the coefficient of static friction between the block and the table top. Then the force of friction $\mathbf{F}$ has a maximum value of $\mu_s mg$, where m is the mass of the block. The condition for slipping is that the inertial force $-m\mathbf{A}_0$ exceeds the frictional force where $\mathbf{A}_0$ is the acceleration of the table. Hence the condition for slipping is

$$|-m\mathbf{A}_0| > \mu_s mg$$

or

$$A_0 > \mu_s g$$ ■

5.2 Rotating Coordinate Systems. Angular Velocity as a Vector Quantity

To discuss the effects of rotation of the coordinate system it will be convenient to first consider the case of pure rotation. The origins of the two coordinate systems then coincide, Figure 5.2, and so $\mathbf{r} = \mathbf{r}'$, or explicitly

$$\mathbf{i}x + \mathbf{j}y + \mathbf{k}z = \mathbf{i}'x' + \mathbf{j}'y' + \mathbf{k}'z' \tag{5.6}$$

When we differentiate with respect to time to find the velocity we must keep in mind the fact that the unit vectors $\mathbf{i}'$, $\mathbf{j}'$, and $\mathbf{k}'$ in the rotating system are *not* constant, whereas the primary unit vectors $\mathbf{i}$, $\mathbf{j}$, and $\mathbf{k}$ are considered constant. Thus we can write

$$\mathbf{i}\frac{dx}{dt} + \mathbf{j}\frac{dy}{dt} + \mathbf{k}\frac{dz}{dt} = \mathbf{i}'\frac{dx'}{dt} + \mathbf{j}'\frac{dy'}{dt} + \mathbf{k}'\frac{dz'}{dt} + x'\frac{d\mathbf{i}'}{dt} + y'\frac{d\mathbf{j}'}{dt} + z'\frac{d\mathbf{k}'}{dt}$$

The three terms on the left side of the above equation clearly give the velocity vector $\mathbf{v}$

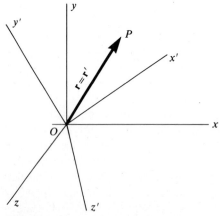

FIGURE 5.2   Rotating coordinate system (primed system).

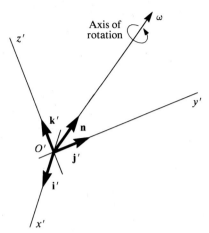

FIGURE 5.3 The angular velocity vector of a rotating coordinate system.

in the fixed system, and the first three terms on the right are the components of the velocity *in* the rotating system, which we shall call $\mathbf{v}'$, so the equation may be written

$$\mathbf{v} = \mathbf{v}' + x'\frac{d\mathbf{i}'}{dt} + y'\frac{d\mathbf{j}'}{dt} + z'\frac{d\mathbf{k}'}{dt} \tag{5.7}$$

The last three terms on the right represent the velocity due to rotation of the primed coordinate system. We must now determine how the time derivatives of the basis vectors are related to the rotation.

At any given instant the rotation of the primed system is specified by some axis of rotation and an angular speed about that axis. Let the *direction* of the axis be designated by a unit vector $\mathbf{n}$, and let the angular speed be ω. We shall call the product $\omega\mathbf{n}$ the *angular velocity vector* of the rotating system:

$$\boldsymbol{\omega} = \omega\mathbf{n} \tag{5.8}$$

The sense of the angular velocity vector is given by the right-hand rule, similar to the definition of the cross product, as shown in Figure 5.3.

In order to find the time derivatives $d\mathbf{i}'/dt$, $d\mathbf{j}'/dt$, and $d\mathbf{k}'/dt$, consider Figure 5.4. Here is shown the change $\Delta\mathbf{i}'$ in the unit vector $\mathbf{i}'$ due to a small rotation $\Delta\theta$ about the axis of rotation. (The vectors $\mathbf{j}'$ and $\mathbf{k}'$ are omitted for clarity.) From the figure we see that the magnitude of $\Delta\mathbf{i}'$ is given by the approximate relation

$$|\Delta\mathbf{i}'| \simeq (\sin\varphi)\Delta\theta$$

where φ is the angle between $\mathbf{i}'$ and $\boldsymbol{\omega}$. Let Δt be the time interval for this change. Then we can write

$$\left|\frac{d\mathbf{i}'}{dt}\right| = \lim_{\Delta t \to 0}\left|\frac{\Delta\mathbf{i}'}{\Delta t}\right| = \sin\varphi\frac{d\theta}{dt} = (\sin\varphi)\omega$$

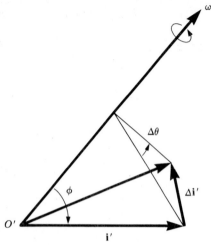

FIGURE 5.4   Change in the unit vector **i′** produced by a small rotation $\Delta\theta$.

Now the direction of $\Delta\mathbf{i}'$ is perpendicular to *both* $\boldsymbol{\omega}$ and $\mathbf{i}'$; consequently, from the definition of the cross product, we can write the above equation in vector form

$$\frac{d\mathbf{i}'}{dt} = \boldsymbol{\omega} \times \mathbf{i}' \tag{5.9}$$

Similarly, we find $d\mathbf{j}'/dt = \boldsymbol{\omega} \times \mathbf{j}'$, and $d\mathbf{k}'/dt = \boldsymbol{\omega} \times \mathbf{k}'$.

We now apply the above result to the last three terms in Equation 5.7 as follows:

$$x'\frac{d\mathbf{i}'}{dt} + y'\frac{d\mathbf{j}'}{dt} + z'\frac{d\mathbf{k}'}{dt} = x'(\boldsymbol{\omega} \times \mathbf{i}') + y'(\boldsymbol{\omega} \times \mathbf{j}') + z'(\boldsymbol{\omega} \times \mathbf{k}')$$
$$= \boldsymbol{\omega} \times (\mathbf{i}'x' + \mathbf{j}'y' + \mathbf{k}'z')$$
$$= \boldsymbol{\omega} \times \mathbf{r}'$$

This is the velocity of P due to rotation of the primed coordinate system. Accordingly, Equation 5.7 can be shortened to read

$$\mathbf{v} = \mathbf{v}' + \boldsymbol{\omega} \times \mathbf{r}' \tag{5.10}$$

or, more explicitly

$$\left(\frac{d\mathbf{r}}{dt}\right)_{fixed} = \left(\frac{d\mathbf{r}'}{dt}\right)_{rot} + \boldsymbol{\omega} \times \mathbf{r}' = \left[\left(\frac{d}{dt}\right)_{rot} + \boldsymbol{\omega} \times \right]\mathbf{r}'$$

that is, the operation of differentiating the position vector with respect to time in the fixed system is equivalent to the operation of taking the time derivative in the rotating system plus the operator $\boldsymbol{\omega} \times$. A little reflection will show that the same applies to *any* vector $\mathbf{Q}$: $d\mathbf{Q}/dt)_{fixed} = d\mathbf{Q}/dt)_{rot} + \boldsymbol{\omega} \times \mathbf{Q}$. In particular, if that vector is the velocity, then we have

$$\left(\frac{d\mathbf{v}}{dt}\right)_{fixed} = \left(\frac{d\mathbf{v}}{dt}\right)_{rot} + \boldsymbol{\omega} \times \mathbf{v}$$

But $\mathbf{v} = \mathbf{v}' + \boldsymbol{\omega} \times \mathbf{r}'$, so

$$\left(\frac{d\mathbf{v}}{dt}\right)_{fixed} = \left(\frac{d}{dt}\right)_{rot} (\mathbf{v}' + \boldsymbol{\omega} \times \mathbf{r}') + \boldsymbol{\omega} \times (\mathbf{v}' + \boldsymbol{\omega} \times \mathbf{r}')$$

$$= \left(\frac{d\mathbf{v}'}{dt}\right)_{rot} + \left[\frac{d(\boldsymbol{\omega} \times \mathbf{r}')}{dt}\right]_{rot} + \boldsymbol{\omega} \times \mathbf{v}' + \boldsymbol{\omega} \times (\boldsymbol{\omega} \times \mathbf{r}')$$

$$= \left(\frac{d\mathbf{v}'}{dt}\right)_{rot} + \left(\frac{d\boldsymbol{\omega}}{dt}\right)_{rot} \times \mathbf{r}' + \boldsymbol{\omega} \times \left(\frac{d\mathbf{r}'}{dt}\right)_{rot} + \boldsymbol{\omega} \times \mathbf{v}'$$
$$+ \boldsymbol{\omega} \times (\boldsymbol{\omega} \times \mathbf{r}')$$

Now concerning the term involving the time derivative of $\boldsymbol{\omega}$, we have $(d\boldsymbol{\omega}/dt)_{fixed} = (d\boldsymbol{\omega}/dt)_{rot} + \boldsymbol{\omega} \times \boldsymbol{\omega}$. But the cross product of any vector with itself vanishes, so $(d\boldsymbol{\omega}/dt)_{fixed} = (d\boldsymbol{\omega}/dt)_{rot} = \dot{\boldsymbol{\omega}}$. Since $\mathbf{v}' = (d\mathbf{r}'/dt)_{rot}$ and $\mathbf{a}' = (d\mathbf{v}'/dt)_{rot}$, we can express the final result as follows:

$$\mathbf{a} = \mathbf{a}' + \dot{\boldsymbol{\omega}} \times \mathbf{r}' + 2\boldsymbol{\omega} \times \mathbf{v}' + \boldsymbol{\omega} \times (\boldsymbol{\omega} \times \mathbf{r}') \qquad (5.11)$$

giving the acceleration in the fixed system in·terms of the position, velocity, and acceleration in the rotating system.

In the general case in which the primed system is undergoing *both* translation and rotation, Figure 5.5, we must add the velocity of translation $\mathbf{V}_0$ to the right-hand side of Equation 5.10 and the acceleration $\mathbf{A}_0$ of the moving system to the right side of Equa-

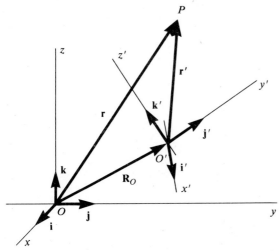

FIGURE 5.5 Geometry for the general case of translation and rotation of the moving coordinate system (primed system).

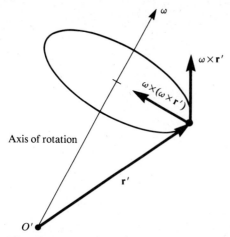

FIGURE 5.6   Illustrating the centripetal acceleration.

tion 5.11. This gives the general equations for transforming from a fixed system to a moving and rotating system:

$$\mathbf{v} = \mathbf{v}' + \boldsymbol{\omega} \times \mathbf{r}' + \mathbf{V}_0 \tag{5.12}$$

$$\mathbf{a} = \mathbf{a}' + \dot{\boldsymbol{\omega}} \times \mathbf{r}' + 2\boldsymbol{\omega} \times \mathbf{v}' + \boldsymbol{\omega} \times (\boldsymbol{\omega} \times \mathbf{r}') + \mathbf{A}_0 \tag{5.13}$$

The term $2\boldsymbol{\omega} \times \mathbf{v}'$ is known as the *Coriolis acceleration*, and the term $\boldsymbol{\omega} \times (\boldsymbol{\omega} \times \mathbf{r}')$ is called the *centripetal acceleration*. The Coriolis acceleration appears whenever a particle *moves* in a rotating coordinate system (except when the velocity $\mathbf{v}'$ is parallel to the axis of rotation), and the centripetal acceleration is the result of the particle being carried around a circular path (for fixed $\mathbf{r}'$) in the rotating system. The centripetal acceleration is always directed toward the axis of rotation and is perpendicular to the axis as shown in Figure 5.6. The term $\dot{\boldsymbol{\omega}} \times \mathbf{r}'$ is sometimes called the *transverse acceleration* since it is perpendicular to the position vector $\mathbf{r}'$. It appears as a result of any angular acceleration of the rotating system, that is, if the angular velocity vector is changing in either magnitude or direction, or both.

Examples

5.2   A wheel of radius b rolls along the ground with constant forward speed V_0. Find the acceleration, relative to the ground, of any point on the rim. Let us choose a coordinate system fixed to the rotating wheel, and let the moving origin be at the center with the x axis passing through the point in question, as shown in Figure 5.7. Then we have

$$\mathbf{r}' = \mathbf{i}'b \qquad \mathbf{a}' = \ddot{\mathbf{r}}' = 0 \qquad \mathbf{v}' = \dot{\mathbf{r}}' = 0$$

The angular velocity vector is given by

$$\boldsymbol{\omega} = \mathbf{k}'\omega = \mathbf{k}'\frac{V_0}{b}$$

for the choice of coordinates shown. Hence all terms in the expression for acceleration vanish except the centripetal term:

$$\mathbf{a} = \boldsymbol{\omega} \times (\boldsymbol{\omega} \times \mathbf{r}') = \mathbf{k}'\boldsymbol{\omega} \times (\mathbf{k}'\boldsymbol{\omega} \times \mathbf{i}'b)$$

$$= \frac{V_0^2}{b}\mathbf{k}' \times (\mathbf{k}' \times \mathbf{i}')$$

$$= \frac{V_0^2}{b}\mathbf{k}' \times \mathbf{j}'$$

$$= \frac{V_0^2}{b}(-\mathbf{i}')$$

Thus **a** is of magnitude V_0^2/b and is always directed toward the center of the rolling wheel. ∎

5.3   A bicycle travels with constant speed around a track of radius ρ. What is the acceleration of the highest point on one of its wheels? Let V_0 denote the speed of the bicycle and b the radius of the wheel. We choose a coordinate system with origin at the center of the wheel and with the x' axis horizontal pointing toward the center of curvature C of the track. Rather than have the moving coordinate system rotate with the wheel, we choose a system in which the z' axis remains vertical as shown in Figure 5.8. Thus the $O'x'y'z'$ system rotates with angular velocity $\boldsymbol{\omega}$ which can be expressed as

$$\boldsymbol{\omega} = \mathbf{k}'\frac{V_0}{\rho}$$

and the acceleration of the moving origin $\mathbf{A}_0$ is given by

$$\mathbf{A}_0 = \mathbf{i}'\frac{V_0^2}{\rho}$$

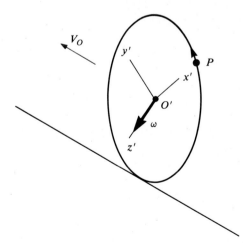

FIGURE 5.7   Rotating coordinates fixed to a rolling wheel.

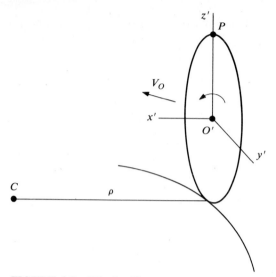

FIGURE 5.8   Wheel rolling on a curved track. The z' axis remains vertical as the wheel turns.

Since each point on the wheel is moving in a circle of radius b with respect to the moving origin, the acceleration in the $O'x'y'z'$ system of any point on the wheel is directed toward O' and has magnitude V_0^2/b. Thus, in the moving system we have

$$\ddot{\mathbf{r}}' = -\mathbf{k}'\frac{V_0^2}{b}$$

for the point at the top of the wheel. Also, the velocity of this point in the moving system is given by

$$\mathbf{v}' = -\mathbf{j}'V_0$$

so the Coriolis acceleration is

$$2\boldsymbol{\omega} \times \mathbf{v}' = 2\left(\frac{V_0}{\rho}\mathbf{k}'\right) \times (-\mathbf{j}'V_0) = 2\frac{V_0^2}{\rho}\mathbf{i}'$$

Since the angular velocity $\boldsymbol{\omega}$ is constant, the transverse acceleration is zero. The centripetal acceleration is also zero, because

$$\boldsymbol{\omega} \times (\boldsymbol{\omega} \times \mathbf{r}') = \frac{V_0^2}{\rho^2}\mathbf{k}' \times (\mathbf{k}' \times b\mathbf{k}') = 0$$

Thus the net acceleration, relative to the ground, of the highest point on the wheel is

$$\mathbf{a} = 3\frac{V_0^2}{\rho}\mathbf{i}' - \frac{V_0^2}{b}\mathbf{k}'$$

∎

5.3   Dynamics of a Particle in a Rotating Coordinate System

Since the primary coordinate system is assumed to be an inertial system, then the fundamental equation of motion is

$$\mathbf{F} = m\mathbf{a}$$

In view of Equation 5.13, we can now write the equation of motion in the moving coordinates as follows:

$$\mathbf{F} - m\mathbf{A}_0 - 2m\boldsymbol{\omega} \times \mathbf{v}' - m\dot{\boldsymbol{\omega}} \times \mathbf{r}' - m\boldsymbol{\omega} \times (\boldsymbol{\omega} \times \mathbf{r}') = m\mathbf{a}' \quad (5.14)$$

The terms have been transposed in order to display them in the form of inertial forces to be added to the physical force $\mathbf{F}$. The inertial forces have been given names corresponding to their respective accelerations, discussed in Section 5.2.

The *Coriolis force:*

$$\mathbf{F}_{\text{Cor}} = -2m\boldsymbol{\omega} \times \mathbf{v}'$$

The *transverse force:*

$$\mathbf{F}_{\text{trans}} = -m\dot{\boldsymbol{\omega}} \times \mathbf{r}'$$

The *centrifugal force:*

$$\mathbf{F}_{\text{cent}} = -m\boldsymbol{\omega} \times (\boldsymbol{\omega} \times \mathbf{r}')$$

The remaining force $-m\mathbf{A}_0$ is the inertial term due to translation of the coordinate system and has been discussed in Section 5.1 above.

Again, as in the previous discussion of the inertial term $-m\mathbf{A}_0$, we can write the equation of motion in the moving system as

$$\text{``}\mathbf{F}\text{''} = m\mathbf{a}'$$

in which the total "force" is given by

$$\text{``}\mathbf{F}\text{''} = \mathbf{F} + \mathbf{F}_{\text{Cor}} + \mathbf{F}_{\text{trans}} + \mathbf{F}_{\text{cent}} - m\mathbf{A}_0$$

The four inertial terms on the right-hand side all depend on the particular coordinate system in which the motion is described. They arise from the inertial properties of matter rather than from the presence of other bodies.

The Coriolis force is particularly interesting. It is present only if a particle is *moving in a rotating coordinate system*. Its direction is always perpendicular to the velocity vector of the particle in the moving system. The Coriolis force thus seems to deflect a moving particle at right angles to its direction of motion. This force is important, for example, in computing the trajectory of a projectile. Coriolis effects are also responsible for the circulation of air around high- or low-pressure areas on the earth's surface. Thus in the case of a high-pressure area the air tends to flow outward and to the right in the northern hemisphere, so that the circulation is clockwise. In the southern hemisphere the reverse is true.

The transverse force is present only if there is an angular acceleration of the

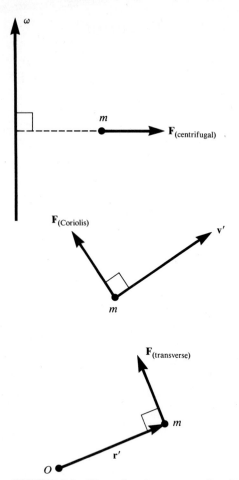

FIGURE 5.9 Illustrating the apparent (inertial) forces arising from rotation. The forces are drawn separately for clarity.

rotating coordinate system. This force is always perpendicular to the radius vector **r′** in the moving system.

Finally, the centrifugal force is the familiar force arising from rotation about an axis. This force is always directed outward away from the axis of rotation and is perpendicular to that axis. If θ is the angle between the radius vector **r′** and the rotation vector $\boldsymbol{\omega}$, then the magnitude of the centrifugal force is clearly $mr'\omega^2 \sin \theta$ or $mp\omega^2$ where ρ is the perpendicular distance from the moving particle to the axis of rotation. The various forces are illustrated in Figure 5.9.

Examples

5.4 A bug crawls outward with constant speed v' along the spoke of a wheel which is rotating with constant angular velocity $\boldsymbol{\omega}$ about a vertical axis. Find all the apparent forces acting on the bug. First, let us choose a coordinate system fixed on the wheel, and let the x' axis point along the spoke in question. Then we have

$$\dot{\mathbf{r}}' = \mathbf{i}\dot{x}' = \mathbf{i}v'$$
$$\ddot{\mathbf{r}}' = 0$$

for the velocity and acceleration of the bug as described in the rotating system. If we choose the z' axis to be vertical, then

$$\boldsymbol{\omega} = \mathbf{k}'\omega$$

The various forces are then given by the following:

Coriolis force

$$-2m\boldsymbol{\omega} \times \dot{\mathbf{r}}' = -2m\omega v' (\mathbf{k}' \times \mathbf{i}') = -2m\omega v'\mathbf{j}'$$

Transverse force

$$-m\dot{\boldsymbol{\omega}} \times \mathbf{r}' = 0 \qquad (\boldsymbol{\omega} = \text{constant})$$

Centrifugal force

$$-m\boldsymbol{\omega} \times (\boldsymbol{\omega} \times \mathbf{r}') = -m\omega^2 [\mathbf{k}' \times (\mathbf{k}' \times \mathbf{i}'x')]$$
$$= -m\omega^2 (\mathbf{k}' \times \mathbf{j}'x')$$
$$= m\omega^2 x'\mathbf{i}'$$

Thus, Equation 5.14 reads

$$\mathbf{F} - 2m\omega v'\mathbf{j}' + m\omega^2 x'\mathbf{i}' = 0$$

Here $\mathbf{F}$ is the real force exerted on the bug by the spoke. The forces are shown in Figure 5.10.   ∎

5.5   In the above problem, find how far the bug can crawl before it starts to slip, given the

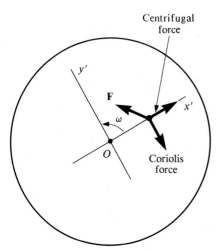

Centrifugal
force

FIGURE 5.10   Forces on an insect crawling outward along a radial line on a rotating wheel.

coefficient of static friction μ_s between the bug and the spoke. Since the force of friction **F** has a maximum value of $\mu_s mg$, slipping will start when

$$|\mathbf{F}| = \mu_s mg$$

or

$$[(2m\omega v')^2 + (m\omega^2 x')^2]^{1/2} = \mu_s mg$$

Upon solving for x', we find

$$x' = \frac{[\mu_s^2 g^2 - 4\omega^2 (v')^2]^{1/2}}{\omega^2}$$

for the distance the bug can crawl before slipping.   ∎

5.4   Effects of the Earth's Rotation

Let us apply the theory developed in the foregoing sections to a coordinate system which is moving with the earth. Since the angular speed of the earth's rotation is 2π radians per day, or about 7.27×10^{-5} radians per sec, we might expect the effects of such rotation to be relatively small. Nevertheless, it is the spin of the earth that produces the equatorial bulge; the equatorial radius is some 13 miles greater than the polar radius.

Static Effects. The Plumb Line

We consider first the case of a particle which is at rest on the surface of the earth. For definiteness, we shall take the particle to be the bob at the end of a plumb line. Let us choose the origin of our coordinate system to be at the position of the bob, so that

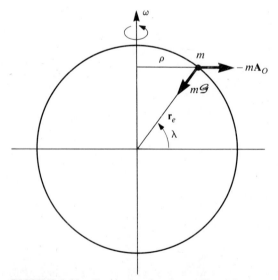

FIGURE 5.11   Gravitational and centrifugal forces on a particle near the earth's surface.

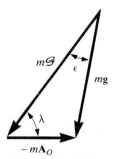

FIGURE 5.12   Vector diagram defining $m\mathbf{g}$.

$\mathbf{r}' = 0$. Now the angular velocity vector $\boldsymbol{\omega}$ is in the direction of the earth's axis and is very nearly constant; that is, the angular acceleration $\dot{\boldsymbol{\omega}}$ is zero. For the static case, then, all terms in the equation of motion Equation 5.14, vanish except the applied force $\mathbf{F}$ and the inertial term $-m\mathbf{A}_0$. The result is

$$\mathbf{F} - m\mathbf{A}_0 = 0$$

The force $\mathbf{F}$ is given by the vector sum of two forces: the true gravitational attraction of the earth (which we shall call $m\mathcal{G}$) and the vertical tension of the plumb line (which we shall denote by $-m\mathbf{g}$). The forces are shown in Figures 5.11 and 5.12. We have then

$$m\mathcal{G} - m\mathbf{g} - m\mathbf{A}_0 = 0 \tag{5.15}$$

or

$$\mathbf{g} = \mathcal{G} - \mathbf{A}_0 \tag{5.15a}$$

Now the vector $m\mathcal{G}$ is in the direction of the center of the earth. The acceleration $\mathbf{A}_0$ is just the centripetal acceleration of our moving origin. Its magnitude is $\rho\omega^2$ or $(r_e \cos \lambda)\omega^2$, where r_e is the radius of the earth, and λ is the *geocentric latitude*. The term $-m\mathbf{A}_0$ (the centrifugal force) is of magnitude $(mr_e \cos \lambda)\omega^2$. It is directed away from and is perpendicular to the earth's axis, as indicated in Figure 5.11. Thus the plumb line does not point to the earth's center, but deviates by a small angle ϵ. From Equation 5.15 the vector $m\mathbf{g}$ may be represented diagrammatically as the third side of a triangle, the other two sides of which are $m\mathcal{G}$ and $-m\mathbf{A}_0$ (Figure 5.12). Applying the law of sines, we have

$$\frac{\sin \epsilon}{mr_e\omega^2 \cos \lambda} = \frac{\sin \lambda}{mg}$$

or, since ϵ is small,

$$\sin \epsilon \simeq \epsilon = \frac{r_e\omega^2}{g} \sin \lambda \cos \lambda = \frac{r_e\omega^2}{2g} \sin 2\lambda$$

Thus ϵ vanishes at the equator ($\lambda = 0$) and at the poles ($\lambda = \pm 90°$), as we would

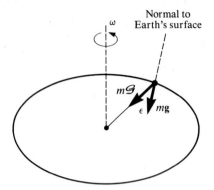

FIGURE 5.13   Exaggerated diagram illustrating the flattening of the earth from rotation.

expect. The maximum deviation of the plumb line from the "true" vertical is at $\lambda = 45°$ where

$$\epsilon_{max} = \frac{r_e\omega^2}{2g} \simeq 1.7 \times 10^{-3} \text{ radian} \simeq \frac{1}{10} \text{ degree}$$

The shape of the earth is such that the plumb line is normal to the surface of the earth at any point. The resulting cross section is approximately elliptical (Figure 5.13). In the above analysis it is assumed that the gravitational force $m\mathcal{G}$ is constant and is directed toward the center of the earth. This assumption is not strictly valid, because the earth is not a true sphere. Local variations owing to mountains, mineral deposits, and so on, also affect the direction of the plumb line to a slight extent.

Dynamic Effects. Motion of a Projectile

The equation of motion Equation 5.14 can be written

$$m\ddot{\mathbf{r}}' = \mathbf{F} + m\mathcal{G} - m\mathbf{A}_0 - 2m\boldsymbol{\omega} \times \dot{\mathbf{r}}' - m\boldsymbol{\omega} \times (\boldsymbol{\omega} \times \mathbf{r}')$$

where $\mathbf{F}$ represents any applied forces other than gravity. But, from the static case considered above, the combination $m\mathcal{G} - m\mathbf{A}_0$ is called $m\mathbf{g}$, hence we can write the equation of motion as

$$m\ddot{\mathbf{r}}' = \mathbf{F} + m\mathbf{g} - 2m\boldsymbol{\omega} \times \dot{\mathbf{r}}' - m\boldsymbol{\omega} \times (\boldsymbol{\omega} \times \mathbf{r}')$$

Let us consider the motion of a projectile. If we neglect air resistance, then $\mathbf{F} = 0$. Furthermore, the term $-m\boldsymbol{\omega} \times (\boldsymbol{\omega} \times \mathbf{r}')$ is very small compared to the other terms, so we shall neglect it. The equation of motion then reduces to

$$m\ddot{\mathbf{r}}' = m\mathbf{g} - 2m\boldsymbol{\omega} \times \dot{\mathbf{r}}' \tag{5.16}$$

in which the last term is the Coriolis force.

To solve the above equation we shall choose the directions of the coordinate axes $O'x'y'z'$ such that the z' axis is vertical (in the direction of the plumb line), the x' axis is to the east, and the y' axis points north (Figure 5.14). With this choice of axes, we have

$$\mathbf{g} = -\mathbf{k'}g$$

The components of $\boldsymbol{\omega}$ in the primed system are

$$\omega_{x'} = 0 \qquad \omega_{y'} = \omega \cos \lambda \qquad \omega_{z'} = \omega \sin \lambda$$

The cross product is therefore given by

$$\boldsymbol{\omega} \times \dot{\mathbf{r}}' = \begin{vmatrix} \mathbf{i'} & \mathbf{j'} & \mathbf{k'} \\ \omega_{x'} & \omega_{y'} & \omega_{z'} \\ \dot{x}' & \dot{y}' & \dot{z}' \end{vmatrix}$$

$$= \mathbf{i}(\omega \dot{z}' \cos \lambda - \omega \dot{y}' \sin \lambda) + \mathbf{j'}(\omega \dot{x}' \sin \lambda) + \mathbf{k'}(-\omega \dot{x}' \cos \lambda)$$

Upon using the above expressions for $\boldsymbol{\omega} \times \dot{\mathbf{r}}'$ in Equation 5.16 and canceling the m's and equating components, we find

$$\ddot{x}' = -2\omega(\dot{z}' \cos \lambda - \dot{y}' \sin \lambda) \tag{5.17}$$

$$\ddot{y}' = -2\omega(\dot{x}' \sin \lambda) \tag{5.18}$$

$$\ddot{z}' = -g + 2\omega \dot{x}' \cos \lambda \tag{5.19}$$

for the component differential equations of motion. These equations are not of the separated type, but we can integrate once with respect to t to obtain

$$\dot{x}' = -2\omega(z' \cos \lambda - y' \sin \lambda) + \dot{x}_0' \tag{5.20}$$

$$\dot{y}' = -2\omega x' \sin \lambda + \dot{y}_0' \tag{5.21}$$

$$\dot{z}' = -gt + 2\omega x' \cos \lambda + \dot{z}_0' \tag{5.22}$$

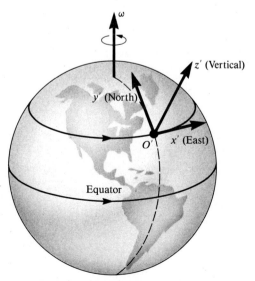

FIGURE 5.14   Coordinate axes for analyzing projectile motion.

The constants of integration $\dot{x}_0'$, $\dot{y}_0'$, and $\dot{z}_0'$ are the initial components of the velocity. The values of $\dot{y}'$ and $\dot{z}'$ from the last two equations above may be substituted into Equation 5.17. The result is

$$\ddot{x}' = 2\omega g t \cos \lambda - 2\omega(\dot{z}_0' \cos \lambda - \dot{y}_0' \sin \lambda) \qquad (5.23)$$

where terms involving ω^2 have been neglected. We now integrate again to get

$$\dot{x}' = \omega g t^2 \cos \lambda - 2\omega t(\dot{z}_0' \cos \lambda - \dot{y}_0' \sin \lambda) + \dot{x}_0'$$

and finally, by a third integration, we find x' as a function of t:

$$x'(t) = \tfrac{1}{3}\omega g t^3 \cos \lambda - \omega t^2 (\dot{z}_0' \cos \lambda - \dot{y}_0' \sin \lambda) + \dot{x}_0' t + x_0' \qquad (5.24)$$

The above expression for x' may be inserted into Equations 5.21 and 5.22. The resulting equations, when integrated, yield

$$y'(t) = \dot{y}_0' t - \omega \dot{x}_0' t^2 \sin \lambda + y_0' \qquad (5.25)$$

$$z'(t) = -\tfrac{1}{2}g t^2 + \dot{z}_0' t + \omega \dot{x}_0' t^2 \cos \lambda + z_0' \qquad (5.26)$$

where, again, terms of order ω^2 have been ignored.

In each of the above three equations, the terms involving ω express the effect of the earth's rotation on the motion of a projectile in a coordinate system fixed to the earth.

Examples

5.6 *Falling body.* Suppose a body is dropped from rest at a height h above the ground. Then at time $t = 0$ we have $\dot{x}_0' = \dot{y}_0' = \dot{z}_0' = 0$ and we shall set $x_0' = y_0' = 0$, $z_0' = h$ for the initial position. Equations 5.24, 5.25, and 5.26 then reduce to

$$x'(t) = \tfrac{1}{3}\omega g t^3 \cos \lambda$$
$$y'(t) = 0$$
$$z'(t) = -\tfrac{1}{2}g t^2 + h$$

Thus, as it falls, the body drifts to the *east*. When it hits the ground ($z' = 0$) we see that $t^2 = 2h/g$, and the eastward drift is given by the corresponding value of $x'(t)$, namely

$$x_h' = \frac{1}{3}\omega\left(\frac{8h^3}{g}\right)^{1/2} \cos \lambda$$

For a height of, say, 100 meters at a latitude of 45°, the drift is

$$\tfrac{1}{3}(7.27 \times 10^{-5}s^{-1})(8 \times 100^3 m^3/9.8 \text{ ms}^{-2})^{1/2} \cos 45°$$
$$= 1.55 \times 10^{-2} \text{ m} = 1.55 \text{ cm}.$$

Since the earth turns to the east, common sense would seem to say that the body should drift westward. Can the reader think of an explanation? ∎

5.7 *Deflection of a rifle bullet.* Consider a projectile that is fired with high initial speed v_0 in a nearly horizontal direction, and suppose this direction is east. Then $\dot{x}_0' = v_0$ and $\dot{y}_0' = \dot{z}_0' = 0$. If we take the origin to be the point from which the projectile is fired, then $x_0' = y_0' = z_0' = 0$ at time $t = 0$. Equation 5.25 then gives

$$y'(t) = -\omega v_0 t^2 \sin \lambda$$

which says that the projectile veers to the *south* or to the right in the northern hemisphere ($\lambda > 0$), and to the left in the southern hemisphere ($\lambda < 0$). If H is the horizontal range of the projectile, then we know that $H \simeq v_0 t_1$ where t_1 is the time of flight. The transverse deflection is then found by setting $t = t_1 = H/v_0$ in the above expression for $y'(t)$. The result is

$$\Delta \simeq \frac{\omega H^2}{v_0} |\sin \lambda|$$

for the magnitude of the deflection. It can be shown that this is the same for *any* direction in which the projectile is initially aimed, provided the trajectory is flat. This follows from the fact that the magnitude of the horizontal component of the Coriolis force on a body traveling parallel to the ground is independent of the direction of motion. (See Problem 5.9.) Since the deflection is proportional to the square of the horizontal range it becomes of considerable importance in long-range gunnery.   ∎

5.5   The Foucault Pendulum

In this section we shall study the effect of the earth's rotation on the motion of a pendulum that is free to swing in any direction, the so called *spherical pendulum*. As shown in Figure 5.15, the applied force acting on the pendulum bob is the vector sum of the weight $m\mathbf{g}$ and the tension $\mathbf{S}$ in the cord. The differential equation of motion is then

$$m\ddot{\mathbf{r}}' = m\mathbf{g} + \mathbf{S} - 2m\boldsymbol{\omega} \times \dot{\mathbf{r}}' \tag{5.27}$$

Here we have neglected the term $-m\boldsymbol{\omega} \times (\boldsymbol{\omega} \times \mathbf{r}')$ as we did in the previous section.

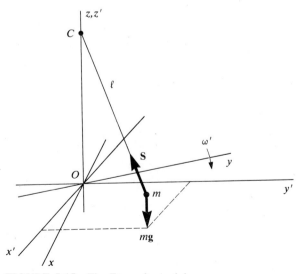

FIGURE 5.15   The Foucault pendulum.

We also worked out the components of the cross product $\boldsymbol{\omega} \times \dot{\mathbf{r}}'$, given just above Equation 5.17. Now the x' and y' components of the tension can be found simply by noting that the direction cosines of the vector $\mathbf{S}$ are $-x'/l$, $-y'/l$, and $-(l - z')/l$, respectively. Consequently $S_x = -x'S/l$, $S_y = -y'S/l$, and the corresponding components of the differential equation of motion (5.27) are

$$m\ddot{x}' = \frac{-x'}{l}S - 2m\omega(\dot{z}' \cos \lambda - \dot{y}' \sin \lambda) \qquad (5.27a)$$

$$m\ddot{y}' = \frac{-y'}{l}S - 2m\omega\dot{x}' \sin \lambda \qquad (5.27b)$$

We are interested in the case where the amplitude of oscillation of the pendulum is small so that the magnitude of the tension S is very nearly constant and equal to mg. Also, we shall neglect $\dot{z}'$ compared to $\dot{y}'$ in Equation 5.27a. The $x'y'$ motion is then governed by the following differential equations:

$$\ddot{x}' = -\frac{g}{l}x' + 2\omega'\dot{y}' \qquad (5.28a)$$

$$\ddot{y}' = -\frac{g}{l}y' - 2\omega'\dot{x}' \qquad (5.28b)$$

in which we have introduced the quantity $\omega' = \omega \sin \lambda = \omega_{z'}$, which is *the local vertical component of the earth's angular velocity*.

Again we are confronted with a set of differential equations of motion that are not in separated form. A heuristic method of solving the equations is to transform to a new coordinate system $Oxyz$ that rotates relative to the primed system in such a way as to cancel the vertical component of the earth's rotation, namely, with angular rate $-\omega'$ about the vertical axis as shown in Figure 5.14. Thus the unprimed system has no rotation about the vertical axis. The equations of transformation are

$$x' = x \cos \omega't + y \sin \omega't$$
$$y' = -x \sin \omega't + y \cos \omega't$$

Upon substituting the expressions for the primed quantities and their derivatives from the above equations into Equations 5.28a and 5.28b, the following result is obtained, after collecting terms and dropping terms involving ω'^2,

$$(\ddot{x} + \frac{g}{l}x) \cos \omega't + (\ddot{y} + \frac{g}{l}y) \sin \omega't = 0 \qquad (5.29)$$

and an identical equation, except that the sine and cosine are reversed. Clearly, the above equation is satisfied if the coefficients of the sine and cosine terms both vanish, namely

$$\ddot{x} + \frac{g}{l}x = 0$$

$$\ddot{y} + \frac{g}{l}y = 0$$

These are the differential equations of a two-dimensional harmonic oscillator. Thus the path, projected on the xy plane, is an ellipse with *fixed orientation in the unprimed system*. In the primed system the path is an ellipse which undergoes a steady precession with angular speed $\omega' = \omega \sin \lambda$.

In addition to the above type of precession there is another *natural* precession of the spherical pendulum which is ordinarily much larger than the rotational precession under discussion. However, if the pendulum is carefully started by drawing it aside with a thread and letting it start from rest by burning the thread, the natural precession is rendered negligibly small.[1]

The rotational precession is clockwise in the northern hemisphere and counterclockwise in the southern. The period is $2\pi/\omega' = 2\pi/(\omega \sin \lambda) = \dfrac{24}{\sin \lambda}$ hours. Thus, at a latitude of 45° the period is $(24/0.707)$ hr $= 33.94$ hr. The result was first demonstrated by the French physicist Jean Foucault in Paris in the year 1851. The Foucault pendulum has come to be a traditional display in major planetariums throughout the world.

PROBLEMS

5.1   A 120 lb person stands on a bathroom spring scale while riding in an elevator. If the elevator has (a) upward, and (b) downward acceleration of $g/4$, what is the weight indicated on the scale in each case?

5.2   An ultracentrifuge has a rotational speed of 500 rps. (a) Find the centrifugal force on a one-microgram particle in the sample chamber if the particle is 5 cm from the rotational axis. (b) Express the result as the ratio of the centrifugal force to the weight of the particle.

5.3   A plumb line is held steady while being carried along in a moving train. If the mass of the plumb bob is m, find the tension in the cord and the deflection from the local vertical if the train is accelerating forward with constant acceleration $g/10$. (Neglect any effects of the earth's rotation.)

5.4   If, in the above problem, the plumb line is not held steady but oscillates as a simple pendulum, find the period of oscillation for small amplitude.

5.5   A hauling truck is traveling on a level road. The driver suddenly applies the brakes causing the truck to decelerate by an amount $g/2$. This causes a box in the rear of the truck to slide forward. If the coefficient of sliding friction between the box and the truckbed is 1/3, find the acceleration of the box relative to (a) the truck, and (b) the road.

5.6   A cockroach crawls with constant speed in a circular path of radius b on a phonograph turntable rotating with constant angular speed ω. The circular path is concentric with the center of the turntable. If the mass of the insect is m and the coefficient of static friction with the surface of the turntable is μ_s, how fast, relative to the turntable, can the cockroach crawl before it starts to slip if it goes (a) in the direction of rotation and (b) opposite to the direction of rotation.

---

[1] The natural precession will be discussed briefly in Chapter 10. For a quantitative treatment of the relative amounts of the two types of precession, see J. L. Synge and B. A. Griffith, *Principles of Mechanics*, McGraw-Hill, New York, 1959.

5.7   In the problem of the bicycle wheel rounding a curve, Example 5.3, what is the acceleration relative to the ground of the point at the very front of the wheel.

5.8   On the salt flats at Bonneville, Utah (latitude = 41°N) the British auto racer John Cobb in 1947 became the first man to travel at a speed of 400 mph on land. If he was headed due north at this speed, find the ratio of the magnitude of the Coriolis force on the racing car to the weight of the car. What is the direction of the Coriolis force?

5.9   A particle moves in a horizontal plane on the surface of the earth. Show that the magnitude of the horizontal component of the Coriolis force is independent of the direction of the motion of the particle.

5.10 If a pebble were dropped down an elevator shaft of the Empire State building (h = 1250 ft, latitude = 41°N) find the deflection of the pebble due to Coriolis force.

5.11 In Yankee stadium, New York, a baseball is driven a distance of 200 ft in a fairly flat trajectory. Is the amount of deflection due to Coriolis force alone of much importance? (Let the angle of elevation be 15°.)

5.12 Show that the third derivative with respect to time of the position vector (jerk) of a particle moving in a rotating coordinate system in terms of appropriate derivatives in the rotating system is given by

$$\dddot{\mathbf{r}} = \dddot{\mathbf{r}}' + 3\boldsymbol{\omega} \times \ddot{\mathbf{r}}' + 3\boldsymbol{\omega} \times \dot{\mathbf{r}}' + \ddot{\boldsymbol{\omega}} \times \mathbf{r}' + 3\boldsymbol{\omega} \times (\boldsymbol{\omega} \times \dot{\mathbf{r}}') + \dot{\boldsymbol{\omega}} \times (\boldsymbol{\omega} \times \mathbf{r}')$$
$$+ 2\boldsymbol{\omega} \times (\dot{\boldsymbol{\omega}} \times \mathbf{r}') - \omega^2 (\boldsymbol{\omega} \times \mathbf{r}')$$

5.13 A bullet is fired straight up with initial speed v_0'. Assuming g is constant and neglecting air resistance, show that the bullet will hit the ground *west* of the initial point of upward motion by an amount $4\omega v_0'^3 \cos\lambda/3g^2$ where λ is the latitude and ω is the earth's angular velocity.

5.14 The force on a charged particle in an electric field $\mathbf{E}$ and a magnetic field $\mathbf{B}$ is given by

$$\mathbf{F} = q(\mathbf{E} + \mathbf{v} \times \mathbf{B})$$

in an inertial system where q is the charge and $\mathbf{v}$ is the velocity of the particle in the inertial system. Show that the differential equation of motion referred to a rotating coordinate system with angular velocity $\boldsymbol{\omega} = -(q/2m)\mathbf{B}$ is, for small ω,

$$m\ddot{\mathbf{r}}' = q\mathbf{E}$$

that is, the term involving $\mathbf{B}$ is eliminated. This result is known as *Larmor's Theorem*.

5.15 Complete the steps leading to Equation 5.29 for the differential equation of motion of the Foucault pendulum.

5.16 The latitude of Mexico City is approximately 19°N. What is the period of precession of a Foucault pendulum there?

5.17 Work Example 5.3 using a coordinate system that is fixed to the bicycle wheel and rotates with it, as in Example 5.2.

6

Central Forces and Celestial Mechanics

6.1 Introduction. Newton's Law of Gravity

A force whose lines of action pass through a single point or center is called a *central force*. If the magnitude of the force depends only on the distance from that center and not on the direction, it is called *isotropic*. Central forces are of fundamental importance in physics, for they include such forces as gravity, electrostatic forces, and others. The forces of interaction between the fundamental particles of nature are mostly central in the sense that, for two particles, either particle acts as a center of force for the other. The main purpose of the present chapter is to study the motion of a particle in isotropic central force fields with particular emphasis on gravitational fields.

Gravity

Newton announced his law of universal gravitation in 1666. It is no exaggeration to state that this marked the beginning of modern astronomy, for the law of gravity accounts for the motions of the planets of the solar system, their satellites, binary or double stars, and even stellar systems. The law may be stated:

Every particle in the universe attracts every other particle with a force that varies directly as the product of the masses of the two particles and inversely as the square of their distance apart. The direction of the force is along the straight line joining the two particles.

133

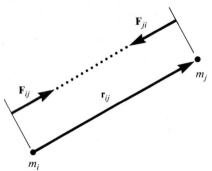

FIGURE 6.1   Action and reaction in Newton's law of gravity.

We can express the law vectorially by the equation

$$\mathbf{F}_{ij} = G\frac{m_i m_j}{r_{ij}^2}\left(\frac{\mathbf{r}_{ij}}{r_{ij}}\right)$$ (6.1)

where $\mathbf{F}_{ij}$ is the force on particle i, of mass m_i exerted by particle j, of mass m_j. The vector $\mathbf{r}_{ij}$ is the directed line segment running from particle i to particle j, as shown in Figure 6.1. The law of action and reaction requires that $\mathbf{F}_{ij} = -\mathbf{F}_{ji}$. The constant of proportionality G is known as the *universal constant of gravitation*. Its value is determined in the laboratory by carefully measuring the force between two bodies of known mass. The internationally accepted value at present is, in SI units,

$$G = (6.672 \pm 0.004) \times 10^{-11} \mathrm{Nm}^2\,\mathrm{kg}^{-2}$$

All of our present knowledge of the masses of astronomical bodies, including the earth, is based on the value of this fundamental constant.[1]

6.2   Gravitational Force Between a Uniform Sphere and a Particle

In Chapter 2, where we discussed the motion of a falling body, it was asserted that the gravitational force of the earth on a particle above the earth's surface is inversely proportional to the square of the particle's distance from the center of the earth; that is, the earth attracts as if all of its mass were concentrated at a single point. We shall now prove that this is true for any uniform spherical body, or any spherically symmetric distibution of matter.

Consider first a thin uniform shell of mass M and radius R. Let r be the distance from the center O to a test particle P of mass m (Figure 6.2). It is assumed that $r > R$. We shall divide the shell into circular rings of width $R\,\Delta\theta$ where, as shown in the

[1] G is the least accurately known of all the basic physical constants. This stems from the fact that the gravitational force between two bodies of laboratory size is extremely small. For a review of the current situation regarding the determination of G, see an article by J. Maddox, *Nature*, *30*, 723 (1984).

figure, the angle POQ is denoted by θ, Q being a point on the ring. The circumference of our representative ring element is therefore $2\pi R \sin \theta$, and its mass ΔM is given by

$$\Delta M \simeq \rho 2\pi R^2 \sin \theta \, \Delta\theta$$

where ρ is the mass per unit area of the shell.

Now the gravitational force exerted on P by a small subelement Q of the ring (which we shall regard as a particle) is in the direction PQ. Let us resolve this force $\Delta\mathbf{F}_q$ into two components, one component along PO, of magnitude $\Delta F_q \cos \phi$, the other perpendicular to PO, of magnitude $\Delta F_q \sin \phi$. Here ϕ is the angle OPQ, as shown in the figure. From symmetry we can easily see that the vector sum of all of the perpendicular components exerted on P by the whole ring vanishes. The force $\Delta\mathbf{F}$ exerted by the entire ring is therefore in the direction PO, and its magnitude ΔF is obtained by summing the components $\Delta F_q \cos \phi$. The result is clearly

$$\Delta F = G\frac{m\Delta M}{u^2}\cos \phi = G\frac{m2\pi\rho R^2 \sin \theta \cos \phi}{u^2}\Delta\theta$$

where u is the distance PQ (the distance from the particle P to the ring) as shown. The magnitude of the force exerted on P by the whole shell is then obtained by taking the limit of $\Delta\theta$ and integrating:

$$F = Gm2\pi\rho R^2 \int_0^\pi \frac{\sin \theta \cos \phi \, d\theta}{u^2}$$

The integral is most easily evaluated by expressing the integrand in terms of u. From the triangle OPQ we have, from the law of cosines,

$$r^2 + R^2 - 2rR \cos \theta = u^2$$

Differentiating, we have, since both R and r are constant,

$$rR \sin \theta \, d\theta = u \, du$$

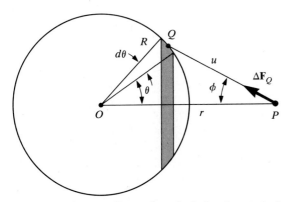

FIGURE 6.2   Coordinates for calculating the gravitational field of a spherical shell.

Also, in the same triangle OPQ, we can write

$$\cos \phi = \frac{u^2 + r^2 - R^2}{2ru}$$

Upon performing the substitutions given by the above two equations, we obtain

$$
\begin{aligned}
F &= Gm2\pi\rho R^2 \int_{\theta=0}^{\theta=\pi} \frac{u^2 + r^2 - R^2}{2Rr^2u^2}\,du \\
&= \frac{GmM}{4Rr^2} \int_{r-R}^{r+R} \left(1 + \frac{r^2 - R^2}{u^2}\right) du \\
&= \frac{GmM}{r^2}
\end{aligned}
$$

where $M = 4\pi\rho R^2$ is the mass of the shell. We can then write vectorially

$$\mathbf{F} = -G\frac{Mm}{r^2}\mathbf{e}_r \tag{6.2}$$

where $\mathbf{e}_r$ is the unit radial vector from the origin O. The above result means that a uniform spherical shell of matter attracts an external particle as if the whole mass of the shell were concentrated at its center. This will be true for every concentric spherical portion of a solid uniform sphere. *A uniform spherical body, therefore, attracts an external particle as if the entire mass of the sphere were located at the center.* The same is true also for a nonuniform sphere provided the density depends only on the radial distance r.

It can be shown that the gravitational force on a particle located *inside* a uniform spherical shell is zero. The proof is left as an exercise.

6.3   Potential Energy in a Gravitational Field. Gravitational Potential

In Chapter 2, Section 2.3, we proved that the inverse-square law of force leads to an inverse first power law for the potential energy function. In this section we shall derive this same relationship in a more physical way.

Let us consider the work W required to move a test particle of mass m along some prescribed path in the gravitational field of another particle of mass M.

We shall place the particle of mass M at the origin of our coordinate system, as shown in Figure 6.3(a). Since the force $\mathbf{F}$ on the test particle is given by $\mathbf{F} = -(GMm/r^2)\mathbf{e}_r$, then, to overcome this force, an external force $-\mathbf{F}$ must be applied. The work dW done in moving the test particle through a distance $d\mathbf{r}$ is thus given by

$$dW = -\mathbf{F} \cdot d\mathbf{r} = \frac{GMm}{r^2}\mathbf{e}_r \cdot d\mathbf{r} \tag{6.3}$$

Now we can resolve $d\mathbf{r}$ into two components: $\mathbf{e}_r \, dr$ parallel to $\mathbf{e}_r$ (the radial component) and the other at right angles to $\mathbf{e}_r$ [Figure 6.3(b)]. Clearly,

$$\mathbf{e}_r \cdot d\mathbf{r} = dr$$

and so W is given by

$$W = GMm \int_{r_1}^{r_2} \frac{dr}{r^2} = -GMm \left(\frac{1}{r_2} - \frac{1}{r_1} \right) \tag{6.4}$$

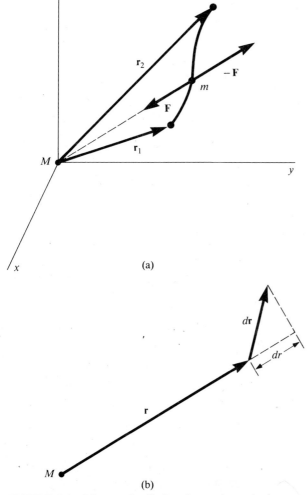

(a)

(b)

FIGURE 6.3   Diagram for finding the work required to move a test particle in a gravitational field.

where r_1 and r_2 are the radial distances of the particle at the beginning and end, respectively, of the path. Thus the work is independent of the particular path taken; it depends only on the end points. This verifies a fact we already knew, namely that the inverse-square law of force is conservative.

We can define the potential energy of a particle of mass at a given point in the gravitational field of another particle as the work done in moving the test particle from some (arbitrary) reference position to the point in question. It is convenient to take the reference position at infinity.[2] Putting $r_1 = \infty$ and $r_2 = r$ in Equation 6.4, we have

$$V(r) = GMm \int_{\infty}^{r} \frac{dr}{r^2} = -\frac{GMm}{r} \tag{6.5}$$

It is sometimes convenient to define a quantity Φ, called the *gravitational potential*, as the gravitational potential energy per unit mass:

$$\Phi = \frac{V}{m}$$

Thus the gravitational potential in the field of a particle of mass M is given by

$$\Phi = -\frac{GM}{r} \tag{6.6}$$

If we have a number of particles $M_1, M_2, \ldots M_i, \ldots$ located at the positions $\mathbf{r}_1, \mathbf{r}_2, \ldots \mathbf{r}_i \ldots$, then the gravitational potential at the point (x, y, z) is the sum of the gravitational potentials of all the particles, that is

$$\Phi(x, y, z) = \Sigma\Phi_i = -G\Sigma \frac{M_i}{u_i} \tag{6.7}$$

in which u_i is the distance from the particle i, of mass M_i, to the field point $\mathbf{r}(x, y, z)$. Thus

$$u_i = |\mathbf{r} - \mathbf{r}_i|$$

The ratio of the gravitational force on a given particle to the mass of that particle is called the *gravitational field intensity*. It is denoted by $\mathcal{G}$. Then

$$\mathcal{G} = \frac{\mathbf{F}}{m}$$

The relationship between field intensity and the potential is the same as that between the force $\mathbf{F}$ and the potential energy V, namely

$$\mathcal{G} = -\nabla\Phi \tag{6.8}$$
$$\mathbf{F} = -\nabla V$$

The gravitational field intensity can be calculated by first finding the potential function from Equation 6.7 and then calculating the gradient. This method is usually simpler

---

[2] It is important to note that it is not legitimate to *define* potential energy as the integral of $\mathbf{F} \cdot d\mathbf{r}$ unless we know in advance that $\mathbf{F}$ is conservative, that is, that a potential function exists.

than the method of calculating the field directly from the inverse-square law. The reason is that the potential energy is a scalar sum whereas the field is given by a vector sum. The situation is quite analogous to the theory of electrostatic fields. In fact, one can apply any of the corresponding results from electrostatics to find gravitational fields and potentials with the proviso, of course, that there are no negative masses.

Examples

6.1   *Potential of a uniform spherical shell*

As an example, let us find the potential function for a uniform spherical shell. By using the same notation as that of Figure 6.2, we have

$$\Phi = -G\int \frac{dM}{u} = -G\int \frac{2\pi\rho R^2 \sin\theta \, d\theta}{u}$$

From the same relation between u and θ that we used earlier, we find that the above equation may be simplified to read

$$\Phi = -G\frac{2\pi\rho R^2}{rR}\int_{r-R}^{r+R} du = -\frac{GM}{r} \tag{6.9}$$

where M is the mass of the shell. This is the same potential function as that of a single particle of mass M located at O. Hence the gravitational field outside the shell is the same as if the entire mass were concentrated at the center. It is left as a problem to show that, with an appropriate change of the integral and its limits, the potential inside the shell is constant and hence that the field there is zero.   ∎

6.2   *Potential and field of a thin ring*

We now wish to find the potential function and the gravitational field intensity in the plane of a thin circular ring. Let the ring be of radius R and mass M. Then, for an exterior point lying in the plane of the ring, Figure 6.4, we have

$$\Phi = -G\int \frac{dM}{u} = -G\int_0^{2\pi} \frac{\mu R \, d\theta}{u}$$

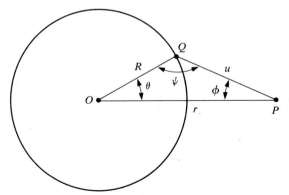

FIGURE 6.4   Coordinates for calculating the gravitational field of a ring.

in which μ is the linear density of the ring. In order to evaluate the integral, we shall express the integrand in terms of the angle ψ shown. In the triangle OPQ we have

$$R \sin \psi = r \sin \phi$$

Differentiating,

$$R \cos \psi \, d\psi = r \cos \phi \, d\phi = r \cos \phi (-d\theta - d\psi)$$

The last step follows from the fact that $\theta + \phi + \psi = \pi$. Upon transposing terms and using the relation $u = R \cos \psi + r \cos \phi$, we obtain

$$u \, d\psi = -r \cos \phi \, d\theta = -(r^2 - R^2 \sin^2 \psi)^{1/2} \, d\theta$$

Hence the integral above becomes

$$\Phi = -G\mu R 4 \int_0^{\pi/2} (r^2 - R^2 \sin^2 \psi)^{-1/2} \, d\psi \tag{6.10}$$

By expanding the integrand as a series and integrating term by term, we obtain

$$\Phi = -G \frac{4\mu R}{r} \int_0^{\pi/2} \left(1 + \frac{1}{2} \frac{R^2}{r^2} \sin^2 \psi + \ldots \right) d\psi$$

$$= -G \frac{4\mu R}{r} \left(\frac{\pi}{2} + \frac{\pi R^2}{8r^2} + \ldots \right)$$

$$= -\frac{GM}{r} \left(1 + \frac{R^2}{4r^2} + \ldots \right)$$

The field intensity at a distance r from the center of the ring is then in the radial direction (since Φ is not a function of θ), and is given by

$$\mathscr{G} = -\frac{\partial \Phi}{\partial r} \mathbf{e}_r = \left(-\frac{GM}{r^2} - \frac{3GMR^2}{4r^4} - \ldots \right) \mathbf{e}_r$$

Thus the field is *not* given by an inverse-square law. If r is very large compared to R, however, the first term predominates, and the field is approximately of the inverse-square type. In fact, the same is true for a finite body of any shape; that is, *for distances large compared to the linear dimensions of the body, the field tends to become predominantly inverse square.*   ∎

6.4   Potential Energy in a General Central Field

We have previously shown that a central field of the inverse-square type is conservative. Let us now consider the question as to whether or not *any* (isotropic) central field of force is conservative. A general isotropic central field can be expressed in the following way:

$$\mathbf{F} = f(r)\mathbf{e}_r \tag{6.11}$$

in which $\mathbf{e}_r$ is the unit radial vector. To apply the test for conservativeness, we calculate the curl of $\mathbf{F}$. It is convenient here to employ spherical coordinates for which the curl is given in Appendix F. We find

$$\nabla \times \mathbf{F} = \frac{1}{r^2 \sin \theta} \begin{vmatrix} \mathbf{e}_r & \mathbf{e}_\theta r & \mathbf{e}_\phi r \sin \theta \\ \dfrac{\partial}{\partial r} & \dfrac{\partial}{\partial \theta} & \dfrac{\partial}{\partial \phi} \\ F_r & rF_\theta & rF_\phi \sin \theta \end{vmatrix}$$

For our central force $F_r = f(r)$, $F_\theta = 0$, $F_\phi = 0$. The curl then reduces to

$$\nabla \times \mathbf{F} = \frac{\mathbf{e}_\theta}{r \sin \theta} \frac{\partial f}{\partial \phi} - \frac{\mathbf{e}_\phi}{r} \frac{\partial f}{\partial \theta} = 0$$

The two partial derivatives both vanish since $f(r)$ does not depend on the angular coordinates ϕ and θ. Thus the curl vanishes and so the general central field defined by Equation 6.11 is conservative. We recall that the same test was applied to the inverse-square field in Section 4.2, Example 4.5.

We can now define a potential energy function

$$V(r) = -\int_{r_{ref}}^{r} \mathbf{F} \cdot d\mathbf{r} = -\int_{r_{ref}}^{r} f(r) \, dr \tag{6.12}$$

where the lower limit r_{ref} is the reference value of r at which the potential energy is *defined* to be zero. For inverse-power type forces, r_{ref} is often taken to be at infinity. This allows us to calculate the potential energy function, given the force function. Conversely, if we know the potential energy function, we have

$$f(r) = -\frac{dV(r)}{dr} \tag{6.13}$$

giving the force function for a central field.

6.5 Angular Momentum in Central Fields

We previously proved in Section 4.1 that the time rate of change of the quantity $\mathbf{r} \times \mathbf{p}$, the angular momentum, is equal to the moment of the force acting on a particle about a given origin. Let us denote the angular momentum by the symbol $\mathbf{L}$. Then the angular momentum theorem states that

$$\frac{d\mathbf{L}}{dt} = \mathbf{r} \times \mathbf{F}$$

Let us apply the above general rule to the particular case of a particle moving in a central field. Here the force $\mathbf{F}$ acts in the direction of the radius vector $\mathbf{r}$. Hence the cross product $\mathbf{r} \times \mathbf{F}$ vanishes, that is, there is zero moment. Consequently, for any central field

$$\frac{d\mathbf{L}}{dt} = 0$$

and therefore

$$\mathbf{L} = \text{constant vector}$$

The angular momentum of a particle moving in a central field always remains constant.

As a corollary, it follows that the path of motion of a particle in a central field remains in a *single plane*, because the constant angular momentum vector **L** is normal to both **r** and **v**, and therefore is normal to the plane in which the particle moves. Thus it is possible, without loss of generality, to employ plane polar coordinates in treating central motion.

Magnitude of the Angular Momentum

In order to determine the magnitude of the angular momentum, it is convenient to resolve the velocity vector **v** into radial and transverse components in polar coordinates. Thus we can write

$$\mathbf{v} = \dot{r}\mathbf{e}_r + r\dot{\theta}\mathbf{e}_\theta$$

in which $\mathbf{e}_r$ is the unit radial vector and $\mathbf{e}_\theta$ is the unit transverse vector. The magnitude of the angular momentum is then given by

$$L = |\mathbf{r} \times m\mathbf{v}| = |r\mathbf{e}_r \times m(\dot{r}\mathbf{e}_r + r\dot{\theta}\mathbf{e}_\theta)|$$

Since $|\mathbf{e}_r \times \mathbf{e}_r| = 0$ and $|\mathbf{e}_r \times \mathbf{e}_\theta| = 1$, we find

$$L = |mr^2\dot{\theta}| = \text{constant} \qquad (6.14)$$

for a particle moving in a central field of force.

6.6   The Law of Areas. Kepler's Laws of Planetary Motion

The angular momentum of a particle is related to the rate at which the position vector sweeps out area. To show this, consider Figure 6.5 which illustrates two successive

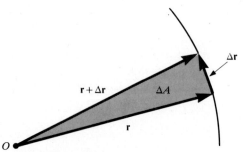

FIGURE 6.5   Area swept out by the radius vector.

position vectors $\mathbf{r}$ and $\mathbf{r} + \Delta\mathbf{r}$ representing the motion of a particle in a time interval Δt. The area ΔA of the shaded triangular segment lying between the two vectors is expressible as

$$\Delta A = \tfrac{1}{2}|\mathbf{r} \times \Delta\mathbf{r}|$$

Upon division by Δt and taking the limit, we have

$$\frac{dA}{dt} = \frac{1}{2}|\mathbf{r} \times \mathbf{v}| \qquad (6.15)$$

From the definition of $\mathbf{L}$, we can further write

$$\frac{dA}{dt} = \frac{1}{2m}|\mathbf{r} \times m\mathbf{v}| = \frac{L}{2m} \qquad (6.16)$$

for the rate at which the radius vector sweeps out area. Since the angular momentum $\mathbf{L}$ is constant in any central field, it follows that the *areal velocity dA/dt* is also constant in a central field.

Kepler's Laws

The fact that the planets move about the sun in such a way that the areal velocities are constant was discovered empirically by Johannes Kepler in 1609. Kepler deduced this rule, and two others,[3] from a painstaking study of planetary positions recorded by Tycho Brahe. Kepler's three laws are:

I.   *Each planet moves in an ellipse with the sun as a focus.*
II. *The radius vector sweeps out equal areas in equal times.*
III. *The square of the period of revolution about the sun is proportional to the cube of the major axis of the orbit.*

Newton showed that Kepler's three laws are consequences of the law of gravity. From the argument leading to Equation 6.16, we see that the second law comes about from the fact that the gravitational field of the sun is central. The other two laws, as we shall show later, are consequences of the fact that the force varies as the inverse square of the distance.

6.7   Orbit of a Particle in a Central-Force Field

To study the motion of a particle in an isotropic central field, it is convenient to express the differential equation of motion

$$m\ddot{\mathbf{r}} = f(r)\mathbf{e}_r$$

in polar coordinates. As shown in Chapter 1, the radial component of $\ddot{\mathbf{r}}$ is $\ddot{r} - r\dot{\theta}^2$, and

---

[3] The third law was announced in 1619.

the transverse component is $2\dot{r}\dot{\theta} + r\ddot{\theta}$. The component differential equations of motion are then

$$m(\ddot{r} - r\dot{\theta}^2) = f(r) \tag{6.17}$$
$$m(2\dot{r}\dot{\theta} + r\ddot{\theta}) = 0 \tag{6.18}$$

From the latter equation it follows that

$$\frac{d}{dt}(r^2\dot{\theta}) = 0$$

or

$$r^2\dot{\theta} = \text{constant} = l \tag{6.19}$$

From Equation 6.14 we see that

$$|l| = \frac{L}{m} = |\mathbf{r} \times \mathbf{v}| \tag{6.20}$$

Thus l is the angular momentum per unit mass. Its constancy is simply a restatement of a fact which we already know, namely, that the angular momentum of a particle is constant when it is moving under the action of a central force.

Given a certain radial force function $f(r)$, we could, in theory, solve the pair of differential equations (Equations 6.17 and 6.18) to obtain r and θ as functions of t. It is often the case that one is interested only in the path in space (the *orbit*) without regard to the time t. To find the equation of the orbit, we shall use the variable u defined by

$$r = \frac{1}{u} \tag{6.21}$$

Then

$$\dot{r} = -\frac{1}{u^2}\dot{u} = -\frac{1}{u^2}\dot{\theta}\frac{du}{d\theta} = -l\frac{du}{d\theta} \tag{6.22}$$

The last step follows from the fact that

$$\dot{\theta} = lu^2 \tag{6.23}$$

according to Equations 6.19 and 6.21.

Differentiating a second time, we have

$$\ddot{r} = -l\frac{d}{dt}\frac{du}{d\theta} = -l\dot{\theta}\frac{d^2u}{d\theta^2} = -l^2u^2\frac{d^2u}{d\theta^2} \tag{6.24}$$

From these values of r, $\dot{\theta}$, and $\ddot{r}$, we readily find that Equation 6.17 transforms to

$$\frac{d^2u}{d\theta^2} + u = -\frac{1}{ml^2u^2}f(u^{-1}) \tag{6.25}$$

The above equation is the *differential equation of the orbit* of a particle moving under a central force. The solution gives u (hence r) as a function of θ. Conversely, if one is given the polar equation of the orbit, namely, $r = r(\theta) = u^{-1}$, then the force function can be found by differentiating to get $d^2u/d\theta^2$ and inserting this into the differential equation.

Examples

6.3   A particle in a central field moves in the spiral orbit

$$r = c\theta^2$$

Determine the form of the force function. We have

$$u = \frac{1}{c\theta^2}$$

and

$$\frac{du}{d\theta} = \frac{-2}{c}\theta^{-3} \qquad \frac{d^2u}{d\theta^2} = \frac{6}{c}\theta^{-4} = 6cu^2$$

Then, from Equation 6.25,

$$6cu^2 + u = -\frac{1}{mh^2u^2}f(u^{-1})$$

Hence

$$f(u^{-1}) = -mh^2(6cu^4 + u^3)$$

and

$$f(r) = -mh^2\left(\frac{6c}{r^4} + \frac{1}{r^3}\right)$$

Thus the force is a combination of an inverse cube and inverse fourth power law.

6.4   In the above problem, determine how the angle θ varies with time. Here we use the fact that $h = r^2\dot{\theta}$ is constant. Thus

$$\dot{\theta} = hu^2 = h\frac{1}{c^2\theta^4}$$

or

$$\theta^4\,d\theta = \frac{h}{c^2}dt$$

and so, by integrating, we find

$$\frac{\theta^5}{5} = hc^{-2}t$$

where the constant of integration is taken to be zero, so that $\theta = 0$ at $t = 0$. Then we can write

$$\theta = \alpha t^{1/5}$$

where $\alpha = \text{constant} = (5hc^{-2})^{1/5}$.   ∎

Energy Equation of the Orbit

The square of the speed is given in polar coordinates by

$$v^2 = \dot{r}^2 + r^2\dot{\theta}^2$$

Since a central force is conservative, the total energy $T + V$ is constant and is given by

$$\tfrac{1}{2}m(\dot{r}^2 + r^2\dot{\theta}^2) + V(r) = E = \text{constant} \tag{6.26}$$

We can also write the above equation in terms of the variable $u = 1/r$. From Equations 6.22 and 6.23 we obtain

$$\frac{1}{2}mh^2\left[\left(\frac{du}{d\theta}\right)^2 + u^2\right] + V(u^{-1}) = E \tag{6.27}$$

In the above equation the only variables occurring are u and θ. We shall call this equation, therefore, *the energy equation of the orbit.*

Example

6.5   In the previous example we had for the spiral orbit $r = c\theta^2$:

$$\frac{du}{d\theta} = \frac{-2}{c}\theta^{-3} = -2c^{1/2}u^{3/2}$$

so the energy equation of the orbit is

$$\tfrac{1}{2}mh^2(4cu^3 + u^2) + V = E$$

Thus

$$V(r) = E - \frac{1}{2}mh^2\left(\frac{4c}{r^3} + \frac{1}{r^2}\right)$$

This readily gives the force function of the example above, since $f(r) = -dV/dr$.   ∎

6.8   Orbits in an Inverse-Square Field

The most important type of central field is that in which the force varies inversely as the square of the radial distance:

$$f(r) = -\frac{k}{r^2}$$

In the above equation, since we have included a minus sign, the constant of proportionality k is positive for an attractive force, and vice versa. As we have seen in Section 6.2, $k = GMm$ for a gravitational field. (In this chapter, we shall always assume that the source of the field remains fixed at the origin. The slight modification required when the source is of finite mass and is therefore not fixed will be treated in Chapter 7.) The equation of the orbit (Equation 6.25) then becomes

$$\frac{d^2u}{d\theta^2} + u = \frac{k}{ml^2} \tag{6.28}$$

The general solution is clearly

$$u = A\cos(\theta - \theta_0) + \frac{k}{ml^2}$$

or

$$r = \frac{1}{A\cos(\theta - \theta_0) + k/ml^2} \tag{6.29}$$

The constants of integration A and θ_0 are determined from the initial conditions. The value of θ_0 merely determines the orientation of the orbit, so we can, without loss of generality in discussing the form of the orbit, choose $\theta_0 = 0$. Then

$$r = \frac{1}{A\cos\theta + k/ml^2} \tag{6.30}$$

This is the polar equation of the orbit. It is the equation of a conic section (ellipse, parabola, or hyperbola) with the origin at a focus. The equation can be written in the standard form (see Appendix C):

$$r = r_0\frac{1 + e}{1 + e\cos\theta} \tag{6.31}$$

where

$$e = \frac{Aml^2}{k} \tag{6.32}$$

and

$$r_0 = \frac{ml^2}{k(1 + e)} \tag{6.33}$$

The constant e is called the *eccentricity*. The different cases, illustrated in Figure 6.6 for constant r_0, are as follows:

$$
\begin{aligned}
&e < 1 &&\textit{ellipse} \\
&e = 0 &&\textit{circle (special case of an ellipse)} \\
&e = 1 &&\textit{parabola} \\
&e > 1 &&\textit{hyperbola}
\end{aligned}
$$

From Equation 6.31, r_0 is the value of r for $\theta = 0$. The value of r for elliptic orbits at $\theta = \pi$ is given by

$$r_1 = r_0\frac{1 + e}{1 - e} \tag{6.34}$$

In reference to the elliptic orbits of the planets around the sun, the distance r_0 is called the *perihelion* distance (closest to the sun) and the distance r_1 is called the *aphelion* distance (farthest from the sun). The corresponding distances for the orbit of

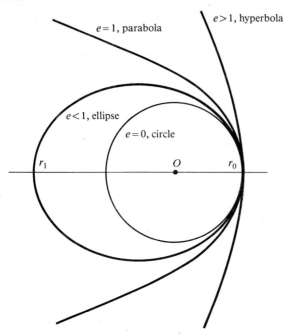

FIGURE 6.6 The family of central conics.

the moon around the earth—and for the orbits of the earth's artificial satellites—are called the *perigee* and *apogee* distances, respectively.

The orbital eccentricities of the planets are quite small. (See Table 6.1, Section 6.11.) For example, in the case of the earth's orbit $e = 0.017$, $r_0 = 91,000,000$ miles, and $r_1 = 95,000,000$ miles. On the other hand, the comets generally have large orbital eccentricities (highly elongated orbits). Halley's comet, for instance, has an orbital eccentricity of 0.967 with a perihelion distance of only 55,000,000 miles, while at aphelion it is beyond the orbit of Neptune. Many comets (the nonrecurring type) have parabolic or hyperbolic orbits.

Orbital Parameters from the Conditions at Closest Approach

From Equation 6.33 we find the eccentricity can be expressed as

$$e = \frac{ml^2}{kr_0} - 1 \tag{6.35}$$

Let v_0 be the speed of the particle at $\theta = 0$. Then, from the definition of the constant l we have

$$l = r^2\dot{\theta} = r_0^2\dot{\theta}_0 = r_0v_0$$

The eccentricity is then given by

$$e = \frac{mr_0 v_0^2}{k} - 1 \tag{6.35a}$$

For a circular orbit $(e = 0)$ we have then $k = mr_0 v_0^2$ or

$$\frac{k}{r_0^2} = \frac{mv_0^2}{r_0} \tag{6.36}$$

Now let us denote the quantity k/mr_0 by v_c^2, so that if $v_0 = v_c$, the orbit is a circle. The expression for the eccentricity, Equation 6.35a, can then be written, for $v_0 \geq v_c$, as

$$e = (v_0/v_c)^2 - 1 \tag{6.37}$$

and the equation of the orbit can be written

$$r = r_0 \frac{(v_0/v_c)^2}{1 + [(v_0/v_c)^2 - 1] \cos \theta} \tag{6.38}$$

The value of r_1 is given by setting $\theta = \pi$, thus

$$r_1 = r_0 \frac{(v_0/v_c)^2}{2 - (v_0/v_c)^2}$$

[*Note:* Equation 6.38 is also valid when $v_0 < v_c$, in which case $r_1 < r_0$ and the eccentricity is given by $e = 1 - (v_0/v_c)^2$, and $\theta_0 = \pi$ in Equation 6.29.]

Example

6.6(a)   In the earth's gravitational field the force constant $k = GM_e m$ in which M_e is the mass of the earth and m is the mass of the body. Thus, for circular orbits of earth satellites we have

$$v_c^2 = \frac{k}{mr_0} = \frac{GM_e}{r_0}$$

Now, as pointed out in Example 2.3, the product GM_e can be found simply by noting that the force of gravity at the earth's surface is $mg = GM_e m/R_e^2$ or $GM_e = gR_e^2$ where R_e is the earth's radius. Hence the speed for a circular orbit around the earth is

$$v_c = \left(\frac{gR_e^2}{r_0}\right)^{1/2}$$

In particular, for satellites in circular orbits very near the earth's surface $r_0 \approx R_e$, so the speed for such orbits is simply

$$v_c = (gR_e)^{1/2} = (9.8 \text{ ms}^{-2} \times 6.4 \times 10^6 \text{ m})^{1/2} = 7{,}920 \text{ m/s}$$

or about 8 km/s.

(b)   A rocket satellite is going around the earth in a circular orbit of radius r_0. A sudden blast of the rocket motor increases the speed by 15 percent. Find the equation of the new

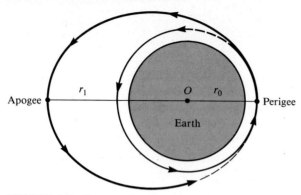

FIGURE 6.7   Space rocket changing from a circular orbit to an elliptical orbit.

orbit, and compute the apogee distance. Let v_c be the speed in the circular orbit, and let v_0 be the new initial speed; that is

$$v_0/v_c = 1.15$$

Equation 6.38 for the new orbit then reads

$$r = r_0 \frac{1.3225}{1 + 0.3225 \cos \theta}$$

and the apogee distance is

$$r_1 = r_0 \frac{1.3225}{2 - 1.3225} = 1.95 r_0$$

The orbits are shown in Figure 6.7.   ■

6.9   Orbital Energies in the Inverse-Square Field

Since the potential energy function $V(r)$ for an inverse-square force field is given by

$$V(r) = -\frac{k}{r} = -ku$$

the energy equation of the orbit, Equation 6.27, then reads

$$\frac{1}{2}ml^2\left[\left(\frac{du}{d\theta}\right)^2 + u^2\right] - ku = E$$

or, upon separating variables,

$$d\theta = \left(\frac{2E}{ml^2} + \frac{2ku}{ml^2} - u^2\right)^{-1/2} du$$

Upon integrating, we find

$$\theta = \sin^{-1}\left[\frac{ml^2u - k}{(k^2 + 2Eml^2)^{1/2}}\right] + \theta_0$$

where θ_0 is a constant of integration. If we let $\theta_0 = -\pi/2$ and solve for u, we obtain

$$u = \frac{k}{ml^2}[1 + (1 + 2Eml^2k^{-2})^{1/2} \cos \theta]$$

or

$$r = \frac{ml^2k^{-1}}{1 + (1 + 2Eml^2k^{-2})^{1/2} \cos \theta} \tag{6.39}$$

This is the polar equation of the orbit. If we compare it with Equations 6.31 and 6.32, we see that the eccentricity is given by

$$e = (1 + 2Eml^2k^{-2})^{1/2} \tag{6.40}$$

The above expression for the eccentricity allows us to classify the orbits according to the total energy E as follows

$$
\begin{array}{lll}
E < 0 & e < 1 & \textit{closed orbits (ellipse or circle)} \\
E = 0 & e = 1 & \textit{parabolic orbit} \\
E > 0 & e > 1 & \textit{hyperbolic orbit}
\end{array}
$$

Since $E = T + V$ and is constant, the closed orbits are those for which $T < |V|$, and the open orbits are those for which $T \geq |V|$.

In the sun's gravitational field the force constant $k = GMm$ where M is the mass of the sun and m is the mass of the body. The total energy is then

$$\frac{mv^2}{2} - \frac{GMm}{r} = E = \text{constant}$$

so the orbit is an ellipse, a parabola, or a hyperbola depending on whether v^2 is less than, equal to, or greater than the quantity $2GM/r$, respectively.

Example

6.7   A comet is observed to have a speed v_{com} when it is a distance r_{com} from the sun, and its direction of motion makes an angle φ with the radius vector from the sun, Figure 6.8. Find the eccentricity of the comet's orbit.

Solution:

To use the formula for the eccentricity, Equation 6.40, we need the square of the angular momentum constant l. It is given by

$$l^2 = |\mathbf{r} \times \mathbf{v}|^2 = (r_{com}v_{com} \sin \varphi)^2$$

The eccentricity therefore has the value

$$e = \left[1 + \left(v_{com}^2 - \frac{2GM}{r_{com}}\right)\left(\frac{r_{com}v_{com} \sin \varphi}{GM}\right)^2\right]^{1/2}$$

Note that the mass m of the comet cancels out. Now the product GM can be expressed in terms of the earth's speed v_e and orbital radius a_e (assuming a circular orbit), namely

$$GM = a_e v_e^2$$

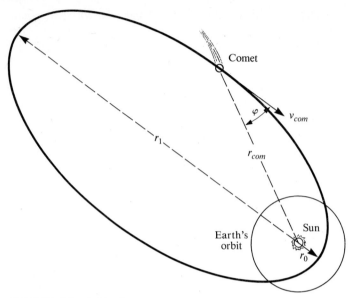

FIGURE 6.8   Orbit of a comet.

The above expression for the eccentricity then becomes

$$e = \left[1 + \left(\mathsf{V}^2 - \frac{2}{\mathsf{R}}\right)(\mathsf{RV} \sin \varphi)^2\right]^{1/2}$$

where we have introduced the *dimensionless ratios*

$$\mathsf{V} = \frac{v_{com}}{v_e} \qquad \mathsf{R} = \frac{r_{com}}{a_e}$$

which simplify the computation of e.

As a numerical example, let v_{com} be one-half the earth's speed, let r_{com} be four times the earth-sun distance, and $\varphi = 30°$. Then $\mathsf{V} = 0.5$ and $\mathsf{R} = 4$, so the eccentricity is

$$e = [1 + (0.25 - 0.5)(4 \times 0.5 \times 0.5)^2]^{1/2} = (0.75)^{1/2} = 0.866$$

For an ellipse the quantity $(1 - e^2)^{-1/2}$ is equal to the ratio of the major (long) axis to the minor (short) axis. For the orbit of the comet in this example this ratio is $(1 - 0.75)^{-1/2} = 2$, or 2:1, as shown in Figure 6.8.   ∎

6.10   Limits of the Radial Motion. Effective Potential

We have seen that the angular momentum of a particle moving in *any* isotropic central field is a constant of the motion, as expressed by Equations 6.19 and 6.20 defining l. This fact allows us to write the general energy equation 6.26 in the following form

$$\frac{m}{2}\left(\dot{r}^2 + \frac{l^2}{r^2}\right) + V(r) = E$$

or

$$\frac{m}{2}\dot{r}^2 + U(r) = E \qquad (6.41)$$

in which

$$U(r) = \frac{ml^2}{2r^2} + V(r) \qquad (6.42)$$

The function $U(r)$ defined above is called the "effective potential". The term $ml^2/2r^2$ is sometimes called the "centrifugal potential". Looking at Equation 6.41 we see that, as far as the radial motion is concerned, the particle behaves in exactly the same way as a particle of mass m moving in one-dimensional motion under a potential energy function $U(r)$. As in Section 3.3 where we discussed harmonic motion, the limits of the radial motion (turning points) are given by setting $\dot{r} = 0$ in Equation 6.41. These limits are therefore the roots of the equation

$$U(r) - E = 0 \qquad (6.43)$$

or

$$\frac{ml^2}{2r^2} + V(r) - E = 0 \qquad (6.43a)$$

Furthermore, the *allowed* values of r are those for which $U(r) \leq E$, since $\dot{r}^2$ is necessarily positive or zero.

Thus it is possible to determine the range of the radial motion without knowing anything about the orbit. A plot of $U(r)$ is shown in Figure 6.9. Also shown are the radial limits r_0 and r_1 for a particular value of the total energy E. The graph is drawn for the inverse-square law, namely

$$U(r) = \frac{ml^2}{2r^2} - \frac{k}{r} \qquad (6.44)$$

In this case Equation 6.43, upon rearranging terms, becomes

$$-2Er^2 - 2kr + ml^2 = 0$$

which is a quadratic equation in r. The two roots are

$$r_{1,0} = \frac{k \pm (k^2 + 2Eml^2)^{1/2}}{-2E} \qquad (6.45)$$

giving the maximum (upper sign) and minimum (lower sign) values of the radial distance r under the inverse-square law of force. Since the energy E is a negative quantity for all bound orbits, the two roots are both positive, as they should be.

Now we have already shown that closed orbits under the inverse-square law are ellipses for which the major axis $2a$ is the sum $r_1 + r_0$. Thus, by adding the two roots above, we have

$$2a = r_1 + r_0 = \frac{k}{-E} \qquad (6.46)$$

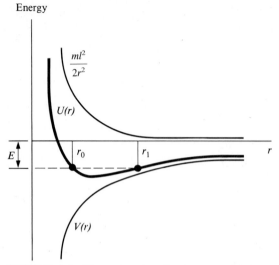

Energy

$\dfrac{ml^2}{2r^2}$

$U(r)$

E

r_0

r_1

r

$V(r)$

FIGURE 6.9 Illustrating the effective potential and limits of the radial motion for the inverse-square law of force.

This result shows that the value of a, the semimajor axis, is determined entirely by the force constant k and the total energy E.

Example

6.8 Find the semimajor axis of the orbit of the comet of Example 6.7.

Solution:
    Equation 6.46 gives directly

$$a = \frac{k}{-2E} = \frac{GMm}{-2\left(\dfrac{mv_{com}^2}{2} - \dfrac{GMm}{r_{com}}\right)}$$

where m is the mass of the comet. Clearly, m again cancels out. Also, as stated above $GM = a_e v_e^2$. So the final result is the simple expression

$$a = \frac{a_e}{\dfrac{2}{R} - V^2}$$

where R and V are as defined in the previous example.
    For the previous numerical values, $R = 4$ and $V = 0.5$, we find $a = a_e/[0.5 - (0.5)^2] = 4a_e$ ∎

    The above two examples bring out an important fact, namely that the orbital parameters are independent of the mass of a body. Given the same initial position, speed, and direction of motion, a grain of sand, a coasting spaceship, or a comet would all have identical orbits, provided that no other bodies came near enough to have an effect on the motion of the body. (We also assume, of course, that the mass of the body in question is small compared to the sun's mass.)

6.11 Periodic Time of Orbital Motion

In Section 6.6 we showed that the areal velocity $\dot{A}$ of a particle moving in any central field is constant. Consequently, from Equations 6.16 and 6.20, the time t_{12} required for a particle to move from one point P_1 to any other point P_2 (Figure 6.10) is given by

$$t_{12} = \frac{A_{12}}{\dot{A}} = A_{12}\frac{2m}{L} = A_{12}\frac{2}{|l|}$$

where A_{12} is the area swept out by the radius vector between P_1 and P_2.

Let us apply the above result to the case of an elliptic orbit of a particle in an inverse-square field. Since the area of an ellipse is πab, where a and b are the semimajor and the semiminor axes, respectively, then the time τ required for the particle to complete one orbital path is expressed by

$$\tau = \frac{2\pi ab}{l}$$

But for an ellipse (see Appendix C)

$$\frac{b}{a} = \sqrt{1 - e^2}$$

where e is the eccentricity. Thus we can write

$$\tau = \frac{2\pi a^2}{l}\sqrt{1 - e^2}$$

Furthermore, if we refer to Equations 6.33 and 6.34, we find that the major axis is given by

$$2a = r_0 + r_1 = \frac{ml^2}{k}\left(\frac{1}{1 + e} + \frac{1}{1 - e}\right) = \frac{2ml^2}{k(1 - e^2)}$$

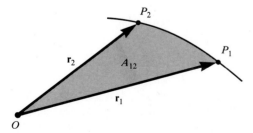

FIGURE 6.10 Area swept out by the radius vector for an orbiting particle.

TABLE 6.1 Planetary Data

Planet	Semimajor Axis in Astronomical Units	Period in Years	Eccentricity
Mercury	0.387	0.241	0.206
Venus	0.723	0.615	0.007
Earth	1.000	1.000	0.017
Mars	1.524	1.881	0.093
Jupiter	5.203	11.86	0.048
Saturn	9.539	29.46	0.056
Uranus	19.19	84.02	0.047
Neptune	30.06	164.8	0.009
Pluto	39.46	247.7	0.249

We can therefore express the period as

$$\tau = 2\pi \left(\frac{m}{k}\right)^{1/2} a^{3/2} \tag{6.47}$$

Thus, for a given inverse-square force field, the period depends only on the size of the major axis of an elliptical orbit.

Since, for a planet, or *any* body, of mass m moving in the sun's gravitational field, $k = GMm$, we can write for the period of orbital motion

$$\tau = ca^{3/2} \tag{6.47a}$$

where $c = 2\pi(GM)^{-1/2}$. Clearly, c is the same for all planets. Equation 6.47a is a mathematical statement of Kepler's third law. If a is expressed in astronomical units (93,000,000 miles $= a_{earth} = 1$ astronomical unit) and τ is in years, then the numerical value of c is unity. In Table 6.1 are listed the periods, semimajor axes in astronomical units, and the orbital eccentricities of the planets of the solar system. Notice that most planets have nearly circular orbits, the exceptions being Pluto, Mercury, and Mars, in order of decreasing eccentricity.

Example

6.9 Find the period of the comet of Example 6.8.

Solution:

Using the previous result that $a = 4a_e = 4$ a.u. (astronomical units) together with Equation 6.47a with $c = 1$, we have simply

$$\tau = 4^{3/2} \text{ yr} = 8 \text{ yr}$$

Actually, there are about 20 comets in the solar system that have periods of about this value (5 to 10 years). They are called *Jupiter's family of comets* because their aphelia all lie close to Jupiter's orbit, and their periods are roughly one-half of Jupiter's period around the sun. (Halley's comet is *not* a member of Jupiter's family.)   ∎

6.12   Motion in an Inverse-Square Repulsive Field. Scattering of Atomic Particles

There is an important physical application involving motion of a particle in a central field in which the law of force is of the inverse-square *repulsive* type, namely the deflection of high-speed atomic particles (protons, alpha particles, and so on) by the positively charged nuclei of atoms. The basic investigations underlying our present knowledge of atomic and nuclear structure are scattering experiments, the first of which were carried out by the British physicist Lord Rutherford in the early part of this century.

Consider a particle of charge q and mass m (the incident high-speed particle) passing near a heavy particle of charge Q (the nucleus, assumed fixed). The incident particle is repelled with a force given by Coulomb's law:

$$f(r) = \frac{Qq}{r^2}$$

where the position of Q is taken to be the origin. (We shall use cgs electrostatic units for Q and q. Then r is in centimeters, and the force is in dynes.) The differential equation of the orbit then takes the form

$$\frac{d^2u}{d\theta^2} + u = -\frac{Qq}{ml^2}$$

and so the equation of the orbit is

$$u^{-1} = r = \frac{1}{A \cos (\theta - \theta_0) - Qq/ml^2}$$

We can also write the equation of the orbit in the form given by Equation 6.39, namely

$$r = \frac{ml^2Q^{-1}q^{-1}}{-1 + (1 + 2Eml^2Q^{-2}q^{-2})^{1/2} \cos (\theta - \theta_0)} \tag{6.48}$$

since $k = -Qq$. The orbit is a hyperbola. This may be seen from the physical fact that the energy E is always greater than zero in a repulsive field of force. (In our case $E = \frac{1}{2}mv^2 + Qq/r$.) Hence the eccentricity e, the coefficient of $\cos (\theta - \theta_0)$, is greater than unity, which means that the orbit must be hyperbolic.

The incident particle approaches along one asymptote and recedes along the other, as shown in Figure 6.11. We have chosen the direction of the polar axis such that the initial position of the particle is $\theta = 0$, $r = \infty$. It is clear from either of the two equations of the orbit that r assumes its minimum value when $\cos (\theta - \theta_0) = 1$, that is, when $\theta = \theta_0$. Since $r = \infty$ when $\theta = 0$, then r is also infinite when $\theta = 2\theta_0$. Hence the angle between the two asymptotes of the hyperbolic path is $2\theta_0$, and the angle θ_s through which the incident particle is deflected is given by

$$\theta_s = \pi - 2\theta_0$$

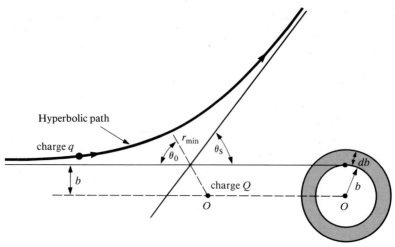

FIGURE 6.11   Hyperbolic path (orbit) of a charged particle moving in the inverse-square repulsive force field of another charged particle.

Furthermore, in Equation 6.48 the denominator on the right vanishes at $\theta = 0$ and $\theta = 2\theta_0$. Thus,

$$-1 + (1 + 2Eml^2Q^{-2}q^{-2})^{1/2} \cos \theta_0 = 0$$

from which we readily find

$$\tan \theta_0 = (2Em)^{1/2}lQ^{-1}q^{-1} = \cot \frac{\theta_s}{2} \qquad (6.49)$$

The last step follows from the angle relationship given above.

In applying the above equation to scattering problems, it is convenient to express the constant l in terms of another quantity b called the *impact parameter*. The impact parameter is the perpendicular distance from the origin (scattering center) to the initial line of motion of the particle, as shown in Figure 6.11. We have then

$$|l| = |\mathbf{r} \times \mathbf{v}| = bv_0$$

where v_0 is the initial speed of the particle. We know also that the energy E is constant and is equal to the initial kinetic energy $\frac{1}{2}mv_0^2$, because the initial potential energy is zero ($r = \infty$). Accordingly, we can write the scattering formula, Equation 6.49, in the form

$$\cot \frac{\theta_s}{2} = \frac{bmv_0^2}{Qq} = \frac{2bE}{Qq} \qquad (6.50)$$

giving the relationship between the scattering angle and the impact parameter.

In a typical scattering experiment a beam of particles is projected at a target, such as a thin foil. The nuclei of the target atoms are the scattering centers. The fraction of incident particles that are deflected through a given angle θ_s can be expressed in terms of a *differential scattering cross section* $\sigma(\theta_s)$ defined by the equation

$$\frac{dN}{N} = n \, \sigma(\theta_s) \, d\Omega$$

Here dN is the number of incident particles scattered through an angle between θ_s and $\theta_s + d\theta_s$, N is the total number of incident particles, n is the number of scattering centers per unit area of the target foil, and $d\Omega$ is the element of solid angle corresponding to the increment $d\theta_s$. Thus $d\Omega = 2\pi \sin \theta_s \, d\theta_s$.

Now an incident particle approaching a scattering center will have an impact parameter lying between b and $b + db$ if the projection of its path lies in a ring of inner radius b and outer radius $b + db$, Figure 6.11. The area of this ring is $2\pi b \, db$. The total number of such particles must correspond to the number scattered through a given angle, that is

$$dN = Nn\sigma(\theta_s)2\pi \sin \theta_s \, d\theta_s = Nn2\pi b \, db$$

Thus

$$\sigma(\theta_s) = \frac{b}{\sin \theta_s} \left| \frac{db}{d\theta_s} \right| \qquad (6.51)$$

To find the scattering cross section for charged particles, we differentiate with respect to θ_s in Equation 6.50:

$$\frac{1}{2 \sin^2\left(\dfrac{\theta_s}{2}\right)} = \frac{2E}{Qq} \left| \frac{db}{d\theta_s} \right| \qquad (6.52)$$

(The absolute value sign is inserted because the derivative is negative.) By eliminating b and $|db/d\theta_s|$ among Equations 6.50, 6.51, and 6.52, and using the identity $\sin \theta_s = 2 \sin(\theta_s/2) \cos(\theta_s/2)$ we find the following result:

$$\sigma(\theta_s) = \frac{Q^2 q^2}{16E^2} \frac{1}{\sin^4\left(\dfrac{\theta_s}{2}\right)} \qquad (6.53)$$

This is the famous Rutherford scattering formula. It shows that the differential cross section varies as the inverse fourth power of $\sin(\theta_s/2)$. Its experimental verification in the first part of this century marked one of the early milestones of nuclear physics.

Examples

6.10   An alpha particle emitted by radium ($E = 5$ million electron volts $= 5 \times 10^6 \times 1.6 \times 10^{-12}$ erg) suffers a deflection of $90°$ upon passing near a gold nucleus. What is the value of the impact parameter? For alpha particles $q = 2e$, and for gold $Q = 79e$, where e is the elementary charge. (The charge carried by a single electron is $-e$.) In our units $e = 4.8 \times 10^{-10}$ esu. Thus, from Equation 6.50,

$$b = \frac{Qq}{2E} \cot 45° = \frac{2 \times 79 \times (4.8)^2 \times 10^{-20} \text{ cm}}{2 \times 5 \times 1.6 \times 10^{-6}}$$

$$= 2.1 \times 10^{-12} \text{ cm} \qquad ∎$$

6.11 Calculate the distance of closest approach of the alpha particle in the above problem. The distance of closest approach is given by the equation of the orbit (Equation 6.48) for $\theta = \theta_0$, thus

$$r_{\min} = \frac{ml^2 Q^{-1} q^{-1}}{-1 + (1 + 2Eml^2 Q^{-2} q^{-2})^{1/2}}$$

Upon using Equation 6.50, the above equation, after a little algebra, can be written

$$r_{\min} = \frac{b \cot (\theta_s/2)}{-1 + [1 + \cot^2 (\theta_s/2)]^{1/2}} = \frac{b \cos (\theta_s/2)}{1 - \sin (\theta_s/2)}$$

Thus, for $\theta_s = 90$ degrees, we find $r_{\min} = 2.41 \, b = 5.1 \times 10^{-12}$ cm.

Notice that the expressions for $r_{\min}$ become indeterminate when $l = b = 0$. In this case the particle is aimed directly at the nucleus. It approaches the nucleus along a straight line, and, being continually repelled by the coulomb force, its speed is reduced to zero when it reaches a certain point, $r_{\min}$, from which point it returns along the same straight line. The angle of deflection is 180°. The value of $r_{\min}$ in this case is found by using the fact that the energy E is constant. At the turning point the potential energy is $Qq/r_{\min}$, and the kinetic energy is zero. Hence $E = \frac{1}{2}mv_0^2 = Qq/r_{\min}$, and

$$r_{\min} = \frac{Qq}{E}$$

For radium alpha particles and gold nuclei we find $r_{\min} \simeq 10^{-12}$ cm when the angle of deflection is 180°. The fact that such deflections are actually observed shows that the order of magnitude of the radius of the nucleus is at least as small as 10^{-12} cm. ∎

6.13 Nearly Circular Orbits in Central Fields. Stability

A circular orbit is possible under any attractive central force, but not all central forces result in *stable* circular orbits. We wish to investigate the following question: If a particle traveling in a circular orbit suffers a sight disturbance, will the ensuing orbit remain close to the original circular path? In order to answer the query, we refer to the radial differential equation of motion (6.17). Since $\dot\theta = l/r^2$, we can write the radial equation as follows:

$$m\ddot{r} = \frac{ml^2}{r^3} + f(r)$$

[This is the same as the differential equation for one-dimensional motion under the effective potential $U(r) = (ml^2/2r^2) + V(r)$, so that $m\ddot{r} = -dU(r)/dr = (ml^2/r^3) - dV(r)/dr$.]

Now for a circular orbit, r is constant, and $\ddot{r} = 0$. Thus, calling a the radius of the circular orbit, we have

$$-\frac{ml^2}{a^3} = f(a) \tag{6.54}$$

for the force at $r = a$. It will be convenient to express the radial motion in terms of the variable x defined by

$$x = r - a$$

The differential equation for radial motion then becomes

$$m\ddot{x} = ml^2(x + a)^{-3} + f(x + a)$$

Expanding the two terms involving $x + a$ as power series in x, we obtain

$$m\ddot{x} = ml^2 a^{-3}\left(1 - 3\frac{x}{a} + \ldots\right) + [f(a) + f'(a)x + \ldots]$$

The above equation, by virtue of the relation shown in Equation 6.54, reduces to

$$m\ddot{x} + \left[\frac{-3}{a}f(a) - f'(a)\right]x = 0 \tag{6.55}$$

if we neglect terms involving x^2 and higher powers of x. Now, if the coefficient of x (the quantity in brackets) in the above equation is positive, then the equation is the same as that of the simple harmonic oscillator. In this case the particle, if perturbed, oscillates harmonically about the circle $r = a$, so the circular orbit is a stable one. On the other hand, if the coefficient of x is negative, the motion is nonoscillatory, and the result is that x eventually increases exponentially with time; the orbit is unstable. (If the coefficient of x is zero, then higher terms in the expansion must be included in order to determine the stability.) Hence we can state that a circular orbit of radius a is stable if the force function $f(r)$ satisfies the inequality

$$f(a) + \frac{a}{3}f'(a) < 0 \tag{6.56}$$

For example, if the radial force function is a power law, namely,

$$f(r) = -cr^n$$

then the condition for stability reads

$$-ca^n - \frac{a}{3}cna^{n-1} < 0$$

which reduces to

$$n > -3$$

Thus the inverse-square law ($n = -2$) gives stable circular orbits, as does the law of direct distance ($n = 1$). The latter case is that of the two-dimensional isotropic harmonic oscillator. For the inverse fourth power ($n = -4$) circular orbits are unstable. It can be shown that circular orbits are also unstable for the inverse cube law of force ($n = -3$). To show this it is necessary to include terms of higher power than one in the radial equation. (See Problem 6.22.)

6.14 Apsides and Apsidal Angles for Nearly Circular Orbits

An *apsis*, or *apse*, is a point in an orbit at which the radius vector assumes an extreme value (maximum or minimum). The perihelion and aphelion points are the apsides of planetary orbits. The angle swept out by the radius vector between two consecutive apsides is called the *apsidal angle*. Thus the apsidal angle is π for elliptic orbits under the inverse square law of force.

In the case of motion in a nearly circular orbit, we have seen that r oscillates about the circle $r = a$ (if the orbit is stable). From Equation 6.55 it follows that the period τ_r of this oscillation is given by

$$\tau_r = 2\pi \left[\frac{m}{-\dfrac{3}{a}f(a) - f'(a)} \right]^{1/2}$$

The apsidal angle in this case is just the amount by which the polar angle θ increases during the time that r oscillates from a minimum value to the succeeding maximum value. This time is clearly $\frac{1}{2}\tau_r$. Now $\dot{\theta} = l/r^2$, therefore $\dot{\theta}$ remains approximately constant, and we can write

$$\dot{\theta} \simeq \frac{l}{a^2} = \left[-\frac{f(a)}{ma} \right]^{1/2}$$

The last step above follows from Equation 6.54. Hence the apsidal angle is given by

$$\psi = \frac{1}{2}\tau_r\dot{\theta} = \pi\left[3 + a\frac{f'(a)}{f(a)}\right]^{-1/2} \tag{6.57}$$

Thus for the power law of force $f(r) = -cr^n$, we obtain

$$\psi = \pi(3 + n)^{-1/2}$$

The apsidal angle is independent of the size of the orbit in this case. The orbit is *re-entrant*, or repetitive, in the case of the inverse-square law ($n = -2$) for which $\psi = \pi$ and also in the case of the linear law ($n = 1$) for which $\psi = \pi/2$. If, however, say $n = 2$, then $\psi = \pi/\sqrt{5}$ which is an irrational multiple of π, and so the motion does not repeat itself.

If the law of force departs slightly from the inverse-square law, then the apsides will either advance or regress steadily, depending on whether the apsidal angle is slightly greater or slightly less than π. (See Figure 6.12.)

Example

6.12 Let us suppose that the force is of the form

$$f(r) = -\frac{k}{r^2} - \frac{\epsilon}{r^4}$$

where ϵ is very small. (This is the form of the force function in the plane of a ring, as shown in Example 6.2.) The apsidal angle, from Equation 6.57, is

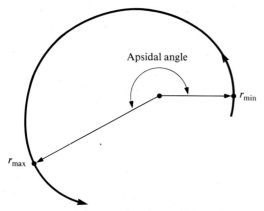

FIGURE 6.12   Illustrating the apsidal angle.

$$\psi = \pi\left(3 + a\frac{2ka^{-3} + 4\epsilon a^{-5}}{-ka^{-2} - \epsilon a^{-4}}\right)^{-1/2}$$

$$= \pi\left(\frac{1 - \epsilon k^{-1}a^{-2}}{1 + \epsilon k^{-1}a^{-2}}\right)^{-1/2}$$

$$\approx \pi\left(1 + \frac{\epsilon}{ka^{2}}\right)$$

In the last step above we have neglected powers of the quantity ϵ/ka^{2} higher than one. We see that the apsides advance if ϵ is positive, whereas they regress if ϵ is negative.

∎

For a given planet, the gravitational perturbation owing to the other planets in the solar system is indeed approximated by a term of the form ϵ/r^{4}. (The cumulative effect of one planet may be considered to be approximately the same as if that planet were smeared out into a ring.) For the innermost planet, Mercury, the calculated perturbations are such as to cause an advance of Mercury's perihelion of 531 sec of arc per century. The observed advance is 574 sec per century. The discrepancy of 43 sec per century is apparently explained by Einstein's general theory of relativity.

The gravitational field near the earth departs slightly from the inverse-square law. This is due to the fact that the earth is not quite a true sphere. As a result, the perigee of an artificial satellite whose orbit lies near the earth's equatorial plane will advance steadily in the direction of the satellite's motion. The observation of this advance is, in fact, one method of accurately determining the shape of the earth. Such observations have shown that the earth is slightly pear-shaped. In addition to causing an advance of the perigee of an orbiting satellite, the earth's oblateness also causes the plane of the orbit to precess if the orbit is not in the plane of the earth's equator.

PROBLEMS

6.1   Find the gravitational attraction between two solid lead spheres of one kilogram mass each if the spheres are almost in contact. Express the answer as a fraction of the weight of either sphere. (The density of lead is 11.35 g/cm^{3}.)

6.2   Show that the gravitational force on a test particle inside a thin spherical shell is zero (a) by finding the force directly, and (b) by showing that the gravitational potential is constant.

6.3   Assuming the earth to be a uniform solid sphere, show that if a straight hole were drilled from pole to pole, a particle dropped into the hole would execute simple harmonic motion. Show also that the period of this oscillation depends only on the density of the earth and is independent of the size. What is the period in hours? ($r_{earth} = 6.38 \times 10^6$ m).

6.4   Show that the motion is simple harmonic with the same period as the previous problem for a particle sliding in a straight smooth tube passing obliquely through the earth. (Neglect any effects of rotation.)

6.5   Assuming a circular orbit, show that Kepler's Third Law follows directly from Newton's Second Law and his law of gravity: $GMm/r^2 = mv^2/r$.

6.6   (a)   Show that the radius for a circular orbit of a synchronous (24 hr) earth satellite is about seven earth radii.

(b)   The distance to the moon is about sixty earth radii. From this calculate the length of the month (period of the moon's orbital revolution).

6.7   Show that the orbital period for an earth satellite in a circular orbit just above the earth's surface is the same as the period of oscillation of the particle dropped into a hole drilled through the earth (Problem 6.3.)

6.8   If the solar system were embedded in a uniform dust cloud of density ρ, show that the law of force on a planet a distance r from the center of the sun would be given by

$$F(r) = -GMm/r^2 - (4/3)\pi\rho mGr$$

6.9   A particle moving in a central field describes the spiral orbit $r = r_0 e^{k\theta}$. Show that the force law is inverse-cube and that θ varies logarithmically with t.

6.10   A particle moves in an inverse-cube field of force. Show that, in addition to the exponential spiral orbit of Problem 6.9, there are two other possible types of orbit, and give their equations.

6.11   The orbit of a particle moving in a central field is a circle passing through the origin, namely $r = r_0 \cos \theta$. Show that the force law is inverse-fifth power.

6.12   A particle moves in a spiral orbit given by $r = a\theta$. If θ increases linearly with t, is the force a central field? If not, determine how θ would have to vary with t for a central force.

6.13   A rocket ship is initially going in a circular orbit close to the earth. It is desired to place the ship into a new orbit such that the apogee distance is equal to the radius of the moon's orbit around the earth. (a) If a single rocket thrust is used to accomplish this, determine the ratio of the final and initial speeds. Assume that the radius of the original circular orbit is $\frac{1}{60}$ the distance to the moon. (b) Find the new orbit if the speed ratio is 1 percent too great. This problem illustrates the extreme accuracy needed to achieve a circumlunar orbit.

6.14   Compute the period of Halley's comet from the data given in the text, Section 6.8. Find also the comet's speed at perihelion and aphelion.

6.15   A comet is first seen at a distance of d astronomical units from the sun and it is traveling with a speed of q times the earth's speed. Show that the orbit of the comet is hyperbolic, parabolic, or elliptic, depending on whether the quantity $q^2 d$ is greater than, equal to, or less than 2, respectively.

6.16   A particle moves in an elliptic orbit in an inverse-square force field. Prove that the product of the minimum and maximum speeds is equal to $(2\pi a/\tau)^2$ where a is the semimajor axis and τ is the periodic time.

6.17   Prove that the time average of the potential energy of a particle describing an elliptic orbit, in the inverse-square force field $f(r) = -k/r^2$, is $-k/a$ where a is the semimajor axis of the ellipse.

6.18 Find the apsidal angle for nearly circular orbits in a central field for which the law of force is

$$f(r) = -k\frac{e^{-br}}{r^2}$$

6.19 If the solar system were embedded in a uniform dust cloud (Problem 6.8) what would the apsidal angle of a planet be for motion in a nearly circular orbit? This was once suggested as a possible explanation for the advance of the perihelion of mercury.

6.20 Show that the stability condition for a circular orbit of radius a is equivalent to the condition that $d^2U/dr^2 > 0$ for $r = a$ where $U(r)$ is the "effective potential" defined in Section 6.10.

6.21 Find the condition for which circular orbits are stable if the force function is of the form in Example 6.12, namely

$$f(r) = -\frac{k}{r^2} - \frac{\epsilon}{r^4}$$

6.22 (a) Show that a circular orbit of radius r is stable in Problem 6.18 if r is less than b^{-1}.
(b) Show that circular orbits are unstable in an inverse-cube force field.

6.23 A comet is going in a parabolic orbit lying in the plane of the earth's orbit. Regarding the earth's orbit as circular of radius a, show that the points where the comet intersects the earth's orbit are given by

$$\cos\theta = -1 + \frac{2p}{a}$$

where p is the perihelion distance of the comet defined at $\theta = 0$.

6.24 Use the result of the above problem to show that the time interval that the comet remains inside the earth's orbit is the fraction

$$\frac{2^{1/2}}{3\pi}\left(\frac{2p}{a} + 1\right)\left(1 - \frac{p}{a}\right)^{1/2}$$

of a year, and that the maximum value of this time interval is $2/3\pi$ year, or 77.5 days, corresponding to $p = a/2$. Compute the time interval for Halley's comet ($p = 0.6a$).

6.25 In advanced texts on potential theory it is shown that the potential energy of a particle of mass m in the gravitational field of an oblate spheroid, like the earth, is approximately

$$V(r) = -\frac{k}{r}\left(1 + \frac{\epsilon}{r^2}\right)$$

where r refers to distances in the equatorial plane, $k = GMm$ as before, and $\epsilon = (\frac{2}{5})R\Delta R$ in which R is the equatorial radius and ΔR is the difference between the equatorial and polar radii. From this, find the apsidal angle for a satellite moving in a nearly circular orbit in the equatorial plane of the earth where $R = 4000$ mi, $\Delta R = 13$ mi.

6.26 According to the special theory of relativity, a particle moving in a central field with potential energy $V(r)$ will describe the same orbit that a particle with a potential energy

$$V(r) - \frac{[E - V(r)]^2}{2m_0c^2}$$

would describe according to nonrelativistic mechanics. Here E is the total energy, m_0 is the rest mass of the particle, and c is the speed of light. From this, find the apsidal angle for motion in an inverse-square force field, $V(r) = -k/r$.

6.27 A comet is observed to have a speed v_{com} when it is a distance r_{com} from the sun, and its direction of motion makes an angle φ with the radius vector from the sun. Show that the major axis of the elliptical orbit of the comet makes an angle θ with the initial radius vector of the comet given by

$$\theta = \cot^{-1}\left(\tan \varphi - \frac{2}{V^2R} \csc 2\varphi\right)$$

where $V = v_{com}/v_{earth}$ and $R = r_{com}/a_e$ are dimensionless ratios as defined in Example 6.7. Apply the result to the numerical values of Example 6.7.

7

Dynamics of Systems of Particles

7.1 Introduction. Center of Mass and Linear Momentum of a System

We now expand our study of mechanics to systems of many particles (two or more). These particles may or may not move independently of one another. Special systems, called rigid bodies, in which the relative positions of all the particles are fixed will be taken up in the next two chapters. For the present, we shall develop some general theorems that apply to *all* systems. These will then be applied to some simple systems of free particles.

Our general system consists of n particles of masses $m_1, m_2, \ldots, m_n$ whose position vectors are, respectively, $\mathbf{r}_1, \mathbf{r}_2, \ldots, \mathbf{r}_n$. We define the *center of mass* of the system as the point whose position vector $\mathbf{r}_{cm}$ (Figure 7.1) is given by

$$\mathbf{r}_{cm} = \frac{m_1\mathbf{r}_1 + m_2\mathbf{r}_2 + \ldots + m_n\mathbf{r}_n}{m_1 + m_2 + \ldots + m_n} = \frac{\sum\limits_i m_i\mathbf{r}_i}{m} \tag{7.1}$$

where $m = \Sigma\, m_i$ is the total mass of the system. The above definition is clearly equivalent to the three equations

$$x_{cm} = \frac{\sum\limits_i m_i x_i}{m} \qquad y_{cm} = \frac{\sum\limits_i m_i y_i}{m} \qquad z_{cm} = \frac{\sum\limits_i m_i z_i}{m}$$

We define the *linear momentum* $\mathbf{p}$ of the system as the vector sum of the linear momenta of the individual particles, namely,

$$\mathbf{p} = \sum_i \mathbf{p}_i = \sum_i m_i \mathbf{v}_i \tag{7.2}$$

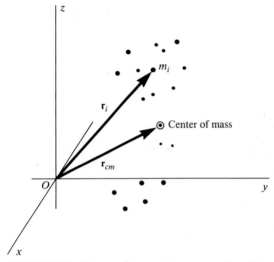

FIGURE 7.1   Center of mass of a system of particles.

Upon calculating $\dot{\mathbf{r}}_{cm} = \mathbf{v}_{cm}$ from Equation 7.1 and comparing with Equation 7.2, it readily follows that

$$\mathbf{p} = m\mathbf{v}_{cm} \tag{7.3}$$

that is, *the linear momentum of a system of particles is equal to the velocity of the center of mass multiplied by the total mass of the system.*

Suppose now that there are external forces $\mathbf{F}_1, \mathbf{F}_2, \ldots, \mathbf{F}_i, \ldots, \mathbf{F}_n$, acting on the respective particles. In addition, there may be internal forces of interaction between any two particles of the system. We shall denote these internal forces by $\mathbf{F}_{ij}$, meaning the force exerted on particle i by particle j, with the understanding that $\mathbf{F}_{ii} = 0$. The equation of motion of particle i is then

$$\mathbf{F}_i + \sum_{j=1}^{n} \mathbf{F}_{ij} = m_i \ddot{\mathbf{r}}_i = \dot{\mathbf{p}}_i \tag{7.4}$$

where $\mathbf{F}_i$ means the total external force acting on particle i. The second term in the above equation represents the vector sum of all the internal forces exerted on particle i by all other particles of the system. Adding Equation 7.4 for the n particles, we have

$$\sum_{i=1}^{n} \mathbf{F}_i + \sum_{i=1}^{n}\sum_{j=1}^{n} \mathbf{F}_{ij} = \sum_{i=1}^{n} \dot{\mathbf{p}}_i \tag{7.5}$$

In the double summation above, for every force $\mathbf{F}_{ij}$ there is also a force $\mathbf{F}_{ji}$, and these two forces are equal and opposite

$$\mathbf{F}_{ij} = -\mathbf{F}_{ji} \tag{7.6}$$

from the law of action and reaction, Newton's third law. Consequently, the internal forces cancel in pairs, and the double sum vanishes. We can therefore write Equation 7.5 in the following way:

$$\sum_i \mathbf{F}_i = \dot{\mathbf{p}} = m\mathbf{a}_{cm} \qquad (7.7)$$

In words: *The acceleration of the center of mass of a system of particles is the same as that of a single particle having a mass equal to the total mass of the system and acted upon by the sum of the external forces.*

Consider, for example, a swarm of particles moving in a *uniform* gravitational field. Then, since $\mathbf{F}_i = m_i\mathbf{g}$ for each particle,

$$\sum_i \mathbf{F}_i = \Sigma m_i\mathbf{g} = m\mathbf{g}$$

The last step follows from the fact that $\mathbf{g}$ is constant. Hence

$$\mathbf{a}_{cm} = \mathbf{g} \qquad (7.8)$$

This is the same as the equation for a single particle or projectile. Thus the center of mass of the shrapnel from an artillery shell that has burst in mid-air will follow the same parabolic path that the shell would have taken had it not burst (until any of the pieces strikes something).

In the special case in which there are *no* external forces acting on a system (or if $\Sigma \mathbf{F}_i = 0$), then $\mathbf{a}_{cm} = 0$ and $\mathbf{v}_{cm} =$ constant. Thus the linear momentum of the system remains constant:

$$\sum_i \mathbf{p}_i = \mathbf{p} = m\mathbf{v}_{cm} = \text{constant} \qquad (7.9)$$

This is the *principle of conservation of linear momentum*. In Newtonian mechanics the constancy of the linear momentum of an isolated system is directly related to, and is in fact a consequence of, the third law. But even in those cases in which the forces between particles do not directly obey the law of action and reaction, such as the magnetic forces between moving charges, the principle of conservation of linear momentum still holds when due account is taken of the total linear momentum of the particles and the electromagnetic field.[1]

Example

7.1 At some point in its trajectory a ballistic missile (ICBM) of mass m breaks into three fragments of mass $m/3$ each. One of the fragments continues on with an initial velocity of one-half the velocity $\mathbf{v}_0$ of the missile just before breakup. The other two pieces go off at right angles to each other with equal speeds. Find the initial speeds of the latter two fragments in terms of v_0.

---

[1] See, for example, W. T. Scott, *The Physics of Electricity and Magnetism*, 2d ed., John Wiley and Sons, Inc., New York, 1966.

Solution:

At the point of breakup, conservation of linear momentum is expressed as

$$m\mathbf{v}_{cm} = m\mathbf{v}_0 = \frac{m}{3}\mathbf{v}_1 + \frac{m}{3}\mathbf{v}_2 + \frac{m}{3}\mathbf{v}_3$$

The given conditions are: $\mathbf{v}_1 = \mathbf{v}_0/2$, $\mathbf{v}_2 \cdot \mathbf{v}_3 = 0$, and $v_2 = v_3$. From the first we get, upon cancellation of the m's, $3\mathbf{v}_0 = (\mathbf{v}_0/2) + \mathbf{v}_2 + \mathbf{v}_3$, or

$$\frac{5}{2}\mathbf{v}_0 = \mathbf{v}_2 + \mathbf{v}_3$$

Taking the dot product of each side with itself, we have

$$\frac{25}{4}v_0^2 = (\mathbf{v}_2 + \mathbf{v}_3) \cdot (\mathbf{v}_2 + \mathbf{v}_3) = v_2^2 + 2\mathbf{v}_2 \cdot \mathbf{v}_3 + v_3^2 = 2v_2^2$$

Therefore

$$v_2 = v_3 = \frac{5}{2\sqrt{2}}v_0 = 1.77\, v_0$$

■

7.2 Angular Momentum and Kinetic Energy of a System

We previously stated that the angular momentum of a single particle is defined as the cross product $\mathbf{r} \times m\mathbf{v}$. The angular momentum $\mathbf{L}$ of a system of particles is defined accordingly, as the vector sum of the individual angular momenta, namely

$$\mathbf{L} = \sum_{i=1}^{n} (\mathbf{r}_i \times m_i\mathbf{v}_i)$$

Let us calculate the time derivative of the angular momentum. Using the rule for differentiating the cross product, we find

$$\frac{d\mathbf{L}}{dt} = \sum_{i=1}^{n} (\mathbf{v}_i \times m_i\mathbf{v}_i) + \sum_{i=1}^{n} (\mathbf{r}_i \times m_i\mathbf{a}_i) \tag{7.10}$$

Now the first term on the right vanishes, because $\mathbf{v}_i \times \mathbf{v}_i = 0$ and, since $m_i\mathbf{a}_i$ is equal to the total force acting on particle i, we can write

$$\frac{d\mathbf{L}}{dt} = \sum_{i=1}^{n} \left[\mathbf{r}_i \times \left(\mathbf{F}_i + \sum_{j=1}^{n} \mathbf{F}_{ij} \right) \right]$$

$$= \sum_{i=1}^{n} \mathbf{r}_i \times \mathbf{F}_i + \sum_{i=1}^{n}\sum_{j=1}^{n} \mathbf{r}_i \times \mathbf{F}_{ij} \tag{7.11}$$

where, as in Section 7.1, $\mathbf{F}_i$ denotes the total external force on particle i, and $\mathbf{F}_{ij}$ denotes the (internal) force exerted on particle i by any other particle j. Now the double summation on the right consists of pairs of terms of the form

$$(\mathbf{r}_i \times \mathbf{F}_{ij}) + (\mathbf{r}_j \times \mathbf{F}_{ji}) \tag{7.12}$$

Denoting the vector displacement of particle j relative to particle i by $\mathbf{r}_{ij}$, we see from the triangle shown in Figure 7.2 that

$$\mathbf{r}_{ij} = \mathbf{r}_j - \mathbf{r}_i \tag{7.13}$$

Therefore, since $\mathbf{F}_{ji} = -\mathbf{F}_{ij}$, expression 7.12 reduces to

$$-\mathbf{r}_{ij} \times \mathbf{F}_{ij}$$

which clearly vanishes if the internal forces are central, that is, if they act along the lines connecting pairs of particle. Hence the double sum in Equation 7.11 vanishes. Now the cross product $\mathbf{r}_i \times \mathbf{F}_i$ is the moment of the external force $\mathbf{F}_i$. The sum $\Sigma \mathbf{r}_i \times \mathbf{F}_i$ is therefore the total moment of all the external forces acting on the system. If we denote the total external torque, or moment of force, by $\mathbf{N}$, Equation 7.11 takes the form

$$\frac{d\mathbf{L}}{dt} = \mathbf{N} \tag{7.14}$$

That is, *the time rate of change of the angular momentum of a system is equal to the total moment of all the external forces acting on the system.*

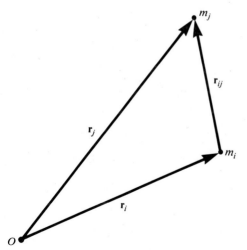

FIGURE 7.2   Definition of the vector $\mathbf{r}_{ij}$.

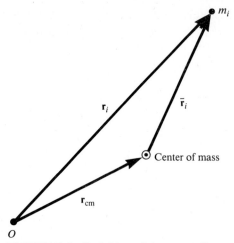

FIGURE 7.3   Definition of the vector $\bar{\mathbf{r}}_i$.

If a system is isolated, then $\mathbf{N} = 0$, and the angular momentum remains constant in both magnitude and direction:

$$\mathbf{L} = \sum_i \mathbf{r}_i \times m_i \mathbf{v}_i = \text{constant vector} \qquad (7.15)$$

This is a statement of the *principle of conservation of angular momentum*. It is a generalization for a single particle in a central field. Like the constancy of linear momentum discussed in the preceding section, the angular momentum of an isolated system is also constant in the case of a system of moving charges when the angular momentum of the electromagnetic field is considered.[2]

It is sometimes convenient to express the angular momentum in terms of the motion of the center of mass. As shown in Figure 7.3, we can express each position vector $\mathbf{r}_i$ in the form

$$\mathbf{r}_i = \mathbf{r}_{cm} + \bar{\mathbf{r}}_i \qquad (7.16)$$

where $\bar{\mathbf{r}}_i$ is the position of particle i relative to the center of mass. Taking the derivative with respect to t, we have

$$\mathbf{v}_i = \mathbf{v}_{cm} + \bar{\mathbf{v}}_i \qquad (7.17)$$

Here $\mathbf{v}_{cm}$ is the velocity of the center of mass and $\bar{\mathbf{v}}_i$ is the velocity of particle i relative to the center of mass. The expression for $\mathbf{L}$ can therefore be written

$$\mathbf{L} = \sum_i (\mathbf{r}_{cm} + \bar{\mathbf{r}}_i) \times m_i (\mathbf{v}_{cm} + \bar{\mathbf{v}}_i)$$

[2] See footnote 1.

$$= \sum_i (\mathbf{r}_{cm} \times m_i \mathbf{v}_{cm}) + \sum_i (\mathbf{r}_{cm} \times m_i \bar{\mathbf{v}}_i) + \sum_i (\bar{\mathbf{r}}_i \times m_i \mathbf{v}_{cm}) + \sum_i (\bar{\mathbf{r}}_i \times m_i \bar{\mathbf{v}}_i)$$

$$= \mathbf{r}_{cm} \times \left(\sum_i m_i \right) \mathbf{v}_{cm} + \mathbf{r}_{cm} \times \sum_i m_i \bar{\mathbf{v}}_i + \left(\sum_i m_i \bar{\mathbf{r}}_i \right) \times \mathbf{v}_{cm} + \sum_i (\bar{\mathbf{r}}_i \times m_i \bar{\mathbf{v}}_i)$$

Now, from Equation 7.16, we have

$$\sum_i m_i \bar{\mathbf{r}}_i = \sum_i m_i (\mathbf{r}_i - \mathbf{r}_{cm}) = \sum_i m_i \mathbf{r}_i - m \mathbf{r}_{cm} = 0$$

Similarly, we obtain

$$\sum_i m_i \bar{\mathbf{v}}_i = \sum_i m_i \mathbf{v}_i - m \mathbf{v}_{cm} = 0$$

by differentiation with respect to t. (These two equations merely state that the position and velocity of the center of mass, relative to the center of mass, are both zero.) Consequently, the second and third summations in the expansion of **L** vanish, and we can write

$$\mathbf{L} = \mathbf{r}_{cm} \times m \mathbf{v}_{cm} + \sum_i \bar{\mathbf{r}}_i \times m_i \bar{\mathbf{v}}_i \qquad (7.18)$$

expressing the angular momentum of a system in terms of an "orbital" part (motion of the center of mass) and a "spin" part (motion about the center of mass).

Kinetic Energy of a System

The total kinetic energy T of a system of particles is given by the sum of the individual energies, namely

$$T = \sum_i \frac{1}{2} m_i v_i^2 = \sum_i \frac{1}{2} m_i (\mathbf{v}_i \cdot \mathbf{v}_i) \qquad (7.19)$$

As before, we can express the velocities relative to the mass center giving

$$T = \sum_i \frac{1}{2} m_i (\mathbf{v}_{cm} + \bar{\mathbf{v}}_i) \cdot (\mathbf{v}_{cm} + \bar{\mathbf{v}}_i)$$

$$= \sum_i \frac{1}{2} m_i v_{cm}^2 + \sum_i m_i (\mathbf{v}_{cm} \cdot \bar{\mathbf{v}}_i) + \sum_i \frac{1}{2} m_i \bar{v}_i^2$$

$$= \frac{1}{2} v_{cm}^2 \sum_i m_i + \mathbf{v}_{cm} \cdot \sum_i m_i \bar{\mathbf{v}}_i + \sum_i \frac{1}{2} m_i \bar{v}_i^2$$

Since the second summation $\sum_i m_i \bar{\mathbf{v}}_i$ vanishes, we can express the kinetic energy as follows:

$$T = \frac{1}{2} m v_{cm}^2 + \sum_i \frac{1}{2} m_i \bar{v}_i^2 \tag{7.20}$$

The first term is the kinetic energy of translation of the whole system, and the second is the kinetic energy of motion relative to the mass center.

The separation of angular momentum and kinetic energy into a center-of-mass part and a relative-to-center-of-mass part finds important applications in atomic and molecular physics and also in astrophysics. We shall find the above two theorems useful in the study of rigid bodies in the following chapters.

7.3   Motion of Two Interacting Bodies. The Reduced Mass

Let us consider the motion of a system consisting of two bodies, treated here as particles, that interact with one another by a central force. We shall assume the system is isolated, and hence the center of mass moves with constant velocity. For simplicity, we shall take the center of mass as the origin. We have then

$$m_1 \bar{\mathbf{r}}_1 + m_2 \bar{\mathbf{r}}_2 = 0 \tag{7.21}$$

where, as shown in Figure 7.4, the vectors $\bar{\mathbf{r}}_1$ and $\bar{\mathbf{r}}_2$ represent the positions of the

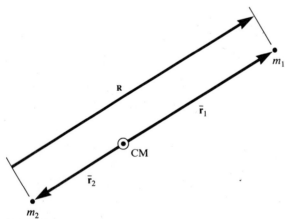

FIGURE 7.4   Showing the definition of the relative position vector for the two-body problem.

particles m_1 and m_2, respectively, relative to the center of mass. Now, if $\mathbf{R}$ is the position vector of particle 1 relative to particle 2, then

$$\mathbf{R} = \bar{\mathbf{r}}_1 - \bar{\mathbf{r}}_2 = \bar{\mathbf{r}}_1\left(1 + \frac{m_1}{m_2}\right) \tag{7.22}$$

The last step follows from Equation 7.21.

The differential equation of motion of particle 1 relative to the center of mass is

$$m_1\frac{d^2\bar{\mathbf{r}}_1}{dt^2} = \mathbf{F}_1 = f(R)\frac{\mathbf{R}}{R} \tag{7.23}$$

in which $|f(R)|$ is the magnitude of the mutual force between the two particles. By using Equation 7.22, we can write

$$\mu\frac{d^2\mathbf{R}}{dt^2} = f(R)\frac{\mathbf{R}}{R} \tag{7.24}$$

where

$$\mu = \frac{m_1 m_2}{m_1 + m_2} \tag{7.25}$$

The quantity μ is called the *reduced mass*. The new equation of motion, 7.24, gives the motion of particle 1 relative to particle 2, and an exactly similar equation gives the motion of particle 2 relative to particle 1. This equation is precisely the same as the ordinary equation of motion of a single particle of mass μ moving in a central field of force given by $f(R)$. Thus the fact that both particles are moving relative to the center of mass is automatically accounted for by replacing m_1 by the reduced mass μ. If the bodies are of equal mass m, then $\mu = m/2$. On the other hand, if m_2 is very much greater than m_1, so that m_1/m_2 is very small, then μ is nearly equal to m_1.

For two bodies attracting one another by gravitation

$$f(R) = -\frac{Gm_1 m_2}{R^2} \tag{7.26}$$

In this case the equation of motion is

$$\mu\ddot{\mathbf{R}} = -\frac{Gm_1 m_2}{R^2}\mathbf{e}_R \tag{7.27}$$

or, equivalently

$$m_1\ddot{\mathbf{R}} = -\frac{G(m_1 + m_2)m_1}{R^2}\mathbf{e}_R \tag{7.28}$$

where $\mathbf{e}_R = \mathbf{R}/R$ is a unit vector in the direction of $\mathbf{R}$.

In Chapter 6, Section 6.11, we derived an equation giving the periodic time of orbital motion of a planet of mass m moving in the sun's gravitational field, namely $\tau = 2\pi(GM)^{-1/2}a^{3/2}$ where M is the sun's mass and a is the semimajor axis of the elliptical orbit of the planet about the sun. In this derivation it was assumed that the sun was stationary with the origin of our coordinate system at the center of the sun. To account for the sun's motion about the common center of mass, the correct equation is 7.28 in which $m = m_1$, and $M = m_2$. The force constant k, which was taken to be GMm in the earlier treatment, should therefore be replaced by $G(M + m)m$ so that the correct equation for the period is

$$\tau = 2\pi[G(M + m)]^{-1/2}a^{3/2} \tag{7.29}$$

or, for *any* two-body system held together by gravity the orbital period is

$$\tau = 2\pi[G(m_1 + m_2)]^{-1/2}a^{3/2} \tag{7.29a}$$

If m_1 and m_2 are expressed in units of the sun's mass, and a is in astronomical units (the mean distance from the earth to the sun), then the orbital period *in years* is given by

$$\tau = (m_1 + m_2)^{-1/2}a^{3/2} \tag{7.29b}$$

For most planets in our solar system the added mass term in the above expression for the period makes very little difference—the earth's mass is only 1/330,000 the sun's mass. The most massive planet, Jupiter, has a mass of about 1/1000 the mass of the sun, so the effect of the reduced-mass formula is to change the earlier calculation in the ratio $(1.001)^{-1/2} = 0.9995$ for the period of Jupiter's revolution about the sun.

Binary Stars. White Dwarfs and Black Holes

It is known that about half of all the stars in the galaxy in the vicinity of the sun are binary or double, that is, they occur in pairs held together by their mutual gravitational attraction, with each member of the pair revolving about their common center of mass. From the above analysis we can infer that either member of a binary system revolves about the other in an elliptical orbit for which the orbiting period is given by Equations 7.29a and 7.29b, where a is the semimajor axis of the ellipse, and m_1 and m_2 are the masses of the two stars. Values of a for known binary systems range from the very least (*contact binaries* in which the stars touch each other) to values so large that the period is measured in millions of years. A typical example is the brightest star in the night sky, Sirius, which consists of a very luminous star with a mass of about three solar masses and a very small dim star, called a *white dwarf*, which can only be seen in large telescopes. The mass of this small companion is about the same as the sun's mass, but its size is roughly that of a large planet, so its density is extremely large (30,000 times the density of water). The value of a for the Sirius system is approximately 20 astronomical units (about the distance from the sun to the planet Uranus) and the period, as calculated from Equation 7.29b, should be

$$\tau = (3 + 1)^{-1/2}(20)^{3/2}\,\text{yr} = 44.7 \text{ yr}$$

The observed period is about 49 yr.

A binary system that has received considerable attention in recent years is the one known as Cygnus X-1. One component of this system is a massive luminous star of about ten solar masses. The other component has about the same mass as the visible member, as determined by the latter's motion, but is invisible in even the largest telescopes. Many astronomers and astrophysicists now believe that this invisible component is a *black hole*: an object that is so massive and dense that nothing, not even light, can escape its gravitational field. Black holes are predicted mathematically by the general theory of relativity[3] and convincing proof that they actually exist would constitute a milestone in the science of astrophysics.

7.4 Collisions

Whenever two bodies undergo a collision, the force that either exerts on the other during the contact is an internal force, if the bodies are regarded together as a single system. The total linear momentum is therefore unchanged. We can therefore write

$$\mathbf{p}_1 + \mathbf{p}_2 = \mathbf{p}_1' + \mathbf{p}_2' \tag{7.30}$$

or, equivalently

$$m_1\mathbf{v}_1 + m_2\mathbf{v}_2 = m_1\mathbf{v}_1' + m_2\mathbf{v}_2' \tag{7.30a}$$

The subscripts 1 and 2 refer to the two bodies, and the primes indicate the respective momenta and velocities *after* the collision. The above equations are quite general. They apply to any two bodies regardless of their shapes, rigidity, and so on.

With regard to the energy balance, we can write

$$\frac{p_1^2}{2m_1} + \frac{p_2^2}{2m_2} = \frac{p_1'^2}{2m_1} + \frac{p_2'^2}{2m_2} + Q \tag{7.31}$$

or

$$\frac{1}{2}m_1v_1^2 + \frac{1}{2}m_2v_2^2 = \frac{1}{2}m_1v_1'^2 + \frac{1}{2}m_2v_2'^2 + Q \tag{7.31a}$$

Here the quantity Q is introduced to indicate the net loss or gain in kinetic energy, that occurs as a result of the collision.

In the case of an *elastic* collision, there is no change in the total kinetic energy, so that $Q = 0$. If there is an energy loss, then Q is positive. This is called an *exoergic* collision. It may happen that there is an energy gain. This would occur, for example, if an explosive was present on one of the bodies at the point of contact In this case Q is negative, and the collision is called *endoergic*.

The study of collisions is of particular importance in atomic and nuclear physics. Here the bodies involved may be atoms, nuclei, or various elementary particles, such as electrons, protons, and so on.

---

[3] According to the theory, a spherical body of mass m becomes a black hole if it is compressed to a radius r_B, known as the *Schwarzschild radius*, where

$$r_B = \frac{2Gm}{c^2}$$

in which c is the speed of light. The earth would become a black hole if it were compressed to the size of a small marble. For the sun r_B is about 3 km which is much smaller than the white dwarf companion of Sirius.

Direct Collisions

Let us consider the special case of a head-on collision of two bodies, or particles, in which the motion takes place entirely on a single straight line, the x axis, as shown in Figure 7.5. In this case the momentum balance equation, Equation 7.30a, can be written

$$m_1\dot{x}_1 + m_2\dot{x}_2 = m_1\dot{x}_1' + m_2\dot{x}_2' \tag{7.32}$$

The direction along the line of motion is given by the signs of the $\dot{x}$'s.

In order to compute the values of the velocities after the collision, given the values before the collision, we can use the above momentum equation together with the energy balance equation, Equation 7.31a, if we know the value of Q. It is often convenient in this kind of problem to introduce another parameter ϵ called the *coefficient of restitution*. This quantity is defined as the ratio of the speed of separation v' to the speed of approach v. In our notation, ϵ may be written as

$$\epsilon = \frac{|\dot{x}_2' - \dot{x}_1'|}{|\dot{x}_2 - \dot{x}_1|} = \frac{v'}{v} \tag{7.33}$$

The numerical value of ϵ depends primarily on the composition and physical makeup of the two bodies. It is easy to verify that in an elastic collision, the value of $\epsilon = 1$. To do this, we set $Q = 0$ in Equation 7.31a, and solve it together with Equation 7.32, for the final velocities. The steps are left as an exercise.

In the case of a *totally inelastic* collision, the two bodies stick together after colliding, so that $\epsilon - 0$. For most real bodies, ϵ has a value somewhere between the two extremes of 0 and 1. For ivory billiard balls, it is about 0.95. The value of the coefficient of restitution may also depend on the speed of approach. This is particularly evident in the case of a silicone compound known under a trade name as "silly putty." A ball of this material bounces when it strikes a hard surface at high speed, but at low speeds it acts like ordinary putty.

We can calculate the values of the final velocities from Equation 7.32 together with the definition of the coefficient of restitution, Equation 7.33. The result is

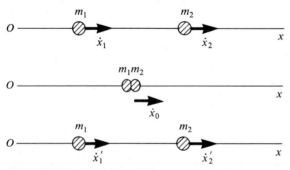

FIGURE 7.5   Head-on collision of two particles.

$$\dot{x}_1' = \frac{(m_1 - \epsilon m_2)\dot{x}_1 + (m_2 + \epsilon m_2)\dot{x}_2}{m_1 + m_2} \tag{7.34}$$

$$\dot{x}_2' = \frac{(m_1 + \epsilon m_1)\dot{x}_1 + (m_2 - \epsilon m_1)\dot{x}_2}{m_1 + m_2}$$

Taking the totally inelastic case by setting $\epsilon = 0$, we find, as we should, that $\dot{x}_1' = \dot{x}_2'$, that is, there is no rebound. On the other hand, in the special case that the bodies are of equal mass, $m_1 = m_2$, and are perfectly elastic, $\epsilon = 1$, then we obtain

$$\dot{x}_1' = \dot{x}_2$$
$$\dot{x}_2' = \dot{x}_1$$

The two bodies, therefore, just *exchange* their velocities as a result of the collision.

In the general case of a direct nonelastic collision, it is easily verified that the energy loss Q is related to the coefficient of restitution by the equation

$$Q = \frac{1}{2}\mu v^2(1 - \epsilon^2)$$

in which $\mu = m_1 m_2/(m_1 + m_2)$ is the reduced mass, and $v = |\dot{x}_2 - \dot{x}_1|$ is the relative speed before impact. The derivation is left as an exercise.

Impulse in Collisions

Forces of extremely short duration in time, such as those exerted by bodies undergoing collisions, are called *impulsive forces*. If we confine our attention to one body, or particle, the differential equation of motion, as we know, is $\frac{d(m\mathbf{v})}{dt} = \mathbf{F}$, or, in differential form $d(m\mathbf{v}) = \mathbf{F}\,dt$. Let us take the time integral over the interval $t = t_1$ to $t = t_2$. This is the time during which the force is considered to act. Then we have

$$\Delta(m\mathbf{v}) = \int_{t_1}^{t_2} \mathbf{F}\,dt \tag{7.35}$$

The time integral of the force is the impulse, previously defined in Section 2.4. It is customarily denoted by the symbol $\hat{\mathbf{P}}$. The above equation is, accordingly, expressed as

$$\Delta(m\mathbf{v}) = \hat{\mathbf{P}} \tag{7.35a}$$

We can think of an *ideal impulse* as produced by a force that tends to infinity but lasts for a time interval which approaches zero in such a way that the integral $\int \mathbf{F}\,dt$ remains finite. Such an ideal impulse would produce an instantaneous change in the momentum and velocity of a body without producing any displacement.

Relationship Between Impulse and Coefficient of Restitution in Direct Collisions

Let us apply the concept of impulse to the case of the direct collision of two bodies. We shall divide the impulse into two parts, namely, the impulse of compression, $\hat{P}_c$, and the impulse of restitution, $\hat{P}_r$. We are concerned only with direct collisions along the x axis, as before. Therefore, for the compression we can write

$$m_1\dot{x}_0 - m_1\dot{x}_1 = \hat{P}_c \qquad (7.36)$$
$$m_2\dot{x}_0 - m_2\dot{x}_2 = -\hat{P}_c$$

where $\dot{x}_0$ is the common velocity of both particles at the instant their relative speed is zero. Similarly, for the restitution, we have

$$m_1\dot{x}_1' - m_1\dot{x}_0 = \hat{P}_r \qquad (7.37)$$
$$m_2\dot{x}_2' - m_2\dot{x}_0 = -\hat{P}_r$$

Upon eliminating $\dot{x}_0$ from Equations 7.36 and also from Equations 7.37, we obtain the following pair of equations:

$$m_1 m_2(\dot{x}_2 - \dot{x}_1) = \hat{P}_c(m_1 + m_2) \qquad (7.38)$$
$$m_1 m_2(\dot{x}_1' - \dot{x}_2') = \hat{P}_r(m_1 + m_2)$$

Division of the second equation by the first yields the relation

$$\frac{|\dot{x}_2' - \dot{x}_1'|}{|\dot{x}_1 - \dot{x}_2|} = \frac{\hat{P}_r}{\hat{P}_c} \qquad (7.39)$$

But the left-hand side is just the definition of the coefficient of restitution ϵ. Hence we have

$$\epsilon = \frac{\hat{P}_r}{\hat{P}_c} \qquad (7.40)$$

The coefficient of restitution is thus equal to the ratio of the impulse of restitution to the impulse of compression.

Example

7.2 *Determining the speed of a bullet.* A gun is fired horizontally point-blank at a block of wood which is initially at rest on a horizontal floor. The bullet becomes imbedded in the block, and the impact causes the system to slide a certain distance s before coming to rest. Given m, the mass of the bullet, M, the mass of the block, and μ, the coefficient of sliding friction between the block and the floor, find the initial speed (*muzzle velocity*) of the bullet.

Solution:
First, from conservation of linear momentum, we can write

$$m\dot{x}_0 = (M + m)\dot{x}_0'$$

where $\dot{x}_0$ is the initial velocity of the bullet and $\dot{x}_0'$ is the velocity of the system (block + bullet) immediately after impact. (Note that the coefficient of restitution ϵ is zero in this case.) Second, we know that the magnitude of the retarding frictional force is equal to $(M + m)\mu g = (M + m)a$ where $a = -\ddot{x}$ is the deceleration of the system after impact, so $a = \mu g$. Now, from Chapter 2 we recall that $s = v_0^2/2a$ for the case of uniform acceleration in one dimension. Thus, in our problem

$$s = \frac{\dot{x}_0'^2}{2\mu g} = \left(\frac{m\dot{x}_0}{M + m}\right)^2 \left(\frac{1}{2\mu g}\right)$$

Solving for $\dot{x}_0$ we obtain

$$\dot{x}_0 = \left(\frac{M + m}{m}\right)(2\mu g s)^{1/2}$$

for the initial velocity of the bullet in terms of the given quantities.

As a numerical example, let the mass of the block be 4 kg, and that of the bullet 10 g = 0.01 kg (about that of a .38 calibre slug). For the coefficient of friction (wood-on-wood) let us take $\mu = 0.4$. If the block slides a distance of 15 cm = 0.15 m, then we find

$$\dot{x}_0 = \frac{4.01}{0.01}(2 \times 0.4 \times 9.8 \text{ ms}^{-2} \times 0.15 \text{ m})^{1/2} = 435 \text{ m/sec} \qquad \blacksquare$$

7.5 Oblique Collisions and Scattering. Comparison of Laboratory and Center-of-Mass Coordinates

We now turn our attention to the more general case of collisions in which the motion is not confined to a single straight line. Here the vectorial form of the momentum equations must be employed. Let us study the special case of a particle of mass m_1 with initial velocity $\mathbf{v}_1$ (the incident particle) that strikes a particle of mass m_2 that is initially at rest (the target particle). This is a typical problem found in nuclear physics. The momentum equations in this case are

$$\mathbf{p}_1 = \mathbf{p}_1' + \mathbf{p}_2' \qquad (7.41)$$

$$m_1\mathbf{v}_1 = m_1\mathbf{v}_1' + m_2\mathbf{v}_2' \qquad (7.41a)$$

The energy balance condition is

$$\frac{p_1^2}{2m_1} = \frac{p_1'^2}{2m_1} + \frac{p_2'^2}{2m_2} + Q \qquad (7.42)$$

or

$$\tfrac{1}{2}m_1v_1^2 = \tfrac{1}{2}m_1v_1'^2 + \tfrac{1}{2}m_2v_2'^2 + Q \qquad (7.42a)$$

Here, as before, the primes indicate the velocities and momenta after the collision, and Q represents the net energy that is lost or gained as a result of the impact. The quantity Q is of fundamental importance in atomic and nuclear physics, since it represents the energy released or absorbed in atomic and nuclear collisions. In many cases the target particle is broken up or changed by the collision. In such cases, the particles that leave the collision are different from the particles that enter. This is easily taken into account by assigning different masses, say m_3 and m_4 to the particles leaving the collision. In any case, the law of conservation of linear momentum is always assumed to be valid.

Consider the particular case in which the masses of the incident and target particles are the same. Then the energy balance equation (7.42) can be written

$$p_1^2 = p_1'^2 + p_2'^2 + 2mQ \tag{7.43}$$

where $m = m_1 = m_2$. Now if we take the dot product of each side of the momentum equation (7.41) with itself, we get

$$p_1^2 = (\mathbf{p}_1' + \mathbf{p}_2') \cdot (\mathbf{p}_1' + \mathbf{p}_2') = p_1'^2 + p_2'^2 + 2\mathbf{p}_1' \cdot \mathbf{p}_2'$$

Comparing the above two equations, we see that

$$\mathbf{p}_1' \cdot \mathbf{p}_2' = mQ \tag{7.44}$$

For an elastic collision ($Q = 0$) we have therefore

$$\mathbf{p}_1' \cdot \mathbf{p}_2' = 0 \tag{7.44a}$$

so the two particles emerge from the collision at right angles to one another.

Center-of-Mass Coordinates

Theoretical calculations in nuclear physics are often done in terms of quantities referred to a coordinate system in which the center of mass of the colliding particles is at rest. On the other hand, the experimental observations on scattering of particles are carried out in terms of the laboratory coordinates. It is of interest, therefore, to consider briefly the problem of conversion from one coordinate system to the other.

The velocity vectors in the laboratory system and in the center-of-mass system are illustrated diagramatically in Figure 7.6. In the figure, ϕ_1 is the angle of deflection of the incident particle after it strikes the target particle and ϕ_2 is the angle that the line of motion of the target particle makes with the line of motion of the incident particle. Both ϕ_1 and ϕ_2 are measured in the laboratory system. In the center-of-mass system, since the center of mass must lie on the line joining the two particles at all times, both

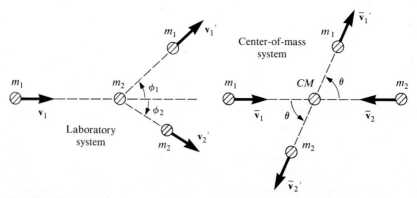

FIGURE 7.6   Comparison of laboratory and center-of-mass coordinates.

particles approach the center of mass, collide, and recede from the center of mass in opposite directions. The angle θ denotes the angle of deflection of the incident particle in the center-of-mass system as indicated.

From the definition of the center of mass, the linear momentum in the center-of-mass system is zero both before and after the collision. Hence we can write

$$\bar{\mathbf{p}}_1 + \bar{\mathbf{p}}_2 = 0 \tag{7.45}$$
$$\bar{\mathbf{p}}_1' + \bar{\mathbf{p}}_2' = 0$$

The bars are used to indicate that the quantity in question is referred to the center-of-mass system. The energy balance equation reads

$$\frac{\bar{p}_1^2}{2m_1} + \frac{\bar{p}_2^2}{2m_2} = \frac{\bar{p}_1'^2}{2m_1} + \frac{\bar{p}_2'^2}{2m_2} + Q \tag{7.46}$$

We can eliminate $\bar{p}_2$ and $\bar{p}_2'$ from the energy equation by using the momentum relations. The result, which is conveniently expressed in terms of the reduced mass, is

$$\frac{\bar{p}_1^2}{2\mu} = \frac{\bar{p}_1'^2}{2\mu} + Q \tag{7.47}$$

The momentum relations, Equations 7.45 expressed in terms of velocities, read

$$m_1\bar{\mathbf{v}}_1 + m_2\bar{\mathbf{v}}_2 = 0 \tag{7.48}$$
$$m_1\bar{\mathbf{v}}_1' + m_2\bar{\mathbf{v}}_2' = 0$$

The velocity of the center of mass is

$$\mathbf{v}_{cm} = \frac{m_1\mathbf{v}_1}{m_1 + m_2} \tag{7.49}$$

Hence we have

$$\bar{\mathbf{v}}_1 = \mathbf{v}_1 - \mathbf{v}_{cm} = \frac{m_2\mathbf{v}_1}{m_1 + m_2} \tag{7.50}$$

The relationships among the velocity vectors $\mathbf{v}_{cm}$, $\mathbf{v}_1'$, and $\bar{\mathbf{v}}_1'$ are shown in Figure 7.7. From the figure, we see that

$$v_1' \sin \phi_1 = \bar{v}_1' \sin \theta \tag{7.51}$$
$$v_1' \cos \phi_1 = \bar{v}_1' \cos \theta + v_{cm}$$

Hence, by dividing, we find the equation connecting the scattering angles to be expressible in the form

$$\tan \phi_1 = \frac{\sin \theta}{\gamma + \cos \theta} \tag{7.52}$$

in which γ is a numerical parameter whose value is given by

$$\gamma = \frac{v_{cm}}{\bar{v}_1'} = \frac{m_1 v_1}{\bar{v}_1'(m_1 + m_2)} \tag{7.53}$$

The last step follows from Equation 7.49.

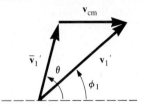

FIGURE 7.7   Velocity vectors in the laboratory system and the center-of-mass system.

Now we can readily calculate the value of $\bar{v}'_1$ in terms of the initial energy of the incident particle from the energy equation, Equation 7.47. This gives us the necessary information to find γ and thus determine the relationship between the scattering angles. For example, in the case of an elastic collision, $Q = 0$, we find from the energy equation that $\bar{p}_1 = \bar{p}'_1$, or $\bar{v}_1 = \bar{v}'_1$. This result, together with Equation 7.50, yields the value

$$\gamma = \frac{m_1}{m_2} \tag{7.54}$$

for an elastic collision.

Two special cases of such elastic collisions are instructive to consider. First, if the mass m_2 of the target particle is very much greater than the mass m_1 of the incident particle, then γ is very small. Hence $\tan \phi_1 \approx \tan \theta$, or $\phi_1 \approx \theta$. That is, the scattering angles as seen in the laboratory and in the center-of-mass systems are nearly equal.

The second special case is that of equal masses of the incident and target particles $m_1 = m_2$. In this case $\gamma = 1$, and the scattering relation reduces to

$$\tan \phi_1 = \frac{\sin \theta}{1 + \cos \theta} = \tan \frac{\theta}{2} \tag{7.55}$$

$$\phi_1 = \frac{\theta}{2}$$

That is, the angle of deflection in the laboratory system is just half that in the center-of-mass system. Furthermore, since the angle of deflection of the target particle is $\pi - \theta$ in the center-of-mass system, as shown in Figure 7.6, then the same angle in the laboratory system is $(\pi - \theta)/2$. Therefore the two particles leave the point of impact at right angles to each other as seen in the laboratory system, in agreement with Equation 7.44a.

In the general case of nonelastic collisions, it is left as a problem to show that γ is expressible as

$$\gamma = \frac{m_1}{m_2} \left[1 - \frac{Q}{T} \left(1 + \frac{m_1}{m_2} \right) \right]^{-1/2} \tag{7.56}$$

in which T is the kinetic energy of the incident particle as measured in the laboratory system.

Example

7.3   (a)   In a nuclear scattering experiment a beam of 4 MeV α-particles (helium nuclei) strikes a target consisting of helium gas, so that the incident and the target particles have equal mass. If a certain incident α-particle is scattered through an angle of 30° in the laboratory system, find its kinetic energy, and also the kinetic energy of recoil of the target particle, as a fraction of the initial kinetic energy T of the incident α-particle. (Assume that the target particle is at rest and that the collision is elastic.)

Solution:

For elastic collisions with particles of equal mass, we know from Equation 7.44a that $\phi_1 + \phi_2 = 90°$ (Figure 7.6). Hence, if we take components parallel to and perpendicular to the momentum of the incident particle, the momentum balance equation (7.41) becomes

$$p_1 = p_1' \cos \phi_1 + p_2' \sin \phi_1$$
$$0 = p_1' \sin \phi_1 - p_2' \cos \phi_1$$

in which $\phi_1 = 30°$. Solving the above pair of equations for the primed components, we find

$$p_1' = p_1 \cos \phi_1 = p_1 \cos 30° = p_1 \frac{\sqrt{3}}{2}$$

$$p_2' = p_1 \sin \phi_1 = p_1 \sin 30° = p_1 \frac{1}{2}.$$

Therefore, the kinetic energies after impact are

$$T_1' = \frac{p_1'^2}{2m_1} = \frac{3}{4} \frac{p_1^2}{2m_1} = \frac{3}{4} T = 3 \text{ MeV}$$

$$T_2' = \frac{p_2'^2}{2m_2} = \frac{1}{4} \frac{p_1^2}{2m_1} = \frac{1}{4} T = 1 \text{ MeV}$$

(b)   What is the scattering angle in the center-of-mass system for the above problem?

Solution:

Here Equation 7.55 gives the answer directly, namely

$$\theta = 2\phi_1 = 60°$$ ∎

7.6   Motion of a Body with Variable Mass. Rocket Motion

In the case of a body whose mass changes with time, it is necessary to use care in setting up the differential equations of motion. The concept of impulse can be helpful in this type of problem.

Consider the general case of the motion of a body with changing mass. Let $\mathbf{F}_{ext}$ denote the external force acting on the body at a given time, and let Δm denote the increment of the mass of the body that occurs in a short time interval Δt. Then $\mathbf{F}_{ext}\Delta t$ is the impulse delivered by the external force, and we have

$$\mathbf{F}_{ext}\Delta t = (\mathbf{p}_{total})_{t+\Delta t} - (\mathbf{p}_{total})_t \tag{7.57}$$

for the change in the total linear momentum of the system. Hence if $\mathbf{v}$ denotes the velocity of the body and $\mathbf{V}$ the velocity of the mass increment Δm relative to the body, then we can write

$$\mathbf{F}_{ext}\Delta t = (m + \Delta m)(\mathbf{v} + \Delta \mathbf{v}) - [m\mathbf{v} + \Delta m(\mathbf{v} + \mathbf{V})]$$

This reduces to

$$\mathbf{F}_{ext}\Delta t = m\Delta \mathbf{v} + \Delta m\Delta \mathbf{v} - \mathbf{V}\Delta m \tag{7.58}$$

or, by dividing by Δt, we can write

$$\mathbf{F}_{ext} = (m + \Delta m)\frac{\Delta \mathbf{v}}{\Delta t} - \mathbf{V}\frac{\Delta m}{\Delta t} \tag{7.58a}$$

Thus, in the limit as Δt approaches zero, we have the general equation

$$\mathbf{F}_{ext} = m\dot{\mathbf{v}} - \mathbf{V}\dot{m} \tag{7.59}$$

Here the force $\mathbf{F}_{ext}$ may represent gravity, air resistance, and so on. In the case of rockets, the term $\mathbf{V}\dot{m}$ represents the thrust.

Let us apply the equation to two special cases. First, suppose that a body is moving through a fog or mist so that it collects mass as it goes. In this case the initial velocity of the accumulated matter is zero. Hence $\mathbf{V} = -\mathbf{v}$, and we get

$$\mathbf{F}_{ext} = m\dot{\mathbf{v}} + \mathbf{v}\dot{m} = \frac{d(m\mathbf{v})}{dt} \tag{7.60}$$

for the equation of motion. It applies *only* if the initial velocity of the matter that is being swept up is zero. Otherwise the general equation (7.59) must be used.

For the second case, consider the motion of a rocket. In this instance the sign of $\dot{m}$ is negative, because the rocket is losing mass in the form of ejected fuel. Hence $\mathbf{V}\dot{m}$ is opposite to the direction of $\mathbf{V}$, the relative velocity of the ejected fuel. For simplicity we shall solve the equation of motion for the case in which the external force $\mathbf{F}_{ext}$ is zero, that is, we neglect gravity, air resistance, and so on. Then we have

$$m\dot{\mathbf{v}} = \mathbf{V}\dot{m} \tag{7.61}$$

We can now separate the variables and integrate to find $\mathbf{v}$ as follows:

$$\int d\mathbf{v} = \int \frac{\mathbf{V}\,dm}{m} \tag{7.61a}$$

If it is assumed that $\mathbf{V}$ is constant, then we can integrate between limits to find the *speed* as a function of m:

$$\int_{v_0}^{v} dv = -V\int_{m_0}^{m} \frac{dm}{m}$$

$$v = v_0 + V\ln\frac{m_0}{m} \tag{7.62}$$

Here m_0 is the initial mass of the rocket plus unburned fuel, m is the mass at any time, and V is the speed of the ejected fuel relative to the rocket. Owing to the nature of the logarithmic function, it is necessary to have a large fuel to payload ratio in order to attain the large speeds needed for satellite launching.

Example

7.4   *Launching an Earth-satellite from Cape Canaveral.* We know from the preceding chapter, Example 6.6(a), that the speed of a satellite in a circular orbit near the earth is about 8 km/sec. Satellites are launched toward the east in order to take advantage of the earth's rotation. For a point on the earth near the equator the rotational speed is approximately $R_{earth}\omega_{earth}$ which is about 0.5 km/sec. For most rocket fuels the effective ejection speed is of the order of 2 to 4 km/sec. For example, if we take $V = 2.5$ km/sec, then we find that the mass ratio calculated from Equation 7.62 is

$$\frac{m_0}{m} = \exp\left(\frac{v - v_0}{V}\right) = \exp\left(\frac{8.0 - 0.5}{2.5}\right) = e^3 = 20.1$$

to achieve orbital speed from the ground. Thus only about five percent of the total initial mass m_0 is payload.

PROBLEMS

7.1   A system consists of three particles, each of unit mass, with positions and velocities as follows:

$$
\begin{aligned}
\mathbf{r}_1 &= \mathbf{i} + \mathbf{j} & \mathbf{v}_1 &= 2\mathbf{i} \\
\mathbf{r}_2 &= \mathbf{j} + \mathbf{k} & \mathbf{v}_2 &= \mathbf{j} \\
\mathbf{r}_3 &= \mathbf{k} & \mathbf{v}_3 &= \mathbf{i} + \mathbf{j} + \mathbf{k}
\end{aligned}
$$

Find the position and velocity of the center of mass. Find also the linear momentum of the system.

7.2   (a) Find the kinetic energy of the above system. (b) Find the value of $mv_{cm}^2/2$. (c) Find the angular momentum about the origin.

7.3   A bullet of mass m is fired from a gun of mass M. If the gun can recoil freely and the muzzle velocity of the bullet (velocity relative to the gun as it leaves the barrel) is v_0, show that the actual velocity of the bullet relative to the ground is $v_0/(1 + \gamma)$ and the recoil velocity for the gun is $-\gamma v_0/(1 + \gamma)$ where $\gamma = m/M$.

7.4   A block of wood rests on a smooth horizontal table. A gun is fired horizontally at the block and the bullet passes through the block emerging with half its initial speed just before it entered the block. Show that the fraction of the initial kinetic energy of the bullet that is lost as frictional heat is $\dfrac{3}{4} - \dfrac{1}{4}\gamma$ where γ is the ratio of the mass of the bullet to the mass of the block. ($\gamma < 1$).

7.5   An artillery shell is fired at an angle of elevation of 60° with initial speed v_0. At the uppermost part of its trajectory the shell bursts into two equal fragments, one of which moves directly upward, relative to the ground, with initial speed $v_0/2$. What is the direction and speed of the other fragment immediately after the burst?

7.6   A ball is dropped from a height h onto a horizontal pavement. If the coefficient of restitution is ϵ, show that the total vertical distance the ball goes before the rebounds cease is $h(1 + \epsilon^2)/(1 - \epsilon^2)$. Find also the total length of time that the ball bounces.

7.7   A small car of a mass m and initial speed v_0 collides head-on on an icy road with a truck of mass $4m$ going toward the car with initial speed $\frac{1}{2}v_0$. If the coefficient of restitution in the collision is 1/4, find the speed and direction of each vehicle just after colliding.

7.8   Show that the kinetic energy of a two-particle system is $\frac{1}{2}mv_{cm}^2 + \frac{1}{2}\mu v^2$ where $m = m_1 + m_2$, v is the relative speed, and μ is the reduced mass.

7.9   If two bodies undergo a direct collision, show that the loss in kinetic energy is equal to

$$\tfrac{1}{2}\mu v^2(1 - \epsilon^2)$$

where μ is the reduced mass, v is the relative speed before impact, and ϵ is the coefficient of restitution.

7.10   A moving particle of mass m_1 collides elastically with a target particle of mass m_2 which is initially at rest. If the collision is head-on, show that the incident particle loses a fraction $4\mu/m$ of its original kinetic energy where μ is the reduced mass and $m = m_1 + m_2$.

7.11   Show that the angular momentum of a two-particle system is

$$\mathbf{r}_{cm} \times m\mathbf{v}_{cm} + \mathbf{R} \times \mu\mathbf{v}$$

where $m = m_1 + m_2$, μ is the reduced mass, $\mathbf{R}$ is the relative position vector, and $\mathbf{v}$ is the relative velocity of the two particles.

7.12   The observed period of the binary system Cygnus X-1, presumed to be a bright star and a black hole, is 5.6 days. If the mass of the visible component is 15 solar masses, and the black hole has a mass of 8 solar masses, show that the semimajor axis of the orbit of the black hole relative to the visible star is roughly 1/5 the distance from the earth to the sun.

7.13   A proton of mass m_p with initial velocity $\mathbf{v}_0$ collides with a helium atom, mass $4m_p$, that is initially at rest. If the proton leaves the point of impact at an angle of 45° with its original line of motion, find the final velocities of each particle. Assume that the collision is perfectly elastic.

7.14   Work the above problem for the case that the collision is inelastic and that Q is equal to $\frac{1}{4}$ of the initial energy of the proton.

7.15   Referring to Problem 7.13, find the scattering angle of the proton in the center-of-mass system.

7.16   Find the scattering angle of the proton in the center-of-mass system for Problem 7.14.

7.17   A particle of mass m with initial momentum p_1 collides with a particle of equal mass at rest. If the magnitudes of the final momenta of the two particles are p_1' and p_2', respectively, show that the energy loss of the collision is given by

$$Q = \frac{p_1'p_2'}{m} \cos \psi$$

where ψ is the angle between the paths of the two particles after colliding.

7.18   A uniform chain lies in a heap on a table. If one end is raised vertically with uniform velocity v, show that the upward force that must be exerted on the end of the chain is equal to the weight of a length $z + (v^2/g)$ of the chain where z is the length that has been uncoiled at any instant.

7.19   Find the differential equation of motion of a raindrop falling through a mist collecting mass as it falls. Assume that the drop remains spherical and that the rate of accretion is proportional to the cross-sectional area of the drop multiplied by the speed of fall. Show that if the drop starts from rest when it is infinitely small, then the acceleration is constant and equal to $g/7$.

7.20   A uniform heavy chain of length a hangs initially with a part of length b hanging over the edge of a table. The remaining part, of length $a - b$, is coiled up at the edge of the table. If the chain is released, show that the speed of the chain when the last link leaves the end of the table is $[2g(a^3 - b^3)/3a^2]^{1/2}$.

7.21   A rocket traveling through the atmosphere experiences a linear air resistance $-k\mathbf{v}$. Find the differential equation of motion when all other external forces are negligible. Integrate the equation and show that if the rocket stars from rest, the final speed is given by $v = V$ $\alpha[1 - (m/m_0)^{1/\alpha}]$ where V is the relative speed of the exhaust fuel, $\alpha = |\dot{m}/k| =$ constant, m_0 is the initial mass of the rocket plus fuel, and m is the final mass of the rocket.

7.22   Find the equation of motion for a rocket fired vertically upward, assuming g is constant. Find the ratio of fuel to payload to achieve a final spced equal to the escape speed v_e from the earth if the speed of the exhaust gas is kv_e where k is a given constant, and the fuel burning rate is $|\dot{m}|$. Compute the numerical value of the fuel-payload ratio for $k = \frac{1}{4}$, and $|\dot{m}|$ equal to 1 percent of the mass of the fuel, per second.

8

Mechanics of Rigid Bodies. Planar Motion

A rigid body may be regarded as a system of particles whose *relative* positions are fixed, or, in other words, the distance between any two particles is constant. This definition of a rigid body is idealized. In the first place, as pointed out in the definition of a particle, there are no true particles in nature. Secondly, real extended bodies are not strictly rigid; they become more or less deformed (stretched, compressed, or bent) when external forces are applied. We shall for the present, however, neglect such deformations. In this chapter we take up the study of rigid-body motion for the case in which the direction of the axis of rotation does not change. The general case, which involves more extensive calculation, will be treated in the next chapter.

8.1 Center of Mass of a Rigid Body

We have already defined the center of mass (Section 7.1) of a system of particles as the point (x_{cm}, y_{cm}, z_{cm}) where

$$x_{cm} = \frac{\sum_i x_i m_i}{\sum_i m_i} \qquad y_{cm} = \frac{\sum_i y_i m_i}{\sum_i m_i} \qquad z_{cm} = \frac{\sum_i z_i m_i}{\sum_i m_i}$$

For a rigid extended body, we can replace the summation by an integration over the volume of the body, namely,

$$x_{cm} = \frac{\int_v \rho x \, dv}{\int_v \rho \, dv} \qquad y_{cm} = \frac{\int_v \rho y \, dv}{\int_v \rho \, dv} \qquad z_{cm} = \frac{\int_v \rho z \, dv}{\int_v \rho \, dv} \qquad (8.1)$$

where ρ is the density, and dv is the element of volume.

If a rigid body is in the form of a thin shell, the equations for the center of mass become

$$x_{cm} = \frac{\int_s \rho x \, ds}{\int_s \rho \, ds} \qquad y_{cm} = \frac{\int_s \rho y \, ds}{\int_s \rho \, ds} \qquad z_{cm} = \frac{\int_s \rho z \, ds}{\int_s \rho \, ds} \qquad (8.2)$$

where ds is the element of area, and ρ is the mass per unit area, the integration extending over the area of the body.

Similarly, if the body is in the form of a thin wire, we have

$$x_{cm} = \frac{\int_l \rho x \, dl}{\int_l \rho \, dl} \qquad y_{cm} = \frac{\int_l \rho y \, dl}{\int_l \rho \, dl} \qquad z_{cm} = \frac{\int_l \rho z \, dl}{\int_l \rho \, dl} \qquad (8.3)$$

In this case ρ is the mass per unit length, and dl is the element of length.

For uniform homogeneous bodies, the density factors ρ are constant in each case and therefore may be canceled out in each equation above.

If a body is composite, that is, if it consists of two or more parts whose centers of mass are known, then it is clear, from the definition of the center of mass, that we can write

$$x_{cm} = \frac{x_1 m_1 + x_2 m_2 + \ \cdots}{m_1 + m_2 + \cdots} \qquad (8.4)$$

with similar equations for y_{cm} and z_{cm}. Here (x_1, y_1, z_1) is the center of mass of the part m_1, and so on.

Symmetry Considerations

If a body possesses symmetry, it is possible to take advantage of that symmetry in locating the center of mass. Thus, if the body has a plane of symmetry, that is, if each particle m_i has a mirror image of itself m_i' relative to some plane, then the center of mass lies in that plane. To prove this, let us suppose that the xy plane is a plane of symmetry. We have then

$$z_{cm} = \frac{\sum_i (z_i m_i + z_i' m_i')}{\sum_i (m_i + m_i')}$$

But $m_i = m_i'$ and $z_i = -z_i'$. Hence the terms in the numerator cancel in pairs, and so $z_{cm} = 0$; that is, the center of mass lies in the xy plane.

Similarly, if the body has a line of symmetry, it is easy to show that the center of mass lies on that line. The proof is left as an exercise.

Solid Hemisphere

To find the center of mass of a solid homogeneous hemisphere of radius a, we know from symmetry that the center of mass lies on the radius that is normal to the plane face. Choosing coordinate axes as shown in Figure 8.1, we have that the center of mass lies on the z axis. To calculate z_{cm} we use a circular element of volume of thickness dz and radius $(a^2 - z^2)^{1/2}$, as shown. Thus

$$dv = \pi(a^2 - z^2)\,dz$$

Therefore

$$z_{cm} = \frac{\displaystyle\int_0^a \rho\pi z(a^2 - z^2)\,dz}{\displaystyle\int_0^a \rho\pi(a^2 - z^2)\,dz} = \frac{3}{8}a \tag{8.5}$$

Hemispherical Shell

For a hemispherical shell of radius a we use the same axes as in the previous problem (Figure 8.1). Again, from symmetry, the center of mass is located on the z axis. For our element of surface we choose a circular strip of width $a\,d\theta$. Hence we can write

$$ds = 2\pi(a^2 - z^2)^{1/2}a\,d\theta$$

But $\theta = \sin^{-1}(z/a)$, so $d\theta = (a^2 - z^2)^{-1/2}\,dz$. Therefore

$$ds = 2\pi a\,dz$$

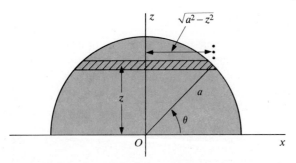

FIGURE 8.1 Coordinates for calculating the center of mass of a hemisphere.

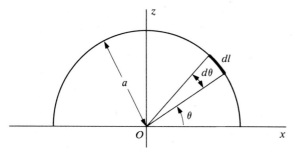

FIGURE 8.2   Coordinates for calculating the center of mass of a wire bent into the form of a semicircle.

The location of the center of mass is accordingly given by

$$z_{cm} = \frac{\int_0^a \rho 2\pi a z \, dz}{\int_0^a \rho 2\pi a \, dz} = \frac{1}{2} a \qquad (8.6)$$

Semicircle

To find the center of mass of a thin wire bent into the form of a semicircle of radius a, we use axes as shown in Figure 8.2. We have

$$dl = a \, d\theta$$

and

$$z = a \sin \theta$$

Hence

$$z_{cm} = \frac{\int_0^\pi \rho (a \sin \theta) a \, d\theta}{\int_0^\pi \rho a \, d\theta} = \frac{2}{\pi} a \qquad (8.7)$$

Semicircular Lamina

In the case of a uniform semicircular lamina, the center of mass is on the z axis (Figure 8.2). It is left for the student to verify that

$$z_{cm} = \frac{4}{3\pi} a \qquad (8.8)$$

8.2   Rotation of a Rigid Body About a Fixed Axis. Moment of Inertia

The simplest type of rigid-body motion, other than pure translation, is that in which the body is constrained to rotate about a fixed axis. Let us choose the z axis of an appropriate coordinate system as the axis of rotation. The path of a representative particle m_i located at the point (x_i, y_i, z_i) is then a circle of radius $(x_i^2 + y_i^2)^{1/2} = R_i$ centered on the z axis. A representative cross section parallel to the xy plane is shown in Figure 8.3.

The speed v_i of particle i is given by

$$v_i = R_i\omega = (x_i^2 + y_i^2)^{1/2}\omega$$

where ω is the angular speed of rotation. From a study of the figure, we see that the velocity has components as follows:

$$\begin{aligned}
\dot{x}_i &= -v_i \sin \phi_i = -\omega y_i \\
\dot{y}_i &= v_i \cos \phi_i = \omega x_i \\
\dot{z}_i &= 0
\end{aligned} \qquad (8.9)$$

where ϕ_i is defined as shown in the figure. The above equations can also be obtained by taking the components of

$$\mathbf{v}_i = \boldsymbol{\omega} \times \mathbf{r}_i \qquad (8.10)$$

where $\boldsymbol{\omega} = \mathbf{k}\omega$.

Let us calculate the kinetic energy of rotation of the body. We have

$$T_{rot} = \sum_i \tfrac{1}{2}m_i v_i^2 = \tfrac{1}{2}\left(\sum_i m_i R_i^2\right)\omega^2 = \tfrac{1}{2}I_z\omega^2 \qquad (8.11)$$

where

$$I_z = \sum_i m_i R_i^2 = \sum_i m_i(x_i^2 + y_i^2) \qquad (8.12)$$

The quantity I_z, defined by the above equation, is of particular importance in the study of the motion of rigid bodies. It is called the *moment of inertia* about the z axis.

To show how the moment of inertia further enters the picture, let us next calculate the angular momentum about the axis of rotation. Since the angular momentum of a single particle is, by definition, $\mathbf{r}_i \times m_i \mathbf{v}_i$, the z component is

$$m_i(x_i \dot{y}_i - y_i \dot{x}_i) = m_i(x_i^2 + y_i^2)\omega = m_i R_i^2 \omega \qquad (8.13)$$

where we have made use of Equations 8.9. The total z component of the angular momentum, which we shall call L_z, is then given by summing over all the particles, namely,

$$L_z = \sum_i m_i R_i^2 \omega = I_z\omega \qquad (8.14)$$

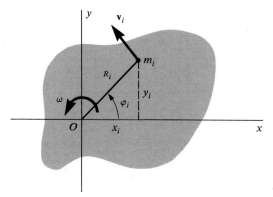

FIGURE 8.3   Cross section of a rigid body rotating about the z axis. (The z axis is out of the page.)

In Section 7.2 we found that the rate of change of angular momentum for any system is equal to the total moment of the external forces. For a body constrained to rotate about a fixed axis, taken here as the z axis, then

$$N_z = \frac{dL_z}{dt} = \frac{d(I_z\omega)}{dt} \tag{8.15}$$

where N_z is the total moment of all the applied forces about the axis of rotation (the component of $\mathbf{N}$ along the z axis). If the body is rigid, then I_z is constant, and we can write

$$N_z = I_z\frac{d\omega}{dt} \tag{8.16}$$

The analogy between the equations for translation and for rotation about a fixed axis is shown below:

Translation along x axis		*Rotation about z axis*	
Linear momentum	$p_x = mv_x$	Angular momentum	$L_z = I_z\omega$
Force	$F_x = m\dot{v}_x$	Torque	$N_z = I_z\dot{\omega}$
Kinetic energy	$T = \frac{1}{2}mv^2$	Kinetic energy	$T_{rot} = \frac{1}{2}I_z\omega^2$

Thus the moment of inertia is analogous to mass; it is a measure of the rotational inertia of a body relative to some fixed axis of rotation, just as mass is a measure of translational inertia of a body.

8.3   Calculation of the Moment of Inertia

In actual calculations of the moment of inertia $\Sigma m_i R_i^2$ for extended bodies, we can replace the summation by an integration over the body, just as we did in calculation of the center of mass. Thus we may write for *any* axis

$$I = \int R^2 \, dm \tag{8.17}$$

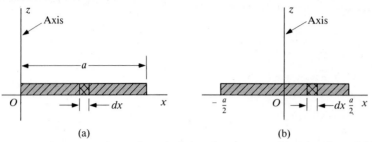

FIGURE 8.4   Coordinates for calculating the moment of inertia of a rod (a) about one end and (b) about the center of the rod.

where dm the element of mass, is given by a density factor multiplied by an appropriate differential (volume, area, or length). It is important to remember that R is the perpendicular distance from the element of mass to the axis of rotation.

In the case of a composite body, it is clear, from the definition of the moment of inertia that we may write

$$I = I_1 + I_2 + \ldots \tag{8.18}$$

where I_1, I_2, etc., are the moments of inertia of the various parts about the particular axis chosen.

Let us calculate the moments of inertia for some important special cases.

Thin Rod

For a thin uniform rod of length a and mass m, we have, for an axis perpendicular to the rod at one end [Figure 8.4(a)],

$$I_z = \int_0^a x^2 \rho \, dx = \tfrac{1}{3}\rho a^3 = \tfrac{1}{3}ma^2 \tag{8.19}$$

The last step follows from the fact that $m = \rho a$.

If the axis is taken at the center of the rod [Figure 8.4(b)], we have

$$I_z = \int_{-a/2}^{a/2} x^2 \rho \, dx = \tfrac{1}{12}\rho a^3 = \tfrac{1}{12}ma^2 \tag{8.20}$$

Hoop or Cylindrical Shell

In the case of a thin circular hoop or cylindrical shell, for the central or *symmetry* axis all particles lie at the same distance from the axis. Thus

$$I_{axis} = ma^2 \tag{8.21}$$

where a is the radius, and m is the mass.

Circular Disc or Cylinder

To calculate the moment of inertia of a uniform circular disc of radius a and mass m, we shall use polar coordinates. The element of mass, a thin ring of radius r and thickness dr, is given by

$$dm = \rho 2\pi r\, dr$$

where ρ is the mass per unit area. The moment of inertia about an axis through the center of the disc normal to the plane faces (Figure 8.5) is obtained as follows:

$$I_{axis} = \int_0^a \rho(r^2)(2\pi r\, dr) = 2\pi\rho\frac{a^4}{4} = \frac{1}{2}ma^2 \qquad (8.22)$$

The last step results from the relation $m = \rho\pi a^2$.

Clearly, the above formula also applies to a uniform right-circular cylinder of radius a and mass m, the axis being the central axis of the cylinder.

Sphere

Let us find the moment of inertia of a uniform solid sphere of radius a and mass m about an axis (the z axis) passing through the center. We shall divide the sphere into thin circular discs, as shown in Figure 8.6. The moment of inertia of a representative disc of radius y, from Equation 8.22, is $\frac{1}{2}y^2\, dm$. But $dm = \rho\pi y^2\, dz$, hence

$$I_z = \int_{-a}^a \tfrac{1}{2}\pi\rho y^4\, dz = \int_{-a}^a \tfrac{1}{2}\pi\rho(a^2 - z^2)^2\, dz = \tfrac{8}{15}\pi\rho a^5 \qquad (8.23)$$

The last step above should be filled in by the student. Since the mass m is given by

$$m = \tfrac{4}{3}\pi a^3\rho$$

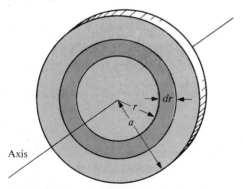

FIGURE 8.5   Coordinates for finding the moment of inertia of a disc.

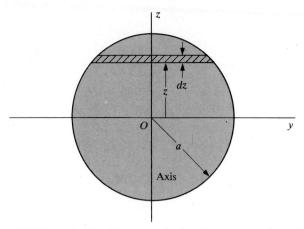

FIGURE 8.6   Coordinates for finding the moment of inertia of a sphere.

we have

$$I_z = \tfrac{2}{5}ma^2 \qquad (8.24)$$

for a solid uniform sphere. Clearly also, $I_x = I_y = I_z$.

Spherical Shell

The moment of inertia of a thin uniform spherical shell can be found very simply by application of Equation 8.23. If we differentiate with respect to a, namely,

$$dI_z = \tfrac{8}{3}\pi\rho a^4 \, da$$

the result is the moment of inertia of a shell of thickness da and radius a. The mass of the shell is $4\pi a^2 \rho \, da$. Hence we can write

$$I_z = \tfrac{2}{3}ma^2 \qquad (8.25)$$

for the moment of inertia of a thin shell of radius a and mass m. The student should verify the above result by direct integration.

Perpendicular-Axis Theorem for a Plane Lamina

Consider a rigid body which is in the form of a plane lamina of any shape. Let us place the lamina in the xy plane (Figure 8.7). The moment of inertia about the z axis is given by

$$I_z = \sum_i m_i(x_i^2 + y_i^2) = \sum_i m_i x_i^2 + \sum_i m_i y_i^2$$

But the sum $\sum m_i x_i^2$ is just the moment of inertia I_y about the y axis, because z_i is zero

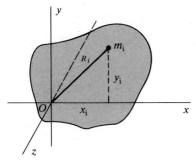

FIGURE 8.7 The perpendicular axis theorem for a lamina.

for all particles. Similarly, $\sum_i m_i y_i^2$ is the moment of inertia I_x about the x axis. The above equation can therefore be written

$$I_z = I_x + I_y \tag{8.26}$$

This is the perpendicular-axis theorem. In words: *The moment of inertia of any plane lamina about an axis normal to the plane of the lamina is equal to the sum of the moments of inertia about any two mutually perpendicular axes passing through the given axis and lying in the plane of the lamina.*

As an example of the use of this theorem, let us consider a thin circular disc in the xy plane (Figure 8.8). From Equation 8.22 we have

$$I_z = \tfrac{1}{2}ma^2 = I_x + I_y$$

In this case, however, we know from symmetry that $I_x = I_y$. Therefore we must have

$$I_x = I_y = \tfrac{1}{4}ma^2 \tag{8.27}$$

for the moment of inertia about any axis in the plane of the disc passing through the center. The above result can also be obtained by direct integration.

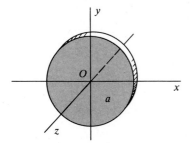

FIGURE 8.8 Circular disc.

Parallel-Axis Theorem for any Rigid Body

Consider the equation for the moment of inertia about some axis, say the z axis,

$$I_z = \sum_i m_i(x_i^2 + y_i^2)$$

Now we can express x_i and y_i in terms of the coordinates of the center of mass (x_{cm}, y_{cm}, z_{cm}) and the coordinates *relative* to the center of mass $(\bar{x}_i, \bar{y}_i, \bar{z}_i)$ (Figure 8.9) as follows:

$$x_i = x_{cm} + \bar{x}_i \qquad y_i = y_{cm} + \bar{y}_i \qquad (8.28)$$

We have, therefore, after substituting and collecting terms,

$$I_z = \sum_i m_i(\bar{x}_i^2 + \bar{y}_i^2) + \sum_i m_i(x_{cm}^2 + y_{cm}^2) + 2x_{cm}\sum_i m_i\bar{x}_i + 2y_{cm}\sum_i m_i\bar{y}_i \qquad (8.29)$$

The first sum on the right is just the moment of inertia about an axis parallel to the z axis and passing through the center of mass. We shall call it I_{cm}. The second sum is clearly equal to the mass of the body multiplied by the square of the distance between the center of mass and the z axis. Let us call this distance l. That is, $l^2 = x_{cm}^2 + y_{cm}^2$.

Now, from the definition of the center of mass,

$$\sum_i m_i\bar{x}_i = \sum_i m_i\bar{y}_i = 0$$

Hence, the last two sums on the right of Equation 8.29 vanish. The final result may be written in the general form for *any* axis

$$I = I_{cm} + ml^2 \qquad (8.30)$$

This is the *parallel-axis* theorem. It is applicable to any rigid body, solid as well as

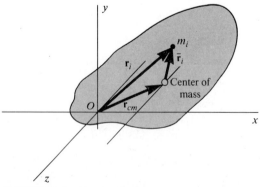

FIGURE 8.9   The parallel axis theorem for any rigid body.

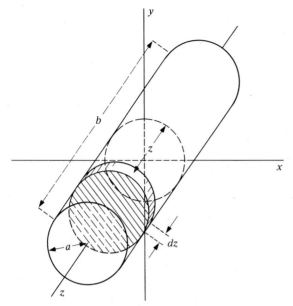

FIGURE 8.10 Coordinates for finding the moment of inertia of a circular cylinder.

laminar. The theorem states, in effect, that *the moment of inertia of a rigid body about any axis is equal to the moment of inertia about a parallel axis passing through the center of mass plus the product of the mass of the body and the square of the distance between the two axes.*

Applying the above theorem to a circular disc, we have, from Equations 8.22 and 8.30,

$$I = \tfrac{1}{2}ma^2 + ma^2 = \tfrac{3}{2}ma^2 \tag{8.31}$$

for the moment of inertia of a uniform circular disc about an axis *perpendicular* to the plane of the disc and passing through the edge. Furthermore, from Equations 8.27 and 8.30, we find

$$I = \tfrac{1}{4}ma^2 + ma^2 = \tfrac{5}{4}ma^2 \tag{8.32}$$

for the moment of inertia about an axis in the plane of the disc and *tangent* to the edge.

As a second example, let us find the moment of inertia of a uniform circular cylinder of length b and radius a about an axis through the center and *perpendicular* to the central axis, namely I_x or I_y in Figure 8.10. For our element of integration we choose a disc of thickness dz located a distance z from the xy plane. Then, from the previous result for a thin disc, Equation 8.27, together with the parallel-axis theorem, we have

$$dI_x = \frac{1}{4}a^2 \, dm + z^2 \, dm$$

in which $dm = \rho \pi a^2 \, dz$. Thus

$$I_x = \rho \pi a^2 \int_{-b/2}^{b/2} \left(\frac{1}{4}a^2 + z^2\right) dz = \rho \pi a^2 \left(\frac{1}{4}a^2 b + \frac{1}{12}b^3\right)$$

But the mass of the cylinder is $m = \rho \pi a^2 b$, therefore

$$I_x = I_y = m\left(\frac{1}{4}a^2 + \frac{1}{12}b^2\right) \tag{8.33}$$

Radius of Gyration

For some purposes it is convenient to express the moment of inertia of a rigid body in terms of a distance k called the *radius of gyration*, where k is defined by the equation

$$I = mk^2 \quad \text{or} \quad k = \sqrt{\frac{I}{m}} \tag{8.34}$$

For example, we find for the radius of gyration of a thin rod about an axis passing through one end (refer to Equation 8.19)

$$k = \sqrt{\frac{\frac{1}{3}ma^2}{m}} = \frac{a}{\sqrt{3}}$$

Moments of inertia for various objects can be tabulated simply by listing the squares of their radii of gyration, Table 8.1.

8.4   The Physical Pendulum

A rigid body which is free to swing under its own weight about a fixed horizontal axis of rotation is known as a *physical pendulum* or *compound pendulum*. A physical pendulum is shown in Figure 8.11. Here *CM* is the center of mass, and *O* is the point on the axis of rotation that is in the vertical plane of the circular path of the center of mass.

Denoting the angle between the line *OCM* and the vertical line *OA* by θ, the moment of the gravitational force (acting at *CM*) about the axis of rotation is of magnitude

$$mgl \sin \theta$$

The fundamental equation of motion $N = I\dot{\omega}$ then takes the form $- mgl \sin \theta = I\ddot{\theta}$ or

$$\ddot{\theta} + \frac{mgl}{I} \sin \theta = 0 \tag{8.35}$$

The above equation is identical in form to the equation of motion of a simple pendu-

Table 8.1   Values of k^2 of Various Bodies (Moment of Inertia = Mass $\times$ k^2)

Body	Axis	k^2
Thin rod, length a	Normal to rod at its center	$\dfrac{a^2}{12}$
	Normal to rod at one end	$\dfrac{a^2}{3}$
Thin rectangular lamina, sides a and b	Through the center, parallel to side b	$\dfrac{a^2}{12}$
	Through the center, normal to the lamina	$\dfrac{a^2 + b^2}{12}$
Thin circular disc, radius a	Through the center, in the plane of the disc	$\dfrac{a^2}{4}$
	Through the center, normal to the disc	$\dfrac{a^2}{2}$
Thin hoop (or ring) radius a	Through the center, in the plane of the hoop	$\dfrac{a^2}{2}$
	Through the center, normal to the plane of the hoop	a^2
Thin cylindrical shell, radius a, length b	Central longitudinal axis	a^2
Uniform solid right circular cylinder radius a, length b	Central longitudinal axis	$\dfrac{a^2}{2}$
	Through center, perpendicular to longitudinal axis	$\dfrac{a^2}{4} + \dfrac{b^2}{12}$
Thin spherical shell, radius a	Any diameter	$\dfrac{2}{3}a^2$
Uniform solid sphere, radius a	Any diameter	$\dfrac{2}{5}a^2$
Uniform solid rectangular parallelepiped, sides a, b, and c	Through center, normal to face ab, parallel to edge c	$\dfrac{a^2 + b^2}{12}$

lum. For small oscillations, as in the case of the simple pendulum, we can replace $\sin\theta$ by θ:

$$\ddot{\theta} + \frac{mgl}{I}\theta = 0 \tag{8.36}$$

The solution, as we know from Chapter 3, can be written

$$\theta = \theta_0 \cos(2\pi f_0 t - \epsilon) \tag{8.37}$$

where θ_0 is the amplitude and ϵ is a phase angle. The frequency of oscillation is given by

$$f_0 = \frac{1}{2\pi}\sqrt{\frac{mgl}{I}} \tag{8.38}$$

The period is therefore given by

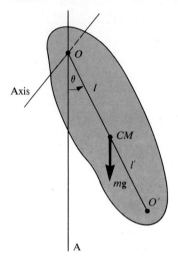

FIGURE 8.11   The physical pendulum.

$$T_0 = \frac{1}{f_0} = 2\pi \sqrt{\frac{I}{mgl}} \tag{8.39}$$

(To avoid confusion, we shall not use a specific symbol to designate the angular frequency $2\pi f_0$.) We can also express the period in terms of the radius of gyration k, namely,

$$T_0 = 2\pi \sqrt{\frac{k^2}{gl}} \tag{8.40}$$

Thus the period is the same as that of a simple pendulum of length k^2/l.

Consider as an example a thin uniform rod of length a swinging as a physical pendulum about one end: $k^2 = a^2/3$, $l = a/2$. The period is then

$$T_0 = 2\pi \sqrt{\frac{a^2/3}{ga/2}} = 2\pi \sqrt{\frac{2a}{3g}}$$

which is the same as that of a simple pendulum of length $\frac{2}{3}a$.

Center of Oscillation

By use of the parallel-axis theorem, we can express the radius of gyration k in terms of the radius of gyration about the center of mass k_{cm}, as follows:

$$I = I_{cm} + ml^2$$

or

$$mk^2 = mk_{cm}^2 + ml^2$$

Canceling the m's, we get

$$k^2 = k_{cm}^2 + l^2 \tag{8.41}$$

Equation 8.40 can therefore be written as

$$T_0 = 2\pi \sqrt{\frac{k_{cm}^2 + l^2}{gl}} \tag{8.42}$$

Suppose that the axis of rotation of a physical pendulum is shifted to a different position O' at a distance l' from the center of mass, as shown in Figure 8.11. The period of oscillation T_0' about this new axis is given by

$$T_0' = 2\pi \sqrt{\frac{k_{cm}^2 + l'^2}{gl'}}$$

It follows that the periods of oscillation about O and about O' will be equal, provided

$$\frac{k_{cm}^2 + l^2}{l} = \frac{k_{cm}^2 + l'^2}{l'}$$

The above equation readily reduces to

$$ll' = k_{cm}^2 \tag{8.43}$$

The point O', related to O by the above equation, is called the *center of oscillation* for the point O. It is clear that O is also the center of oscillation for O'. Thus, for a rod of length a swinging about one end, we have $k_{cm}^2 = a^2/12$ and $l = a/2$. Hence, from Equation 8.43, $l' = a/6$, and so the rod will have the same period when swinging about an axis located a distance $a/6$ from the center as it does for an axis passing through one end.

The "Upside-down Pendulum". Elliptic Integrals

When the amplitude of oscillation of a pendulum is so large that the approximation $\sin \theta = \theta$ is not valid, the formula for the period, Equation 8.39, is not accurate. Earlier, in Chapter 3, Example 3.9, we obtained an improved formula for the period of a simple pendulum by using a method of successive approximations. That result also applies to the physical pendulum with l replaced by I/ml, but it is still an approximation and is completely erroneous when the amplitude approaches $180°$ (vertical position), Figure 8.12.

To find the period for large amplitude we start with the energy equation for the physical pendulum

$$\frac{1}{2}I\dot{\theta}^2 + mgh = E \tag{8.44}$$

where h is the vertical distance of the center of mass from the equilibrium position, that is $h = l(1 - \cos \theta)$. Let θ_0 denote the amplitude of the pendulum's oscillation. Then $\theta = 0$ when $\theta = \theta_0$, so that $E = mgl(1 - \cos \theta_0)$. The energy equation can then be written

$$\frac{1}{2}I\dot{\theta}^2 + mgl(1 - \cos \theta) = mgl(1 - \cos \theta_0) \tag{8.44a}$$

Solving for $\dot{\theta}$ gives

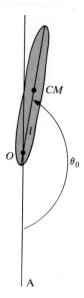

FIGURE 8.12   The "upside down" pendulum.

$$\frac{d\theta}{dt} = \pm\left[\frac{2mgl}{I}(\cos\theta - \cos\theta_0)\right]^{1/2} \qquad (8.44b)$$

Thus, by taking the positive root, we can write

$$t = \sqrt{\frac{I}{2mgl}}\int_0^\theta \frac{d\theta}{(\cos\theta - \cos\theta_0)^{1/2}} \qquad (8.45)$$

from which we can, in principle, find t as a function of θ. Also, we note that θ increases from 0 to θ_0 in just one quarter of a complete cycle. The period T can therefore be expressed as

$$T = 4\sqrt{\frac{I}{2mgl}}\int_0^{\theta_0} \frac{d\theta}{(\cos\theta - \cos\theta_0)^{1/2}} \qquad (8.46)$$

Unfortunately, the integrals in the above expressions cannot be evaluated in terms of elementary functions. However, they can be expressed in terms of special functions known as *elliptic integrals*. For this purpose it is convenient to introduce a new variable of integration φ which is defined as follows:

$$\sin\varphi = \frac{\sin(\theta/2)}{\sin(\theta_0/2)} = \frac{1}{k}\sin(\theta/2)$$

where

$$k = \sin(\theta_0/2)$$

Thus, when $\theta = \theta_0$ we have $\sin\varphi = 1$ and so $\varphi = \pi/2$. The result of making the above substitutions in Equations 8.45 and 8.46 yields

$$t = \sqrt{\frac{I}{mgl}} \int_0^{\varphi} \frac{d\varphi}{(1 - k^2 \sin^2 \varphi)^{1/2}} \tag{8.47}$$

$$T = 4\sqrt{\frac{I}{mgl}} \int_0^{\pi/2} \frac{d\varphi}{(1 - k^2 \sin^2 \varphi)^{1/2}} \tag{8.48}$$

The steps are left as an exercise and involve use of the identity $\cos \theta = 1 - 2 \sin^2 (\theta/2)$.

Tabulated values of the integrals in the above expressions can be found in various handbooks and mathematical tables. The first integral

$$\int_0^{\varphi} \frac{d\varphi}{(1 - k^2 \sin^2 \varphi)^{1/2}} = F(k,\varphi) \tag{8.49}$$

is called the *incomplete elliptic integral of the first kind*. In our problem, given a value of the amplitude θ_0, we can find the relationship between θ and t through a series of steps involving the definitions of k *and* φ. We are more interested in finding the period of the pendulum, which involves the second integral

$$\int_0^{\pi/2} \frac{d\varphi}{(1 - k^2 \sin^2 \varphi)^{1/2}} = F(k,\pi/2) \tag{8.50}$$

known as the *complete elliptic integral of the first kind*. [It is also variously listed as $K(k)$ or $F(k)$ in many tables.] In terms of it, the period is

$$T = 4\sqrt{\frac{I}{mgl}} F(k,\pi/2) \tag{8.51}$$

A short table of selected values of $F(k,\pi/2)$ is given below. Also listed is the period T as a factor multiplied by the period for zero amplitude: $T_0 = 2\pi(I/mgl)^{1/2}$.

A glance at the table shows the trend as the amplitude approaches $180°$ at which value the elliptic integral diverges and the period becomes infinitely large. This means that, *theoretically,* a physical pendulum, such as a rigid rod, if placed exactly in the vertical position with absolutely zero initial angular velocity, would remain in that same unstable position indefinitely.

TABLE 8.2 Selected Values of the Complete Elliptic Integral and Corresponding Period of Oscillation of a Physical Pendulum.[1]

Amplitude θ_0	$k = \sin(\theta_0/2)$	$F(k,\pi/2)$	Period T
0°	0	$1.5708 = \pi/2$	T_0
10°	0.0872	1.5738	$1.0019\ T_0$
45°	0.3827	1.6336	$1.0400\ T_0$
90°	0.7071	1.8541	$1.1804\ T_0$
135°	0.9234	2.4003	$1.5281\ T_0$
178°	0.99985	5.4349	$3.5236\ T_0$
179°	0.99996	7.2660	$4.6002\ T_0$
180°	1	∞	∞

[1]For more extensive tables and other information on elliptic integrals, consult any treatise on elliptic functions, such as L. M. Milne-Thomson, *Jacobian Elliptic Function Tables*, Dover, New York, 1950. See also Appendix E.

8.5   A General Theorem Concerning Angular Momentum

In order to study the more general case of rigid-body motion, that in which the axis of rotation is *not* fixed, we need to develop a fundamental theorem about angular momentum. In Section 7.2 we showed that the time rate of change of angular momentum of any system is equal to the applied torque:

$$\frac{d\mathbf{L}}{dt} = \mathbf{N}$$

or, explicitly

$$\frac{d}{dt}\sum_i (\mathbf{r}_i \times m_i\mathbf{v}_i) = \sum_i (\mathbf{r}_i \times \mathbf{F}_i) \tag{8.52}$$

In the above equation all quantities are referred to some inertial coordinate system.

Let us now introduce the center of mass by expressing the position vector of each particle $\mathbf{r}_i$ in terms of the position of the center of mass $\mathbf{r}_{cm}$ and the position vector of particle i relative to the center of mass $\bar{\mathbf{r}}_i$ (as in Section 7.2), namely,

$$\mathbf{r}_i = \mathbf{r}_{cm} + \bar{\mathbf{r}}_i$$

and

$$\mathbf{v}_i = \mathbf{v}_{cm} + \bar{\mathbf{v}}_i$$

Equation 8.52 then becomes

$$\frac{d}{dt}\sum_i [(\mathbf{r}_{cm} + \bar{\mathbf{r}}_i) \times m_i(\mathbf{v}_{cm} + \bar{\mathbf{v}}_i)] = \sum_i (\mathbf{r}_{cm} + \bar{\mathbf{r}}_i) \times \mathbf{F}_i \tag{8.53}$$

Upon expanding and using the fact that $\Sigma m_i\bar{\mathbf{r}}_i$ and $\Sigma m_i\bar{\mathbf{v}}_i$ both vanish, we find that the above equation reduces to

$$\mathbf{r}_{cm} \times \sum_i m_i\mathbf{a}_{cm} + \frac{d}{dt}\sum_i \bar{\mathbf{r}}_i \times m_i\bar{\mathbf{v}}_i = \mathbf{r}_{cm} \times \sum_i \mathbf{F}_i + \sum_i \bar{\mathbf{r}}_i \times \mathbf{F}_i \tag{8.54}$$

where $\mathbf{a}_{cm} = \dot{\mathbf{v}}_{cm}$.

In Section 7.1 we showed that the translation of the center of mass of any system of particles obeys the equation

$$\sum_i \mathbf{F}_i = \sum_i m_i\mathbf{a}_i = m\mathbf{a}_{cm}$$

Consequently, the first term on the left of Equation 8.54 cancels the first term on the right. The final result is

$$\frac{d}{dt}\sum_i \bar{\mathbf{r}}_i \times m_i\bar{\mathbf{v}}_i = \sum_i \bar{\mathbf{r}}_i \times \mathbf{F}_i \tag{8.55}$$

The sum on the left in the above equation is just the angular momentum of the system about the center of mass, and the sum on the right is the total moment of the external forces about the center of mass. Calling these quantities $\bar{\mathbf{L}}$ and $\bar{\mathbf{N}}$, respectively, we have

$$\frac{d\bar{\mathbf{L}}}{dt} = \bar{\mathbf{N}} \tag{8.56}$$

This important result states that the time rate of change of angular momentum about the center of mass of any system is equal to the total moment of the external forces about the center of mass. This is true even if the center of mass is accelerating. If we choose any point *other* than the center of mass as a reference point, then that point must be at rest in an inertial coordinate system (except for certain special cases which we shall not attempt to discuss). An example of the use of the above theorem is given in the next section.

8.6 Laminar Motion of a Rigid Body

If the motion of a body is such that all particles move parallel to some fixed plane, then that motion is called *laminar*. In laminar motion the axis of rotation may change position, but it does not change in direction. Rotation about a fixed axis is a special case of laminar motion. The rolling of a cylinder on a plane surface is another example of laminar motion.

If a body undergoes a laminar displacement, that displacement can be specified as follows: Choose some reference point of the body, for example, the center of mass. The reference point undergoes some displacement $\Delta\mathbf{r}$. In addition, the body rotates about the reference point through some angle $\Delta\phi$. Clearly, any laminar displacement can be so specified. Consequently, laminar motion can be specified by giving the translational velocity of a convenient reference reference point together with the angular velocity.

The fundamental equation governing translation of a rigid body is

$$\mathbf{F} = m\ddot{\mathbf{r}}_{cm} = m\dot{\mathbf{v}}_{cm} = m\mathbf{a}_{cm} \tag{8.57}$$

where $\mathbf{F}$ represents the sum of all the external forces acting on the body, m is the mass, and $\mathbf{a}_{cm}$ is the acceleration of the center of mass.

Application of Equation 8.14 to the case of laminar motion of a rigid body yields

$$\bar{L}_C = I_{cm}\omega \tag{8.58}$$

for the component of the angular momentum about an axis C passing through the center of mass where ω is the angular speed of rotation about that axis. The fundamental equation governing the rotation of the body, Equation 8.56, then becomes

$$\frac{d\bar{L}_C}{dt} = I_{cm}\dot{\omega} = \bar{N}_C \tag{8.59}$$

where $\bar{N}_C$ is the total moment of the applied forces about the axis C.

Body Rolling Down an Inclined Plane

As an illustration of laminar motion, we shall study the motion of a round object (cylinder, ball, and so on) rolling down an inclined plane. As shown in Figure 8.13, there are three forces acting on the body. These are (1) the downward force of gravity, (2) the normal reaction of the plane: $\mathbf{F}_N$, and (3) the frictional force parallel to the plane: $\mathbf{F}_P$. Choosing axes as shown, the component equations of the translation of the center of mass are

$$m\ddot{x}_{cm} = mg \sin \theta - F_P \tag{8.60}$$
$$m\ddot{y}_{cm} = -mg \cos \theta + F_N \tag{8.61}$$

where θ is the inclination of the plane to the horizontal. Since the body remains in contact with the plane, we have

$$y_{cm} = \text{constant}$$

Hence

$$\ddot{y}_{cm} = 0$$

Therefore, from Equation 8.61,

$$F_N = mg \cos \theta \tag{8.62}$$

The only force which exerts a moment about the center of mass is the frictional force $\mathbf{F}_P$. The magnitude of this moment is $F_P a$ where a is the radius of the body. Hence the rotational equation, Equation 8.59, becomes

$$I_{cm}\dot{\omega} = F_P a \tag{8.63}$$

To discuss the problem further, we need to make some assumptions regarding the contact between the plane and the body. We shall solve the equations of motion for two cases.

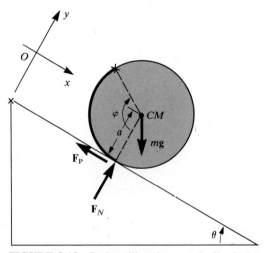

FIGURE 8.13   Body rolling down an inclined plane.

Motion with No Slipping

If the contact is very rough so that no slipping can occur, that is, if $F_P \leq \mu_s F_N$ where μ_s is the coefficient of *static* friction we have the following relations:

$$\dot{x}_{cm} = a\dot{\phi} = a\omega$$
$$\ddot{x}_{cm} = a\ddot{\phi} = a\dot{\omega}$$

(8.64)

where ϕ is the angle of rotation. Equation 8.63 can then be written

$$\frac{I_{cm}}{a^2}\ddot{x}_{cm} = F_P$$

(8.65)

Substituting the above value for F_P into Equation 8.60 yields

$$m\ddot{x}_{cm} = mg \sin\theta - \frac{I_{cm}}{a^2}\ddot{x}_{cm}$$

Solving for $\ddot{x}_{cm}$, we find

$$\ddot{x}_{cm} = \frac{mg \sin\theta}{m + (I_{cm}/a^2)} = \frac{g \sin\theta}{1 + (k_{cm}^2/a^2)}$$

(8.66)

where k_{cm} is the radius of gyration about the center of mass. The body therefore rolls down the plane with constant linear acceleration and also with constant angular acceleration by virtue of Equations 8.64.

For example, the acceleration of a uniform cylinder ($k_{cm}^2 = a^2/2$) is

$$\frac{g \sin\theta}{1 + \frac{1}{2}} = \frac{2}{3}g \sin\theta$$

whereas that of a uniform sphere ($k_{cm}^2 = 2a^2/5$) is

$$\frac{g \sin\theta}{1 + \frac{2}{5}} = \frac{5}{7}g \sin\theta$$

Energy Considerations

The above results can also be obtained from energy considerations. In a uniform gravitational field the potential energy V of a rigid body is given by the sum of the potential energies of the individual particles, namely,

$$V = \sum_i (m_i g z_i) = mg z_{cm}$$

where z_{cm} is the vertical distance of the center of mass from some (arbitrary) reference plane. Now if the forces, other than gravity, acting on the body do no work, then the motion is conservative, and we can write

$$T + V = T + mg z_{cm} = E = \text{constant}$$

where T is the kinetic energy.

In the case of the body rolling down the inclined plane, Figure 8.13, the kinetic energy of translation is $\frac{1}{2}m\dot{x}_{cm}^2$ and that of rotation is $\frac{1}{2}I_{cm}\omega^2$, so the energy equation reads

$$\tfrac{1}{2}m\dot{x}_{cm}^2 + \tfrac{1}{2}I_{cm}\omega^2 + mgz_{cm} = E$$

But $\omega = \dot{x}_{cm}/a$ and $z_{cm} = -x_{cm}\sin\theta$. Hence

$$\frac{1}{2}m\dot{x}_{cm}^2 + \frac{1}{2}mk_{cm}^2\frac{\dot{x}_{cm}^2}{a^2} - mgx_{cm}\sin\theta = E$$

In the case of pure rolling motion the frictional force does not appear in the energy equation since no mechanical energy is converted into heat unless slipping occurs. Thus the total energy E is constant. Differentiating with respect to t and collecting terms yields

$$m\dot{x}_{cm}\ddot{x}_{cm}\left(1 + \frac{k_{cm}^2}{a^2}\right) - mg\dot{x}_{cm}\sin\theta = 0$$

Canceling the common factor $\dot{x}_{cm}$ (assuming, of course, that $\dot{x}_{cm} \neq 0$) and solving for $\ddot{x}_{cm}$, we find the same result as that obtained previously using forces and moments, Equation 8.66.

Occurrence of Slipping

Let us now consider the case in which the contact with the plane is not perfectly rough but has a certain coefficient of *sliding* friction μ. If slipping occurs, then the magnitude of the frictional force $\mathbf{F}_P$ is given by

$$F_P = \mu F_N = \mu mg\cos\theta \tag{8.67}$$

The equation of translation, Equation 8.60, then becomes

$$m\ddot{x}_{cm} = mg\sin\theta - \mu mg\cos\theta \tag{8.68}$$

and the rotational equation, Equation 8.63, is

$$I_{cm}\dot{\omega} = \mu mga\cos\theta \tag{8.69}$$

From Equation 8.68 we see that again the center of mass undergoes constant acceleration:

$$\ddot{x}_{cm} = g(\sin\theta - \mu\cos\theta) \tag{8.70}$$

and, at the same time, the angular acceleration is constant:

$$\dot{\omega} = \frac{\mu mga\cos\theta}{I_{cm}} = \frac{\mu ga\cos\theta}{k_{cm}^2} \tag{8.71}$$

Let us integrate these two equations with respect to t, assuming that the body starts from rest, that is, at $t = 0$, $\dot{x}_{cm} = 0$, $\dot{\phi} = 0$. We obtain

$$\dot{x}_{cm} = g(\sin\theta - \mu\cos\theta)t$$
$$\omega = \dot{\phi} = g(\mu a\cos\theta/k_{cm}^2)t \tag{8.72}$$

Consequently, the linear speed and the angular speed have a constant ratio, and we can write

$$\dot{x}_{cm} = \gamma a \omega$$

where

$$\gamma = \frac{\sin \theta - \mu \cos \theta}{\mu a^2 \cos \theta / k_{cm}^2} = \frac{k_{cm}^2}{a^2} \left(\frac{\tan \theta}{\mu} - 1 \right) \tag{8.73}$$

Now $a\omega$ cannot be greater than $\dot{x}_{cm}$, so γ cannot be less than unity. The limiting case, that for which we have pure rolling, is given by $\dot{x}_{cm} = a\omega$, that is,

$$\gamma = 1$$

Solving for μ in Equation 8.73 with $\gamma = 1$, we find that the critical value of the coefficient of friction is given by

$$\mu_{crit} = \frac{\tan \theta}{1 + (a/k_{cm})^2} \tag{8.74}$$

(Actually this is the critical value for the coefficient of *static* friction μ_s.) If μ_s is greater than that given above, then the body rolls without slipping.

For example, if a ball is placed on a 45° plane, it will roll without slipping provided μ_s is greater than tan 45°/(1 + $\frac{5}{2}$) or $\frac{2}{7}$.

8.7 Impulse and Collisions Involving Rigid Bodies

In the previous chapter we considered the case of an impulsive force acting on a particle. In this section we shall extend the notion of impulsive force to the case of laminar motion of a rigid body. First, we know that the translation of the body, assuming constant mass, is governed by the general equation $\mathbf{F} = m d\mathbf{v}_{cm}/dt$, so that if $\mathbf{F}$ is an impulsive type of force the change of linear momentum of the body is given by

$$\int \mathbf{F} \, dt = \hat{\mathbf{P}} = m \Delta \mathbf{v}_{cm} \tag{8.75}$$

Thus, the result of an impulse $\hat{\mathbf{P}}$ is to produce a sudden change in the velocity of the center of mass by an amount

$$\Delta \mathbf{v}_{cm} = \frac{\hat{\mathbf{P}}}{m} \tag{8.76}$$

Secondly, the rotational part of the motion of the body obeys the equation $N = \dot{L} = I d\omega/dt$, so the change in angular momentum is

$$\int N dt = I \Delta \omega \tag{8.77}$$

The integral $\int N dt$ is called the *rotational impulse*. Let us use the symbol $\hat{L}$ to designate it. Now if the primary impulse $\hat{\mathbf{P}}$ is applied to the body in such a way that its line of action is a distance l from the reference axis about which the angular momentum is calculated, then $N = Fl$ and we have

$$\hat{L} = \hat{P}l \tag{8.78}$$

Consequently, the change in angular velocity produced by an impulse $\hat{\mathbf{P}}$ acting on a rigid body in laminar motion is given by

$$\Delta\omega = \frac{\hat{P}l}{I} \tag{8.79}$$

For the general case of free laminar motion the reference axis must be taken through the center of mass, and the moment of inertia $I = I_{cm}$. On the other hand, if the body is constrained to rotate about a fixed axis, then the rotational equation alone suffices to determine the motion, and I is the moment of inertia about the fixed axis.

In collisions involving rigid bodies, the forces, and therefore the impulses, that the bodies exert on one another during the collision are always equal and opposite. Thus the principles of conservation of linear and angular momentum apply.

Center of Percussion: The "Baseball Bat Theorem"

As an example of the above theory, let us discuss the collision of a ball of mass m, treated as a particle, with a rigid body (bat) of mass M. For simplicity we shall assume that the body is initially at rest on a smooth horizontal surface and is free to move in laminar-type motion. Let $\hat{\mathbf{P}}$ denote the impulse delivered to the body by the ball. Then the equations for translation are

$$\hat{\mathbf{P}} = M\mathbf{v}_{cm} \tag{8.80}$$

$$-\hat{\mathbf{P}} = m\mathbf{v}_1 - m\mathbf{v}_0 \tag{8.81}$$

where $\mathbf{v}_0$ and $\mathbf{v}_1$ are, respectively, the initial and final velocities of the ball, and $\mathbf{v}_{cm}$ is the velocity of the mass center of the body after the impact. Clearly, the above two equations imply conservation of linear momentum.

Since the body is initially at rest, the rotation about the center of mass, as a result of the impact, is given by

$$\omega = \frac{\hat{P}l}{I_{cm}} \tag{8.82}$$

in which l is the distance OC from the center of mass C to the line of action of $\hat{\mathbf{P}}$, as shown in Figure 8.14. Let us now consider a point O' located a distance l' from the center of mass such that the line CO' is the extension of OC, as shown. The (scalar) velocity of O' is obtained by combining the translational and rotational parts, namely

$$v_{O'} = v_{cm} - \omega l' = \frac{\hat{P}}{M} - \frac{\hat{P}l}{I_{cm}}l' = \hat{P}\left(\frac{1}{M} - \frac{ll'}{I_{cm}}\right) \tag{8.83}$$

In particular, the velocity of O' will be zero if the quantity in parentheses vanishes, that is, if

$$ll' = \frac{I_{cm}}{M} = k_{cm}^2 \tag{8.84}$$

where k_{cm} is the radius of gyration of the body about its center of mass. In this case the

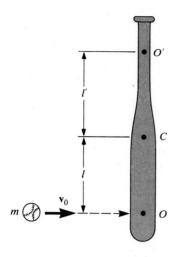

FIGURE 8.14   Baseball colliding with a bat.

point O' is the instantaneous center of rotation of the body just after impact. O is called the *center of percussion* about O'. The two points are related in the same way as the centers of oscillation, defined previously in our analysis of the physical pendulum, Equation 8.43.

Anyone who has played baseball knows that if the ball hits the bat in just the right spot there will be no "sting" upon impact. This "right spot" is just the center of percussion about the point at which the bat is held.

PROBLEMS

8.1   Find the center of mass of each of the following:
   (a) A thin wire bent into the form of a block "⊔" with each segment of equal length b.
   (b) A quadrant of a uniform circular lamina of radius b.
   (c) The area bounded by parabola $y = x^2/b$ and the line $y = b$.
   (d) The volume bounded by paraboloid of revolution $z = (x^2 + y^2)/b$ and the plane $z = b$.
   (e) A solid uniform right circular cone of height b.

8.2   The linear density of a thin rod is given by $\rho = cx$ where c is a constant and x is the distance measured from one end. If the rod is of length b, find the center of mass.

8.3   A solid uniform sphere of radius a has a spherical cavity of radius $a/2$ centered at a point $a/2$ from the center of the sphere. Find the center of mass.

8.4   Find the moments of inertia of each of the objects in Problem 8.1 about their symmetry axes.

8.5   Find the moment of inertia of the sphere in Problem 8.3 about an axis passing through the center of the sphere and the center of the cavity.

8.6   Show that the moment of inertia of a solid uniform octant of a sphere of radius a is $(2/5)ma^2$ about an axis along one of the straight edges. [*Note:* This is the same formula as that for a solid sphere of the same radius.]

8.7   Show that the moments of inertia of a solid uniform rectangular parallelepiped, elliptic cylinder, and ellipsoid are, respectively, $(m/3)(a^2 + b^2)$, $(m/4)(a^2 + b^2)$, and $(m/5)(a^2 + b^2)$, where m is the mass, and $2a$ and $2b$ are the principal diameters of the solid at right angles to the axis of rotation, the axis being through the center in each case.

8.8   Show that the period of a physical pendulum is equal to $2\pi(d/g)^{1/2}$, where d is the distance between the point of suspension O and the center of oscillation O'.

8.9   A circular hoop of radius a swings as a physical pendulum about a point on the circumference. Find the period of oscillation for small amplitude if the axis of rotation is (a) normal to the plane of the hoop, and (b) in the plane of the hoop.

8.10   A uniform solid ball has a few turns of light string wound around it. If the end of the string is held steady, and the ball is allowed to fall under gravity, what is the acceleration of the center of the ball? (Assume the string remains vertical.)

8.11   Two men are holding the ends of a uniform plank of length l and mass m. Show that if one man suddenly lets go, the load supported by the other man suddenly drops from $mg/2$ to $mg/4$. Show also that the initial downward acceleration of the free end is $\frac{3}{2}g$.

8.12   A uniform solid ball contains a hollow spherical cavity at its center, the radius of the cavity being $\frac{1}{2}$ the radius of the ball. Show that the acceleration of the ball rolling down a rough inclined plane is just $\frac{98}{101}$ of that of a uniform solid ball with no cavity. [*Note:* This suggests a method for nondestructive testing.]

8.13   Two weights of mass m_1 and m_2 are tied to the ends of a light inextensible cord. The cord passes over a rough pulley of radius a and moment of inertia I. Find the accelerations of the weights, assuming $m_1 > m_2$ and neglecting friction in the axle of the pulley.

8.14   A uniform right-circular cylinder of radius a is balanced on the top of a perfectly rough fixed cylinder of radius $b(b > a)$, the axes of the two cylinders being parallel. If the balance is slightly disturbed, show that the rolling cylinder leaves the fixed one when the line of centers makes an angle with the vertical of $\cos^{-1}(4/7)$.

8.15   A uniform ladder leans against a smooth vertical wall. If the floor is also smooth, and the initial angle between the floor and the ladder is θ_0, show that the ladder, in sliding down, will lose contact with the wall when the angle between the floor and the ladder is $\sin^{-1}(\frac{2}{3}\sin\theta_0)$.

8.16   At Cape Canaveral a Saturn V rocket stands in a vertical position ready for launch. Unfortunately, before firing, a slight disturbance causes the rocket to fall over. Find the horizontal and vertical components of the reaction on the launch pad as functions of the angle θ between the rocket and the vertical at any instant. Show from this that the rocket will tend to slide backward for $\theta < \cos^{-1}(2/3)$ and forward for $\theta > \cos^{-1}(2/3)$. (Assume the rocket to be a thin uniform rod.)

8.17   A ball is initially projected, without rotation, at a speed v_0 up a rough inclined plane of inclination θ and coefficient of sliding friction μ. Find the position of the ball as a function of time, and determine the position of the ball when pure rolling begins. Assume that μ is greater than $\frac{2}{7}\tan\theta$.

8.18   A billiard ball of radius a is initially spinning about a horizontal axis with angular speed ω_0, and with zero forward speed. If the coefficient of sliding friction between the ball and the billiard table is μ, find the distance the ball travels before slipping ceases to occur.

8.19   A thin uniform plank of length l lies at rest on a horizontal sheet of ice. If the plank is given a kick at one end in a direction normal to the plank, show that the plank will begin to rotate about a point located a distance $l/6$ from the center.

8.20   Show that the edge (cushion) of a billiard table should be at a height of 7/10 of the diameter of the billiard ball in order that no reaction occurs between the table surface and the ball when the ball strikes the cushion.

8.21   A ballistic pendulum is made of a long plank of length l and mass m. It is free to swing about one end O, and is initially at rest in a vertical position. A bullet of mass m' is fired horizontally into the pendulum at a distance l' below O, the bullet coming to rest in the plank. If the resulting amplitude of oscillation of the pendulum is θ_0, find the speed of the bullet.

8.22   Two uniform rods AB and BC of equal mass m and equal length l are smoothly joined at B. The system is initially at rest on a smooth horizontal surface, the points A, B, and C lying in a straight line. If an impulse $\hat{\mathbf{P}}$ is applied at A at right angles to the rod, find the initial motion of the system. [*Hint:* Isolate the rods.]

9

Motion of Rigid Bodies in Three Dimensions

In the motion of a rigid body constrained either to rotate about a fixed axis or to move parallel to a fixed plane, the direction of the axis does not change. In the more general cases of rigid body motion, which we take up in this chapter, the direction of the axis may vary. Compared to the previous chapter, the analysis here is considerably more involved. In fact, even in the case of a freely rotating body on which no external forces whatever are acting, the motion, as we shall see, is not simple.

9.1 Rotation of a Rigid Body About an Arbitrary Axis. Moments and Products of Inertia. Angular Momentum and Kinetic Energy

We begin the study of the general motion of a rigid body with some mathematical preliminaries. First, we shall give a calculation of the moment of inertia about an axis whose direction is arbitrary. The axis passes through a fixed point O, Figure 9.1, taken as the origin of our coordinate system. We shall apply the fundamental definition

$$I = \sum_i m_i R_i^2$$

where R_i is the perpendicular distance from the particle of mass m_i to the axis of rotation. The direction of the axis of rotation is defined by the unit vector $\mathbf{n}$. Then

$$R_i = |r_i \sin \theta_i| = |\mathbf{r}_i \times \mathbf{n}|$$

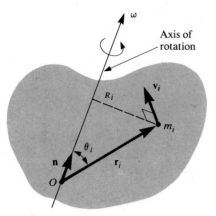

FIGURE 9.1 The velocity vector of a representative particle of a rotating rigid body.

in which θ_i is the angle between $\mathbf{r}_i$ and $\mathbf{n}$, and

$$\mathbf{r}_i = \mathbf{i}x_i + \mathbf{j}y_i + \mathbf{k}z_i$$

is the position vector of the i-th particle. Let the direction cosines of the axis be $\cos \alpha$, $\cos \beta$, and $\cos \gamma$. Then

$$\mathbf{n} = \mathbf{i} \cos \alpha + \mathbf{j} \cos \beta + \mathbf{k} \cos \gamma \qquad (9.1)$$

and so

$$R_i^2 = |\mathbf{r}_i \times \mathbf{n}|^2$$
$$= (y_i \cos \gamma - z_i \cos \beta)^2 + (z_i \cos \alpha - x_i \cos \gamma)^2 + (x_i \cos \beta - y_i \cos \alpha)^2$$

Upon rearranging terms, we can write

$$R_i^2 = (y_i^2 + z_i^2) \cos^2 \alpha + (z_i^2 + x_i^2) \cos^2 \beta + (x_i^2 + y_i^2) \cos^2 \gamma$$
$$-2y_iz_i \cos \gamma \cos \beta - 2z_ix_i \cos \alpha \cos \gamma - 2x_iy_i \cos \alpha \cos \beta$$

The moment of inertia about our general axis of rotation is then give by the rather lengthy expression

$$I = \sum_i m_i(y_i^2 + z_i^2) \cos^2 \alpha + \sum_i m_i(z_i^2 + x_i^2) \cos^2 \beta + \sum_i m_i(x_i^2 + y_i^2) \cos^2 \gamma$$

$$-2\sum_i m_iy_iz_i \cos \gamma \cos \beta - 2\sum_i m_iz_ix_i \cos \alpha \cos \gamma - 2\sum_i m_ix_iy_i \cos \alpha \cos \beta \quad (9.2)$$

As we shall see later, the formula can be simplified. First, we immediately recognize the sums involving the squares of the coordinates as the moments of inertia of the body about the three coordinate axes. We shall use a slightly modified notation for them as follows:

$$\sum_{i} m_i(y_i^2 + z_i^2) = I_{xx} \qquad \text{\textit{moment of inertia about the x axis}}$$

$$\sum_{i} m_i(z_i^2 + x_i^2) = I_{yy} \qquad \text{\textit{moment of inertia about the y axis}}$$

$$\sum_{i} m_i(x_i^2 + y_i^2) = I_{zz} \qquad \text{\textit{moment of inertia about the z axis}}$$

The sums involving the products of the coordinates are new to us. They are called *products of inertia*. These quantities will be designated as follows:

$$-\sum_{i} m_i x_i y_i = I_{xy} = I_{yx} \qquad \text{\textit{xy product of inertia}}$$

$$-\sum_{i} m_i y_i z_i = I_{yz} = I_{zy} \qquad \text{\textit{yz product of inertia}}$$

$$-\sum_{i} m_i z_i x_i = I_{zx} = I_{xz} \qquad \text{\textit{zx product of inertia}}$$

Notice that our definition includes the minus sign. (In some textbooks the minus sign is not included.) Products of inertia have the same physical dimensions as moments of inertia, namely, mass $\times$ (length)^2, and their values are determined by the mass distribution and orientation of the body relative to the coordinate axes. They make their appearance here because we wish to allow the axis of rotation to have an arbitrary direction, whereas in the previous chapter one of the coordinate axes was taken as the axis of rotation. In order for the moments and products of inertia to be constant quantities, it will generally be necessary to employ a coordinate system that is fixed to the body and rotates with it.

In actually computing the moments and products of inertia of an extended rigid body, we replace the summations by integrations over the volume, as we have done previously:

$$I_{zz} = \int (x^2 + y^2) \, dm$$

$$I_{xy} = -\int xy \, dm$$

with similar expressions for the other I's. We have already found the moments of inertia for a number of cases in the previous chapter. It is important to remember that the values of the moments and products of inertia depend on the choice of the coordinate system.

Using the above notation, the general expression (9.2) for the moment of inertia about an arbitrary axis becomes

$$I = I_{xx} \cos^2 \alpha + I_{yy} \cos^2 \beta + I_{zz} \cos^2 \gamma \qquad (9.3)$$
$$+ \ 2I_{yz} \cos \gamma \cos \beta \quad + \ 2I_{zx} \cos \alpha \cos \gamma \quad + 2I_{xy} \cos \alpha \cos \beta$$

Although the above equation seems rather cumbersome for obtaining the moment of inertia, it is nevertheless useful for certain applications. Furthermore, the calculation is included here in order to show how the products of inertia enter into the general problem of rigid body dynamics.

Angular Momentum Vector

We next proceed to calculate the angular momentum of the rigid body shown in Figure 9.1. To do this we make use of the fact that the rotational velocity of any constituent particle of the body is expressible as a cross product

$$\mathbf{v}_i = \boldsymbol{\omega} \times \mathbf{r}_i$$

Thus, the angular momentum about the origin is

$$\mathbf{r}_i \times m_i \mathbf{v}_i = \mathbf{r}_i \times (m_i \boldsymbol{\omega} \times \mathbf{r}_i)$$

for particle i. Consequently, for all particles, the total angular momentum is given by the summation

$$\mathbf{L} = \sum_i [m_i \mathbf{r}_i \times (\boldsymbol{\omega} \times \mathbf{r}_i)]$$

Consider the x component of the triple cross product

$$\mathbf{r}_i \times (\boldsymbol{\omega} \times \mathbf{r}_i)$$

Now $\mathbf{r}_i = \mathbf{i}x_i + \mathbf{j}y_i + \mathbf{k}z_i$, and $\boldsymbol{\omega} = \mathbf{i}\omega_x + \mathbf{j}\omega_y + \mathbf{k}\omega_z$. We then find

$$[\mathbf{r}_i \times (\boldsymbol{\omega} \times \mathbf{r}_i)]_x = \omega_x(y_i^2 + z_i^2) - \omega_y x_i y_i - \omega_z x_i z_i$$

The student should verify this as an exercise. The x component of the total angular momentum is therefore

$$L_x = \sum_i m_i [\omega_x(y_i^2 + z_1^2) - \omega_y x_i y_i - \omega_z x_i z_i]$$

$$= \omega_x \sum_i m_i (y_i^2 + z_i^2) - \omega_y \sum_i m_i x_i y_i - \omega_z \sum_i m_i x_i z_i \qquad (9.4)$$

Analogous expressions hold for the y and z components which can be obtained by cyclic permutation: $x \rightarrow y, y \rightarrow z, z \rightarrow x$. Again we see that the sums appearing are just the moments and products of inertia as defined above. Hence we can write

$$L_x = \omega_x I_{xx} + \omega_y I_{xy} + \omega_z I_{xz} \qquad (9.5)$$

for the x component of the angular momentum vector. The final expression for the total angular momentum is as follows:

$$\mathbf{L} = \mathbf{i}L_x + \mathbf{j}L_y + \mathbf{k}L_z \qquad (9.6)$$

$$= \mathbf{i}(\omega_x I_{xx} + \omega_y I_{xy} + \omega_z I_{xz}) + \mathbf{j}(\omega_x I_{yx} + \omega_y I_{yy} + \omega_z I_{yz})$$

$$+ \mathbf{k}(\omega_x I_{zx} + \omega_y I_{zy} + \omega_z I_{zz})$$

An important and fundamental fact should now be apparent, namely that *the angular momentum vector is not necessarily in the same direction as the axis of rotation* (direction of $\boldsymbol{\omega}$). For example, let the x axis be the axis of rotation. Then $\omega_x = \omega$, $\omega_y = 0$, and $\omega_z = 0$. In this particular case the above expression for $\mathbf{L}$ reduces to

$$\mathbf{L} = \mathbf{i}\omega I_{xx} + \mathbf{j}\omega I_{xy} + \mathbf{k}\omega I_{xz}$$

so that $\mathbf{L}$ may have components perpendicular to the x axis (axis of rotation). However, the component of $\mathbf{L}$ along the axis of rotation is ωI_{xx} in agreement with the previous chapter. More generally, the component of the angular momentum along the axis of rotation is given by the dot product $\mathbf{L} \cdot \mathbf{n}$ where $\mathbf{n}$ is the unit vector, defined by Equation 9.1, specifying the direction of $\boldsymbol{\omega}$. Hence $\cos\alpha = \omega_x/\omega$, $\cos\beta = \omega_y/\omega$, and $\cos\gamma = \omega_z/\omega$. As a consequence, it is quite straightforward to verify that

$$\mathbf{L} \cdot \mathbf{n} = I\omega \qquad (9.7)$$

where $\mathbf{L}$ is given by the general expression 9.6 and I is the moment of inertia about the axis of rotation given by Equation 9.3.

Examples

9.1   Find the moment of inertia of a uniform square lamina of side a and mass m about a diagonal.

Solution:

Let us choose coordinate axes as shown in Figure 9.2 with the lamina lying in the xy plane with a corner at the origin. Then, from the last chapter, we have $I_{xx} = I_{yy} = ma^2/3$, and $I_{zz} = I_{xx} + I_{yy} = 2ma^2/3$. Now $z = 0$ for all points in the lamina, therefore the xz and yz products of inertia vanish: $I_{xz} = I_{yz} = 0$. The xy product of inertia is found by integrating as follows:

$$I_{xy} = I_{yx} = -\int_0^a\int_0^a xy\rho\,dx dy = -\rho\int_0^a \frac{a^2}{2}y\,dy = -\rho\frac{a^4}{4}$$

where ρ is the mass per unit area, that is $\rho = m/a^2$. Therefore, we get

$$I_{xy} = -\frac{1}{4}ma^2$$

For the diagonal axis we have $\alpha = \beta = 45°$, and $\gamma = 90°$. The direction cosines are then $\cos\alpha = \cos\beta = 1/\sqrt{2}$, $\cos\gamma = 0$. Equation 9.3 then gives

$$I = \frac{1}{2}I_{xx} + \frac{1}{2}I_{yy} + I_{xy} = \frac{1}{6}ma^2 + \frac{1}{6}ma^2 - \frac{1}{4}ma^2 = \frac{1}{12}ma^2$$

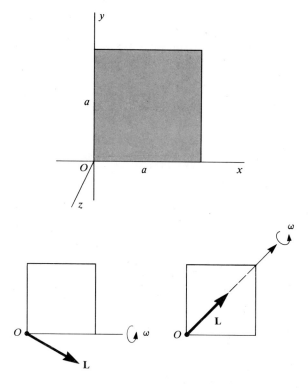

FIGURE 9.2   Square lamina.

for the moment of inertia about a diagonal. The same result can also be obtained by direct integration. The student may wish to verify this as an exercise; the calculation is quite straightforward. See also Problem 9.2(c).

9.2   Find the angular momentum about the origin for the above square plate when it is rotating with angular speed ω about (a) the x-axis, and (b) about the diagonal through the origin.

Solution:

   (a)   For rotation about the x-axis we have

$$\omega_x = \omega \qquad \omega_y = \omega_z = 0$$

   The general expression for angular momentum, Equation 9.6, then gives

$$\mathbf{L} = \mathbf{i}I_{xx}\omega + \mathbf{j}I_{yx}\omega = \mathbf{i}\frac{ma^2}{3}\omega - \mathbf{j}\frac{ma^2}{4}\omega$$

   (b)   About the diagonal the components of ω are

$$\omega_x = \omega_y = \omega \cos 45° = \omega/\sqrt{2} \qquad \omega_z = 0$$

Therefore

$$\mathbf{L} = \mathbf{i}\left(I_{xx}\frac{\omega}{\sqrt{2}} + I_{xy}\frac{\omega}{\sqrt{2}}\right) + \mathbf{j}\left(I_{yx}\frac{\omega}{\sqrt{2}} + I_{yy}\frac{\omega}{\sqrt{2}}\right)$$

$$= \mathbf{i}\left(\frac{ma^2}{3} - \frac{ma^2}{4}\right)\frac{\omega}{\sqrt{2}} + \mathbf{j}\left(-\frac{ma^2}{4} + \frac{ma^2}{3}\right)\frac{\omega}{\sqrt{2}}$$

$$= (\mathbf{i} + \mathbf{j})\frac{ma^2}{12}\frac{\omega}{\sqrt{2}}$$

Notice that the angular momentum vector in case (a) does not point in the same direction as the angular velocity vector, but points downward as shown in Figure 9.2. In case (b) however, the angular velocity vector $\boldsymbol{\omega} = (\mathbf{i} + \mathbf{j})\dfrac{\omega}{\sqrt{2}}$ so that the angular momentum is in the same direction as $\boldsymbol{\omega}$.

The magnitude of the angular momentum is given by $L = (L_x^2 + L_y^2 + L_z^2)^{1/2}$. Thus, for case (a) we find

$$L = ma^2\omega\sqrt{\frac{1}{9} + \frac{1}{16}} = ma^2\omega\frac{5}{12}$$

and for case (b)

$$L = ma^2\omega\frac{1}{12}$$

Rotational Kinetic Energy of a Rigid Body

We next calculate the kinetic energy of rotation of our general rigid body of Figure 9.1. As in our calculation of the angular momentum, we use the fact that the velocity of a representative particle is given by $\mathbf{v}_i = \boldsymbol{\omega} \times \mathbf{r}_i$. The rotational kinetic energy is therefore given by the summation

$$T_{rot} = \sum_i \frac{1}{2}m_i\mathbf{v}_i \bullet \mathbf{v}_i = \frac{1}{2}\sum_i (\boldsymbol{\omega} \times \mathbf{r}_i) \bullet m_i\mathbf{v}_i$$

Now in any triple scalar product we can exchange the dot and the cross: $(\mathbf{A} \times \mathbf{B}) \bullet \mathbf{C} = \mathbf{A} \bullet (\mathbf{B} \times \mathbf{C})$. (See Section 1.7.) Hence

$$T_{rot} = \frac{1}{2}\sum_i \boldsymbol{\omega} \bullet (\mathbf{r}_i \times m_i\mathbf{v}_i) = \frac{1}{2}\boldsymbol{\omega} \bullet \sum_i (\mathbf{r}_i \times m_i\mathbf{v}_i)$$

But, by definition, the sum $\sum_i (\mathbf{r}_i \times m_i\mathbf{v}_i)$ is the angular momentum $\mathbf{L}$. Thus we can write

$$T_{rot} = \frac{1}{2}\boldsymbol{\omega} \bullet \mathbf{L} \tag{9.8}$$

for the kinetic energy of rotation of a rigid body. We recall from Chapter 7 that the translational kinetic energy of any system is equal to the expression $\frac{1}{2}\mathbf{v}_{cm} \cdot \mathbf{p}$ where $\mathbf{p} = m\mathbf{v}_{cm}$ is the linear momentum of the system and $\mathbf{v}_{cm}$ is the velocity of the mass center. For a rigid body the total kinetic energy is accordingly

$$T = T_{rot} + T_{trans} = \frac{1}{2}\boldsymbol{\omega} \cdot \mathbf{L} + \frac{1}{2}\mathbf{v}_{cm} \cdot \mathbf{p} \tag{9.9}$$

where $\mathbf{L}$ is the angular momentum about the center of mass.

By expressing the angular momentum explicitly in terms of components we can write the rotational kinetic energy as

$$T_{rot} = \frac{1}{2}\boldsymbol{\omega} \cdot \mathbf{L} = \frac{1}{2}(\omega_x L_x + \omega_y L_y + \omega_z L_z) \tag{9.10}$$

$$= \frac{1}{2}(I_{xx}\omega_x^2 + I_{yy}\omega_y^2 + I_{zz}\omega_z^2 + 2I_{xy}\omega_x\omega_y + 2I_{xz}\omega_x\omega_z + 2I_{yz}\omega_y\omega_z)$$

The last step follows from Equations 9.5 and 9.6 and should be verified by the reader.

Example

9.3 Find the rotational kinetic energy of the square plate of the previous example.

Solution:
For the case (a) of rotation about the x-axis, we have simply

$$T_{rot} = \frac{1}{2}I_{xx}\omega_x^2 = \frac{1}{2}\frac{ma^2}{3}\omega^2 = \frac{1}{6}ma^2\omega^2$$

For rotation about a diagonal, case (b), we find

$$T_{rot} = \frac{1}{2}\boldsymbol{\omega} \cdot \mathbf{L} = \frac{1}{2}\left[(\mathbf{i} + \mathbf{j})\frac{\omega}{\sqrt{2}}\right] \cdot \left[(\mathbf{i} + \mathbf{j})\frac{ma^2}{12}\frac{\omega}{\sqrt{2}}\right]$$

Now $(\mathbf{i} + \mathbf{j}) \cdot (\mathbf{i} + \mathbf{j}) = 2$, hence

$$T_{rot} = \frac{1}{2}\frac{ma^2}{12}\omega^2 = \frac{1}{24}ma^2\omega^2$$

Notice that we could also have obtained the same answer by using the result of Example 9.1 for the moment of inertia about the diagonal. The student should verify this. See also Problem 9.2(c).

9.2 Principal Axes of a Rigid Body. Dynamic Balancing

A considerable simplification in the above-derived mathematical formulas for rigid body motion results if we employ a coordinate system such that the products of inertia all vanish. It turns out that such a coordinate system does in fact exist for *any* rigid body and for *any* point taken as the origin. The axes of this coordinate system are said to be *principal axes* for the body at the point O, the origin of the coordinate system in question. (Often we shall choose O to be the center of mass.)

Explicitly, if the coordinate axes are principal axes of the body, then $I_{xy} = I_{xz} = I_{yz} = 0$. In this case we shall employ the following notation:

$$
\begin{aligned}
I_{xx} &= I_1 & \omega_x &= \omega_1 & \mathbf{i} &= \mathbf{e}_1 \\
I_{yy} &= I_2 & \omega_y &= \omega_2 & \mathbf{j} &= \mathbf{e}_2 \\
I_{zz} &= I_3 & \omega_z &= \omega_3 & \mathbf{k} &= \mathbf{e}_3
\end{aligned}
$$

The three moments of inertia I_1, I_2, and I_3 are known as *principal moments* of the body at the point O. For principal axes the general formulas for moment of inertia, angular momentum, and rotational kinetic energy, Equations 9.3, 9.6, and 9.10, respectively, reduce to

$$ I = I_1 \cos^2 \alpha + I_2 \cos^2 \beta + I_3 \cos^2 \gamma \tag{9.11} $$

$$ \mathbf{L} = \mathbf{e}_1 I_1 \omega_1 + \mathbf{e}_2 I_2 \omega_2 + \mathbf{e}_3 I_3 \omega_3 \tag{9.12} $$

$$ T_{rot} = \frac{1}{2}(I_1 \omega_1^2 + I_2 \omega_2^2 + I_3 \omega_3^2) \tag{9.13} $$

Existence of Principal Axes

Let us now investigate the question of finding the principal axes. First, if the body possesses some symmetry, then it is usually possible to choose a set of coordinate axes by inspection such that one or more of the three products of inertia consists of two parts of equal magnitude and opposite algebraic sign and therefore vanishes. For example the rectangular block and the symmetric laminar body (ping-pong paddle) have the principal axes at O as indicated in Figures 9.3 (a) and (b).

A body does not have to be symmetric, however, in order that the products of inertia vanish for an appropriately-chosen coordinate system. For example, consider a plane lamina of *any shape* (Figure 9.4). If the xy plane is the plane of the lamina, then $z = 0$ for all parts of the body and so $I_{zy} = -\int zy \, dm$ and $I_{zx} = -\int zx \, dm$ both vanish. Now, relative to any given origin in the plane of the lamina, we can easily prove that there always exists a set of axes such that $I_{xy} = -\int xy \, dm$ also vanishes. To show this, we observe that the integral changes sign as the Oxy system is rotated through an angle of $90°$, because the lamina passes from one quadrant to the next, as shown. Consequently, the integral must vanish for some angle between $0°$ and $90°$. This angle defines a set of coordinate axes for which *all* products of inertia vanish. By definition, this is a set of principal axes.

It can be argued in a similar way that for any rigid body there always exists, at any given point, at least one set of three mutually orthogonal axes such that all products of inertia vanish, that is, there always exists at least one set of principal axes at the point in question. A method of determining principal axes is discussed below.

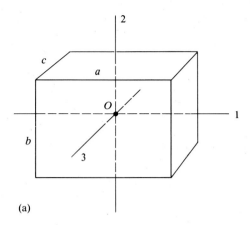

(a)

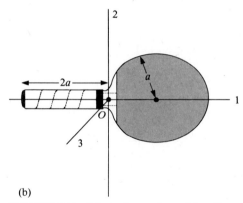

(b)

FIGURE 9.3 Principal axes for a (a) uniform rectangular block and (b) ping-pong paddle.

Examples

9.4 (a) For the rectangular block shown in Figure 9.3(a) the principal moments at the center of mass O are clearly just those indicated in Table 8.1 of the previous chapter, namely

$$I_1 = \frac{m}{12}(b^2 + c^2)$$

$$I_2 = \frac{m}{12}(a^2 + c^2)$$

$$I_3 = \frac{m}{12}(a^2 + b^2)$$

in which m is the mass of the block and a, b, and c are the edge lengths. The moment of inertia about *any* axis passing through O is then given by Equation 9.11. Note in

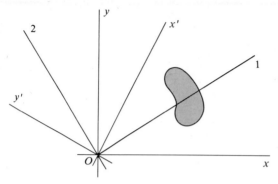

FIGURE 9.4   Showing the existence of principal axes for a laminar body of any shape.

particular that for a *cubical* block ($a = b = c$) the three principal moments at O are all equal. In this case, since $\cos^2 \alpha + \cos^2 \beta + \cos^2 \gamma = 1$, then the moment of inertia about any axis through the center of the block is independent of the direction of the axis and is given by $I = \dfrac{1}{6}ma^2$.

(b)   To find the principal moments of the ping-pong paddle at the point O indicated in Figure 9.3(b), we shall assume for simplicity that the paddle is a circular lamina of radius a and mass $m/2$ attached to a thin rod for a handle of mass $m/2$ and length $2a$. Again we borrow from the results of the previous chapter, Section 8.3. The principal moments are each calculated by adding the moments about the respective axes for the two parts, namely

$$I = I_{rod} + I_{disc}$$

$$I_1 = 0 + \frac{1}{4}\frac{m}{2}a^2 = \frac{1}{8}ma^2$$

$$I_2 = \frac{1}{3}\frac{m}{2}(2a)^2 + \frac{5}{4}\frac{m}{2}a^2 = \frac{31}{24}ma^2$$

$$I_3 = \frac{1}{3}\frac{m}{2}(2a)^2 + \frac{3}{2}\frac{m}{2}a^2 = \frac{17}{12}ma^2$$

We note that $I_3 = I_1 + I_2$ since the object is assumed to be laminar.

Suppose that a body is rotating about one of its principal axes, say the *1*-axis. Then $\omega = \omega_1$, $\omega_2 = \omega_3 = 0$. The expression for the angular momentum, Equation 9.12, then reduces to just one term, namely

$$\mathbf{L} = \mathbf{e}_1 I_1 \omega_1$$

or, equivalently

$$\mathbf{L} = I_1 \boldsymbol{\omega}$$

Thus, in this circumstance the angular momentum vector is in the same direction as the angular velocity vector or axis of rotation. We have therefore the following important fact: *The angular momentum vector is either in the same direction as the axis of rotation, or is not, depending on whether the axis of rotation is, or is not, a principal axis.*

Dynamic Balancing

The above rule finds application in the case of a rotating device such as an automobile wheel or fan blade. If the device is *statically balanced,* the center of mass lies on the axis of rotation. To be *dynamically balanced* the axis of rotation must also be a principal axis so that, as the body rotates, the angular momentum vector **L** will lie along the axis. Otherwise, if the rotational axis is not a principal one, the angular momentum vector varies in direction: it describes a cone as the body rotates (Figure 9.5). Then, since $d\mathbf{L}/dt$ is equal to the applied torque, there must be a torque exerted on the body. The direction of this torque is at right angles to the axis. The result is a reaction on the bearings. Thus in the case of a dynamically unbalanced wheel or rotator, there may be violent vibration and wobbling, even if the wheel is statically balanced.

Determination of the Other Two Principal Axes When One is Known

In many instances a body possesses sufficient symmetry so that at least one principal axis can be found by inspection, that is, axes can be chosen so as to make two of the three products of inertia vanish. If such is the case, then the other two principal axes can be determined as follows.

Suppose the z axis is known to be a principal axis at the origin in a certain coordinate system. Then, by definition

$$I_{zx} = I_{zy} = 0$$

The other two principal axes are each perpendicular to the z axis and so they must lie in the xy plane. Suppose the body is rotating about one or the other of these two, as yet, unknown principal axes. Then we know that the angular momentum vector must be in the same direction as the angular velocity vector, so we can write

$$\mathbf{L} = I_p\boldsymbol{\omega} \qquad\qquad (9.14)$$

in which I_p is one of the two principal moments of inertia in question. In components the above equation reads

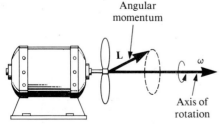

Angular momentum

FIGURE 9.5   A rotating fan blade. The angular momentum vector L describes a cone about the axis of rotation if the blade is not dynamically balanced.

$$I_{xx}\omega_x + I_{xy}\omega_y = I_p\omega_x \qquad\qquad (9.14a)$$

$$I_{xy}\omega_x + I_{yy}\omega_y = I_p\omega_y \qquad\qquad (9.14b)$$

(There is no z component.) Now let θ denote the angle between the x axis and the particular principal axis about which the body is rotating. Then $\omega_y/\omega_x = \tan\theta$, so, upon dividing by ω_x we have

$$I_{xx} + I_{xy}\tan\theta = I_p$$
$$I_{xy} + I_{yy}\tan\theta = I_p\tan\theta$$

Elimination of I_p between the two equations yields

$$(I_{yy} - I_{xx})\tan\theta = I_{xy}(\tan^2\theta - 1)$$

from which θ can be found. In this calculation it is helpful to employ the trigonometric identity $\tan 2\theta = 2\tan\theta/(1 - \tan^2\theta)$. This gives

$$\tan 2\theta = \frac{2I_{xy}}{I_{xx} - I_{yy}} \qquad\qquad (9.15)$$

In the interval $0°$ to $180°$ there are two values of θ, differing by $90°$, that satisfy the above equation, and these give the directions of the two principal axes in the xy plane.

Note that in the case $I_{xx} = I_{yy}$, $\tan 2\theta = \infty$ so that the two values of θ are $45°$ and $135°$. (This is the case for the square lamina of Example 9.1 when the origin is at a corner.) Also, if $I_{xy} = 0$ the equation is satisfied by the two values $\theta = 0°$ and $\theta = 90°$, that is, the x and y axes are already principal axes.

Example

9.5   *Balancing a crooked wheel.* Suppose an automobile wheel, through some defect or accident, has its axis of rotation (axle) slightly bent relative to the symmetry axis of the wheel. The situation can be remedied by use of counterbalance weights suitably located on the rim so as to make the axle a principal axis for the total system: wheel plus weights. For simplicity we shall treat the wheel as a thin uniform circular disc of radius a and mass m, Figure 9.6. We choose $Oxyz$ axes such that the disc lies in the yz plane, with the x axis as the symmetry axis of the disc. The axis of rotation (axle) is taken as the *1*-axis inclined by an angle θ relative to the x axis and lying in the xy plane, as shown. Two balancing weights, each of mass m', are attached to the wheel by means of light supports of length b. The weights both lie in the xy plane, as indicated. The wheel will be dynamically balanced if the *1, 2, 3* coordinate axes are principal axes for the total system.

Now, from symmetry relative to the xy plane, we see that the z axis is a principal axis for the wheel plus weights: z is zero for the weights, and the xy plane divides the wheel into two equal parts having opposite signs for the products zx and zy. Consequently, we can use Equation 9.15 to find the relationship between θ and the other parameters.

From the previous chapter we know that for the wheel alone the moments of inertia about the x and the y axes are $\frac{1}{2}ma^2$ and $\frac{1}{4}ma^2$, respectively. Thus, for the wheel plus weights

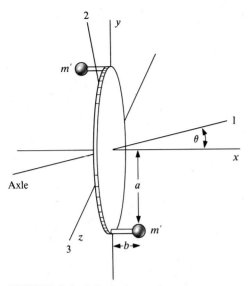

FIGURE 9.6   Principal axes for a bent wheel with balancing weights.

$$I_{xx} = \frac{1}{2}ma^2 + 2m'a^2$$

$$I_{yy} = \frac{1}{4}ma^2 + 2m'b^2$$

Now the xy product of inertia for the wheel alone is zero, and so we need only consider the weights for finding I_{xy} for the system, namely

$$I_{xy} = -\Sigma x_i y_i m_i' = -[(-b)am' + b(-a)m'] = 2abm'$$

Notice that this is a positive quantity for our choice of coordinate axes. Equation 9.15 then gives the inclination of the 1-axis:

$$\tan 2\theta = \frac{2I_{xy}}{I_{xx} - I_{yy}} = \frac{4abm'}{\frac{1}{4}ma^2 + 2m'(a^2 - b^2)}$$

If, as is typical, θ is very small, and also m' is small compared to m, then we can express the above relation in approximate form by neglecting the second term in the denominator and using the fact that $\tan u \approx u$ for small u. The result is

$$\theta \approx 8\frac{bm'}{am}$$

As a numerical example, let $\theta = 1° = 0.017$ rad, $a = 7$ inches, $b = 2$ inches, $m = 20$ lb. Solving for m', we find

$$m' = \theta\frac{am}{8b} = 0.017\frac{7\text{in.} \times 20\text{lb}}{8 \times 2\text{in.}} = 0.15 \text{ lb} = 2.4 \text{ oz}$$

for the required balance weights.

9.3   Euler's Equations of Motion of a Rigid Body

We come now to what we may call the essential physics of the present chapter, namely the actual three-dimensional rotation of a rigid body under the action of external forces. As we have learned from Chapter 7, the fundamental equation governing the rotational part of the motion of any system, referred to an inertial coordinate system, is

$$\mathbf{N} = \frac{d\mathbf{L}}{dt}$$

in which $\mathbf{N}$ is the net applied torque and $\mathbf{L}$ is the angular momentum. For a rigid body, we have seen that $\mathbf{L}$ is most simply expressed if the coordinate axes are principal axes for the body. Thus, in general, we must employ a coordinate system that is fixed in the body and rotates with it. That is, the angular velocity of the body and the angular velocity of the coordinate system are one and the same. (There is an exception: If *two* of the three principal moments I_1, I_2, and I_3 are equal to each other, then the coordinate axes need not be fixed in the body in order to be principal axes. This case will be considered later.) In any case, our coordinate system is not an inertial one.

Referring to the theory of rotating coordinate systems developed in Chapter 5, we know that the time rate of change of the angular momentum vector in a fixed (inertial) system versus a rotating system is given by the formula

$$\left(\frac{d\mathbf{L}}{dt}\right)_{fixed} = \left(\frac{d\mathbf{L}}{dt}\right)_{rot} + \boldsymbol{\omega} \times \mathbf{L}$$

Thus, the equation of motion in the rotating system is

$$\mathbf{N} = \left(\frac{d\mathbf{L}}{dt}\right)_{rot} + \boldsymbol{\omega} \times \mathbf{L} \tag{9.16}$$

In components along the directions of the principal axes, the above equation reads

$$N_1 = \dot{L}_1 + (\boldsymbol{\omega} \times \mathbf{L})_1$$
$$N_2 = \dot{L}_2 + (\boldsymbol{\omega} \times \mathbf{L})_2 \tag{9.16a}$$
$$N_3 = \dot{L}_3 + (\boldsymbol{\omega} \times \mathbf{L})_3$$

or, more explicitly

$$N_1 = I_1\dot{\omega}_1 + \omega_2\omega_3(I_3 - I_2)$$
$$N_2 = I_2\dot{\omega}_2 + \omega_3\omega_1(I_1 - I_3) \tag{9.16b}$$
$$N_3 = I_3\dot{\omega}_3 + \omega_1\omega_2(I_2 - I_1)$$

These are known as Euler's equations for the motion of a rigid body.

Body Constrained to Rotate About a Fixed Axis

As a first application of Euler's equations, we take up the special case of a rigid body that is constrained to rotate about a fixed axis and with *constant angular velocity*.

Then

$$\dot{\omega}_1 = \dot{\omega}_2 = \dot{\omega}_3 = 0$$

and Euler's equations reduce to

$$N_1 = \omega_2\omega_3(I_3 - I_2)$$
$$N_2 = \omega_3\omega_1(I_1 - I_3) \qquad (9.17)$$
$$N_3 = \omega_1\omega_2(I_2 - I_1)$$

These give the components of the torque that must be exerted on the body by the constraining support.

In particular, suppose that the axis of rotation is a principal axis, say the *1*-axis. Then $\omega_2 = \omega_3 = 0$, $\omega = \omega_1$. In this case all three components of the torque vanish:

$$N_1 = N_2 = N_3 = 0$$

That is, there is no torque at all. This agrees with our previous discussion concerning dynamic balancing in the previous section.

9.4   Free Rotation of a Rigid Body. Geometric Description of the Motion

Let us consider the case of a rigid body that is free to rotate in any direction about a certain point O. There are no torques acting on the body. This is the case of free rotation and is exemplified, for example, by a body supported on a smooth pivot at its center of mass. Another example is that of a rigid body moving freely under no forces or falling freely in a uniform gravitational field so that there are no torques. The point O in this case is the center of mass.

With zero torque the angular momentum of the body, as seen from the outside, must remain constant in direction and magnitude according to the general principle of conservation of angular momentum. However, with respect to rotating axes fixed in the body, the direction of the angular momentum vector may change, although its magnitude must remain constant. This fact can be expressed by the equation

$$\mathbf{L} \cdot \mathbf{L} = \text{constant} \qquad (9.18)$$

In terms of components referred to the principal axes of the body, the above equation reads

$$I_1^2\omega_1^2 + I_2^2\omega_2^2 + I_3^2\omega_3^2 = L^2 = \text{constant} \qquad (9.18a)$$

As the body rotates, the components of $\boldsymbol{\omega}$ may vary, but they must always satisfy the above equation.

A second relation is obtained by considering the kinetic energy of rotation. Again, since there is zero torque, the total rotational kinetic energy must remain constant. This may be expressed as

$$\boldsymbol{\omega} \cdot \mathbf{L} = 2T_{rot} = \text{constant} \qquad (9.19)$$

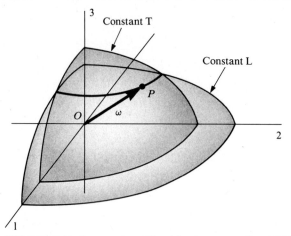

FIGURE 9.7 Intersecting ellipsoids of constant L and T for a rigid body undergoing torque-free rotation. (Only one octant is shown for clarity.)

or, equivalently in terms of components,

$$I_1\omega_1^2 + I_2\omega_2^2 + I_3\omega_3^2 = 2T_{rot} = \text{constant} \tag{9.19a}$$

We now see that the components of $\boldsymbol{\omega}$ must simultaneously satisfy two different equations expressing the constancy of kinetic energy and of magnitude of angular momentum. (These two equations can also be obtained by use of Euler's equations. See Problem 9.7.) These are the equations of two ellipsoids whose principal axes coincide with the principal axes of the body. The first ellipsoid, Equation 9.18a, has principal diameters in the ratios $I_1^{-1}{:}I_2^{-1}{:}I_3^{-1}$. The second ellipsoid, Equation 9.19a, has principal diameters in the ratios $I_1^{-1/2}{:}I_2^{-1/2}{:}I_3^{-1/2}$. It is known as the *Poinsot ellipsoid*. As the body rotates, the extremity of the angular velocity vector thus describes a curve which is the intersection of the two ellipsoids. This is illustrated in Figure 9.7.

From the equations of the intersecting ellipsoids, it can be shown that in the case where the initial axis of rotation coincides with one of the principal axes of the body, then the curve of intersection diminishes to a point. In other words, the two ellipsoids just touch at a principal diameter, and the body rotates steadily about this axis. This is true, however, only if the initial rotation is about the axis of either the largest or the smallest moment of inertia. If it is about the intermediate axis, say the 2-axis where $I_3 > I_2 > I_1$, then the intersection of the two ellipsoids is not a point, but a curve that goes entirely around both, as illustrated in Figure 9.8. In this case the rotation is unstable since the axis of rotation precesses all around the body. See Problem 9.19. (If the initial axis of rotation is almost, but not exactly, along one of the two stable axes, then the angular velocity vector describes a tight cone about the corresponding axis.) These facts can easily be illustrated by tossing an oblong block, a book, or a ping-pong paddle into the air.

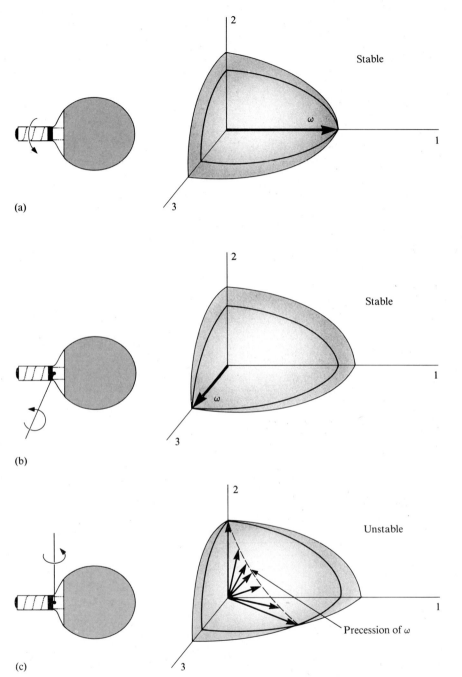

FIGURE 9.8 Ellipsoids of constant L and constant T for a rigid body rotating freely about the axis of (a) least, (b) greatest, and (c) intermediate moment of inertia.

9.5   Free Rotation of a Rigid Body with an Axis of Symmetry. Analytical Treatment. The Eulerian Angles

Although the geometric description of the motion of a rigid body given in the preceding section is helpful in visualizing free rotation under no torques, the method does not immediately give numerical values. We now proceed to augment that description with an analytical approach based on the direct integration of Euler's equations.

We shall solve Euler's equations for the special case in which the body possesses an axis of symmetry, so that two of the three principal moments of inertia are equal.

Let us choose the 3-axis as the axis of symmetry. We introduce the following notation:

$$I_s = I_3 \quad \textit{(moment of inertia about the symmetry axis)}$$
$$I = I_1 = I_2 \quad \textit{(moment about the axes normal to the symmetry axis)}$$

For the case of zero torque, Euler's equations then read

$$I\dot{\omega}_1 + \omega_2\omega_3(I_s - I) = 0 \tag{9.20}$$
$$I\dot{\omega}_2 + \omega_3\omega_1(I - I_s) = 0$$
$$I_s\dot{\omega}_3 = 0$$

From the last equation it follows that

$$\omega_3 = \text{constant}$$

Let us now define a constant Ω as

$$\Omega = \omega_3 \frac{I_s - I}{I} \tag{9.21}$$

Then the first two of Equations 9.20 may be written

$$\dot{\omega}_1 + \Omega\omega_2 = 0 \tag{9.22}$$
$$\dot{\omega}_2 - \Omega\omega_1 = 0 \tag{9.23}$$

To separate the variables in the above pair of equations, we differentiate the first with respect to t and obtain

$$\ddot{\omega}_1 + \Omega\dot{\omega}_2 = 0$$

Upon solving for $\dot{\omega}_2$ and inserting the result into Equation 9.23, we find

$$\ddot{\omega}_1 + \Omega^2\omega_1 = 0$$

This is the equation for simple harmonic motion. A solution is

$$\omega_1 = \omega_0 \cos\Omega t \tag{9.24}$$

in which ω_0 is a constant of integration. To find ω_2, we differentiate the above equation with respect to t and insert the result into Equation 9.22. We can then solve for ω_2 to obtain

$$\omega_2 = \omega_0 \sin\Omega t \tag{9.25}$$

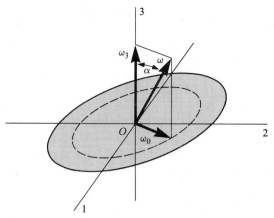

FIGURE 9.9   Angular velocity vector and its components for the free precession of a disc.

Thus ω_1 and ω_2 vary harmonically in time with angular frequency Ω, and their phases differ by $\pi/2$. It follows that the projection of $\boldsymbol{\omega}$ on the 1, 2 plane describes a circle of radius ω_0 at the angular frequency Ω.

We can summarize the above results as follows: In the free rotation of a rigid body with an axis of symmetry, the angular velocity vector describes a conical motion (precesses) about the symmetry axis. It describes a surface called the *body cone*. (See Figure 9.11.) The angular frequency of this precession is the constant Ω defined by Equation 9.21. Let α denote the angle between the symmetry axis (*3*-axis) and the axis of rotation (direction of $\boldsymbol{\omega}$) as shown in Figure 9.9. Then $\omega_3 = \omega \cos \alpha$, and so

$$\Omega = \left(\frac{I_s}{I} - 1\right)\omega \cos \alpha \qquad (9.26)$$

giving the rate of precession of the angular velocity vector about the axis of symmetry. (Some specific examples are discussed at the end of the present section.)

We can now see the connection between the above analysis of the torque-free rotation of a rigid body and the geometric description of the previous section. The circular path of radius ω_0 traced out by the extremity of the angular velocity vector is just the intersection of the two ellipsoids of Figure 9.7.

Description of the Rotation of a Rigid Body Relative to a Fixed Coordinate System. The Eulerian Angles

In the foregoing analysis of the free rotation of a rigid body, the precessional motion was relative to a set of principal axes fixed in the body and rotating with it. In order to describe the motion relative to an observer outside the body we must use a fixed coordinate system. In Figure 9.10(a) the coordinate system $Oxyz$ has a fixed orientation in space. The numbered system $O123$ is our previously defined set of principal axes which is fixed in the body and rotates with it. A third system $Ox'y'z'$ is defined as follows: The z' axis coincides with the *3*-axis or symmetry axis of the body, and the x' axis is the line of intersection of the *1, 2* plane with the fixed *xy* plane. The angle between the x and the x' axes is denoted by φ, and the angle between the z and z' or *3* axes is θ. The turning of the body about the *3*-axis is determined by the angle between the *1*-axis and the x'axis, denoted by ψ as shown. The three angles φ, θ, and ψ completely define the orientation of the body in space and are called the *Eulerian angles*.

Now, from a study of the figure we see that $\boldsymbol{\omega}$, the angular velocity of the body (numbered system) consists of a turning about the z' axis or *3*-axis with angular rate $\dot{\psi}$ superimposed on the rotation of the primed system $Ox'y'z'$. Let us call $\boldsymbol{\omega}'$ the angular velocity of the primed coordinate system. $\boldsymbol{\omega}'$ is not shown in the figure because it would clutter the diagram. [It is shown in Figure 9.10(b).] However, it should be clear that the actual rotation of the primed system consists of two parts: an angular rate $\dot{\theta}$ about the x' axis, and an angular rate $\dot{\varphi}$ about the fixed z axis. The components of $\boldsymbol{\omega}'$ in the $Ox'y'z'$ system are therefore

$$
\begin{aligned}
\omega'_{x'} &= \dot{\theta} \\
\omega'_{y'} &= \dot{\varphi}_{y'} = \dot{\varphi}\sin\theta \\
\omega'_{z'} &= \dot{\varphi}_{z'} = \dot{\varphi}\cos\theta
\end{aligned}
\tag{9.27}
$$

Now $\boldsymbol{\omega}$ differs from $\boldsymbol{\omega}'$ only in the turning with angular rate $\dot{\psi}$ about the z' axis. Therefore, for the components of $\boldsymbol{\omega}$ in the primed system we can write

$$
\begin{aligned}
\omega_{x'} &= \dot{\theta} \\
\omega_{y'} &= \dot{\varphi}\sin\theta \\
\omega_{z'} &= \dot{\varphi}\cos\theta + \dot{\psi}
\end{aligned}
\tag{9.28}
$$

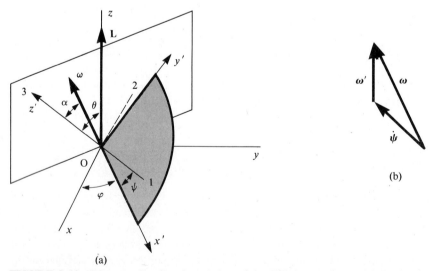

FIGURE 9.10 Diagram showing the relation of the Eulerian angles to the fixed and the rotating coordinate axes.

We can now express the components of ω in the $O123$ system. They are as follows:

$$\omega_1 = \omega_{x'} \cos \psi + \omega_{y'} \sin \psi = \dot{\theta} \cos \psi + \dot{\varphi} \sin \theta \sin \psi$$
$$\omega_2 = \omega_{x'}(-\sin \psi) + \omega_{y'} \cos \psi = -\dot{\theta} \sin \psi + \dot{\varphi} \sin \theta \cos \psi \qquad (9.29)$$
$$\omega_3 = \omega_{z'} = \dot{\varphi} \cos \theta + \dot{\psi}$$

(We shall not need to use Equations 9.29 at present but will refer to them later.)

Now in the present case in which there is zero torque acting on the body, the angular momentum vector $\mathbf{L}$ is constant in magnitude *and* direction in the fixed system $Oxyz$. Let us choose the z axis to be the direction of $\mathbf{L}$. This is known as the *invariable line*. From the figure, we see that the components of $\mathbf{L}$ in the primed system are

$$L_{x'} = 0$$
$$L_{y'} = L \sin \theta \qquad (9.30)$$
$$L_{z'} = L \cos \theta$$

We again restrict ourselves to the case of a body with an axis of symmetry, the *3* axis. Since the x' and y' axes lie in the *1, 2* plane, and the z' axis coincides with the *3*-axis, then the primed axes are *also* principal axes. In fact, the principal moments are the same: $I_1 = I_2 = I_{x'x'} = I_{y'y'} = I$ and $I_3 = I_{z'z'} = I_s$.

Now consider the first of Equations 9.28 and 9.30 giving the x' component of the angular velocity and angular momentum of the body, namely zero. From these we see that $\dot{\theta} = 0$. Hence θ is constant and ω, having no x' component, must lie in the $y'z'$ plane, as shown. Let α denote the angle between the angular velocity vector ω and the z' axis. Then, in addition to equations 9.28 and 9.30 we also have the following:

$$\omega_{y'} = \omega \sin \alpha \qquad \omega_{z'} = \omega \cos \alpha$$
$$L_{y'} = I\omega \sin \alpha \qquad L_{z'} = I_s\omega \cos \alpha \qquad (9.31)$$

It readily follows that

$$\frac{L_{y'}}{L_{z'}} = \tan \theta = \frac{I}{I_s} \tan \alpha \qquad (9.32)$$

giving the relation between the angles θ and α.

According to the above result, θ is less than or greater than α, depending on whether I is less than I_s or greater than I_s, respectively. In other words, the angular momentum vector lies between the symmetry axis and the axis of rotation in the case of a flattened body ($I < I_s$), whereas in the case of an elongated body ($I > I_s$) the axis of rotation lies between the axis of symmetry and the angular momentum vector. The two cases are illustrated in Figure 9.11. In either case, as the body rotates, the axis of symmetry (z' axis or *3*-axis) describes a conical motion or precesses about the constant angular momentum vector $\mathbf{L}$. At the same time the axis of rotation (ω vector) precesses about $\mathbf{L}$ with same frequency. The surface traced out by ω about $\mathbf{L}$ is called the *space cone*, as indicated.

Referring to Figure 9.10, we see that the angular speed of rotation of the $y'z'$ plane about the z axis is equal to the time rate of change of the angle φ. Thus $\dot{\varphi}$ is the angular rate of precession of the symmetry axis, and also of the axis of rotation about the invariable line ($\mathbf{L}$ vector) as viewed from outside the body. This precession appears

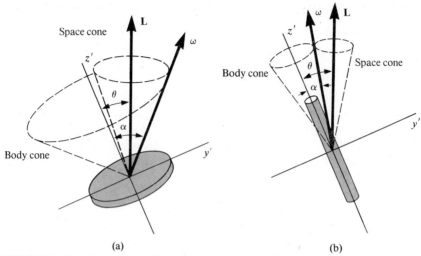

FIGURE 9.11   Free rotation of a (a) disc and (b) rod. The space cones and body cones are shown dotted.

as a "wobble" such as that seen in an imperfectly thrown football or discus. From the second of Equations 9.28 and the first of Equations 9.31 we have $\dot{\varphi}$ sin $\theta = \omega$ sin α, or

$$\dot{\varphi} = \omega \frac{\sin \alpha}{\sin \theta} \tag{9.33}$$

for the rate of precession. The above equation can be put into a somewhat more useful form by using the relation between α and θ given by Equation 9.32. After a little algebra, we obtain

$$\dot{\varphi} = \omega \left[1 + \left(\frac{I_s^2}{I^2} - 1 \right) \cos^2 \alpha \right]^{1/2} \tag{9.34}$$

for the wobble rate in terms of the angular speed ω of the body about its axis of rotation and the inclination α of the axis of rotation to the symmetry axis of the body.

To summarize our analysis of the free rotation of a rigid body with an axis of symmetry, there are three basic angular rates: the magnitude ω of the angular velocity, the precession of angular rate Ω of the axis of rotation (direction of $\boldsymbol{\omega}$) about the symmetry axis of the body, and the precession (wobble) of angular rate $\dot{\varphi}$ of the symmetry axis about the invariable line (constant angular momentum vector).

Examples

9.6   *Precession of a Frisbee.* As an example of the above theory we consider the case of a thin disc, or any symmetric and fairly "flat" object such as a china plate or a Frisbee. The perpendicular axis theorem for principal axes is $I_1 + I_2 = I_3$, and, for a symmetric body $I_1 = I_2$, so that $2I_1 = I_3$. In our present notation this is $2I = I_s$, so the ratio

$$\frac{I_s}{I} = 2$$

to a good approximation. If our object is thrown into the air in such a way that the angular velocity $\boldsymbol{\omega}$ is inclined to the symmetry axis by an angle α, then Equation 9.26 gives

$$\Omega = \omega \cos \alpha$$

for the rate of precession of the rotational axis about the symmetry axis.

For the precession of the symmetry axis about the invariable line, the "wobble" as seen from the outside, Equation 9.34 yields

$$\dot{\varphi} = \omega(1 + 3 \cos^2 \alpha)^{1/2}$$

In particular, if α is quite small so that $\cos \alpha$ is very nearly unity, then we have approximately

$$\Omega \approx \omega$$

$$\dot{\varphi} \approx 2\omega$$

Thus the wobble rate is very nearly twice the angular speed of rotation.

9.7   *Free precession of the earth.* In the motion of the earth, it is known that the axis of rotation is very slightly inclined with respect to the geographic pole defining the axis of symmetry. The angle α is about 0.2 sec of arc (shown exaggerated in Figure 9.12). It is

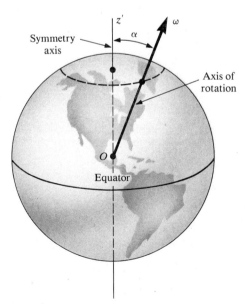

FIGURE 9.12   Showing the symmetry axis and the rotational axis of the earth. (The angle α is greatly exaggerated.)

also known that the ratio of the moments of inertia I_s/I is about 1.00327 as determined from the earth's oblateness. From Equation 9.26 we have therefore

$$\Omega = 0.00327\omega$$

Then, since $\omega = 2\pi/\text{day}$, the period of the above precession is calculated to be

$$\frac{2\pi}{\Omega} = \frac{1}{0.00327}\text{days} = 305 \text{ days}$$

The observed period of precession of the earth's axis of rotation about the pole is about 440 days. The disagreement between the observed and calculated values is attributed to the fact that the earth is not perfectly rigid.

With regard to the precession of the earth's symmetry axis as viewed from space, Equation 9.34 gives

$$\dot{\varphi} = 1.00327\omega$$

The associated period of the earth's wobble is thus

$$\frac{2\pi}{\dot{\varphi}} = \frac{2\pi}{\omega}\frac{1}{1.00327} \simeq 0.997 \text{ day}$$

This free precession of the earth's axis in space is superimposed upon a very much longer gyroscopic precession of 26,000 years, the latter resulting from the fact that there is actually a torque exerted on the earth (because of its oblateness) by the sun and the moon. The fact that the period of gyroscopic precession is so much longer than that of the free precession justifies the neglect of the external torques in calculating the period of the free precession.

9.6 Gyroscopic Precession. Motion of a Top

In this section we shall study the motion of a symmetrical rigid body which is free to turn about a fixed point and on which there is exerted a torque, instead of no torque, as in the case of free precession. The case is exemplified by a simple gyroscope (or top).

The notation for our coordinate axes is shown in Figure 9.13(a). For clarity, only the z', y', and z axes are shown in Figure 9.13(b), the x' axis being normal to the paper. The origin O is the fixed point about which the body turns.

The torque about O resulting from the weight is of magnitude $mgl \sin \theta$, l being the distance from O to the center of mass C. This torque is about the x' axis, so that

$$\begin{aligned} N_{x'} &= mgl \sin \theta \\ N_{y'} &= 0 \\ N_{z'} &= 0 \end{aligned} \tag{9.35}$$

The components of the angular velocity of the body $\boldsymbol{\omega}$ are given by Equations 9.28. Hence the angular momentum of the gyroscope has the following components in the primed system:

$$\begin{aligned} L_{x'} &= I_{x'x'}\omega_{x'} = I\dot{\theta} \\ L_{y'} &= I_{y'y'}\omega_{y'} = I\dot{\varphi} \sin \theta \\ L_{z'} &= I_{z'z'}\omega_{z'} = I_s(\dot{\varphi} \cos \theta + \dot{\psi}) = I_s S \end{aligned} \tag{9.36}$$

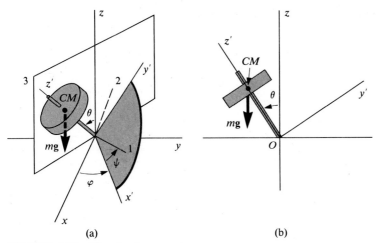

FIGURE 9.13   The simple gyroscope.

Here we use the same notation for the moments of inertia as in the previous section, and in the last equation above we have abbreviated the quantity $\omega_{z'} = \dot{\varphi}\cos\theta + \dot{\psi}$ by the letter S, called the *spin*.

The fundamental equation of motion in the primed system is

$$\mathbf{N} = \left(\frac{d\mathbf{L}}{dt}\right)_{rot} + \boldsymbol{\omega}' \times \mathbf{L} \tag{9.37}$$

in which the components of $\mathbf{N}$, $\mathbf{L}$, and $\boldsymbol{\omega}'$, are given by Equations 9.35, 9.36, and 9.27, respectively. Consequently, the component equations of motion are found to be the following:

$$mgl\sin\theta = I\ddot{\theta} + I_s S\dot{\varphi}\sin\theta - I\dot{\varphi}^2\cos\theta\sin\theta \tag{9.37a}$$

$$0 = I\frac{d}{dt}(\dot{\varphi}\sin\theta) - I_s S\dot{\theta} + I\dot{\theta}\dot{\varphi}\cos\theta \tag{9.37b}$$

$$0 = I_s\dot{S} \tag{9.37c}$$

The last equation shows that S, the spin of the body about the symmetry axis, remains constant. Also, of course, the component of the angular momentum along that axis is constant

$$L_{z'} = I_s S = \text{constant} \tag{9.38}$$

The second equation is then equivalent to

$$0 = \frac{d}{dt}(I\dot{\varphi}\sin^2\theta + I_s S\cos\theta) \tag{9.39}$$

so that

$$I\dot{\varphi}\sin^2\theta + I_s S\cos\theta = B = \text{constant} \tag{9.40}$$

Steady Precession of a Gyroscope

At this point we shall discuss a simple special case of gyroscopic motion, namely that of steady precession in a horizontal plane. This is the common "demonstration" case in which the axis remains horizontal and precesses at a constant rate around a vertical line, the z axis in our notation. Then we have $\theta = 90° = $ constant, $\dot{\theta} = \ddot{\theta} = 0$. Equation 9.37a then reduces to the simple relation

$$mgl = I_s S \dot{\phi} \tag{9.41}$$

Now it is easy to see that the quantity mgl is just the (scalar) torque about the x' axis. Furthermore, the horizontal (vector) component of the angular momentum has a magnitude of $I_s S$ and it describes a circle in the horizontal plane. Consequently, the extremity of the $\mathbf{L}$ vector has a velocity (time rate of change) of magnitude $I_s S \dot{\phi}$ *and a direction which is parallel to the x' axis.* Thus Equation 9.41 is simply a statement of the general relation $\mathbf{N} = d\mathbf{L}/dt$ for the special case in point.

The more general case of steady precession in which the angle θ is constant but has a value *other* than 90° is still handled by use of Equation 9.37a which gives, upon setting $\ddot{\theta} = 0$ and cancelling the common factor $\sin \theta$,

$$mgl = I_s S \dot{\phi} - I \dot{\phi}^2 \cos \theta \tag{9.42}$$

This is a quadratic equation in the unknown $\dot{\phi}$. Solving it yields two roots

$$\dot{\phi} = \frac{I_s S \pm (I_s^2 S^2 - 4mglI \cos \theta)^{1/2}}{2I \cos \theta} \tag{9.43}$$

Thus, for a given value of θ there are two possible rates of steady precession of the gyroscope: a fast precession (upper sign) and a slow precession (lower sign). Which of the two occurs depends on the initial conditions. Usually, it is the slower one that takes place in the motion of a simple top or gyroscope. In either case, the quantity in parentheses must be zero or positive for a physically possible solution, that is

$$I_s^2 S^2 \geq 4mglI \cos \theta \tag{9.44}$$

Sleeping Top

Anyone who has played with a top knows that if the top is set spinning sufficiently fast and is started in a vertical position, the axis of the top will remain steady in the upright position, a condition called *sleeping*. This corresponds to a constant value of zero for θ in the above equations. Since $\dot{\phi}$ must be real, we conclude that the criterion for stability of the sleeping top is given by

$$I_s^2 S^2 \geq 4mglI \tag{9.45}$$

If the top slows down through friction so that the above condition no longer holds, then it will begin to fall and will eventually topple over.

Examples

9.8   A toy gyroscope has a mass of 100 g and is made in the form of a uniform disc of radius $a = 2$ cm fastened to a light spindle, the center of the disc being 2 cm from the pivot. If the gyroscope is set spinning at a rate of 20 revolutions per second, find the period for steady horizontal precession.

Solution:

Using cgs units we have $I_s = \frac{1}{2}ma^2 = \frac{1}{2} \times 100 \text{ g} \times (2 \text{ cm})^2 = 200 \text{ g cm}^2$. For the spin we must convert revolutions per second to radians per second, that is, $S = 20 \times 2\pi$ radians per sec. Equation 9.41 then gives the precession rate

$$\dot{\varphi} = \frac{mgl}{I_s S} = \frac{100 \text{ g} \times 980 \text{ cms}^{-2} \times 2 \text{ cm}}{200 \text{ g cm}^2 \times 40 \times 3.142 \text{ s}^{-1}} = 7.8 \text{ s}^{-1}$$

in radians per second. The associated period is then

$$\frac{2\pi}{\dot{\varphi}} = \frac{2 \times 3.142}{7.8 \text{ s}^{-1}} = 0.81 \text{ sec}$$

9.9   Find the minimum spin of the above gyroscope in order that it can "sleep" in the vertical position.

Solution:

We need, in addition to the above values, the moment of inertia I about the x' or y' axes. By the parallel-axis theorem, we have $I = I_{x'x'} = I_{y'y'} = \frac{1}{4}ma^2 + ml^2 = \frac{1}{4}100 \text{ g} \times (2 \text{ cm})^2 + 100 \text{ g} \times (2 \text{ cm})^2 = 500 \text{ g cm}^2$.

From Equation 9.45, we can then write

$$S \geq \frac{2}{I_s}(mgII)^{1/2} = \frac{2}{200}(200 \times 980 \times 2 \times 500)^{1/2}\text{s}^{-1} = 140 \text{ s}^{-1}$$

or, in revolutions per second, the minimum spin is

$$S = \frac{140}{2\pi} = 22.3 \text{ rps}$$

The Energy Equation and Nutation

If there are no frictional forces acting on the gyroscope to dissipate its energy, then the total energy $T_{rot} + V$ remains constant:

$$\tfrac{1}{2}(I\omega_{x'}^2 + I\omega_{y'}^2 + I_s S^2) + mg\,h = E$$

or equivalently, in terms of the Eulerian angles,

$$\tfrac{1}{2}(I\dot{\theta}^2 + I\dot{\varphi}^2 \sin^2\theta + I_s S^2) + mgl \cos\theta = E \qquad (9.46)$$

From Equation 9.40, we can solve for $\dot{\varphi}$ and substitute into the above equation. The result is

$$\frac{1}{2}I\dot{\theta}^2 + \frac{(B - I_s S \cos\theta)^2}{2I \sin^2\theta} + \frac{1}{2}I_s S^2 + mgl \cos\theta = E \qquad (9.47)$$

which is entirely in terms of θ. This equation allows us, in principle, to find θ as a function of t by integration. Let us make the substitution

$$u = \cos\theta$$

Thus $\dot{u} = -(\sin \theta)\dot{\theta} = -(1 - u^2)^{1/2}\dot{\theta}$. We find that Equation 9.47 then becomes

$$\dot{u}^2 = (1 - u^2)(2E - I_s S^2 - 2mglu)I^{-1} - (B - I_s Su)^2 I^{-2} \qquad (9.47a)$$

or

$$\dot{u}^2 = f(u) \qquad (9.47b)$$

from which u (hence θ) can be found as a function of t by integration:

$$t = \int \frac{du}{\sqrt{f(u)}} \qquad (9.48)$$

Here $f(u)$ is a cubic polynomial, and the integration can be carried out in terms of elliptic functions.[1]
We need not actually perform the integration, however, to discuss the general properties of the motion. We see that $f(u)$ must be positive in order that t be real. Hence the limits of the motion in θ are determined by the roots of the equation $f(u) = 0$. Since θ must lie between 0 and 90 degrees, then u must take values between 0 and $+1$. A plot of $f(u)$ is shown in Figure 9.14a for the case in which there are two distinct roots u_1 and u_2 between 0 and $+1$. The corresponding values of θ, namely θ_1, and θ_2, are then the limits of the vertical motion. The axis of the top oscillates back and forth between these two values of θ as the top precesses about the vertical, Figure 9.15. This oscillation is called *nutation*. If we have a double root, that is, if $u_1 = u_2$, then there is no nutation and the top precesses steadily, Figure 9.14(b). The "sleeping" case is shown in Figure 9.14(c).

9.7   The Gyrocompass

Let us consider the motion of a gyroscope that is mounted on a gimbal support that constrains the spin axis to remain horizontal, but the axis is otherwise free to turn in any direction. The situation is diagrammed in Figure 9.16 which is taken from Figure 9.13 except that now $\theta = 90°$ and the unprimed axes are labeled to correspond to directions on the earth's surface as shown. The gyroscope is centrally mounted so that $l = 0$.
We know from Chapter 5 that the earth's angular velocity, here denoted by ω_e, has components $\omega_e \cos \lambda$ (north) and $\omega_e \sin \lambda$ (vertical) where λ is the latitude. In the primed coordinate system we can then write

$$\omega_e = \mathbf{i}'\omega_e \cos \lambda \cos \varphi + \mathbf{j}'\omega_e \sin \lambda + \mathbf{k}'\omega_e \cos \lambda \sin \varphi \qquad (9.49)$$

Now the primed system is turning about the vertical with angular rate $\dot{\varphi}$ so the angular velocity of the primed system is

$$\boldsymbol{\omega}' = \boldsymbol{\omega}_e + \mathbf{j}'\dot{\varphi} = \mathbf{i}'\omega_e \cos \lambda \cos \varphi + \mathbf{j}'(\dot{\varphi} + \omega_e \sin \lambda) + \mathbf{k}'\omega_e \cos \lambda \sin \varphi \qquad (9.50)$$

---

[1] See reference cited in footnote 1 (Table 8.2) in previous chapter.

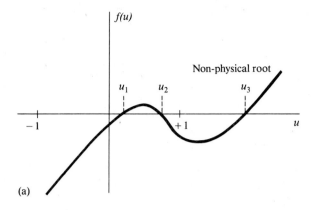

(a)

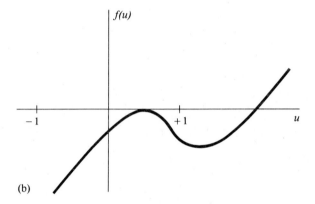

(b)

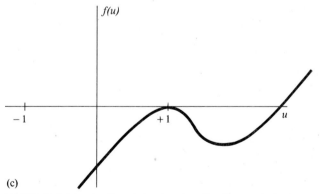

(c)

FIGURE 9.14   Graphs of the function $f(u)$ for a spinning top or simple gyroscope. (a) Two distinct roots: regular nutation. (b) Two equal roots: steady precession. (c) Condition for the "sleeping top."

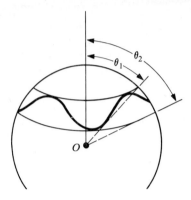

FIGURE 9.15   Illustrating nutation.

Similarly, the gyroscope itself is turning about the z' axis at a rate $\dot{\psi}$ superimposed on the above components so that the angular velocity of the gyroscope, referred to the primed system, is

$$\boldsymbol{\omega} = \boldsymbol{\omega}' + \mathbf{k}'\dot{\psi} = \mathbf{i}'\omega_e \cos\lambda \cos\varphi + \mathbf{j}'(\dot{\varphi} + \omega_e \sin\lambda) + \mathbf{k}'(\dot{\psi} + \omega_e \cos\lambda \sin\varphi) \tag{9.51}$$

The principal moments of inertia of the gyroscope are, as before, $I_1 = I_2 = I$, $I_3 = I_s$. Hence the angular momentum can be expressed as

$$\mathbf{L} = \mathbf{i}'I\omega_e \cos\lambda \cos\varphi + \mathbf{j}'I(\dot{\varphi} + \omega_e \sin\lambda) + \mathbf{k}'I_s S \tag{9.52}$$

where, in the last term, the total spin S is

$$S = \dot{\psi} + \omega_e \cos\lambda \sin\varphi$$

Now, since the gyroscope is free to turn about both the vertical (y' axis) and the spin or z' axis, the applied torque required to keep the axis horizontal must be about the x' axis: $\mathbf{N} = \mathbf{i}'N$. The equation of motion

$$\mathbf{N} = \left(\frac{d\mathbf{L}}{dt}\right)_{rot} + \boldsymbol{\omega}' \times \mathbf{L} \tag{9.53}$$

thus has components referred to the primed system as follows:

$$N = I\frac{d}{dt}(\omega_e \cos\lambda \cos\varphi) + (\boldsymbol{\omega}' \times \mathbf{L})_{x'} \tag{9.53a}$$

$$0 = I\frac{d}{dt}(\dot{\varphi} + \omega_e \sin\lambda) + (\boldsymbol{\omega}' \times \mathbf{L})_{y'} \tag{9.53b}$$

$$0 = I_s\frac{dS}{dt} + (\boldsymbol{\omega}' \times \mathbf{L})_{z'} \tag{9.53c}$$

From the expressions for $\boldsymbol{\omega}'$ and $\mathbf{L}$, we find that $(\boldsymbol{\omega}' \times \mathbf{L})_{z'} = 0$, so the last equation becomes $dS/dt = 0$. Thus S is constant. Further, we find that the second equation becomes

$$0 = I\ddot{\varphi} + I\omega_e^2 \cos^2\lambda \cos\varphi \sin\varphi - I_s S\omega_e \cos\lambda \cos\varphi \tag{9.54}$$

It is convenient at this point to express the angle φ in terms of its complement $\chi = 90° - \varphi$, so $\cos \varphi = \sin \chi$ and $\ddot{\varphi} = -\ddot{\chi}$. Furthermore, we can neglect the term involving ω_e^2 in the above equation because $S \gg \omega_e$ in the present case. Consequently, the equation reduces to

$$\ddot{\chi} + \left(\frac{I_s S \omega_e \cos \lambda}{I} \right) \sin \chi = 0 \tag{9.54a}$$

This is similar to the differential equation for a pendulum. The variable χ oscillates

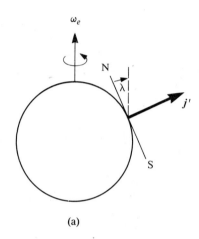

(a)

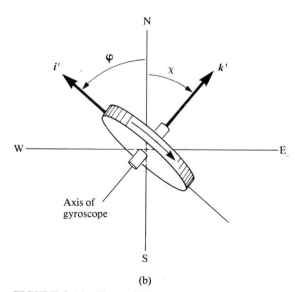

(b)

FIGURE 9.16   The gyrocompass.

about the value $\chi = 0$, and the presence of any damping will cause the axis of the gyroscope to "seek" and eventually settle down to a north-south direction. For small amplitude the period of the oscillation is

$$T_0 = 2\pi \left(\frac{I}{I_s \omega_e S \cos \lambda} \right)^{1/2} \tag{9.55}$$

Since the ratio I_s/I is very nearly 2 for any "flat-type" symmetric object, the period of oscillation is essentially independent of the mass and dimensions of the gyroscope. Further, since ω_e is very small the spin S must be fairly large in order to have a reasonably small period. For example, let $S = 60$ revolutions per second $= 2\pi \times 60$ rad/sec. Then, for a flat-type gyroscope, we find for a latitude of 45° N

$$T_0 = 2\pi \left(\frac{24 \times 60 \times 60}{2 \times 2\pi \times 60 \times 2\pi \times 0.707} \right)^{1/2} \sec = \left(\frac{12 \times 60}{0.707} \right)^{1/2} s = 31.9 \text{ s}$$

or about 1/2 min. In the above calculation we have used the fact that $\omega_e = 2\pi/(24 \times 60 \times 60)$ rad per sec so that the factors 2π all cancel.

9.8   General Motion of a Rigid Body. Rolling Wheel

As we have seen, the general motion of any system can be resolved into two parts: (1) the translational motion of the center of mass, governed by the equation $\mathbf{F} = m d\mathbf{v}_{cm}/dt$, and (2) the rotation about the center of mass, determined by $\mathbf{N} = d\mathbf{L}/dt$. As an example we shall discuss the motion of a wheel or disc rolling on a perfectly rough horizontal surface. The external forces are the weight $m\mathbf{g}$ acting at the center and the reaction $\mathbf{F}_P$ at the point of contact, Figure 9.17. The general equations of motion are then $\mathbf{F}_P + m\mathbf{g} = m d\mathbf{v}_{cm}/dt$ and $\mathbf{r}_{OP} \times \mathbf{F}_P = d\mathbf{L}/dt$. Elimination of $\mathbf{F}_P$ between the two equations yields the single equation

$$\mathbf{r}_{OP} \times \left(m\frac{d\mathbf{v}_{cm}}{dt} - m\mathbf{g} \right) = \frac{d\mathbf{L}}{dt} \tag{9.56}$$

If $\boldsymbol{\omega}$ is the angular velocity of the wheel, then the velocity of the mass center is given by

$$\mathbf{v}_{cm} = \boldsymbol{\omega} \times \mathbf{r}_{PO} = \boldsymbol{\omega} \times (-\mathbf{r}_{OP})$$

Now, in the primed coordinate system $\mathbf{r}_{OP} = -\mathbf{j}'a$, and $\mathbf{g} = -g(\mathbf{j}' \sin \theta + \mathbf{k}' \cos \theta)$, in which a is the radius and θ is the inclination of the wheel's axis to the vertical, as shown. Further, we have a rotating coordinate system, so we must write $d/dt = d/dt)_{rot} + \boldsymbol{\omega}' \times$ where $\boldsymbol{\omega}'$ is the angular velocity of the primed system. Equation 9.56 then becomes

$$-ma^2\mathbf{j}' \times \left[\left(\frac{d\boldsymbol{\omega}}{dt} \right)_{rot} \times \mathbf{j}' + \boldsymbol{\omega}' \times (\boldsymbol{\omega} \times \mathbf{j}') \right] - mga[\mathbf{j}' \times (\mathbf{j}' \sin \theta + \mathbf{k}' \cos \theta)]$$

$$= \left(\frac{d\mathbf{L}}{dt} \right)_{rot} + \boldsymbol{\omega}' \times \mathbf{L} \tag{9.57}$$

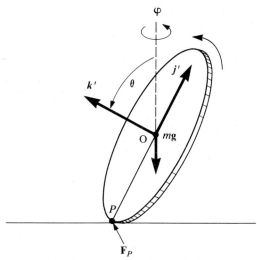

FIGURE 9.17   Coordinates for analyzing the motion of a rolling wheel.

We shall not attempt to solve the above general equation of motion. Rather, we wish to discuss a special case, namely that for which the wheel stays very nearly vertical and the direction of the rolling motion is constant or nearly constant: *steady rolling*. This means that θ remains close to 90° so that the complement $\chi = 90° - \theta$ and the angle φ both remain small. Under these assumptions $\sin \chi = \chi$ and $\sin \varphi = \varphi$, approximately, and the general expressions for the components of $\boldsymbol{\omega}'$, $\boldsymbol{\omega}$, and $\mathbf{L}$, as given by Equations 9.27, 9.28, and 9.36, simplify to give

$$\boldsymbol{\omega}' = -\mathbf{i}'\dot{\chi} + \mathbf{j}'\dot{\varphi} \tag{9.58}$$

$$\boldsymbol{\omega} = -\mathbf{i}'\dot{\chi} + \mathbf{j}'\dot{\varphi} + \mathbf{k}'S \tag{9.59}$$

$$\mathbf{L} = -\mathbf{i}'I\dot{\chi} + \mathbf{j}'I\dot{\varphi} + \mathbf{k}'I_sS \tag{9.60}$$

Inserting these into Equation 9.57 and performing the indicated operations and dropping higher order terms in the small quantities χ and φ, the following result is obtained:

$$ma^2(\mathbf{i}'\ddot{\chi} - \mathbf{k}'\dot{S} - \mathbf{i}'S\dot{\varphi}) - mgai'\chi = \mathbf{i}'(I\ddot{\chi} + T_sS\dot{\varphi})$$
$$+ \mathbf{j}'(I\ddot{\varphi} + I_sS\dot{\chi}) + \mathbf{k}'I_s\dot{S} \tag{9.61}$$

Equating the three components gives

$$ma^2(\ddot{\chi} - S\dot{\varphi}) - mga\chi = -I\ddot{\chi} + I_sS\dot{\varphi} \tag{9.61a}$$

$$0 = I\ddot{\varphi} + I_sS\dot{\chi} \tag{9.61b}$$

$$-ma^2\dot{S} = I_s\dot{S} \tag{9.61c}$$

The last of the three equations shows that $\dot{S} = 0$ so S is constant. The second equation can then be integrated to yield $I\dot{\varphi} + I_sS\chi = 0$ provided we assume that $\chi = \dot{\varphi} = 0$ for the initial condition. Then $\dot{\varphi} = -I_sS\chi/I$, which, inserted into the first equation gives the following separated differential equation for χ:

$$I(I + ma^2)\ddot{\chi} + [I_s(I_s + ma^2)S^2 - Imga]\chi = 0 \tag{9.62}$$

It follows that the assumed stable rolling will take place if the quantity in brackets is positive. Thus the stability criterion is

$$S^2 > \frac{Imga}{I_s(I_s + ma^2)} \tag{9.63}$$

Example

9.10 *Rolling Penny.* How fast must a penny ($a = 0.95$ cm) roll in order to remain upright?

Solution:

Assuming the penny to be a uniform thin lamina, we have $I_s = 2I = \frac{1}{2}ma^2$, so the criterion for stable rolling is

$$S^2 > \frac{mga}{2\left(\frac{1}{2}ma^2 + ma^2\right)} = \frac{g}{3a}$$

Since the rolling speed is $v = v_{cm} = aS$, the above criterion can be expressed alternatively as

$$v^2 > \frac{ga}{3}$$

Thus

$$v > \left(\frac{980 \text{ cm s}^{-2} \times 0.95 \text{ cm}}{3}\right)^{1/2} = 17.6 \text{ cm/sec}$$

*9.9   Use of Matrices in Rigid Body Dynamics. The Inertia Tensor

Many of the equations that have been derived in this chapter can be simply and conveniently written in matrix form. Thus, consider the general expression for the angular momentum, Equation 9.6. In matrix notation this equation reads

$$\begin{bmatrix} L_x \\ L_y \\ L_z \end{bmatrix} = \begin{bmatrix} I_{xx} & I_{xy} & I_{xz} \\ I_{yx} & I_{yy} & I_{yz} \\ I_{zx} & I_{zy} & I_{zz} \end{bmatrix} \begin{bmatrix} \omega_x \\ \omega_y \\ \omega_z \end{bmatrix} \tag{9.64}$$

Here, as in the treatment of coordinate transformations in Section 1.8, vectors are represented by column matrices. The 3×3 matrix involving the moments and products of inertia embodies a complete characterization of a rigid body with respect to its rotational properties. This matrix is called the *inertia tensor*. Let us introduce the symbol **I** for the inertia tensor. Then the above equation for the angular momentum may be written simply as

$$\mathbf{L} = \mathbf{I}\boldsymbol{\omega} \tag{9.65}$$

in which it is understood that the vectors **L** and $\boldsymbol{\omega}$ are column matrices.

Kinetic Energy

The general expression for rotational kinetic energy of a rigid body, Equation 9.10, is easily shown to be given by the matrix expression

$$T_{rot} = \tfrac{1}{2}[\omega_x \omega_y \omega_z] \begin{bmatrix} I_{xx} & I_{xy} & I_{xz} \\ I_{yx} & I_{yy} & I_{yz} \\ I_{zx} & I_{zy} & I_{zz} \end{bmatrix} \begin{bmatrix} \omega_x \\ \omega_y \\ \omega_z \end{bmatrix} \tag{9.66}$$

or, in abbreviated form,

$$T_{rot} = \tfrac{1}{2}\boldsymbol{\omega}^{\mathrm{T}}\mathbf{I}\boldsymbol{\omega} \tag{9.67}$$

Here the row matrix $\boldsymbol{\omega}^{\mathrm{T}}$ is the transpose matrix of the column matrix $\boldsymbol{\omega}$, and $\mathbf{I}$ is the inertia tensor defined above.

Principal Axes

If the coordinate axes are principal axes of the body, then the inertia tensor takes the diagonal form

$$\mathbf{I} = \begin{bmatrix} I_1 & 0 & 0 \\ 0 & I_2 & 0 \\ 0 & 0 & I_3 \end{bmatrix} \tag{9.68}$$

Evidently, the general problem of finding the principal axes of a rigid body is equivalent to the mathematical problem of diagonalizing a 3×3 matrix. From matrix theory, it is known that any symmetric square matrix can be diagonalized. In our case $I_{xy} = I_{yx}$, and similarly for the other pairs. Hence the matrix is symmetric, and so there must exist a set of principal axes at any point.

The diagonalization is accomplished by finding the roots of the determinantal equation

$$|\mathbf{I} - \lambda\mathbf{1}| = 0$$

where $\mathbf{1}$ is the unit matrix. Explicitly, this equation reads

$$\begin{vmatrix} I_{xx} - \lambda & I_{xy} & I_{xz} \\ I_{yx} & I_{yy} - \lambda & I_{yz} \\ I_{zx} & I_{zy} & I_{zz} - \lambda \end{vmatrix} = 0 \tag{9.69}$$

It is a cubic in λ, namely

$$-\lambda^3 + A\lambda^2 + B\lambda + C = 0 \tag{9.70}$$

in which A, B, and C are simple functions of the I's. The three roots, λ_1, λ_2, and λ_3 are the three principal moments of inertia.

In order to find the orientation of the principal axes, we make use of the physical fact that when the body is rotating about one of its principal axes, the angular momentum vector is in the same direction as the angular velocity vector. Let the direction angles of one of the principal axes be α, β, and γ, and let the body rotate with angular velocity $\boldsymbol{\omega}$ about this axis. The angular momentum is then given by

$$\mathbf{L} = \lambda\boldsymbol{\omega} = \mathbf{I}\boldsymbol{\omega} \tag{9.71}$$

in which λ is one of the three roots λ_1, λ_2, or λ_3. Explicitly, the above equation reads

$$\begin{bmatrix} \lambda\omega\cos\alpha \\ \lambda\omega\cos\beta \\ \lambda\omega\cos\gamma \end{bmatrix} = \begin{bmatrix} I_{xx} & I_{xy} & I_{xz} \\ I_{yx} & I_{yy} & I_{yz} \\ I_{zx} & I_{zy} & I_{zz} \end{bmatrix} \begin{bmatrix} \omega\cos\alpha \\ \omega\cos\beta \\ \omega\cos\gamma \end{bmatrix} \tag{9.72}$$

In turn, this equation is equivalent to the three scalar equations

$$\begin{aligned} (I_{xx} - \lambda)\cos\alpha + I_{xy}\cos\beta + I_{xz}\cos\gamma &= 0 \\ I_{yx}\cos\alpha + (I_{yy} - \lambda)\cos\beta + I_{yz}\cos\gamma &= 0 \\ I_{zx}\cos\alpha + I_{zy}\cos\beta + (I_{zz} - \lambda)\cos\gamma &= 0 \end{aligned} \tag{9.73}$$

in which the common factor ω has been cancelled out. Thus the direction cosines of the principal axes can be found by solving the above equations. The roots are not independent, for they must clearly satisfy the condition

$$\cos^2\alpha + \cos^2\beta + \cos^2\gamma = 1 \tag{9.74}$$

Notice that Equation 9.69 is just the vanishing of the determinant of the coefficients of the cosines in Equations 9.73, i.e., the condition that a solution for the direction cosines exists.

Examples

9.11 **(a)** Find the inertia tensor for a square plate of side a and mass m in a coordinate system $Oxyz$ where O is at one corner and the x and y axes are along the two edges. Utilizing the results of Example 9.1, we have $I_{xx} = I_{yy} = ma^2/3$, $I_{zz} = 2ma^2/3$, $I_{xy} = -ma^2/4$, $I_{xz} = I_{yz} = 0$. Hence the inertia tensor is

$$\mathbf{I} = \begin{bmatrix} ma^2/3 & -ma^2/4 & 0 \\ -ma^2/4 & ma^2/3 & 0 \\ 0 & 0 & 2ma^2/3 \end{bmatrix} = \frac{ma^2}{3} \begin{bmatrix} 1 & -\frac{3}{4} & 0 \\ -\frac{3}{4} & 1 & 0 \\ 0 & 0 & 2 \end{bmatrix}$$

(b) Find the angular momentum of the above plate when it is rotating about a diagonal. In this case, the angular velocity vector can be expressed as the column matrix

$$\boldsymbol{\omega} = \begin{bmatrix} \omega_x \\ \omega_y \\ \omega_z \end{bmatrix} = \begin{bmatrix} \omega/\sqrt{2} \\ \omega/\sqrt{2} \\ 0 \end{bmatrix} = \frac{\omega}{\sqrt{2}} \begin{bmatrix} 1 \\ 1 \\ 0 \end{bmatrix}$$

Consequently, the angular momentum is

$$\mathbf{L} = \mathbf{I}\boldsymbol{\omega} = \frac{ma^2\omega}{3\sqrt{2}} \begin{bmatrix} 1 & -\frac{3}{4} & 0 \\ -\frac{3}{4} & 1 & 0 \\ 0 & 0 & 2 \end{bmatrix} \begin{bmatrix} 1 \\ 1 \\ 0 \end{bmatrix}$$

$$= \frac{ma^2\omega}{3\sqrt{2}} \begin{bmatrix} \frac{1}{4} \\ \frac{1}{4} \\ 0 \end{bmatrix} = \frac{ma^2\omega}{12\sqrt{2}} \begin{bmatrix} 1 \\ 1 \\ 0 \end{bmatrix}$$

(c) Find the kinetic energy of rotation in the above problem. Using the above results, we have

$$T_{rot} = \frac{1}{2} \boldsymbol{\omega}^T \mathbf{I} \boldsymbol{\omega} = \frac{1}{2} \boldsymbol{\omega}^T \mathbf{L} = \frac{ma^2\omega^2}{48} [1 \quad 1 \quad 0] \begin{bmatrix} 1 \\ 1 \\ 0 \end{bmatrix}$$

$$= \frac{ma^2\omega^2}{24}$$

9.12 **(a)** Find the principal moments of inertia of a square plate about a corner. Here Equation 9.69 reads

$$\begin{vmatrix} \tfrac{1}{3}ma^2 - \lambda & -\tfrac{1}{4}ma^2 & 0 \\ -\tfrac{1}{4}ma^2 & \tfrac{1}{3}ma^2 - \lambda & 0 \\ 0 & 0 & \tfrac{2}{3}ma^2 - \lambda \end{vmatrix} = 0$$

or

$$[(\tfrac{1}{3}ma^2 - \lambda)^2 - (\tfrac{1}{4}ma^2)^2](\tfrac{2}{3}ma^2 - \lambda) = 0$$

The second factor gives

$$\lambda = \tfrac{2}{3}ma^2$$

for one of the principal moments. The first factor gives

$$\tfrac{1}{3}ma^2 - \lambda = \pm \tfrac{1}{4}ma^2$$

or

$$\lambda = \tfrac{7}{12}ma^2$$

and

$$\lambda = \tfrac{1}{12}ma^2$$

These three values of λ are the three principal moments.

(b) Find the directions of the principal axes for the above problem. Equations 9.73 give

$$(\tfrac{1}{3}ma^2 - \lambda) \cos \alpha - \tfrac{1}{4}ma^2 \cos \beta = 0$$
$$-\tfrac{1}{4}ma^2 \cos \alpha + (\tfrac{1}{3}ma^2 - \lambda) \cos \beta = 0$$
$$(\tfrac{2}{3}ma^2 - \lambda) \cos \gamma = 0$$

From the last equation we see that $\gamma = 90°$ is one root. If we set λ equal to $\tfrac{1}{12}ma^2$, the first equation becomes

$$\cos \alpha - \cos \beta = 0$$

This, together with Equation 9.74 gives

$$2 \cos^2 \alpha = 1$$

or, taking the positive root, we have $\alpha = 45°$ for one principal axis. The other is given by taking the negative root, that is $\alpha = 135°$. Thus one principal axis is along the diagonal, the other perpendicular to the diagonal and in the plane of the plate, and the third principal axis is normal to the plate. If we label these the *1*, *2*, and *3* axes, respectively, then the inertia tensor in these axes is

$$\mathbf{I} = \begin{bmatrix} \tfrac{1}{12} & 0 & 0 \\ 0 & \tfrac{7}{12} & 0 \\ 0 & 0 & \tfrac{2}{3} \end{bmatrix} ma^2$$

PROBLEMS

9.1   A thin uniform rectangular plate (lamina) is of mass m and dimensions $2a$ by a. Choose a coordinate system $Oxyz$ such that the plate lies in the xy plane with origin at a corner, the long dimension being along the x axis. Find the following:

(a) The moments and products of inertia.
(b) The moment of inertia about the diagonal through the origin.
(c) The angular momentum about the origin if the plate is spinning with angular rate ω about the diagonal through the origin.
(d) The kinetic energy in part (c).

9.2   A "rigid body" consists of three thin uniform rods, each of mass m and length $2a$, held mutually perpendicular at their midpoints. Choose a coordinate system with axes along the rods. **(a)** Find the angular momentum and kinetic energy of the body if it rotates with angular velocity $\boldsymbol{\omega}$ about an axis passing through the origin and the point $(1,1,1)$. **(b)** Show that the moment of inertia is the same for *any* axis passing through the origin. **(c)** Show that the moment of inertia of a uniform square lamina is that given in Example 9.1 for *any* axis passing through the center of the lamina and lying in the plane of the lamina.

9.3   Find a set of principal axes for the lamina of Problem 9.1 in which the origin is **(a)** at a corner, and **(b)** at the center of the lamina.

9.4   A uniform block of mass m and dimensions a by $2a$ by $3a$ spins about a long diagonal with angular velocity $\boldsymbol{\omega}$. Find **(a)** the kinetic energy and **(b)** the angle between the angular velocity vector and the angular momentum vector about the origin, using a coordinate system with origin at the center of the block.

9.5   A thin uniform rod of length l and mass m is constrained to rotate with constant angular velocity $\boldsymbol{\omega}$ about an axis passing through the center O of the rod and making an angle α with the rod. **(a)** Show that the angular momentum $\mathbf{L}$ about O is perpendicular to the rod and is of magnitude $(ml^2\omega/12) \sin \alpha$. **(b)** Show that the torque vector $\mathbf{N}$ is perpendicular to the rod and to $\mathbf{L}$, and is of magnitude $(ml^2\omega^2/12) \sin \alpha \cos \alpha$.

9.6   Find the magnitude of the torque that must be exerted on the block in Problem 9.4 if the angular velocity $\boldsymbol{\omega}$ is constant in magnitude and direction.

9.7   A rigid body of arbitrary shape rotates freely under zero torque. By means of Euler's equations show that both the rotational kinetic energy and the magnitude of the angular momentum are constant, as stated in Section 9.4. [*Hint:* For $\mathbf{N} = 0$, multiply Euler's equations (9.16b) by ω_1, ω_2, and ω_3, respectively, and add the three equations. The result indicates the constancy of kinetic energy. Next, multiply by $I_1\omega_1$, $I_2\omega_2$, and $I_3\omega_3$, respectively, and add. The result shows that L^2 is constant.]

9.8   A lamina of arbitrary shape rotates freely under zero torque. Use Euler's equations to show that the sum $\omega_1^2 + \omega_2^2$ is constant if the *1, 2* plane is the plane of the lamina. This means that the projection of $\boldsymbol{\omega}$ on the plane of the lamina is constant in magnitude, although the component ω_3 normal to the plane is not necessarily constant. (*Hint:* Use the perpendicular axis theorem.) What kind of lamina gives $\omega_3 = $ constant as well?

9.9   A square plate of side a and mass m is thrown into the air so that it rotates freely under zero torque. The rotational period $2\pi/\omega$ is 1 sec. If the axis of rotation makes an angle of $45°$ with the symmetry axis of the plate, find the period of the precession of the axis of rotation about the symmetry axis and the period of wobble of the symmetry axis about the invariable line for two cases **(a)** a thin plate and **(b)** a thick plate of thickness $a/4$.

9.10 A rigid body having an axis of symmetry rotates freely about a fixed point under no torques. If α is the angle between the axis of symmetry and the instantaneous axis of rotation, show that the angle between the axis of rotation and the invariable line (the **L** vector) is

$$\tan^{-1}\left[\frac{(I_s - I)\tan\alpha}{I_s + I\tan^2\alpha}\right]$$

where I_s (the moment of inertia about the symmetry axis) is greater than I (the moment of inertia about an axis normal to the symmetry axis).

9.11 Since the greatest value of the ratio $I_s/I = 2$ (symmetrical lamina), show from the result of the above problem that the angle between $\boldsymbol{\omega}$ and **L** cannot exceed $\tan^{-1}(1/\sqrt{8})$ or about 19.5°, and that the corresponding value of α is $\tan^{-1}\sqrt{2}$ or about 54.7°.

9.12 Find the angle between $\boldsymbol{\omega}$ and **L** for the two cases in Problem 9.9.

9.13 Find the same angle for the earth.

9.14 A space platform in the form of a thin circular disc of radius a and mass m (flying saucer) is initially rotating steadily with angular velocity $\boldsymbol{\omega}$ about its symmetry axis. A meteorite strikes the platform at the edge, imparting an impulse $\hat{\mathbf{P}}$ to the platform. The direction of $\hat{\mathbf{P}}$ is parallel to the axis of the platform, and the magnitude of $\hat{\mathbf{P}}$ is equal to $ma\omega/4$. Find the resulting values of the precessional rate Ω, the wobble rate $\dot{\phi}$, and the angle α between the symmetry axis and the new axis of rotation.

9.15 A Frisbee is thrown into the air in such a way that it has a definite wobble. If air friction exerts a frictional torque $-c\boldsymbol{\omega}$ on the rotation of the frisbee, show that the component of $\boldsymbol{\omega}$ in the direction of the symmetry axis decreases exponentially with time. Show also that the angle α between the symmetry axis and the angular velocity vector $\boldsymbol{\omega}$ decreases with time if I_s is larger than I, which is the case for a flat-type object. Thus the degree of wobble steadily diminishes if there is air friction.

9.16 A simple gyroscope consists of a heavy circular disc of mass m and radius a mounted at the center of a thin rod of mass $m/2$ and length a. If the gyroscope is set spinning at a given rate S, and with the axis at an angle of 45° with the vertical, there are two possible values of the precession rate $\dot{\phi}$ such that the gyroscope precesses steadily at a constant value of $\theta = 45°$. **(a)** Find the two numerical values of $\dot{\phi}$ when $S = 900$ rpm and $a = 10$ cm. **(b)** How fast must the gyroscope spin in order to "sleep" in the vertical position? Express the results in rpm.

9.17 A pencil is set spinning in an upright position. How fast must the spin be in order that the pencil will remain in the upright position? Assume that the pencil is a uniform cylinder of length a and diameter b. Find the value of the spin in revolutions per second for $a = 20$ cm and $b = 1$ cm.

9.18 A bicycle wheel of diameter 30 in. rolls along the ground. How fast must it roll in order to remain upright? Assume that half the mass of the wheel is on the periphery (rim), one fourth of the mass is in the spokes, and the remainder is concentrated at the center (hub). Compare the result with that obtained if the spokes and hub are neglected.

9.19 A rigid body rotates freely under zero torque. By differentiating the first of Euler's equations with respect to t, and eliminating $\dot{\omega}_2$ and $\dot{\omega}_3$ by means of the second and third of Euler's equations, show that the following result is obtained:

$$\ddot{\omega}_1 + K_1\omega_1 = 0$$

in which the function K_1 is given by

$$K_1 = -\omega_2^2[(I_3 - I_2)(I_2 - I_1)/I_1 I_3] + \omega_3^2[(I_3 - I_2)(I_3 - I_1)/I_1 I_2]$$

Two similar pairs of equations are obtained by cyclic permutations: $1 \rightarrow 2, 2 \rightarrow 3, 3 \rightarrow 1$. In the above expression for K_1 both quantities in brackets are *positive constants* if $I_1 < I_2 < I_3$, or if $I_1 > I_2 > I_3$. Discuss the question of the growth of ω_1 (stability) if initially ω_1 is very small and (a) $\omega_2 = 0$ and ω_3 is large: initial rotation is very nearly about the 3-axis, and (b) $\omega_3 = 0$ and ω_2 is large: initial rotation is nearly about the 2-axis. (*Note:* This is an analytical method of deducing the stability criteria illustrated in Figure 9.8.)

9.20 A "rigid body" consists of six particles, each of mass m, fixed to the ends of three light rods of length $2a$, $2b$, and $2c$, respectively, the rods being held mutually perpendicular to one another at their midpoints. (a) Show that a set of coordinate axes defined by the rods are principal axes, and write down the inertia tensor for the system in these axes. (b) Use matrix algebra to find the angular momentum and the kinetic energy of the system when it is rotating with angular velocity $\boldsymbol{\omega}$ about an axis passing through the origin and the point (a,b,c).

9.21 Work Problems 9.1 and 9.4 using matrix methods.

9.22 A uniform rectangular block of dimensions $2a$ by $2b$ by $2c$ and mass m spins about a long diagonal. Find the inertia tensor for a coordinate system with origin at the center of the block and with axes normal to the faces. Find also the angular momentum and the kinetic energy. Find also the inertia tensor for axes with origin at one corner.

10

Lagrangian
Mechanics

The direct application of Newton's laws to the motion of simple systems will now be supplemented by a general, more sophisticated approach—a very elegant and useful method for finding the equations of motion for all dynamical systems, invented by the French mathematician Joseph Louis Lagrange.

10.1 Generalized Coordinates

We have seen that the position of a particle in space can be specified by three coordinates. These may be Cartesian, spherical, cylindrical, or, in fact, any three suitably chosen parameters. If the particle is constrained to move in a plane or on a fixed surface, only two coordinates are needed to specify the particle's position, whereas if the particle moves on a straight line or on a fixed curve, then one coordinate is sufficient.

In the case of a system of N particles we need, in general, $3N$ coordinates to specify completely the simultaneous positions of all the particles—the *configuration* of the system. If there are constraints imposed on the system, however, the number of coordinates actually needed to specify the configuration is less than $3N$. For instance, if the system is a rigid body, we need give only the position of some convenient reference point of the body (for example, the center of mass) and the orientation of the body in space in order to specify the configuration. In this case only six coordinates are needed—three for the reference point and three more (say the Eulerian angles) for the orientation.

In general, a certain minimum number n of coordinates is required to specify the configuration of a given system. We shall designate these coordinates by the symbols

$$q_1, \ q_2, \ \ldots, \ q_n$$

called *generalized coordinates*. A given coordinate q_k may be either an angle or a distance. If, in addition to specifying the configuration of the system, each coordinate can vary independently of the others, the system is said to be *holonomic*. The number of coordinates n in this case is also the number of *degrees of freedom* of the system.

In a nonholonomic system the coordinates cannot all vary independently; that is, the number of degrees of freedom is less than the minimum number of coordinates needed to specify the configuration. An example of a nonholonomic system is a sphere constrained to roll on a perfectly rough plane. Five coordinates are required to specify the configuration—two for the position of the center of the sphere and three for its orientation. But the coordinates cannot all vary independently, for, if the sphere rolls, at least two coordinates must change. For the present, we shall consider only holonomic systems.

If the system is a single particle, the Cartesian coordinates are expressible as functions of the generalized coordinates:

$$x = x(q) \qquad \text{\textit{(one degree of freedom—motion on a curve)}}$$

$$
\begin{aligned}
x &= x(q_1, q_2) \\
y &= y(q_1, q_2)
\end{aligned}
\qquad \text{\textit{(two degrees of freedom—motion on a surface)}}
$$

$$
\begin{aligned}
x &= x(q_1, q_2, q_3) \\
y &= y(q_1, q_2, q_3) \\
z &= z(q_1, q_2, q_3)
\end{aligned}
\qquad \text{\textit{(three degrees of freedom—motion in space)}}
$$

Suppose that the q's change from initial values $(q_1, q_2, \ldots)$ to the neighboring values $(q_1 + \delta q_1, q_2 + \delta q_2, \ldots)$. The corresponding changes in the Cartesian coordinates are given by

$$\delta x = \frac{\partial x}{\partial q_1}\delta q_1 + \frac{\partial x}{\partial q_2}\delta q_2 + \ \cdots$$

$$\delta y = \frac{\partial y}{\partial q_1}\delta q_1 + \frac{\partial y}{\partial q_2}\delta q_2 + \ \cdots$$

and so on. The partial derivatives $\partial x / \partial q_1$, and so on, are functions of the q's. As a specific example, consider the motion of a particle in a plane. Let us choose polar coordinates

$$q_1 = r \qquad q_2 = \theta$$

Then

$$
\begin{aligned}
x &= x(r, \theta) = r \cos \theta \\
y &= y(r, \theta) = r \sin \theta
\end{aligned}
$$

and

$$\delta x = \frac{\partial x}{\partial r}\,\delta r + \frac{\partial x}{\partial \theta}\,\delta\theta = \cos\theta\,\delta r - r\sin\theta\,\delta\theta$$

$$\delta y = \frac{\partial y}{\partial r}\,\delta r + \frac{\partial y}{\partial \theta}\,\delta\theta = \sin\theta\,\delta r + r\cos\theta\,\delta\theta$$

giving the changes in x and y that correspond to small changes in r and θ.

Consider now a system consisting of a large number of particles. Let the system have n degrees of freedom and generalized coordinates

$$q_1, q_2, \ldots, q_n$$

Then, in a change from the configuration $(q_1, q_2, \ldots, q_n)$, to the neighboring configuration $(q_1 + \delta q_1, \ldots, q_n + \delta q_n)$, a representative particle i moves from the point (x_i, y_i, z_i) to the neighboring point $(x_i + \delta x_i, y_i + \delta y_i, z_i + \delta z_i)$ where

$$\delta x_i = \sum_{k=1}^{n} \frac{\partial x_i}{\partial q_k}\,\delta q_k$$

$$\delta y_i = \sum_{k=1}^{n} \frac{\partial y_i}{\partial q_k}\,\delta q_k$$

$$\delta z_i = \sum_{k=1}^{n} \frac{\partial z_i}{\partial q_k}\,\delta q_k$$

The partial derivatives are again functions of the q's. We shall adopt the convention of letting the subscript i refer to the rectangular coordinates, and the subscript k refer to the generalized coordinates. Let us further adopt the convenient notation of letting the symbol x_i refer to *any* rectangular coordinate. Thus, for a system of N particles, i would take on values between 1 and $3N$.

10.2   Generalized Forces

If a particle undergoes a displacement $\delta \mathbf{r}$ under the action of a force $\mathbf{F}$, then we know that the work δW done by the force is given by

$$\delta W = \mathbf{F}\cdot\delta\mathbf{r} = F_x\delta x + F_y\delta y + F_z\delta z$$

In our newly adopted notation, the expression for the work is given by

$$\delta W = \sum_i F_i\delta x_i \qquad (10.1)$$

It is clear that the above formula holds not only for a single particle, but also for a system of many particles. For one particle, i goes from 1 to 3. For N particles, i ranges from 1 to $3N$.

Now let us express the increments δx_i in terms of the generalized coordinates. Then

$$\delta W = \sum_i \left(F_i \sum_k \frac{\partial x_i}{\partial q_k} \delta q_k \right)$$

$$= \sum_i \left(\sum_k F_i \frac{\partial x_i}{\partial q_k} \delta q_k \right)$$

By reversing the order of summation, we have

$$\delta W = \sum_k \left(\sum_i F_i \frac{\partial x_i}{\partial q_k} \right) \delta q_k$$

This can be written

$$\delta W = \sum_k Q_k \delta q_k \tag{10.2}$$

where

$$Q_k = \sum_i \left(F_i \frac{\partial x_i}{\partial q_k} \right) \tag{10.3}$$

The quantity Q_k defined by the above equation is called the *generalized force* associated with the coordinate q_k. Since the product $Q_k \delta q_k$ has the dimensions of work, then Q_k has the dimensions of force if q_k is a distance, and the dimensions of torque if q_k is an angle.

It is usually unnecessary, and even impractical, to use Equation 10.3 to calculate the actual value of Q_k; rather, each generalized force Q_k can be found directly from the fact that $Q_k \delta q_k$ is the work done on the system by the external forces when the coordinate q_k changes by the amount δq_k (the other generalized coordinates remaining constant). For example, if the system is a rigid body, the work done by the external forces when the body turns through an angle $\delta\theta$ about a given axis is $N_\theta \delta\theta$, where N_θ is the magnitude of the total moment of all the forces about the axis. In this case N_θ is the generalized force associated with the coordinate θ.

Generalized Forces for Conservative Systems

We have seen in Chapter 4 that the rectangular components of the force acting on a particle in a conservative field of force are given by

$$F_i = -\frac{\partial V}{\partial x_i}$$

where V is the potential energy function. Accordingly, our formula for the generalized force becomes

$$Q_k = -\left(\sum_i \frac{\partial V}{\partial x_i} \frac{\partial x_i}{\partial q_k}\right)$$

Now the expression in parentheses is just the partial derivative of the function V with respect to q_k. Hence

$$Q_k = -\frac{\partial V}{\partial q_k} \tag{10.4}$$

For example, if we use polar coordinates $q_1 = r$, $q_2 = \theta$, then the generalized forces are $Q_r = -\partial V/\partial r$; $Q_\theta = -\partial V/\partial \theta$. If V is a function of r alone (central force), then $Q_\theta = 0$.

10.3   Lagrange's Equations

In order to find the differential equations of motion in terms of the generalized coordinates, we could start with the equation

$$F_i = m_i \ddot{x}_i$$

and try to write it directly in terms of the q's. It turns out, however, to be simpler to use a different approach based on energy considerations. We shall first calculate the kinetic energy T in terms of Cartesian coordinates and shall then express it as a function of the generalized coordinates and their time derivatives. Thus, the kinetic energy T of a system of N particles, which we have previously expressed as

$$T = \sum_{i=1}^{N} [\tfrac{1}{2}m_i(\dot{x}_i^2 + \dot{y}_i^2 + \dot{z}_i^2)]$$

will now be written simply

$$T = \sum_{i=1}^{3N} \tfrac{1}{2}m_i \dot{x}_i^2 \tag{10.5}$$

The Cartesian coordinates x_i are functions of the generalized coordinates q_k. For generality, we shall also include the possibility that the functional relationship between the x's and the q's may also involve the time t explicitly. This would be the case if there were moving constraints, such as a particle constrained to move on a surface which itself is moving in some prescribed manner. We can write

$$x_i = x_i(q_1, q_2, \ldots, q_n, t)$$

Thus

$$\dot{x}_i = \sum_k \frac{\partial x_i}{\partial q_k} \dot{q}_k + \frac{\partial x_i}{\partial t} \tag{10.6}$$

In the above equation and in all that follows, unless stated to the contrary, we shall assume that the range of i is $1, 2, \ldots, 3N$, where N is the number of particles in the system, and the range of k is $1, 2, \ldots, n$, where n is the number of generalized coordinates (degrees of freedom) of the system. In view of the above equation, we see that we can regard T as a function of the generalized coordinates, their time derivatives, and possibly the time. In the usual case the time t is not explicitly involved in the relation between the x_i's and the q_k's so that $\partial x_i / \partial t = 0$. In this case it is clear that *the kinetic energy T is a homogeneous quadratic function of the generalized velocities $\dot{q}_k$.*

From the expression for $\dot{x}_i$, we see that

$$\frac{\partial \dot{x}_i}{\partial \dot{q}_k} = \frac{\partial x_i}{\partial q_k} \tag{10.7}$$

Now let us multiply by $\dot{x}_i$ and differentiate with respect to t. We then have

$$\frac{d}{dt}\left(\dot{x}_i \frac{\partial \dot{x}_i}{\partial \dot{q}_k}\right) = \frac{d}{dt}\left(\dot{x}_i \frac{\partial x_i}{\partial q_k}\right)$$

$$= \ddot{x}_i \frac{\partial x_i}{\partial q_k} + \dot{x}_i \frac{\partial \dot{x}_i}{\partial q_k}$$

or

$$\frac{d}{dt}\left(\frac{\partial}{\partial \dot{q}_k} \frac{\dot{x}_i^2}{2}\right) = \ddot{x}_i \frac{\partial x_i}{\partial q_k} + \frac{\partial}{\partial q_k}\left(\frac{\dot{x}_i^2}{2}\right)$$

The last step follows from the fact that the order of differentiation with respect to t and q_k or $\dot{q}_k$ can be reversed. If we next multiply by m_i and set $m_i \ddot{x}_i = F_i$, we can write

$$\frac{d}{dt} \frac{\partial}{\partial \dot{q}_k}\left(\frac{m_i \dot{x}_i^2}{2}\right) = F_i \frac{\partial x_i}{\partial q_k} + \frac{\partial}{\partial q_k}\left(\frac{m_i \dot{x}_i^2}{2}\right)$$

Hence, by summing over i, we find

$$\frac{d}{dt} \frac{\partial T}{\partial \dot{q}_k} = \sum_i \left(F_i \frac{\partial x_i}{\partial q_k}\right) + \frac{\partial T}{\partial q_k} \tag{10.8}$$

Finally from the definition of the generalized force Q_k, we obtain the result

$$\frac{d}{dt} \frac{\partial T}{\partial \dot{q}_k} = Q_k + \frac{\partial T}{\partial q_k} \tag{10.9}$$

These are the differential equations of motion in the generalized coordinates. They are known as *Lagrange's equations of motion.*

In case the motion is conservative so that the Q's are given by Equation 10.4, then Lagrange's equations can be written

$$\frac{d}{dt} \frac{\partial T}{\partial \dot{q}_k} = \frac{\partial T}{\partial q_k} - \frac{\partial V}{\partial q_k} \tag{10.10}$$

The equations can be written even more compactly by defining a function L, known as the *Lagrangian function,* such that

$$L = T - V$$

where it is understood that T and V are expressed in terms of the generalized coordinates. Thus, since $V = V(q_k)$ and $\partial V/\partial \dot{q}_k = 0$, we have

$$\frac{\partial L}{\partial \dot{q}_k} = \frac{\partial T}{\partial \dot{q}_k} \quad \text{and} \quad \frac{\partial L}{\partial q_k} = \frac{\partial T}{\partial q_k} - \frac{\partial V}{\partial q_k}$$

Lagrange's equations can then be written

$$\frac{d}{dt}\frac{\partial L}{\partial \dot{q}_k} = \frac{\partial L}{\partial q_k} \tag{10.11}$$

Thus the differential equations of motion for a conservative system are readily obtained if we know the Lagrangian function in terms of an appropriate set of coordinates.

If part of the generalized forces are not conservative, say Q'_k, and part are derivable from a potential function V, we can write

$$Q_k = Q'_k - \frac{\partial V}{\partial q_k} \tag{10.12}$$

We can then also define a Lagrangian function $L = T - V$, and write the differential equations of motion in the form

$$\frac{d}{dt}\frac{\partial L}{\partial \dot{q}_k} = Q'_k + \frac{\partial L}{\partial q_k} \tag{10.13}$$

The above form is a convenient one to use, for example, when frictional forces are present.

Lagrange's equations have the same form for *any* coordinates. They give us a uniform way of finding the differential equations of motion of a system in whatever kind of coordinate system is the most convenient.

10.4 Some Applications of Lagrange's Equations

In this section we shall illustrate the remarkable versatility of Lagrange's equations by applying them to a number of specific cases. The general procedure for finding the differential equations of motion for a system is as follows:

I. Select a suitable set of coordinates to represent the configuration of the system.
II. Obtain the kinetic energy T as a function of these coordinates and their time derivatives.
III. If the system is conservative, find the potential energy V as a function of the coordinates, or, if the system is not conservative, find the generalized forces Q_k.
IV. The differential equations of motion are then given by Equations 10.9, 10.11, or 10.13.

Examples

10.1 *Harmonic Oscillator*

Consider the case of a one-dimensional harmonic oscillator, and suppose that there is a damping force which is proportional to the velocity. The system is thus nonconservative. If x is the displacement coordinate, then the Lagrangian function is

$$L = T - V = \tfrac{1}{2}m\dot{x}^2 - \tfrac{1}{2}Kx^2$$

in which m is the mass and K is the usual stiffness parameter. Hence

$$\frac{\partial L}{\partial \dot{x}} = m\dot{x} \qquad \frac{\partial L}{\partial x} = -Kx$$

Now since there is a nonconservative force present, Lagrange's equations in the form of Equation 10.13 can be used. Thus $Q' = -c\dot{x}$, and the equation of motion reads

$$\frac{d}{dt}(m\dot{x}) = -c\dot{x} + (-Kx)$$

or

$$m\ddot{x} + c\dot{x} + Kx = 0$$

This is the familiar equation of the damped harmonic oscillator that we studied earlier.

10.2   *Single Particle in a Central Field*

Let us find Lagrange's equations of motion for a particle moving in a plane under a central force. We shall choose polar coordinates $q_1 = r$, $q_2 = \theta$. Then

$$T = \tfrac{1}{2}mv^2 = \tfrac{1}{2}m(\dot{r}^2 + r^2\dot{\theta}^2)$$
$$V = V(r)$$
$$L = \tfrac{1}{2}m(\dot{r}^2 + r^2\dot{\theta}^2) - V(r)$$

The relevant partial derivatives are as follows:

$$\frac{\partial L}{\partial \dot{r}} = m\dot{r} \qquad \frac{\partial L}{\partial r} = mr\dot{\theta}^2 - \frac{\partial V}{\partial r} = mr\dot{\theta}^2 + f(r)$$

$$\frac{\partial L}{\partial \theta} = 0 \qquad \frac{\partial L}{\partial \dot{\theta}} = mr^2\dot{\theta}$$

This is a conservative system, and the equations of motion are

$$\frac{d}{dt}\frac{\partial L}{\partial \dot{r}} = \frac{\partial L}{\partial r} \qquad \frac{d}{dt}\frac{\partial L}{\partial \dot{\theta}} = \frac{\partial L}{\partial \theta}$$

$$m\ddot{r} = mr\dot{\theta}^2 + f(r) \qquad \frac{d}{dt}(mr^2\dot{\theta}) = 0$$

These are equivalent to the equations found in Section 6.7 for the motion of a particle in a central field.

10.3   *Atwood's Machine*

A mechanical system known as Atwood's machine consists of two weights of mass m_1 and m_2, respectively, connected by a light inextensible cord of length l which passes over a pulley (Figure 10.1). The system has one degree of freedom. We shall let the variable x represent the configuration of the system, where x is the vertical distance from the pulley to m_1, as shown. The angular speed of the pulley is clearly $\dot{x}/a$, where a is the radius. The kinetic energy of the system is therefore given by

$$T = \frac{1}{2}m_1\dot{x}^2 + \frac{1}{2}m_2\dot{x}^2 + \frac{1}{2}I\frac{\dot{x}^2}{a^2}$$

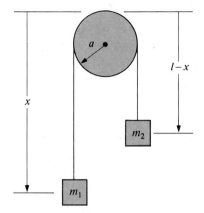

FIGURE 10.1 A simple Atwood machine.

where I is the moment of inertia of the pulley. The potential energy is given by

$$V = -m_1gx - m_2g(l - x)$$

Assuming that there is no friction, we have the Lagrangian function

$$L = \frac{1}{2}\left(m_1 + m_2 + \frac{I}{a^2}\right)\dot{x}^2 + g(m_1 - m_2)x + m_2gl$$

and Lagrange's equation

$$\frac{d}{dt}\frac{\partial L}{\partial \dot{x}} = \frac{\partial L}{\partial x}$$

then reads

$$\left(m_1 + m_2 + \frac{I}{a^2}\right)\ddot{x} = g(m_1 - m_2)$$

or

$$\ddot{x} = g\frac{m_1 - m_2}{m_1 + m_2 + I/a^2}$$

giving the acceleration of the system. We see that if $m_1 > m_2$, then m_1 descends with constant acceleration, whereas if $m_1 < m_2$, then m_1 ascends with constant acceleration. The inertial effect of the pulley shows up in the term I/a^2 in the denominator.

10.4 *The Double Atwood Machine*

Consider the system shown in Figure 10.2. Here we have replaced one of the weights in the simple Atwood machine by another pulley supporting two weights connected by another cord. The system now has two degrees of freedom. We shall specify its configuration by the two coordinates x and x', as shown. For simplicity, let us neglect the masses of the pulleys in this case. We have

$$T = \tfrac{1}{2}m_1\dot{x}^2 + \tfrac{1}{2}m_2(-\dot{x} + \dot{x}')^2 + \tfrac{1}{2}m_3(-\dot{x} - \dot{x}')^2$$
$$V = -m_1gx - m_2g(l - x + x') - m_3g(l - x + l' - x')$$

where m_1, m_2, and m_3 are the three masses, and l and l' are the lengths of the two connecting cords. Then

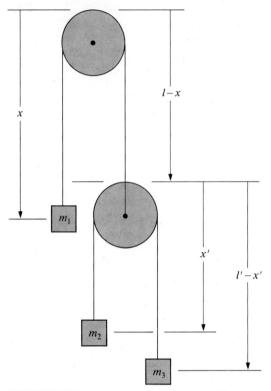

FIGURE 10.2 A compound Atwood machine.

$$L = \tfrac{1}{2}m_1\dot{x}_1^2 + \tfrac{1}{2}m_2(-\dot{x} + \dot{x}')^2 + \tfrac{1}{2}m_3(\dot{x} + \dot{x}')^2$$
$$+ g(m_1 - m_2 - m_3)x + g(m_2 - m_3)x' + \text{constant}$$

The equations of motion

$$\frac{d}{dt}\frac{\partial L}{\partial \dot{x}} = \frac{\partial L}{\partial x} \qquad \frac{d}{dt}\frac{\partial L}{\partial \dot{x}'} = \frac{\partial L}{\partial x'}$$

read

$$m_1\ddot{x} + m_2(\ddot{x} - \ddot{x}') + m_3(\ddot{x} + \ddot{x}') = g(m_1 - m_2 - m_3)$$
$$m_2(-\ddot{x} + \ddot{x}') + m_3(\ddot{x} + \ddot{x}') = g(m_2 - m_3)$$

from which the accelerations $\ddot{x}$ and $\ddot{x}'$ are found by simple algebra.

10.5 *Particle Sliding on a Movable Inclined Plane*

Let us consider the case of a particle sliding on a smooth inclined plane which, itself, is free to slide on a smooth horizontal surface, as shown in Figure 10.3. In this problem there are two degrees of freedom, so we need two coordinates to specify the configuration. We shall choose the coordinates x and x', the horizontal displacement of the plane from some reference point and the displacement of the particle from some reference point on the plane, respectively, as shown.

From a study of the velocity diagram, shown to the right of the figure, we see that the square of the speed of the particle is given by the law of cosines

$$v^2 = \dot{x}^2 + \dot{x}'^2 + 2\dot{x}\dot{x}' \cos \theta$$

Hence the kinetic energy T of the system is given by

$$T = \tfrac{1}{2}mv^2 + \tfrac{1}{2}M\dot{x}^2 = \tfrac{1}{2}m(\dot{x}^2 + \dot{x}'^2 + 2\dot{x}\dot{x}' \cos \theta) + \tfrac{1}{2}M\dot{x}^2$$

where M is the mass of the inclined plane, θ is the wedge angle as shown, and m is the mass of the particle. The potential energy of the system does not involve x, since the plane is on a horizontal surface. Hence we can write

$$V = -mgx' \sin \theta + \text{constant}$$

and

$$L = \tfrac{1}{2}m(\dot{x}^2 + \dot{x}'^2 + 2\dot{x}\dot{x}' \cos \theta) + \tfrac{1}{2}M\dot{x}^2 + mgx' \sin \theta + \text{constant}$$

The equations of motion

$$\frac{d}{dt}\frac{\partial L}{\partial \dot{x}} = \frac{\partial L}{\partial x} \qquad \frac{d}{dt}\frac{\partial L}{\partial \dot{x}'} = \frac{\partial L}{\partial x'}$$

then become

$$m(\ddot{x} + \ddot{x}' \cos \theta) + M\ddot{x} = 0 \qquad m(\ddot{x}' + \ddot{x} \cos \theta) = mg \sin \theta$$

Solving for $\ddot{x}$ and $\ddot{x}'$ we find

$$\ddot{x} = \frac{-g \sin \theta \cos \theta}{\dfrac{m+M}{m} - \cos^2 \theta} \qquad \ddot{x}' = \frac{g \sin \theta}{1 - \dfrac{m \cos^2 \theta}{m+M}}$$

The above result can be obtained by analyzing the forces and reactions involved, but that method is much more tedious than the above method of using Lagrange's equations.

10.6 *Derivation of Euler's equations for the free rotation of a rigid body.* Lagrange's method can be used to derive Euler's equations for the motion of a rigid body. We shall consider the case of torque-free rotation. We know that the kinetic energy is given by

$$T = \frac{1}{2}(I_1\omega_1^2 + I_2\omega_2^2 + I_3\omega_3^2)$$

where the ω's are referred to principal axes of the body. In Section 9.5 we showed that the ω's can be expressed in terms of the Eulerian angles θ, ϕ, and ψ as follows:

$$\omega_1 = \dot{\theta} \cos \psi + \dot{\phi} \sin \theta \sin \psi$$
$$\omega_2 = -\dot{\theta} \sin \psi + \dot{\phi} \sin \theta \cos \psi$$
$$\omega_3 = \dot{\psi} + \dot{\phi} \cos \theta$$

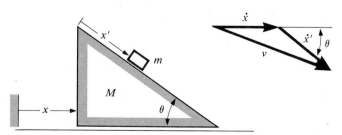

FIGURE 10.3   A block sliding down a movable wedge or inclined plane.

Regarding the Eulerian angles as the generalized coordinates, the equations of motion are

$$\frac{d}{dt}\frac{\partial T}{\partial \dot{\theta}} = \frac{\partial T}{\partial \theta} \tag{10.14}$$

$$\frac{d}{dt}\frac{\partial T}{\partial \dot{\phi}} = \frac{\partial T}{\partial \phi} \tag{10.15}$$

$$\frac{d}{dt}\frac{\partial T}{\partial \dot{\psi}} = \frac{\partial T}{\partial \psi} \tag{10.16}$$

because the Q's (the generalized forces) are all zero. Now, by the chain rule,

$$\frac{\partial T}{\partial \dot{\psi}} = \frac{\partial T}{\partial \omega_3}\frac{\partial \omega_3}{\partial \dot{\psi}} = I_3\omega_3$$

so

$$\frac{d}{dt}\frac{\partial T}{\partial \dot{\psi}} = I_3\dot{\omega}_3$$

Again, using the chain rule, we have

$$\frac{\partial T}{\partial \psi} = I_1\omega_1\frac{\partial \omega_1}{\partial \psi} + I_2\omega_2\frac{\partial \omega_2}{\partial \psi}$$

$$= I_1\omega_1(-\dot{\theta}\sin\psi + \dot{\phi}\sin\theta\cos\psi) + I_2\omega_2(-\dot{\theta}\cos\psi - \dot{\phi}\sin\theta\sin\psi)$$

$$= I_1\omega_1\omega_2 - I_2\omega_2\omega_1$$

Consequently, Equation 10.16 becomes

$$I_3\dot{\omega}_3 = \omega_1\omega_2(I_1 - I_2)$$

which, as we showed in Section 9.3, is the third of Euler's equations for the rotation of a rigid body under zero torque. The other two of Euler's equations can be obtained by cyclic permutation of the subscripts: $1 \rightarrow 2,\ 2 \rightarrow 3,\ 3 \rightarrow 1$. This is valid because we have not designated any particular principal axis as being preferred.

10.5 Generalized Momenta. Ignorable Coordinates

Consider the motion of a single particle moving in a straight line (rectilinear motion). The kinetic energy is

$$T = \tfrac{1}{2}m\dot{x}^2$$

where m is the mass of the particle, and x is its positional coordinate. Now rather than define the momentum p of the particle as the product $m\dot{x}$, we could define p as the quantity $\partial T/\partial \dot{x}$, namely,

$$p = \frac{\partial T}{\partial \dot{x}} = m\dot{x}$$

In the case of a system described by generalized coordinates $q_1, q_2, \ldots, q_k, \ldots,$ q_n, the quantities p_k defined by

$$p_k = \frac{\partial L}{\partial \dot{q}_k} \tag{10.17}$$

are called the *generalized momenta*.[1] Lagrange's equations for a conservative system can then be written

$$\dot{p}_k = \frac{\partial L}{\partial q_k} \tag{10.18}$$

Suppose, in particular, that one of the coordinates, say q_λ, is not explicitly contained in L. Then

$$\dot{p}_\lambda = \frac{\partial L}{\partial q_\lambda} = 0 \tag{10.19}$$

so that

$$p_\lambda = \text{constant} = c_\lambda \tag{10.20}$$

The coordinate q_λ is said to be *ignorable* in this case. The generalized momentum associated with an ignorable coordinate is therefore a constant of the motion of the system.

For example, in the problem of the particle sliding on the smooth inclined plane (treated in the previous section), we found that the coordinate x, the position of the plane, was not contained in the Lagrangian function L. Thus x is an ignorable coordinate, and

$$p_x = \frac{\partial L}{\partial \dot{x}} = (M + m)\dot{x} + m\dot{x}' \cos \theta = \text{constant}$$

We can see, as a matter of fact, that p_x is the total horizontal component of the linear momentum of the system, and, since there is no external horizontal force acting on the system, the horizontal component of the linear momentum must be constant.

Another example of an ignorable coordinate is found in the case of the motion of a particle in a central field. In polar coordinates

$$L = \tfrac{1}{2}m(\dot{r}^2 + r^2\dot{\theta}^2) - V(r)$$

as shown in Example 10.2 above. In this case θ is an ignorable coordinate, and

$$p_\theta = \frac{\partial L}{\partial \theta} = mr^2\dot{\theta} = \text{constant}$$

which, as we know from Chapter 6, is the angular momentum about the origin.

---

[1] If the potential energy function V does not explicitly involve the $\dot{q}$'s, then $p_k = \partial L/\partial \dot{q}_k = \partial T/\partial \dot{q}_k$.

Example

10.7 *The spherical pendulum, or bar of soap in a bowl.* A classic problem in mechanics is that of a particle which is constrained to stay on a smooth spherical surface under gravity, such as a small mass sliding around inside a smooth spherical bowl. The case is also illustrated by a simple pendulum which is free to swing in *any* direction, Figure 10.4. This is the so-called spherical pendulum, mentioned earlier in Section 5.5.

There are two degrees of freedom, and we shall use generalized coordinates θ and ϕ, as shown. These are actually equivalent to spherical coordinates with $r = l =$ constant in which l is the length of the pendulum cord. The two components of the velocity are $v_\theta = l\dot\theta$ and $v_\phi = l \sin \theta \,\dot\phi$. The height of the bob, measured from the xy plane, is l-$l \cos \theta$, so the Lagrangian function is

$$L = \frac{1}{2}ml^2(\dot\theta^2 + \sin^2 \theta \,\dot\phi^2) - mgl(1 - \cos \theta)$$

The coordinate ϕ is ignorable, so we have immediately

$$p_\phi = \frac{\partial L}{\partial \dot\phi} = ml^2 \sin^2 \theta \,\dot\phi = \text{constant}$$

This is the angular momentum about the vertical or z axis. We are left with just the equation in θ:

$$\frac{d}{dt}\frac{\partial L}{\partial \dot\theta} = \frac{\partial L}{\partial \theta}$$

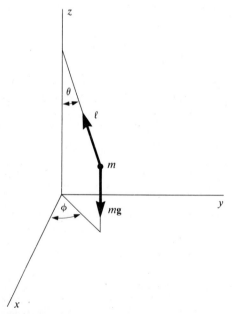

FIGURE 10.4   The spherical pendulum.

which reads

$$ml^2\ddot{\theta} = ml^2 \sin\theta \cos\theta \, \dot{\phi}^2 - mgl \sin\theta$$

Let us introduce the constant L, defined by

$$L = \sin^2\theta \, \dot{\phi} = \frac{p_\phi}{ml^2} \tag{10.21}$$

(This is the angular momentum divided by ml^2.)
The differential equation of motion for θ then becomes

$$\ddot{\theta} + \frac{g}{l}\sin\theta - L^2\frac{\cos\theta}{\sin^3\theta} = 0 \tag{10.22}$$

It is instructive to consider some special cases at this point. First, if the angle ϕ is constant, then $\dot{\phi} = 0$, and so $L = 0$. Consequently, the above equation reduces to

$$\ddot{\theta} + \frac{g}{l}\sin\theta = 0$$

which, of course, is just the differential equation of the simple pendulum. The motion takes place in the plane $\phi = \phi_0 = $ constant.

The second special case is that of the *conical pendulum*. Here the bob describes a horizontal circle, so $\theta = \theta_0 = $ constant. In this case $\dot{\theta} = 0$ and $\ddot{\theta} = 0$, so Equation 10.22 reduces to

$$\frac{g}{l}\sin\theta_0 - L^2\frac{\cos\theta_0}{\sin^3\theta_0} = 0$$

or

$$L^2 = \frac{g}{l}\sin^4\theta_0 \sec\theta_0 \tag{10.23}$$

From the value of l given by the above equation, we find from Equation 10.21 that

$$\dot{\phi}_0^2 = \frac{g}{l}\sec\theta_0 \tag{10.24}$$

as the condition for conical motion of the pendulum.

Let us now consider the case in which the motion is *almost* conical; that is, the value of θ remains close to the value θ_0. If we insert the expression for L^2 given in Equation 10.23 into the separated differential equation of θ, Equation 10.22, the result is

$$\ddot{\theta} + \frac{g}{l}\left(\sin\theta - \frac{\sin^4\theta_0}{\cos\theta_0}\frac{\cos\theta}{\sin^3\theta}\right) = 0$$

It is convenient at this point to introduce the new variable ξ defined as

$$\xi = \theta - \theta_0$$

The expression in parentheses, which we shall call $f(\xi)$, may be expanded as a power series in ξ according to the standard formula

$$f(\xi) = f(0) + f'(0)\xi + f''(0)\frac{\xi^2}{2!} + \cdots$$

We find, after performing the indicated operations, that $f(0) = 0$ and $f'(0) =$

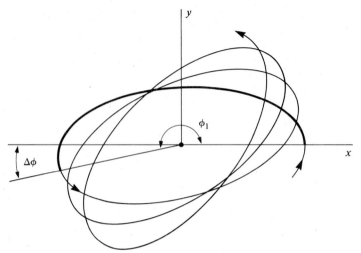

FIGURE 10.5   Projection on the xy plane of the path of motion of the spherical pendulum.

$3 \cos \theta_0 + \sec \theta_0$. Since we are concerned with the case of small values of ξ, we shall neglect higher powers of ξ than the first, and so we can write

$$\ddot{\xi} + \frac{g}{l}(3 \cos \theta_0 + \sec \theta_0)\xi = 0$$

Thus ξ oscillates harmonically about $\xi = 0$, or equivalently, θ oscillates harmonically about the value θ_0 with a period

$$T_1 = 2\pi\sqrt{\frac{l}{g(3 \cos \theta_0 + \sec \theta_0)}}$$

Now the value of $\dot{\phi}$ does not vary greatly from the value given by the purely conical motion $\dot{\phi}_0$, so ϕ increases steadily during the oscillation of θ about θ_0. During one complete oscillation of θ the value of the azimuth angle ϕ increases by the amount.

$$\phi_1 \cong \dot{\phi}_0 T_1$$

From the values of $\dot{\phi}_0$ and T_1 given above, we readily find

$$\phi_1 = 2\pi(3 \cos^2 \theta_0 + 1)^{-1/2}$$

Now the quantity in parentheses is less than 4, for non-zero θ_0, so ϕ_1 is greater than π (180°). The excess $\Delta\phi$ is shown in Figure 10.5 which is a plot of the projection of the path of the pendulum bob on the xy plane. As the pendulum swings, it precesses in the direction of increasing ϕ, as indicated.

Finally, for the general case we can go back to the differential equation of motion, Equation 10.22, and integrate once with respect to θ by using the fact that $\ddot{\theta} = \dot{\theta}d\dot{\theta}/d\theta = \frac{1}{2}d\dot{\theta}^2/d\theta$. The result is

$$\frac{1}{2}\dot{\theta}^2 = \frac{g}{l}\cos\theta - \frac{L^2}{2\sin^2\theta} + C = -U(\theta) + C$$

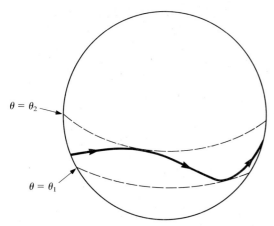

$\theta = \theta_2$

$\theta = \theta_1$

FIGURE 10.6   Illustrating the limits of the motion of the spherical pendulum.

in which C is the constant of integration and

$$U(\theta) = -\frac{g}{l}\cos\theta + \frac{L^2}{2\sin^2\theta}$$

is the "effective potential". Actually, the integrated equation of motion is just the energy equation where the total energy $E = C\,ml^2$. For a given initial condition, the motion of the pendulum is such that the bob oscillates between two horizontal circles. These circles define the turning points of the θ-motion for which $\dot{\theta} = 0$ or $U(\theta) = C$. This is illustrated in Figures 10.6 and 10.7.

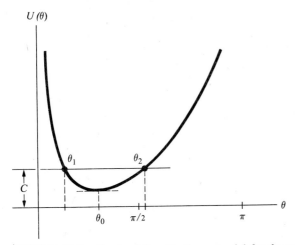

$U(\theta)$

θ_1 θ_2

C

θ_0 $\pi/2$ π θ

FIGURE 10.7   Graph of the effective potential for the spherical pendulum.

10.6   Hamilton's Variational Principle: An Alternative Way to Derive Lagrange's Equations

Thus far, our study of mechanics has been based largely on the Newtonian laws of motion. In fact, in the first part of this chapter when we derived Lagrange's equations we used Newton's second law as one of the basic assumptions. In this section we shall investigate an alternative way of deriving Lagrange's equations. This method is based on a postulate that has proved to be most far-reaching in its consequences—Hamilton's variational principle.

This principle, first announced in 1834 by the Irish mathematician Sir William R. Hamilton, states that the motion of any system takes place in such a way that the integral

$$\int_{t_1}^{t_2} L \, dt$$

always assumes an extreme value, where $L = T - V$ is the Lagrangian function of the system. Stated in other words, Hamilton's principle declares that out of all possible ways a system can change in a given finite time interval $t_2 - t_1$, that particular motion which will occur is the one for which the above integral is either a maximum or a minimum. The statement can be expressed in mathematical form as

$$\delta \int_{t_1}^{t_2} L \, dt = 0 \tag{10.25}$$

in which δ denotes a small variation. This variation results from taking different paths of integration by varying the generalized coordinates and generalized velocities as functions of t, Figure 10.8.

To show that the above equation leads directly to Lagrange's equations of motion, let us compute the variation explicitly, assuming that L is a known function of the generalized coordinates q_k and their time derivatives $\dot{q}_k$. We have

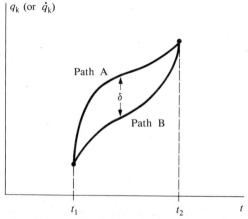

FIGURE 10.8   Illustrating the variation of q_k or $\dot{q}_k$ in Hamilton's variational principle.

$$\delta \int_{t_1}^{t_2} L \, dt = \int_{t_1}^{t_2} \delta L \, dt = \int_{t_1}^{t_2} \sum_k \left(\frac{\partial L}{\partial q_k} \delta q_k + \frac{\partial L}{\partial \dot{q}_k} \delta \dot{q}_k \right) dt = 0$$

Now δq_k is equal to the difference between two slightly different functions of the time t. Therefore,

$$\delta \dot{q}_k = \frac{d}{dt} \delta q_k$$

Hence, upon integrating the last term in the integrand by parts, we find

$$\int_{t_1}^{t_2} \sum_k \frac{\partial L}{\partial \dot{q}_k} \delta \dot{q}_k \, dt = \left[\sum_k \frac{\partial L}{\partial \dot{q}_k} \delta q_k \right]_{t_1}^{t_2} - \int_{t_1}^{t_2} \sum_k \frac{d}{dt} \frac{\partial L}{\partial \dot{q}_k} \delta q_k \, dt$$

But, for fixed values of the limits t_1 and t_2, the variation $\delta q_k = 0$ at t_1 and t_2, hence the integrated term vanishes. It follows that

$$\delta \int_{t_1}^{t_2} L \, dt = \int_{t_1}^{t_2} \sum_k \left[\frac{\partial L}{\partial q_k} - \frac{d}{dt} \frac{\partial L}{\partial \dot{q}_k} \right] \delta q_k \, dt = 0 \qquad (10.26)$$

Now if the generalized coordinates q_k are all independent, then their variations δq_k are also independent. Therefore each term in brackets in the integrand must vanish in order that the integral itself vanish. Thus

$$\frac{\partial L}{\partial q_k} - \frac{d}{dt} \frac{\partial L}{\partial \dot{q}_k} = 0 \qquad (k = 1, 2, \ldots, n)$$

These are precisely Lagrange's equations of motion that we found earlier.

In the above derivation it has been assumed that a potential function exists, that is, that the system under consideration is a conservative one. The method of variations can be made to include nonconservative systems by replacing L in the variational integral by the quantity $T + W$ in which W is the work done by *all* forces, whether conservative or nonconservative. The generalized force Q_k is then introduced as defined earlier, Section 10.2, and the same procedure as above leads to the general form of Lagrange's equations, Equation 10.9.

10.7   The Hamiltonian Function. Hamilton's Equations

Consider the following function of the generalized coordinates:

$$H = \sum_k \dot{q}_k p_k - L$$

For simple dynamic systems the kinetic energy T is a homogeneous quadratic function of the $\dot{q}$'s, and the potential energy V is a function of the q's alone, so that

$$L = T(q_k, \dot{q}_k) - V(q_k)$$

Now, from Euler's theorem for homogeneous functions,[2] we have

$$\sum_k \dot{q}_k p_k = \sum_k \dot{q}_k \frac{\partial L}{\partial \dot{q}_k} = \sum_k \dot{q}_k \frac{\partial T}{\partial \dot{q}_k} = 2T$$

Therefore

$$H = \sum_k \dot{q}_k p_k - L = 2T - (T - V) = T + V \qquad (10.27)$$

That is, the function H is equal to the total energy for the type of system we are considering.

Suppose we regard the n equations

$$p_k = \frac{\partial L}{\partial \dot{q}_k} \qquad (k = 1, 2, \ldots, n)$$

as solved for the $\dot{q}$'s in terms of the p's and the q's:

$$\dot{q}_k = \dot{q}_k(p_k, q_k)$$

With these equations we can then express H as a function of the p's and the q's:

$$H(p_k, q_k) = \sum_k p_k \dot{q}_k(p_k, q_k) - L \qquad (10.28)$$

Let us calculate the variation of the function H corresponding to a variation δp_k, δq_k. We have

$$\delta H = \sum_k \left[p_k \, \delta \dot{q}_k + \dot{q}_k \, \delta p_k - \frac{\partial L}{\partial \dot{q}_k} \delta \dot{q}_k - \frac{\partial L}{\partial q_k} \delta q_k \right]$$

The first and third terms in the brackets cancel, because $p_k = \partial L / \partial \dot{q}_k$ by definition. Also, since Lagrange's equations can be written as $\dot{p}_k = \partial L / \partial q_k$, we can write

$$\delta H = \sum_k [\dot{q}_k \, \delta p_k - \dot{p}_k \, \delta q_k]$$

Now the variation of H must be given by the equation

$$\delta H = \sum_k \left[\frac{\partial H}{\partial p_k} \delta p_k + \frac{\partial H}{\partial q_k} \delta q_k \right]$$

It follows that

$$\frac{\partial H}{\partial p_k} = \dot{q}_k \qquad (10.29)$$

$$\frac{\partial H}{\partial q_k} = -\dot{p}_k$$

[2] Euler's theorem states that for a homogeneous function f of degree n in the variables $x_1, x_2, \ldots, x_r$

$$x_1 \frac{\partial f}{\partial x_1} + x_2 \frac{\partial f}{\partial x_2} + \ldots + x_r \frac{\partial f}{\partial x_r} = nf$$

These are known as *Hamilton's canonical equations of motion*. They consist of $2n$ first-order differential equations, whereas Lagrange's equations consist of n second-order equations. We have derived Hamilton's equations for simple conservative systems. It can be shown that Equations 10.29 also hold for more general systems, for example, nonconservative systems, systems in which the potential-energy function involves the $\dot{q}$'s, and for systems in which L involves the time explicitly, but in these cases the total energy is no longer necessarily equal to H.

Hamilton's equations will be encountered by the student when he studies quantum mechanics (the fundamental theory of atomic phenomena). Hamilton's equations also find application in celestial mechanics. For further reading the student is referred to the Selected References (under *Advanced Mechanics*) at the end of the book.

Examples

10.8   Obtain Hamilton's equations of motion for a one-dimensional harmonic oscillator. We have

$$T = \tfrac{1}{2}m\dot{x}^2 \qquad\qquad V = \tfrac{1}{2}Kx^2$$

$$p = \frac{\partial T}{\partial \dot{x}} = m\dot{x} \qquad \dot{x} = \frac{p}{m}$$

Hence

$$H = T + V = \frac{1}{2m}p^2 + \frac{K}{2}x^2$$

The equations of motion

$$\frac{\partial H}{\partial p} = \dot{x} \qquad\qquad \frac{\partial H}{\partial x} = -\dot{p}$$

then read

$$\frac{p}{m} = \dot{x} \qquad Kx = -\dot{p}$$

The first equation merely amounts to a restatement of the momentum-velocity relationship in this case. Using the first equation, the second can be written

$$Kx = -\frac{d}{dt}(m\dot{x})$$

or, upon rearranging terms,

$$m\ddot{x} + Kx = 0$$

which is the familiar equation of the harmonic oscillator.

10.9   Find the Hamiltonian equations of motion for a particle in a central field. Here we have

$$T = \frac{m}{2}(\dot{r}^2 + r^2\dot{\theta}^2)$$

$$V = V(r)$$

in polar coordinates. Hence

$$p_r = \frac{\partial T}{\partial \dot{r}} = m\dot{r} \qquad \dot{r} = \frac{p_r}{m}$$

$$p_\theta = \frac{\partial T}{\partial \dot{\theta}} = mr^2\dot{\theta} \qquad \dot{\theta} = \frac{p_\theta}{mr^2}$$

Consequently

$$H = \frac{1}{2m}\left(p_r^2 + \frac{p_\theta^2}{r^2}\right) + V(r)$$

The Hamiltonian equations

$$\frac{\partial H}{\partial p_r} = \dot{r} \qquad \frac{\partial H}{\partial r} = -\dot{p}_r \qquad \frac{\partial H}{\partial p_\theta} = \dot{\theta} \qquad \frac{\partial H}{\partial \theta} = -\dot{p}_\theta$$

then read

$$\frac{p_r}{m} = \dot{r}$$

$$\frac{\partial V(r)}{\partial r} - \frac{p_\theta^2}{mr^3} = -\dot{p}_r$$

$$\frac{p_\theta}{mr^2} = \dot{\theta}$$

$$0 = -\dot{p}_\theta$$

The last two equations yield the constancy of angular momentum:

$$p_\theta = \text{constant} = mr^2\dot{\theta} = ml$$

from which the first two give

$$m\ddot{r} = \dot{p}_r = \frac{ml^2}{r^3} - \frac{\partial V(r)}{\partial r}$$

for the radial equation of motion. This, of course, is equivalent to that found earlier in Example 10.2.

PROBLEMS

Lagrange's method should be used in *all* of the following, unless stated otherwise.

10.1   Find the differential equations of motion of a projectile in a uniform gravitational field without air resistance.

10.2   Find the acceleration of a solid uniform sphere rolling down a perfectly rough fixed inclined plane. Compare with the result derived earlier in Section 8.6.

10.3   Two blocks of equal mass m are connected by a flexible cord. One block is placed on a smooth horizontal table, the other block hangs over the edge. Find the acceleration of the system assuming (a) the mass of the cord is negligible, and (b) the cord is heavy, of mass m'.

10.4   Set up the equations of motion of a "double-double" Atwood machine consisting of one Atwood machine (with masses m_1 and m_2) connected by means of a light cord passing over a pulley to a second Atwood machine with masses m_3 and m_4. Neglect the masses of all pulleys. Find the actual accelerations for the case $m_1 = m$, $m_2 = 4m$, $m_3 = 2m$, and $m_4 = m$.

10.5   A ball of mass m rolls down a movable wedge of mass M. The angle of the wedge is θ, and it is free to slide on a smooth horizontal surface. The contact between the ball and the wedge is perfectly rough. Find the acceleration of the wedge.

10.6   A particle slides on a smooth inclined plane whose inclination θ is increasing at a constant rate ω. If $\theta = 0$ at time $t = 0$, at which time the particle starts from rest, find the subsequent motion of the particle.

10.7   Show that Lagrange's method automatically yields the correct equations of motion for a particle moving in a plane in a rotating coordinate system Oxy. [*Hint: $T = \frac{1}{2}m\mathbf{v} \cdot \mathbf{v}$*, where $\mathbf{v} = \mathbf{i}(\dot{x} - \omega y) + \mathbf{j}(\dot{y} + \omega x)$, and $F_x = -\partial V/\partial x$, $F_y = -\partial V/\partial y$.]

10.8   Repeat the above problem for motion in three dimensions.

10.9   Find the differential equations of motion for an "elastic pendulum": a particle of mass m attached to an elastic string of stiffness K and unstretched length l_0. Assume that the motion takes place in a vertical plane.

10.10   The point of support of a simple pendulum is being elevated at a constant acceleration a, so that the height of the support is $\frac{1}{2}at^2$, and its vertical velocity is at. Find the differential equation of motion for small oscillations of the pendulum by Lagrange's method. Show that the period of the pendulum is $2\pi[l/(g + a)]^{1/2}$ where l is the length of the pendulum.

10.11   Work Problem 8.10 by using Lagrange's equations. Show that the acceleration of the ball is $\frac{5}{7}g$.

10.12   A heavy elastic spring of uniform stiffness and density supports a block of mass m. If m' is the mass of the spring and k its stiffness, show that the period of vertical oscillations is

$$2\pi\sqrt{\frac{m + (m'/3)}{k}}$$

This problem shows the effect of the mass of the spring on the period of oscillation. [*Hint:* To set up the Lagrangian function for the system, assume that the velocity of any part of the spring is proportional to its distance from the point of suspension.]

10.13   (a) Find the general differential equations of motion for a particle in cylindrical coordinates: R, φ, z. Use the relation

$$v^2 = v_R^2 + v_\varphi^2 + v_z^2$$

$$= \dot{R}^2 + R^2\dot{\varphi}^2 + \dot{z}^2$$

(b) Find the general differential equations of motion for a particle in spherical coordinates: r, θ, φ. Use the relation

$$v^2 = v_r^2 + v_\theta^2 + v_\varphi^2$$

$$= \dot{r}^2 + r^2\dot{\theta}^2 + r^2 \sin^2 \theta\, \dot{\varphi}^2$$

[*Note:* Compare your results with the result derived in Chapter 1, Equations 1.52 and 1.60 by setting $\mathbf{F} = m\mathbf{a}$ and taking components.]

10.14   Find the differential equations of motion in *three* dimensions for a particle in a central field using spherical coordinates.

10.15   A bar of soap slides in a smooth bowl in the shape of an inverted right circular cone of apex angle 2α. The axis of the cone is vertical. Treating the bar of soap as a particle of mass m, find the differential equations of motion using spherical coordinates with $\theta = \alpha = $ constant. As is the case with the spherical pendulum. Example 10.7, show that the particle, given an initial motion with $\dot{\varphi}_0 \neq 0$, must remain between two horizontal circles on the cone. [*Hint:* Show that $\dot{r}^2 = f(r)$ where $f(r) = 0$ has two roots that define the turning points of the motion in r.] What is the "effective potential" for this problem?

10.16   In the above problem, find the value of $\dot{\varphi}_0$ such that the particle remains on a *single* horizontal circle: $r = r_0$. Find also the period of small oscillations about this circle if $\dot{\varphi}_0$ is not quite equal to the required value.

10.17   As stated in Chapter 4, the differential equation of motion of a particle of mass m and electric charge q moving with velocity $\mathbf{v}$ in a static magnetic field $\mathbf{B}$ is given by

$$m\ddot{\mathbf{r}} = q(\mathbf{v} \times \mathbf{B})$$

Show that the Lagrangian function

$$L = \tfrac{1}{2}mv^2 + q\mathbf{v} \cdot \mathbf{A}$$

yields the correct equation of motion where $\mathbf{B} = \nabla \times \mathbf{A}$. The quantity $\mathbf{A}$ is called the *vector potential*. [*Hint:* In this problem it will be necessary to employ the general formula $df(x, y, z)/dt = \dot{x}\partial f/\partial x + \dot{y}\partial f/\partial y + \dot{z}\partial f/\partial z$. Thus, for the part involving $\mathbf{v} \cdot \mathbf{A}$, we have

$$\frac{d}{dt}\left[\frac{\partial(\mathbf{v} \cdot \mathbf{A})}{\partial \dot{x}} \right] = \frac{d}{dt}\left[\frac{\partial}{\partial \dot{x}}(\dot{x}A_x + \dot{y}A_y + \dot{z}A_z) \right] = \frac{d}{dt}(A_x)$$

$$= \dot{x}\frac{\partial A_x}{\partial x} + \dot{y}\frac{\partial A_x}{\partial y} + \dot{z}\frac{\partial A_x}{\partial z}$$

and similarly for the other derivatives.]

10.18   Write down the Hamiltonian function and find Hamilton's canonical equations for the three-dimensional motion of a projectile in a uniform gravitational field with no air resistance. Show that these equations lead to the same equations of motion as found in Chapter 4.

10.19   Find Hamilton's canonical equations for
(a) A simple pendulum
(b) A simple Atwood machine
(c) A particle sliding down a smooth inclined plane

10.20   As we know, the kinetic energy of a particle in one-dimensional motion is $\tfrac{1}{2}m\dot{x}^2$. If the potential energy is proportional to x^2, say $\tfrac{1}{2}kx^2$, show by direct application of Hamilton's variational principle, $\delta\int L\,dt = 0$, that the equation of motion of the simple harmonic oscillator is obtained.

11

Dynamics of
Oscillating Systems

In the preceding chapters we have studied some simple systems that can undergo oscillations about a configuration of equilibrium, including a simple pendulum, a particle suspended on an elastic spring, a physical pendulum, and so on, all being cases of one degree of freedom characterized by a single frequency of oscillation. When we consider more complicated systems—systems with several degrees of freedom—we shall find that not one but several different frequencies of oscillation are possible. In our analysis of oscillating systems, we shall find it very convenient to use generalized coordinates and to employ Lagrange's method for finding the equations of motion in terms of those coordinates.

11.1 Potential Energy and Equilibrium. Stability

Before we take up the study of the motion of a system about an equilibrium configuration, let us examine briefly the equilibrium itself. Consider a system with n degrees of freedom, and let the generalized coordinates $q_1, q_2, \ldots, q_n$ specify the configuration. We shall assume that the system is conservative and that the potential energy V is a function of the q's alone:

$$V = V(q_1, q_2, \ldots, q_n)$$

Now we have shown that the generalized forces Q_k are given by

$$Q_k = -\frac{\partial V}{\partial q_k} \qquad (k = 1, 2, \ldots, n) \tag{11.1}$$

283

An equilibrium configuration is defined as a configuration for which all of the generalized forces vanish,

$$Q_k = -\frac{\partial V}{\partial q_k} = 0 \tag{11.2}$$

These equations constitute a necessary condition for the system to remain at rest if, initially, it is at rest. If the system is given a small displacement, however, it may or may not return to equilibrium. If a system always tends to return to equilibrium, given a sufficiently small displacement, the equilibrium is *stable;* otherwise, the equilibrium is *unstable.* (If the system has no tendency to move either toward or away from equilibrium, the equilibrium is said to be *neutral.*)

A ball placed (1) at the bottom of a spherical bowl, (2) on top of a spherical cap, and (3) on a plane horizontal surface are examples of stable, unstable, and neutral equilibrium, respectively.

Intuition tells us that the potential energy must be a *minimum* in all cases for stable equilibrium. That this is so can be argued from energy considerations. If the system is conservative the total energy $T + V$ is constant, so for a small change near equilibrium $\Delta T = -\Delta V$; thus T will decrease if V increases, that is, the motion tends to slow down and return to the equilibrium position, given a small displacement. The reverse is true if the potential energy is *maximum,* that is, any displacement causes V to decrease and T to increase, so the system tends to move away from the equilibrium position at an ever-increasing rate.

Extended Criteria for Stable Equilibrium

We consider first a system with one degree of freedom. Suppose we expand the potential energy function $V(q)$ as a Taylor series about the point $q = 0$, namely

$$V(q) = V_0 + qV_0' + \frac{q^2}{2!}V_0'' + \frac{q^3}{3!}V_0''' + \cdots + \frac{q^n}{n!}V_0^{(n)} + \cdots \tag{11.3}$$

where we use the notation $V_0' = (dV/dq)_{q=0}$, and so on. Now if $q = 0$ is a position of equilibrium, then $V_0' = 0$. This eliminates the linear term in the expansion. Furthermore, the term V_0 is a constant whose value depends on the arbitrary choice of the zero of the potential energy, so without incurring any loss of generality we can set $V_0 = 0$. Consequently, the expression for $V(q)$ simplifies to

$$V(q) = \frac{q^2}{2}V_0'' + \cdots \tag{11.3a}$$

If V_0'' is not zero, then for a small displacement q from equilibrium the force is approximately linear in the displacement:

$$F(q) = -\frac{dV}{dq} = -qV_0''$$

This will be of a "restorative" or "stabilizing" type if V_0'' is positive, whereas, if V_0'' is negative, the force will be antirestoring and the equilibrium is unstable. If $V_0'' = 0$,

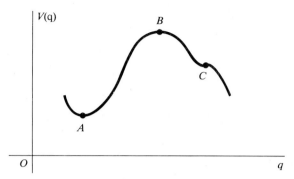

FIGURE 11.1 Graph of a one-dimensional potential energy function. The point A is one of stable equilibrium. Points B and C are unstable.

then we must examine the first nonvanishing term in the expansion. If this term is of even order in n, then the equilibrium is again stable, or unstable, depending on whether the derivative $V_0^{(n)} = (d^n V/dq^n)_{q=0}$ is positive or negative, respectively. If the first nonvanishing derivative is of odd order in n, then the equilibrium is always unstable regardless of the sign of the derivative; this corresponds to the situation at point C in Figure 11.1. Clearly, if *all* derivatives vanish then the potential energy function is a constant, and the equilibrium is neutral.

Similarly, for the case of a system with several degrees of freedom, we can effect a linear transformation so that $q_1 = q_2 = \cdots = q_n = 0$ is configuration of equilibrium, if an equilibrium configuration exists. The potential-energy function can then be expanded in the form

$$V(q_1, q_2, \ldots, q_n) = \tfrac{1}{2}(\kappa_{11}q_1^2 + 2\kappa_{12}q_1q_2 + \kappa_{22}q_2^2 + \cdots) \tag{11.4}$$

where

$$\kappa_{11} = \left(\frac{\partial^2 V}{\partial q_1^2}\right)_{q_1 = q_2 = \cdots = q_n = 0}$$

$$\kappa_{12} = \left(\frac{\partial^2 V}{\partial q_1 \partial q_2}\right)_{q_1 = q_2 = \cdots = q_n = 0}$$

and so on. We have arbitrarily set $V(0, 0, \ldots, 0) = 0$. The linear terms in the expansion are absent because the expansion is about an equilibrium configuration.

The expression in parentheses in Equation 11.4 is known as a *quadratic form*. If this quadratic form is positive definite,[1] that is, either zero or positive for all values of the q's, then the equilibrium configuration $q_1 = q_2 = \cdots = q_n = 0$ is stable.

---

[1] The necessary and sufficient conditions that the quadratic form in Equation 11.4 be positive definite are

$$\kappa_{11} > 0 \qquad \begin{vmatrix} \kappa_{11} & \kappa_{12} \\ \kappa_{21} & \kappa_{22} \end{vmatrix} > 0 \qquad \begin{vmatrix} \kappa_{11} & \kappa_{12} & \kappa_{13} \\ \kappa_{21} & \kappa_{22} & \kappa_{23} \\ \kappa_{31} & \kappa_{32} & \kappa_{33} \end{vmatrix} > 0 \qquad \text{and so on}$$

Example

11.1 *Stability of rocking chairs, pencils-on-end, etc.*

Let us examine the equilibrium of a body having a rounded (spherical or cylindrical) base which is balanced on a plane horizontal surface. Let a be the radius of curvature of the base, and let the center of mass CM be a distance b from the initial point of contact, as shown in Figure 11.2(a). In Figure 11.2(b) the body is shown in a displaced position, where θ is the angle between the vertical and the line OCM (O being the center of curvature), as shown. Let h denote the distance from the plane to the center of mass. Then the potential energy is given by

$$V = mgh = mg[a - (a - b)\cos\theta]$$

where m is the mass of the body. We have

$$V' = \frac{dV}{d\theta} = mg(a - b)\sin\theta$$

which gives, for $\theta = 0$

$$V_0' = 0$$

Thus $\theta = 0$ is a position of equilibrium. Furthermore, the second derivative is

$$V'' = mg(a - b)\cos\theta$$

so, for $\theta = 0$

$$V_0'' = mg(a - b)$$

Hence the equilibrium is stable if $a > b$, that is, if the center of mass lies below the center of curvature O. If $a < b$ the second derivative is negative and the equilibrium is unstable, such as with a pencil standing on end. If $a = b$ the potential energy function is constant, and the equilibrium is neutral. In this latter case, the center of mass coincides with the center of curvature.

11.2   Oscillation of a System with One Degree of Freedom about a Position of Stable Equilibrium

If a system has one degree of freedom, the kinetic energy may be expressed as

$$T = \frac{1}{2}M\dot{q}^2$$

where the coefficient M may be a constant, or may be a function of the generalized coordinate q. In any case, if $q = 0$ is a position of equilibrium, we shall consider q small enough so that $M = M(0) = constant$ is a valid approximation. From the expression for the potential energy, Equation 11.3a we can write the Lagrangian function as

$$L = T - V = \frac{1}{2}M\dot{q}^2 - \frac{1}{2}V_0''q^2 \tag{11.5}$$

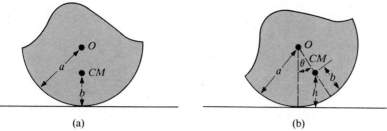

(a)   (b)

FIGURE 11.2   Coordinates for analyzing the stability of equilibrium of a round-bottomed object.

Lagrange's equation of motion

$$\frac{d}{dt}\frac{\partial L}{\partial \dot{q}} - \frac{\partial L}{\partial q} = 0$$

then becomes

$$M\ddot{q} + V_0''q = 0 \tag{11.6}$$

Thus, if $q = 0$ is a position of stable equilibrium, that is, if $V_0'' > 0$, then the system oscillates harmonically about the equilibrium position with angular frequency

$$\omega = \sqrt{\frac{V_0''}{M}} \tag{11.7}$$

Examples

11.2   Consider the motion of the round-bottomed object discussed in the example of the preceding section (Figure 11.2). If the contact is perfectly rough, we have pure rolling, and the speed of the center of mass is approximately $b\dot{\theta}$ for small θ. The kinetic energy T is accordingly given by

$$T = \tfrac{1}{2}m(b\dot{\theta})^2 + \tfrac{1}{2}I_{cm}\dot{\theta}^2$$

where I_{cm} is the moment of inertia about the center of mass. Also, we can express the potential-energy function V as follows:

$$V(\theta) = mg[a - (a - b)\cos\theta]$$
$$= mg\left[a - (a - b)\left(1 - \frac{\theta^2}{2!} + \frac{\theta^4}{4!} - \cdots\right)\right]$$
$$= \tfrac{1}{2}mg(a - b)\theta^2 + \text{constant} + \text{higher terms}$$

We can then write

$$L = \tfrac{1}{2}(mb^2 + I_{cm})\dot{\theta}^2 - \tfrac{1}{2}mg(a - b)\theta^2$$

neglecting constants and higher terms. Comparing with Equation 11.5, we see that

$$M = mb^2 + I_{cm}$$
$$V_0'' = mg(a - b)$$

The motion about the equilibrium position $\theta = 0$ is therefore approximately simple harmonic with angular frequency

$$\omega = \sqrt{\frac{mg(a - b)}{mb^2 + I_{cm}}}$$

11.3 *Attitude stability and oscillation of an orbiting satellite.* In this example we shall analyze the oscillatory motion of a non-spherical satellite travelling in a circular orbit. For simplicity, we shall consider the satellite to be a "dumbbell" consisting of two small spheres, of mass $m/2$ each, connected by a light rod of length $2a$, Figure 11.3. Polar coordinates r, θ specify the center of mass CM (center of the rod), and the angle ϕ gives the "attitude" of the satellite axis relative to the radius vector OCM, O being the center of the earth. We shall treat the two end spheres as particles and assume that the motion is in a single plane, the plane of the orbit. For a circular orbit $r = r_0 = $ constant, and $\dot{\theta} = \omega_0 = v_{cm}/r_0 = $ constant.

The most important quantity to calculate in this example is the potential energy function of the satellite. It is given by

$$V = -\frac{GM_e m}{2}\left(\frac{1}{r_1} + \frac{1}{r_2}\right)$$

in which M_e is the earth's mass and r_1 and r_2 are the distances from O to the respective end spheres, as shown. From the law of cosines we have

$$r_{1,2} = (r_0^2 + a^2 \pm 2r_0 a \cos \phi)^{1/2} = (r_0^2 + a^2)^{1/2}(1 \pm \epsilon \cos \phi)^{1/2}$$

where $\epsilon = 2r_0 a/(r_0^2 + a^2)$. Now $a \ll r_0$, so ϵ is a very small quantity. We shall therefore express the potential energy function by use of the binomial series $(1 + x)^{-1/2} = 1 -$

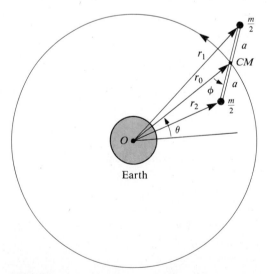

FIGURE 11.3   Dumbell-shaped satellite in a circular orbit.

$\dfrac{1}{2}x + \dfrac{3}{8}x^2 + \cdots$ where $x = \pm\,\epsilon\cos\phi$. The result, after collecting and cancelling terms, is

$$V(\phi) = -\frac{GM_e m}{r_0}\left(1 + \frac{3a^2}{2r_0^2}\cos^2\phi + \cdots\right)$$

where we have neglected a^2 compared to r_0^2 in all terms involving the quantity $r_0^2 + a^2$. Taking the first and second derivatives with respect to ϕ, we find

$$V'(\phi) = \frac{GM_e m}{r_0^3}\,3a^2\sin\phi\cos\phi$$

$$V''(\phi) = \frac{GM_e m}{r_0^3}\,3a^2\cos(2\phi)$$

Thus we have $\phi = 0$ and $\phi = \pi/2$ as two positions of equilibrium: $V'(0) = V'(\pi/2) = 0$. The first is stable, since $V''(0) > 0$. In this case the attitude of the satellite is such that the satellite's axis (line connecting the two masses) is along the radius vector OCM. The second position is an unstable equilibrium since $V''(\pi/2) < 0$; here the axis is at right angles to the radius vector.

The rocking motion of the satellite about the position of stable equilibrium is given by Equation 11.6 with $q = \phi$, $M = I_{cm} = ma^2$, and $V_0'' = 3a^2 GM_e m/r_0^3$. Thus the angular frequency of the oscillation is

$$\omega = \sqrt{\frac{V_0''}{I_{cm}}} = \sqrt{\frac{3GM_e}{r_0^3}}$$

(Note that this is independent of m and a.) Now the angular frequency of the circular orbit around the earth is given by $\omega_0^2 = v_{cm}^2/r_0^2 = GM_e/r_0^3$. [See Example 6.6(a).] Thus we can write

$$\omega = \omega_0\sqrt{3}$$

For a synchronous earth satellite the orbital period $2\pi/\omega_0 = 24$ hr. Consequently, the rocking period of our dumbbell satellite in a synchronous orbit would be

$$\frac{2\pi}{\omega} = \frac{24}{\sqrt{3}}\text{ hr} = 13.86\text{ hr}$$

11.3   Coupled Harmonic Oscillators. Normal Coordinates

Prior to developing the general theory of oscillating systems with any number of degrees of freedom, we shall study a simple specific example, namely, a system consisting of two harmonic oscillators that are coupled together.

For definiteness we use a model comprised of particles attached to elastic springs, although any type of oscillator could be used. For simplicity we assume that the oscillators are identical and are restricted to move in a straight line, Figure 11.4. The coupling is represented by a spring of stiffness K' as shown. The system has two

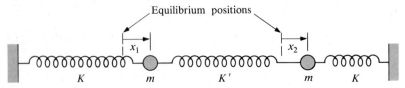

FIGURE 11.4 Model of two coupled harmonic oscillators.

degrees of freedom. We shall choose coordinates x_1 and x_2, the displacements of the particles from their respective equilibrium positions, to represent the configuration of the system.

The kinetic energy of the system is

$$T = \tfrac{1}{2}m\dot{x}_1^2 + \tfrac{1}{2}m\dot{x}_2^2$$

and the potential energy is

$$V = \tfrac{1}{2}Kx_1^2 + \tfrac{1}{2}K'(x_2 - x_1)^2 + \tfrac{1}{2}Kx_2^2$$

Hence the Lagrangian function L is given by

$$L = \tfrac{1}{2}m\dot{x}_1^2 + \tfrac{1}{2}m\dot{x}_2^2 - \tfrac{1}{2}Kx_1^2 - \tfrac{1}{2}K'(x_2 - x_1)^2 - \tfrac{1}{2}Kx_2^2 \tag{11.8}$$

Lagrange's equations

$$\frac{d}{dt}\frac{\partial L}{\partial \dot{x}_1} - \frac{\partial L}{\partial x_1} = 0 \qquad \frac{d}{dt}\frac{\partial L}{\partial \dot{x}_2} - \frac{\partial L}{\partial x_2} = 0$$

then read

$$m\ddot{x}_1 + Kx_1 - K'(x_2 - x_1) = 0$$
$$m\ddot{x}_2 + Kx_2 + K'(x_2 - x_1) = 0 \tag{11.9}$$

If it were not for the coupling spring K', the two equations would be separated, and each particle would move independently with simple harmonic motion of frequency $\sqrt{K/m}$. It is reasonable, therefore, to try a solution for which x_1 and x_2 both depend on time through a factor $\cos \omega t$, where ω is to be determined. Our trial solution is

$$x_1 = A_1 \cos \omega t$$
$$x_2 = A_2 \cos \omega t \tag{11.10}$$

By direct substitution into Equations 11.9 we find

$$-m\omega^2 A_1 \cos \omega t + KA_1 \cos \omega t - K'(A_2 - A_1) \cos \omega t = 0$$
$$-m\omega^2 A_2 \cos \omega t + KA_2 \cos \omega t + K'(A_2 - A_1) \cos \omega t = 0$$

Cancelling the common factor $\cos \omega t$ and collecting terms gives

$$(-m\omega^2 + K + K')A_1 - K'A_2 = 0$$
$$-K'A_1 + (-m\omega^2 + K + K')A_2 = 0 \tag{11.11}$$

These two equations give the conditions on the coefficients A_1 and A_2 that must be satisfied if our trial solution is valid. Thus, either we have a trivial solution for which $A_1 = A_2 = 0$, or the determinant of the coefficients of the A's must vanish:

$$\begin{vmatrix} -m\omega^2 + K + K' & -K' \\ -K' & -m\omega^2 + K + K' \end{vmatrix} = 0 \qquad (11.12)$$

This is known as the *secular equation*. Upon expanding the determinant, the secular equation reads

$$(-m\omega^2 + K + K')^2 - K'^2 = 0 \qquad (11.12a)$$

or

$$-m\omega^2 + K + K' = \pm K' \qquad (11.12b)$$

Thus there are *two* possible frequencies of oscillation, which we shall denote by ω_a and ω_b, given by

$$\omega_a = \left(\frac{K}{m}\right)^{1/2} \qquad \omega_b = \left(\frac{K + 2K'}{m}\right)^{1/2}$$

The two frequencies ω_a and ω_b are called the *normal frequencies* of the system. We now have two possible solutions:

(a) $x_1 = A_1 \cos \omega_a t$ $x_2 = A_2 \cos \omega_a t$ (11.13)

and

(b) $x_1 = B_1 \cos \omega_b t$ $x_2 = B_2 \cos \omega_b t$ (11.14)

Notice that the negative roots of the secular equation do not give different solutions, since $\cos \omega t = \cos (-\omega t)$. The amplitudes A_1, A_2, B_1, and B_2 are not independent, however. If we substitute the values of ω back into Equations 11.11, we find the following:

(a) for $\omega = \omega_a$

$$\left[-m\left(\frac{K}{m}\right) + K + K'\right]A_1 - K'A_2 = 0$$

which reduces, upon cancellation, to

$$A_1 = A_2$$

(b) for $\omega = \omega_b$

$$\left[-m\left(\frac{K + 2K'}{m}\right) + K + K'\right]B_1 - K'B_2 = 0$$

which reduces to

$$B_1 = -B_2$$

Thus our solutions (Equations 11.13 and 11.14) can be expressed

$$x_1 = A \cos \omega_a t \qquad x_2 = A \cos \omega_a t \qquad (11.15)$$
$$x_1 = B \cos \omega_b t \qquad x_2 = -B \cos \omega_b t \qquad (11.16)$$

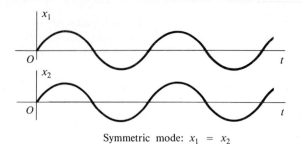

Symmetric mode: $x_1 = x_2$

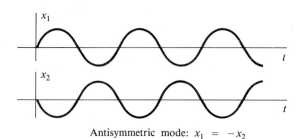

Antisymmetric mode: $x_1 = -x_2$

FIGURE 11.5 Graphs of displacement versus time for the two normal modes of two coupled harmonic oscillators.

The subscripts for A and B are no longer necessary. The oscillations represented by the above solutions are called *normal modes*. The normal modes are characterized by the condition that all coordinates oscillate with the same frequency. In our case the oscillation at the frequency ω_a is such that

$$x_1 = x_2$$

This is called the *symmetric* mode. The oscillation at the frequency ω_b is such that

$$x_1 = -x_2$$

This is known as the *antisymmetric mode*. Graphs illustrating the two normal modes are shown in Figure 11.5.

The Complete Solution

Let us go back now and consider the original differential equations of motion, Equations 11.9. We can easily see that a trial solution in which the x's depend on time through a factor $\sin \omega t$ rather than $\cos \omega t$ would have yielded essentially the same results as those we have already obtained—we would have found the same normal frequencies and the same normal modes. That is,

$$x_1 = A' \sin \omega_a t \qquad x_2 = A' \sin \omega_a t$$

and

$$x_1 = B' \sin \omega_b t \qquad x_2 = -B' \sin \omega_b t$$

are also solutions. Now, since the differential equations are linear, we know that solutions may be added together to yield other solutions. Hence we can write the complete solution in the form

$$x_1(t) = A \cos \omega_a t + A' \sin \omega_a t + B \cos \omega_b t + B' \sin \omega_b t$$
$$x_2(t) = A \cos \omega_a t + A' \sin \omega_a t - B \cos \omega_b t - B' \sin \omega_b t$$

(11.17)

or, equivalently, as in Section 3.2,

$$x_1(t) = \mathscr{A} \cos (\omega_a t - \varphi_a) + \mathscr{B} \cos (\omega_b t - \varphi_b)$$
$$x_2(t) = \mathscr{A} \cos (\omega_a t - \varphi_a) - \mathscr{B} \cos (\omega_b t - \varphi_b)$$

(11.17a)

(We could also have used a trial solution of the complex exponential type $e^{-i\omega t}$ with the same final result.)

Initial Conditions

The amplitudes and phases are determined from the initial conditions. Thus at time $t = 0$, we have from Equations 11.17

$$x_1(0) = A + B \qquad x_2(0) = A - B$$

Also, by differentiating with respect to t, we have at time $t = 0$, the relations

$$\dot{x}_1(0) = A'\omega_a + B'\omega_b \qquad \dot{x}_2(0) = A'\omega_a - B'\omega_b$$

We can now solve for the amplitudes to find

$$A = \tfrac{1}{2}[x_1(0) + x_2(0)] \qquad B = \tfrac{1}{2}[x_1(0) - x_2(0)] \qquad (11.18)$$

$$A' = \frac{1}{2\omega_a}[\dot{x}_1(0) + \dot{x}_2(0)] \qquad B' = \frac{1}{2\omega_b}[\dot{x}_1(0) - \dot{x}_2(0)] \qquad (11.19)$$

These equations allow us to find the excitations of the two normal modes from the initial conditions. Suppose, for example, that initially the two particles are pulled from their equilibrium positions by equal amounts in the same direction and released so that the initial conditions are $x_1(0) = x_2(0)$, $\dot{x}_1(0) = \dot{x}_2(0) = 0$. The result is that the symmetric mode alone is excited, since all the constants except A vanish. On the other hand, if the motion is started by pulling the two particles equally in opposite directions and releasing them, the initial conditions are $x_1(0) = -x_2(0)$, $\dot{x}_1(0) = \dot{x}_2(0) = 0$. In this case all constants except B are zero, so the antisymmetric alone is excited. In general, the oscillation of the system consists of a mixture of the two modes.

Normal Coordinates

Upon inspection of the complete solution of the coupled harmonic oscillators, Equations 11.17 and 11.17a, we see that it is possible to construct linear combinations $c_1 x_1 + c_2 x_2$ such that the combination involves only *one* of the normal frequencies. In our present example in which the two oscillators are identical, the required combination is particularly simple, namely the sum and the difference, or any constant multiple of the sum and the difference. We shall choose the constant to be 1/2 so that

$$\frac{1}{2}(x_1 + x_2) = X_a = \mathscr{A}\cos(\omega_a t - \varphi_a)$$

$$\frac{1}{2}(x_1 - x_2) = X_b = \mathscr{B}\cos(\omega_b t - \varphi_b)$$

(11.20)

The quantities X_a and X_b are called *normal coordinates*. If the initial condition is such that the symmetric mode alone is excited, then X_a is active and X_b is zero. Similarly, if only the antisymmetric mode is excited, then X_a is zero and X_b is active. In general, both normal coordinates are active simultaneously.

It is instructive to go back to the Lagrangian function and express it in terms of the normal coordinates. To do this we first express x_1 and x_2 in terms of the normal coordinates. In the present case, from Equations 11.20 we have

$$x_1 = X_a + X_b \qquad x_2 = X_a - X_b \tag{11.21}$$

Upon substitution of these expressions, and their time derivatives, into our original Lagrangian function, Equation 11.8, we find

$$L = 2\left(\frac{m}{2}\dot{X}_a^2 - \frac{K_a}{2}X_a^2\right) + 2\left(\frac{m}{2}\dot{X}_b^2 - \frac{K_b}{2}X_b^2\right) \tag{11.22}$$

The result of transforming to normal coordinates is that the cross terms involving the products $X_a X_b$ and $\dot{X}_a \dot{X}_b$ all cancel out so that the kinetic energy and potential energy both reduce to sums of squares. Consequently, Lagrange's equations in the normal coordinates

$$\frac{d}{dt}\frac{\partial L}{\partial \dot{X}_a} - \frac{\partial L}{\partial X_a} = 0 \qquad \frac{d}{dt}\frac{\partial L}{\partial \dot{X}_b} - \frac{\partial L}{\partial X_b} = 0$$

are simply

$$m\ddot{X}_a + K_a X_a = 0 \qquad m\ddot{X}_b + K_b X_b = 0 \tag{11.23}$$

These are in separated form, and the solution is clearly that expressed by Equations 11.20.

Thus the normal coordinates act as though they are the coordinates of two *independent* harmonic oscillators, each with its own frequency, amplitude, and phase. Clearly, if we knew in advance the normal coordinates and frequencies of a system of coupled oscillators, we could write down the equations of motion immediately. However, it is not the usual case that we know beforehand what particular linear combinations of the original coordinates make up the normal coordinates in a given situation. Fortunately, it is *not* necessary to find the normal coordinates in order to determine the frequencies. *The normal frequencies are always given by the roots of the secular determinant regardless of the particular coordinates used to specify the configuration of the system.*

Example

11.4 *The double pendulum, or two mountain climbers dangling on a single rope.* Let us
consider the motion of the so-called "double pendulum" consisting of a light inextensible
cord of length $2l$ with one end fixed, the other supporting a bob (treated here as a particle)
of mass m, and with a second bob, also of mass m, at the center as shown in Figure 11.6a.
Assuming that the system stays in a single plane, we can specify the configuration by two
angles, θ and ϕ as shown. For small oscillations about the equilibrium position, the
speeds of the two particles are approximately $l\dot{\theta}$ and $l(\dot{\theta} + \dot{\phi})$, and their potential energies are $-mgl \cos \theta$ and $-mgl(\cos \theta + \cos \phi)$. The Lagrangian function for the system
is then

$$L = \frac{m}{2} l^2 \dot{\theta}^2 + \frac{m}{2} l^2 (\dot{\theta} + \dot{\phi})^2 + 2mgl \cos \theta + mgl \cos \phi$$

Lagrange's equations of motion

$$\frac{d}{dt} \frac{\partial L}{\partial \dot{\theta}} - \frac{\partial L}{\partial \theta} = 0 \qquad \frac{d}{dt} \frac{\partial L}{\partial \dot{\phi}} - \frac{\partial L}{\partial \phi} = 0$$

then read

$$ml^2 \ddot{\theta} + ml^2 (\ddot{\theta} + \ddot{\phi}) - 2mgl \sin \theta = 0$$
$$ml^2 (\ddot{\theta} + \ddot{\phi}) - mgl \sin \phi = 0$$

Assuming that $\sin \theta \approx \theta$, $\sin \phi \approx \phi$, we find

$$2\ddot{\theta} + \frac{2g}{l} \theta + \ddot{\phi} = 0$$

(11.24)

$$\ddot{\theta} + \ddot{\phi} + \frac{g}{l} \phi = 0$$

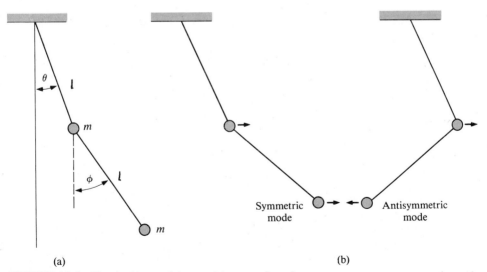

(a)   (b)

FIGURE 11.6 The double pendulum and its normal modes.

The secular determinant for the system is then

$$
\begin{vmatrix}
-2\omega^2 + \dfrac{2g}{l} & -\omega^2 \\[4mm]
-\omega^2 & -\omega^2 + \dfrac{g}{l}
\end{vmatrix} = 0
$$

or

$$
\omega^4 - 4\omega^2 \left(\frac{g}{l} \right) + 2\left(\frac{g}{l} \right)^2 = 0
$$

The two normal frequencies are thus

$$
\omega_a = \left[\frac{g}{l}(2 - \sqrt{2}) \right]^{1/2} \quad \omega_b = \left[\frac{g}{l}(2 + \sqrt{2}) \right]^{1/2} \tag{11.25}
$$

If the system is oscillating at either of its normal frequencies, then the first of Equations 11.24 yields

$$
\left(-2\omega^2 + 2\frac{g}{l} \right)\theta = \omega^2 \phi
$$

Upon substituting the two values of ω into the above equation, we find the following relations between ϕ and θ for the normal modes:

$$
\begin{aligned}
\phi &= +\sqrt{2}\,\theta & \omega &= \omega_a & \textit{(symmetric mode)} \\
\phi &= -\sqrt{2}\,\theta & \omega &= \omega_b & \textit{(antisymmetric mode)}
\end{aligned}
$$

The normal modes are shown in Figure 11.6b. The ratio of the two normal frequencies is independent of the length l, and is given by

$$
\frac{\omega_b}{\omega_a} = \left(\frac{2 + \sqrt{2}}{2 - \sqrt{2}} \right)^{1/2} = 2.414
$$

so the oscillation in the fast (antisymmetric) mode is almost two and one-half times the frequency of the slow (symmetric) mode. The complete solution can now be written down as follows:

$$
\begin{aligned}
\theta(t) &= \mathcal{A}\cos(\omega_a t - \epsilon_a) + \mathcal{B}\cos(\omega_b t - \epsilon_b) \\
\phi(t) &= \sqrt{2}\mathcal{A}\cos(\omega_a t - \epsilon_a) - \sqrt{2}\mathcal{B}\cos(\omega_b t - \epsilon_b)
\end{aligned} \tag{11.26}
$$

A set of normal coordinates can then be found by inspection, namely

$$
X_a = \frac{1}{2}\left(\theta + \frac{\phi}{\sqrt{2}} \right) = \mathcal{A}\cos(\omega_a t - \epsilon_a)
$$

$$
X_b = \frac{1}{2}\left(\theta - \frac{\phi}{\sqrt{2}} \right) = \mathcal{B}\cos(\omega_b t - \epsilon_b)
$$

(11.27)

where ω_a and ω_b are given by Equations 11.25. It is left as a problem to show that the kinetic and potential energies reduce to sums of squares when θ and ϕ are expressed in terms of the above normal coordinates.

11.4 General Theory of Vibrating Systems

Turning now to a general system with n degrees of freedom, we have shown in the last chapter (Section 10.3) that the kinetic energy T is a homogeneous quadratic function of the generalized velocities, namely,

$$T = \frac{1}{2}M_{11}\dot{q}_1^2 + M_{12}\dot{q}_1\dot{q}_2 + \frac{1}{2}M_{22}\dot{q}_2^2 + \cdots = \sum_j \sum_k \frac{1}{2}M_{jk}\dot{q}_j\dot{q}_k$$

provided there are no moving constraints. Since we are concerned with motion about an equilibrium configuration, we shall assume, as in Section 11.2, that the M's are constant and equal to their values at the equilibrium configuration. We shall further assume that the coordinate origins have been chosen such that the equilibrium configuration is given by

$$q_1 = q_2 = \cdots = q_n = 0$$

Accordingly, the potential energy V, from Equation (11.4), is given by

$$V = \frac{1}{2}K_{11}q_1^2 + K_{12}q_1q_2 + \frac{1}{2}K_{22}q_2^2 + \cdots = \sum_j \sum_k \frac{1}{2}K_{jk}q_jq_k$$

The Lagrangian function then assumes the form

$$L = \sum_j \sum_k \frac{1}{2}(M_{jk}\dot{q}_j\dot{q}_k - K_{jk}q_jq_k) \tag{11.28}$$

and the equations of motion

$$\frac{d}{dt}\frac{\partial L}{\partial \dot{q}_k} - \frac{\partial L}{\partial q_k} = 0$$

then read

$$\sum_j (M_{jk}\ddot{q}_j + K_{jk}q_j) = 0 \qquad (k = 1, 2, \ldots n) \tag{11.29}$$

If a solution of the form

$$q_k = A_k \cos \omega t \qquad (k = 1, 2, \ldots n) \tag{11.30}$$

exists, then by direct substitution the following equations must be satisfied:

$$\sum_j (-M_{jk}\omega^2 + K_{jk})A_j = 0 \qquad (k = 1, 2, \ldots n) \tag{11.31}$$

A nontrivial solution requires that the determinant of the coefficients of the A's vanish:

$$\begin{vmatrix} -M_{11}\omega^2 + K_{11} & -M_{12}\omega^2 + K_{12} & \cdots \\ -M_{21}\omega^2 + K_{21} & -M_{22}\omega^2 + K_{22} & \cdots \\ \cdots & \cdots & \cdots \end{vmatrix} = 0 \qquad (11.32)$$

The above secular equation is an equation of the nth degree in ω^2. The n roots are the squares of the normal frequencies of the system.

Thus, if a given system has n degrees of freedom there are, in general, n different possible frequencies of oscillation about the equilibrium configuration, each characterized by its own normal mode. The calculation of these normal frequencies often entails the tedious task of solving a high-order algebraic equation, cubic for $n = 3$, biquadratic for $n = 4$, and so on. There are some special situations for which the roots of the secular equation are either *repeated* or *zero,* or both. In such cases the mathematical problem of finding the normal frequencies may be simplified. An example will be given at the end of this section. In the next section we shall give a method of determining the normal frequencies for a linear array of coupled oscillators for which n may have *any* value.

As in the previous case of two coupled oscillators, the complete solution for n oscillators is given by a superposition of sinusoidal oscillations at the normal frequencies ω_N, namely

$$q_k(t) = \sum_{N=1}^{n} \mathcal{A}_{kN} \cos (\omega_N t - \varphi_N) \qquad (k = 1, 2, \ldots, n)$$

The amplitudes $\mathcal{A}_{kN}$ are not independent, but are related by the fact that for *each* normal frequency ω_N a set of equations of the type 11.31 must be satisfied. This allows us, in principle, to determine the amplitude ratios $\mathcal{A}_{1N}:\mathcal{A}_{2N}: \ldots :\mathcal{A}_{nN}$, and thus to construct linear combinations

$$c_{1N}q_1 + c_{2N}q_2 + \cdots + c_{nN}q_n = X_N = \mathcal{A}_N \cos (\omega_N t - \varphi_N)$$
$$(N = 1, 2, \ldots n)$$

defining the normal coordinates X_N of the system, as we did above. For $n > 2$ this is not the most efficient method, as a rule. In the general case the transformation coefficients c_{kN} are best found by matrix algebra. This involves the diagonalizing of the matrix of the determinant of Equation 11.32. We shall not pursue this question further at this point. (See Appendix H.)

Example

11.5 *Linear motion of a triatomic molecule.* Let us consider the motion of a three-particle system in which the particles all lie in a straight line. An example of such a collinear system is the carbon dioxide molecule CO_2 which has the chemical structure O—C—O. For simplicity we shall consider only motion in one dimension, the x-axis (Figure 11.7). The two end particles, each of mass m, are bound to the central particle, mass M, through a potential function that is equivalent to two springs of stiffness K, as shown. Our coordinates are x_1, x_2, and x_3. The Lagrangian function for the system is clearly

$$L = T - V$$

$$= \left(\frac{m}{2}\dot{x}_1^2 + \frac{M}{2}\dot{x}_2^2 + \frac{m}{2}\dot{x}_3^2\right) - \left[\frac{K}{2}(x_2 - x_1)^2 + \frac{K}{2}(x_3 - x_2)^2\right]$$

and Lagrange's three equations of motion read

$$
\begin{aligned}
m\ddot{x}_1 + Kx_1 \quad\quad\quad -Kx_2 \quad\quad\quad\quad\quad\quad\quad &= 0 \\
-Kx_1 \quad + M\ddot{x}_2 + 2Kx_2 \quad\quad -Kx_3 \quad &= 0 \\
-Kx_2 \quad + m\ddot{x}_3 + Kx_3 &= 0
\end{aligned}
\tag{11.33}
$$

If a solution of the form $x_1 = A_1 \cos \omega t$, $x_2 = A_2 \cos \omega t$, $x_3 = A_3 \cos \omega t$ exists, then

$$
\begin{aligned}
(-m\omega^2 + K)A_1 \quad\quad -KA_2 \quad\quad\quad\quad\quad\quad &= 0 \\
-KA_1 \quad + (-M\omega^2 + 2K)A_2 \quad\quad -KA_3 \quad &= 0 \\
-KA_2 \quad + (-m\omega^2 + K)A_3 &= 0
\end{aligned}
\tag{11.34}
$$

The secular equation is thus

$$
\begin{vmatrix}
-m\omega^2 + K & -K & 0 \\
-K & -M\omega^2 + 2K & -K \\
0 & -K & -m\omega^2 + K
\end{vmatrix} = 0
\tag{11.35}
$$

which, upon expanding the determinant and collecting terms, fortuitously becomes the product of three factors

$$\omega^2(-m\omega^2 + K)(-mM\omega^2 + KM + 2Km) = 0$$

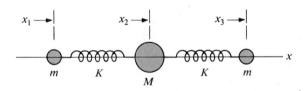

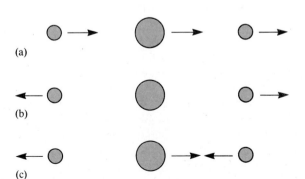

(a)

(b)

(c)

FIGURE 11.7 Model of a triatomic molecule and its three normal modes for motion in a single line.

Equating each of the three factors to zero gives the three normal frequencies of the system:

$$\omega_a = 0 \qquad \omega_b = \left(\frac{K}{m}\right)^{1/2} \qquad \omega_c = \left(\frac{K}{m} + 2\frac{K}{M}\right)^{1/2}$$

Let us discuss the modes corresponding to these three roots.

(a) The first mode is no oscillation at all, but is *pure translation* of the system as a whole. If we set $\omega = 0$ in Equations 11.34 we find that $A_1 = A_2 = A_3$ for this mode.
(b) Setting $\omega = \omega_b$ in Equations 11.34 gives $A_2 = 0$ and $A_1 = -A_3$. In this mode the center particle is at rest while the two end particles vibrate in opposite directions (antisymmetrically) with the same amplitude.
(c) Finally, setting $\omega = \omega_c$ in Equations 11.34 we obtain the following relations: $A_1 = A_3$ and $A_2 = -2A_1(m/M) = -2A_3(m/M)$. Thus, in this mode the two end particles vibrate in unison while the center particle vibrates oppositely with a different amplitude. The three modes are illustrated in Figure 11.7.

It is interesting to note that the ratio ω_c/ω_b is independent of the constant K, namely

$$\frac{\omega_c}{\omega_b} = \left(1 + 2\frac{m}{M}\right)^{1/2}$$

In the carbon dioxide molecule the mass ratio m/M is very nearly 16:12 for ordinary CO_2 (C_{12} and O_{16} atoms). Thus the frequency ratio

$$\frac{\omega_c}{\omega_b} = \left(1 + 2 \times \frac{16}{12}\right)^{1/2} = \left(\frac{11}{3}\right)^{1/2} = 1.915$$

11.5 Vibration of a Loaded String or Linear Array of Coupled Harmonic Oscillators: One-dimensional Crystal

In this section we consider the motion of a simple mechanical system consisting of a light elastic string that is clamped at both ends and loaded with a given number n of particles equally spaced along the length of the string, each being of equal mass m. The problem illustrates the general theory of vibrations and also leads naturally into the theory of wave motion, briefly treated in the next section.

Let us label the displacements of the various particles from their equilibrium positions by the coordinates $q_1, q_2, \ldots, q_n$. Actually, there are two types of displacement that can occur, namely a longitudinal displacement in which the particle moves along the direction of the string, and a transverse displacement in which the particle moves at right angles to the length of the string. These are illustrated in Figure 11.8. For simplicity we shall assume that the motion is either purely longitudinal or purely transverse, although in the actual physical situation a combination of the two could occur. The kinetic energy of the system is then given by

$$T = \frac{m}{2}(\dot{q}_1^2 + \dot{q}_2^2 + \cdots + \dot{q}_n^2)$$

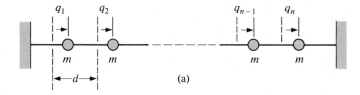

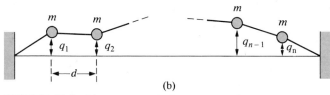

(b)

FIGURE 11.8   Linear array of vibrating particles or the loaded string. (a) Longitudinal motion. (b) Transverse motion.

If we use the letter k to denote any given particle, then, in the case of longitudinal motion, the stretch of the section of string between particle k and particle $k + 1$ is

$$q_{k+1} - q_k$$

Hence the potential energy of this section of the string is

$$\frac{1}{2}K(q_{k+1} - q_k)^2$$

in which K is the elastic stiffness coefficient of the section of string connecting the two adjacent particles.

For the case of transverse motion, the distance between particle k and $k + 1$ is

$$[d^2 + (q_{k+1} - q_k)^2]^{1/2} = d + \frac{1}{2d}(q_{k+1} - q_k)^2 + \cdots$$

in which d is the equilibrium distance between two adjacent particles. The stretch of the section of string connecting the two particles is then approximately

$$\Delta l = \frac{1}{2d}(q_{k+1} - q_k)^2$$

Thus, if S is the tension in the string, the potential energy of the section under consideration is given by

$$S\Delta l = \frac{S}{2d}(q_{k+1} - q_k)^2$$

It follows that the total potential energy of the system in either the longitudinal or the transverse type of motion is expressible as a quadratic function of the form

$$V = \frac{K}{2}[q_1^2 + (q_2 - q_1)^2 + \cdots + (q_n - q_{n-1})^2 + q_n^2]$$

in which

(1) $K = \dfrac{S}{d} = \dfrac{\text{tension}}{\text{separation}}$ (*transverse vibration*)

or

(2) $K = \text{elastic constant}$ (*longitudinal vibration*)

The Lagrangian function for either case is thus given by

$$L = \frac{1}{2}\sum_k [m\dot{q}_k^2 - K(q_{k+1} - q_k)^2] \tag{11.36}$$

The Lagrangian equations of motion

$$\frac{d}{dt}\frac{\partial L}{\partial \dot{q}_k} = \frac{\partial L}{\partial q_k}$$

then become

$$m\ddot{q}_k = -K(q_k - q_{k-1}) + K(q_{k+1} - q_k) \tag{11.37}$$

where $k = 1, 2, \ldots, n$.

To solve the above system of n equations, we use a trial solution in which the q's are assumed to vary harmonically with time:

$$q_k = a_k \cos(\omega t)$$

where a_k is the amplitude of vibration of the kth particle. Substitution of the above trial solution into the differential equations (11.37) yields the following recursion formula for the amplitudes:

$$-m\omega^2 a_k = K(a_{k-1} - 2a_k + a_{k+1}) \tag{11.38}$$

This formula will include the end points of the string if we set

$$a_0 = a_{n+1} = 0$$

The secular determinant is thus

$$\begin{vmatrix} -m\omega^2 + 2K & -K & 0 & \cdots & 0 \\ -K & -m\omega^2 + 2K & -K & \cdots & 0 \\ 0 & -K & -m\omega^2 + 2K & \cdots & 0 \\ \cdots & \cdots & \cdots & \cdots & \cdots \\ 0 & 0 & 0 & \cdots & -m\omega^2 + 2K \end{vmatrix} = 0$$

The determinant is of the nth order and there are thus n values of ω that satisfy the equation. However, rather than find these n roots by algebra, it turns out that we can find them by working directly with the recursion relation, Equation 11.38.

To this end, we define a quantity φ related to the amplitudes a_k by the following equation

$$a_k = A \sin(k\varphi) \tag{11.39}$$

Direct substitution into the recursion formula then yields

$$-m\omega^2 A \sin(k\varphi) = KA[\sin(k\varphi - \varphi) - 2 \sin(k\varphi) + \sin(k\varphi + \varphi)]$$

which easily reduces to

$$m\omega^2 = K(2 - 2 \cos \varphi) = 4K \sin^2 \frac{\varphi}{2}$$

or

$$\omega = 2\omega_0 \sin \frac{\varphi}{2} \tag{11.40}$$

in which

$$\omega_0 = \left(\frac{K}{m}\right)^{1/2} \tag{11.41}$$

Equation 11.40 gives the normal frequencies in terms of the quantity φ which we have not, as yet determined. Now, as a matter of fact, the same relation would have been obtained by any of the following substitutions for the amplitude a_k: $A \cos (k\varphi)$, $Ae^{ik\varphi}$, $Ae^{-ik\varphi}$, or any linear combination of these. However, only the substitution $a_k = A \sin (k\varphi)$ satisfies the end condition $a_0 = 0$. In order to determine the actual value of the parameter φ, and thus find the normal frequencies of the vibrating string, we use the other end condition, namely $a_{n+1} = 0$. This condition will be met if we set

$$(n + 1)\varphi = N\pi \tag{11.42}$$

in which N is an integer, because we then have

$$a_{n+1} = A \sin(N\pi) = 0$$

Having found φ, we can now calculate the normal frequencies. They are given by

$$\omega_N = 2\omega_0 \sin \left(\frac{N\pi}{2n + 2}\right) \tag{11.43}$$

Furthermore, from Equations 11.39 and 11.42 we see that the amplitudes for the normal modes are given by

$$a_k = A \sin \left(\frac{N\pi k}{n + 1}\right) \tag{11.44}$$

Here the value of $k = 1, 2, \ldots, n$ denotes a particular particle in the linear array, and the value of $N = 1, 2, \ldots, n$ refers to the normal mode in which the system is oscillating.

The different normal modes are illustrated graphically by plotting the amplitudes

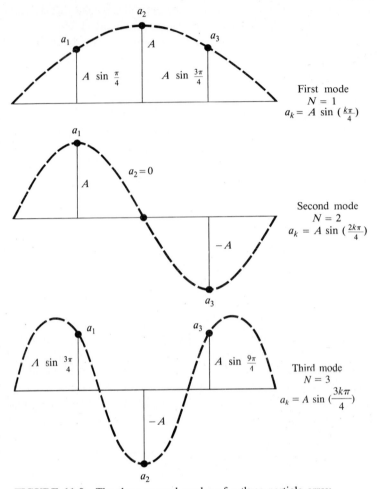

FIGURE 11.9   The three normal modes of a three-particle array.

as given by Equation 11.44. These fall on a sine curve as shown in Figure 11.9 which shows the case of three particles, $n = 3$. The actual motion of the system, when it is vibrating in a single pure mode is given by the equation

$$q_k = a_k \cos (\omega_N t) = A \sin \left(\frac{\pi N k}{n + 1} \right) \cos (\omega_N t) \tag{11.45}$$

The general type of motion is a linear combination of all the normal modes. This can be expressed as

$$q_k = \sum_{N=1}^{n} A_N \sin \left(\frac{N \pi k}{n + 1} \right) \cos (\omega_N t - \epsilon_N) \tag{11.46}$$

in which the values of A_N and ϵ_N are determined from the initial conditions.

In the event that the number n of particles is large compared to the mode number N, so that the ratio $N\pi/(2n + 2)$ is small, we can replace the sine term in Equation 11.43 by the argument. Thus we have approximately

$$\omega_N \approx N\left(\frac{\pi\omega_0}{n + 1}\right) \tag{11.47}$$

This means that the normal frequencies are approximately integral multiples of the lowest frequency $\pi\omega_0/(n + 1)$. In other words, we can regard the different normal frequencies as the fundamental, the second harmonic, the third harmonic, and so on. The accuracy of this integral harmonic relationship is improved as the number of particles is made larger.

11.6   Vibration of a Continuous System. The Wave Equation

Let us consider the motion of a linear array of connected particles in which the number of particles is made indefinitely large and the distance between adjacent particles indefinitely small. In other words, we have a continuous heavy cord or rod. To analyze this type of system it is convenient to rewrite the differential equations of motion of a finite system, Equation 11.37, in the following form:

$$m\ddot{q} = Kh\left[\left(\frac{q_{k+1} - q_k}{d}\right) - \left(\frac{q_k - q_{k-1}}{d}\right)\right]$$

in which d is the distance between the equilibrium positions of any two adjacent particles. Now if the variable x represents general distances in the longitudinal direction, and if the number n of particles is very large so that d is small compared to the total length, then we can write

$$\frac{q_{k+1} - q_k}{d} \approx \left(\frac{\partial q}{\partial x}\right)_{x=kd+d/2}$$

$$\frac{q_k - q_{k-1}}{d} \approx \left(\frac{\partial q}{\partial x}\right)_{x=kd-d/2}$$

Consequently the difference between the above two expressions is equal to the second derivative multiplied by d, namely,

$$\frac{q_{k+1} - q_k}{d} - \frac{q_k - q_{k-1}}{d} \approx d\left(\frac{\partial^2 q}{\partial x^2}\right)_{x=kd}$$

The equation of motion can therefore be written

$$\frac{\partial^2 q}{\partial t^2} = \frac{Kd^2}{m}\frac{\partial^2 q}{\partial x^2}$$

or

$$\frac{\partial^2 q}{\partial t^2} = v^2\frac{\partial^2 q}{\partial x^2} \tag{11.48}$$

FIGURE 11.10   A running wave.

in which we have introduced the abbreviation

$$v^2 = \frac{Kd^2}{m} \qquad (11.49)$$

Equation 11.48 is a well-known differential equation of mathematical physics. It is called the *one-dimensional wave equation*. It is encountered in many different places. Solutions of the wave equation represent traveling disturbances of some sort. It is easy to verify that a very general type of solution of the wave equation is given by

$$q = f(x + vt)$$

or

$$q = f(x - vt)$$

where f is *any* differentiable function of the argument $x \pm vt$. The first solution represents a disturbance that is propagating in the negative x direction with speed v, and the second equation represents a disturbance moving with speed v in the positive x direction. In our particular problem, the disturbance q is a *displacement* of a small portion of the system from its equilibrium configuration, Figure 11.10. For the cord, this displacement could be a kink that travels along the cord; and for a solid rod, it could be a region of compression or of rarefaction moving along the length of the rod.

Evaluation of the Wave Speed

In the preceding section we found that the constant K, for transverse motion of a loaded string, is equal to the ratio S/d where S is the tension in the string. For the continuous string this ratio would, of course, become infinite as d approaches zero. However, if we introduce the linear density or mass per unit length ρ, we have

$$\rho = \frac{m}{d}$$

Consequently, the expression for v^2, Equation 11.49, can be written

$$v^2 = \frac{(S/d)d^2}{\rho d} = \frac{S}{\rho}$$

so that d cancels out. The speed of propagation for transverse waves in a continuous string is then

$$v = \left(\frac{S}{\rho}\right)^{1/2} \qquad (11.50)$$

For the case of longitudinal vibrations, we introduce the elastic modulus Y which is defined as the ratio of the force to the elongation per unit length. Thus K, the stiffness of a small section of length d, is given by

$$K = \frac{Y}{d}$$

Consequently, Equation 11.49 can be written as

$$v^2 = \frac{(Y/d)d^2}{\rho d} = \frac{Y}{\rho}$$

and again we see that d cancels out. Hence the speed of propagation of longitudinal waves in an elastic rod is

$$v = \left(\frac{Y}{\rho}\right)^{1/2} \tag{11.51}$$

Sinusoidal Waves

In the study of wave motion, those particular solutions of the wave equation

$$\frac{\partial^2 q}{\partial t^2} = v^2 \frac{\partial^2 q}{\partial x^2}$$

in which q is a sinusoidal function of x and t, namely

$$q = A \frac{\sin}{\cos}\left[\frac{2\pi}{\lambda}(x + vt)\right] \tag{11.52}$$

$$q = A \frac{\sin}{\cos}\left[\frac{2\pi}{\lambda}(x - vt)\right] \tag{11.53}$$

are of fundamental importance. These solutions represent traveling disturbances in which the displacement, at a given point x, varies harmonically in time. The amplitude of this motion is the constant A, and the *frequency f* is given by

$$f = \frac{\omega}{2\pi} = \frac{v}{\lambda}$$

Furthermore, at a given value of the time t, say $t = 0$, the displacement varies sinusoidally with the distance x. The distance between two successive maxima, or minima, of the displacement is the constant λ, called the *wavelength*. The waves represented by Equation 11.52 propagate in the negative x direction, and those represented by Equation 11.53 propagate in the positive x direction, as shown in Figure 11.11. They are special cases of the general type of solution mentioned earlier.

Standing Waves

Since the wave equation, Equation 11.48, is linear, we can build up any number of solutions by making linear combinations of known solutions. One possible linear combination which is of particular significance is obtained by adding together two

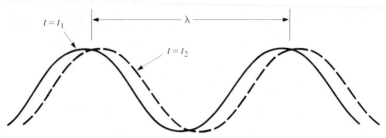

FIGURE 11.11   A sinusoidal wave.

waves of equal amplitude that are traveling in opposite directions. In our notation, such a solution is given by

$$q = \frac{1}{2}A \sin\left[\frac{2\pi}{\lambda}(x + vt)\right] + \frac{1}{2}A \sin\left[\frac{2\pi}{\lambda}(x - vt)\right] \qquad (11.54)$$

By using the appropriate trigonometric identity and collecting terms, we find that the equation reduces to

$$q = A \sin\left(\frac{2\pi}{\lambda}x\right) \cos(\omega t) \qquad (11.54a)$$

in which $\omega = 2\pi v/\lambda$. The above equation represents what are known as *standing waves*. Here we see that the amplitude of the displacement is no longer constant, but varies with the value of x. Thus, for $x = 0$, $\lambda/2$, λ, $3\lambda/2$, . . . , the displacement is always zero since the sine term vanishes at these points. The points of zero displacement are called *nodes*. On the other hand, at those values of x for which the absolute value of the sine term is unity, namely, $x = \lambda/4$, $3\lambda/4$, $5\lambda/4$, . . . , the amplitude of the harmonic oscillation has its maximum value of A. These points are called *antinodes*. The distance between two successive nodes, or two successive antinodes, is just one half of the wavelength. The above facts are illustrated in Figure 11.12.

Interpretation of the Motion of a Loaded String in Terms of Standing Waves

If we compare the equation for a standing wave, Equation 11.54a, with our previous solution for the motion of a loaded string, Equation 11.45, we observe that the two expressions are very similar. The similarity can be brought out even more by noting that the standing wave solution will satisfy the boundary conditions of our original problem, namely

$$q = 0: x = 0 \qquad \text{and} \qquad x = l$$

provided that the end points of the string correspond to nodes of the standing wave.

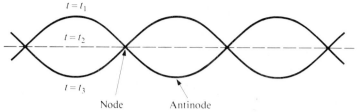

Node   Antinode

FIGURE 11.12   Standing waves.

This condition is met if the length l of the string is an integral number N of half wavelengths, that is

$$l = (n + 1)d = N\frac{\lambda}{2}$$

Solving for λ and substituting in Equation 11.54a yields

$$q = A \sin\left[\frac{\pi Nx}{(n + 1)d}\right] \cos (\omega t) \tag{11.55}$$

This agrees with our previous solution, Equation 11.45, since at the positions of the various particles we have

$$x_k = kd \qquad (k = 1, 2, \ldots , n)$$

Thus the vibration of a loaded string can be regarded as a standing wave. Each normal mode contains a certain integral number of nodes in the standing-wave pattern.

PROBLEMS

11.1   A particle of mass m moves in one-dimensional motion with the following potential energy functions:

(a) $V(x) = \dfrac{k}{2}x^2 + \dfrac{k^2}{x}$

(b) $V(x) = kxe^{-bx}$

(c) $V(x) = k(x^4 - b^2x^2)$

where all constants are real and positive. Find the equilibrium positions for each case and determine their stability.

(d) Find the angular frequency ω for small oscillations about the respective positions of *stable* equilibrium for parts (a), (b), and (c), and find the period in seconds for each case if $m = 1$ gram, and k and b are each of unit value in cgs units.

11.2   A particle moves in two dimensions under the potential energy function

$$V(x,y) = k(x^2 + y^2 - 2bx - 4by)$$

where k is a positive constant. Show that there is one position of equilibrium. Is it stable or unstable?

11.3   The potential energy function of a particle of mass m in one-dimensional motion is given by

$$V(x) = -\frac{k}{2}x^2$$

and so the force is of the antirestoring type

$$F(x) = kx$$

with $x = 0$ as a position of unstable equilibrium when k is a positive constant. If the initial conditions are $t = 0$, $x = x_0$, and $\dot{x} = 0$, show that the ensuing motion is given by an exponential "runaway"

$$x(t) = x_0(e^{\alpha t} + e^{-\alpha t})/2$$

where the constant $\alpha = \sqrt{k/m}$.

11.4   A light elastic cord of length $2l$ and stiffness k is held with the ends fixed a distance $2l$ apart in a horizontal position. A block of mass m is then suspended from the midpoint of the cord. Show that the potential energy of the system is given by the expression

$$V(y) = 2k[y^2 - 2l(y^2 + l^2)^{1/2}] - mgy$$

where y is the vertical sag of the center of the cord. From this show that the equilibrium position is given by a root of the equation

$$u^4 - 2au^3 + a^2u^2 - 2au + a^2 = 0$$

where $u = y/l$ and $a = mg/4kl$.

11.5   A uniform cubical block of mass m and sides $2a$ is balanced on top of a rough sphere of radius b. Show that the potential energy function can be expressed as

$$V(\theta) = mg[(a + b) \cos \theta + b\theta \sin \theta]$$

where θ is the angle of tilt. From this, show that the equilibrium at $\theta = 0$ is stable, or unstable, depending on whether a is less than or greater than b, respectively.

11.6   Expand the potential energy function of the above problem as a power series in θ. From this determine the stability for the case $a = b$.

11.7   A solid homogeneous hemisphere of radius a rests on top of a rough hemispherical cap of radius b, the curved faces being in contact. Show that the equilibrium is stable if a is less than $3b/5$.

11.8   Determine the frequency of vertical oscillations about the equilibrium position in Problem 11.4.

11.9   Determine the period of oscillation of the block in Problem 11.5.

11.10   Determine the period of oscillation of the hemisphere in Problem 11.7.

11.11   A small steel ball rolls back and forth about its equilibrium position in a rough spherical bowl. Show that the period of oscillation is $2\pi[7(b - a)/5\ g]^{1/2}$ where a is the radius of the ball and b is the radius of the bowl. Find the period in seconds if $b = 1$ meter and $a = 1$ centimeter.

11.12   For an orbiting satellite in the form of a thin rod, show that the stable equilibrium attitude and period of oscillation are the same as those found in Example 11.3 for the dumbell satellite.

11.13   In the system of two identical coupled oscillators shown in Figure 11.4, one oscillator is started with initial amplitude A_0 while the other is at rest at its equilibrium position, so that the initial conditions are:

$$t = 0, \qquad x_1(0) = A_0, \quad x_2(0) = 0, \qquad \dot{x}_1(0) = \dot{x}_2(0) = 0$$

Show that the amplitude of the symmetric component is equal to the amplitude of the antisymmetric component in this case and that the complete solution can be expressed as follows:

$$x_1(t) = \frac{1}{2}A_0(\cos \omega_a t + \cos \omega_b t) = A_0 \cos \bar{\omega} t \cos \Delta t$$

$$x_2(t) = \frac{1}{2}A_0(\cos \omega_a t - \cos \omega_b t) = A_0 \sin \bar{\omega} t \sin \Delta t$$

in which $\bar{\omega} = (\omega_a + \omega_b)/2$ and $\Delta = (\omega_b - \omega_a)/2$. Thus, if the coupling is very weak so that $K' \ll K$, then $\bar{\omega}$ will be very nearly equal to $\omega_a = (K/m)^{1/2}$, and Δ is very small. Consequently, under the stated initial conditions, the first oscillator will eventually come to rest while the second oscillator oscillates with amplitude A_0. Later, the system will return to the initial condition, and so on. Thus the energy passes back and forth between the two oscillators indefinitely.

11.14   In the above problem, show that for weak coupling, the period at which the energy trades back and forth is approximately equal to $T_a(K/2K')$ where $T_a = 2\pi/\omega_a = 2\pi/(m/K)^{1/2}$ is the period of the symmetric oscillation.

11.15   Two identical simple pendulums are coupled together by a very weak force of attraction that varies as the inverse square of the distance between the two particles. (This force might be the gravitational attraction between the two particles, for instance.) Show that, for *small* departures from the equilibrium configuration, the Lagrangian can be reduced to the same mathematical form, with appropriate constants, as that of the two identical coupled oscillators treated in Section 11.3 and in Problems 11.13 and 11.14 above. [*Hint:* Consider Equation (11.4).]

11.16   Find the normal frequencies of the coupled harmonic oscillator system, Figure 11.4, for the general case in which the two particles have unequal mass, and the springs have different stiffness. In particular, find the frequencies for the case $m_1 = m$, $m_2 = 2m$, $K_1 = K$, $K_2 = 2K$, $K' = 2K$. Express the result in terms of the quantity $\omega_0 = (K/m)^{1/2}$.

11.17   A light elastic spring of stiffness K is clamped at its upper end and supports a particle of mass m at its lower end. A second spring of stiffness K is fastened to the particle and, in turn, supports a particle of mass $2m$ at its lower end. Find the normal frequencies of the system for vertical oscillations about the equilibrium configuration. Find also the normal coordinates.

11.18   Consider the case of a double pendulum, Figure 11.6(a), in which the two sections are of different length, the upper one being of length l_1, and the lower of length l_2. Both particles are of equal mass m. Find the normal frequencies of the system and the normal coordinates.

11.19   Set up the secular equation for the case of three coupled particles in a linear array and show that the normal frequencies are the same as those given by Equation 11.43.

11.20   Illustrate the normal modes for the case of four particles in a linear array. Find the numerical values of the ratios of the 2nd, 3rd, and 4th normal frequencies to the lowest or first normal frequency.

11.21   A light elastic cord of natural length l and stiffness K is stretched out to a length $l + \Delta l$ and loaded with a number n of particles evenly spaced along its length. If m is the total mass of all n particles, find the speed of transverse and of longitudinal waves in the cord.

11.22   Work the above problem for the case in which, instead of being loaded, the cord is heavy with linear density ρ.

Selected References

Mechanics

Barger, V., and Olsson, M., *Classical Mechanics,* McGraw-Hill, New York, 1973.

Becker, R. A., *Introduction to Theoretical Mechanics,* McGraw-Hill, New York, 1954.

Lindsay, R. B., *Physical Mechanics,* Van Nostrand, Princeton, N. J., 1961.

Rossberg, K., *A First Course in Analytical Mechanics,* Wiley, New York, 1983.

Rutherford, D. E., *Classical Mechanics,* Interscience, New York, 1951.

Slater, J. C., and Frank, N. H., *Mechanics,* McGraw-Hill, New York, 1947.

Symon, K., *Mechanics,* 3rd ed., Addison-Wesley, Reading, Mass., 1971.

Synge, J. L., and Griffith, B. A., *Principles of Mechanics,* McGraw-Hill, New York, 1959.

Advanced Mechanics

Corbin, H. C., and Stehle, P., *Classical Mechanics,* Wiley, New York, 1950.

Desloge, E., *Classical Mechanics* (two volumes), Wiley-Interscience, New York, 1982.

Goldstein, H., *Classical Mechanics,* 2nd ed., Addison-Wesley, Reading, Mass., 1980.

Hauser, W., *Introduction to the Principles of Mechanics,* Addison-Wesley, Reading, Mass., 1965.

Landau, L. D., and Lifshitz, E. M., *Mechanics,* Addison-Wesley, Reading, Mass., 1960.

Marion, J. B., *Classical Dynamics,* Academic Press, New York, 1965.

Moore, E. N., *Theoretical Mechanics,* Wiley, New York, 1983.

Wells, D. A., *Lagrangian Dynamics,* Shaum, New York, 1967.

Whittaker, E. T., *Advanced Dynamics,* Cambridge University Press, London and New
     York, 1937.

Mathematical Methods
Churchill, R. V., *Fourier Series and Boundary Value Problems,* McGraw-Hill, New
     York, 1963.
Jeffreys, H., and Jeffreys, B. S., *Methods of Mathematical Physics,* Cambridge Uni-
     versity Press, London and New York, 1946.
Kaplan, W., *Advanced Calculus,* Addison-Wesley, Reading, Mass., 1952.
Mathews, J., and Walker, R. L., *Methods of Mathematical Physics,* W. A. Benjamin,
     New York, 1964.
Margenau, J., and Murphy, G. M., *The Mathematics of Physics and Chemistry,* 2nd
     ed., Van Nostrand, New York, 1956.
Wylie, C. R., Jr., *Advanced Engineering Mathematics,* McGraw-Hill, New York,
     1951.

Tables
Dwight, H. B., *Mathematical Tables,* Dover, New York, 1958.
Pierce, B. O., *A Short Table of Integrals,* Ginn, Boston, 1929.
Handbook of Chemistry and Physics, Mathematical Tables, Chemical Rubber Co.,
     Cleveland, Ohio, 1962 or after.

Appendix A

UNITS

Basic SI (Système International) Units

Unit	Symbol	Physical Quantity
meter	m	length
kilogram	kg	mass
second	s	time
ampere	A	electric current
Kelvin	K	temperature
mole	mol	amount of substance
candela	cd	luminous intensity

Derived SI Units (not a complete list)

Unit	Symbol	Physical Quantity	Equivalent
newton	N	force	$kg \cdot m/s^2$
joule	J	work or energy	$N \cdot m$
watt	W	power	J/s
pascal	Pa	pressure	N/m^2
volt	V	electric potential difference	W/A
couloumb	C	electric charge	$A \cdot s$

Some Other Common Units

Unit	Metric Equivalent
inch	2.540 centimeters
foot (12 in)	0.3048 meter
yard (3 ft)	0.9144 meter
mile (5280 ft)	1.609 kilometers
feet/second	0.3048 meters/second
miles/hour	0.4470 meters/second
pound (mass)	0.4536 kilogram
gallon	3.785 liters (10^{-3} m^3)
cubic foot	0.02832 cubic meter
horsepower	746 watts

Prefixes for Multiplication by a Power of Ten

Name	Symbol	Factor	Name	Symbol	Factor
			centi	c	10^{-2}
kilo	k	10^{3}	milli	m	10^{-3}
mega	M	10^{6}	micro	μ	10^{-6}
giga	G	10^{9}	nano	n	10^{-9}
tera	T	10^{12}	pico	p	10^{-12}
peta	P	10^{15}	femto	f	10^{-15}
exa	E	10^{18}	atto	a	10^{-18}

Appendix B

Complex Numbers

The quantity

$$z = x + iy$$

is said to be a *complex number* if x and y are real and $i = \sqrt{-1}$. The *complex conjugate* is defined as

$$z^* = x - iy$$

The *absolute value* $|z|$ is given by

$$|z|^2 = zz^* = x^2 + y^2$$

The following are true

$$z + z^* = 2x = 2\,\text{Re}\,z$$
$$z - z^* = 2y = 2\,\text{Im}\,z$$

Exponential Notation

$$z = x + iy = |z|e^{i\theta} = |z|(\cos\theta + i\sin\theta)$$
$$z^* = x - iy = |z|e^{-i\theta} = |z|(\cos\theta - i\sin\theta)$$

where

$$\tan\theta = \frac{y}{x}$$

316

(For a proof of the relation $e^{i\theta} = \cos \theta + i \sin \theta$ see under Series Expansions in Appendix D below.)

Circular and Hyperbolic Functions
The following relations are often useful

$$\cos \theta = \frac{e^{i\theta} + e^{-i\theta}}{2}$$

$$\sin \theta = \frac{e^{i\theta} - e^{-i\theta}}{2i}$$

$$\cosh \theta = \frac{e^{\theta} + e^{-\theta}}{2} \qquad \text{(hyperbolic cosine)}$$

$$\sinh \theta = \frac{e^{\theta} - e^{-\theta}}{2} \qquad \text{(hyperbolic sine)}$$

$$\tanh \theta = \frac{\sinh \theta}{\cosh \theta} = \frac{e^{\theta} - e^{-\theta}}{e^{\theta} + e^{-\theta}} \qquad \text{(hyperbolic tangent)}$$

Relations Between Circular and Hyperbolic Functions

$$\sin i\theta = i \sinh \theta$$
$$\cos i\theta = \cosh \theta$$
$$\sinh i\theta = i \sin \theta$$
$$\cosh i\theta = \cos \theta$$

Derivatives

$$\frac{d}{d\theta} \sin \theta = \cos \theta \qquad \frac{d}{d\theta} \sinh \theta = \cosh \theta$$

$$\frac{d}{d\theta} \cos \theta = -\sin \theta \qquad \frac{d}{d\theta} \cosh \theta = \sinh \theta$$

Identities

$\cos^2 \theta + \sin^2 \theta = 1$

$\sin (\theta + \phi) = \sin \theta \cos \phi + \cos \theta \sin \phi$

$\cos (\theta + \phi) = \cos \theta \cos \phi - \sin \theta \sin \phi$

$\cosh^2 \theta - \sinh^2 \theta = 1$

$\sinh (\theta + \phi) = \sinh \theta \cosh \phi + \cosh \theta \sinh \phi$

$\cosh (\theta + \phi) = \cosh \theta \cosh \phi + \sinh \theta \sinh \phi$

Appendix C

Conic Sections

Cartesian Coordinates

Ellipse:

$$\frac{x^2}{a^2} + \frac{y^2}{b^2} = 1 \qquad \text{area} = \pi a b$$

$$\text{eccentricity } e = \sqrt{1 - \frac{b^2}{a^2}}, \, a > b$$

distance from
origin to focus $= \sqrt{a^2 - b^2}$
major axis $= 2a$
minor axis $= 2b$

Circle: Special case of ellipse with $a = b$ and $e = 0$.

Parabola:

$$y^2 = 4px \qquad \text{eccentricity } e = 1$$

distance from
origin to focus $= p$

Hyperbola:

$$\frac{x^2}{a^2} - \frac{y^2}{b^2} = 1 \qquad \text{eccentricity } e = \sqrt{1 + \frac{b^2}{a^2}}$$

distance from origin
to focus $= \sqrt{a^2 + b^2}$

Polar Coordinates

All cases:

$$r = \frac{r_0(1 + e)}{1 + e \cos \theta} \qquad \begin{array}{l} \text{focus is at the origin;} \\ r_0 \text{ is minimum value of } |r| \end{array}$$

Ellipse: $e < 1$, Parabola: $e = 1$, Hyperbola: $e > 1$, Circle: $e = 0$

For the ellipse the semimajor axis

$$a = \frac{r_0}{1 - e}$$

and the semiminor axis

$$b = a\sqrt{1 - e^2}$$

Appendix D

Series Expansions

Taylor's Series

$$f(x + a) = f(a) + xf'(a) + \frac{x^2}{2!}f''(a) + \cdots + \frac{x^n}{n!}f^n(a) + \cdots$$

$$f(x) = f(0) + xf'(0) + \frac{x^2}{2!}f''(0) + \cdots + \frac{x^n}{n!}f^n(0) + \cdots$$

where

$$f^n(a) = \frac{d^n}{dx^n}f(x)\bigg|_{x=a}$$

Often-Used Expansions

$$e^x = 1 + x + \frac{x^2}{2!} + \cdots + \frac{x^n}{n!} + \cdots$$

$$\sin x = x - \frac{x^3}{3!} + \frac{x^5}{5!} - \cdots$$

$$\cos x = 1 - \frac{x^2}{2!} + \frac{x^4}{4!} - \cdots$$

$$\sinh x = x + \frac{x^3}{3!} + \frac{x^5}{5!} + \cdots$$

$$\cosh x = 1 + \frac{x^2}{2!} + \frac{x^4}{4!} + \cdots$$

$$\ln (1 + x) = x - \frac{x^2}{2} + \frac{x^3}{3} - \cdots \qquad |x| < 1$$

$$\tan x = x + \frac{x^3}{3} + \frac{2}{15}x^5 + \cdots \qquad |x| < \frac{\pi}{2}$$

Complex Exponential

Setting $x = i\theta$ in the expansion for e^x gives

$$e^{i\theta} = 1 + i\theta + \frac{i^2\theta^2}{2!} + \frac{i^3\theta^3}{3!} + \cdots + \frac{i^n\theta^n}{n!} + \cdots$$

Since $i = \sqrt{-1}$

$$i^n = \begin{matrix} +1: n = 0, 4, \ldots \\ -1: n = 2, 6, \ldots \\ +i: n = 1, 5, \ldots \\ -i: n = 3, 7, \ldots \end{matrix}$$

then

$$e^{i\theta} = (1 - \frac{\theta^2}{2!} + \frac{\theta^4}{4!} - \cdots) + i(\theta - \frac{\theta^3}{3!} + \frac{\theta^5}{5!} - \cdots)$$

$$= \cos \theta + i \sin \theta$$

from the series for the cosine and sine above.

Binomial Series

$$(a + x)^n = a^n + na^{n-1}x + \frac{n(n-1)}{2!}a^{n-2}x^2 + \cdots + \binom{n}{m}a^{n-m}x^m + \cdots$$

where the binomial coefficient is

$$\binom{n}{m} = \frac{n!}{(n-m)!m!}$$

The series converges for $|x/a| < 1$.

Useful Approximations

For small x, the following approximations are often used

$$e^x \simeq 1 + x$$

$$\sin x \simeq x$$

$$\cos x \simeq 1 - \tfrac{1}{2}x^2$$

$$\sqrt{1 + x} \simeq 1 + \tfrac{1}{2}x$$

$$\frac{1}{1 + x} \simeq 1 - x$$

$$\frac{1}{1 - x} \simeq 1 + x$$

The last three are based on the binomial series, and the list can be extended for other values of the exponent:

$$(1 + x)^n = 1 + nx + \frac{1}{2}n(n - 1)x^2 + \cdots$$

Appendix E

Special Functions

Elliptic Integrals

The elliptic integral of the *first kind* is given by the expressions

$$F(k,\phi) = \int_0^\phi \frac{d\phi}{(1 - k^2 \sin^2 \phi)^{1/2}}$$

$$= \int_0^x \frac{dx}{(1 - x^2)^{1/2}(1 - k^2x^2)^{1/2}}$$

and the elliptic integral of the *second kind* by

$$E(k,\phi) = \int_0^\phi (1 - k^2 \sin^2 \phi)^{1/2} \, d\phi$$

$$= \int_0^x \frac{(1 - k^2x^2)^{1/2}}{(1 - x^2)^{1/2}} \, dx$$

Both converge for $|k| < 1$. They are called *incomplete* if $x = \sin \phi < 1$, and *complete* if $x = \sin \phi = 1$. The complete integrals have the following series expansions

$$F(k) = F\left(k, \frac{\pi}{2}\right) = \frac{\pi}{2}\left(1 + \frac{k^2}{4} + \frac{9}{64}k^4 + \cdots\right)$$

$$E(k) = E\left(k, \frac{\pi}{2}\right) = \frac{\pi}{2}\left(1 - \frac{k^2}{4} - \frac{9}{64}k^4 - \cdots\right)$$

Gamma Function

The gamma function is defined as

$$\Gamma(n) = \int_0^\infty x^{n-1} e^{-x} \, dx$$

For any value of n

$$n\Gamma(n) = \Gamma(n + 1)$$

If n is a positive integer

$$\Gamma(n) = (n - 1)!$$

Special values

$$\Gamma(\tfrac{1}{2}) = \sqrt{\pi}$$
$$\Gamma(1) = 1$$
$$\Gamma(\tfrac{3}{2}) = \tfrac{1}{2}\sqrt{\pi}$$
$$\Gamma(2) = 1$$

Integrals expressible in terms of gamma functions

$$\int_0^1 \frac{dx}{\sqrt{1 - x^n}} = \frac{\sqrt{\pi}}{n} \frac{\Gamma(1/n)}{\Gamma[(1/2) + (1/n)]}$$

$$\int_0^1 (1 - x^2)^n x^m \, dx = \frac{\Gamma(n + 1)\Gamma[(m + 1)/2]}{2\Gamma[(2n + m + 3)/2]}$$

Appendix F

Curvilinear Coordinates

We consider a general orthogonal system of coordinates u, v, and w with unit vectors $\mathbf{e}_1$, $\mathbf{e}_2$, and $\mathbf{e}_3$. The volume element is

$$dV = h_1 h_2 h_3 du\ dv\ dw$$

and the line element is

$$d\mathbf{s} = \mathbf{e}_1 h_1\ du + \mathbf{e}_2 h_2\ dv + \mathbf{e}_3 h_3\ dw$$

The gradient, divergence, and curl are as follows

$$\operatorname{grad} f = \frac{\mathbf{e}_1}{h_1} \frac{\partial f}{\partial u} + \frac{\mathbf{e}_2}{h_2} \frac{\partial f}{\partial v} + \frac{\mathbf{e}_3}{h_3} \frac{\partial f}{\partial w}$$

$$\operatorname{div} \mathbf{Q} = \frac{1}{h_1 h_2 h_3} \left[\frac{\partial}{\partial u}(h_2 h_3 Q_1) + \frac{\partial}{\partial v}(h_3 h_1 Q_2) + \frac{\partial}{\partial w}(h_1 h_2 Q_3) \right]$$

$$\operatorname{curl} \mathbf{Q} = \frac{1}{h_1 h_2 h_3} \begin{vmatrix} h_1 \mathbf{e}_1 & h_2 \mathbf{e}_2 & h_3 \mathbf{e}_3 \\ \dfrac{\partial}{\partial u} & \dfrac{\partial}{\partial v} & \dfrac{\partial}{\partial w} \\ h_1 Q_1 & h_2 Q_2 & h_3 Q_3 \end{vmatrix}$$

325

The *h* functions for some common coordinate systems are listed below.

Rectangular Coordinates: x, y, z

$$h_x = 1 \qquad h_y = 1 \qquad h_z = 1$$

Cylindrical Coordinates: R, ϕ, z

$$x = R \cos \phi \qquad y = R \sin \phi$$
$$h_R = 1 \qquad h_\phi = R \qquad h_z = 1$$

Spherical Coordinates: r, θ, ϕ

$$x = r \sin \theta \cos \phi \qquad y = r \sin \theta \sin \phi \qquad z = r \cos \theta$$
$$h_r = 1 \qquad h_\theta = r \qquad h_\phi = r \sin \theta$$

Parabolic Coordinates: u, v, θ

$$x = uv \cos \theta \qquad y = uv \sin \theta \qquad z = \tfrac{1}{2}(u^2 - v^2)$$
$$h_u = h_v = \sqrt{u^2 + v^2} \qquad h_\theta = uv$$

Example: The curl in spherical coordinates is

$$\text{curl } \mathbf{Q} = \begin{vmatrix} \mathbf{e}_r & r\mathbf{e}_\theta & r \sin \theta \, \mathbf{e}_\phi \\ \dfrac{\partial}{\partial r} & \dfrac{\partial}{\partial \theta} & \dfrac{\partial}{\partial \phi} \\ Q_r & rQ_\theta & r \sin \theta \, Q_\phi \end{vmatrix} \dfrac{1}{r^2 \sin \theta}$$

Appendix G

Fourier Series

To find the coefficients of the terms in the trigonometric expansion

$$f(t) = \frac{a_0}{2} + \sum_{n=1}^{\infty} [a_n \cos (n\omega t) + b_n \sin (n\omega t)]$$

multiply both sides of the equation by $\cos (n'\omega t)$ and integrate over the interval $-\pi/\omega$ to $+\pi/\omega$:

$$\int_{-\pi/\omega}^{\pi/\omega} f(t) \cos (n'\omega t) \, dt = \frac{a_0}{2} \int_{-\pi/\omega}^{\pi/\omega} \cos (n'\omega t) \, dt$$

$$+ \sum_{n=1}^{\infty} [a_n \int_{-\pi/\omega}^{\pi/\omega} \cos (n'\omega t) \cos (n\omega t) \, dt + b_n \int_{-\pi/\omega}^{\pi/\omega} \cos (n'\omega t) \sin (n\omega t) \, dt]$$

Now if n' and n are integers, we have the general formulas

$$\int_{-\pi/\omega}^{\pi/\omega} \cos (n'\omega t) \, dt = 2\pi/\omega \qquad n' = 0$$

$$= 0 \qquad n' \neq 0$$

$$\int_{-\pi/\omega}^{\pi/\omega} \cos (n'\omega t) \cos (n\omega t) \, dt = \pi/\omega \qquad n' = n$$

$$= 0 \qquad n' \neq n$$

$$\int_{-\pi/\omega}^{\pi/\omega} \cos (n'\omega t) \sin (n\omega t) \, dt = 0 \qquad \text{for all } n' \text{ and } n$$

Thus, for a given n', all of the definite integrals in the summation vanish except the one for which $n' = n$. Consequently we can write

$$a_n = \frac{\omega}{\pi} \int_{-\pi/\omega}^{\pi/\omega} f(t) \cos (n\omega t) \, dt \qquad \text{for } n = 0, 1, 2, \ldots$$

Similarly, if the equation for $f(t)$ is multiplied by $\sin (n'\omega t)$ and integrated term by term, we use the general formula

$$\int_{-\pi/\omega}^{\pi/\omega} \sin (n'\omega t) \sin (n\omega t) \, dt = \pi/\omega \qquad n' = n$$
$$= 0 \qquad n' \neq n$$

in addition to the ones above. As before, all of the definite integrals vanish except for $n' = n$, and so we get

$$b_n = \frac{\omega}{\pi} \int_{-\pi/\omega}^{\pi/\omega} f(t) \sin (n\omega t) \, dt \qquad n = 1, 2, \ldots$$

Since the period $T = 2\pi/\omega$, the limits of integration can also be expressed as $-T/2$ to $T/2$. For more detailed information concerning continuity conditions, integrability, and so on, the reader should consult a text on Fourier series, such as R. V. Churchill, *Fourier Series and Boundary Value Problems*, McGraw-Hill, New York, 1963.

Appendix H

Matrices

A *matrix* **A** is an array of elements a_{ij} arranged thus

$$
\mathbf{A} = \begin{bmatrix}
a_{11} & a_{12} & \cdots & a_{1j} & \cdots & a_{1m} \\
a_{21} & a_{22} & \cdots & a_{2j} & \cdots & a_{2m} \\
\vdots & \vdots & & \vdots & & \vdots \\
a_{i1} & a_{i2} & \cdots & a_{ij} & \cdots & a_{im} \\
\vdots & \vdots & & \vdots & & \vdots \\
a_{n1} & a_{n2} & \cdots & a_{nj} & \cdots & a_{nm}
\end{bmatrix}
$$

If $n = m$, it is called a *square* matrix. Unless stated otherwise, we shall consider only square matrices in this Appendix. A *symmetric* matrix is one such that $a_{ij} = a_{ji}$. If $a_{ij} = -a_{ji}$, it is *antisymmetric*.

The sum of two matrices is defined as

$$(\mathbf{A} + \mathbf{B})_{ij} = a_{ij} + b_{ij}$$

The product of two matrices is defined as

$$(\mathbf{AB})_{ij} = a_{i1}b_{1j} + a_{i2}b_{2j} + \cdots = \sum_{k} a_{ik}b_{kj}$$

The product **AB** is not, in general, equal to **BA**. If **AB** = **BA**, the two matrices are said to *commute*. A *diagonal matrix* is one whose nondiagonal elements are zero, $a_{ij} = 0$ for $i \neq j$. The *identity* matrix[1] is a diagonal matrix with all diagonal elements equal to unity,

$$\mathbf{1} = \begin{bmatrix} 1 & 0 & 0 & \cdots & 0 \\ 0 & 1 & 0 & \cdots & 0 \\ 0 & 0 & 1 & \cdots & 0 \\ \cdot & \cdot & \cdot & \cdots & \\ 0 & 0 & 0 & \cdots & 1 \end{bmatrix}$$

From the definition of the product, it is easily shown that

$$\mathbf{A1} = \mathbf{1A}$$

The *inverse* $\mathbf{A}^{-1}$ of a matrix **A** is defined by

$$\mathbf{AA}^{-1} = \mathbf{1} = \mathbf{A}^{-1}\mathbf{A}$$

The *transpose* $\mathbf{A}^T$ of a matrix **A** is defined as

$$(\mathbf{A}^T)_{ij} = (\mathbf{A})_{ji}$$

For two matrices **A** and **B**, $(\mathbf{AB})^T = \mathbf{B}^T\mathbf{A}^T$.

The determinant of a matrix is the determinant of its elements,

$$\det \mathbf{A} = \begin{vmatrix} a_{11} & a_{12} & \cdots \\ a_{21} & a_{22} & \cdots \\ \cdot & \cdot & \cdots \end{vmatrix}$$

The determinant of the product of two matrices is equal to the product of the respective determinants,

$$\det \mathbf{AB} = \det \mathbf{A} \det \mathbf{B}$$

It can be shown that the inverse of a matrix **A** is given by the formula

$$\mathbf{A}^{-1} = \begin{bmatrix} \dfrac{\det \mathbf{A}_{11}}{\det \mathbf{A}} & \dfrac{\det \mathbf{A}_{21}}{\det \mathbf{A}} & \cdots \\ \dfrac{\det \mathbf{A}_{12}}{\det \mathbf{A}} & \dfrac{\det \mathbf{A}_{22}}{\det \mathbf{A}} & \cdots \\ \cdots & \cdots & \cdots \end{bmatrix}$$

where the matrix $\mathbf{A}_{ij}$ is the matrix left after the ith row and jth column have been removed from the matrix **A**.

Matrix Representation of Vectors

A matrix with one row, or one column, defines a *row vector,* or *column vector,* respectively. If **a** is a column vector, then $\mathbf{a}^T$ is the corresponding row vector,

[1]This should not be confused with the inertia tensor defined in Chapter 9.

$$
\mathbf{a} = \begin{bmatrix} a_1 \\ a_2 \\ \cdot \\ \cdot \\ \cdot \\ a_n \end{bmatrix} \qquad \mathbf{a}^T = [a_1, a_2, \ldots, a_n]
$$

For two column vectors $\mathbf{a}$ and $\mathbf{b}$ with the same number of elements, the product $\mathbf{a}^T\mathbf{b}$ is a scalar, analogous to the dot product,

$$
\mathbf{a}^T\mathbf{b} = [a_1, a_2, \ldots] \begin{bmatrix} b_1 \\ b_2 \\ \cdot \\ \cdot \\ \cdot \end{bmatrix} = a_1 b_1 + a_2 b_2 + \cdots
$$

Two vectors $\mathbf{a}$ and $\mathbf{b}$ are *orthogonal* if $\mathbf{a}^T\mathbf{b} = 0$.

Matrix Transformations

A matrix $\mathbf{Q}$ is said to *transform* a vector $\mathbf{a}$ into another vector $\mathbf{a}'$ according to the rule

$$
\mathbf{a}' = \mathbf{Q}\mathbf{a} = \begin{bmatrix} q_{11} & q_{12} & \cdots \\ q_{21} & q_{22} & \cdots \\ \cdot & \cdot & \cdots \\ \cdot & \cdot & \cdots \\ \cdot & \cdot & \cdots \end{bmatrix} \begin{bmatrix} a_1 \\ a_2 \\ \cdot \\ \cdot \end{bmatrix} = \begin{bmatrix} q_{11}a_1 + q_{12}a_2 + \cdots \\ q_{21}a_1 + q_{22}a_2 + \cdots \\ \cdot & \cdot & \cdots \\ \cdot & \cdot & \cdots \end{bmatrix}
$$

The transpose of $\mathbf{a}'$ is then

$$
\mathbf{a}'^T = \mathbf{a}^T\mathbf{Q}^T = [a_1, a_2, \ldots] \begin{bmatrix} q_{11} & q_{12} & \cdots \\ q_{21} & q_{22} & \cdots \\ \cdot & \cdot & \cdots \end{bmatrix}
$$

$$
= [q_{11}a_1 + q_{12}a_2 + \ldots, q_{21}a_1 + q_{22}a_2 + \ldots, \ldots]
$$

A matrix $\mathbf{Q}$ is said to be *orthogonal* if $\mathbf{Q}^T = \mathbf{Q}^{-1}$. It defines an *orthogonal transformation*. It leaves $\mathbf{a}^T\mathbf{b}$ unchanged, since $\mathbf{a}'^T\mathbf{b}' = \mathbf{a}^T\mathbf{Q}^T\mathbf{Q}\mathbf{b} = \mathbf{a}^T\mathbf{Q}^{-1}\mathbf{Q}\mathbf{b} = \mathbf{a}^T\mathbf{b}$.

The transformation defined by the matrix product $\mathbf{Q}^{-1}\mathbf{A}\mathbf{Q}$ is called a *similarity transformation*. The transformation defined by the product $\mathbf{Q}^T\mathbf{A}\mathbf{Q}$ is called a *congruent transformation*.

If the elements of $\mathbf{Q}$ are complex, then $\mathbf{Q}$ is called *Hermitian* if $q_{ij}{}^* = q_{ji}$, that is, $\mathbf{Q}^{T*} = \mathbf{Q}$. If $\mathbf{Q}^{T*} = \mathbf{Q}^{-1}$, then $\mathbf{Q}$ is called a *unitary* matrix, and the transformation $\mathbf{Q}^{-1}\mathbf{A}\mathbf{Q}$ is called a *unitary transformation*.

Eigenvectors of a Matrix

An *eigenvector* $\mathbf{a}$ of a matrix $\mathbf{Q}$ is a vector such that

$$
\mathbf{Q}\mathbf{a} = \lambda\mathbf{a}
$$

or

$$
(\mathbf{Q} - \mathbf{1}\lambda)\mathbf{a} = 0
$$

where λ is a scalar, called the *eigenvalue*. The eigenvalues are found by solving the *secular equation*

$$\det(\mathbf{Q} - \mathbf{1}\lambda) = \begin{vmatrix} q_{11} - \lambda & q_{12} & \cdots \\ q_{21} & q_{22} - \lambda & \cdots \\ \cdot & \cdot & \cdots \end{vmatrix} = 0$$

which is an algebraic equation of degree n (the number of rows or columns or order of the matrix.)

If the matrix $\mathbf{Q}$ is diagonal, then the eigenvalues are its elements.

Consider two different eigenvectors $\mathbf{a}_\alpha$ and $\mathbf{a}_\beta$ of a symmetric matrix $\mathbf{Q}$. Then

$$\mathbf{Q}\mathbf{a}_\alpha = \lambda_\alpha \mathbf{a}_\alpha$$
$$\mathbf{Q}\mathbf{a}_\beta = \lambda_\beta \mathbf{a}_\beta$$

where λ_α and λ_β are the eigenvalues. Multiply the first by $\mathbf{a}_\beta^T$ and the second, transposed, by $\mathbf{a}_\alpha$. Then

$$\mathbf{a}_\beta^T \mathbf{Q}\mathbf{a}_\alpha = \lambda_\alpha \mathbf{a}_\beta^T \mathbf{a}_\alpha$$
$$\mathbf{a}_\beta^T \mathbf{Q}^T \mathbf{a}_\alpha = \lambda_\beta \mathbf{a}_\beta^T \mathbf{a}_\alpha$$

But if $\mathbf{Q}$ is symmetric, then $\mathbf{Q}^T = \mathbf{Q}$, so the two expressions on the left are equal. Hence

$$(\lambda_\beta - \lambda_\alpha)\mathbf{a}_\beta^T \mathbf{a}_\alpha = 0$$

If the eigenvalues are different, then the two eigenvectors must be orthogonal.

Reduction to Diagonal Form

Given a matrix $\mathbf{Q}$, we seek a matrix $\mathbf{A}$ such that

$$\mathbf{A}^{-1}\mathbf{Q}\mathbf{A} = \mathbf{D}$$

where $\mathbf{D}$ is diagonal. Now

$$\mathbf{D} - \lambda\mathbf{1} = \mathbf{A}^{-1}\mathbf{Q}\mathbf{A} - \lambda\mathbf{1} = \mathbf{A}^{-1}(\mathbf{Q} - \lambda\mathbf{1})\mathbf{A}$$

Hence the eigenvalues of $\mathbf{Q}$ are the same as those of $\mathbf{D}$, namely, the elements of $\mathbf{D}$. Let λ_k be a particular eigenvalue, found by solving the secular equation $\det(\mathbf{Q} - \lambda\mathbf{1}) = 0$. Then the corresponding eigenvector $\mathbf{a}_k$ satisfies the equation

$$\mathbf{Q}\mathbf{a}_k = \lambda_k \mathbf{a}_k$$

which is equivalent to n linear homogeneous algebraic equations

$$\sum_j q_{ij}a_{jk} = \lambda_k a_{ik} \qquad (i = 1, 2, \ldots, n)$$

These may be solved for the ratios of the a's to yield the components of the eigenvector $\mathbf{a}_k$. The same procedure is repeated for each eigenvalue in turn. We then form the matrix $\mathbf{A}$ whose columns are the eigenvectors $\mathbf{a}_k$, that is, $[\mathbf{A}]_{ik} = a_{ik}$. Thus the matrix $\mathbf{A}$ must satisfy

$$\mathbf{QA} = \mathbf{A}\begin{bmatrix} \lambda_1 & 0 & \cdot\ \cdot\ \cdot \\ 0 & \lambda_2 & \cdot\ \cdot\ \cdot \\ \cdot & \cdot & \cdot\ \cdot\ \cdot \\ 0 & 0 & \cdot\ \cdot\ \lambda_n \end{bmatrix} = \mathbf{AD}$$

so that $\mathbf{A}^{-1}\mathbf{QA} = \mathbf{D}$ as required. The above method can always be done if $\mathbf{Q}$ is symmetric and the eigenvalues are all different.

Application to Oscillating Systems

For a system with n degrees of freedom, the generalized displacement vector is

$$\mathbf{q} = \begin{bmatrix} q_1 \\ q_2 \\ \cdot \\ \cdot \\ \cdot \\ q_n \end{bmatrix}$$

In matrix notation the kinetic and potential energies (defined in Section 11.4 of the text) take the compact forms

$$T = \tfrac{1}{2}\dot{\mathbf{q}}^T\mathbf{M}\dot{\mathbf{q}} \qquad V = \tfrac{1}{2}\mathbf{q}^T\mathbf{K}\mathbf{q}$$

in which

$$\mathbf{M} = \begin{bmatrix} M_{11} & M_{12} & \cdot\ \cdot\ \cdot \\ M_{21} & M_{22} & \cdot\ \cdot\ \cdot \\ \cdot & \cdot & \cdot\ \cdot\ \cdot \end{bmatrix}$$

$$\mathbf{K} = \begin{bmatrix} \kappa_{11} & \kappa_{12} & \cdot\ \cdot\ \cdot \\ \kappa_{21} & \kappa_{22} & \cdot\ \cdot\ \cdot \\ \cdot & \cdot & \cdot\ \cdot\ \cdot \end{bmatrix}$$

We note that both $\mathbf{M}$ and $\mathbf{K}$ are symmetric matrices. The differential equations of motion of the system given by Equation 11.29 can then be written

$$\mathbf{M}\ddot{\mathbf{q}} + \mathbf{K}\mathbf{q} = 0$$

If a harmonic solution of the form

$$q_k = A_k \cos \omega t \qquad (k = 1, 2, \ldots, n)$$

exists, then $\ddot{q}_k = -\omega^2 q_k$ that is

$$\ddot{\mathbf{q}} = -\omega^2\mathbf{q}$$

Consequently

$$(-\mathbf{M}\omega^2 + \mathbf{K})\mathbf{q} = 0$$

A nontrivial solution requires the secular determinant to vanish

$$\det (-\mathbf{M}\omega^2 + \mathbf{K}) = 0$$

or

$$\left| -M_{ij}\omega^2 + \kappa_{ij} \right| = 0$$

The roots give the normal frequencies and the associated eigenvectors define the normal modes. For further reading, see any of the first seven titles under *Advanced Mechanics* in Selected References.

Answers to Selected Odd-Numbered Problems

Chapter 1

1.1   (a) $\sqrt{6}$, (b) $3\mathbf{i} + \mathbf{j} - 2\mathbf{k}$, (c) 1, (d) $\mathbf{i} - \mathbf{j} + \mathbf{k}$

1.3 $\cos^{-1}\sqrt{5/14} \approx 53.3°$

1.5 $q = 1$ or 2

1.11 $3.232\mathbf{i}' + 1.598\mathbf{j}' - \mathbf{k}'$

1.13 $b\omega(\sin^2 \omega t + 4\cos^2 \omega t)^{1/2}$, $2b\omega$, $b\omega$

1.17 $b\omega[\cos^2(\dfrac{\pi}{8}\cos 4\omega t) + \dfrac{\pi^2}{4}\sin^2(4\omega t)]^{1/2}$

1.21 For Problem 1.15 $a_n = bc(k^2 + c^2)^{1/2}e^{kt}$, $a_\tau = bk(k^2 + c^2)^{1/2}e^{kt}$

Chapter 2

2.1   (a) $\dot{x} = (F_0/m)t + (c/2m)t^2$, $x = (F_0/2m)t^2 + (c/6m)t^3$

    (b) $\dot{x} = (F_0/cm)(1 - \cos ct)$, $x = (F_0/c^2m)(ct - \sin ct)$

    (c) $\dot{x} = -(F_0/cm)(1 - e^{ct})$, $x = -(F_0/c^2m)(ct - e^{ct} + 1)$

2.3   (a) $V = -F_0x - (c/2)x^2 + C$, (b) $V = (F_0/c)e^{-cx} + C$,

    (c) $V = -(F_0/c)\sin cx + C$

Chapter 3

3.1   6.43 m/s, 2.07×10^4 m/s^2

3.3 $x(t) = 0.25 \cos(20\pi t) + 0.00159 \sin(20\pi t)$ in meters

3.5 $[(\dot{x}_2^2 - \dot{x}_1^2)/(x_1^2 - x_2^2)]^{1/2}$, $[(x_1^2\dot{x}_2^2 - x_2^2\dot{x}_1^2)/(\dot{x}_2^2 - \dot{x}_1^2)]^{1/2}$

3.17 (a) $T = 2\pi(l/g)^{1/2} \times 1.041$, (b) g will come out to be about 8 percent low, (c) $B/A = 0.0032$

Chapter 4

4.1   (a) $\mathbf{F} = -c(yz\mathbf{i} + xz\mathbf{j} + xy\mathbf{k})$, (b) $\mathbf{F} = -2(\alpha x\mathbf{i} + \beta y\mathbf{j} + \gamma z\mathbf{k})$
      (c) $\mathbf{F} = ce^{-(\alpha x + \beta y + \gamma z)}(\alpha\mathbf{i} + \beta\mathbf{j} + \gamma\mathbf{k})$, (d) $\mathbf{F} = -cnr^{n-1}\mathbf{e}_r$

4.3   (a) $c = 1/2$, (b) $c = -1$

4.9 $m\ddot{x} = -c_2\dot{x}\dot{s}$, $m\ddot{y} = -c_2\dot{y}\dot{s}$, $m\ddot{z} = -mg - c_2\dot{z}\dot{s}$

4.11 Long axis: $\psi = 80.8°$, Short axis: $\psi = -9.2°$

4.17 $v = (2gb)^{1/2}$, $R = 3mg$

Chapter 5

5.1   Up: 150 lb, Down: 90 lb

5.3   1.005 mg, about 5.7°

5.5   (a) $g/6$ forward, (b) $g/3$ toward rear

5.7 $(V_0^2/\rho)\mathbf{i}' + [(V_0^2/b) + (V_0^2b/\rho^2)]\mathbf{j}'$

Chapter 6

6.1   About 2×10^{-9}

6.3   About 1.4 h

6.13 $(120/61)^{1/2} = 1.4026$. Orbit is hyperbolic: $v_0^2/v_c^2 > 2$.

6.19 $\psi = \pi(1 + c/1 + 4c)^{1/2}$ where $c = \rho 4\pi a^3/3M_{sun}$

6.21 $a > (\epsilon/k)^{1/2}$

6.25 $\psi = 180.7°$ for orbits near the earth.

6.27 $\theta = -30°$

Chapter 7

7.1 $\mathbf{r}_{cm} = (\mathbf{i} + 2\mathbf{j} + 2\mathbf{k})/3$, $\mathbf{v}_{cm} = (3\mathbf{i} + 2\mathbf{j} + \mathbf{k})/3$, $\mathbf{p} = 3\mathbf{i} + 2\mathbf{j} + \mathbf{k}$

7.5   Direction: downward at an angle of 26.6° with the horizontal, Speed: 1.118 v_0

7.7   Car: $v_0/2$, Truck: $v_0/8$. Both final velocities are in the direction of the initial velocity of the truck.

7.13 Proton: $v'_x = v'_y = 0.657 v_0$, Helium: $v'_x = 0.086 v_0$, $v'_y = -0.164 v_0$

7.15 Approximately 55.2°

7.19 $\ddot{z} = g - 3\dot{z}^2/(z_1 + z)$ where z_1 is a constant proportional to the initial radius of the drop. ($z_1 = 0$ for this problem.)

Chapter 8

8.1   (a) $b/3$ from center section, (b) $x_{cm} = y_{cm} = 4b/3\pi$ where lamina is in xy plane, (c) $x_{cm} = 0$, $y_{cm} = 3b/5$, (d) $x_{cm} = y_{cm} = 0$, $z_{cm} = 2b/3$, (e) $b/4$ from base

8.3 $a/14$ from center of large sphere

8.5 $(31/70)ma^2$

8.9 $2\pi (2a/g)^{1/2}$, $2\pi (3a/2g)^{1/2}$

8.13 $g(m_1 - m_2)/(m_1 + m_2 + I/a^2)$

8.17 $v_0t - \dfrac{1}{2}gt^2(\sin\theta + \mu\cos\theta)$

      $(2v_0^2/g)(\sin\theta + 6\mu\cos\theta)/(2\sin\theta + 7\mu\cos\theta)^2$

8.21 $[2g(1 - \cos\theta_0)(\dfrac{m}{3}l^2 + m'l'^2)(\dfrac{m}{2}l + m'l')]^{1/2}/m'l'$

Chapter 9

9.1 (a) $I_{xx} = \dfrac{m}{3}a^2$, $I_{yy} = \dfrac{4m}{3}a^2$, $I_{zz} = \dfrac{5m}{3}a^2$

$I_{xz} = I_{yz} = 0$, $I_{xy} = -\dfrac{m}{2}a^2$

(b) $\dfrac{2}{15}ma^2$, (c) $\mathbf{L} = (ma^2\omega/6\sqrt{5})(\mathbf{i} + 2\mathbf{j})$, (d) $T = \dfrac{1}{15}ma^2\omega^2$

9.3 (a) Inclination of the I-axis is $\dfrac{1}{2}\tan^{-1} 1 = 22.5°$

(b) Principal axes in the xy plane are parallel to the edges of the lamina.

9.9 (a) 1.414 s, 0.632 s; (b) 1.603 s, 0.663 s

9.13 $\alpha - \tan^{-1}[(I/I_s)\tan \alpha] \simeq \alpha(I_s - I)/I_s \simeq 0.00065$ arc sec

9.17 $S > \left[\dfrac{128\ ga}{b^4}\left(\dfrac{a^2}{3} + \dfrac{b^2}{16}\right)\right]^{1/2} \simeq 2910$ rps

Chapter 10

10.1 Use $L = \dfrac{m}{2}(\dot{x}^2 + \dot{y}^2 + \dot{z}^2) - mgz$

10.3 (a) $g/2$, (b) $g(m + m'z/b)/(2m + m')$ where b is the length of the cord, and z is the length hanging over the table at any instant.

10.5 $-mg \sin \theta \cos \theta/[(7/5)(m + M) - m \cos^2 \theta]$

10.9 $d^2r/dt^2 = r\dot{\theta}^2 + g \cos \theta - (k/m)(r - l_0)$
$d(r^2\dot{\theta})/dt = -gr \sin \theta$

10.15 $U(r) = \dfrac{mh^2 \sin^2 \alpha}{2r^2} + mgr \cos \alpha$ where $h = r^2\dot{\phi} = constant$

10.19 (a) $\dot{\theta} = p_\theta/ml^2$, $\dot{p}_\theta = -mgl \sin \theta$
(b) $\dot{x} = p_x/(m_1 + m_2)$, $\dot{p}_x = g(m_1 - m_2)$
(c) $\dot{x} = p_x/m$, $\dot{p}_x = mg \sin \theta$

Chapter 11

11.1 (a) $x = k^{1/3}$ stable
(b) $x = b$ unstable
(c) $x = 0$ unstable, $x = \pm b/\sqrt{2}$ stable
(d) $(3k/m)^{1/2}$, 3.628 sec; $b(k/m)^{1/2}$, 6.283 sec for parts (a) and (c), respectively.

11.9 $2\pi\ a[5/3g(b - a)]^{1/2}$

11.11 2.363 sec

11.17 $\omega = (k/m)^{1/2}\dfrac{(5 \pm \sqrt{17})^{1/2}}{2}$

11.21 $v_{long} = (K/m)^{1/2}(l + \Delta l)$, $v_{trans} = (K/m)^{1/2}[(l + \Delta l)\ \Delta l]^{1/2}$

Index